CONGRESSIONAL POLITICS

CONGRESSIONAL POLITICS

Leroy N. Rieselbach

Professor of Political Science

Indiana University

McGraw-Hill Book Company

New York   St. Louis   San Francisco   Düsseldorf   Johannesburg
Kuala Lumpur   London   Mexico   Montreal   New Delhi
Panama   Rio de Janeiro   Singapore   Sydney   Toronto

CONGRESSIONAL POLITICS

Copyright © 1973 by McGraw-Hill, Inc. All rights reserved.
Printed in the United States of America. No part of this
publication may be reproduced, stored in a retrieval system,
or transmitted, in any form or by any means, electronic,
mechanical, photocopying, recording, or otherwise, without
the prior written permission of the publisher.
1234567890DODO798765432

This book was set in English by University Graphics, Inc.
The editors were Robert P. Rainier and Sally Mobley;
the designer was J. E. O'Connor;
and the production supervisor was Ted Agrillo.
The printer and binder was R. R. Donnelley & Sons
Company.

Library of Congress Cataloging in Publication Data

Rieselbach, Leroy N
Congressional politics.

1. United States. Congress.
JK1061.R48   328.73   72-5203
ISBN: 0-07-052725-3

Contents

Preface   xi

Chapter 1   Congress as a Political System   1

The Systems Approach: An Overview
  The System
  Environment and Inputs to the System
  System Outputs
  Feedback
  Summary
The Congressional System
  The Congressional System
  Inputs to the Congressional System
  Congressional Outputs
  Feedback
  Summary

Part 1   **The Congressional System**

Chapter 2   The Men of Congress   27

The Legislators: Background Characteristics
  Social Background Attributes
  Personality Characteristics
The Electoral Gamut
  Apportionment
  Nominations
  Campaigns
  Election Results

Life in Washington

Summary and Discussion

Chapter 3   Congressional Committees   57

Committees: General Considerations
  Committees in Congress
  Types of Committees
Committee Assignments
  Methods of Assignment
  Criteria for Committee Assignment
The Committee Chairman
  Powers of the Chairman
  Seniority
Subcommittees
Committee Staff
Relations among Committees
Summary and Discussion

Chapter 4   Political Parties in Congress   86

The Functions of the Congressional Party

Assets and Liabilities of the Congressional Party

The Party Machinery
  The Speaker of the House
  Floor Leaders
  The Whips
  Party Conferences and Committees
The Party in Action
  The Techniques of Leadership
  Conditions for Party Leadership
  Leadership Change
Summary

Chapter 5   The Rules and Procedures   113

Rules and Procedures in the House
  Introduction
  Committee Consideration
  To the Floor: Privileged Matter
  To the Floor: The Rules Committee
  On the Floor
Rules and Procedures in the Senate
  Introduction
  Committee Consideration
  On the Floor
Rules and Procedures Pertaining to Conference Committees
Summary

Chapter 6 Informal Norms and Organization   140

Folkways of the House and Senate
  The Norms
  Functions of the Norms
  The "Inner-Club" Controversy
Norms Relating to Legislative Subsystems
  Norms about Committees
  Norms about Parties
Committee Norms
Informal Organizations
Summary

Part 2   Inputs to the Congressional System

Chapter 7 The Executive and Congress   167

The President as "Chief Legislator"
Presidential Involvement in the Legislative Process
  Limits on Presidential Leadership
  Opportunities for Presidential Leadership
  Formal Bases of Presidential Power
  Informal Bases of Presidential Influence: The Power to Persuade
  The President and Foreign Policy
  Some Additional Caveats
Executive Agencies and Congress
  Administrative Lobbying
  Intraexecutive Differences
Executive Supports for Congress
Summary

Chapter 8 The Lobbyists and Congress   194

The Classic Image
Contemporary Lobbying
  Lobbyists versus Legislators
  "Lobbying as a Communications Process"
Legislative Use of Lobbies
The Regulation of Lobbying
Pressure-group Support for the Legislative System
Summary

Chapter 9 Intermittent Pressures: Public Opinion and the Courts   214

Public Demands on Congress
  Policy Demands

The "Information Gap"
Role Orientations
Public Supports for Congress
Demands from the Supreme Court
Judicial Supports for Congress
Summary

Part 3 Outputs of the Congressional System

Chapter 10 Lawmaking 1: Getting to the Floor   235

Lawmaking: Some General Considerations
Role Orientations toward Lawmaking
Drafting the Bill
  What to Ask For?
  The Form of the Legislation
  How Specific a Bill?
In Committee: Hearings
  Purposes
  Closed Hearings
  The Role of the Chairman
  The Testimony
  Participation
In Committee: The "Mark-up"
Committee Decisions
The Committee Report
Summary

Chapter 11 Lawmaking 2: On the Floor   261

From Committee to Floor: A Review
Debate and Amendment
Congressional Voting
  Individual Votes
  Voting Patterns
  Committee Success
Conference Committees
The Substance of Congressional Policy Outputs
Summary

Chapter 12 Congressional Oversight   295

Oversight: Some General Considerations
Techniques of Oversight

Statutory Controls
The Legislative Veto
"Power of the Purse": Appropriations and the Audit
Controls over Personnel
Control through Investigation
Informal Controls

Congressional Oversight: Some Limitations

Summary

Chapter 13   Legislative Representation   326

Policy Representation
Who Is to Represent?
Representation in Action: Focus and Style
Policy Representation: An Overview

Constituent Services
Casework
The Congressional Office
Publicity and Constituent Education

Role Conflict

Feedback

Summary

Part 4   Congress and the Future

Chapter 14   Congressional Reform: Proposals and Prospects   359

Some Perspectives on the Congressional System
Presidential-dominance Models
Congressional-supremacy Models
Intermediate Positions: Bargaining Models

Congressional Reforms
Strengthening the President
Strengthening Congress
Incremental Change
General Problems: Staff and Information

Support: Issues of Secrecy and Ethics

Conclusion

Bibliography   397
Index   413

Preface

During the 1960s, scholars rediscovered the legislative process. More correctly, perhaps, they brought to an old and abiding interest in legislatures, particularly the United States Congress, a renewed set of concerns and a refined body of research methods. Social scientists have adapted the interview technique, so successful in analyzing voting behavior, to eliciting perceptual and attitudinal data about lawmakers. They extended and developed modes of participant observation in order to gain insight into the operation of legislative institutions. They have applied quantitative techniques—especially statistical treatment of roll call data and, to a lesser extent, content analysis of public documents—to a variety of legislatures and legislative situations. The upshot of these and other developments has been the generation of a considerably larger body of information on legislative politics than has been available in the past. This book seeks to integrate and present in a coherent fashion some of this recent scholarship.

The framework employed here, and set forth more fully in Chapter 1, is the systems approach, pioneered by David Easton and others. This conceptual scheme permits the orderly organization of a diverse body of research on a variety of aspects of the legislative process; it is intended to enable the reader to see interconnections among the multitude of legislative behaviors that might otherwise go unnoticed. The notion of role conflict, for instance, should highlight the individual legislator's need to allocate his time and energy, and that of his staff, among various activities which are not mutually exclusive except that together they demand more resources than the legislator has to commit. What the legislature does, in a sense, reflects the distribution of its members' resolutions of their role conflicts.

Moreover, the systems paradigm should suggest a variety of avenues for further investigation of the legislative process. Throughout the present volume, gaps in our knowledge appear, interstices that have been ignored or filled with pure speculation. Again, to cite a single but prominent example, there is considerable evidence to suggest that lawmakers orient themselves toward particular aspects of their legislative jobs in distinctive fashions; at the same time, however, there is virtually no data on the specific ways in which these role orientations influence the day-to-day behavior of individual representatives. Some hypotheses are offered in the pages which follow, but they are in need of verification through careful research.

In short, the systems approach seems to offer advantages in organizing a sprawling body of material and in pointing the way toward the acquisition of much-needed but presently unavailable information. At the same time, however, in keeping with the intent to present a broad overview of the legislative process, the chapters of the present volume are organized along conventional lines. They present detailed descriptions and discussions of the standard features of the legislative process: its party and committee structures; the involvement of the executive branch and political interest groups; and the floor consideration of, and vote on, legislation. Thus, the intent is both to cast the U.S. Congress in a systems framework in a reasonably novel fashion and to provide full, up-to-date coverage of the standard topics of interest.

The present focus is exclusively on Congress for several reasons. First, there has been considerably more investigation of the national legislature than of any, perhaps all, of the state assemblies. Few, if any, state legislatures have been studied with the same intensity and over the same extended period as the Congress, and it is difficult if not impossible to characterize them on the basis of insufficient research. In addition, since one goal of this text is to illustrate the utility of a systems framework, it seems reasonable to treat a single system fully rather than many systems partially. If the systems approach proves fruitful, if it serves well to organize the extant literature and to suggest topics for additional study, then it can be extended to other legislatures. Finally, an attempt to integrate the scattered materials on state legislative politics and processes would have made the book inordinately long.

This book was conceived and written over an extended period during which I incurred a number of obligations which I happily acknowledge here. My interest in the "systems perspective" dates to a year spent as a Postdoctoral Fellow at the Mental Health Research Institute of the University of Michigan. Although what appears here will not satisfy the more rigorous "general systems" theorists at the institute, nonetheless it is highly unlikely that it would have been written without the stimulation and the freedom to follow one's inclinations that the institute provided. I was able to gather some original data presented here because of a grant from the American Political Science Association's The Study of Congress project, funded by the Carnegie Corporation. Indiana University also assisted with research and secretarial support. In addition, several chapters were drafted during my tenure as Research Associate, Center for International Affairs, Harvard University. Chapter 1 is a slightly revised version of the Editor's Introduction to my *The Congressional System: Notes and Readings* (Duxbury Press, 1970).

A number of individuals also contributed aid and comfort. Charles O. Jones and Randall B. Ripley read the entire manuscript; their comments were incisive, and those I have chosen to incorporate have improved the book. Others, including Richard F. Fenno, Bernard C. Hennessy, Charles F. Levine, Morris S. Ogul, and Raymond E. Wolfinger, read various sections of the text and made perceptive and useful suggestions for needed changes. I have benefited from the able research assistance of Tom Wisnowski and Peter Schneider and from the superb secretarial help of Pam Hussen, Linda Smith, and Darlyne Sowder. Finally, the editors and staff at the McGraw-Hill Book Company have provided helpful and efficient aid in producing the completed text.

Needless to say, none of these institutions or individuals bears any responsibility for what appears here. All commentary, favorable or otherwise, should be directed to the author.

Finally, I dedicate this book to the smallest system to which I belong, my family: my wife Helen and our children, Karen, Alice, Kurt, and Erik. Without their inputs of patient tolerance and affectionate encouragement, the present output would never have been realized.

Leroy N. Rieselbach

CHAPTER ONE

Congress as a Political System

The twentieth century has been described as the age of the executive. In the United States, the President has become the focal point of national politics, and reaction to this fact has taken several forms. Some observers, pleased by increased executive strength and fearful that a revived legislature would block solutions to critical problems, seek to enhance the position of the Chief Executive. Others, alarmed by what they see as the eclipse of the legislature, look to a more powerful Congress, one capable of asserting an independent influence on governmental action. Still another group, displaying a sort of "plague-on-both-your-houses" view of the political process, believes government, executive and legislative branches alike, is simply unresponsive to national needs. Regardless of one's position with respect to these sentiments, it is abundantly clear that Congress is a central participant in American politics, for virtually no federal action can be taken without the consent, explicit or implicit, of the legislative branch. This book will analyze the workings of Congress in order to promote a better understanding of the operation of the institution, to clarify its participation in the making of policy, and to assess its strengths and weaknesses.

To comprehend the contribution of Congress to the formulation of public policy, we must understand more than the formal, codified rules of procedure that define how a bill becomes a law. We also must comprehend the informal, unwritten rules of behavior that often affect the application of the formal rules. The nature and extent of the support emanating outside the legislative halls for any particular bill and the ways in which that support is brought to bear on individual legislators are relevant to any evaluation of the bill's prospects. Whether the President supports the bill and whether or not he works actively to get it out of committee or to solicit votes for it may be crucial to its passage. The fate of a bill also depends upon the activity of the congressional representatives; we should not assume that the representatives are passive occupants of positions in Congress, their behavior determined by the workings of that institution; the attitudes and values which they bring with them to the legislature influence their behavior, what they do to bring about the passage or defeat of a bill. Nor does activity end when a bill is passed, for Congress must watch to see if the bill serves its purposes; it must observe critically the administration of the bill by the executive branch. The opponents of the bill, in Congress and outside, may organize campaigns for its amendment or repeal.

In short, to understand congressional operations we must take into account not only the basic and commonly noted legislative organization and procedures, but also the influence of the informal customs (or norms) of the legislature and the nature of the relationships of those who sit in Congress to a variety of other people who are not members. In recent years, political scientists have borrowed from their colleagues in sociology and have increasingly employed a conceptual scheme, known as systems theory or systems analysis, to encompass and relate a large number of seemingly different forms of activity. Because this approach seems so admirably suited to understanding congressional politics, it will be used in this book.

THE SYSTEMS APPROACH: AN OVERVIEW[1]

The system The systems approach focuses attention on what actually occurs —on the behaviors of those who are a part of the system. Institutional structures are important not because they are formally specified but because they may affect individual behavior in ways quite unintended and unforeseen. We may define a system, in general terms, as the *patterned interactions among two or more actors (variables) which operate persistently over time to produce some form of result (output).*[2] As Easton (1965*a*, pp. 27–28) suggests, there exist

> . . . sets of interdependent actions such that a change in one part will be likely to affect what happens in another part. Included within a system will be only those actions that display a coherence and unity or constitute a whole. Modification in any part of these must have determinate repercussions on other parts. If not for this connectedness of the parts, there would be little point in identifying the behavior as a system.

[1] The ideas in this section are drawn, somewhat eclectically, from David Easton, William C. Mitchell, and through them, Talcott Parsons. See Easton, 1965*a* and 1965*b*, and Mitchell, 1962 and 1967.
[2] In most cases, the actors in a system will be individuals; but with respect to the international political system, nations are the unit of analysis, i.e., the actors.

The kinds of systems which are of interest to social scientists may vary widely: they may consist of two persons, say a husband and wife, or a very large entity, such as the social system of the United States. The important thing is that we can conceive of a set of interrelationships which endure over time and which lead to some persistent forms of activity. We will use "system" to refer to such a web of interactions.

The interacting members of the system can be described as playing *roles*. Such terminology is, in general, consistent with ordinary conversational usage. We are accustomed to talking about individuals playing the roles of husband, father, or citizen. We recognize that a "good" citizen will act in accordance with a set of "rules" which define what kinds of actions he should take and what sorts of actions he should refrain from taking. More formally, we may define role as *"the rights and duties, the normatively approved patterns of behavior" for people in given positions in society.*[3]

Role, thus defined, has both social (or structural) and cultural attributes. A position refers to a specific place in a social structure. The rights and obligations of a position tend to be formalized and codified. A number of behaviors are required or forbidden by law or by some other rules for the occupant of a particular position; engaging in such forbidden activity will lead to the invoking of formal, legal sanctions. Culturally, a role is based upon a set of norms or expectations about how the person who takes the role should act. The members of the system learn that there are some things which they are expected to do, and some things which they must refrain from doing; those who violate the norms, while not subject to formal sanctions, may be punished informally. They may be ignored, socially ostracized, or generally deprived of the rewards which successful role playing brings. In sum, the role concept encompasses a set of legal and extralegal, formal and informal, norms, expectations, values, and beliefs about how the occupant of a given position in a system should behave in a variety of social situations.[4]

A distinction must be made between role and *role behavior.* Role defines how the role player, whoever he may be, should behave. Role behavior consists of what a particular occupant of the role actually does. The behavior he exhibits may or may not correspond with how others expect him to play the role. Inappropriate behavior may occur for a number of reasons.

[3]Yinger, 1965, p. 99. For other discussions of role and "role theory," see Sarbin, 1954; Gross et al., 1958, chaps. 1–4; Stryker, 1964; and Wahlke et al., 1962, especially chap. 1. The present treatment of role draws heavily on these sources.

[4]Talcott Parsons treats the distinctions made in the previous paragraphs in a somewhat different way, using a different terminology. He suggests that to survive a system must solve a number of functional problems. One of these is the question of *integration,* the coordination of the actions of the system members. The formal rules, which allocate the rights and duties of particular positions, serve to promote system integration. A second problem is that of *pattern maintenance,* the need of the system to maintain its basic normative value patterns in order to facilitate appropriate actions. This function is akin to the definition of appropriate role behaviors by the norms and expectations which comprise a given role. In sum integration relates to a structural (formal, legal) component of the role pattern while pattern maintenance refers to the cultural (informal, extralegal) aspects of the system. For a full discussion of the Parsonian schema and complete citation of Parsons' works, see Mitchell, 1967.

In the first place, the occupant of a given role may not know what behaviors are expected of him; he may have to learn by a painful trial-and-error method. This is the process of *socialization,* the learning by the role players of the behaviors that others with whom they must deal expect them to enact. In this socialization process, the role taker may learn that there is no agreement about how he should behave (more formally, that *role consensus* does not exist). That is, the people with whom the role occupant must interact do not agree on what is proper activity for him to engage in. Second, a role player may encounter *role conflict* when he is confronted by incompatible expectations from two or more sources. That is, his role may require him to deal with two or more sets of people each of which wants him to perform different, and mutually exclusive, behaviors. Part of the socialization process involves learning how to cope with such varying expectations. Finally, the occupant of the role may be personally incapable of meeting the demands of the role. We are all familiar with people who seem temperamentally unsuited for marriage, group membership, or citizenship. On occasion, such individuals will be thrust into a particular role and their personalities will render it difficult for them to behave appropriately. For all these reasons, role behavior may depart from the norms and expectations which define the role.

This discussion of system and role suggests a first set of questions which must be answered if we are to understand the actions of any system: Who are the members of the system? What roles make up the system? How do these roles relate to one another? At any point in time, what kinds of people occupy the various roles of the system? What kinds of role behavior do they display?

Environment and inputs to the system We cannot speak of a system, and the roles included in it, without noting that some things are not part of the system. This implies further that there exists a *boundary* which separates the system from all that is outside it, its *environment.* Boundary is, at times, a difficult notion to handle. For some purposes some actors may fall within the system; for other purposes it will be appropriate to exclude them and to treat them as environmental in character. Generally, we include only those actors whom we perceive to be members of the system, i.e., the analyst is free to set somewhat arbitrarily the boundary of his system in order to suit his research purposes.

Despite this ambiguity in definition, there exist some clues as to what to include and what to exclude from a system. The expectations and norms that define the roles will be related to one another and quite distinct from the defining roles in other systems. The members of a system will interact with each other more frequently than they interact with nonmembers. They will tend to form a group displaying evidence of solidarity and group loyalty.[5] In short, though delineations of system boundaries may vary, we can often

---

[5] See Easton, 1965*a,* pp. 68–69, for a discussion of these points.

establish that some people interact sufficiently often and with sufficient intensity to justify including them and excluding others as members of a system.

Simply because some things are not included in a system but are treated as environmental does not, however, eliminate them from consideration. In the social world, few if any systems are self-sufficient, i.e., can survive without any interactions with environmental systems. To put the matter another way, systems of interest tend to be "open," not "closed." Thus, it becomes important to look at the nature of the interchanges between elements in the environment and elements within the system's boundary. The transactions directed from the environment to the system are called *inputs* to the system. These inputs are of two forms: demands and supports. Demands are defined as *requests or requirements originating outside the system that the members of the system behave in given ways.* The demands may create problems and cause stress for the system. The system may not have sufficient resources to deal with any given demand, or there may be too many demands from the environment for the system to cope with. Some demands may originate within the system [Easton (1965a, pp. 114–115) calls these "withinputs"], but their net effect is the same as that of the more numerous external demands. As the character and volume of the demands alter, the structure of the system may prove inadequate, and new processes—formal structures, new role orientations, or some combination of the two—will have to be developed if the system is to survive.

Difficulties for the system may stem from the second type of inputs, supports, as well as from demands. We may define support for a system as *the sentiments, and the actions based on those sentiments, which individuals hold toward the system.* Support may be overt, when it is reflected in specific actions directed toward the system, or covert, when it occurs at the level of attitudes and opinions. Thus support may vary from open, positive activity on behalf of the system, through passive acquiescence or indifference, to overt antagonism toward the system. Obviously, a system cannot survive unchanged if its support falls below some minimum level. If people no longer care enough about its continued existence or openly seek its destruction, the system will be in jeopardy. Support may also, following Easton, be described as diffuse or specific. The former refers to general feelings of attachment to the system; the latter pertains to favorable responses to the system which stem from particular actions (outputs) that the system takes.[6]

The notion of inputs from the environment suggests a second set of questions that must be dealt with in the analysis of any system: Who are the major actors in the environment of the system? What kinds of demands do these environmental actors make on the system? What sorts of supports for

---

[6]For a full treatment of these points, see Easton, 1965b, pp. 153–170.

the system are forthcoming from these environmental actors? What effects do these inputs have on the character of the system itself?

System outputs Internal adaptation is one way in which systems reduce the stress placed upon them by inputs from the environment. Perhaps a more common way is to produce *outputs* that satisfy the demands made upon the system, or produce adequate levels of support for the system, or both. By outputs, we mean *these end results or products which the system generates.* Referring to the total political system, Easton refers to the outputs as "the authoritative allocations of values" for society; for less inclusive systems outputs would include decisions and articulated policies which the system announces and acts upon. [7]

Outputs, like inputs, are exchanges across the boundary of the system between members of the system and actors in the environment. Outputs may serve to satisfy the demands made upon the system and thus facilitate the system's survival by reducing the level of demands upon it. Outputs may also serve to produce support. A system decision that allocates rewards—money, favor, or prestige—to some set of individuals or groups may win, in return, the support of the recipients. Outputs which provide sufficient rewards for enough actors in the environment of the system may engender a good deal of support for the system. In addition, diffuse support may linger on long after the specific output has ceased to be rewarding. It is clear that generation of support will enhance the survival potential of any system.

Any system, then, will seek, through production of outputs, to satisfy the demands made upon it and to create support for itself. To understand a particular system, we need to inquire about the kinds of outputs it produces, the effect of these outputs on demand and support levels, and the consequences of these outputs for the system itself. These sorts of inquiries constitute a third set of questions which the analysis of any system must seek to answer.

Feedback Just as inputs from the environment may affect the internal organization and activity of a system, the outputs from the system may well influence the actors in the environment. A decision that a system makes may satisfy some external actors and produce support; it thus permits the system to take additional actions on the basis of that support. A certain policy enactment may displease groups in the environment, stimulating them to make new demands or to press old demands more vigorously. This is the *feedback cycle,* or loop, *by which future inputs to the system reflect environmental reactions to past outputs.* What the system does presently may influence, via the feedback process, what the system will be subsequently required to face. [8]

[7] See Easton, 1965*b*, pp. 343–362, for a more detailed discussion of outputs.
[8] On feedback, see Easton, 1965*a* and 1965*b*, and Deutsch, 1963, especially pp. 88–97.

The distinction between negative (self-correcting) and positive (self-reinforcing) feedback should be noted. In the former, the responses or the new inputs to the system suggest negative reactions to old outputs, and the system will attempt to adjust its behavior to take these critical reactions into account. To cite a simple example, a national system that embarks on a military build-up may stimulate countermobilization from another country, and upon learning of this, may cease its production of armaments rather than engage in an arms race which it feels it cannot win. The information that is "fed back" to the system, in this instance, produces a change in the system's outputs. Positive feedback, on the other hand, serves to reinforce the system's commitment to its present outputs by communicating the success of present policy. If a weapons development program does not generate counterdevelopments on the part of other nations, the first nation may decide to step up its construction of weapons in the hope of gaining a permanent military advantage vis-a-vis other countries.

The feedback process adds a dynamic element to the systems approach. Because a system seeks to survive in its environment, it will respond to external changes about which it learns through feedback. Its response may be a restructuring of the system itself, or it may take the form of an altered pattern of outputs. These new outputs may change the environmental conditions, thus stimulating still further changes in the type and intensity of the demands and supports which reach the system. Thus a continuous cycle of adaptation and readjustment is established, which, over time, may lead to fundamental changes in the character and outputs of a system. If the feedback process fails, a system may be unable to make functional responses to its environment and may be unable to survive.

Feedback, in short, refers to what a system learns about the reactions of others to its outputs. To understand any system fully, we must attempt to answer a fourth and final set of questions: What is the environmental response to system outputs? What changes in the inputs (demands and supports) to the system does this response engender? How accurately does the system perceive these environmental changes? What alterations in the system does the new input pattern require?

Summary This section has sketched out, in brief and oversimplified form, the basic elements of the systems approach to the analysis of social units. A system, characterized by a particular set of formal structures and role orientations, interacts with elements in its environment. It receives inputs (demands and supports), processes them in some fashion, and produces outputs. The effects of these outputs on the relevant actors in the environment are returned to the system as new inputs through the feedback process. The interrelationships among these four sets of factors—system, inputs, outputs, and feedback—are summarized diagrammatically in Figure 1-1.

Before we move on to look at the congressional system specifically, a note

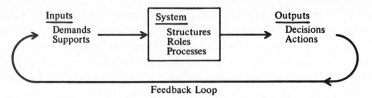

FIGURE 1-1   Schematic model of a system and its environment

of caution needs to be interjected. This has indeed been an oversimplified view of system analysis. We have talked as if there were but a single system operating in an undifferentiated environment. In fact, this is not the case. What for one set of purposes may appear to be unified system may appear, from another perspective, to be only a part, a *subsystem,* of a larger system. In this book, we will treat Congress as the system upon which we will focus our attention. If, however, we were to look at the entire American political system, we would discover that the legislature is merely one subsystem and would have to be considered along with the presidential (or executive), judicial, popular, and other subsystems of the total governmental system. Similarly, when we look at the congressional system, we will find that a number of important subsystems exist within it. The committees of Congress can be treated as distinct subsystems of the legislative system as can the party organizations.

Each of these subsystems can be analyzed as total systems, and from that perspective, we discover distinctive structures and role patterns peculiar to each committee or party. Boundary interchanges—inputs and outputs— occur between subsystems. Put another way, what is internal to a total system is environmental to some subsystem; what is a total system from one point of view may be a subsystem from another point of view. Thus, to repeat a point made earlier, every system is the analytical creation of the researcher who studies it. The true test of any formulation is, of course, the extent to which it fosters understanding of that part of social life under investigation.

THE CONGRESSIONAL SYSTEM

As the foregoing suggests, the systems framework seems well suited for an analysis of the United States Congress. This approach will permit us to see, as a whole, the entire range of activities in which the legislature engages. It will allow us to integrate a vast amount of recent research into as complete a picture of legislative politics as is possible. The purpose of the present section is to explain how the concepts outlined in the first half of this chapter apply to Congress.

The congressional system For present purposes, it seems useful to define the congressional system as including *all the legislators, the senators, the representatives, and their supporting individual and committee staff facilities.* Other important actors such as the executive branch, the courts, and the public will be treated as environmental factors. Drawing the boundary of the legislative system in this way is consistent with the constitutional separation of powers, which defines the independent but overlapping powers of the three branches of government. In addition, it is reasonable to believe that the members of the legislative system interact with one another more frequently than they interact with those who have been excluded from the system. Each of the environmental actors engages in substantial activity that is nonlegislative in character; members of Congress and their staff associates are involved in legislative business almost exclusively. Moreover, there exist a number of specialized norms of behavior that apply directly to those who are identified as members of the congressional system and not to actors in the environment, except as these latter take the norms into account in dealing with the legislature. Finally, in keeping with the definition of a system as the "patterned interactions among actors," there are visible regularities in the interactions among the actors of Congress. The formal rules (for example, the regulation of debate in the House and the absence of such regulation in the Senate), the informal norms (seniority, for example), the operation of particular committees, the activities of the political parties and other features of Congress influence outputs in predictable (or at least in understandable) ways. The parties hold their adherents in line in some circumstances but not in others; committee action reflects unwritten decision rules. Other participants in the congressional process are important, but the interactions among congressmen and their staffs are sufficiently distinctive to justify treating the legislature as a political system, with any remaining actors considered as environmental in character.

In examining the congressional system, it is important to know something about its members. Since the behavior of legislators, like that of other people, reflects their life experiences, it is instructive to see what kinds of people are chosen to serve in Washington. The ease with which a legislator learns (is socialized into) legislative roles and the way he performs those roles may be related to what he is when he arrives in the nation's capital. One facet of these life experiences can be gauged by looking at the *social background characteristics* of the congressman. His family experiences—being raised in an urban or a rural setting, in a rich or poor family, in a particular region of the country; his educational attainments; his occupational choices; the socioeconomic status which he has achieved; the church which he has attended—these and a variety of other background attributes may shape the way in which a senator or representative approaches his job in Congress.[9] Though we have virtually

[9]For an example of how social background characteristics are related to a congressman's roll call vote, see Rieselbach, 1966, chap. 3, pp. 61–82.

no data to confirm our speculations, it nonetheless seems safe to suggest that a representative's *personality,* presumably formed prior to his election, will influence the manner in which he acts in the legislature. Common sense and casual observation permit us to recognize the introverted or shy person, the abrasive or aggressive type, or the rigid, unyielding individual; and it should come as no surprise that different personality types should differ in the ways in which they are able to fit into the roles that constitute the legislative system.[10]

A third feature of the life experiences that may influence a congressman's legislative performance is his *political background,* i.e., his previous involvement in politics. Has he endured the strains of many prior campaigns or is he a relative newcomer to electoral politics? Did he win his congressional contest by a wide or by a narrow margin? If he has had prior exposure to politics, was it in an executive or in a legislative capacity? (Matthews, 1960, pp. 102–117). Finally, a lawmaker's behavior may reflect the nature of the constituency he *represents.* Members from Eastern, urban, relatively poor districts may well behave, in committee and on the floor, in a fashion quite different from that of men from Southern, suburban, relatively well-to-do constituencies (Froman, 1963).

The roles of a system, we noted earlier, have both structural and normative (or cultural) features. The roles of the congressional system reflect bicameralism, the central structural feature of the legislature. There are two central distinctions between the Senate and the House of Representatives that undoubtedly affect the roles played by the members of the two chambers.[11] First and most obvious is the simple matter of size—the House has more than four times as many members as the Senate. Thus, the Senate can conduct its business much less formally than the House; with only 100 members, it requires less formal, hierarchical organization and can provide freer opportunities for individual participation in committee work and debate on the floor. It also allows more senators to gain access to political power. These same features, in turn, lead to a much slower form of activity. The House, on the other hand, depends on formal, centralized organization, minimal individual participation, and less-even distribution of authority to expedite its business. Only in this more organized fashion can a body of 435 members process all the matters which come before it.

The second major difference between the two chambers lies in the types of constituencies the members represent. Senators are elected from entire, often socially heterogeneous states; representatives tend to be selected in smaller, more homogeneous congressional districts. The wider, more diverse

---

[10]Surely the conspicuous differences in style and behavior between Senate Democratic leader Lyndon B. Johnson and his successor, Mike Mansfield, reflect the effects of personality differences. For additional evidence on the relevance of personality, see Huitt, 1961*b.*

[11]Froman (1967) presents a useful summary of the distinctions between the two houses of Congress. See pp. 5–15, especially the summary table at p. 7.

constituencies of the senators tend to make them more visible (they have more constituents, get more attention from the media of communication, develop more prestige) and more liberal (they often have large, urban, liberal-oriented groups of constituents upon whom their reelection may depend). These differences in size and type of constituency represented, and the consequences that flow from the differences, in all probability create differing sets of expectations about how senators and representatives should act.

Within each house, two subsystems command immediate attention: the committees and the party organizations. The former are the main decentralizing force in Congress; each is an independent center of power that competing sources of power can control only with great difficulty. Each committee has its own specific jurisdiction and its own rules of procedure. The chairman, chosen under the seniority rule on the basis of the length of time he has served on the committee, is the most important single figure on the committee; in some cases he rules over the group with nearly autocratic powers. The division of most committees into permanent subcommittees, each of which is to some extent the creature of its chairman, serves to fragment power still further. In sum, the committees divide, and subdivide, authority within the congressional system.

Since the bulk of legislative work is performed within committee, and since each legislator has one or more committee assignments, each member of Congress will develop a role orientation toward committee work.[12] He will decide, if he obtains a committee-leadership position, how he will conduct himself as chairman or ranking minority member of a committee or subcommittee. He will choose whether to devote a substantial amount of his time to mastery of the matters that come before the committee or whether to expend his energies elsewhere. Thus, it may be possible to distinguish *committee leadership, committee specialist,* and *committee indifferent* orientations toward committee work. The committee leader attempts to run his panel from a formal leadership position; the specialist devotes much energy to mastery of the details of the committee's work, in hopes of achieving leader-

[12]Technically speaking, each legislator plays the "role" (singular) of senator or representative. The total role, or role set, is the sum of a set of "role orientations" toward the set of "significant others" with whom the role occupant must deal. Thus the member of Congress will have orientations toward other members of the system—as a member of his party and of one or more committees, for instance—and toward the relevant actors in the environment. In his committee, for example, a representative who has risen to the position of chairman will face his fellow members as a leader; the formal rules of the committee as well as the informal expectations about leadership will shape how leader and followers interact. Similarly, other committee members, because of their thorough knowledge of the substance of committee business, will be recognized as experts and, as such, will have characteristic patterns of interaction with others on the committee. Limitations of space preclude detailed spelling out of all the potential role orientations, but the reader should remember that when for purposes of explication we refer to "roles" or "orientations," the reference is to the complex relationships which may exist between a legislator and some other(s) with respect to some particular segment of his total role as a member of Congress. Nor are the orientations necessarily the product of conscious choice; they may result from simple acceptance of "the way things are done." Nonetheless, the role perspective seeks to understand the various ways in which role players relate to those with whom they must deal.

ship at some point in the future; the indifferent does not concern himself with committee work beyond the minimum, preferring to expend his efforts on other facets of congressional activity.

What the committees rend asunder, the political parties can only partially put together. The parties employ floor leaders, whip organizations, caucuses, and policy committees in an effort to maximize the cohesion of their respective members. And while party may be the most important single influence on an individual lawmaker's behavior, rarely do the parties even approach unity; more often, legislative battles are fought between bipartisan coalitions. In the last analysis, party lacks the sanctions required to enforce discipline among its members. Congressmen may, willingly or unwillingly, defer to the wishes of those outside the legislative system rather than fall into line with party. In any case, the senator or representative will have to devise ways to relate to his party. Jewell and Patterson have identified three basic orientations toward party: the *party man* who "conceives of his job as supporting the program of his party or its leaders, regardless of his own judgments or the consequences of party loyalty"; the *maverick,* who operates independently of his party, often supporting the opposition; and the *party indifferent,* for whom party is of little significance.[13]

Whatever of a personal character they bring with them to Congress, however they choose to relate to the committee and party subsystems, legislators must operate within the framework of a formal set of rules and procedures. Among other things, these rules define the jurisdictions of the committees; the way in which a bill may move from committee to the floor, including its passage through the House Rules Committee; the fashion in which the proposed law may be debated and voted upon; and the mode of resolving differences between the versions of the bill passed by the two chambers.[14] The roles which the congressmen assume, then, will be shaped to an important degree by the formal rules; these rules provide the bounds beyond which legislative behavior cannot go. It should be noted that the rules profoundly influence the way in which Congress works. That is, rules are not neutral in their effects on legislative behavior. In general, the rules favor those who support the status quo; they make more difficult the task of those lawmakers who propose changes and facilitate the job of those who resist changes. Role orientations toward the rules, then, may reflect whether the legislators seek to bring about or to inhibit change.

There are other, informal restraints that may limit the freedom of action within the legislative halls. White has characterized the Senate as a "club" with a set of norms, or folkways, which define the conditions of membership.[15]

---

[13]Jewell and Patterson, 1966, p. 385. This work follows the lead of the pioneering study of state legislatures by Wahlke and associates (1962).

[14]See Riddick, 1949, for the classic exposition of the rules and procedures of Congress.

[15]White, 1956, pp. 81–94. See also Matthews, 1960, pp. 102–117. For a critique of this position, see Polsby, 1964, pp. 32–43, and 1969.

Conformity to these norms—dealing with legislative business and one's legislative colleagues in appropriate fashion—will speed a lawmaker's rise to positions of influence and enhance his legislative effectiveness. The specifics of these folkways will be discussed later; for the present, the emphasis is upon Senate and House mores that impose additional constraints on individual member behavior. There may be risks to the congressman if he chooses to run counter to the norms: he will have to decide whether to be a *conformist* or a *nonconformist* with respect to the unwritten rules of the chamber.

To review, we have defined the congressional system to include all the senators and representatives and their supporting staffs. The roles that these men and women play as congressmen, roles that may differ because of differences between the two houses, will reflect the life experiences of the members as well as the two major subsystems of Congress—the committees and the parties. In addition, the formal rules and the informal norms will contribute to the shape of the role patterns that individual legislators develop. Role orientations may contain conflicting elements, i.e., role conflict may be present. A representative may be unable to play out all his role orientations simultaneously. His role as a committee specialist may lead him to conclusions contrary to those reached by the party leadership and thus make it impossible for him to assume his preferred posture of loyal party man.[16] The series of chapters which make up Part I of this book will explore in some detail these elements of the legislative system.

Inputs to the congressional system If a congressman must, as the above implies, adjust his behavior to the realities of the internal workings of the legislative system, he must also learn to deal with the inputs to that system which emanate in the environment. These inputs—demands upon and support for the congressional system—come from four major sources: the President and the executive branch, the interest (or pressure) groups, the courts, and the public. With respect to public policy, the first two sources tend to be more persistent and reflect, to some degree, the actions of all four. There will also be "withinputs," that is, demands arising within the legislative system itself. Many of these will be the transmission of demands originating in the environment, and in any event, the congressional system will process all demands in similar fashion. Demands tend to be for three major types of congressional action: laws or policy decisions, supervision of the activities of the executive branch, and representation of the public. Supports tend to result from these same categories of action. These outputs will be discussed in the next section.

---

[16]In the language of role analysis, two types of role conflict may occur: interrole and intrarole conflict. The former refers to incompatible expectations emanating from two conflicting role orientations; the example of committee-party conflict is of this sort. Intrarole conflict occurs when inconsistent demands occur within a single role orientation, as when a committee leader is urged to follow one course by the experts on his committee and to adhere to another course by the rank-and-file membership.

Without doubt, the most important single source of demands upon, and thus the chief cause of stress for, the congressional system is the executive branch—the President and the multitude of agencies under his at least nominal control. The Chief Executive towers over American politics; he functions at the center of the political stage. Congress, like other parts of the overall political system, plays its part in support of the star. To a very great extent, the legislature responds to initiatives taken by the President. He sets the agenda of Congress; the great bulk of congressional activity revolves around proposals sent down from the White House. Congress may not accept what the President suggests; it may amend, modify, or even veto his ideas, but it cannot escape the necessity of responding to his suggestions.

In addition to determining the topics on which congressional deliberation will focus, the President may well intervene in the legislative process in an effort to influence the outcome of those deliberations. He has at his disposal a variety of techniques with which he can try to affect the behavior of individual senators and representatives. He can employ positive inducements; he can do favors in the hopes of eliciting favorable responses from the legislators. He can also use, or threaten to use, sanctions to achieve the same result. In short, the President will profoundly influence the subjects with which Congress deals and the manner in which it deals with them. [17]

It would be a serious mistake to treat the President as if he is, or speaks for, the entire executive branch simply because he bears the responsibility, as "chief administrator," for supervision of the executive establishment. The organization chart which places him neatly at the pinnacle of the executive hierarchy is not realistic; in fact, bureaucratic agencies strive for, and often attain, a good deal of independence from presidential control. Their requests for legislative action may differ markedly from the desires of the President. Frequently, for example, agencies lose out during the preparation of the executive budget; they dislike the treatment given to their proposals for new programs and for funds to support existing programs. In such instances, they take their case, on appeal in a sense, to Congress. To the degree that the agencies find legislative allies, they may form relationships with Congress, or specifically, with the congressional committees which handle their requests, that are far more intimate than those they establish within the executive branch. [18]

The roles which the legislators assume, then, will have to relate to the executive branch. A senator or representative will have to decide whether to be *executive-oriented* or *legislative-oriented,* that is, he will have to decide whether he will facilitate or resist the initiatives of the President or of the executive branch agencies and bureaus. The executive-oriented legislator

[17]See, for an overview of some means of Presidential involvement with Congress, Rieselbach, 1966, pp. 181–192.
[18]For examples of the intricacies of these executive-legislative relationships, see Freeman, 1965, and Maass, 1951.

supports executive demands; the legislative-oriented lawmaker opposes them. Where the executive agencies disagree among themselves, the congressman may have to choose sides in an intraexecutive squabble. He may develop an *agency-oriented* role in which he acts as the spokesman for, and defender of, the interests of a particular agency, even if those interests run counter to the notions of the President. On the other hand, he may choose a *President-oriented* role in which he seeks to assist the President in his efforts to control the executive agencies. If the congressman is legislative-oriented, he will prefer to impose legislative priorities on both the Chief Executive and the agencies.[19]

A second persistent source of inputs to the legislative system from the environment comes from the lobbyists. Hundreds of groups, including business, labor, agriculture, the professions, and a nearly infinite variety of subdivisions within these broad categories hire representatives in Washington whose job it is to try to protect the interests of their employers. These interests usually lead to efforts to encourage the enactment of beneficial legislation and to act to block passage of bills seen as detrimental to group goals. The lobbyist seeks to maintain contact with, or access to, a large number of congressmen, and on occasion to persuade them of the wisdom of the group's position. The classic image of interest-group activity is one of unremitting pressure on lawmakers—threats of electoral reprisals, entertainment, and even bribery—in an attempt to command support for the position of the group. Current research suggests that, at present, interest-group activities include far greater efforts than have been employed in the past to earn the goodwill of legislators (e.g., Milbrath, 1963). Far from relying exclusively on blatant pressure, the lobbyists provide needed information to lawmakers otherwise dependent on executive branch sources; they help recruit support in response to legislative initiatives; and they seek to develop open channels of communication with congressmen. The lobbyist hopes to be able to approach the legislator in an atmosphere of trust and mutual confidence so that he can make a persuasive case on the merits of the issue. He feels that such tactful techniques, rather than threats, are likely to make him most effective.

Whatever the manner of group-legislator contact, the senators and representatives have to learn to live in the constant presence of lobbyists. A study of congressional role orientations will have to take account of this virtual omnipresence. Wahlke and his associates have suggested a typology of role orientations toward interest groups which, though developed as a result of investigations at the state level, should apply to the national legislature as well (Wahlke et al., 1962, pp. 311–342). Lawmakers may be classified as pressure-group *facilitators, resisters,* or *neutrals.* The facilitator is a man who is informed about and favorably disposed toward interest groups and their activities; the resister, while knowledgeable, is generally unsympathetic

---

[19] This role pattern departs only slightly from that suggested by Jewell and Patterson, 1966.

to lobbyists and lobbying. The neutral, as the label implies, is relatively uncon-cerned about pressure groups or has no consistent posture either for or against them. Role behavior may reflect these orientations.

A second set of environmental inputs to Congress may be described as intermittent because they do not impinge upon legislative formulation of public policy to the same degree as do those from the executive branch and those from the lobbyists. One source of these inputs is the public—the consti-tuents who send the lawmakers to Washington. It may seem inappropriate to characterize congressman-constituent relations as intermittent in the light of the vast amount of time and effort which legislative offices devote to hand-ling requests which originate in the individual districts, but the fact is that, especially with regard to policy, Congress is not very salient to much of the electorate (Stokes and Miller, 1962). In short, legislators seldom get policy mandates from their constituents.

This does not mean that the "folks back home" are unimportant to their representatives. On the contrary, the congressmen, perhaps because they believe that they operate in public to a much greater extent than they in fact do, struggle to ascertain the views of their constituents. They scan the local press, meet with residents of their states and districts whenever possible, conduct public opinion polls, and keep tabs on the positions expressed in that issue-oriented mail which they do receive. However, the messages that reach them are in all likelihood atypical of actual district sentiment, for typical citizens do not seem inclined to communicate with their representatives. Thus the congressman may well not be accurately informed about the true nature of constituency opinion.

The heavy demand from constituents for services is considerably more time-consuming to the legislator and his staff. Residents of local communities have problems that they believe command the attention of their representa-tives. They need someone to intercede with the bureaucracy. Some desire federal employment. Others want copies of government publications sent to them. Congressional offices, with reelection prospects of their principals firmly in mind, strive to satisfy all such requests. And indeed the importance of this communication between a citizen and his government can hardly be overstressed.

These matters will be discussed in subsequent chapters, but the important point is that each lawmaker will have to decide how he will relate himself and his activities to the geographical unit he represents. In the terminology employed here, his role as legislator will have to include orientations toward his constituency. Three orientational patterns seem possible.[20] The congress-man may focus his attention on his constituency alone, that is, he may be *district- (or state-) oriented.* This posture suggests that the lawmaker sees

---

[20] This discussion follows Jewell and Patterson, 1966, p. 385, which, in turn, is an adaptation of Wahlke et al., 1962, pp. 287–310.

his task as that of promoting the interests of the geographical area from which he was elected. Alternatively, the congressman may adopt a *nation-oriented* position; he may choose to approach policy problems from a national rather than a local perspective. Finally, the legislator may assume an in-between stance, he may be *district- (state-) nation-oriented,* in which case he will give roughly equal consideration to local and national interests.

A final and more clearly intermittent source of inputs to the legislative system is the judiciary, particularly the Supreme Court. While the vast bulk of judicial activity does not concern Congress, occasionally a court decision pertains directly to some congressional action. This direct relation of the Court to Congress has been the case more frequently in recent years as the courts have increasingly taken on a policy-making function. For instance, it is clear that the decisions in *Brown v. Board of Education of Topeka* and subsequent cases enunciated a policy of educational integration that was well within the power of Congress to enact. In other instances, the courts have overturned congressional decisions. Whether or not court action makes policy or inhibits legislative decision making, from time to time the two branches have come into open conflict; and individual legislators must decide how they will react when such clashes come.[21]

We may distinguish two broad role orientations to such interbranch antagonism. The legislator may assume either a *procourt* or *anticourt* position. The former posture reflects a disposition to accept court rulings as binding on the legislature— to see the court as in a sense the final arbiter of constitutional issues. The anticourt stance is indicative of a feeling that congressional action should prevail in the event of conflict with the judiciary. The latter orientation may lead to legislative efforts to overturn court decisions.

In discussing inputs we have concentrated upon demands. This concentration, however, should not blind us to an awareness that a system— the congressional system or any other—cannot survive unless a sufficient level of support from the environment is forthcoming. Supports are sentiments and actions in the affirmative and in the negative, which actors in the environment display toward the system. While there exists very little data about the supports directed toward the congressional system, it is clear that each set of environmental actors that makes demands upon the legislature also contributes to the continued existence of Congress by providing support for it. The President and the executive agencies work with, and through, the legislature; they do not attempt to subvert it. The President is quick to praise the legislative branch when it complies with his requests; the bureaucrats seek to cultivate cooperative relationships with legislators. Similarly, the interest groups support Congress; they provide information and other services to overburdened lawmakers; they respond to requests for aid from a congressman

---

[21] On the Court as policymaker, see Dahl, 1958. Murphy, 1962, illustrates the nature of conflict between the legislative and the judicial branches.

at least as often as they try to influence him. The public continues to consider Congress as a legitimate institution—that is, the public gives it diffuse support; and some segments of the populace may well give specific support in response to particular legislative enactments. Finally, support is also forthcoming from the courts. The Supreme Court upholds legislative actions far more frequently than it overturns them. The justices search for congressional "intent" in dealing with the constitutionality of statutes; their aim is to interpret a law in keeping with the purposes that prompted the lawmakers initially to pass it. On the whole, the congressional system receives sufficient support so that its place in the larger political system remains unchallenged.

In review, the congressional system receives inputs of demands and supports across its boundaries from four major sets of actors in its environment: the President and the executive agencies, interest groups, the public, and the courts. The former two tend to be more immediately involved in legislative policy making than the latter pair. The legislative role will include orientations toward these important environmental forces as well as toward the internal structural characteristics of the congressional system. The chapters of Part 2 of this book will explore the nature of these inputs to Congress and their effects on legislative activity.

Congressional outputs   A system, as we noted earlier, exists for some purpose; some result is associated with the interactions among the system members and between the members and the actors in the environment. These results, or outputs, are in a sense the products of the inputs and the internal systemic processes for converting inputs into outputs. Thus any examination of the congressional system must include some analysis of the functions that the legislature performs. There are three major output activities of Congress which will concern us here.

The first of these is the *lawmaking* function; Congress is expected to play its part in the enactment of public policy. Almost every policy initiative, major or minor, that the national government takes requires a congressional grant of authority, appropriation of funds, or both. Medicare, the government-financed health insurance plan for citizens over sixty-five years of age, exists only because Congress defined its coverage and enacted the tax to pay its benefits; public transportation is desegregated only because the national legislature declared it a crime to segregate transportation facilities in interstate commerce; the United States engages in a foreign-aid program only as a result of congressional funding and only under conditions specified by law. Only the few decisions that are taken by the President under his powers as Commander in Chief escape the necessity for congressional action; all others are scrutinized by Congress.

In addition to making policy choices, the lawmaking activities of Congress perform several useful subsidiary functions. Mere action by the legislature lends legitimacy to governmental decisions; a policy which Congress has examined and debated is more likely to be believed to be appropriate for the nation to pursue. Legislative consideration also contributes to the process of consensus building and conflict resolution. The decisions of Congress emerge from a welter of conflicting interests after each concerned group will have made some concessions to the other interested parties. Thus the policy is likely to embody a compromise that provides some satisfactions for many of those involved and that helps to remove the subject from the area of most intense conflict.

Wahlke and his associates, in their study of four state legislatures, discovered five role orientations toward the lawmaking function that apply to the national legislature as well (Wahlke et al., 1962, pp. 245–266). The first of these purposive orientations, as they have been called, is that of the *ritualist,* the legislator who orients himself "to the job of lawmaking in terms of the parliamentary rules and routines, rather than in terms of legislative functions . . . " (Wahlke et al., p. 247). The ritualist prefers going through the appropriate motions to achieving specific goals. A second orientation, that of the *tribune*, aims at promoting the wishes and desires of the populace; the tribune sees himself as responding to, and acting as spokesman for, public needs. A third posture, that of the *inventor,* seeks to find new solutions to the substantive issues confronting the country; as the name implies, the inventor is concerned with ideas more than with the process by which ideas become policies. In sharp contrast is the *broker,* the lawmaker who strives to find the acceptable solution; he practices the "art of the possible" and tries to compromise and coordinate diverse legislative demands. The fifth and final purposive role orientation is that of the *opportunist,* whose interests are in personal advancement and are thus nonlegislative and whose legislative activities are thereby limited to the barest minimum. Each representative will approach his lawmaking task from one or another of these perspectives.

A second congressional function or output activity is the exercise of *oversight,* or control over the agencies of the executive branch. Congress must see whether its enactments are accomplishing their intended purposes, whether they are efficiently administered, and whether additional legislative action is needed. Therefore, the legislature engages in surveillance over the executive agencies. Investigations permit formal oversight; the bureaucrats testify, and the congressmen may question them closely about the conduct of agency affairs. More often, supervision is carried out informally through consultations between legislators and their staffs on the one hand and agency personnel on the other. In addition, legislation may require the agency to submit periodic reports on its activities to the appropriate congressional committee. Through this surveillance, Congress hopes efficiently to examine current bureaucratic operations.[22]

Oversight can focus on several topics. The most important congressional

---

[22] For an overview of the oversight function, see Harris, 1965.

control is the authority to pass on the budget. While fiscal decisions are clearly policy decisions, for each set of authorization-appropriation choices determines what programs will operate and at what level they will do so, the budget also provides interested legislators with a major opportunity to examine agency performance. At budget hearings, when the agency men request funds for new programs as well as those to continue old ones, they must justify their use of the appropriations that were granted in the past. They must be prepared to defend past policies and to demonstrate past efficiencies. Hearings thus provide the congressmen with the chance to probe executive activities. Oversight also focuses on the personnel who conduct these executive activities. The Constitution requires the Senate to give "advice and consent" to presidential nominees for major administrative posts, and the upper house can use its right of confirmation as a lever to extract commitments for certain future agency or departmental behavior from the appointee. Similarly, the legislature as a whole, through its power to enact civil service requirements, can set the standards for federal employment. By determining who is eligible for government service, Congress can, at least indirectly, influence the direction and the quality of agency performance. Much oversight seems to be carried out informally; bureaucrats contact the appropriate congressmen and gain prior approval for the administrative actions that they propose to take.

Thus, each individual legislator must ask himself how he will conduct his oversight activities. If the congressman is *executive-oriented,* he will see his task as assisting the President in keeping control over the executive bureaus; if he is *legislative-oriented,* he will seek to impose congressional control over agency performance. The lawmaker may, in addition, be *agency-oriented* and will attempt to exert legislative control over a particular agency or seek to protect the administrative unit from congressional intervention in its affairs. Finally, we may distinguish an *oversight-indifferent* position, the occupant of which minimizes the importance of the control function, choosing instead to spend his time on other legislative duties.

The third major aspect of the congressional job is representing the citizenry of the nation; thus we may talk about the *representative* function of Congress. It is clear that to some degree the lawmaker is expected to act on behalf of his constituents, and to seek to promote their interests. We have already noted the very heavy demands from those in the legislator's state or district for him to perform services, as well as the less intensive policy opinions which those "back home" express. We suggested earlier that the congressman was faced with a choice as to which geographical unit—the state or district, the nation, or some combination of the two—will receive the focus of his attention. But such a choice is only half his problem; he must also decide how, in what style, he will represent his constituents. Is he bound to follow their views or is he free to follow his own judgment? How is he to resolve his dilemma when constituent opinion conflicts with his personal opinion?

In their study of four state legislatures, Wahlke et al. (1962, pp. 267–286) identified three basic orientations toward the legislative task of representation; these three orientations probably are found in Congress as well. First, the congressman may adopt a *trustee* stance, seeing himself as free to follow the dictates of his own conscience and to act in keeping with his own notions of what is appropriate behavior. The trustee interprets his election as a vote of confidence in his judgment, not as a set of instructions to be followed slavishly. At the other extreme is the *delegate,* who believes his obligation is to adhere to the desires of his constituents as closely as he possibly can. In the event of a conflict, the delegate is prepared to surrender his personal views in order to act in accordance with the attitudes of those to whom he owes his election. It is possible, of course, to combine these two orientations and, thus, to assume a posture which has been called the *politico.* The politico will oscillate between the trustee and delegate positions according to political conditions. He will take the former position when he feels that the political risks are minimal and the latter position when he feels that a disregard for district sentiment may endanger his political future. In many instances no conflict will arise, for the preferences of congressman and constituents will coincide. In such a case, the legislator need not make the painful choice between his own views and those of the citizens he represents.

There is another facet to the representational role of the congressman. He may not feel that it is sufficient to take the positions of those whom he represents into account when he makes his choices. He may, in addition, feel an obligation to explain his behavior to the residents of his district—that is, to educate them about congressional activities. Thus, through the use of "public relations" devices—newsletters, special mailings, radio and television tapes, appearances in the district, and others—he seeks to justify his legislative performance. The indirect effect of this contact may be a stimulation of communication from the district, so that as a result, he may be better able to gauge local sentiments and thus to make the choice among his representational orientations a more rational one. Moreover, by stimulating public opinion and by focusing it on particular topics and in particular ways, a lawmaker hopes to generate pressure for new policies. In this fashion, he may be able to use the electorate to further his own policy preferences.[23] In any event, much congressional effort goes into constituency relations.

In sum, senators and representatives as members of the congressional system produce outputs of a legislative, oversight, and representational kind; and they must assume role orientations toward each of these activities. Here, as in other aspects of their jobs, they may encounter role conflict, i.e., it may be difficult, if not impossible, for them to play all their parts with equal effectiveness. There may not be time or staff resources available to be both a

---

[23]The hearings on the Indochina war conducted by Senate Foreign Relations Committee Chairman William Fulbright and the outspoken criticism by a number of senators of the proposed deployment of an antiballistic missile system seen to have been motivated, in part at least, by a desire to mobilize public opinion against the nation's foreign policies and thus to compel new policy departures.

policy-making specialist and an efficient overseer; similarly the necessities of policy making and representation may present choices—whether to remain in Washington or to return to the home district—where one alternative must be selected to the exclusion of the other. The lawmakers probably cannot perform all three output functions effectively at the same time and among congressmen different patterns of concern and resulting activity will emerge. Part 3 of this study will examine the output activities of Congress and the problems these activities create for the legislative system.

Feedback While no chapters of this book will deal exclusively with feedback—the process by which present system outputs influence future inputs—it is essential to remember that feedback does affect many congressional operations. What Congress does today will affect what it will be asked to do tomorrow. Outputs that satisfy demands will produce support; those that do not will cause dissatisfaction and diminished support. Failure to deal with national crises may lead the public elsewhere for solutions to major problems. Inability to respond to the President's program may enhance his stature and his domination of the total governmental system. Unwillingness to act upon public or interest-group requests may lead to withdrawal of support and to increased sentiment for presidential leadership.

Total output failure, however, is unlikely; more probable is a mixed record of partial successes and failures. Congress usually manages to satisfy the demands upon it to some degree. Still, the feedback cycle operates. Passage of a medical insurance program for people over sixty-five years of age produces demands for increased benefits or for extension of the plan to the entire population, or at least to some larger segment of it. These new demands may come from the executive branch, the pressure groups, the public, or some combination of the three. If the legislature does not respond to some demands, those making the requests will search for new ways to compel congressional compliance. Thus, while the substance of the demands may remain unchanged, the tactics utilized in support of them may alter markedly and create new sorts of stressful situations for Congress.

Thus, in Parts 2 and 3, understanding of feedback is crucial to the discussion of inputs and outputs. The demands upon and support for Congress that come from the executive branch, the pressure groups, the courts, and the public will reflect earlier congressional activity. The legislative, oversight, and representational outputs of Congress will be necessary, in part, because of earlier decisions and in turn will stimulate problems which will have to be faced subsequently. In short, though we may not have the occasion repeatedly to mention it, feedback is virtually omnipresent and our understanding of the congressional system cannot proceed at any length without taking it into account. Underlying much congressional behavior will be calculations about how others will react to that behavior and what such reactions will entail in the future.

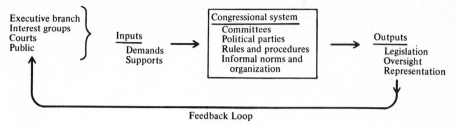

FIGURE 1-2   Schematic model of the congressional system and its environment

Summary The second section of this chapter has attempted to apply the concepts of the systems analysis to the congressional system. We have defined the legislative system to include the 535 senators and representatives and their staffs. The major features of the system include bicameralism, the conduct of congressional operations through a set of highly independent committees, and the party organizations, all of which function within a set of formal rules and procedures. A variety of informal norms of behavior and a set of informal legislative organizations also contribute to the form of the congressional system. This system receives inputs of demands and supports from four major sources: the executive branch, the interest groups, the courts, and the public. The system responds by producing three major types of outputs: legislation, oversight, and representation. These outputs, in turn, are "fed back" to the environment, thus stimulating a new set of inputs with which Congress must deal. The role of congressman includes orientations toward each of these features: the system's attributes; the inputs it receives; and the outputs it is expected to produce. These relationships are summarized in Figure 1-2.

All the role orientations outlined above do not actually exist as they were discussed. Rather the system-role concepts suggest that they may exist, thus the conditional language employed throughout this section. The systems approach provides one way of looking at the complex series of relationships that make up the legislative process, but simply organizing material in this (or any other) fashion does not guarantee an accurate description or understanding of reality. It remains for research to uncover the extent to which role-orientational patterns can be discovered and the degree to which these orientations help to explain how the congressional system processes inputs to produce outputs.

We have developed a series of hypotheses about the ways in which members of Congress handle their roles as lawmakers. The chapters that follow attempt to elaborate these propositions. We would expect to find, with respect to party role orientation, for example, that a "party man" votes in support of his party leaders to a high degree while a "maverick" displays lower levels of party regularity. A committee "expert" is expected to participate more fully in floor debate, since the nonmembers of the committee look to him for guidance; the committee indifferent will have less need to speak and others are not likely to expect him to do so. Finally, to cite one more example, we may hypothesize that those who assume a "delegate" role orientation toward their constituents will spend more time and energy in representational activities, and as a consequence have less opportunity to engage in the lawmaking function than will a "trustee." If inquiry confirms these hypotheses, then, and only then, can we say that the systems-role approach is useful; for then it will help us to explain how the congressional system processes inputs and produces outputs.

Yet even if certain regularities are found to exist, there is no guarantee that they will continue to exist for long periods of time. Role orientations are seldom the result of conscious choice and will change over time. A change in Presidents or the appointment of new Supreme Court justices will mean that congressmen will have to work with, will receive inputs from, new individuals with differing expectations, and new role orientations will certainly result from such changes. Likewise, inputs will alter, sometimes gradually, sometimes dramatically; and this alteration may require new behaviors to deal with changed circumstances. In short, the interactions within the system and between its members and actors in the environment are dynamic, not static; and we will be taxed to keep an accurate picture of them in our minds. Yet when the complexity of the congressional process at any one point in time is noted, the systems approach still seems a sound way to view the totality of congressional politics and a meaningful way to gain perspective on a complex, but crucial, feature of American political life.

PART

1

The Congressional System

CHAPTER TWO

The Men of Congress

Viewing Congress as a political system suggests that each member of the legislature must define his own role, must orient himself toward a number of objects and individuals within and without the system. To put it another way, this means that each senator or representative must decide how to expend his time and energy and that of his staff. He must choose which activities, out of an extensive set, he will undertake and which he will largely ignore. Each legislator must, given the limits to his resources, make such choices; each develops a particular set of role orientations toward the features of the legislative system and the forces in its environment. Knowing these orientations will help us understand the workings of Congress.

Furthermore, most members of the legislature have a good deal of freedom to make these commitments as they personally see fit. There are, of course, pressures which must be taken into account, but they are not nearly so great as is sometimes believed. Congressmen are jealous of their own independence and tolerant of their colleagues' exercise of individual judgment. In the last analysis, the future of a congressman is in his own hands. He must, to be sure, consider many factors in deciding how he will play his legislative role, but no one of these things is likely to be decisive; he has wide latitude to select the specific orientations toward each aspect of the legislative task he will adopt as his own, and to adjust his positions as the situation seems to warrant.

Given this freedom of choice, congressmen will assume role orientations which reflect the kinds of people they are, the kinds of lives they have led prior to election to the national legislature, and the sorts of experiences and strains they endure during their terms of service. In other words, lawmakers do not make role choices unencumbered; rather they bring to those choices beliefs and values developed over their entire lives. There is ample evidence to suggest that Americans learn their political preferences at an early age.[1] The prime sources of political learning appear to be the family, supplemented by the educational system and primary and peer groups. These agents teach notions about politics which tend to persist in adult life and which seem highly resistant to change. Clear also is the fact that adult political behavior, voting choice for example, to a considerable extent reflects social position.[2] Sharp differences in the direction of the vote emerge among racial and religious groups, the various social classes, and residents of different geographical regions. Thus an individual's views about politics and the political process reflect his childhood experiences and the kinds of religious, occupational, and social choices he has made. And what is true for an "average citizen" is no less true for an elected member of Congress. Each congressman brings with him to Washington a set of political beliefs and opinions richly colored by the socialization process and life situations he has experienced.[3]

Moreover, to get to the nation's capital he must undergo the trials of the electoral process. Winning a seat in Congress is seldom an easy task and the experiences involved in campaigning for office will in all likelihood influence legislative performance. Once he gets to Washington, the lawmaker enters into a new way of life, one which provides obvious rewards but also imposes less visible costs. How he adjusts to the strains of public life will also contribute to how he acts as a lawmaker.

From the perspective of the legislative system, what is important is that the beliefs and values he brings with him to office, the nature of his electoral experiences, and the kind of life he leads once he takes his congressional seat will profoundly affect how a lawmaker defines his legislative role. This chapter will examine these extralegislative features of the lives of congressmen and attempt to suggest how these attributes may influence the ways in which senators and representatives conduct the business of Congress.

THE LEGISLATORS: BACKGROUND CHARACTERISTICS

We may conveniently distinguish between the social backgrounds and the personal, or personality, attributes of the legislators. While these categories are related—an individual's early life experiences surely influence the

---

[1] Scholars refer to the study of the acquisition or learning of political attitudes and values as political socialization. For a convenient and thorough review of the burgeoning literature on socialization, see Dawson, 1966.

[2] On voting, see Berelson et al., 1954, and Campbell et al., 1960.

[3] For some preliminary data on the political socialization of American congressmen which indicate that socialization occurs throughout the life cycle, see Kornberg and Thomas, 1965.

traits of personality he develops—they are analytically separable. We shall examine each category in turn, but the point to remember is that both sets of factors contribute to the sort of person a lawmaker is and, most importantly, to the approach he takes to his legislative chores.

Social background attributes An examination of the social experiences of congressmen leads inevitably to the conclusion that our legislators are not typical Americans in the sense that they reflect (or "represent") a good cross section of United States citizens. A pollster taking a sample of 535 Americans would not get a group at all similar to the members of the Senate and the House of Representatives. In the first place, those who find places in the national legislature are not the children of typical American families. Rather they come disproportionately from the middle and upper reaches of the American status pyramid. Of the 180 men and women who served in the Senate in the decade between 1947 and 1957, 24 percent were the children of professionally employed fathers, and another 35 percent had fathers classified as "proprietors and officials," that is, as self-employed, small businessmen or upper-level white-collar workers. The total labor force in 1900—the census year nearest to the birth date of most 1947–1957 senators— had 6 percent and 7 percent, respectively, in these groups. From the reverse perspective, 5 percent of the 1947–1957 senators were the sons of industrial wage earners while 39 percent of the work force was so employed (Matthews, 1960, 1961b). In short, if they are not born with silver spoons in their mouths, United States senators tend to come from families where the head of the household has a larger paycheck in his pocket than most Americans.

In addition to being better off financially, the families of senators tend to live in rural, small-town America. Table 2-1 shows that sparsely populated

TABLE 2-1 *Birthplaces of congressmen compared with population distribution*

Size of place	Senators (1947–1957)		Representatives (90th Congress)	
	Birthplaces %	*Population distribution (1900)* %	*Birthplaces* %	*Population distribution (1910)* %
Rural	52	60	36	54
2,500–4,999	12	4	7	5
5,000–9,999	7	4	10	5
10,000–24,999	8	5	8	6
25,000–49,999	6	4	7	4
50,000–99,999	3	4	6	5
100,000 and over	12	19	26	22
	100	100	100	101
	(N = 177)		(N = 430)	

SOURCE: Matthews, 1961b, *International Social Science Journal,* vol. 13, no. 4. Reproduced by permission of Unesco; Rieselbach, 1970, p. 325.

communities are overrepresented in the Senate. More members of the upper
house were born in towns of 2,500 to 10,000 population than would be
expected from the residences of all United States citizens. On the other hand,
fewer than the expected number of senators were born in cities of over
50,000 people. A similar pattern of overrepresentation of smaller communities
appears to have characterized the House of Representatives in an earlier
period (McKinney, 1942), but more recently, perhaps as a result of court-
induced and enforced reapportionment, the picture seems to have changed.
In the 1960s, as the data in Table 2-1 indicate, cities of all sizes are overrepresented in the House at the expense of the countryside.[4] Their birthplaces
(and hometowns) then, as their families' economic status, distinguish members of Congress and their fellow citizens, and such differing origins may
distinguish their outlooks as well.

Moreover, lawmakers are also atypical in terms of national origins. The
vast majority of congressmen, despite the nation's "melting-pot" traditions,
are native-born Americans. Of all the members who served in Congress to
1949 only 4 percent (374 of 9,618) were foreign-born. And of these four out
of five were immigrants from Canada and Western Europe—notably the
British Isles and Germany (Lawson, 1959). Some of the immigrants' children
do win election to Congress; during the 1947–1957 period, in the Senate,
13 percent of the senators were second-generation Americans (as compared
with 16 percent of the white population of the country). The bulk of these
were of Northern and Central European ancestry; the nations of Eastern
and Southern Europe, from which so many came to the New World, and the
Asian and African continents provide virtually no members of the upper
house (Matthews, 1961b). The older stock—the "Yankees"—dominate the
Senate to a remarkable degree.

In terms of their family origins, then, it appears that members of Congress
are not typical Americans. Much more than those they represent, senators
and representatives are born and raised in America, in affluence, and away
from the major metropolitan centers around which swirl so much conflict
and controversy in modern life. They grow up, in short, in atypical families,
and it should not surprise us, therefore, if they learn atypical views about
politics in those families.[5] It is these views, that, in all likelihood, many
congressmen bring with them to their legislative service and which help to
determine how they approach their jobs.

But family influence, though of central importance, is not the whole
story. Socialization continues throughout the life cycle into adulthood. Thus,

[4]Looking at present residences rather than at birthplaces reveals the same pattern: Senators live more
often than the general population in small and middle-sized cities and less often on the farm or in major
metropolitan centers; representatives reside in cities of all sizes more often and in rural areas less
frequently than average Americans.

[5]For evidence that children learn their basic orientations at an early age in the context of the family,
see Greenstein, 1965; Easton and Hess, 1962; McClosky and Dahlgren, 1959; Hyman, 1959; and Hess
and Torney, 1967.

postadolescent experience must be considered; what the congressman has done, what he has experienced, prior to his election will also contribute to the set of beliefs he possesses as he undertakes a legislative career. What sort of man is he? An examination of the social backgrounds of present-day members of Congress reveals that, in many respects, the typical legislator is his father's son. That is, he is a white man, well educated, and of middle- or upper-class status. Furthermore, he is quite likely to be a lawyer or business-man and to belong to an upper-status Protestant religious denomination. In short, his station in life, like his familial origins, is hardly typical of the people who elect him.

There can be little doubt that legislative service has traditionally been a man's business. Thirteen women—twelve in the House and one in the Senate—were chosen to serve in the Ninety-second Congress (elected in November 1970); this is down somewhat from the feminine high-water mark of seventeen elected to the Eighty-seventh Congress in 1960, but up from the eleven women who served in the Ninety-first Congress. Formerly, the most common route to Congress for a woman was the so-called "widow's succes-sion," whereby the wife was chosen to fill the seat of her deceased husband, often only until the next election; more recently women have begun to carve out independent careers based on talent rather than the marital right to the "family" seat (Werner, 1966).

And if a member is likely to be male, he is also almost certainly a white male. The congressional elections of 1970 saw twelve Negroes emerge as winners in House races, up from six in the Ninetieth Congress and nine in the Ninety-first, to join Sen. Edward Brooke (R., Mass.), the first black senator since the post-Civil War Reconstruction era, giving Negro Americans a total representation of thirteen in the Ninety-second Congress. In 1968 the voters in a new district, carved out of New York City's Bedford-Stuyvesant ghetto, chose Shirley Chisholm to be the first black woman ever to serve in the national legislature. Using a proportional criterion, Negroes, who constitute 11 percent of the population, would have eleven senators and about fifty members of the House.

In addition to being disproportionately male and white, members of Congress are virtually certain to be older than most of their constituents. Senators in the Ninety-second Congress averaged more than fifty-six years old, while the mean for their House colleagues was nearly fifty-two.[6] Table 2-2 compares congressmen and the general population in terms of age. The data make clear that congressmen overrepresent "middle-aged" Americans (those between forty-five and sixty-nine years) and underrepresent the young (below age forty-five). In the Senate, but not the House, the elderly get their fair share of members. In short, to refer to the national lawmakers as "middle-aged" or "elders" is not inappropriate.

[6]*Congressional Quarterly Weekly Report*, Jan. 15, 1971, p. 126. These means differ to no significant degree from those of Congresses of the 1940s and 1950s; see Walker, 1960.

TABLE 2-2   Ages of congressmen and general population

Years of age	Senators (1947–1957) %	Population over 30 (1950) %	Representatives (91st Congress, 1969–1970) %	Population over 30 (1966) %
30–34	1	15	1	12
35–44	11	28	23	26
45–54	32	23	36	24
55–64	35	18	27	19
65–69	8	7	8	7
70–74	8	5	3	6
75 +	5	5	2	7
	100	100	100	100
	(N = 180)		(N = 435)	

SOURCES: Matthews, 1961*b*, *International Social Science, Journal,* vol. 13, no. 4. Reproduction by permission of Unesco; *Statistical Abstract of the United States 1967,* Washington, D.C., 1967; and *Congressional Quarterly Weekly Report,* Jan. 3, 1969, pp. 44–50.

Nor are the legislators typical Americans in terms of their social positions. Many of them held professional, technical, or managerial positions before their entry into politics. Of the members of the Ninety-second Congress, sixty-five senators and 236 (or 54.2 percent) representatives were lawyers (*Congressional Quarterly Weekly Report,* Jan. 15, 1971, p. 129). The law appears to provide relatively easy entry into politics; lawyers, more than other occupations, can "get away," take time off from their practices without suffering irreparable professional damage, to pursue careers in politics. Businessmen and bankers provide another pool of legislative talent: twenty-seven senators and more than one-third of the representatives serving in the Ninety-second Congress reported prior employment in such occupations. Smaller, but still substantial, numbers listed careers in agriculture, education, and journalism. Notable by its absence from such tabulations is employment in the manual labor area; few congressmen worked with their hands, on farms and in factories and mills, prior to legislative service.[7]

As might be expected, prestige occupations rest on high educational attainments. Table 2-3 displays the extent to which members of both chambers outstrip their fellow citizens in years of schooling; the great majority of legislators have some college experience while less than one-fifth of the total population has had a similar opportunity.

In keeping with their upper-status social positions and advanced educational accomplishments, members of Congress tend to belong to a select group of religious denominations. In the Senate (see Table 2-4) especially

[7]*Congressional Quarterly Weekly Report,* Jan. 15, 1971, p. 129. The percentages add to more than 100 percent because some legislators listed several occupations. For additional data illustrating the heavy concentration of congressmen in prestige occupations, see Matthews, 1961*b*.

TABLE 2-3 *Education of congressmen and general population*

Educational level	Senators (1947–1957) %	Population over 25 (1950) %	Representatives (91st Congress 1969–1970) %	Population over 25 (1962) %
Grade school or less	1	48	0	40
High school	14	38	6	44
College or more	84	14	92	17
Unknown	1	0	1	0
	100	100	99	101
	(N = 180)		(N = 435)	

SOURCES: Matthews, 1961*b, International Social Science Journal,* vol. 13, no. 4. Reproduction by permission of Unesco; *Statistical Abstract of the United States 1967,* Washington, D.C., 1967; and *Congressional Quarterly Weekly Report,* Jan. 3, 1969, pp. 44–50.

there appear to be more Protestants and fewer Catholics and Jews than the membership of these broad categories would entitle them to under some proportional scheme. The disparities are not so great in the House. In both chambers, however, there are wide divergences among the Protestant denominations. The so-called "high-status" churches tend to be overrepresented at the expense of the more traditional sects; specifically, there are more Episcopalians and Presbyterians and fewer Lutherans and Baptists than would be expected from the number of adherents to these groups.

TABLE 2-4 *Religious affiliations of congressmen and general population*

	Senators (1947–1957) %	Population (1952) %	Representatives (91st Congress 1969–1970) %	Population over 14 (1957) %
Jewish	1	3	4	3
Catholic	11	21	23	26
Protestant	88	72	71	69
Baptist	(10)	(25)	(10)	(20)
Congregational	(8)	(7)		
Episcopal	(12)	(4)	(11)	(3)
Lutheran	(3)	(7)	(2)	(7)
Methodist	(17)	(16)	(15)	(14)
Presbyterian	(14)	(5)	(15)	(6)
Other	0	3	2	2
	100	99	100	100
	(N = 180)		(N = 428)	

SOURCES: Matthews, 1960, chap. 2, reproduced by permission of the University of North Carolina Press; *Congressional Quarterly Weekly Report,* Jan. 3, 1969, p. 45; *Statistical Abstract of the United States 1967,* Washington, D.C., 1967.

In sum, congressmen are as atypical in the social positions they hold as in their family origins; they tend to occupy social statuses shared by only a small proportion of American citizens. It is possible that middle-class and upper-class values, somewhat slower to envision change, are found more often in Washington than elsewhere around the country.[8] Such uncommon social origins and social backgrounds, thus, may help to explain the charges of Congress's critics that "the leadership of Congress has lacked the incentive to take the legislative initiative in handling emerging national problems" (Huntington, 1965, p. 8).

While there exist little or no data to test these speculations, there is evidence that suggests the relationship of social background to congressional performance. The ultimate products of the legislative system include policy outputs and it seems clear that background attributes are related to legislators' votes on substantive issues. The data displayed in Table 2-5 demonstrate this association; for each category of lawmaker, those born in rural areas or small towns (under 10,000 population) cast a greater proportion of their votes in support of the so-called Republican–Southern Democratic "conservative coalition" than did their colleagues whose birthplace was a medium- or large-sized city.[9] Other social background attributes—e.g., religious affiliation, occupation prior to legislative service, and age—have been found to be related to congressional voting on civil rights, economic, and foreign affairs issues (MacRae, 1958; Andrain, 1964; Rieselbach, 1964; Jones, 1968). Thus, it seems likely that a lawmaker's social background, his experiences in childhood and adult life, contribute to his outlook on matters of public policy.

[8]On the class differences in political opinions and behavior, see the voting studies, cited above, footnote 2; Lipset, 1960; Alford, 1963; and Free and Cantril, 1967.
[9]Data on the adult residences (hometowns) of the congressmen reveal the same pattern: those who live in small-town America average higher support for the coalition than the residents of larger, urban areas. Note, however, that place of birth (or residence) is not the only important factor; party affiliation and region contribute as well. All three factors are related to coalition support which is highest among rural and small-town Republicans and lowest among Northern Democrats from the metropolitan centers (see Table 2-5).

TABLE 2-5   Size of birthplace and support for the conservative coalition, 90th Congress

Size of birthplace (1910)	Northern Democrats	Southern Democrats	Republicans
Rural	22.1 (34)	65.5 (54)	73.4 (68)
2,500–9,999	17.5 (21)	64.3 (15)	70.8 (33)
10,000–99,999	12.0 (24)	54.5 (21)	69.7 (47)
100,000 and over	6.8 (62)	39.6 (8)	59.2 (37)

NOTE: The cell entry is the mean percentage of support for the conservative coalition for each category of congressmen. The number of cases is given in parentheses.
SOURCE: Rieselbach, 1970, p. 325.

Personality characteristics A second set of individual attributes which in all probability help to shape the legislator's orientations toward the various facets of his job consists of the bundle of traits commonly referred to as personality. Personality refers to a characteristic outlook toward the world; whereas an attitude describes a person's feelings about, or orientation toward, a specific object (e.g., a particular person or nation, his political party, a given event), personality describes an individual's orientations toward broad classes of objects (e.g., people, nations, politics, wars, and the like). Thus when we talk about an aggressive person the reference is to an individual who views the world around him with suspicion and distrust, whose response to problems is to strike back at those seen as the source of difficulties. Similarly, there are people who need to be with other people, to feel that they are liked by others, to get a sense of belonging to groups of others. Such individuals have been termed "other-directed" or high in need for affiliation or affection. A number of other politically relevant traits or needs have been identified.

In a pioneering study of the Connecticut Legislature, James D. Barber (1965) has shown how such factors influence legislative orientations and performance. One of the types of legislator which Barber identifies is the "spectator," a political amateur, who appears to have a strong need for acceptance by, and affection from, others. His "need for approval from others . . . appears to spring from his doubts about his own worth" (p. 43). Thus the spectator adapts to his legislative service by becoming a "follower," one who seeks approval from others by going along with those others. Submission serves to satisfy personal needs. At the other extreme is the "lawmaker," whose satisfaction with himself, whose confidence in his own abilities, leads him to take an active part in the legislative process. He thus works to achieve results, certain that rational solutions to the issues at hand can be found, and he stresses the need to accomplish what he sees as desirable. But he is prepared to compromise knowing that he cannot always get precisely what he wants. The needs and personal style of the "lawmaker" fit to a great extent with the requisites of the legislature and he contributes greatly to the viability of the institution (Barber, 1965, chap. 5).

If personality helps explain behavior in one state legislature, there is no reason to doubt that it will help us to understand the role orientations of congressmen. Unfortunately there is little data available, but we can speculate about some possible relationshps between personality factors and role patterns. In line with Barber's analysis, a legislator's "self-concept" may influence his orientation toward lawmaking.[10] A congressman with doubts about his ability to master the world around him may find protection or solace in being a ritualist, in adhering to the relatively predictable patterns of congressional routine. A senator or representative with confidence in himself

[10]See above, pp. 18–19, on orientations toward the lawmaking function.

—with a "strong ego"—will not need the assurance that conforming to the routine provides; he may be expected to have a greater drive to achieve visible results even at the price of sharing the control over those results with others. He may, in the terminology used here, find the broker orientation congenial, for he is personally equipped to search for the solution, inevitably a compromise negotiated with others, which does provide an answer, in the short run at least, to issues of public policy.

Similarly, the personalities of individual lawmakers may relate to their orientations toward the informal norms of Congress.[11] For instance, Ralph K. Huitt (1961b) describes Sen. William Proxmire (D., Wis.), in personality terms, as a man of "driving ambition" and, more decisively, of "compulsive independence." These attributes led Proxmire to violate the expectations of his Senate colleagues and he quickly became an "outsider," or "maverick," in a chamber where conformity to the norms is widely held to be a requisite if power and influence are to be obtained. This is not to say that Proxmire was unconscious of his actions, that they were irrational in any sense, but merely that given his personality, he found the nonconformist orientation a satisfying one, worth the price of deviance.[12]

There are other fragments of evidence in the events of recent years which lend support to the notion that personality is relevant to an understanding of legislative behavior. In 1950, for instance, Sen. Joseph McCarthy (R., Wis.) became chairman of the Permanent Subcommittee on Investigations of the Committee on Government Operations. McCarthy's accession to his chairmanship marked the beginning of an era which saw the committee emerge from obscurity—it was created by the Legislative Reorganization Act of 1946—to become front-page copy. The crucial determinant of the prominence (or notoriety) which the committee gained seems to have been the personality of the Wisconsin Republican. The committee attracted little attention before McCarthy and it largely passed from public view following his censure by the Senate. Nor was it granted new powers or an otherwise altered position in the chamber during McCarthy's tenure. What seems decisive was that a particular senator, with a set of personal needs and goals, and a distinctive set of ideas about how to fulfill those needs and achieve those goals, assumed the direction of the committee.[13] In short, his chairmanship provided McCarthy with an opportunity—also available but unused by his predecessors and successors—to follow his personal political instincts. Knowledge of his personality seems to advance our understanding of the committee's behavior during what we now call the "McCarthy era."

---

[11] On the norms, see above, pp. 12–13.
[12] It may be worthwhile to note here that personality ought not to be equated with pathology. All people, normal and abnormal, have personalities; all individuals develop modes of relating to the environment in which they live. That some persons develop abnormal personalities must not blind us to the fact that most behave well within socially acceptable bounds.
[13] For a critical view of McCarthy, see Rovere, 1959.

In the same vein, the conspicuous differences in the style and behavior of two recent Senate Democratic floor leaders—Lyndon B. Johnson (D., Tex.) and his successor Montana Sen. Mike Mansfield—seem to have roots in personality differences between the two men. Johnson, a man of "overpowering personality," conducted a highly personal leadership. He was reputed to have talked each day with every Democratic senator, and with many of the Republican opposition; his forte was "wheeling and dealing" in an effort to work out solutions acceptable to a majority of his colleagues (Huitt, 1961a). The approach to leadership of Senator Mansfield, by contrast, appears more low-keyed. His activities are neither so breathtakingly paced nor so highly visible as Johnson's; he often seems content to act on behalf of his colleagues rather than to persuade them of the correctness of his own position (Stewart, 1971). This is not to assert the superiority of one style to the other, but rather to suggest that the same job—and one which has not formally changed in character—may well be performed in quite different ways by men of contrasting personalities.

In sum, a congressman arriving in Washington brings with him a set of experiences, rooted in the social positions in which he was raised and which he has occupied during his prelegislative adult life, and a personality, a characteristic way of viewing and responding to the world. Both personality and experience may well help him to define his orientations toward the multiple facets of his congressional role as well as influence the fashion in which he performs his legislative tasks.[14] We should not ignore these possibilities, though much remains to be done to understand the relationships between background and personality, on the one hand, and role orientations and performance, on the other.

THE ELECTORAL GAMUT

Another, and perhaps more immediate, set of experiences which colors the responses of congressmen to their legislative role flows from the need to win elections, initially and periodically thereafter. If he is to rise to a position of power and importance in Congress, a national lawmaker must gain seniority, that is, he must run the electoral gamut successfully a number of times in order to build up the years of consecutive service which are essential for promotion to positions of leadership. Whatever he may wish to accomplish in Washington—in the areas of policy making, oversight, or representation—will be impossible if the voters turn him out of office. Thus, the single most

[14]For an intriguing, though highly speculative attempt to link personality and voting behavior in the House, see Hermann, 1963. This study, using content analysis techniques to assess the legislators' personality attributes, found that congressmen who were personally secure and able to tolerate ambiguity were significantly more likely to vote for an internationalist, as opposed to a nationalistic, position on foreign aid bills.

important task which confronts the senator or representative is the necessity to act—in playing the legislative role—in ways which will protect his electoral position in his constituency. Much of his behavior follows from this requisite. Of importance here are questions of apportionment, the nature of the nomination process, and the conduct of the general election campaign.

Apportionment A lawmaker's opportunity to win and retain office depends in part on the nature of his district: its size, the kind of people who live there, the degree of their political participation, their political preferences, and the extent of competition between the political parties in the constituency. District characteristics reflect, in turn, the way in which state legislators, performing their task of "political cartography," draw district boundaries.[15] How these lines are drawn goes far to determine what types of constituency exist and, indirectly, what kind of candidate is likely to be successful with them.

Since the constitutional provision granting each state two senators has never been seriously challenged, most discussion of congressional apportionment focuses on the House of Representatives. Moreover, the issue of population equality dominates this discussion, for there is general agreement that apportionment should be based on population, even though the precise character of such apportionment remains an area of substantial controversy. There can be little doubt, however, that until the federal judiciary concerned itself with the apportionment issue there were substantial population disparities among the nation's congressional districts. As the data for 1962, displayed in Table 2-6, reveal, population ratios of better than 4 to 1 existed within single states. Some congressmen thus represented four times as many constituents as other members of the lower house. These are, to be sure,

---

[15]The phrase is Andrew Hacker's (1964). His book remains the most convenient and most useful discussion of the issues of congressional districting. See also Dixon, 1968.

TABLE 2-6   *Intrastate population variation in congressional districts (1960 census)*

	1962		1968	
State	*Population*	*Ratio*	*Population*	*Ratio*
Michigan: largest	802,994	4.5:1	417,026	1.03:1
smallest	177,431		403,263	
Maryland: largest	711,045	2.9:1	393,210	1.03:1
smallest:	243,570		382,881	
Texas: largest	951,572	4.4:1	459,050	1.2:1
smallest	216,371		376,200	

SOURCES: 1962 data from Baker, 1966, p. 77, reprinted by permission of the copyright holder, Random House, Inc.; Data for 1968 from Supplements 7, 21, 31 to *Congressional District Data Book (Districts of the 88th Congress),* Washington, D.C., Bureau of the Census, 1965–1967.

extreme cases, but while generally not so severe, the problem of malapportionment was widespread. Using a 15 percent deviation from the population norm to define equitable size, in 1955 only 229 seats (54 percent) were fairly apportioned.[16]

This situation did not exist by accident; rather it reflected successful practice of one of the oldest of the political arts, the gerrymander. The United States Constitution provides only that the *number* of seats to which each state is entitled shall be determined by population; the task of drawing district boundaries is left to the state legislatures. Lawmakers in the states, as politicians with political motivations, could hardly be expected to ignore the possiblity of furthering partisan interests in carrying out their apportionment chores. Thus, the gerrymander—after Elbridge Gerry, Governor of Massachusetts, one of its earliest practitioners—refers to the construction of legislative districts to achieve partisan goals.

There are a number of ways to achieve the objective of gerrymandering, winning the greatest possible number of seats for the dominant political party. First, reapportionment may be postponed indefinitely, allowing population changes within the state to create inequitable districts. In Illinois, to cite an extreme case, the congressional apportionment enacted following the 1900 census was not altered until after World War II. During this period, the up-state metropolitan area around Chicago experienced enormous population growth relative to the rural areas, yet the latter retained a fixed share of congressional seats. This failure to act is often referred to as the "silent" gerrymander.

Other possibilities entail more active participation by the state legislatures. One scheme is to concentrate the opposition's votes in as few districts as possible. To take a hypothetical case of a state with ten legislative districts, the party controlling the state assembly may, if the distribution of partisan preferences permits, draw the lines so that their opponents win three districts by margins of 80 percent or more of the vote. The remaining seven seats can then be won by the party responsible for the apportionment. Another technique is to draw the boundaries to spread the opposition votes in such a way that they are a minority, large but still a minority, in as many districts as possible. Again it may be possible to win 70 percent of the seats with only 45 to 50 percent of the total votes cast. The congressional redistricting of 1951, carried out by the Republican-controlled California Legislature, enabled the GOP to win a "disproportionately high share of the state's delegation for the next decade" (Baker, 1966, p. 85).

One effect of these devices on Congress was to give the rural areas of the nation greater representation than their numbers entitled them to, seats

---

[16]The norm, as defined by Hacker (1964), is the average population of a state's districts. Thus for a state with 4,000,000 population and ten congressional seats the norm would be 400,000. Districts with populations between 340,000 and 460,000 would be equitable constituencies under the 15 percent criterion.

gained at the expense of the cities and, especially, the suburbs. The failure of state legislatures to reapportion themselves led to a rural dominance there which was translated, in turn, into rural overrepresentation in the national House. *Congressional Quarterly* estimated, as of 1963, that an "ideal" apportionment would take twelve seats from rural areas and four from so-called "mixed" districts and redistribute them giving six to urban and ten to suburban areas (*Congressional Quarterly Weekly Report,* Sept. 20, 1963, pp. 1642–1644).

Another effect of the clear population inequities of the 1950s and early 1960s was to bring the courts into the apportionment contest. Though as late as 1946, the Supreme Court had refused to enter the reapportionment "thicket,"[17] by 1962 the situation had changed. Malapportionment was obvious, there was a new Court, a new concern for individual rights, and the result was the landmark decision in *Baker v. Carr* (369 U.S. 186). This case held, with specific reference to Tennessee where 27 percent of the voters could elect a majority of the state senate, that the federal courts would, under the "equal protection of the laws" clause of the Fourteenth Amendment to the federal Constitution, hear cases challenging the fairness of state legislative apportionment. Moreover, rather than waiting to see what would be the indirect effects on congressional districting of the spate of suits challenging state legislative apportionment which followed *Baker v. Carr,* the Court, in the 1964 case of *Wesberry v. Sanders* (376 U.S. 1), ruled that "as nearly as is practicable one man's vote in a congressional election is to be worth as much as another's." Thus, in these and in subsequent decisions, the Court has taken for itself the task of overseeing state legislative performance in apportionment and has laid down the "one man, one vote" doctrine of population equality for legislative districts.

These judicial rulings, however, have not reduced apportionment to settled practice. For one thing, the courts have characteristically refrained from setting precise standards. While recognizing that districts cannot be exactly equal, the justices have not specified how great a deviation from equal populations will satisfy the one man, one vote formula.[18] Nor have criteria other than population been employed to evaluate apportionment. Congress, prior to 1911, directed that districts be "compact," that is, that the constituencies should somehow be "reasonably" shaped. What constitutes reasonable, of course, is a matter of opinion.[19] It is clear that some shapes—e.g., a long, thin district which runs through an entire city or across a whole state— are not compact, but beyond this there is little to guide judgment. Congress

---

[17]In the case of *Colgrove v. Green,* 328 U.S. 549 (1946), the Court ruled by a narrow 4 to 3 vote (two justices not participating) that apportionment was a "political" question to be left to the political branches, the executive and the legislature, to handle.

[18]The court does seem to be moving toward a strict standard of equality, however. In April 1969, by a 6 to 3 vote, it ruled invalid the New York congressional apportionment which had a maximum variation of 6.6 percent from the state norm.

[19]For one effort to measure compactness, see Reock, 1961.

has dropped the requirement and the courts have ignored the issue. Similarly, there is no need for districts to be composed of contiguous territory. Most often they are contiguous, but occasionally widely separated areas are placed in a single constituency.[20]

In short, the requirements of nearly equal population for legislative districts have reduced but by no means eliminated the possibilities for the gerrymander. (See Table 2-6 for evidence of the decrease in population disparities.) For example, the question remains open as to the creation of districts which would virtually guarantee a seat for a member of some racial or ethnic group. For the 1968 elections, perhaps in recognition of the Negro drive for equality in the 1960s, new districts were created in the ghetto areas of New York, Cleveland, and St. Louis which, as expected, sent three additional blacks to Congress. Room for maneuver, thus, still exists. And, however the state legislatures draw the constituency lines, legislative candidates will have to consider the nature of the district in designing their campaign strategies. Moreover, the nature of the district is likely to influence role performance once the electoral hurdles have been overcome; the inputs to the congressman from the "folks back home" will reflect the kinds of people they are—urban or rural, black or white, rich or poor—what they believe as a result, and how they relate to the political process. An incumbent lawmaker can consistently ignore such factors only at great peril to his political future.

Nominations The first step in winning legislative office, whatever the character of the constituency, is to get on the ballot, and the most effective way to do so is to gain the nomination of one of the two major political parties. This necessity serves to highlight the widely noted fact that the American party system is a highly "decentralized" one, where state and local party organizations operate quite independently of one another. The nomination contest will in all likelihood be an "open contest, to be won by a local candidate campaigning on local issues" (Price, 1965, p. 39). Rarely, in other words, is the national Democratic or Republican party a potent force in the choice of candidates for Congress. The nature of the local political situation —which, of course, varies widely from one locality to another—is the crucial factor.

The first thing to note is that not everyone is equally likely to emerge as a potential candidate. To become a candidate often imposes a number of requirements. One pertains to place of residence; the Constitution dictates that a congressman live in the state (though by custom a representative usually resides in the district he represents). The period of residence may be

---

[20] In their 1961 districting, the Republican majority in the New York Legislature attempted to gain a congressional seat by joining Richmond Borough (Staten Island) and a section of Brooklyn considerably removed from the channel separating the two boroughs. See the map in *Congressional Quarterly Weekly Report,* Sept. 16, 1966, Part 1, p. 2087.

short in some areas—witness the recent nominations of sometime-residents Pierre Salinger (California) and the late Robert Kennedy (New York) for Senate seats—but elsewhere, in the South and Midwest especially, lifelong residence in the constituency is a major asset in seeking nomination to the legislature.[21]

In addition, certain features of an individual's personal situation seem conducive to his entering politics. For one thing, the candidate for nomination may be atypical in terms of personality; office seekers may have greater needs for power, prestige, or respect and affection than those who refrain from candidacy.[22] As noted earlier, some occupations provide easier access to the political arena. Lawyers and salesmen, for instance, can "get away" for an electoral fling without doing great harm to their careers; in fact, new contacts made as a candidate may improve business prospects. Beyond this, family and financial considerations enter in. A candidate's wife and children must be prepared to endure a demanding schedule, life in the public eye, and numerous other disruptions of more routine existence. Likewise, a candidate and his family may have to suffer monetary dislocations stemming from the costs of campaigning, especially in the primary, and the need to live at a grand scale on smaller income if successful in winning office. Only those prepared in all these areas are likely to consider running for Congress seriously.[23]

The nominations themselves are, in virtually all cases, made by the party voters in a direct primary election. Much of the character of the primary will be determined by the prospect of the nominee in the general election. Where there is no real competition between the parties, that is, in the "one-party" districts, the primary is, for all practical purposes, the election; the winner of the major party nomination will win easily in the fall. In more competitive ("two-party") areas, the primary victor will face a hard and uncertain campaign in the general election. In fact, as Table 2-7 illustrates, there is a direct connection between the degree of primary competition and the chance for success in the general election: the greater the prospects for victory in the fall, the greater the competition in the spring primary. Specifically, to take the Senate case, where chances for the general election were poor, where the Democratic nominee could expect to get less than 40 percent of the vote, two-thirds of the primary winners garnered at least 90 percent of the ballots, indicating weak or absent opposition. Where, on the other hand, the general election was more promising, with more than 60 percent of the

[21]In the Ninetieth Congress, 211 members of the House lived in the same county in which they had been born and another ninety-eight resided in the state but not the county of their birth. Thus, 71 percent continued to make their homes in their state of birth. On the other hand, Ed Foreman, a Republican representative from Texas in the Eighty-eighth Congress, was elected to the Ninety-first Congress from New Mexico.

[22]On the relevance of personality to political recruitment, see Barber, 1965, and Jacob, 1962.

[23]For a discussion of entry into congressional races, see Leuthold, 1968, chap. 2.

vote likely, only 14 percent of the candidates scored easy primary wins.[24] This relationship holds as well for House Democrats and Republicans in both chambers.

Where there is an incumbent seeking reelection, however, the story may be different. Once in office, a legislator has at his disposal resources—the publicity and attention which focus on a congressman, the ability to provide services, the franking privilege, and the experience to take advantage of these opportunities—which make the task of any challenger a difficult one (Leuthold, 1968; Turner, 1953). Where the sitting senator or representative can be attacked on grounds of age and infirmity—a theme which contributed to the defeat in 1966 of Sen. Paul Douglas (D., Ill.) by his Republican challenger, Charles Percy—or where redistricting creates a substantially new constituency, thus minimizing the incumbent's advantages, the opportunities for the nonincumbent improve measurably. In some parts of the country, notably the South, the parties are so weak and divided into factions so frequently that an officeholder can routinely expect primary opposition. Hence, incumbency does not produce certainty, but it does provide a head start toward holding the nomination.

Another basic fact about the primary campaign is that resources are scarce, that is, those who may be counted on for support in the general election are less likely to be committed to one potential candidate, preferring to make a choice between the eventual nominees. In the first place, the parties find it difficult to control their own primaries. The nature of the direct primary makes it impossible to keep those who want to run out. Also, in the interest of eventual party unity, the organization may choose neutrality in the primary, thus enabling it to work smoothly with the victor. Some organizations are, however, in a strong enough position to "slate" candidates

[24]Mezey (1970) suggests that majority-party winners are likely to have held prior political office. Where general election success is likely, the party is prone to select candidates who have demonstrated ability, or at least acquired experience, in state or local elective posts.

TABLE 2-7 Competition in Democratic congressional primaries: Relation between primary and general election votes in races not involving incumbents

General election vote (%)	Candidates nominated (%) with given proportion of primary vote			
	Senate (1920–1960)		House (1952–1958)	
	Under 60%	Over 90%	Under 60%	Over 90%
0–39.9	20	68	21	67
40–59.9	44	31	40	30
60–100	51	14	73	4

SOURCE: Reprinted with permission from V. O. Key, *Politics, Parties and Pressure Groups*, 5th ed., copyright 1964 by Thomas Y. Crowell Company, Inc.

and ensure their triumphs. For instance, Mayor Richard Daley's Chicago Democratic machine controls the House nominations with an iron hand, using the congressional seats as rewards for those who have rendered faithful service to the party. These "inner-city" representatives are oriented toward obtaining federal monies for the city and, in contrast to the nominees from adjacent suburban areas, are rarely concerned with issues of public policy (Snowiss, 1966). Where the organization dominates, the type of candidate nominated may well differ from the sort chosen in the more common situation where the party can or does not dictate the nominee.

Just as the party may be uninvolved or unable to control the primary outcome, other potential participants—interest groups and politically motivated citizens—may adopt a "hands-off" view of the nomination contest. Studying congressional primaries in the San Francisco Bay area, Leuthold (1968, chap. 3) found interest groups less likely to contribute to the campaign chests of primary candidates than to provide cash for a general election fight. Likewise, public interest in primaries was less than that found in the fall; not only were individuals less likely to work for a candidate but they were less likely to get to the polls and vote on primary day.[25] What this means, of course, is that primary candidates may be required to dig deeply into their own pockets if they are to wage serious campaigns. Resources that are unavailable from outside sources will have to be supplied by the candidates themselves.

In a few states—Connecticut, Delaware, Idaho, Indiana, and New York—and in Southern Republican parties, nominations for United States senator are made in convention rather than by direct primary. These conventions tend to resemble the federal nominations for President. Local leaders search for a candidate who can carry the state in November. If they can agree—as they did on Robert F. Kennedy in New York in 1964—they can confer the nomination on their man; where they cannot, extended bargaining will occur in an effort to cement a coalition in support of a candidate acceptable to those controlling a majority of the convention votes.

In sum, seeking a congressional nomination requires a candidate to face the perils of the direct primary in most every instance. In the absence of anyone with the ability to deliver the nomination to him, as is most often the case, he will have to fall back on his own efforts and resources. This being so, it should come as no surprise that legislators often adopt a local perspective (a state or district as opposed to a national orientation, in the language employed in Chapter 1) toward their representational activities or that many at least claim to believe in the necessity of assuming a delegate style toward their lawmaking responsibilities. It seems reasonable to hypothesize, more generally, that the nomination experiences of the primary influence the role orientations and behaviors of incumbent congressmen.

[25] Key, 1964, pp. 580–581, provides clear evidence of the lower turnout rates in primary elections.

Campaigns With the nomination won, the candidate turns his attention to the general election campaign. If he is running in a one-party district, the worst may be behind him; in a two-party one, it may be still to come. If he has a strong party organization in his constituency, the nominee may fall heir to the resources needed to run an effective campaign. Much more often, in all but a very few metropolitan centers, the fall campaign, like the earlier primary, is basically a "do-it-yourself" operation. While he will get more help than in the primary, these outside efforts will remain marginal; the candidate will in all likelihood have to plan and execute his own campaign independently of the activities of those with whom he shares his party's ticket.[26]

This is especially true for House races. Senate seats are taken more seriously by the party organizations; contests for the lower chamber seem to fall between the national organizations, on the one hand, and the state and local parties, on the other. The former concern themselves with presidential and, to a lesser extent, Senate races while the latter focus on county and other local battles. Thus, except for a small number of strong political machines, as in Chicago for instance, where the candidate can share the resources of the organization, he will have to assume responsibility for whatever direction his campaign gets. There are, however, some virtues that flow from this necessity. As Dexter (1969b, pp. 211–216) suggests, the need for congressional candidates to assume personally the management of independent campaigns can enhance their election prospects; the freedom to maneuver may permit appropriate appeals to decisive voting groups in the district.

The candidate will get some help from the party. Each party maintains Senate and House campaign committees, operating out of Washington, D.C., which assist local candidates. The most immediate and direct support is, of course, supplying the funds to finance the campaign activities. A senatorial candidate can expect a maximum of $10,000 or so from the national party; the contribution to a House nominee will be of the order of $2,000. Since a campaign for senator in a major, urban state may cost $1,000,000 and a House race entail expenditures of $60,000, it is clear that much fund raising remains for the candidate and his personal organization. Additionally, the national party will make available advice, campaign literature, ghostwritten speeches, and similar forms of indirect aid. What use to make of these materials remains for the candidate to decide after assessing his particular local situation.

More generally, the candidate's problem is to design a campaign strategy which will produce a majority of the votes cast on election day. This entails the creation of an electoral coalition composed of locally important interest groups, the mass media, party and volunteer workers, and interested citizens. The specific details of the coalition-building operation will, of course, vary

[26]Only recently has much attention been paid to congressional campaigns. Two recent, and useful, studies are Leuthold, 1968, and Kingdon, 1968. This section relies heavily on these two works as well as on Clapp, 1964, chap. 8. See also Bibby and Davidson, 1967, chap. 2.

from district to district, but some of the considerations involved can be stated in general terms. First, strategy will reflect the nature of the district. If his party dominates the district, the candidate need only get out the vote to mobilize his party's usual majority. Where the opposition controls, he will have to seek ways to detach voters from their customary choices and convert them to his cause. The kinds of voters in the constituency, in short, will shape the nature of the campaign.

So, too, will the presence of interest groups willing to commit some of their resources to the campaign. Democratic candidates can often count on the support of labor groups, while business interests frequently contribute to the cause of Republican nominees. The mass media, the press, and to a growing extent television and radio, tend to back GOP candidates. Whichever candidate they choose, interest groups can supply funds, campaign workers, or public endorsements which will further the cause of the man they back. Much of the candidate's efforts will be directed toward securing the support of the politically potent groups in his state or district. Through them, he may be able to reach voters who would otherwise pay scant attention to his campaign.

A third element in coalition building is the personal popularity or appeal of the candidate himself. To the extent he comes to the campaign with a personal following, usually rooted in some local accomplishments, he has some readymade advantages. His local fame may be directly converted into votes; his popularity may greatly ease the task of recruiting campaign workers; his attainments in one area may lead the media or interest groups to believe he will perform effectively in the legislature. The more favorably regarded he is, the easier his task in assembling a winning coalition.

As might be suspected, incumbents have great advantages in all these respects. To start, they have been through the coalition-building process previously, and their task becomes one of reactivating an old alliance rather than forging a new one. Moreover, having carried the district at least once, they are likely to know the partisan sentiments of their constituents, the predispositions of the important local interests and to be relatively familiar if not popular figures in the eyes of the voters. Furthermore, incumbents do not confine their activities to the campaign period; rather they follow the adage that "elections are won in the off year" (Clapp, 1964, p. 374). They will accept a large number of speaking engagements in the district; they will use the franking privilege to send mailings and newsletters free of charge to the residents of the constituency; they will use the congressional office and staff to perform services for the voters. Using these and other devices, the incumbent enters the formal campaign with an important head start. He can, of course, be defeated, but his constant concern with his reelection prospects makes that a difficult task for any challenger.

In putting together a winning coalition, whether or not he starts with the advantages of incumbency, the candidate tends to stress images rather than issues. That is, he tries to create a favorable impression of himself as an attractive, energetic man who will promote the interests of the district rather than specify precisely what those interests are. If elected, he will "do more" for Massachusetts, New York, or the Seventh District, though he may not clarify what "more" amounts to. The downgrading of issues, except of course in the rare instance when an issue—a major national crisis or a scandal involving the incumbent, for example—takes on a critical importance, stems in large part from the remoteness of public policy matters from the mind of the average voter. Aware that the electorate will not know, and often will not care, where he stands on the issues, the candidate will, in his appearances at the county fairs and baked-bean suppers, in his billboard and other forms of advertising, on his radio and television appearances, picture himself as active, involved, and concerned with the welfare of the district rather than as a crusader for any particular cause.[27]

Yet this, or any, type of campaign costs money, and fund raising remains a central campaign problem. Whatever the content of the candidate's message—whether image or issues or both are stressed—he must get it before the electorate, and this entails substantial expenditures. And this is true regardless of the degree of competitiveness in the district, for the pervasive uncertainty of elections seems to compel virtually all candidates to mount some sort of campaign. Each nominee, then, must confront the necessity of securing contributions from outside sources, or of dipping into his own bank account. A variety of devices are employed, ranging from the private solicitation of individual donors to mass appeals such as media advertisements or telethons. Here again the advantage rests with the incumbent; he will have identified potential contributors and will spend what he raises more efficiently. His challenger may raise and spend as much, but he will invest more effort in securing the funds and get less for his money. Fund raising, then, is both necessary and difficult, and campaign strategy will reflect the candidate's choices about how to use his limited financial resources.

To summarize: Each member of Congress will have had to organize his campaign, assemble his coalition, and raise most of his own funds; his experiences can be expected to color his subsequent behavior as a legislator. Concessions or promises, implicit or explicit, made to gain interest-group or media support or to secure campaign funds may limit future freedom of action. To cite one possibility, it is unreasonable to expect a lawmaker, whose campaign benefited from interest-group backing and money, to assume a resister orientation to the group in question; rather we may expect that he will take a facilitator, or at worst a neutral stance toward the interest. As Kingdon (1968, p. 81) puts it, the coalition-building strategy that a candidate follows "helps

[27]This is not to say that the candidates have no ideological positions. Quite the contrary, as Fishel (1969) makes clear, Democratic challengers assume "liberal" stances while their Republican opposites tend to the "conservative" end of the ideological spectrum. However, the candidate views on the issues seem to have little impact on the election outcome. Thus, there is no need to stress the issues during the campaign.

to set the boundaries within which he must make his decisions and to prescribe the general path he must follow."

Election results Whether the campaign is worth the effort, of course, depends on the results; a candidate's satisfactions are likely to be less than complete if the electorate gives a majority to his opponent. While it is impossible to trace the effect of the primary and general election campaigns on the outcome in each state or district, some data are available on the overall pattern of returns.

In the first place, the degree of competition between the parties should be noted. We are accustomed to close presidential races with each party standing a reasonable chance to win; this type of closely competitive situation characterizes some senatorial contests and a small proportion of House elections. This can be seen using either of two modes of assessing competitiveness. An election can be considered close if the losing candidate runs a strong race; a commonly accepted standard for doing well is to poll more than 45 percent of the vote cast. By this standard, one-third or fewer of the congressional races fall in the category of close, or competitive elections. Key (1964, p. 548) reports that of the nearly 700 senatorial contests between 1920 and 1962, about one in three saw the loser gain more than 45 percent of the vote but fall short of a winning majority. Put another way this means that in two of every three instances the winner polled more than 55 percent of the vote. There are variations by region in this pattern; races in the industrial North and West are far more often competitive than contests in the South where many Democratic candidates have customarily won over at most only token opposition.

The House of Representatives is even less competitive by this standard. As Table 2-8 illustrates, in the 1960s only one-fourth or fewer of the districts saw races where the winner polled less than 55 percent of the vote. At the other extreme, roughly one election in ten, mainly in the South, saw the winner without a major party opponent. In the remaining contests, the winner had opposition which put up a fight that fell far short of the needed majority. Thus control of the House hinges on the results in about 100 marginal districts where the loser runs a respectable race, and where only a relatively small shift among the voters could have reversed the outcome.[28]

But closeness in vote totals is only one indicator of competitiveness; it is possible after all for the nominee of one party to run strong races consistently yet never win. That is, "turnover," the change in control of a seat from one party to the other, is another way of looking at competitiveness. A constit-

[28]The ideological balance in Congress also depends on these few districts. Where the marginal districts swing heavily for one party, as they did for the Democrats in 1964, and where the new legislators tend to share an ideological view—the freshmen Democrats elected in 1964 were largely liberals—the balance of power in Congress may alter. Thus the proximate cause of the liberal legislative output of 1965 to 1966 was the election of an unusual number of liberal Democrats in the swing districts in 1964. On these points, see Fishel (1969) and Weinbaum and Judd (1970).

TABLE 2-8   *Degree of competition in House races, 1962–1970*

	1962	1964	1966	1968	1970
Competitive (won by less than 55% of vote)	18.4%	25.5%	17.0%	16.8%	12.6%
Noncompetitive (won by more than 55% of vote)	70.8	65.5	72.2	73.1	76.4
Uncontested (no major party opposition)	10.8	9.0	10.8	10.1	11.0
	100.0	100.0	100.0	100.0	100.0

SOURCE: Election returns by district reported by *Congressional Quarterly.* 1962: Supplement to *Weekly Report,* Apr. 3, 1963. 1964: *Congressional Quarterly Almanac 1964,* pp. 1024–1068, 1966: Supplement to *Weekly Report,* May 12, 1967. 1968: Supplement to *Weekly Report,* June 6, 1969. 1970: *Weekly Report,* Nov. 6, 1970, pp. 2771–2778.

uency which returns the same party to office year after year can hardly be described as highly competitive. Jones (1964) has investigated House races using this criterion and, as Table 2-9 reveals, finds low levels of competition in terms of turnover. Data on the 1968 and 1970 congressional elections have been added to give a rough indication of more recent trends. The evidence is clear; competition is low and seems to be declining further. The great bulk of the seats are carried by the same party repeatedly, that is, the percent of no change districts is high and getting higher. Moreover, the proportion of seats which shift from party to party, as measured by the percentage of fluidity,[29]

[29] The percentage of fluidity records the degree of actual change as a proportion of the potential change. Thus for any pair of elections, there could be 435 changes if the "in-party" lost in each district. In fact, in 1968 party control was reversed in fourteen instances, yielding a percentage of fluidity of 3.2 (14/435). For a series of elections, the percentage of fluidity need not be the reciprocal of the percentage of no-change districts, though the two measures will be closely related to one another.

TABLE 2-9   *Interparty competition for congressional seats*

Time period	Actual number of changes	% of no-change districts	% of fluidity
1914–1926	308	62.1	11.8
1932–1940	184	69.9	10.6
1942–1950	199	74.0	11.9
1952–1960	135	78.2	7.8
1968–1970	41	91.1	4.7

SOURCES: Jones, 1964a, p. 465, reprinted by permission of the *Western Political Quarterly.* The 1968 and 1970 figures are from *Congressional Quarterly Weekly Reports,* Nov. 8, 1968, pp. 3086–3087, and Nov. 6, 1970, p. 2750.

is shrinking. In short, by either measure, general election competition for congressional positions cannot be said to be very high. Again, the conclusion emerges that control of the House and Senate will reflect what happens in a few districts and states.

All this, together with the discussion of primaries and campaigns, suggests that the incumbent seeking reelection stands an excellent chance of being successful. In 1968, for instance, only nine members of the House of Representatives were defeated, and four of these lost to other incumbents in districts where reapportionment required two members to run against one another. This means that only five representatives lost their seats to nonincumbents. In 1970, thirteen incumbents lost their seats, and one of those lost to a fellow representative in a reapportioned district. In a constituency dominated by voters who prefer his political party and campaigning with a number of advantages, noted previously, the incumbent wins with high frequency. This leads to a Congress with low turnover, long careers, and a considerable degree of institutional stability (Polsby, 1968).

The central factor in this consistency of election results is the sense of attachment that individual voters feel for the party of their choice. Often referred to as "party identification," this feeling indicates that citizens hold fast to their party allegiance, continually voting for the candidates of their party, only rarely crossing over to support the opposition nominee. And even when they back the other side, they view the change as temporary rather than permanent; a vote for an unaccustomed party does not often alter the "I-am-a-Democrat (or Republican)" view of themselves which most voters hold (Campbell et al., 1960, 1966). In short, this tendency to identify strongly with and to vote consistently for one's political party leads to a persistence of results. Reapportionment which alters the partisan makeup of congressional districts or major national crises—such as the Great Depression of the 1930s—which cause individuals to "realign" themselves, that is, to identify with a new political party, may cause election results to change drastically, but such events occur only infrequently.

Yet every two years the results are reversed in some congressional districts, and in discussing the causes of these incumbents' losses a distinction between balloting for Congress held coincidentally with presidential elections and that held at midterm, between presidential contests, is helpful. With presidential candidates on the ballot, public attention focuses on the more glamorous White House aspirants and the nearly 500 congressional races tend to reflect voter sentiment about the main event. Since many voters will vote a straight ticket for all the nominees on the ticket of their presidential choice, according to one school of thought, many congressional candidates will ride into office on the "coattails" of a popular presidential contender. That is, some of the attractiveness of a presidential candidate will be transferred to his ticket mates, giving these legislative nominees larger vote totals than they might otherwise expect.

Yet the evidence points to a limited effect for the coattail effect; it is not at all clear that a presidential candidate, however popular, can deliver his strength to his congressional running mates. The issue, in short, is the conditions under which national trends will reverse the usual partisan complexion of a state or district and lead to the election of the candidate of the usual minority. In a painstaking study of the relationship between voting for President and for Congress, Cummings (1964) suggests some causes of differentials between the outcomes on these two levels. As the above suggests, a landslide victory for one presidential candidate may carry some minority-party candidates into office with him. But he must win a district by a wide margin, as the coattail effect seems minimal. Lyndon Johnson swept Democratic congressional nominees with him in his 1964 rout of Barry Goldwater; Dwight Eisenhower, a comfortable winner in 1956, and Richard Nixon, a narrow victor in 1968, each failed to win even a majority of House seats for the Republican Party.

Incumbents, Cummings finds, are able to withstand a tide toward the opposition presidential candidate better than other nominees, no doubt as the result of the advantages of office noted above. Likewise, the form of the ballot seems relevant. Where state election laws provide for straight-ticket voting with a single mark or pull of the lever, the coattail effect seems more pronounced; by contrast, where the voter must make a separate choice for each office, more split-ticket voting appears and the relationship between presidential and congressional voting is reduced. Finally, on occasion there may be issues which affect the electoral outcome. In 1948, for instance, Republican nominees whose policy views were close to those of President Harry Truman tended to survive in the face of the Truman victory more often than their fellow partisans who took less liberal issue positions.

In short, a number of forces—especially attachment to party and the advantages inherent in incumbency—seem to work against the coattail effect. Moreover, given the one-sided, partisan balance in most congressional districts, the pull of the President's coattails will not be sufficient to alter the usual election result. In the marginal constituencies the effect may operate. What seems to happen is that the drama of the presidential campaign draws some usually uninterested citizens into political participation, and they tend to support the most attractive candidate to a disproportionate extent. Since the concern of these marginal voters is with the nominees for President, they most often vote a straight ticket, thus benefitting the candidates on their favorite's ticket. In competitive districts, this influx of votes tipped heavily to one side may be sufficient to carry into office some congressmen of the President's party who might ordinarily be expected to lose (Campbell, 1960; Miller, 1955–1956; Meyer, 1962). Evidence presented by Press (1958) of an increased tendency for straight-ticket voting in marginal districts supports this interpretation.

In off-year, or midterm elections, the story is different. In the absence of a presidential contest, interest in the campaign falls and turnout declines dramatically. Also, and more importantly, the historical record reveals a clear tendency for the President's party to lose seats. These two facts seem related. Citizens who "drop out" in midterm elections appear to be those with little concern for politics who, as noted, vote in presidential years one-sidedly for the most attractive candidate. Thus, the off-year nonvoters include those who created whatever coattail effect existed two years previously. As they withdraw from the electorate, the basic partisan alignment in the district tends to reassert itself and, in the marginal constituencies, the outcome is reversed once again. For instance, in 1966, the Republicans regained one-half of the forty-eight House seats lost in the party's 1964 debacle.

In the view of some observers, issues play a part in the customary midterm decline of the administration party. The officeholders cannot hope to satisfy the entire citizenry, and, however vague the voters' perception of the issues, the most dissatisfied may respond in the traditional American way and vote to "throw the rascals out."[30] Occasionally, events such as the charges of impropriety which led in 1958 to the resignation of Sherman Adams, Assistant to President Eisenhower, may make such reasoning simpler. In any case, historically the party in office loses seats. This century, only in 1934 did the voters reward the administration, presumably in response to the early New Deal activity, with an increase in both Senate and House seats. The Democrats gained four Senate seats in 1962 and the Republicans picked up two in 1970;[31] in every other instance the "in-party" lost in both chambers.

In short, the need for periodic election leaves psychic scars on the candidates that color their responses to their more immediate surroundings in Congress. Everything hinges on successful running of the electoral gamut, and much legislative behavior reflects this basic fact. To be sure, the advantages lie with the incumbent, but advantage is not certainty. The congressman may have to engage in reapportionment battles to retain a district in which he can win; even where he has a safe, noncompetitive constituency, he may face a stiff primary fight; he must work hard at building and maintaining an electoral coalition in his district, and he commits much time and effort between as well as during campaigns to this end; and despite all his efforts a national tide, well beyond his control, may sweep him out of office.

---

[30]For a study which finds only modest relationships between turnout and congressional election results and thus, implicitly at least, suggests the importance of issues, national and local, see Kabaker, 1969. Cf. also Hinckley, 1967.

[31]The mixed verdict of 1962 is in keeping with the interpretation offered here. The 1960 victory of John F. Kennedy was a case in which the winning presidential candidate had virtually no coattails. Kennedy ran behind his congressional ticket in over 300 of the 435 House districts (*Congressional Quarterly Almanac*, 1961, p. 1026). It can be argued that he attracted few marginal voters into the electorate and thus stood to lose little by their defections two years hence. The Democratic gain in the Senate was accompanied by a small loss of four House seats. Similarly, the narrow presidential victory of Richard Nixon in 1968 created a situation in which, two years later, the Republicans gained two Senate seats and held their House losses to nine, well below the historical average for the administration party.

All these dangers may well affect the legislator's behavior in Congress. For instance, Kingdon (1968, p. 23) finds that those who win elections tend, through the operation of a "congratulation effect," to feel that voters are aware of the issues and knowledgeable about the candidates. Winners "tend more than losers to congratulate the electorate for deciding on the 'right' bases because, after all, the electorate made the right choice." Such beliefs about voters should tend to influence representational role orientations; if voters are interested and watching, it will pay to adopt a district focus and a delegate style of representation, and these orientations may be expected to increase among congressmen who must repeatedly face hard election struggles. Similarly, the nature of the district may require that lines of communication to influential segments of the constituency be kept open at the very least. The need to win primary and general election campaigns, to assemble a victorious coalition, may entail commitments, tacit or otherwise, to those whose support seems essential and may limit subsequent freedom of action. In short, the need to win elections in order to sustain a political career imposes constraints on performance of the legislative role; some actions are safe while others are fraught with peril.

LIFE IN WASHINGTON

One other set of experiences deserves brief mention here. When he arrives in Washington, the lawmaker enters into a way of life which, unless he has had prior experience in a major political post, is new and perhaps just a little terrifying. He must learn that much of what he does, even in moments which he believes should be private, will be deemed newsworthy. As the late Rep. Clem Miller (D., Calif.) put it (1962, p. 55): "A congressman's family, his home, his past and present, his utterances, and his silences are a part of the public domain and will be examined and written about." The legislator must learn to live "on display."

Life in the nation's capital is physically demanding as well; the 14- to 16-hour day, six or seven days a week is not uncommon. Politics becomes the dominating feature of the legislator's existence. As Matthews (1960, pp. 74–75) states:

> There is no escape from politics in Washington. Political "inside-dope" stories, rumors, tips, reports of personal feuds, and party intrigue are its favorite topics of conversation. The Washington "party" is not so much a social as a political occasion, an opportunity to make contacts, to swap gossip, to "find out what's really going on."[32]

[32]Reprinted by permission of the University of North Carolina Press. Representative Miller reported (1962, p. 67) that "a congressman can eat out five and six nights a week if he wishes to. . . .The feeling will not down that behind the tenderloin is the cold and indifferent practicality of the Washington lobby."

And congressmen, among the most important men in Washington, move at the center of this political whirlpool. People seek them out to ascertain their views on a variety of topics; in some cases their mere presence is enough to make an event a success. It is no wonder that legislators find this life attractive, that they are reluctant to give it up, and that they tend to develop a strong sense of their own importance.

If this life of daylong politics has its rewards in prestige and power, it also exacts its price. Family life is strained; congressional wives report that they, and especially their children, sometimes resent the enforced disruption of normal routines which life in Washington requires (Clapp, 1964, pp. 447–455). This exceptional mode of existence also complicates the task of representation; it differs so much from the lives of his constituents that the lawmaker may lose sight of the latter, causing him to behave in ways which the residents of his district may not approve and which give his primary or general election opponent ammunition with which to try to bring him down (Matthews, 1960; Shils, 1950–1951; Mitchell, 1958, 1959).

Washington living, then, provides a set of experiences which color the outlook of senators and representatives toward their more narrowly legislative tasks. It may affect their judgments about lawmaking priorities. The need to sustain financially this sort of life may tempt them to make commitments of one kind or another to potential campaign supporters. Life is both rewarding and demanding; the strains must be accepted to gain the benefits, and the legislator may have to shape his behavior accordingly to strike a satisfactory balance.

SUMMARY AND DISCUSSION

The burden of this chapter is that the extralegislative experiences of a member of Congress influence the ways in which he performs his more typically conceived legislative role as lawmaker, representative, and overseer. He cannot help but bring with him to these functions beliefs and values which reflect his experiences outside the chamber in which he serves. We have seen, first of all, that despite the simple constitutional requirements that a legislator be a citizen, of a certain age, and a resident of his constituency,[33] congress is in no way a typical cross section of those who are eligible to serve. Rather the members are drawn heavily from the upper strata of American society, judged in occupational, educational, or financial terms. Most importantly, the outlook engendered by such social backgrounds appears to relate to legislative role performance.

In the same vein, the necessity to win elections repeatedly and the life in Washington which electoral success enables them to lead create tensions, as

[33] As asserted by the Supreme Court in *Powell v. McCormack* (1969), ruling that the House of Representatives had illegally excluded Rep. Adam Clayton Powell (D., N.Y.) for his alleged misbehavior.

well as provide compensations, which contribute to the modes of behavior which congressmen adopt. If they wish to stay in office, lawmakers will assume outlooks and make commitments that help to shape how they will act in Congress. In other words, to put it as simply as possible, the social backgrounds and personalities of senators and representatives, their experiences in winning and retaining office, and their lives in the nation's capital will influence, in part, how they respond as committee and party members, how they relate to the formal and informal rules of their chambers, how they behave as members of Congress.

Specifically, Fiellin (1967) illustrates the applicability of these notions to the Democratic House delegation from New York City. The beliefs and behavior of the New York Democrats clearly reflect their prelegislative experiences. In sharp contrast to most of their House colleagues, they owe their nomination and election to a strong, centralized local party organization; prior political service, often in the state legislature, has accustomed these men to strict party discipline. Moreover, they typically aspire to judicial positions at home, and they view the House as a way station rather than as their ultimate political destination. All these factors, thus, lead them to look homeward and to perform their congressional duties with one eye focused on New York.

For instance, the New Yorkers give precedence to party over committee. They tend to assume party-loyalist role orientations, especially on those issues of concern to local leaders. By contrast, they are indifferent to their committees; since they do not intend to stay in Congress, they have little incentive to master either the substantive issues within the jurisdiction of their assigned panels or the intricacies of procedure necessary to advance those interests. In addition, they lack strong motivation to conform to the chamber's norms. The New York Democrats' attention lies outside the halls of Congress, and they place a higher premium on constituency than on legislative relations; they have no need to observe the folkways that ease their way in Washington since they are not eager to remain there. With respect to legislative output activities, these congressmen appear to be ritualists with respect to lawmaking, indifferent with regard to oversight, and delegates in matters of serving the district. All these role perspectives flow from the transitory character of the characteristic New York Democrat's congressional career.

Not all New Yorkers fit this pattern, and those who do are hardly typical of all national lawmakers. The far more common type of representative aspires to a permanent place in Washington. He is not beholden to any party organization; rather, he is far more likely to be master of his own. His political experience prior to his legislative career, in all likelihood, has been in fluid, open, not tightly structured situations. Thus, he comes to Congress prepared to assume a sharply contrasting legislative role. While he will be loyal to his national political party when he can, he is more concerned with developing expertise over the subject-matter jurisdiction of his committee; he is eager to assume a subcommittee or even full committee leadership role. He will be willing to conform to the legislative norms in order to advance to influential positions within the chamber. To the same end, he will cultivate friendships with those, across party and committee lines, whose help he may need over the years. On the output side, he is more likely to be a tribune or a broker with regard to policy making; these orientations seem likely to permit him to use his developing substantive expertise. Those same skills will enable him to engage in oversight when he deems it worthwhile to do so. As more the master of his own fate, in the representative sphere he may be expected more willingly to act as a trustee and to focus on interests that extend beyond the borders of his own constituency.

Thus, the lawmaker, it seems, will orient himself toward his congressional duties in a fashion that reflects electoral and other experiences he has endured to become a national legislator. What he seeks to accomplish when he reaches Washington will be influenced by his previous experiences; the values acquired from his family, school, or church and the lessons learned in various forms of employment will contribute to his perception of what is possible to attain in the House or Senate. In short, whether we want to understand how Congress works, what Congress does, or both, knowledge of the kinds of men who serve as legislators and information about the outlooks they bring to that service will enhance our comprehension of congressional politics.

CHAPTER THREE

Congressional Committees

Article 1, section 1 of the United States Constitution declares that "all legislative powers herein granted shall be vested in a Congress. . . . " The exercise of these powers is the raison d'être of Congress; their possession gives shape to the congressional system. The previous chapter has argued that the employment of these powers depends in part on the kinds of beliefs and values which the lawmakers themselves hold. The present chapter begins a series which will explore the ways the congressional system is organized to facilitate the use of this constitutionally granted authority. The topics of concern will be the committees of Congress, the political parties, the formal rules under which the legislature operates, and the informal (i.e., not formally specified) beliefs and expectations which influence so much of what occurs within the halls of Congress.

Before turning to these matters, it is crucial to note that the central feature of the legislative system is its *fragmented* or decentralized character, that is to say, there exist in Congress multiple centers of power, authority, and influence,[1] relatively independent of one another, which only rarely "mesh" together in a smooth operation. We have already noted that our national electoral arrangements lead legislators to pay close attention to

---

[1] These three words—*power, influence,* and *authority*—are used interchangeably here to denote the ability of individuals, singly or in groups, to alter outcomes, that is, to make things happen that would otherwise not occur. On the difficult topic of the meaning of power and its measurement see, *inter alia,* Dahl, 1957; MacRae and Price, 1959; Riker, 1964; and the papers collected in Bell et al., 1969.

state and local rather than to national party organizations; where extralegis-lative and intralegislative pressures collide, the former may well dominate the thinking of the congressmen. Then there is the basic fact of bicameralism: each chamber, Senate and House, is jealous of its own independence and resentful of actions of the other which appear to infringe upon that indepen-dence.[2] And within each house are the committees. Woodrow Wilson (1956, pp. 61–72) referred to them as "little legislatures"; modern writers have described them as "virtually autonomous" (Clapp, 1964, p. 242) and possessed of "power largely independent of the elected leadership of the parent body" (Huitt, 1965, p. 89). Their great freedom from restraint, their ability to operate largely without effective control, and their enormous influence over what the full chamber does marks the committees as the major decentralizing force internal to the congressional system. The committees, then, give the legislative system much of its character; the system's production of outputs would be incomprehensible without reference to its committee subsystems. Thus, it makes good sense to begin our analysis of the structures and processes of the system by examining the nature and function of the legislative committees.

COMMITTEES: GENERAL CONSIDERATIONS

Committees in Congress It is hard to imagine Congress without committees; they seem a natural, as well as indispensable, part of the legislative process; yet nowhere in the Constitution are committees mentioned. It is not difficult to discover the reasons why committees have emerged. First of all, there is a need to find an efficient method of dealing with the vast numbers of bills and resolutions introduced in each legislative session. It is surely unreason-able to expect each legislator to be familiar with, and thus in a position to act intelligently concerning, each of the more than 10,000 pieces of legislation which modern Congresses need to consider in one way or another. Some division of labor is absolutely essential.

Second, and related, is the need to deal effectively with the highly technical and complex subjects which confront the lawmakers. Such topics as the shape of the tax structure, the use and regulation of atomic energy, and the control of pollution require sophisticated treatment, and to develop the necessary expertise is a full-time task. Thus, if he is to master the intricacies of some policy area, the legislator must specialize, must devote much of his energy to learning as much as he can about one subject, and he must do so at the cost of knowing little or nothing about a number of other policy matters. Con-tinued service on a legislative committee charged with responsibility for a particular substantive area provides the means whereby the senator or representative acquires the skills of the expert. Thus committees not only

---

[2]For one instance of such jealousy, personified by a clash between two octogenarian committee chair-men which brought the appropriations process to an almost complete standstill, see Pressman, 1966.

divide the labor of lawmaking into more manageable portions but also allow the legislature as a whole to develop, through specialization, expertise across the entire range of policy areas on which action is needed.

Moreover, in the same view, subdivision into committees facilitates Congress's oversight and representational activities. Each of these functions requires intervention into the affairs of a vast, complicated bureaucratic establishment, the former in the name of efficiency and control, the latter on behalf of constituent interests. For either purpose, legislators need expertise or they would be unable to bring sufficient knowledge to bear on the administration to influence the course of bureaucratic action. To avoid being overwhelmed by executive-branch specialization and sophistication, Congress must, as a counterpoise, possess similar information and know-how. And it is precisely these skills and resources which the committees generate. Freed from any necessity to focus on all subjects, some members concentrate on the topics under the jurisdiction of the committee on which they serve. The knowledge they develop ensures that Congress will have among its numbers men who can effectively challenge administrative behavior; the lawmakers will be experts on the subject in question and will know when and where to intervene to make their views known with telling effect. In short, the division of the legislature into committees guarantees that the legislature will be in a position to conduct its activities—lawmaking, oversight, and representation— possessed of a good deal of expertise. And the subdivision of most committees into subcommittees produces further specialization at the same time it further fragments power and influence within the House and Senate.

It is clear from all this why many committees of Congress have developed substantial autonomy within each of the two houses. To the extent that they include on their rosters lawmakers who bring with them or, as is more likely, have built up over their years of committee service, a reservoir of knowledge equalled only by a few of their committee colleagues, it becomes most difficult for nonmembers, rank-and-file legislators, to mount an effective challenge to a carefully constructed committee position. The committees have the talent and those on the outside have little choice but to defer to the specialists. In fact, as we shall see (in Chapter 6), deference to expertise has often become established practice. Where they are uninformed, congressmen are quite prepared to follow the lead of others; in return they expect similar respect for their views in the areas of their competence.

Types of committees   There are four major kinds of congressional committee: standing, joint, select, and conference. The most important of these is the *standing* committee, a permanent body with fixed jurisdiction.[3] There are presently twenty standing committees in the House and sixteen in the Senate,

[3]The Legislative Reorganization Act of 1946 collapsed the forty-eight House and thirty-three Senate committees into nineteen and fifteen panels, respectively, and defined jurisdiction of each as carefully as possible. Since the passage of the 1946 act, each chamber has added a committee to deal with the emerging topics of science, astronautics, and space.

TABLE 3-1   *The standing committees of Congress*

House	Senate
† Agriculture (7)	*Agriculture and Forestry (8)
*Appropriations (3)	*Appropriations (2)
† Armed Services (4)	*Armed Services (4)
† Banking and Currency (11)	*Banking and Currency (11)
District of Columbia (15)	District of Columbia (16)
† Education and Labor (10)	*Labor and Public Welfare (9)
† Foreign Affairs (5)	*Foreign Relations (1)
Government Operations (18)	Government Operations (13)
House Administration (17)	Rules and Administration (14)
Interior and Insular Affairs (14)	*Interior and Insular Affairs (10)
Internal Security (13)	
† Interstate and Foreign Commerce (8)	*Commerce (7)
† Judiciary (6)	*Judiciary (5)
Merchant Marine and Fisheries (19)	
† Post Office and Civil Service (16)	Post Office and Civil Service (15)
† Public Works (9)	*Public Works (12)
*Rules (1)	Rules and Administration (14)
† Science and Astronautics (12)	Aeronautical and Space Sciences (6)
Veterans' Affairs (20)	
*Ways and Means (2)	*Finance (3)

NOTE: Exclusive House committees are marked with an asterisk (*) and semiexclusive committees with a dagger (†). Major Senate committees are marked with an asterisk (*). The number in parentheses following each committee represents a ranking of its prestige, and is a composite of rankings offered by Goodwin, 1970; Matthews, 1960; Gawthrop, 1966; Morrow, 1969; and Horn, 1970.

as listed in Table 3-1. The structure of the two sets of committees is roughly parallel: the smaller Senate, without the need for a powerful Rules Committee to police the chamber's business, has given jurisdiction over its internal affairs to a single Committee on Rules and Administration; the House has established separate committees on Internal Security (formerly called the Committee on Un-American Activities), Merchant Marine and Fisheries, and Veterans' Affairs which the Senate has not seen fit to emulate.

In each house, the committees vary widely in prestige and importance. The Senate divides its committees into major and minor (major committees are marked with an asterisk in Table 3-1) and the distinction reflects our commonsense notions of which issues are most important. It is not surprising that senators view foreign relations, appropriations, and commerce matters, among others, as more important than such topics as the District of Columbia or rules and administration. The House makes similar distinctions among its committees, singling out Rules, Ways and Means, and Appropriations as "exclusive" committees on which legislators should serve to the exclusion of other assignments. These committees treat the most significant policy issues and they have been the most desirable assignments, eagerly sought by members of the lower house.[4] Thus, standing committees are the devices by which Congress performs its day-to-day lawmaking and oversight chores, and congressional careers rise and fall with success in securing appointment to a powerful, prestigious committee.

The similarity of the committee structure of the two chambers has led some observers to propose greater use of the second type of committee, the *joint* committee. By permitting members of each house with comparable responsibilities to sit together, it is argued, the work of Congress can be simplified and expedited. Witnesses would have to testify only once, and scarce staff resources and talent could be pooled. Yet the idea of joint committees has not caught on in Congress, perhaps out of fear that the Senate would be able to dominate such panels. The few joint committees which have been created are not permitted to report legislation and have thus been reduced to research and oversight tasks. The Joint Economic Committee, for instance, conducts yearly analyses of the President's annual budget messages and forwards recommendations on policy to the Congress.

The one exception to this relative unimportance of House-Senate bodies is the Joint Committee on Atomic Energy, which has been described as "probably the most powerful Congressional committee in the history of the nation" (Green and Rosenthal, 1963, p. 266). Through this committee, Congress has counteracted the vast authority of the military and retained for itself substantial control over national atomic-energy policy. The committee's leaders have secured the right of full participation in executive-branch policy making and they exert their influence through such involvement rather than by imposing their views on a reluctant administration through the passage of legislation.[5] When legislation is required—either to authorize programs or to fund them—the committee has its own way and is seldom challenged, especially when it presents a united front to the full houses. The joint-committee device enhances the ability of the committee to control its congressional colleagues. There is no "other house" to which to take an appeal; the rank-and-file representatives must face a joint-committee proposal on a "take-it-or-leave-it" basis; most often, in deference to expertise, they accept it. Thus, while from one perspective congressional power is preserved, from another vantage point it is very narrowly concentrated in a few hands. Perhaps it is a distrust of the latter situation which has prevented the joint-committee idea from being extended to other matters of legislative concern.

[4] The attractiveness of particular committees is usually assessed by the frequency with which legislators seek to get on, and move off, the panel in question. See the sources listed in the note to Table 3-1.

[5] This is consistent with Huntington's (1961, pp. 146–165) finding that in matters of national defense policy decisions tend to be negotiated by a process which is legislative in character, but which takes place within the executive branch. In the case of atomic energy, as opposed to other subjects, members of Congress are included among the influential decision makers.

The third type of committee, the *select* or *ad hoc* committee, resembles the joint panel in having no authority to report legislation (Vardis, 1962; Vinyard, 1966). Despite this disadvantage, these temporary, special-purpose units have a number of uses. Such committees as those on small business provide recognition for interest groups which may feel neglected by the standing committees. Also they provide opportunities for individual legislators to put their skills to work, to gain some public attention, to receive a reward for services rendered. The select committee, in addition, constitutes a device to bypass the standing committees in the event that they will not act or cannot move because of a jurisdictional conflict. Moreover, the hearings of a select committee serve educational purposes, supplying information to Congress as well as to interested segments of the public. Finally, select panels can engage in oversight and constituent-service activities, thus providing access to the bureaucracy for those in need of it. But without direct influence over legislation, the select committee seldom gains a position of eminence within Congress, or without.

The *conference* committee is, in fact, a special form of select committee, empaneled for the sole purpose of resolving differences in bills on the same subject passed by the House and Senate. The four or five most senior members of the standing committee in each chamber which considered the bill in the first instance usually serve on the conference committee which attains prominence because it determines the legislation's final form; if it cannot agree the bill dies. The conference is also important because despite rules to the contrary, it frequently can include new provisions, not in the bill originally passed by either house, to the final draft. The committee proposal, when reported back to the two chambers, must be accepted or rejected without amendment, a rule which guarantees the conference body a central place in the legislative process.

This, then, is the form which the congressional division of labor into committees takes. It is clear that the standing committees dominate; in the areas of their jurisdiction and concern, they are the chief architects of public policy. Where the members agree, the committee position is virtually impregnable. Yet not all the standing committees concern themselves with subjects of equal importance, and they differ widely in prestige. Thus from the perspective of the individual lawmaker the crucial matter is to be assigned to a committee where he can prosper.

COMMITTEE ASSIGNMENTS

Members of Congress recognize that a "good" committee assignment is of the utmost importance. Lawmakers will differ in specific terms about what constitutes a good assignment, but in general a desirable committee post will advance a congressman's career—it may "greatly enhance his value to his constituents and provide unusual opportunities to publicize his activities . . ." (Clapp, 1964, p. 207). A poor assignment is a setback, for it blocks his opportunities to attain the things—influence in the House, impact on public policy, services for his constituents, and, of course, reelection (Fenno, 1970)—that he seeks from congressional service. Moreover, an undesirable post, from which the lawmaker will seek to move, will postpone the time when he can begin to amass the years of service on an important committee which will sooner or later, if he continues to survive his periodic confrontations with the electorate, move him into a position of leadership on that body. In short, there is a good deal at stake in the assignment decisions, and it is no wonder that legislators compete, often intensely, for choice posts.

Methods of assignment Each party in each chamber has a Committee on Committees which has the formal responsibility for determining the composition of the party's roster on each committee. In the House, the Democrats empower their members of the Ways and Means Committee to act as the Committee on Committees, further enhancing the position of that already powerful body. Each Ways and Means member represents a geographical zone and has a single vote in assignment contests. When committee vacancies occur, they are filled in a way which preserves the regional balance. House Republicans constitute their committee with one member from each state electing GOP congressmen. The interesting wrinkle is that each member can cast votes equal to the number of Republican representatives from his state, thus giving the New York and California members, for instance, upwards of twenty votes each and enabling a small group of legislators—a half dozen or less—to dictate the party's assignment lists.

On the Senate side, the Democratic Steering Committee functions as the Committee on Committees. It is chaired by the majority leader who appoints the majority of its members. The committee is the creature of the leadership and this has led to charges that the "Establishment" uses its powers to exclude those who disagree with it from important committee positions.[6] Under the so-called "Johnson Rule," dating from Lyndon Johnson's tenure as majority leader, each Democratic senator is guaranteed a post on a major committee (see Table 3-1) before anyone will be assigned to two such panels. On the Republican side, the chairman of the party conference, elected by his colleagues, appoints the Committee on Committees. The GOP body seems to have operated more successfully; at least there has not been sustained criticism of its actions. Its adherence to the Johnson Rule, together with the smaller membership of the Republican minority in the Senate, has enabled it to satisfy its party rank and file to a greater degree than its Democratic counterpart. It is to these bodies that the campaigns for desirable committee seats are directed.

[6]Until his defeat in 1968, Joseph Clark of Pennsylvania was one of the most outspoken senatorial critics of the Establishment. See Clark, 1963, 1964.

Criteria for committee assignment[7] In mounting a campaign for a specific committee vacancy, a member of Congress will try to emphasize those things about his record and current status in the chamber which will make him an attractive candidate. A large number of factors contribute in one way or another to assignment decisions, but for important committees the most crucial seems to be the search for the "responsible legislator," the man whose "ability, attitudes, and relationships with his colleagues serve to enhance the prestige and importance" of the chamber (Masters, 1961, p. 352). Legislative responsibility, in this sense, requires consideration of others, acceptance of the rules and norms, moderation on issues of public policy, and in general, a predisposition not to "rock the boat." Responsibility must be demonstrated, and extremely few legislators are appointed to the exclusive House committees—Appropriations, Rules, Ways and Means—until after they have served for a while and their behavior has been observed by those who make the assignment decisions: the Committee on Committees and the party leaders.

It is difficult to assess the place of the party leaders in the assignment process. They tend to concern themselves with the major committees, for within these bodies the fate of the party's program will be determined. The Speaker, floor leaders, and whips, by virtue of their leadership positions, are likely to be good judges of legislative responsibility and their voices will carry weight with the assigning committees. Choice posts may be used by the leadership as a reward for past cooperation or, more likely, as an inducement to secure the future support of influential congressmen. Given their concern for party programs and party cohesion, the leadership will work closely with the Committee on Committees in an attempt to advance their interests as leaders.[8]

Beyond responsibility, and related to it, assignment to a major committee will depend on the nature of the constituency a lawmaker represents. Preference will be given to the man from a safe, noncompetitive district. The representative whose reelection prospects are uncertain will have difficulty in behaving in a responsible fashion; he will feel compelled to pay too much attention to the shifting opinions of his constituents and thus find it hard to engage effectively in the bargaining and compromise essential to committee decision making. Committee work will be facilitated if those free to assume a trustee orientation[9] toward the residents of their districts are appointed.

[7]This section relies heavily on the major research in the area: Masters, 1961. See also Clapp, 1964, pp. 221–237; Fenno, 1966, pp. 24–29; Goodwin, 1970, chaps. 3–4; and Robinson, 1963, chap. 5.

[8]The following often-quoted ditty from the days of the late Rep. Sam Rayburn's Speakership of the House of Representatives attests to the influence attributed to powerful party leaders on matters of committee assignment:

I love Speaker Rayburn, his heart is so warm,
And if I love him he'll do me no harm,
So I won't sass the Speaker, not one little bitty,
And then I'll wind up on a major committee.

[9]See above, pp. 20–21, for a discussion of orientations toward the representational aspects of the congressional role.

Thus, those from safe areas are often deemed the most appropriate candidates for major committee posts.

Geography constitutes a third factor in committee assignment decisions. Many committees seek to have diverging regional viewpoints represented on the panel, and try to spread the seats around on a sectional basis. Often when a vacancy occurs, there are pressures to fill the position with a representative from the same state which previously held the post in order to retain the proper geographical balance on the committee.

Assignments to other, less important committees will involve other criteria. Those making the appointments will try to place a lawmaker on a committee which will enhance his position with his constituents and thus improve his chances for reelection. Thus rural Midwesterners often wind up on the Agriculture Committees while senators and representatives from the Far West are assigned to the Committees on Interior and Insular Affairs. Popular committees in this regard include those like Public Works that, through the operation of the so-called "pork barrel" mechanism, permit members to "do something" for their districts. Occasionally, the legislator's prior experience will be taken into account. Thus Chester Bowles (D., Conn.), a former ambassador to India, was placed on the House Foreign Affairs committee as a freshman representative.[10] Finally, the support of outside groups (interest groups) may be helpful. Where a committee seeks to maintain cordial relations with a "clientele" group (e.g., Agriculture Committees with the major farm organizations; Labor Committees with the large unions) the endorsement of such an outside body may carry some weight.

Seldom is a potential appointee sought out; rather he must apply for the post he desires. His campaign for assignment is carried out through contacts with the party leaders, his "zone" representative on the Committee on Committees, and the chairman of the panel on which he wishes to serve.[11]

---

[10]Such is not always the case, however. John Foster Dulles, for decades a professional diplomat and later President Eisenhower's Secretary of State, was denied a place on the Senate Foreign Relations Committee when he was appointed to the Senate from New York. The decision perhaps reflected the greater prestige of, and importance attached to, the Senate committee.

[11]The committee chairman involved may have a strong voice in who is assigned to his panel. He may insist that the prospective member hold "sound" views on particular issues. A Democrat must favor the reciprocal trade program, Medicare, and the continuation of oil depletion allowances if he is to win a seat on the House Ways and Means Committee (Clapp, 1964, p. 228; Manley, 1970, chap. 2). A chairman may go to great lengths to keep "undesirable" lawmakers off his committee. At the outset of the Ninety-first Congress, Chairman J. William Fulbright (D., Ark.) of the Senate Foreign Relations Committee sought to reduce the size of the panel, apparently to keep Gale McGee (D., Wyo.), a "hawk" with regard to the war in Vietnam, off. This plan went awry at the last moment when Eugene McCarthy (D., Minn.) transferred off the committee, making room for McGee. On the other hand, in 1971, at the beginning of the Ninety-second Congress, the new House leadership—Speaker Carl Albert (D., Okla.) and Majority Leader Hale Boggs (D., La.)—operating through the Ways and Means Democrats sitting as the party's committee on committees, overruled the preferences of two powerful committee chairmen—F. Edward Hébert (D., La.) of Armed Services and George H. Mahon (D., Tex.) of Appropriations—and placed on those panels members opposed by the chairmen. One reporter (Rosenbaum, 1971) wrote that the chairmen "used all their authority, seniority, and prestige to block" the appointment of men they considered too liberal.

The senior man in his own state delegation may act as an intermediary for him, making the presentation on his behalf. A file is often prepared, providing "documentary" evidence that, by the criteria outlined above, the proposed assignment is sound and sensible. When two candidates lay equal claim to a particular assignment, the choice is often made on the basis of seniority, the man with the longer service in the chamber getting the seat. Thus seniority becomes relevant for those with some years of service who wish to transfer to a new committee; it counts for little, of course, in the assignment of new members, all of whom have no seniority.

The specific assignment an individual seeks, whether initially or through a transfer, will reflect his own goals, which in turn may reflect his prelegislative experiences (see Chapter 2). A groundbreaking study by Richard Fenno (1970) indicates that representatives seeking assignment to the House Appropriations and Ways and Means Committees are motivated primarily by a desire for chamber influence; these panels deal with wide-ranging portions of House business, and legislators eager to be "where the action is" find them attractive. To win these coveted seats, of course, they are prepared to assume the posture of the responsible lawmaker. In direct contrast, the House Foreign Affairs and Education and Labor Committees draw from representatives concerned with shaping the substance of public policy in these domains; rather than general influence, these men focus on a specific, but constricted, range of issues. Finally, the Interior and Post Office Committees are constituency service-oriented; their members use the assignment as a means to perform services for clientele groups and, in consequence, to secure their own reelection prospects. In short, the congressman's aspirations seem to lead him to aim for committee posts on those panels which offer significant chances for him to fulfill his personal goals.[12]

The party Committees on Committees, then, together with the party leaders, and using a variety of standards—responsibility, district characteristics, sectional balance, and others—make the committee-assignment decisions that are so important to the careers of individual congressmen. Satisfaction with his assignments, it seems reasonable, will affect the legislator's orientation to his committee work. If he finds the topic of jurisdiction

---

[12]Freshmen, especially in the House where no equivalent of the Senate's "Johnson Rule" operates, tend to get the least desirable assignments. When vacancies occur, the more senior get a chance to transfer, leaving the newcomers to scrap for what is left; the latter, as they in turn acquire seniority, move on to better positions (Bullock and Sprague, 1969; Bullock, 1970). Freshmen usually accept this treatment, but recently some have begun to protest. At the outset of the Ninety-second Congress, Herman Badillo (D., N.Y.), representing a heavily urban Manhattan constituency, successfully maneuvered, with leadership support, to have his initial assignment changed. Arguing that the Agriculture Committee was not a place where he could pursue his interests, Badillo won a place on Education and Labor. At the same time, however, his fellow freshman, Bella Abzug (D., N.Y.), failed in her effort to be placed on Armed Services rather than on Government Operations and Public Works. Both sought to capitalize on the success of their New York colleague, Shirley Chisholm, who won a reversal of the decision to place her on the Agriculture Committee at the start of the Ninety-first Congress in 1969.

challenging, if the post helps him with his constituents, if he feels an opportunity to accomplish important objectives, he may work hard at acquiring expertise, that is, he may adopt a committee-expert orientation. He will in all probability aspire to a leadership position—chairman or ranking minority member—over the long run. If, on the other hand, he finds his assignment offers no promise of reward, he is unlikely to make much of a commitment to committee work, preferring to await a transfer to a better position or seeking his satisfactions in other areas of the legislative system. It is clear from all this why so much emotion and effort get bound up in the politics of committee assignment.

THE COMMITTEE CHAIRMAN

The ultimate hope of any member of Congress who envisions a legislative career for himself is to succeed to the chairmanship of his committee, for such a position will give him great leverage over some aspect of the business of Congress. The committee, we have seen, is a highly independent body with substantial influence over legislative activity; the chairman, in turn, is "usually in virtual control of his committee" (Huitt, 1965, p. 89), and this dominant voice in committee decisions often makes him a major determinant of congressional action. From the chairmanship, then, a legislator can make a major contribution to the governing of the nation.

Powers of the chairman This importance of the chairman flows directly from his vast array of power vis-à-vis the members of his panel. Although the precise situation will vary among the committees, most chairmen can control what their committees do. The chairman decides when the committee shall meet and presides over its sessions, exercising the parliamentary right of recognizing the members. Moreover, he sets the committee's agenda, deciding what the committee will consider, when consideration will take place, and when, and under what conditions, hearings will be held. Subcommittees have become indispensable to committee functioning, and their use is the prerogative of the full committee chairman: he creates them, establishes their jurisdictions, and appoints their members, including the subcommittee chairmen. The committee chairman, additionally, wields substantial influence during floor consideration of his committee's product; he manages the committee's bills on the floor, or appoints someone to do so in his stead; he, in fact, decides who will represent the chamber when the bill goes to a conference committee, often including himself on the delegation. Finally, the committee staff is the creature of the chairman: he determines who will be hired, how much assistance will be provided for the minority side, what the majority staff will do, and often the vigor with which it carries out its assignments. The chairman, in short, has formidable bases of power and influence, and that he can use these levers to help or hinder the goals of his committee members goes without saying.

But possession of such powers is not the same as their exercise. A chairman may be unable, or unwilling, to exploit them to their fullest extent, and the most that can be said is that the chairman has a very high potential for power. A number of limiting forces may be present. In the first place, customary ways of conducting committee business may exist; widely shared norms may require consultation with the ranking minority member, the muting of partisanship,[13] and the observance of other proprieties. About half the committees of Congress have formal rules of procedure which a determined committee majority may invoke against a chairman who, in their view, has not met his responsibilities. An arbitrary chairman may find rules imposed upon him, as did Adam Clayton Powell (D., N.Y.) of the House Education and Labor Committee, whose colleagues chose the waning days of the Eighty-ninth Congress to pass rules limiting some of the practices in which Powell had engaged (*Congressional Quarterly Almanac,* 1966, pp. 521–522).

Moreover, personal factors are relevant; some chairmen may have no interest in exercising a tight rein on their committee colleagues. Bibby and Davidson (1967, pp. 173–179) present an interesting contrast between two chairmen of the Senate Committee on Banking and Currency, J. William Fullbright (D., Ark.) and S. Willis Robertson (D., Va.). The former's interests did not lie with the committee and he was content to exercise a "decentralized and permissive style of leadership" while he pursued his concern with foreign relations. Thus he allowed the subcommittees to work independently, under the direction of their respective chairmen, well funded and well staffed. Under his chairmanship the committee "pretty much ran itself." When Fulbright assumed the chairmanship of the Foreign Relations Committee, the leadership of Banking and Currency passed to Robertson, whose style was in sharp contrast to that of his predecessor. He held policy views at variance with others on the panel and used his powers as chairman to restrain their activities. He juggled the subcommittee structure, limited the expenditure of funds for hearings and staff studies, and generally held down the committee's activities. The chairman's leadership style and his views and interests, in sum, influence the ways in which he puts his powers as chairman to use.[14]

Finally, the nature of the times in which he occupies his post may serve to restrain what a chairman can do with his powers (Huitt, 1965, p.90). He must gauge what his majority will tolerate or insist upon; the greater the crisis or urgency, the more actions may be forced upon him against his will. The size of his majority may make a difference; a small majority may not hold together under great pressure from the chairman. He may be limited

[13]See, for instance, Fenno, 1962, 1966, 1970, and Manley, 1965, 1970. The place of informal norms in the legislative system is treated in Chap. 6.
[14]For other evidence illustrating the impact of the chairman's values and style on the decision-making process he implements on his committee, see Fenno, 1970.

further by what the party leadership will support; he needs their backing especially if he wants his committee to act positively. Thus the chairman will seek to develop working relationships with the members of his committee, using his powers to help them whenever he can and expecting their cooperation and support in return. His ability to assist them with projects of interest, and to withhold such aid, usually dooming the project, no doubt encourages the committee members to seek such working relationships. The precise form of such chairman-member relationships would require examination of each committee, as the factors described will certainly vary among the committees.

In the last analysis, the committee chairman is a force to be reckoned with, possessing vast but not unlimited powers over the business of his panel. The use he makes of his potential for influence will depend on his own abilities, his majority, and the demands and pressures of the day. He is ultimately responsible for his actions to his committee colleagues and to the chamber as a whole.[15] Within those limits, he will work out a modus vivendi which, in most cases, will guarantee him a position among the important leaders of the Senate or House.

Seniority Given that the chairmanship of a committee virtually ensures a position among the congressional leaders, it is no surprise that the way in which chairmen are chosen has become an area of controversy. The seniority rule, by which chairmen have been selected, is simple enough: by custom (rather than by any formal rule) the member of the majority party with the longest continuous service on the *committee* automatically becomes chairman.[16] In 1971, House Democrats and Republicans modified the seniority rule, in theory but not in practice. Both parties agreed that their respective party caucuses might employ criteria other than seniority in passing on the nominations of their committee on committees; each party established rules which would permit challenges to the seniority-determined chairmanship nominations. Put to the test, House Democrats refused to unseat chairman John L. McMillan of the District of Columbia Committee. Defeated in caucus on a 126 to 96 vote, liberal Democrats sought Republican support in a floor vote, and lost again, 258 to 32. Thus the seniority criterion remains fully operative, at least for the Ninety-second Congress.

What remains unclear is whether seniority is an adequate method for designating leaders. Defenders of the system suggest a number of reasons why seniority is a desirable means by which to choose committee leaders

[15] For a full discussion of the ultimate control of committees by the parent chamber, and the constraints on committee autonomy that such control imposes, see Fenno, 1966, and Chap. 6.

[16] The distinction here between *chamber* seniority and *committee* seniority is crucial; the former is a plus in seeking a transfer to a new assignment but is irrelevant with respect to the chairmanship. No matter what a legislator's chamber seniority he goes to the bottom of the committee seniority list when he joins that body. Thus it is clear why winning a good committee post *early* in one's career is so crucial; committee seniority is the means to committee power. On the development of seniority, see Polsby et al., 1969, and Abram and Cooper, 1968.

(Goodwin, 1959). First, it promotes harmony. Other methods, election by committee members for instance, might well lead to endless bickering and ill feeling; seniority makes the decision automatic, and the committee can get down to work without damage to the relationships among its members. In addition, seniority means that the chairman will be experienced in the ways of the committee, knowledgeable about the subjects within its jurisdiction, and as a consequence a capable leader. Finally, and more generally, the proponents of the seniority rule argue that no other method yet proposed gives promise of working more satisfactorily.

The critics of the rule counter with other arguments (Burns, 1949, 1963). Other criteria, such as position on the issues and loyalty to the political party and its leaders, they suggest, are more important than choosing a chairman without friction. Getting a leader who holds more typical views and who is responsive to the party is worth the price of a little disharmony. Moreover, there is no guarantee that length of service will produce capable chairmen; more crucial is the expertise a man has, his commitment to committee work, and his relationships with his colleagues. These requisites do not necessarily flow from years of service. The crux of the critics' position rests on the premise that the seniority rule produces minority (i.e., conservative) chairmen—most often Southern Democrats and Midwestern Republicans—from noncompetitive districts, men insulated from effective electoral challenge who can ignore the temper of the times and views of their party leaders—in Congress and without—with impunity. Those who challenge the practice of seniority, in short, seem most upset because, in their opinion, the rule prevents the enactment of desirable policies; the defenders, on the other hand, are more content to move only within the traditional modes of conducting legislative business. Congressmen themselves, moreover, seem overwhelmingly to be traditionalists with respect to seniority.[17]

What is the relative merit of these positions on seniority? Some data are available which can help us answer this question. First of all, while it is clear that seniority leaders—chairmen and ranking minority members—are older, the gap between them and the nonleaders does not seem as great as is sometimes imagined, especially in the Senate. On the average, a senator need only win two elections before reaching the top of his party's committee seniority ladder. Between 1947 and 1966 Democrats averaged ten years service and Republicans seven before reaching chairman or ranking minority member status. Furthermore, once becoming the senior party man on his committee, the average senator did not hold his position for more than five to ten years. Of the fifty-six men holding the ranking party spot on a Senate committee between 1947 and 1966, only eight served more than twelve years while twenty-six lasted four years or less (Hinckley, 1971, chap. 2). Thus,

---

[17]Davidson et al. (1966, p. 195) found 71 percent of a sample of members of the House of Representatives they interviewed *opposed* to a proposal to select committee chairmen from among "the three senior (majority) members of each committee."

turnover rates are such that it does not take too long to reach the top in terms of committee seniority nor, once there, can the post be held for excessive periods.[18] The upshot of this is that committee leaders are less far removed, in terms of length of service and tenure as leaders, from those with less seniority than the critics of the rule seem to suggest.

Moreover, the charge that the seniority practice distorts the distribution of leadership posts in favor of certain regions seems less severe when the contribution of the sections to the party contingents is considered. As Table 3-2 indicates clearly, Democrats from the South *do* gain a lion's share of chairmanships and ranking minority members (53 percent in the Senate, 61 percent in the House). Midwestern Republicans similarly dominate their party's leadership cadres. But what the critics often overlook is that the parties have their respective centers of balance in these regions, that is, there are more members from these areas eligible to achieve leadership status. Put another way, if chairmen and ranking members were chosen at random,

[18]The figures for the House support the same conclusion: On the average, it takes a representative twelve to sixteen years to gain the top spot on his committee, and he serves in that position most often twelve years or less. Between 1947 and 1966, eighty-two members of the House served as chairmen or ranking minority members; of these twenty served thirteen years or more, thirty-six departed after four years or less (Hinckley, 1971, loc. cit.). These, and the Senate figures as well, are of course, only averages; it is a simple matter to call to mind those congressmen who served as leaders for extended periods.

TABLE 3-2 *Regional representation: committee chairmen and ranking minority members compared to all members 1947–1966*

Chamber and region	Democrats		Republicans	
	All members (%)	Leaders (%)	All members (%)	Leaders (%)
Senate				
East	18	10	38	39
South	42	53	2	1
Midwest	17	3	37	46
West	23	35	23	13
	99	101	100	99
House				
East	25	19	36	35
South	45	61	5	1
Midwest	19	14	43	51
West	11	6	15	14
	100	100	99	101

NOTE: All congressmen are counted once for each election won: representatives, from 1946; senators, from 1942. Only those congressmen elected at regular elections are included. Committee leaders are counted only for those elections which precede their terms in top committee posts. SOURCE: Hinckley, 1971, p. 37. Reprinted by permission of The Indiana University Press.

on a probability basis, Southern Democrats and Midwestern Republicans would get the largest share of these jobs simply because numerically they dominate their respective congressional parties. This is not to deny that some distortion of the sort envisaged by the critics of seniority exists—some sections clearly do have more leadership positions than their numbers entitle them to—but rather to suggest that, given the numbers of legislators elected from the various regions, the distortion is not so gross as is often claimed.

What seems to be important here is the existence and distribution of safe (noncompetitive) seats, for the districts, in whatever region they may be located, that repeatedly return the incumbent to office are the constituencies which produce the chairmen and ranking minority members of the congressional committees. A study by Wolfinger and Heifitz (1965) concludes that there are not greater numbers of safe seats in the South than in other sections. There does exist, however, a "seniority generation" dominated by Southerners, resulting from the 1946 electoral landslide, confined to the North, which led to Republican victories in ordinarily Democratic districts. Since that time Northern Democrats have amassed seniority in proportion to their Southern colleagues and as electoral competition becomes more common south of the Mason-Dixon line, it is likely that these Northern safe seats will produce their fair share of seniority leaders. Thus Southern overrepresentation as chairmen and ranking minority members seems a temporary phenomenon; the more even distribution of noncompetitive constituencies should begin to be reflected in a wider regional dispersion of committee leaders.

The major criticism of seniority—that it elevates to positions of power men more conservative and more often opposed to party and executive programs than the typical party member—may also be tested against empirical data. Such a test—see Table 3-3—reveals that while there is truth to the

TABLE 3-3 *Party support: Senate committee chairmen and ranking minority members compared to all senators, 1955–1966*

Party support score	Democrats		Republicans	
	All members (%)	Leaders (%)	All members (%)	Leaders (%)
0–19	1	3	1	0
20–39	10	21	4	3
40–59	18	23	20	28
60–79	48	41	51	50
80–100	23	12	25	20
	100	101	101	101
	(N = 285)	(N = 75)	(N = 190)	(N = 72)

NOTE: Each senator's score for each Congress he served in during the span of years was counted.
SOURCE: Hinckley, 1971, p. 66. Reprinted by permission of The Indiana University Press.

critics' position the distortion is largely limited to the Democratic party. In that party, 71 percent of the rank-and-file Democrats supported the party position more than 60 percent of the time; only 53 percent of Democratic seniority leaders exceeded that level of party support. Among the Republicans the difference was much smaller: 76 percent of all members and 70 percent of the seniority leaders voted for their party's position in excess of 60 percent of the time. These same findings—Democratic leaders more conservative than nonleaders; both groups very similar among the Republicans—hold in the House of Representatives for party support and in both chambers for presidential support.[19]

In sum, the critics of seniority have a point, though they often exaggerate the extent to which the rule promotes to positions of committee leadership legislators who hold minority opinions and who are able to act irresponsibly. It does not take as long to reach the top of the seniority ladder as is often believed; nor do leaders often hang on to their positions for extended periods. Regional distortions are present, but are not so great when viewed in the light of the regional composition of the party contingents. Chairmen and ranking minority members are more conservative among Democrats but are not significantly so in the Republican party. Reform of the seniority practice, in short, might not make as much difference in legislative outputs as its critics seem to imply.

The committee chairman is indeed the most important man on his panel; his overall position in Congress is enhanced by the autonomous position of the committee within the congressional system. But the powers the chairman possesses are not unlimited; he must strive to establish working relationships with his committee members and to do so may require that he forgo the exercise of some of his perquisites on some occasions. The seniority rule, by which the chairman is chosen, does introduce some biases into the selection process, but these distortions are not as pronounced as some critics believe, and are not sufficient to justify the epithet "senility rule" often attached to the seniority device. Reform of the practice would change the *content* of committee decisions in the degree that the changes produced more liberal chairmen, but unless coupled with alterations in the chairman's powers they would not change the *mode* of committee action. It is this latter, the ability of the chairman to dominate committee business if he chooses to do so, which leads so many legislators to look forward to and to work for the day when they will be able to assume positions of committee leadership.

---

[19] Hinckley, 1971, chap. 5. Party and presidential support scores are measures calculated by *Congressional Quarterly*. The former refers to the percent of time that an individual congressman votes with his party on a "party vote," that is, when a majority of one party is arrayed against a majority of the other. Presidential support refers to the percent of time an individual congressman votes consistently with the announced position of the Chief Executive.

SUBCOMMITTEES

The Legislative Reorganization Act of 1946 succeeded in reducing the number of committees in Congress, but it seems, only at the cost of proliferating the number of subcommittees (Goodwin, 1962; Jones, 1962). Only three committees in the House of Representatives do not use subcommittees and these—Internal Security, Rules, and Ways and Means—are among those most tightly controlled by their chairmen. Refusal to countenance any subdivision of authority enables the chairman to retain the maximum control over committee activity. The remaining committees are divided, roughly equally, between those with ad hoc subcommittees and those which have created standing bodies. The former, usually unnamed, are created by the full-committee chairman to deal with a single piece of legislation, enabling him to keep a close rein on subcommittee activity. The latter, the standing subcommittee, is a permanent panel with fixed jurisdiction and often carves out substantial power and independence with respect to some subset of issues within jurisdiction of the full committee.

The use of subcommittees, especially of the standing type, has profound effects on the structure of the legislative system. In the first place, it permits greater specialization; a legislator may become an expert not on all topics within the jurisdiction of the full committee but rather on the more limited range of questions which his subcommittee treats. Table 3-4 lists the subcommittees of the House Appropriations panel and suggests the extent to which such subdivisions may increase the division of labor and permit greater compartmentalization of function. Notice that there were in 1964 only eighty-two subcommittee assignments for the fifty members of the full committee; each member had no more than two subcommittees to work on and could devote his time and energy to a narrow range of topics within the larger area of appropriations decisions. Since, in Fenno's words, "if there is any generalization about Appropriations Committee activity that is fully supported by past research, it is the proposition that the tasks of the Appropriations Committee are accomplished by its subcommittees" (Fenno, 1966, p. 134), a few legislators, specializing in one or two areas, wield substantial authority over what the committee, and the House as well, does.

The further division of labor made possible by the use of subcommittees, as the preceding suggests, creates greater opportunity for a larger number of lawmakers to exercise power and influence and to show their abilities and expertise to good advantage, albeit over a limited range of subjects. This is all the more true as seniority can sometimes be bypassed in the selection of subcommittee chairmen. The man of talent, then, long before he can expect to accede to leadership on the full committee, can put his expertise to good use and carve out a niche for himself on his subcommittee. Such a possibility may account for the attractiveness of the committee-expert role orientation to so many members of Congress.

Another effect of the use of subcommittees is to provide more specific targets, more precise points of access, for outside interest groups. To the extent that the decisions of Congress are made by subcommittees, the task of the pressure group seeking to influence the content of those decisions is made clearer. The group knows at which hearings to appear, which legislators and staff members to cultivate, and where to focus its attention. If the group can persuade a relatively small number of men—the largest Appropriations subcommittee in 1964 had only a dozen members—that its views are sound, its influence on policy can be substantial. Having its own way will not be easy (as we shall see in Chapter 8), but the subcommittee structure indicates the crucial places to which influence efforts must be directed if they are to have a chance of success.

Finally, from the perspective of the legislative system as a whole, there may be difficulties inherent in the dispersion of influence points created by the vast number of subcommittees. If Congress has difficulty in pulling together its various subunits, in integrating committee products into some reasonable formulation of public policy, the problem is certainly exacerbated by further fragmenting decision-making power into subcommittees. The number of separate entities which must participate in the negotiations, the

TABLE 3-4   Subcommittees of the House Appropriations Committee, 1964

Subcommittee	Size	Democrats	Republicans
Department of Agriculture and Related Agencies	5	3	2
Department of Defense	12	7	5
District of Columbia	5	3	2
Foreign Operations	11	7	4
Independent Offices	7	4	3
Department of Interior and Related Agencies	5	3	2
Departments of Labor, HEW, and Related Agencies	5	3	2
Legislative	5	3	2
Military Construction	5	3	2
Public Works	10	6	4
Departments of State, Justice, and Commerce; the Judiciary; Related Agencies	7	4	3
Departments of Treasury and Post Office; Executive Office	5	3	2
	82		

SOURCE: Richard F. Fenno, *The Power of the Purse,* pp. 131–133. Copyright © 1966, Little, Brown and Co. (Inc.). Reprinted by permission.

"logrolling" by which decisions, inevitably compromises, are reached is vast, so great, it can be argued, that the most likely outcome is a decision *not* to act. Or alternatively, the need to defer to the experts may leave effective decision making in the hands of an atypical group. Much research is needed on the powers actually in the hands of individual subcommittees. In any event, the power of subcommittees is not unlimited; ultimate authority lies with the full committee and the parent chamber. But, as in the relationship between full committee and House or Senate, the prospects are good that the smaller body, capitalizing on the need for a division of labor and expertise, can win considerable autonomy for itself.

Whether this happens depends to a large extent on the behavior of the full committee chairman. In most cases, as Goodwin (1962, p. 598) puts it, subcommittees are the creatures of the chairman—"his personality, his political ideology, and his concept of his role." As already noted, some chairmen refuse to use subcommittees at all while others maintain control by using only ad hoc, temporary units. Even where subcommittees are permanent, the full committee chairman may exercise a good deal of authority if he chooses to do so. Senator Robertson's restriction of the freedom which his predecessor had permitted in the Senate Banking and Currency subcommittees has been noted. A similar case occurred in the House Appropriations Committee with regard to foreign aid. Under Clarence Cannon's (D., Mo.) chairmanship, Rep. Otto Passman (D., La.) was allowed, as chairman of the Foreign Operations subcommittee, to reduce the President's foreign assistance requests substantially; both Cannon and Passman had deep reservations about the efficacy of the program. Upon Cannon's death, George Mahon (D., Tex.) succeeded to the chairmanship and maneuvered successfully to bring the foreign aid decisions more nearly into line with the views of his fellow-Texan, President Lyndon B. Johnson (Drew, 1964).

The committee chairman can manage the subcommittee structure of his committee in a number of ways. He decides whether there will be subcommittees at all. Where they are needed or already exist he can control them through his powers of appointment. The full committee chairman determines who will serve on, and who will chair, any subcommittees he creates. He may appoint himself as ex officio member of any, or all, subcommittees he sets up; his involvement, or even mere presence, may go a long way toward determining what the panel will do. Given the chairman's ability to do favors for, or hinder considerably, individual committee members, they may be loath to incur his wrath by too independent subcommittee behavior. Finally the chairman decides how much financial and staff support a subcommitte will get; units which go along with him will get help, those which act contrary to his wishes may find their resources reduced. Again, it is impossible to predict precisely what pattern of chairman-subcommittee relationships will emerge in any given instance; what is likely, however, is that an acceptable modus vivendi will be worked out, an arrangement which reflects the traditions of the committee, the chairman's desire and ability to control, and the countervailing need of the subcommittee members to free themselves from that control. In short, the chairman has a high potential to control his subcommittees, but he will not always be willing or able to capitalize on it.[20]

To summarize: The use of subcommittees, especially of the standing variety, further fragments power in Congress. Many subcommittees attain, upon the sufferance of the full committee chairman and by developing unmatched expertise, a good deal of freedom in effect to make policy. While such decentralization serves to make the integration of policy more difficult, at the same time it provides opportunities for a number of congressmen, closed out from full committee leadership by the seniority rule, to exercise influence over subcommittee business. Such possibilities may account for the attractiveness of the committee-expert role orientation. The extent to which such opportunities exist will depend on the use which the full committee chairman makes of his potential for control of subcommittee affairs.

COMMITTEE STAFF

There can be little doubt, in the light of the specialization of function and the complexity of the issues which Congress must treat, that the lawmakers need expert help. It may come as a surprise that modern staff practices date only to the 1946 Legislative Reorganization Act, which provided for the hiring of professionals and clerks by each standing committee. (On staffing, see Kofmehl, 1962; Kammerer, 1949, 1951; Patterson, 1970.) In theory, the staff should permit the committee to develop its own information, thus avoiding nearly total dependence on the bureaucracy. If Congress is to evaluate both executive proposals for legislation and bureaucratic operations — that is to perform its legislative and oversight functions— it must have independent sources of data, for the administration is hardly likely freely to confess its own inadequacies. In fact, however, the record of the committees in utilizing their staff resources is mixed.

Staff men can perform a number of useful services for the committees. They can conduct valuable research,[21] or they can become subject-matter specialists, experts on some or all of the matters within the jurisdiction of the committee. Staffers can render legal services, drafting legislation or con-

[20]As Fenno (1970) points out, where subcommittees gain a high degree of autonomy and independence, as those of the House Appropriations Committee possess, the chairman's potential for control is sharply curtailed. He can make initial appointments to the various subcommittees, he can move members to more desirable subcommittee assignments when vacancies occur, and he can create new subcommittees where it seems appropriate, but he has little control over the day-to-day operations of ongoing subcommittees. On other committees, for instance House Interior or Education and Labor, the chairman has been able to regulate the flow of committee business by keeping a tight rein on the subcommittees.
[21]Committee members may also draw upon the resources of the Legislative Reference Service of the Library of Congress, which has been available to perform research since 1914.

ducting hearings and investigations. Finally the committee members may use their staff resources for political, often partisan, duties such as speech writing and handling constituent complaints. Jewell and Patterson (1966, p. 232) suggest a useful distinction between "professional" staffs, which emphasize fact-finding and other research-related activities, and "house-keeping" staffs, which limit themselves to more routine clerical and record-keeping tasks. Only the former serves the purpose which the 1946 Reorganization Act envisaged for congressional staffs.

There are problems with the more professionally oriented staffs as well. First is the question of the purpose to which staff resources are to be committed. There is an ambiguity built into the position of the committee staffer, stemming largely from the great control which the committee chairman exercises over the committee's employees. Though the 1946 act envisaged nonpartisan, professional staffs, and despite some movement in this direction, most committees continue to organize their staffs on a partisan basis, with the chairman, in consultation with the ranking minority member, making the hiring and firing decisions. The staff man faces a dilemma as a result of this situation: should he act as an impartial research man, getting "all the facts" regardless of their implications, or should he assume a partisan orientation, working to build a case which will buttress the position held by the chairman or some other committee member to whom he feels a sense of responsibility? Faced with job insecurity, the staff man may feel a need to follow a safe course and avoid activities which are likely to displease his employer.

Related to this is the position of the minority party.[22] The partisan character of the staff organization on most committees means that the full committee chairman is likely to keep most of the staff for his personal use or that of the majority and to assign only a few persons to assist the minority in developing positions at variance with his. The extent of this practice can be seen in Table 3-5. On the thirty (of the thirty-six) congressional committees which organize their staffs along partisan lines, nearly nine out of ten employees work for the majority. Such an important committee as the House Ways and

[22]This paragraph relies heavily on Cochrane (1964).

TABLE 3-5   *Majority and minority staff assignments, 1962*

Chamber	Committees with partisan staff organization	Employees	Employees assigned to majority	Employees assigned to minority
House	15	413	370 (89.3%)	43 (10.7%)
Senate	15	486	432 (88.8%)	54 (11.2%)

SOURCE: Cochrane, 1964. Reprinted by permission of the author and *Western Political Quarterly.*

Means Committee assigned seventeen of its twenty-one staffers to the majority; comparable figures for the Senate Appropriations Committee were thirty-three majority employees and two minority positions. The minority may be hard put to generate alternatives to the proposals advanced by the majority. By contrast, a few committees, the foreign policy panels in each chamber for example, do not differentiate between majority and minority staff, and maintain technically competent professional staffs accessible to all committee members.

Other issues pertaining to the staffing of congressional committees remain. One is the question of size: of how much assistance can a congressional committee profitably take advantage? It is clear that expertise independent of the executive branch is needed, and that staff work can help provide such data, but staff expansion alone cannot meet the information needs of Congress. Legislators cannot create bureaucracies equal to the executive; they have neither the time nor the inclination to manage such an establishment, and they will continue to rely on executive agencies to a large extent. Moreover, as Gross (1953, pp. 421–423) points out, a large and talented staff may discover more that needs to be done and thus place greater demands on the congressman rather than relieve him of some of his burdens. In addition, there remains the question of the pool of talent available on committee staffs. Staff employees are well educated—nearly all have college training—and many have had valuable legal and political experience (Jewell and Patterson, 1966, pp. 237–241), but it is not clear that the ideal mix of skills has been obtained. Finally, it seems possible that better management practices might help committees organize their staffs to handle more effectively whatever duties are assigned to them.

The issue of staff influence is also worth noting at this point. Another dilemma the staffer must face is the definition of his job: should he serve his committee or should he, as an expert, seek to influence committee decisions? A highly competent staff, such as that of the Joint Committee on Internal Revenue Taxation, a staff used by the House Ways and Means and Senate Finance Committees (Manley, 1968), can wield great power. The more complex the issues, the greater the need of the lawmakers for technical expertise and the greater the opportunity for staff to press its own views. Less directly, a sound staff maintaining good relationships with committee leaders may, as Horn (1970) suggests the Senate Appropriations Committee staff does, "largely determine" the focus of committee attention by the way in which it conducts its research and information-processing activities. On the other hand, norms of professionalism, stressing nonpartisanship, objectivity and neutrality, and loyalty to committee members reduce the temptation for staff men to "play God" (Manley, 1968; Patterson, 1970). In general, such influence as professional staffs may have seems to reflect shared values; staff men and women work to help those lawmakers with whom they agree advance their substantive positions.

In sum, committee staffs can do much to assist their principals by performing a wide range of needed services from technical research to routine filing. Yet because of their dependence in many instances on the committee chairman, because they do not often provide adequate support for the minority members, and because they are not always utilized as effectively as possible by the majority, the committee staffs do not uniformly perform at the level which the 1946 Reorganization Act envisaged. They range from fully professional bodies able to render great assistance through mixed partisan-professional groups less capable of technical activities to housekeeping bodies employed mostly for routine business. The availability of some professional staff assistance seems essential for adequate performance of leadership and committee-expert roles, and the absence of such help may contribute to the avoidance of such orientations.

RELATIONS AMONG COMMITTEES

If the central feature of the committee structure of the two houses of Congress is, as we have suggested, the high degree of independence which each committee possesses and which each jealously seeks to protect, then to discover that the relations among the various committees are not always harmonious should come as no surprise. Attempts by one committee to consider new topics inevitably leads to resentment on the part of another panel which sees the shift as an intrusion on its preserve. Thus intercommittee relationships are characterized by tensions which, in turn, contribute to the uncoordinated pattern which the activities of independent committees often present.

One area of conflict pertains to jurisdictional quarrels. Despite the efforts to define committee jurisdictions more precisely which accompanied the reduction, in 1946, of the number of committees, proposed legislation is almost always so complex, composed of titles dealing with related but separable matters, that seldom does it fit neatly into the defined jurisdiction of a single committee. In the foreign-policy sphere, to cite a recent example, the Senate Foreign Relations and Armed Services Committees often compete to influence the shape of American international relations; each may hold separate hearings on the same topic, requiring executive-branch personnel to appear, making the same presentation, before both bodies. The tension between these two committees has been particularly acute in the 1960s because of a sharp disagreement over the wisdom of national policy with regard to the Vietnam war. The Foreign Relations Committee has been openly critical of American intervention in Southeast Asia while Armed Services has been a staunch defender of American presence there. With regard to foreign affairs more generally, Carroll (1966, pp. 25–26) reports:

The Committee on Foreign Affairs now competes with eighteen other standing committees and miscellaneous select and special units for the foreign policy business of the House of Representatives. All of these committees are at least indirectly concerned with foreign affairs. More than half of them regularly consider important foreign policy matters usually in jealous isolation from one another.

Similar dispersion of related topics among a number of committees is common in domestic affairs as well; transportation policy, for example, is treated by at least six of the standing panels in each house.

Steps to alleviate the difficulties created by unclear, overlapping jurisdictions are seldom effective. Occasionally, a select committee will be established to handle a bill or conduct an investigation when other committees cannot resolve their squabbles. Even less often, two committees will agree to handle the matter of conflict jointly. Members of one committee, however, may be invited to participate in the deliberations of another unit, thus reducing, but not eliminating, the conflict between the two panels. In short, cooperation among committees is not great; the rivalries among the subdivisions tend to be severe enough to prevent them from working together effectively.

Another form of intercommittee tension stems from the division of lawmaking into *authorization* and *appropriations* phases. Congress acts first to authorize programs, that is, to set the substantive guidelines for the application of policy. The subject-matter standing committees handle this stage of action. Even though authorized, programs require funding; without money they cannot be put into operation. Money decisions are the province of the appropriations committees and their behavior often leads to conflict with the substantive committees. These latter, having authorized programs, expect them to be financed properly; the appropriations bodies, eager to save money, seek to spend as little as possible.[23] Failure to appropriate adequate funds, in effect, reverses earlier decisions. Moreover, the appropriations panel may, informally, attempt to influence the authorization phase by suggesting in advance the purposes for which it is willing to expend public money and those for which it is not. These activities are resented by the standing committees as infringements on their prerogatives and inevitably lead to tensions among the committees.

The lack of cooperation which results from these jurisdictional sensitivities contributes to the independence of congressional committees and to a lack of policy coordination. Carroll's (1966, p. 89) presentation of national security affairs as "a picture of the uncoordinated control of interrelated foreign policy matters by a host of little governments upon which the House had devolved vast powers" seems an accurate portrayal of the situation in other

---

[23]For a discussion of the conflicting sets of expectations held by the Appropriations and substantive committees, see Fenno, 1966.

areas as well. Moreover, "cooperation between the staffs of the committees is deterred by the same obstacles which discourage other cooperative arrangements between committees" (Carroll, 1966, p. 230). In short, if Congress seems unable or unwilling to produce integrated policy, it may be because the legislators do not wish to work together to achieve that goal.

SUMMARY AND DISCUSSION

This chapter has attempted to identify and discuss the structural factors which contribute to a legislative system in which power is widely distributed among highly autonomous standing committees. Among the important considerations in this regard are (1) the kinds of people who win assignment to the committees and the things— personal interest in the matters within the panel's jurisdiction and the prestige of the committee, for instance— which lead the members to aspire to leadership and expert roles within the unit; (2) the position of the committee chairman: his powers and how he chooses to use them; (3) the nature of the subcommittee structure; and (4) the competence of the committee staff, and the uses to which staff resources are put. The success of the committees in developing power and independence guarantees that relations among the bodies will be less than harmonious.

Identifying these important elements suggests only the broad limits within which committee behavior may vary, and in fact, there are wide variations in the ways in which the committees do act. To illustrate the differing patterns which committees may be expected to follow, it may be instructive, following Eulau and Hinckley (1966), to examine briefly three types of committee structure which exist in the House of Representatives. First is the *oligarchic* structure, typified by the Rules Committee.[24] This body has substantial influence over the business of the House, stemming from its ability to regulate the conditions under which legislation will be considered on the floor of the chamber, an ability which permits committee members to make their views felt in the deliberations of the standing committee involved. The latter, desiring to get its bill to the floor under circumstances in which it will pass, may well try to write a bill which can gain Rules Committee clearance.

This power has made Rules an attractive assignment (see Table 3-1); its ability to shape policy across a broad spectrum of issues has given it high prestige and earned the panel a strong commitment from its members. Recent Rules chairmen, Reps. Howard Smith (D., Va.) and William Colmer (D., Miss.), have exercised strong control, which most often takes the form of preventing bills opposed by the frequently conservative committee majority from reaching the floor. The committee, small in size, has not used subcommittees, preferring to handle its business in full committee sessions. In short,

[24]Data on the Rules Committee are from Robinson (1963).

the Rules Committee possesses both procedural and policy influence, has developed a substantial esprit de corps under the leadership of strong chairmen, and has as a result been a major force in the legislative system. Even the 1961 enlargement of the committee from twelve to fifteen members which was designed to bring the committee more nearly into line with the majority-party leadership seems to have left the powers and position of Rules virtually unchanged (Robinson, 1963, pp. 71–81; Cummings and Peabody, 1963; Peabody, 1963).[25] Fenno's (1970) description of the Interior Committee of the House, under the chairmanship of Wayne Aspinall (D., Colo.), indicates that it approximates the oligarchic structural pattern.

At the other extreme, the Education and Labor Committee presents an *anarchic* pattern.[26] This body treats two relatively separate topics and frequently draws members interested in one but not the other. Moreover it has attracted legislators of heterogeneous background who tend to assume an ideological posture toward the issues under consideration. Further complicating matters, the chairmanship has until recently been in the hands of strong-willed personalities, Reps. Graham Barden (D., N.C.) and Adam Clayton Powell, who did not develop consensus within the committee on procedures much less on the substance of policy. Thus the panel has operated in a "fiercely competitive" fashion which "encourages decision making by free-for-all" (Fenno, 1963, pp. 205–209; Fenno, 1970). Subcommittees are frequently rearranged and their membership altered. As a result the committee's patchwork bills are often lost on the floor. In the light of these difficulties, committee prestige is relatively low, member interest in committee work only moderate, and turnover among members relatively high; these factors, in turn, make the attainment of even a modicum of agreement on the "rules of the game" difficult.

The *bargaining* structure which the Agriculture Committee displays is an intermediate type.[27] Despite diverging interests, the committee has been successful in developing procedures which make it possible for agreement to be reached and legislation passed. Attractive to representatives from farming areas, the unit has used its subcommittee structure as a means for resolving its difficulties. The subcommittees are organized along commodity lines—for cotton, dairy products, wheat, peanuts, and so on—and each member gravitates to the subcommittees which handle the chief products of his district. The subcommittees are given great leeway to write the law for their commodities. Agriculture bills thus tend to be compromises, each subcommittee getting its proposals included and yielding to the desires of the others. The task of the chairman has been to facilitate the negotiations by which a bill

---

[25] In 1961, the House also imposed a "21-Day Rule" on the committee which allowed bills to move to the floor if no committee action was taken in twenty-one days; this power was allowed to lapse in 1963.
[26] The description of Education and Labor draws heavily from Fenno (1963, 1970). See also McAdams, 1964, and Tyler, 1959.
[27] The source of data on the Agriculture Committee is Jones (1961).

acceptable to the full committee is drafted. While there remain dissatisfactions and a tendency for votes to divide along party lines, this bargaining style has enabled the committee to get its legislation passed on the floor and to earn moderate prestige as a place where a representative can work effectively on behalf of his constituents. The House Ways and Means Committee, though it does not use subcommittees, reaches agreement through a negotiation process. The chairman and ranking minority member—Wilbur Mills (D., Ark.) and John W. Byrnes (R., Wis.)—dominate the bargaining, however, and the committee thus has features of both the bargaining and the oligarchic types (Manley, 1970; Fenno, 1970).

Congressional committees, as these examples amply illustrate, operate in a number of ways. In assessing his personal commitment to the committee arrangement, the individual lawmaker is likely to ask himself several questions: Can I get assigned to a committee where I can advance my personal interests? Those congressmen with policy concerns—inventors and tribunes— will seek places on policy-oriented committees like Education and Labor or Foreign Affairs. Those interested in power for its own sake—brokers and, in some cases, ritualists—will look to influential and prestigious panels like Appropriations and Ways and Means. Others, opportunists or those with delegate-representational styles or district- (state-) representational focuses, may look to committees, like Interior, Public Works, or Post Office, where constituency service and reelection goals go hand-in-hand.

Once assigned to a committee the questions become: Does my committee possess the power, and the high regard which goes with power, to permit me, as a member, to work on important matters and for the benefit of my constituents? Does the committee operate in a fashion—using subcommittees and adequate staff under the direction of a sympathetic or at least tolerant chairman—to facilitate these purposes? To the extent that committee work seems attractive, the congressman may adopt expert—and leadership—role orientations toward the panel; to the degree that it appears to lack promise, he may assume an orientation of indifference and work for his transfer to a committee which looks more hopeful.

While individually the committees display substantial structural variability,[28] as a whole they remain the major decentralizing forces in the legislative system. Each exercises considerable influence over the affairs within its jurisdiction regardless of the pattern of behavior adopted. Because each committee, and sometimes an individual subcommittee, is an independent locus of power, it becomes necessary to find ways to overcome these fragmenting tendencies if an integrated program is to be produced. In other

---

[28]We have stressed structural features in this chapter. Each committee operates within a set of written rules (see Chapter 5), a set of informal norms or folkways (Chapter 6), and a host of environmental forces (Chapters 7–9), all of which bear somewhat differently on individual committees. When all these factors are considered (as Chapter 10 seeks to do) the range of committee variability is considerably widened.

words, centripetal forces must counteract the centrifugal force of the committees. One such force is the political party; if the party can command support when in conflict with committees, then it can integrate policy proposals and act as a centralizing force in Congress. To a discussion of the ability of the party to perform as a countervailing, and thus integrating, institution we now turn.

CHAPTER FOUR

Political Parties in Congress

The preceding chapter attempted to suggest that the character of the legislative system reflects to a very large degree the development of highly autonomous and powerful congressional committees. This fragmented, decentralized feature of the congressional system requires that most decisions be reached through a process of bargaining and compromise. Unstructured negotiation is unlikely to be productive and will rarely lead to acceptable outputs unless there is some force which will mediate among the conflicting interests and pressures which play among the members of Congress. The political party, operating through its leaders, seeks to provide this focus, the centralizing force which will permit a meaningful set of decisions to be reached. The party, as we shall see, is incapable of counteracting entirely the fragmenting tendencies created by the committees and other features of the system, but it is the major internal force for order and integration of decisions within the system.[1]

It should be remembered that we are using the term political party in a limited fashion, to refer to the party machinery *within* Congress. But the American political party is not a monolith; the federal system ensures that state and local organizations will have substantial independence from the national party. A senator or representative may respond to the *national*

---

[1]Chapter 7 will suggest that the President, though external to the legislative system, will provide a unifying focus for members of his political party and to an extent, in a negative fashion, for the opposition as well.

party, symbolized by the National Committee and led by the President or by the titular leader of the party out of power; to the *local* party, which as we have seen may be crucial to his electoral prospects; or to the *congressional* party, the leadership of his party within the national legislature. If he does not support the leaders in Congress, if he votes against them, he may be doing so in response to a different conception of party loyalty (Huitt, 1969, p. 227). The concern of this chapter is the degree to which the congressional party apparatus can provide the leadership required to produce the outputs it seeks to generate. Where party fails, and it often does not succeed, it may be because there exist more powerful demands from outside the system, including demands from other types of party organization.

THE FUNCTIONS OF THE CONGRESSIONAL PARTY

The basic goal of the party in the legislature is to "make a record," to "implement the party's vision of what is good for the nation,"[2] to convince the citizenry to vote for it at the ensuing election. The majority party seeks to retain that status while the majority hopes to win sufficient seats to gain control of the legislature. In the last analysis, the party seeks to pass desirable, or to block unacceptable, legislation, and the acid test of leadership is to produce the legislative votes to achieve these purposes. Its accomplishments in this respect provide the core of the argument with which the party takes its case to the people.

In seeking these goals, the party performs a number of useful functions for the legislature.[3] First of all, it is the chief organizing force in Congress. The major leaders, who assume responsibility for advancing the business of the House or Senate, are chosen by the political party, and they, in turn, guide the selection of other, subsidiary leaders. Committee assignments, as described in Chapter 3, are made by the parties. Next, the parties, especially the majority, schedule the activity of the chamber; the leadership decides, often after considering the wishes of the President, the relevant committee chairman, or the rank-and-file membership, and when and how to move the issues up for decision toward resolution. Third, the parties, as they seek to persuade their members to support the party position, serve as important agencies for the collection and distribution of information; through the communications channels of the party, lawmakers learn what their leaders propose to do and can transmit their own views to the top of the party hierarchy. The leaders, in addition, are the chief agents of liaison with the executive, and can feed its views into the congressional communications network. Finally, the parties

---

[2]Ripley, 1969*a*, p. 2. Ripley is perhaps the closest student of congressional party leadership and much in this chapter relies on his excellent work. For an extensive listing of works relevant to the study of the congressional party, see Jones and Ripley, 1966.
[3]This paragraph draws heavily from Ripley, 1969*a*, chap. 3.

do much to promote attendance at congressional sessions; if they are to unify their members, they must get them to the floor to back party programs. The congressional party, in short, provides much of the impetus for the legislature to act.

ASSETS AND LIABILITIES OF THE
CONGRESSIONAL PARTY

As it attempts to generate cohesive support for particular positions on legislative issues, and thus to make a record which will serve it well electorally, the party in Congress has some advantages and encounters some obstacles. On the positive side, party has meaning for its members. Most personal friendships are within the lawmaker's party; members of Congress generally agree that "it is much easier to become acquainted with party colleagues than political opponents" (Clapp, 1964, p. 15). Association with fellow partisans creates a sense of belonging which may be expected to translate into a feeling of loyalty and a desire to help the party if it is at all possible to do so. Failure to act with party may be met with antagonism. Describing an instance when some forty Southern Democrats voted with the Republicans to pass some restrictive amendments to a housing bill, the late Rep. Clem Miller (D., Calif.) reports (1962, p. 111):

> The hostility on the part of other Democrats to this action was as visible as an unsheathed knife. Then, as each amendment came along fewer Southerners arose with the Republicans, till at last there were only five left, conspicuously self-conscious. [Quoted by permission of Charles Scribner's Sons.]

In short, as they attempt to rally support for their position, the party leadership can draw upon a psychological predisposition on the part of most members to go along if there are no strong reasons to the contrary. Put another way, most congressmen assume a loyalist rather than a maverick orientation toward their party.

The data in Table 4-1 indicate the extent of party loyalty. Nearly six out of ten congressmen, Democrats and Republicans alike, would prefer, other things being equal, to support their party; conversely, only 20 percent espouse a basically nonloyalist, or maverick, orientation. Not surprisingly, Davidson (1969, pp. 152–160) finds that leaders have strong feelings of loyalty to their parties; indeed, unswerving support of party may help to propel them to leadership position in the first place. Additionally, seniority appears to erode partisan commitment. While freshmen lawmakers, newly arrived in Washington, need and use party as a focal point for their period of adjustment to legislative life, seniors, familiar with the ways of Congress, have less need to lean on party and evince less loyalty. Finally, the representatives of safe districts, many of which are in the South, seem less positively oriented toward party. Their electoral futures secure, these legislators are relatively immune to the modest pressures that party can bring to bear upon them. There exists, then, considerable goodwill toward the political parties which provides the basis for loyalist appeals to stand with the party.

If they can capitalize on these feelings the party leaders are in a position to produce some centralization. Party is the chief basis of legislative organization, as previously noted, and to the extent that party majorities can be unified in committee and subcommittee and on the floor, the party-sponsored decisions should move through the various stages of the legislative process without hindrance. It is obvious, of course, that this does not always happen; majorities exist more often in name than in fact. This is so for a number of reasons. First, the party is largely without sanctions and can do little to compel a recalcitrant member to back the party position. Because his political future will not be determined in Congress but rather in his state or district, the individual lawmaker will often look outside the legislature for guidance. The congressional party leaders can only seek to persuade their followers to support the party views when these sentiments conflict with the desires of competing centers of influence.

Second, a number of competitors for the loyalty of congressmen do, in fact, exist, and they often possess more means of influence than does the congressional party. There are, of course, the committees within the legislature. The committee-expert role often takes precedence over the party-loyalist orientation; the substantive specialist may well feel he knows more about the topic than the party leaders and may act accordingly when his views conflict with theirs. Constituency is another focus for loyalty; political survival is more crucial to most legislators than a vote for party. Local politics—the party organization and the opinions, real or imagined, of any crucial segment of the electorate—may be sufficient to lead senators or representatives to desert to the opposition. Finally, other, informal groups—ideological groups such as the Democratic Study Group, state delegations, and social clubs such as the Republican Wednesday Club (liberal) and the

TABLE 4-1 Party role orientations among congressmen

Orientation	All (%)	Democrats (%)	Republicans (%)
Loyalist	59	59	59
Neutral	21	19	24
Maverick	20	21	18
Total	100	99	101
N	(86)	(52)	(34)

SOURCE: Data collected by Roger H. Davidson, David M. Kovenock, and Michael K. O'Leary and made available through the Interuniversity Consortium for Political Research.

Democratic Boll Weevils (conservative)—often make a claim on the loyalty of legislators and the leadership may have to deal with them, making concessions to win their support. And, to repeat, the ultimate recourse of the party leaders to counteract these divisive features of the system is mainly persuasion and not compulsion.

One other set of general considerations is relevant to any assessment of the congressional party: its status as majority or minority, with or without control of the White House. For one thing, the leaders of the party whose national ticket captured the Presidency have a special problem; they need to decide whether they will act primarily as the President's men on Capitol Hill, seeking to assist the Chief Executive to pass his legislative proposals, or whether they will work to convey congressional sentiments to the President, and to have these opinions incorporated into the executive program. Such a choice is not an "either-or" decision, however. Party leaders will do both, sometimes urging their followers to support the executive, on other occasions attempting to persuade the President to respect legislative attitudes. And a particular leader's emphasis can be discerned: during the Ninetieth Congress, for instance, Speaker of the House John McCormack (D., Mass.) sought to promote the program of the President while his Senate counterpart, Democratic Floor Leader Mike Mansfield (Mont.), seemed less directly an agent of the executive in Congress.[4]

Moreover, the sort of majority-presidential relationship is crucial to the congressional party's position and activities. Ripley (1969a, pp. 11–14) suggests that four configurations are possible, and that each has existed frequently during the twentieth century. One possibility is a "presidential-partisan" majority where the Chief Executive has the support of an overwhelming majority of his fellow partisans in Congress and has little need to woo the opposition. The 100 Days of the New Deal and the Eighty-ninth Congress, which bore the stamp of the Republican disaster of 1964, are recent examples of this situation. Such arrangements are usually marked by strong presidential leadership in the legislature and by the passage of an unusually large number of bills, with the President's party providing the necessary votes. The task of the party leadership is to mobilize the existing party majority.

A second configuration is the "presidential-bipartisan" majority, where the President's congressional party is a nominal majority but cannot count on the support of all its members and must seek votes from the minority in order to advance its legislative program. Since he is more dependent on the legislative leadership, which must cross party lines for support, the Chief Executive is likely to give his party leaders a greater voice in policy making. The presidential-bipartisan arrangement characterized much of the Democratic era of the 1960s, with the exception of the Eighty-ninth Congress (1965 to

---

[4]As Mansfield once put it: "I'm not the leader, really. They don't do what I tell them. I do what they tell me." Russell Baker, *The New York Times,* July 17, 1961, quoted in Robinson, 1967, p. 188.

1966). Ordinarily Presidents Kennedy and Johnson could not count on sufficient loyalty from Southerners in their own party and were required to appeal for Republican support if their programs were to pass.

At some periods, though they seem to be becoming increasingly rare, the President may leave his congressional party leaders on their own, that is, he assumes a relatively passive stance vis-à-vis the legislature, preferring to make only a limited number of requests and to let Congress proceed with minimum pressure from the White House. Ripley designates this a "congressional" majority and cites the early Eisenhower administration (1953 to 1954) as its most recent occurrence. In this situation, the leaders in Congress must set their own priorities and can exercise substantial control over the actions of the House and Senate.

Finally, it has frequently been the case that the President's party has been the minority in at least one chamber of Congress or, from the reverse perspective, the majority in the legislature must operate confronting a Chief Executive of the opposition. Following Truman (1959, pp. 312–316), Ripley has labeled this a "truncated" majority to indicate its incomplete character. When facing a President of the other party, as the Democratic majority in the Ninety-second Congress was required to do, the congressional leaders must make their record on their own, often in the face of presidential hostility. Table 4-2 summarizes these configurations.

The minority party must also make some difficult choices, though the options open to its leaders are somewhat limited. When facing a presidential-partisan majority, the votes of the minority are not needed and it has little to bargain with; as a result there is little to do but oppose, thus enabling the party to capitalize on errors of the majority. In the presidential-bipartisan and congressional-majority situations, the alternatives are greater. The minority can, of course, continue to oppose, stating its objections to, and seeking to defeat, the proposals which the majority advances.[5] House Minority Leader Charles Halleck (R., Ind.), who held his post from 1959 to 1965, favored this

---

[5] See, on the minority party, Jones, 1968, 1970, and Peabody, 1967, 1969.

TABLE 4-2   The majorities of Congress: 1901–1972

Type	Years of occurrence	Most recent occurrence
Presidential-partisan	24	89th Congress (1965–1966)
Presidential-bipartisan	16	90th Congress (1967–1968)
Congressional	14	83rd Congress (1953–1954)
Truncated	18	92nd Congress (1971–1972)

SOURCE: Ripley, 1969a, p. 13. (The Ninetieth Congress has been assigned to the presidential-bipartisan category; the Ninety-first and Ninety-second are clearly of the truncated type.)

tactic; in part this contributed to his replacement by Gerald Ford (R., Mich.). More frequently, the minority will try to influence the decisions of the majority in a more positive fashion. It can offer the votes which the nominal majority needs to enact its policy choices; in return for this cooperation it can expect to have some influence over the substance of policy. The Senate Republican minority, under Floor Leader Everett M. Dirksen of Illinois, had the necessary votes to close off debate and pass the civil rights bills of the 1960s. In these circumstances, the content of the legislation was designed, in close consultation with Senator Dirksen, to secure the crucial minority cooperation.

Alternatively, in the presidential-bipartisan or congressional-majority situations, the minority can take the approach, favored by House Minority Leader Gerald Ford in the 1965-1969 period, of offering "constructive alternatives" to the proposals of the President. This tactic aims at showing that the minority has a "better idea" and perhaps at encouraging sufficient defections from the majority to enact the outparty's preferences. Finally, a truncated minority—most recently with control of the White House but of neither house of Congress[6]—will have to try to help the President pass his legislative program, but will require some compromise to win sufficient majority votes to do so. In 1969, for example, the Republican minority successfully passed President Nixon's income tax surcharge extension by attaching tax reform provisions attractive to the majority Democrats; the extension passed by a 210 to 205 vote, the majority casting more than fifty of the necessary votes.

In sum, political parties are "the principal agents of centralization in a decentralized political arena" (Bibby and Davidson, 1967, p. 113). In seeking to make a record and to enhance their electoral prospects, they can draw upon extensive resources. The party is the central focus of most legislators' loyalties; the men of Congress want to support their parties. Moreover, if such support is forthcoming, the parties are strategically placed in the structure of the legislative system to perform their unifying function. But the desire to assume a loyalist orientation toward political party meets counter-vailing pressures from committee, constituency, and a variety of informal groups, and in the last analysis party is powerless to enforce discipline. It must capitalize on its potential through persuasion, and its ability to do so will depend in part on its position as majority or minority and its relationship to the President, in part on the kinds of men who occupy the positions of party leadership and their ability to piece together the "fragments of power" of which the legislative system consists, and in part on what the times demand.

[6]This has been the case in the three most recent instances of the truncated majority situation: The Eightieth Congress where a Democratic President (Truman) faced a Republican congressional majority, and the Eighty-fourth through Eighty-sixth Congresses (Eisenhower) and the Ninety-first and Ninety-second Congresses (Nixon) where a GOP Chief Executive had to deal with Democratic majorities in the House and Senate.

The party, in Truman's (1959, p. 95) words, is "mediate and supplementary rather than immediate and inclusive in function"; it is often important but seldom crucial to the congressman; it is a major, but by no means the only, competitor for the loyalty of senators and representatives.

THE PARTY MACHINERY

To this point the discussion has dealt with the party leadership in general and undifferentiated form; in this section we will treat the specific structures of the party apparatus, attempting to suggest what resources the party leaders possess, and the limitations on those resources, as they seek to provide some counterpoise to the divisive, decentralizing tendencies which the committees introduce. For present purposes, the party leadership will include the Speaker of the House, the floor leaders, the whip apparatus, and the various committees which the parties maintain. What should be clear from the descriptions which follow is that the party is without real power to enforce its wishes; what it can do depends in very large part on the men who man its leadership posts, on their skills of persuasion and on their personal styles in general.

The Speaker of the House The Speaker is the single most important party leader in the House. In his person are combined the leadership of the majority party and the powers of the chamber's presiding officer. Though the seniority rule does not apply to the selection of party leaders, the Speaker has, recently at least, served for long years before elevation to his post; during the present century no representative has attained the Speakership with fewer than sixteen years of prior service, and the twelve men who have held the position have averaged twenty-four years (Ripley, 1967, pp. 14–15). During such a lengthy period of House membership, the Speaker can be expected to have built up a network of friendships with his colleagues, to have earned their respect through diligence and conformity to the norms of the system, and to have, as a result, gained some influence with many of his fellow partisans. It is these qualities, plus demonstrated loyalty to party, which lead the party conference, the full membership of the party, to select him for the major leadership post.[7]

As chief partisan, the Speaker plays an important part in the production of the party's record. He participates, along with other members of the

[7]For example, Carl Albert (D., Okla.), who succeeded to the Speakership upon the retirement of John McCormack in 1971, was a veteran of twenty-four years of House service, had "travelled a careful political road that . . . earned him almost no enemies and . . . made him acceptable to all factions of the Democratic party" (*Congressional Quarterly Weekly Report,* Dec. 25, 1970, p. 3071).

In practice, each party conference nominates its leader for the Speakership. In a straight party vote on the floor of the House, the majority elects its man. The losing minority candidate serves as his party's floor leader.

leadership circle, in deliberations with the President when they are of the same political affiliation, presenting his views on what the House will or will not be able to produce and carrying the sentiments of the Chief Executive to Congress. As leader, the Speaker is among the chief architects of legislative strategy; he, together with his majority floor leader, decides how best to advance his party's purposes. Once a program has been determined, it becomes the responsibility of the Speaker and other leaders to move that program through the various stages of the legislative process. Moreover, the Speaker is influential in his party's committee assignments. According to one recent Speaker, during his tenure "no Republican went on an important committee without [his] approval" (Martin, 1960, p. 181). Thus, as previously noted, aspirants for choice committee posts carry their campaigns to the party leaders, including the Speaker.

The Speaker has other resources as well (Ripley, 1967, pp. 23–24). Over and above the ability to influence the allocation of committee seats, he can provide intangible rewards, friendship, recognition of a colleague's accomplishments, trust and respect for another's integrity. Judicious use of these rewards—including invitations to informal discussions of party and policy matters—will enable the Speaker to retain the maximum loyalty of his followers. He can also use his central position in the party's network of communications to good advantage. He, more than most legislators, knows what is going on, and he can supply this information to others who need it as he chooses, in a fashion to suit his own ends. The Speaker, in short, has what Ripley calls "the resources of psychological preferment" with which he can impart a feeling of belonging or of ostracism to the members of his party. The widely shared desire for preferment gives the representatives an incentive to cooperate with the leadership.

As the presiding officer in the House, the Speaker possesses other useful powers. The chair must, under the rules of the House, refer bills to the appropriate committee, and since in some cases committee jurisdiction is unclear he will occasionally have discretion which he can use to further his party's program. When bills are under consideration on the floor, congressmen participate in the debate on recognition from the Speaker; this parliamentary power can be used at times to advance the cause favored by his party. Finally, the Speaker interprets the rules of the House, deciding whether and when they apply.[8] Yet the presiding-officer facet of the Speaker's position is of minimal value to him as a party leader, for there exist congressional expectations of impartiality. Thus the Speaker's exploitation of the rules is likely to be restrained, and his rulings, in any case, can be reversed by a majority vote.

---

[8] The 21-Day Rule, in effect during the Eighty-ninth Congress, empowered the Speaker to call bills to the floor if the Rules Committee had not acted within the three-week period. When centralized power is needed, there seems to be a tendency to look to the majority party, and the Speaker in particular, for its exercise.

In short, as a highly regarded party member of long standing, the contemporary Speaker begins with a potential for personal influence; to this he adds the prerequisites of his office. Yet these resources, and his skill in employing them, permit him only to try to lead; they do not guarantee his success, for there is little he can do to compel a recalcitrant committee or subcommittee chairman or even a reluctant lawmaker to place party above the other competitors for loyalty. The Speaker can, in other words, *urge* behavior in keeping with a loyalist orientation toward party, but he cannot enforce party discipline.

The Senate, it should be noted in passing, has no figure directly comparable to the Speaker of the House. The majority party leadership and presiding-officer functions are separate; the floor leader handles the former while the Constitution gives the duty to preside to the Vice President. The Vice President seldom takes this chore seriously, however; since he can vote only in the rare event of a tie, there is little incentive to be present. And in the more relaxed and smaller Senate, decisions of the chair are less likely to be crucial, and his presence is not often required. A visitor to the Senate will most often find a freshman senator in the chair; as is frequently the case the routine chores fall to the lot of junior senators.

Floor leaders In three of the four congressional parties—both in the Senate and the minority in the House—the floor leader operates as the principal party leader. The exception, of course, is the House majority leader who shares leadership responsibility with the Speaker, and who in most cases ranks in practice as well as theory as number two in his party. Like the Speaker, the floor leaders tend to be chosen because of the widely held confidence in them; they have served for extended periods, and have earned the respect of their colleagues as trustworthy spokesmen for the party.[9] The leaders are men who abide by the informal norms (see Chapter 6) and who have avoided extreme ideological positions; they can treat all factions within the party with fairness if not impartiality.[10]

The main function of the floor leaders is to guide the party as it seeks to create a record on which to stand at subsequent elections. This involves

[9] In the House, for instance, in the twentieth century no majority leader had served fewer than twelve years prior to assuming his post, and no minority leader had fewer than ten years' service (Ripley, 1967, pp. 26 and 30–31). Thus, Hale Boggs (D., La.), chosen in 1971 to succeed Carl Albert as majority leader, had served fourteen terms in the House, and had, according to Congressional Quarterly (*Weekly Report,* Jan. 22, 1971, p. 178), "built a successful House career by supporting the legislative goals of the national Democratic Party. . . ." Moreover, his middle-of-the-road stands on the issues "won him acceptance among urban and Northern Democrats that has distinguished him from more orthodox Southerners and . . . helped him build the coalition he needed to become Majority Leader."

[10] Where a substantial segment of the party believes it is denied a fair chance to present its views, it may look to a change in leadership to redress its grievances. The replacement as Republican leader of Charles Halleck by Gerald Ford in 1965 was in part triggered by a feeling among the younger, often more liberal, Republicans that the strategy of outright opposition favored by Halleck, a self-styled "gut fighter," did not allow them sufficient influence within the councils of the party. See Peabody, 1966, and his other works, cited above, footnote 5.

determining party strategy: What provisions should proposed legislation contain? What is the best method to secure passage of the desired bills? How can voting strength be mustered in support of such legislation? Once these decisions are made, the leaders have some resources at their disposal with which to implement their strategic choices, but, as with the Speaker, these provide a basis on which to negotiate arrangements rather than a means to compel compliance. Leadership remains an art, an ability to persuade those who can easily choose an independent course of action to defer to the wishes of the party, as determined by its leaders.

The majority floor leaders possess the same sorts of tools as the Speaker. They can offer tangible rewards for compliance: they are involved in the committee-assignment process; they can share the knowledge which comes to them as centers in the circulation of information as they see fit; and they can try to take advantage of the more intimate relationship with the President which they gain as leaders. Other favors are also available; the floor leaders can aid individual legislators in a number of ways. They can help congressmen with their constituents by providing support for a pet project, support which may entail making sure a bill that has no chance to pass receives a respectable number of votes. The leaders can try to secure favorable treatment, from the perspective of the party member, of constituency-oriented proposals such as public works projects like parks, dams, and post offices. By helping in patronage matters, the leaders may assist the representative in securing his political situation in his state or district. They may also provide campaign assistance when election time rolls around. Beyond these, there are less obvious ways for the leadership to provide benefits; their involvement in the scheduling of chamber business, especially in the Senate,[11] permits them, for instance, to try to arrange a roll call vote at a time when a legislator will be present; they have a voice in the allocation of office space, which comes in unequal size and quality; they control desirable overseas assignments as the chamber's representative at international meetings.

The majority floor leaders are able to confer psychological, or intangible, rewards as well. By paying attention to their followers—speaking to them, communicating with them, including them in meetings and group discussions —the leaders can make them feel important cogs in the party machinery, vital to its success. Beginning with the respect which led initially to their accession to leadership and adding to this their ability to gratify the legislators' need to belong, the floor leaders can capitalize on the initial feelings of party loyalty which the rank and file often bring to congressional service. They can, through judicious dispensation of their largesse—tangible and intangible—make the party-loyalist orientation attractive to many lawmakers.

This extensive arsenal should not lead us to forget that the leaders have

[11] In the House, where the Rules Committee has considerable influence over the conditions under which a bill is considered, the leadership has less flexibility in arranging schedules to suit individual convenience.

no way to ensure that bargains with congressmen are consummated. The techniques of one of the most successful floor leaders, Senate Majority Leader Lyndon B. Johnson, amply illustrate the essential negotiating and compromise methods which characterize the conduct of leadership.[12] Senator Johnson, possessed with these weapons and with a mastery of parliamentary procedure, took a highly personal approach to leadership; he is reported to have talked with every Democratic senator, and many Republicans, daily. In these conversations he followed a number of strategic imperatives. First, he sought to shape situations in a way that would permit each member to stand with the party. Next, he "exploited every opportunity to get his colleagues to think, not as Northerners or Southerners, liberals or conservatives, but as Democrats" (Huitt, 1961a, p. 340). To cite one instance, Johnson managed to hold his party together in opposition to an Eisenhower appointment to the National Labor Relations Board by casting the issue not in ideological terms, which was certain to divide the party, but rather, on the basis of some inconsistent testimony by the nominee, as a question of shabby treatment of the Senate. All Democrats, he hoped, would unite to object to the "flouting of the dignity of the Senate."

This same case reveals another Johnson tactic: focusing on a few "key" senators in order, by gaining their support, to win the backing of other men who follow the lead of their influential colleagues. In the NLRB controversy Sen. Walter George (D., Ga.) was the crucial man; once he was led to see the issue as Johnson wished him to, he led his followers to vote against confirmation of a nominee with whom they had a good deal of ideological sympathy. Finally, Johnson sought to frame each issue as a compromise, to suggest that his proposal was the best possible legislation *that could pass,* and that it constituted a common ground on which party men could stand united. In sum, Johnson saw his leadership task as emphasizing the party orientation at the expense of competing focuses of loyalty, and he used personal contact and persuasion to seek this goal.

It is interesting to note that Johnson's success came during a truncated majority situation where he was free to operate without the constraints imposed by a President of his own party. In the other, more common situations (see pp. 90–92), the choices of the majority leadership will have to take presidential preferences into account, and this will inevitably, even if the Chief Executive is relatively indifferent, restrict its range of alternatives. This should serve as a reminder that situational factors, including the party's relationship to the President, impose limitations on the leader's ability to maneuver. So, too, does the "temper of the times"—the national condition and mood—which may stimulate or retard the exercise of party leadership. The New Deal period (1933–1939) and the mid-1960s were periods where

---

[12]The classic study of the Johnson leadership is Huitt, 1961a. What follows draws heavily on his descriptions and insights. See also Evans and Novak, 1966, pp. 88–118, reprinted in Pettit and Keynes, 1969, pp. 177–199; and Stewart, 1971.

circumstances coalesced to permit party leaders to generate high levels of party cohesion; both periods were presidential-partisan majorities, obviating the need to negotiate with the minority. The Eisenhower administration, and perhaps that of Richard Nixon, appear to be periods of reevaluation and consolidation rather than innovation, making leadership more difficult. Finally, the personality, style, and skills of the individual party leaders are related to their success in mobilizing their followers. Lyndon Johnson had the drive and interpersonal abilities to make effective use of his bargaining advantages; other leaders appear less forceful, more reticent, and as a result less able to harmonize the discordant voices of their partisans. These kinds of considerations, thus, fix the boundaries within which majority leadership operates, and within which the more specific inducements can be used to generate support for party positions.

The minority leaders face roughly similar leadership tasks, though their opportunities are somewhat more limited and their resources less extensive. They must, as previously noted, decide whether to offer alternatives to the majority's proposals; barter support, if the majority needs it, for concessions; or simply resist what the majority desires. To rally support for whatever choices they make, the minority leaders can employ inducements similar to those which the opposition possesses: substantial items—committee assignments, information, campaign assistance, and the like—or more ephemeral satisfactions such as the gratification which comes from proffered friendship and respect. The range of choice is more limited, however: The minority has less control over the scheduling of chamber business; it seldom has the ability to enlist the President in causes dear to the hearts of rank-and-file legislators; it has fewer opportunities to provide district-oriented partronage and projects. Moreover, situational considerations—the national mood, the desires of the President, and the personal attributes of individual leaders— constrain the minority in much the same fashion as they inhibit the majority. This weakened position of the minority leaders vis-à-vis their followers goes a long way to account for Truman's (1959, pp. 91–93 and 191–192) finding of lessened unity in the minority party.

The whips The floor leaders of each congressional party have the assistance of elaborate whip organizations (Ripley, 1964; 1967, esp. pp. 33–41). These agencies perform a variety of useful services. In the first place, they serve as the chief channels of leadership-member communication, keeping representatives "and office staff informed as to the legislative programs for the week" (House Republican Conference, p. 19), and informing them of the party position on the major issues. Second, the whips seek to ensure the presence on the floor, when needed, of party members, using "the telephone, telegrams, and letters . . . to determine their presence or absence for a vote" (House Republican Conference, p. 19). The whips seem successful in promoting attendance; Ripley (1964, p. 571) found that in 1963 Democratic voting participation averaged 94 percent when the whips were active and only 84 percent when the members were not contacted.

A third function which the whips perform is to provide the leadership with intelligence about the voting intentions of the rank-and-file partisans. Polls are taken, with an error ratio of about 10 percent, which help guide the strategy of the leaders. On the basis of the sentiments which the polls uncover, targets among the undecided or uncertain lawmakers are selected. It is a waste of the leaders' time and energy to try to sway those whose minds are made up; the data which the whips produce indicate where bargaining or pressure may find needed votes or support. The whip organization can, in short, inform the members, urge their attendance, and transmit their views to the leadership. It cannot do more than transmit communications; in the words of the Republican party, "it can suggest and then it is up to the Member's party loyalty and personal responsibility" to respond as he sees fit (House Republican Conference, p. 19).

The whip machinery is organized along regional lines in the House. The Republican whip, most recently Rep. Leslie Arends of Illinois, has since 1965 been formally appointed by a vote of the full-party membership, sitting as the party conference;[13] he, in turn, appoints three regional whips—for the East, the Midwest, and the West and South—and from three to six assistant regional whips to support his regional choices. Thus the Republican whip organization is the creature of the chief whip; to the extent that he cooperates with the floor leaders there will be a relatively clear "chain of command" from leader to assistant whips. On the Democratic side, the whip organization is, at the top, part of the leadership structure: the floor leader (in consultation with the Speaker when the party is the majority) appoints the whip, who in turn selects his deputy whips. The potential for unity breaks down, however, in the selection of assistant whips with responsibility for geographical zones, for the leadership does not determine who will serve in these posts. These decisions are made either by the dean (the member with the greatest chamber seniority) of the zone which the assistant whip will serve or by election by all the Democrats from the zone. In the Eighty-eighth Congress (1963–1964), twelve of the eighteen assistant whips were elected and six appointed (Ripley, 1967, p. 38). This independent selection of the assistant whips creates an organization in which nominal subordinates can flaunt the wishes of their superiors at a minimum risk; there has, in fact, been criticism of the whips for limiting their activities to communications and for not providing sufficient guidance (or pressure) (Clapp, 1964, pp. 340–342).

In the smaller Senate, there is less need for an elaborate whip organization; each party selects a man as chief assistant to its leader. The Republicans label

---

[13]Originally, when the whip organization was established in 1897, the whip was appointed by the Speaker, and this selection by Speaker or minority leader continued until 1919. From 1919 to 1965, the Committee on Committees made the choice. Thus there has been a tendency to involve a greater proportion of Republican representatives in the appointment process. See Ripley, 1967, p. 33.

their choice the *whip* while the Democrats call their man *assistant floor leader*. Whatever the name, the official tasks of the assistant include the transmission of information and the recruiting of voting support for party positions. In each party, the whip or assistant is chosen by the party conference (or caucus), a procedure which may lead to a wide divergence in views between the two chief party leaders. Truman (1959, pp. 117–122) documents the contrasting beliefs between Republican leader Kenneth Wherry (Neb.) and his whip, Leverett Saltonstall (Mass.) during the 1949–1951 period, suggesting that they "appeared as leading members of opposing wings of the party"; the clear differences in the late 1960s between Minority Leader Everett M. Dirksen (Ill.) and Whip Hugh Scott (Pa.) indicate the problem continues to plague the Republicans in the 1960s.[14] The second post may be a pawn in an intraparty struggle within the Democratic party as well, witness the successful 1969 challenge by Northern liberal Edward M. Kennedy (Mass.) for more conservative Russell Long's (La.) post as assistant majority leader.[15] The Senate whips, in short, may subordinate their leadership roles to other orientations with the result that party organization is less cohesive in the upper chamber than in the House.

The record of the whip organizations, as the above discussion indicates, is mixed.[16] They have been successful as communications devices; they provide the leaders with a point of direct contact with party members. The information they transmit does give cues about the leadership's desires and strategy and thus may have contributed, to an uncertain extent, to party cohesion. The data which the whips collect about member sentiments and vote intentions help guide tactical decisions by locating the representatives who, with the application of suitable pressures and/or inducements. might provide needed votes. Similarly the whip apparatus has increased attendance by a factor of about 10 percent. The effectiveness of all this on the marshaling of votes for party positions is difficult to assess in the absence of information on what would have happened had the whips been inactive, but at the very least the whip network permits the leaders to undertake negotiations with reluctant members and provides the latter with a record of agreements reached. Through these activities, it appears that the whip machinery may help persuade and surely cannot hurt the efforts of the party leaders to build majorities. Where the whip organizations cooperate fully with the leadership they serve to enhance the possibility of party cohesion.

Party conferences and committees Each congressional party also maintains a party *conference* (or caucus as the Democrats call it) and a set of party

[14]Upon Dirksen's death in 1969, Scott succeeded to the minority leader's post. The selection of Robert P. Griffin (Mich.) as whip indicates a diminution of the tension between the principal Republican leaders.

[15]Kennedy, in turn, was defeated in 1971 for the assistant leader position by Robert C. Byrd (W. Va.), indicating a reassertion of authority by the Southern Democrats.

[16]This paragraph draws heavily on Ripley, "The Whip Organizations in the United States House of Representatives" (1964).

committees, designed to serve a variety of purposes but generally less important than the individual leaders previously discussed. The conference, composed of all party members, is theoretically the principal governing body of the party; in fact, it is more often used by the elected leaders for their own purposes. This is the case particularly in the House, because the conference is too large, with upwards of 140 eligible to participate, to sustain meaningful debate. As a result, while some efforts have been made, the conference has not developed into the deliberative body some observers foresaw as its potential. Moreover, the conference cannot make binding decisions. The rules of the House Democratic caucus permit issuance of binding instructions by a two-thirds vote, but the heterogeneity of party membership has precluded the invocation of this rule for more than thirty years. Finally, the elected leaders have been unwilling to share their authority with the conference and have resisted any developments which might limit their freedom to act as they see fit. They seem to believe that any necessity to find or generate consensus among large parties of diverse perspectives would impose serious restraints on their room to maneuver. They seem to share Lyndon Johnson's view that "not much" can be accomplished by the conference, that to try to use it to establish substantive positions would probably exacerbate differences rather than create unity (Huitt, 1961*a,* p. 341).

Yet the conference is not without some value, and there is general reluctance to permit it to wither away entirely. At its initial meeting in each Congress, the caucus does play a role in the selection of party leaders, and the outcome of such contests is not always a foregone conclusion, as the changes in Republican leadership in 1959 and 1965 and the Democratic fights for assistant leader in 1969 and 1971 suggest (Peabody, 1967; Polsby, 1963). It is, thus, true that the full membership can decide who it wants to lead the party and the conference is free to make an unencumbered choice, especially if the vote is by secret ballot which negates the possibilities for reprisals against those who backed the loser. Once these choices have been made, however, the main effects of the conference are less tangible. When and if it is convened, it provides a supplementary channel of communication from the leaders, and from the committee experts, to the rank and file. The meeting has what Clapp has called a "psychological effect"; the discussion may influence a few undecided legislators, cues may be transmitted to others, and as a result some coordination may follow (Clapp, 1964, p. 337). But the conference rarely meets, it appears, because from the leaders' point of view the disadvantages have outweighed the potential benefit from its sessions. Dissident members, seeking ways to control the party leaders, have often sought increased caucus meetings.

The effort to coordinate party strategy and tactics has led periodically to the creation of *policy* (or steering) *committees.* The most recent effort in this direction was stimulated by the discussions that led to the Legislative Reorganization Act of 1946; an act that in its initial form included provisions for the creation of such bodies.[17] The House rejected the idea, but the Senate created policy panels, and the parties in the House eventually followed suit. The pressure to make something of these committees has come from junior legislators who feel unable to influence the course of party policy; it has been resisted by the party leaders who are understandably reluctant to share their authority with a potentially independent body. The House Democratic committee has never had more than a nominal existence, and while the others have had a more concrete substance, their record indicates that they have seldom resolved issues dividing the party or enhanced party unity.

In the Senate, the policy committees, especially on the Democratic side, have remained creatures of the leaders. Under Lyndon Johnson's floor leadership, the committee resembled a council of elders since Johnson appointed those closest to him to serve on it. Southern and Western senators, of above-average seniority, held as many as seven of the nine places on the committee; moreover their appointments were for indefinite terms; presumably they continued to sit as long as they remained senators. In 1961, most likely as a reaction to the tight hold which Johnson held over the committee, the Democratic conference imposed some restrictions upon the new leader, Mike Mansfield; it adopted a motion calling for geographical balance among committee members and asserting the right of the conference to approve the leader's committee appointments. But there has been no sign that the committee is emerging as an alternative center of influence. It continues to function at the leader's discretion—he remains its chairman—and provides a place where the leadership can work out its positions, a locus of bargaining and accommodation for the most influential party members. Mansfield used the committee effectively in his successful 1969 fight against simple extension of the income tax surcharge; assisted by several committee meetings, he was able to unify the Democrats in support of his insistence that extension of the tax be linked with reform of the overall tax structure.

The Senate Republican policy committee is somewhat more independent of the floor leader, but like its Democratic counterpart, has not developed as a center of power. The chairman and half of the members (currently there are fifteen) are elected by the conference while the remainder are party leaders— floor leader, whip, chairmen of the Committee on Committees, and the like— serving ex officio. This latter contingent is in a position to dominate committee proceedings, virtually ensuring that the policy panel will be coordinated with overall strategy. The elected members serve only for two-year terms; thus there is some circulation of membership among the various factions and geographical interests of the party. This permits the unit to serve as another supplementary communications link, over which the leaders can present their views to, and request support from, the party rank and file. Moreover,

---

[17]On policy committees, see Bone, 1956 and 1958, chap. 6; Jewell, 1959b; and Jones, 1964b and 1970, chap. 8.

the relatively institutionalized character of the Republican committee, with some staff resources, allows it to perform useful research and publicity work.

The House Republicans have made the most notable use of their policy committee. According to Jones's (1964*b,* p. 139) detailed study, beginning in 1959 the panel began to be effective as a device "to discover a basis (both substantive and procedural) for consensus, or to discover that there is no such basis." The committee has been most successful in finding agreement to oppose the majority's proposals and least able to agree to support Democratic ideas. The committee is broadly based—composed in the Ninetieth Congress of eight regional members, chosen on a secret ballot by the representatives from each region; representatives of the two most recent "classes" (freshmen in the Eighty-ninth and Ninetieth Congresses); ten party leaders (floor leader, whip, chairman of the policy committee itself, etc.) nominated by a resolution of the party conference; and seven members at large chosen by the minority leader—thus permitting wide-ranging discussion and full opportunities for communicating all points of view. Despite this breadth of membership, the selection process gives a unified leadership ample opportunity to control the committee's deliberations. Nonetheless, junior Republicans have found the committee attractive as a place where they can advance their alternatives to the positions staked out by the elected, more senior, leaders, and they have sought to use it as a forum in which to fight out issues of party policy.[18]

Finally, each congressional party has a congressional (campaign) committee, designed mainly to render campaign assistance to party members. A recent description of the House Republican committee is perhaps typical of what the other committees do (House Republican Conference, pp. 15–17). The GOP unit provides financial aid for "public relations expenses, such as newsletters, questionnaires, radio tapes," and the like, but not for travel expenses, office equipment, entertainment, and other costs of a more personal nature. Staff resources are available to help the members with any public relations problems they may encounter. Other services—newsletters, research, roll call voting records, data on the performance of the opposition candidate, and ghost-written speeches—are also provided. Such assistance can perhaps be used by the leadership as a lever to bargain for support from reluctant members, but the evidence on this point is far from clear. What is clear, however, is that these services make only a marginal contribution to the candidate's election prospects; as indicated in Chapter 3, the party

[18] In this connection, it is interesting to note that in 1965 the House Republicans established a Committee on Research and Planning, composed of eight members, to coordinate the work of various task forces—on agriculture, congressional reform, crime, East-West trade, and Western alliances. This step is in keeping with the restlessness of the junior members, who have been eager to see the party do more to develop serious alternatives to the proposals which the majority Democrats advance. See Jones, 1970.

nominee will have to produce most of his own resources, a necessity which reduces his dependence upon the congressional party to a minimal level.

This section has outlined the structure of the congressional party machinery from the most to the least important, from the Speaker and floor leaders through the whip organizations and the various conferences and committees. The party apparatus possesses a number of bargaining advantages with which it can seek to develop party cohesion and to produce a coherent party record; these advantages are especially useful where the leaders work together rather than at cross purposes. In general, the greater the number of independently selected leaders, the greater the probability that divergent interests will prevent or inhibit the creation of party unity. And even if the leadership is cohesive and thus able to make full use of its levers of power, it merely strengthens its bargaining position vis-à-vis the rank and file and does not remove the need to rely on persuasion rather than on compulsion as the means to the end of party harmony.

Furthermore, the *pattern* of centralization, the extent to which a few major leaders dominate their party, relates to success in mobilizing the rank and file and passing legislation. Ripley (1967, Chap. 4) identifies four patterns of majority party leadership. The most common situation, occurring more than half the time during the twentieth century, is leadership by the Speaker, who plays the major part in the determination of party strategy and tactics, though of course he will consult with others. On occasion, the Speaker will yield this power to his majority leaders, as did William B. Bankhead in the 1937–1940 period when Democratic Majority Leader Sam Rayburn assumed the position of chief strategist. At other times the Speaker will share his authority, by choice or necessity, with his chief lieutenants, forming with them a collegial ruling element in the party. Following the death of Speaker Rayburn, for twenty years the dominating figure in the party, the Democrats in the 1960s, with John McCormack as Speaker, shifted to the collegial pattern, as McCormack involved majority leader Carl Albert (Okla.) and Whip Hale Boggs (La.) in tactical decision making. Rarely, as a fourth pattern, the legislative majority leadership will defer entirely to the President, as did the Democrats in the early years of the New Deal. While the evidence is not conclusive, the highly centralized patterns, where a single figure dominates the party machinery, are most productive of legislative results (Ripley, 1967, pp. 112–113).

The minority party reveals similar patterns. Lacking the Speaker, leadership most often falls to the minority leader, a situation comparable to majority leadership by the Speaker or floor leader. Almost as frequently, however, no center of minority leadership emerges, and the opposition acts in a disorganized fashion without structured, purposeful leadership. Recently, and for the first time, the minority—the Republicans from 1959 onwards— has developed a collegial, shared leadership core, thus averting the obvious difficulties inherent in disorganization. Only leadership by the floor leader has been sufficiently centralized to develop sufficient minority cohesion to block the program which the majority advanced.[19] Party unity, in sum, seems to follow when centralized leadership possesses enough "fragments of power" to negotiate successfully with the rank-and-file party members.

THE PARTY IN ACTION

To this point, our discussion has advanced the proposition that the legislative party, as the major centralizing force in a decentralized political system, has a number of resources on which to draw as it seeks to implement its purposes. The effectiveness of these bargaining levers is limited by situational forces— the identity and intentions of the President and the events of the times—and by the ability of the leaders to pool their resources, to centralize their "pieces of power." The advantages which the party leadership possesses do not guarantee success in unifying the party, but rather ensure only a basis on which to negotiate with individual partisans; the leaders have something to give in return for support for party positions.

The techniques of leadership How can party leaders best overcome the countervailing pulls of committee and constituency on their fellow partisans? Their resources, as we have seen, include the ability to give tangible and intangible preferment—to provide committee assignments, needed information, "pork barrel" constituency projects, and other specific rewards as well as the psychic gratification which follows from attention and involvement. These inducements are almost always used in a positive fashion, that is, if rank-and-file lawmakers go along they will receive some quid pro quo in return. Rarely are sanctions invoked; seldom are punishments meted out to those who pursue overly independent courses. In 1965, the House Democrats, fresh from their massive electoral sweep of the previous November and eager to remove all hindrances to enactment of a liberal legislative program, stripped two conservative Southerners—Albert Watson (S.C.) and John Bell Williams (Miss.)—of their seniority in retribution for supporting the Republican presidential candidate.[20] Such discipline is the exception to the rule, however, and positively oriented persuasion remains the basic tactic of the party leaders.

The core of the party leadership—the Speaker, floor leaders, and those others who may participate in a collegial leadership arrangement—most often operates through personal contact, either directly or indirectly through

---

[19]Ripley, 1967, p. 113. These conclusions apply only to the House of Representatives, though similar findings probably hold for the Senate as well.

[20]In the aftermath of these sanctions, Watson became a Republican, but without regaining his seniority, and Williams left the House to run successfully for the governorship of Mississippi. For comparable instances in the Senate, see Huitt, 1957.

intermediaries such as the whips.[21] In these conversations the leaders may request support on the merits of the legislation, i.e., because it embodies "sound" policy; on the basis of party loyalty, because the party "needs" the bill for partisan political purposes; in return for some desirable reward; or on the basis of some combination of these forms of inducement. Such contacts often cross party lines; a vote from the other side counts as much as one from a party colleague, and presidential-bipartisan, congressional, and truncated majorities cannot work their will without opposition votes. In 1969, for instance, Senate Republicans, seeking to pass President Nixon's Antiballistic Missile (ABM) system in a closely divided chamber, lavished a good deal of attention on Democrat Warren Magnuson (Wash.), holding out a supersonic transport plane to be built by a Washington state firm as the bait for a pro-ABM vote.[22]

Moreover, contacts with certain key individuals assume great importance to the degree that those individuals have influence with other lawmakers. Committee chairmen or the leaders of state delegations and other informal groups, if won over to the party's cause, may bring with them their committee or group colleagues. Medicare, for example, could not be enacted until the conditions were such that Chairman Wilbur Mills (Ark.) of the House Ways and Means Committee would support his Democratic party leaders. Once Mills went along, the Medicare bill moved through the House without a serious hitch. To win support from such crucial members, the leaders may have to make concessions; they will tailor the legislation to make it fit the demands of those whose support is required. To cite one case, in 1964 the Senate Democratic leadership agreed, as the price to gain Republican support for their civil rights bill, to certain concessions which GOP floor leader Everett M. Dirksen (Ill.) insisted upon.[23] This strategy of using influential congressmen as a means to win over blocs of votes is enhanced if the key man can be induced to speak out in behalf of the bill; if the leaders can arrange to have such lawmakers take the floor, the message to their followers will be clear.

A variation on this line of strategy is for the leaders to encourage their partisans on the relevant committee or subcommittee to develop agreement on the substance of a program as early as possible in the process. Because these men are the party's experts on the topic in question, any unanimity which characterizes them will be likely to have a telling effect on the remainder of the party contingent in the chamber, for if the specialists are agreed, and are supported by the leadership of the party, rank-and-file members will be exposed to the maximum pressure and will defect only under

[21]On the techniques of leadership, see Ripley, 1967, chap. 5 and 1969, pp. 176–180.
[22]See Finney, 1969. The blandishments failed and Magnuson finally announced his opposition to the ABM.
[23]Sundquist, 1968, chap. 6, concludes that "the show of negotiations with Dirksen and the concessions made to him, however minor, won the entire center bloc of uncommitted Republicans . . ." (p. 269).

great pressure. No doubt bargains will have to be struck in order to generate such committee consensus.

Other techniques are also available. Majority leaders can take advantage of their control over parliamentary procedures to alter the rules under which business is conducted or, more simply, they can control much of what occurs under existing rules. As an example of the changing of the rules, the House Democratic leadership, on a temporary basis in 1961 and permanently two years later, increased the size of the Rules Committee from twelve to fifteen members in order to prevent that body from blocking proposals favored by the elected party leaders. The enlarged committee became a somewhat more reliable partner of the leaders where previously it had been more of an obstacle to party cohesion (Peabody, 1963). And, as noted, the majority, particularly the Speaker and floor leader in the House, can use the existing rules for partisan ends; they can schedule matters to suit their own convenience, they can arrange for the speakers they desire to have the floor at the proper moment, and they can (in the House with the cooperation of the Rules Committee) control the amending process to prevent effective challenge to their proposals.

Finally, the leaders can try to utilize the desire of their followers to be loyal if they can by taking "official" party positions. Through statements on the floor or in the mass media, through letters to all members, or through adoption by the party conference or policy committee of a party position, the leaders hope to reach the rank and file. Dissent from the official line is made more difficult under these circumstances, for to defect will publicly embarrass the leadership which has put its prestige on the line. On the other hand, the greater the attention paid to a particular matter, the greater the likelihood that other, competing interests—local party, interest, and other constituency organizations—will become active, increasing the pressures on congressmen to defect from the leadership position.

Conditions for party leadership Given the availability of the resources, noted earlier, and these techniques for their application, we may inquire about the degree of success in unifying their party which the leaders attain and about the factors which contribute to, and detract from, party cohesion. Froman and Ripley (1965), investigating the House Democrats, advance a number of propositions. First, they suggest, the leadership will attract more support for its position when it is committed, informed, and active, that is, when it makes a concerted effort to employ its bargaining advantages. In such circumstances, the elected leaders can usually find eight to ten votes, so-called "pocket votes," which they can get if the balloting is close. A small number of members will hold themselves ready to change their position to support their leaders rather than to let the party go down to defeat. Yet there are limits to success even under optimum conditions: on the average 9.5 percent of votes which House Democrats cast were contrary to the intentions which they had reported to the whips; and over a series of roll calls, more than half (52 percent) went back on their word on at least one occasion.

Second, leadership success in maximizing party unity is related to the visibility of the step to be taken. This means, for one thing, that greater loyalty is likely to be forthcoming on procedural as opposed to substantive matters. Perfect cohesion is always attained in the selection of chamber leaders such as the Speaker of the House. While decisions on procedure have profound implications for later substantive decisions, it may appear that these are matters internal to the chamber, to be left to the members to decide free of outside pressure. The more the issue at hand deals with basic policy, the harder the leaders will have to work to keep their troops in line; they tend to be more successful on the passage of legislation than on amendments to the bill or on acceptance of conference reports.

In the same vein, party cohesion is higher on issues of low visibility than when the matter up for decision commands a great deal of public attention. The more important an issue is, the more demands from outside the legislative system will be stimulated, and the more the lawmakers will be tempted to give greater weight to some nonparty facet of the legislative role. The visibility of the action taken has similar effects on party cohesion; roll call and, more recently, teller votes, recorded and publicized in the mass media, less often evoke party loyalty than do the voice or division votes on which individual positions go unrecorded.[24] To the extent that the party leaders can manipulate the frame of reference in which an issue is placed—trying to keep it out of the public eye—or the mode of resolution—attempting to avoid roll call votes where issue visibility is high—they can expect to increase the amount of loyalist behavior which their members display.

Following directly from these factors, as a third proposition, leaders will be able to generate more cohesion when competing pressures are absent or inconsistent. Low visibility retards the emergence of such pressures, high activity seeks to overcome them, of course, but their nature is relevant as well. Where committees, local political interests and groups, the public, and informal units such as state delegations are indifferent and thus uninvolved, party loyalty may well follow from party appeals and pressure; where these outside demands are inconsistent, the lawmaker can resolve his role conflict

[24] On a voice vote, members shout out the "ayes" and "nays"; a division is a standing vote where the members rise and are counted by the presiding officer. The 1970 Legislative Reorganization Act altered the character of the teller vote. Prior to the passage of the bill, a teller vote saw the affirmative and negative votes, in turn, march up the aisle to be tabulated by tellers. Since total votes, not individual choices, were recorded, it was possible but improbable that any legislator's position would be discovered on these votes. Beginning in 1971, however, upon the demand of twenty representatives, the tellers will record individual votes as well. Indeed, the reform was credited (see Hunter, 1971) with contributing to the surprising defeat of an appropriation for continued development of the supersonic transport plane (SST). The net impact of the procedural change, following the Froman and Ripley argument, will be to attenuate further the party's ability to hold its members in line. Unable to support the party quietly, in effect privately, members may feel compelled, by constituency or other pressures, to bolt the party traces.

in favor of party and at the same time satisfy some of those interested in how he acts. But where demands are heavy and mostly on one side of the issue, the legislator may feel a necessity to protect himself politically by bolting his congressional party. Moreover, the parties themselves recognize this need; they are quite often prepared to go along, without invoking sanctions, with those who feel they must defect for reasons of constituency or conscience (Clapp, 1964, pp. 352–361). Party leaders, in short, recognize clearly the limits to their powers.

These limits can be seen most clearly at the roll call voting stage, where even within a general issue area such as foreign policy, levels of party cohesion vary widely. Table 4-3 shows the relative pro and con vote in the Eighty-eighth Congress on three topics pertaining to the international position of the United States. The foreign aid question was clearly a party issue; about three-fourths of the Democrats supported the aid program while an equal proportion of Republicans opposed it. The matter of providing funds for the Arms Control and Disarmament Agency found the Democrats heavily in favor, by a four-to-one margin, but split the Republicans sharply. Both parties were deeply divided over whether to build a new, larger and more elaborate, manned military bombing plane, the RS-70. The point here is that on almost every issue, even one like foreign aid which clearly divides the parties from one another, a sizable minority in each party is likely to dissent from the position of the majority of their fellow partisans, and presumably from the viewpoint espoused by their party leaders.

Leadership change The fact remains that party leaders serve upon the sufferance of their colleagues, and if the latter become dissatisfied with their leaders' performance there may well be a "revolution" which elevates new men, with new ideas about the substance of policy and different tactical plans, to the leadership positions (Peabody, 1967). The problem seems less acute for the majority party—the Democrats for most of the recent period—whose

TABLE 4-3 *Party loyalty on foreign policy issues, Eighty-eighth Congress*

		Issue		
		Foreign aid (%)	*Disarmament Agency funds* (%)	*RS-70 bomber funds* (%)
Republicans:	Pro	25.8	47.2	55.3
	Con	74.2	52.8	44.7
Democrats:	Pro	74.0	80.4	44.6
	Con	26.0	19.6	55.4

SOURCE: *Congressional Quarterly Weekly Reports* for 1963, roll calls numbered 8, 61, 62, 95, 100, and 112; and for 1964, roll calls numbered 51, 52, 61, and 62.

leaders have greater resources and are thus able to satisfy, or at least placate, the bulk of their followers. Under these circumstances, a clearer pattern of advancement develops, with lower-level leaders moving up the ladder a rung at a time. Thus when House Speaker Rayburn died, Majority Leader Mc-Cormack became Speaker and Whip Carl Albert succeeded to the floor leadership, easily rebuffing a challenge from Richard Bolling (Mo.); similarly, when McCormack retired, Albert moved up to the Speakership and was succeeded as floor leader by Whip Hale Boggs. Peabody (1967) identifies this pattern as "routine advancement." Contests for leadership posts seem less frequent in the majority and where they do occur they are confined to the lower levels. Dissatisfaction with Senate Democratic leadership in the late 1950s and early 1960s, spearheaded by such dissidents as Wayne Morse (Ore.), Joseph Clark (Pa.), and William Proxmire (Wis.), focused on the policy committee, in an effort to give the rank and file a louder voice in its deliberations, rather than attack the top echelon leaders directly.

The minority leadership faces a more serious set of problems. We have already noted that, depending on the personalities of its leaders and the circumstances under which they hold their positions, the minority must choose among strategies of partisan opposition, cooperation with the majority, and offering "constructive alternatives" to the majority's proposals. If the leaders make choices which displease their followers change is highly likely. Minority leadership may be hard put to satisfy its partisans; the leaders have fewer resources than their majority counterparts with which to bargain with their party colleagues. Moreover, continued minority status, brought about, of course, by repeated election losses, may create frustration among the members, who, looking about for ways to become the majority, may come to believe that the new image of new leaders may enhance their party's standing with the electorate.

The Republican minority in the House has suffered through two revolutions in recent years, both ostensibly designed to bring fresher, more imaginative leadership to the party (Peabody, 1966, 1969; Jones, 1970). In 1959, Joseph Martin, whose basic leadership strategy was cooperation with the opposition, was replaced by Charles Halleck, who was inclined toward tactics of partisan opposition. Six years later, Gerald Ford, a man inclined toward the constructive alternatives position, unseated Halleck as minority leader. Other contests, as for lesser posts such as chairman of the Republican conference, accompanied the struggles for the top spot.

Changes in party leadership, especially through revolution or open competition, produce alterations in the operation of the legislative system (Peabody, 1967). Most directly affected are individual careers; new men move into positions of influence, others find themselves further from the centers of power. In the aftermath of his victory over Halleck, new Republican leader Ford sought to reward his allies in that struggle by moving them into the inner circle of party leadership. Change affects legislation as well;

the policies, and the strategies and tactics employed in pursuit of those policies, favored by the new leaders will be advanced while the desires of those removed from positions of authority will face greatly diminished prospects. Finally, the effects of change, especially that in a minority party opposing a presidential majority, may spill out into the larger political arena. In the absence of a President, national party leadership falls to the congressional leaders; the support of GOP leaders Dirksen and Halleck for a fellow legislator, Sen. Barry Goldwater (Ariz.), substantially aided his drive for the party's 1964 presidential nomination and, a step further removed, the Democratic victory which followed the success of that drive. The 1964 election was a disaster for the congressional Republicans as well—their numbers were reduced to 140 in the House—and led directly to Halleck's ouster. Change in leadership, in short, may bring in its wake unintended and unforeseen consequences.

SUMMARY

The thrust of this chapter has been to suggest that the congressional party, despite its possession of seemingly formidable weapons of persuasion, has only mixed success in its efforts to overcome the divisive tendencies inherent in the legislative system. In the final analysis, party leaders must put together a coalition by judicious use of the fragments of power available to them; they cannot compel, but rather must assemble their majorities on each issue under consideration through bargains and compromises with those over whom they have few real sanctions. The power of the leaders is, thus, in Truman's (1959, p. 245) words "interstitial and personal rather than formal and authorized."

To the extent that the party leaders can reach agreements among themselves and, most importantly, with the seniority leaders on the standing committees, thus creating a unified party posture, they may produce substantial party cohesion. More often, however, the party leaders are divided among themselves or are unable to find a basis on which to unify the various blocs—regional, ideological, informal—into which their followers divide. Committee leaders insist on their own views, rooted in their status as substantive specialists. Some rank-and-file members, especially on highly visible matters of controversy, may feel constrained to follow the President or some constituency interest instead of adhering to the party position; others, with fewer electoral worries, may simply refuse to follow where the party seeks to lead them.

In short, if the party leaders are to succeed in making the record they seek to build, they must make do with inadequate resources. Beginning with those who willingly assume and act upon a loyalist orientation toward their party, the leadership must, through the use of friendship, influence, and the ability to confer rewards—tangible and psychological—add enough votes from those subject to competing pulls and pressures to build a majority and thus carry the day for their positions. To attain this end regularly, given the tools available for the job, is more than can reasonably be expected from even the most skilled leaders, except under circumstances which almost never occur.

CHAPTER FIVE

The Rules and Procedures

The two preceding chapters have dealt with the two chief features of the congressional system—the committees and the political parties—and have suggested that they provide the major forces for fragmentation and centralization, respectively. Neither the committees nor the parties operate unencumbered; rather both function within an institutional framework in large part established by the formal rules and procedures of the House and Senate. It is obvious that no body of 100, much less of 435, men and women can accomplish much of anything without some guidelines about *how* things should be done; without rules of procedure chaos would soon follow. Any system, if it is to produce outputs at a satisfactory level, must be characterized by a minimum level of stability and predictability (Jewell and Patterson, 1966, pp. 255–266). The rules contribute to this end, for they provide a set of fairly regularized ways of conducting legislative business which permit the business of Congress to go forward. Thus certain forms of behavior are forbidden under the rules, and the members of the system know what kinds of action they may reasonably expect and what sorts are not permissible. The rules, in short, set forth the limits of acceptable behavior and procedures under which the congressional system can perform the lawmaking, oversight, and representational activities expected of it.

If our common sense tells us that anarchy is undesirable, that rules are essential for the orderly conduct of legislative affairs, it does not always reveal that the rules are not neutral in the ways they affect what specific outputs the system produces. Put another way, procedures influence outcomes; the way things must be done under the rules often goes far to determine what in fact is done. In Congress, as this chapter will illustrate, those with an interest in seeing the legislature attain certain ends, or who desire to prevent the taking of certain actions, will try to take advantage of the opportunities which the rules afford them to advance these aims. This fact helps to explain the reluctance of many lawmakers to change the rules: the procedures represent power to those expert in putting them to use and few are willing readily to yield the advantages they possess. Thus the rules become ends in themselves; they develop a "life of their own" highly resistant to alteration and defended vigorously by representatives and senators who make good use of them. Not only do procedural rules promote order and routine, they embody a division of authority and influence as well.

More specifically, in Congress, the rules contribute directly to the fragmented, decentralized character of the legislature. The task of the parties, as the chief centralizing force, is vastly complicated by the rules which institutionalize a process for decision making that contains many "veto points," that is, many distinct places at which proposals may be delayed or defeated.[1] To pass even one house of Congress, a bill must move across a number of barriers. It must be acted upon affirmatively by subcommittee and full committee; inaction or negative action at either point may well doom the legislation. In the House, the proposal must survive the possibility of being ignored or defeated by the Rules Committee, acting as legislative "traffic cop." The bill may meet its demise on the chamber floor as well. The full house may refuse to consider it, may amend it virtually out of existence, may return it to committee, or may simply vote it down on final passage. The rules, thus, incorporate and make relatively permanent the division of labor and specialization which, as previously noted, are essential to the conduct of legislative business. They also create difficult conditions for centralization; the party leaders, to advance their program, must use their limited resources to move their proposals past each potential danger point.

Similarly, the rules ensure that bargaining will be the chief mode of congressional resolution. Since they lack effective sanctions over those who control these decision centers—the committee and subcommittee chairmen, the rank-and-file committee members, the Rules Committee, and so on—the party leaders will have to negotiate with the power holders, using the devices outlined in the previous chapter. How difficult this task is will depend upon how many veto points are held by opponents of the leadership, how willing the opponents are to compromise, how unified is the support, and how eager are those supporters to work for passage (Froman, 1967, pp. 21–22). It may be that one location holds the key; once Chairman Wilbur Mills of the House Ways and Means Committee moved into the camp of Medicare proponents,

---

[1]Froman, 1967, chap. 2. This excellent study is easily the best available treatment of the rules and their potential effects on legislative outcomes. For an earlier treatment, see Riddick, 1949.

the program's prospects were enhanced tremendously. Alternatively, a whole series of tests may have to be met, as in the case of the 1969 antiballistic missile controversy where opponents of the weapons system mounted heavy attacks against it in committee and on the floor of the Senate.

In sum, rules of procedure are essential; there must be accepted modes of doing business if the legislative system is to operate at all. The form that such rules take, however, is not a matter of indifference, for the specific provisions of the rules are crucial to any understanding of how any institution, Congress included, accomplishes its purposes. In the American national legislature, the rules contribute to a fragmentation of power—they institutionalize and legitimize multiple centers of influence—and impose a requirement that decisions will not be hierarchically imposed but rather will be produced through a process of negotiation and compromise among those who hold legislative power. As a result, the rules are important to those whose power and influence they enhance, and a source of dismay to those whom they exclude from authority. To understand Congress, then, requires knowledge of the rules themselves, how they can be used to restrict legislative outputs, and how they can be circumvented by lawmakers eager to overcome procedural hurdles.

RULES AND PROCEDURES IN THE HOUSE

The House of Representatives, four times as large as the Senate, has, not surprisingly, a more complex set of rules; its size requires that it have more elaborate procedures to expedite its work. Each and every stage of the legislative process in the House—from the introduction of a bill to the time it goes, in final form, to the President for his signature is governed by a number of potentially applicable rules. As this suggests, the rules are not always applied; under "unanimous-consent" agreements, things are often done which the rules do not allow. Lawmakers recognize the need to act and frequently, most often on noncontroversial matters, do not invoke the rules. Yet the rules are binding and frequently will be invoked when important substantive interests are at stake. When such interests are blocked, moreover, there are other rules which may provide alternative ways to advance them.

Introduction In the House, anyone can introduce legislation. Unlike the Senate, there is no need to gain recognition from the presiding officer to introduce a bill; it need only be filed with the Clerk of the House. The result of this is to increase enormously the number of bills and resolutions introduced; in recent years the total has exceeded the 15,000 mark.

Once introduced, the Speaker refers the bill to the appropriate committee. In doing so, he is formally bound by rule X, which specifies the committee jurisdictions, but, as previously noted, he may have discretion in referral when there exists ambiguity or overlap in the areas of jurisdiction. In 1963, for example, the civil rights bill, containing provisions based on the commerce clause of the Constitution, was referred to the Judiciary Committee, chaired by Emanuel Celler (D., N.Y.), rather than to the Interstate and Foreign Commerce Committee, led by Oren Harris of Arkansas. [In the Senate, the strategy was reversed: the bill went to Warren Magnuson's (Wash.) Commerce Committee, not to the Judiciary Committee of Chairman James Eastland (Miss.)] (Froman, 1967, pp. 36–37). The point is clear; it does make a difference to which committee a bill goes, and the Speaker's use of his discretion, when it exists, may determine the fate of the legislation. Such instances are rare, however, and for the most part committee jurisdictions are clear and protected by the rules.

Committee consideration Committees are, of course, the chief screening bodies in Congress. Most bills are allowed to expire quietly, without serious objection from most nonmembers, in the committee. On the important matters, hearings are held, the bill is rewritten to the extent the committee deems necessary, and the bill is reported out to the floor (via the Rules Committee) for debate, amendment, and the ultimate vote on final passage. The fact that in recent Congresses from 1,500 to 2,000 bills and resolutions (about 10 to 15 percent of those introduced) have been reported by the committees testifies to the effectiveness with which unimportant bills are weeded out and the congressional workload reduced to manageable proportions. Occasionally, however, an important bill, favored by substantial interests, languishes in committee, and unusual measures can be attempted to remove the bill from committee control.

One such device is the *discharge petition*. The rules of the House provide that after a bill has been in committee for more than thirty days without having been reported, it can be removed and brought to the floor upon the petition of a majority (218) of the members. The petition lies in the House for signatures, and when enough are collected, the committee in question is discharged of the bill, which then goes on a discharge calendar from which it can be called up for consideration (after seven days on the calendar) on the second and fourth Mondays of the month.

The discharge procedure has seldom worked to bypass the standing committees. Between 1937 and 1960, at least 212 petitions were filed; twenty-two (about 10 percent) obtained the required signatures, placing the bill in question on the calendar; fourteen of these measures passed the House, but only two—the Wage and Hour Act (1938) and the Federal Pay Raise Act (1960)— became law (Robinson, 1963, pp. 4–6). These two bills, in fact, are the only cases in which the discharge process aided in the passage of legislation since the rule providing for it was adopted in 1910. In all other instances, the Senate or the President blocked final enactment. In short, as Robinson puts it, the discharge petition "is in reality little more than a formal guarantee that the majority of the House will not be thwarted in its attempt to express itself on a given issue. As a practical matter it is rarely used and even more rarely successful in enacting legislation" (Robinson, 1963, p. 5).

The reasons for this are not hard to see. In the first place, as already suggested, specialization is an important norm in Congress;[2] lawmakers feel an obligation to respect one another's expertise. Thus to challenge the experts on one committee is to invite attacks on one's own panel, and the ultimate result would be to undermine the legislative division of labor. Moreover, the discharge petition may be filed without any real prospects for success, as a means to dramatize a cause. Pressure for action seldom reaches the point where all the major steps can be taken within a single Congress; rather support builds slowly over a period of years.[3] Thus the proponents of a bill may not be a majority but merely a minority with hopes of generating support sufficient to make them a majority, and discharge may serve as a tactical weapon of a minority rather than as a device to guarantee majority rule in the House (Froman, 1967, pp. 92–93). Finally, it is worth noting that the impact of the discharge petition may be felt as much in the threat of success as in success itself. That is, a committee, fearing that it will be discharged, may report a bill to avoid having it removed from the panel. Unfortunately, there is no available evidence by which to judge how often, as the signatures on a petition mount toward 218, committees have been induced to act in situations where inaction was their preferred course of action.

Other paths around the standing committees are also available under the House rules, but the prospects for their successful use are even more remote than the employment of the discharge petition. For one thing, on the first and third Mondays each month, motions to *suspend the rules* and pass legislation are in order. Any bill, at any stage of consideration, even one not formally introduced, can in theory be treated under suspension of the rules, but passage requires the vote of a two-thirds majority. Because it takes two-thirds of those voting to pass a bill in this fashion, the suspension device is useful only to expedite consideration of noncontroversial measures. Recognition of a member to offer such a motion is at the discretion of the Speaker, who is unlikely to allow many measures to come to a decision in this fashion. Moreover, since suspension is an extraordinary device, members prefer to operate through more regular channels, especially on important legislative issues.

The committee on rules has the authority, under House rules, to report any bill, whether or not it has been introduced or considered by a standing committee. It seldom utilizes this power, in part because the committee has often been less than eager to expedite matters, acting frequently as a brake on a more liberal party leadership. Occasionally, however, the committee will act,

---

[2]See Chapter 6 for fuller treatment of the informal norms of Congress.
[3]On the "stages" through which an issue may have to pass on its way to resolution and acceptance of the solution enacted, see Key, 1964, pp. 222–227.

as it did twice in 1964, sending to the floor two bills which the Judiciary Committee had refused to support. The first was a constitutional amendment to permit one house of a state legislature to be apportioned by nonpopulation criteria; the second was a measure to deny the Supreme Court any jurisdiction to hear state reapportionment cases. The proposed amendment could not muster the required two-thirds vote; the second item passed the House only to be rejected in the Senate. These instances, and two other occasions when the committee took similar action, indicate the committee can, though it seldom does, exert independent authority under the rules when it chooses to do so (Froman, 1967, p. 94; Robinson, 1963, p. 29).

The House rules, in sum, serve to insulate the committees, to make it very difficult to circumvent them. As a result, the standing panels remain autonomous centers of influence; if they do not choose to act there is little comfort to nonmembers in the discharge, suspension, and Rules Committee report procedures. The rules protect and defend the power of the committees, the informal norms buttress committee independence, and the legislative system remains a fragmented one.

To the floor: privileged matter In the ordinary course of events, a bill, once reported by a standing committee, may proceed to the floor by a number of alternative routes. It may be placed on one of four calendars: (1) the Union Calendar, for all legislation involving the raising or expenditure of funds; (2) the House Calendar, for all other nonmoney bills of a public character; (3) the Private Calendar, for bills relating to specific individuals; or (4) the Consent Calendar, for noncontroversial matters. Some items on these calendars receive privileged status, that is, they go directly to the floor without consideration by the House Rules Committee and become the chief order of business, superseding other items on the agenda.

First of all are matters on the Private Calendar, usually involving payments to individuals who have suffered personal injury or property damage at the hands of the federal government, or waivers of provisions of the immigration laws to permit persons not otherwise qualified to remain in the country. Froman (1967, p. 44) reports that in the Eighty-eighth Congress 360 private bills were passed—about 35 percent of all bills and resolutions enacted. On the first Tuesday of each month, bills on the Private Calendar are treated, to the exclusion of all other business; the third Tuesday may also be used for this calendar at the discretion of the Speaker. Debate is limited to ten minutes on each bill and if two legislators object the bill is returned to committee. To facilitate consideration of private legislation, each party assigns a few of its members to act as "official objectors," thus eliminating the need for many lawmakers to attend the sessions. Unless a private bill can command virtually unanimous consent it cannot be enacted.

Bills on the Consent Calendar are treated in similar fashion. Representatives may request that any bill on the Union or House Calendars be transferred to the Consent Calendar, and on the first and third Mondays of the month such bills are privileged business. Bills involving substantial sums or major policy changes will, by general agreement, not be placed on the Consent Calendar. As with private legislation, bills on the Consent Calendar require almost total agreement: on first call, one objection requires that the bill be passed over, and three objections on the subsequent call defeat the bill. Each party maintains "official objectors" to act on behalf of its members. The harshness of these procedural requirements means, in effect, that only relatively unimportant matters, about which there is no disagreement, will be passed through the Consent Calendar procedure.

Other privileged matters also exist. As previously discussed, the suspension of the rules procedure may be used twice monthly. Also, since Congress governs the District of Columbia,[4] it sets aside two days each month (the second and fourth Mondays) to deal with district business. Finally, the rules make certain kinds of bills reported by particular committees privileged business. Among the most important of such provisions are the privileges granted the Appropriations Committee for reporting general appropriations bills, Ways and Means for revenue measures, Rules for its resolutions, Public Works for rivers and harbors legislation, and Veterans' Affairs for pension bills. These committees, however, especially the first two named, often do not take advantage of their opportunity to avoid the Rules Committee, preferring to let the latter determine the conditions of floor consideration. In this way, these committees hope to enhance their ability to pass their bills without substantial change. All in all, privileged status is granted to, and used to pass, relatively inconsequential or noncontroversial legislation. These matters account for nearly 90 percent of all bills that the House enacts.

To the floor: the Rules Committee The remaining bills—those not privileged under the House rules—go to the Rules Committee. While this legislation constitutes, relatively speaking, a small proportion of House business, it includes virtually all important bills from the Union and House Calendars; these are the measures which contain the major items of the year's legislative program and around which most legislative controversy swirls. Without approval from the Rules Committee, a bill cannot ordinarily pass and, thus, the committee becomes a major element in the power relationships of the chamber. As such, it is no cause for wonder that the committee's authority has aroused substantial antagonism among those who find their proposals thwarted by the committee's action.[5]

The procedures of the committee are straightforward. The chairman of the

[4]The House has resisted efforts to give the district home rule, largely because the Southerners who control the District of Columbia Committee and the District subcommittee of the Appropriations Committee are unwilling to establish a Negro city government in Washington, a virtual certainty given the city's large black population.

[5]The best source on the Rules Committee is Robinson, 1963, from which much of what follows is drawn. See also Fox and Clapp, 1970*a* and 1970*b*, for confirming evidence from a more recent period. Other useful works include Cummings and Peabody, 1963; Peabody, 1963; Kravitz, 1965; Smith, 1965; McKaye, 1963; and Price, 1962.

standing committee reporting the bill requests "a hearing for the purpose of obtaining a 'rule' to have the bill considered in the House" (Robinson, 1963, p. 10). The rule, when and if granted, specifies the conditions under which floor consideration will occur. Put another way, the Rules Committee both influences the agenda, by deciding *what* will be considered, and regulates the debate, by determining *how* each bill will be considered. With respect to the former, Robinson (1963) and Fox and Clapp (1970*a*) report that in each Congress about twenty requests for hearings will be denied and another twelve bills, on the average, will be denied a rule after hearings have been held. Thus more than thirty measures approved by legislative committees fail to reach the floor in a two-year period as a result of adverse Rules Committee action. Moreover, the Rules panel may, by threatening delay or negative action, exert influence on the substance of a bill; suggestions to a standing committee about what kind of legislation is most likely to clear the Rules Committee hurdle are not apt to go unheeded. In fact, the substantive committees will no doubt seek to write bills that will clear Rules as a matter of common practice, quite apart from any direct communication with members of the Rules panel.

As for regulating debate, the rule which the committee grants will specify how much time shall be allotted for debate; which members will control that time; how, if at all, the bill may be amended, and under what conditions final passage may occur. An example of the text of such a rule—which is in fact a resolution that can be rejected—appears in Figure 5-1. Debate may run for various lengths of time, though the average is a period of from one to four hours. The time is assigned to the respective floor managers, often the chairman and ranking minority member of the standing committee which originally handled and reported the bill. With respect to the amending process, the rule may be of an "open" or "closed" sort. The former permits amendment from the floor, usually under the "five-minute rule" whereby any member may offer an amendment and speak in support of it for five minutes.[6] A closed rule limits the opportunity to amend the bill; sometimes no amendments at all are allowed, reducing the choice to acceptance or rejection of the committee text; on other occasions only amendments sponsored by the standing committee involved are permitted. Closed rules (often designated "gag rules" by critics of the practice) are usually reserved for tax, financial, and other complicated issues and are justified in terms of a need to prevent bargaining ("logrolling") on the floor from disrupting agreements negotiated in committee. In any case, closed rules are rarely used; of the 1,215 rules adopted between 1939 and 1960, only eighty-seven (or 7.2 percent) were of the closed variety (Robinson, 1963, p. 44).

One other power of the committee should be noted: its rules may "waive"

---

[6]The five-minute rule is often used to extend debate when the time allotted under the rule has elapsed. Members will introduce a pro forma amendment "to strike out the last word" and use the five minutes to speak on the general issues involved.

H. Res. 527

Resolved, That upon the adoption of this resolution it shall be in order to move that the House resolve itself into the Committee of the Whole House on the State of the Union for the consideration of the bill (H.R. 11039) to amend further the Peace Corps Act (75 Stat. 612), as amended. After general debate, which shall be confined to the bill and shall continue not to exceed one hour, to be equally divided and controlled by the chairman and ranking minority member of the Committee on Foreign Affairs, the bill shall be read for amendment under the five-minute rule. At the conclusion of the consideration of the bill for amendment, the Committee shall rise and report the bill to the House with such amendments as may have been adopted, and the previous question shall be considered as ordered on the bill and amendments thereto to final passage without intervening motion except one motion to recommit.

FIGURE 5-1   Rule on Peace Corps Bill, 1969.
SOURCE: *Congressional Record* (daily ed.), Sept. 8, 1969, p. H7644.

points of order against the pending legislation. Under House rules, nonprivileged matter is not permitted in bills otherwise privileged. On occasion, the Appropriations Committee, for instance, may report a bill containing legislative (substantive) rather than financial provisions. Such tactics should cause the bill to lose its privileged status; members can object to the practice by raising points of order against the bill. The Rules Committee, by including a "waiver of points of order" in the rule, removes the possibility of such an objection, with the result that the committee version is protected. Such waivers are rare; sixty-five were reported in the 1939–1960 period (Robinson, 1963, p. 47).

While the Rules Committee, thus, does a great deal to decide what the House will consider, how the consideration will take place, and what the results of the consideration will be, the panel's power is not entirely unlimited. In the first place, the discharge process is available, but is used against the committee only rarely. Similarly, suspension of the rules is appropriate, though the requirement of a two-thirds vote makes successful application very difficult. Beyond this, the House need not accept the rule proposed by the committee. By majority vote it can reject the resolution embodying the committee's views, refusing to consider the bill at all or dealing with it under its own terms. Such defeats of the committee are rare, occurring on the average only once a year.[7] When a rule does not pass, it is almost always because defeating the rule is part of the strategy of those opposed to the substance of the bill in question; the measure's foes hope, by changing the ground rules for consideration, to advance their own purposes.

There remains one other extraordinary practice, the *Calendar Wednesday* procedure, for circumventing the Rules Committee and getting nonprivileged

[7]Robinson, 1963, p. 37. None of those defeated were closed rules or waivers of points of order.

legislation to the floor. Each Wednesday, the committees are called alphabetically and when its turn comes, a committee may call up any bill from the Union or House Calendars. In practice, the device is surrounded by procedural technicalities, and is often dispensed with by unanimous consent. The alphabetical call means that some committees may have to wait many weeks for their turn to come up; if the committee has two bills to bring to the floor, it must wait until all the committees have been called before it gets its second turn. Under the rules, the bill brought up under Calendar Wednesday proceedings must be considered in one day only, and the existence of such delaying tactics as requiring a full reading of the previous day's *Journal* makes it most difficult to complete action in a single day. Moreover, only the committee chairman is empowered to call up a bill and without his cooperation the practice is of no value. Since the Eighty-third Congress (1953–1955) only three bills or resolutions have been brought to the floor through Calendar Wednesday (Robinson, 1963, p. 9; Froman, 1967, p. 96); the procedure, in short, does not provide a realistic path around the Rules Committee.

Twice in recent years—in the Eighty-first (1949–1951) and Eighty-ninth (1965–1967) Congresses—a realistic circumvention of the Rules Committee has been incorporated into the House rules. Under the 21-Day Rule, on the second and fourth Mondays of each month, the Speaker was empowered to recognize the chairman, or any other member, of a standing committee for the purpose of calling up any resolution pending for more than twenty-one days before the Rules panel. Armed with this power, the Speaker, as party leader, was put in a position to advance proposals which constituted part of his party's program. In each of these Congresses, eight bills reached the floor and seven eventually passed under the 21-Day Rule. The rule, thus, provided an important antidote to delay and defeat in the committee on rules. In each instance, however, the ensuing congressional election produced renewed Republican and conservative strength, and these groups, eager to use the Rules Committee as a brake on liberal legislation, succeeded in repealing the 21-Day Rule.

The controversy which surrounds the Rules panel centers not on whether to abolish or even drastically curtail the committee's power—there is widely shared agreement that the committee is needed—but rather on the relationship of Rules to the leaders of the party which has a nominal majority on the committee. As already noted, the committee performs useful functions in screening legislation and regulating debate. In connection with the former, Rules often acts as a "heat shield" for nonmembers, taking the responsibility for keeping measures which might embarrass representatives from reaching the floor (Peabody, 1963, pp. 143–144). Outside demands—from interest groups, the public, and the executive—may be inconsistent, and if he does not have to vote on a bill because it is "bottled up" in the Rules Committee a lawmaker may avoid alienating one or another group of his political supporters.

Rules Committee consideration, additionally, may provide rank-and-file lawmakers with much-needed time (Peabody, 1963, pp. 139–143). During the period that a bill is before the committee for hearings and discussion, representatives can seek to discover the sentiments of constituency interests, and can evaluate more carefully the potential consequences of their contemplated actions. Similarly, they may benefit from the substance of committee deliberation, which may provide information about the content and implications of the bill as well as additional time to assess the positions of the legislative specialists. Difficulties in the bill may be uncovered and corrected, changes which will enable it to pass the House, during the period the bill is before the Rules Committee. What may seem to be unnecessary delay from one perspective, from another vantage point may appear as an essential opportunity to study, understand, and perfect legislation prior to floor consideration.

Conflict between the committee, often more conservative than the full chamber, and the party leadership underlies reform proposals such as the 21-Day Rule. The issue lies dormant most of the time when cooperation, not antagonism, characterizes committee-leadership relations; only rarely does major conflict break out. One such instance occurred during the late 1950s when the two ranking Democrats—Chairman Howard Smith (Va.) and William Colmer (Miss.)—voted frequently with the four Republican members, all conservatives, to deadlock the twelve-man committee at 6 to 6, thus defeating bills desired by the Democratic leadership. Following the 1960 election, which returned the Democratic party to the White House, the liberal bloc in the House, using the full resources of President Kennedy and Speaker Rayburn, successfully led a close fight to enlarge the committee to fifteen members. A liberal coalition of nearly all the Northern and border state Democrats, about one-third of the Southern Democrats, and decisively, twenty-two Republicans eked out a 217 to 212 victory; a shift of three votes would have retained the twelve-man membership of the Rules panel.

The new, enlarged committee, continuing the customary 2 to 1 ratio between the parties, was intended to be a more reliable instrument of party leadership. The appointment of party loyalists to the two newly created Democratic positions, coupled with the six holdover liberals, was to provide the administration with a narrow, but hopefully consistent 8 to 7 majority on the committee. It is significant that enlargement, while giving the Democratic leaders temporary control of the panel, left the broader powers of Rules untouched; it continued to permit the committee to perform its basic functions. Nor did the larger size seem to make much difference in committee behavior. The eight-member majority proved undependable on the federal aid to education issue; a Catholic representative defected on proposals that failed to assist parochial schools while a Protestant Southerner, ordinarily a liberal, refused to vote out any bill that included aid for private schools. In the Eighty-seventh Congress (1961-1963), the first in which the enlarged committee operated, the Rules panel refused to grant rules in thirty-four instances; of these three measures, including a constitutional amendment to abolish the poll tax, were eventually passed under suspension of the rules (Kravitz, 1965, pp. 129–133).

In short, the Rules Committee remains a powerful body, performing functions accepted as necessary, but able to delay and defeat measures favored by the party leaders and perhaps by a majority of the members of the House. The rules of the chamber protect the committee's position, for none of the alternative procedures, with the exception of the now defunct 21-Day Rule, serve as practical devices for bypassing the panel. Yet it is absolutely essential to note that the power to obstruct is not often used; as Froman (1967, p. 58) puts it: "There are some rules which operate in favor of the status quo in the House, but they are employed only sporadically." The committee on rules works, in the last analysis, on the sufferance of the House and if it goes too far afield, steps—enlargement is only one example—can be taken to restore the balance. Ordinarily such action is not required, for the committee usually cooperates with the leadership. There remains an area between what the House itself will tolerate and what the party leaders want in which the Rules Committee exercises considerable influence.

On the floor Under its rules, the House is to meet six days a week, but it seldom holds Friday or Saturday sessions. By unanimous consent, these sessions are usually dispensed with, though the objection of a single member would require that they be held. Given the heavy workload in Washington and the strongly felt need to return to the district for political purposes, it is not surprising that there exist norms that discourage meeting beyond Thursday. Legislative business would grind to a halt if all rules were strictly adhered to, and there are informal pressures to avoid enforcement of all the procedures. On occasion, however, opponents want to delay consideration of a bill and they may insist that the previous day's *Journal* be read in full or that a quorum (218 members, a majority of the House) be actually present. The former may take several hours; the latter will consume at least twenty minutes and may be repeated at frequent intervals.[8] To cite one recent example, on October 8–9, 1968, after a twenty-seven-hour session, marked by a record forty-five roll calls, and which saw the doors of the House locked to sustain a quorum while the full reading of the *Journal* was concluded, House Democrats finally passed a bill permitting televised debates between the two major-party candidates for President [*Congressional Record* (daily ed.), Oct. 8, 1968, pp. *H*9591–*H*9604, and Oct. 9, 1968, pp. *H*9605–*H*9639]. Such is assuredly not a common occurrence, but illustrates what is possible if the rules are followed to the letter.

Ordinarily, reading of the *Journal* is dispensed with by unanimous consent and quorum calls are reserved for periods immediately prior to consideration

---

[8]If a member makes "the point of order that a quorum is not present" and requests "a call of the House," the roll must be called. The 1970 Legislative Reorganization Act eliminated the ability of a single member to compel a full reading of the *Journal*. The reform may prevent extreme instances, but is not likely to have any major impact on House proceedings.

of major legislation, when both sides want to get their allies to the floor. After a brief period for "morning business," during which members may introduce bills or resolutions, make one-minute speeches, and place material in the *Congressional Record,* the House turns to the business of the day. This may be a special day—the Consent Calender or District of Columbia affairs, for instance—or it may be in order to take up major legislation. In the latter event, if the bill is not privileged, the first step is for the Rules Committee to report its rule (resolution) specifying the conditions under which the bill is to be considered. As previously noted, such rules fail only about once a year, and in most cases, the rule is accepted and the House proceeds to consideration of the bill.

Under the rule adopted or on otherwise privileged legislation, the House handles the bill in the initial stage sitting as the Committee of the Whole House on the State of the Union, a procedural device designed to facilitate consideration. In the Committee of the Whole, the Speaker steps down after appointing another member to preside; he can attend to other facets of the Speaker's job: planning strategy, meeting with his fellow leaders, and dealing with the White House. As another advantage, a quorum in the Committee of the Whole is 100, not 218, members; this provision clearly makes the conduct of business easier, though a member intent on delay can compel the roll to be called. Debate proceeds, with the time under the control of the floor manager of the bill and its chief opponent; these men usually use part of the time available to them for introductory speeches and then yield the remainder, in small blocks, to other representatives, especially the committee experts, for additional presentations.

Under the rules, a bill must be read for amendment (unless it is being considered under a closed rule), with changes proposed at the appropriate points, but it is possible by unanimous consent to ignore these provisions. The bill may be read by titles only or simply be treated as if it had been read. Any member can be recognized, propose his amendment (providing it is germane to the bill),[9] and discuss it under the five-minute rule. Debate on any amendment may be extended by the practice of offering a pro forma amendment "to strike out the last word" and using the time available (the extra five minutes) for general discussion. Given the relatively short periods in which debate may occur, it is required to be to the point, to be germane, and members are forbidden to discuss extraneous matters. Debate, which may continue for considerable periods under amendments to strike the last word, may be terminated by unanimous consent, by agreement between the two sides, or by the passage by majority vote of a motion calling for an end to debate at a specific time.

Amendments in the Committee of the Whole are voted upon in three ways,

[9]A nongermane amendment (a "rider") can be attached only if the rule from the Rules Committee waives points of order against the bill. Otherwise, such a point of order would prevent consideration of the amendment. Germaneness is determined by the presiding officer (aided by the parliamentarian) and his decision may be (though it seldom is) appealed and reversed by a majority vote.

but not by a formal roll call. First of all, a voice vote is taken and the presiding officer states his opinion about whether the "ayes" or "nays" have won; this is frequently not difficult to ascertain because amendments opposed by the floor manager, and by the standing committee or original jurisdiction, have little chance of acceptance. Any member may demand a division, a standing vote. Opponents and proponents of the amendment rise in turn; the chair counts and announces the decision. Any member, at this point, may ask for a teller vote, a request which must be granted if supported by twenty members (one-fifth of a quorum). In this event, those in favor march down the aisle and are counted by members serving as tellers, those opposed follow, and the result is announced.[10] The 1970 Reorganization Act permits twenty members to demand that the tellers record individual votes, thus reducing that extent to which the Committee of the Whole acts outside of public scrutiny. Under these sequential procedures, the losing side can get another vote on its amendment, and can seek to reverse the outcome by getting its supporters to the floor for the subsequent voting. A bill can be defeated in the Committee of the Whole by the passage of a motion "to strike the enacting clause" of the legislation. This is a preferential motion, in order at any time, which has the effect of amending the bill out of existence.

When it has finished going over the bill, the Committee of the Whole "rises," and the House sits again; the Speakers returns to the chair and the quorum reverts to 218. The House then acts on the report of the Committee of the Whole. Amendments passed in Committee of the Whole can be reconsidered, but those rejected cannot. The effect of this rule is to give a decided advantage to the committee of original jurisdiction and the floor manager acting on its behalf, for if they defeat an amendment it is permanently lost, but if they lose, they can seek to restore their bill in the full House, after the Committee of the Whole rises.[11] The leadership has the advantage of being able to recoup its losses, a privilege denied to its opponents.

As a first step, the amendments approved in the Committee of the Whole are voted upon; usually all are acted upon at once. Next in order[12] is a motion to recommit the bill, to send it back to committee. This motion can be

---

[10]It is possible to get a roll call vote in the Committee of the Whole, but only under unusual circumstances. If fewer than 100 votes are cast on a division or teller vote, a quorum is absent and a call of the House is in order. On such a call, however, rather than simply indicate their presence, the members vote "aye" or "nay" on the amendment in question. This vote, a so-called "automatic roll call," is the final vote on the amendment.

[11]It is interesting to note that the rules for voting may preclude the determination of the existence of a majority in favor of some specific provision. For instance, if an amendment is offered and is defeated there is no vote on the part of the bill at which the amendment aimed. That is, it is assumed that the original text is the preferred one. This may not be the case, however, and all that is certain is that the original was preferred to the amendments offered. See Riker, 1958.

[12]It is in order, under the rules, for a majority to demand that an engrossed copy—the exact text, printed on parchment—of the bill be physically present. This is seldom done. Until 1965, however, when the rules were changed, a single member could make such a demand, causing the House to adjourn for a day while the engrossed copy was prepared. In such cases, if the contest was close, a day's time to try to sway a few needed votes might prove of great strategic value.

with or without instructions. In the first case, passage of the recommittal motion defeats the bill in most instances, although if circumstances become more propitious at a later date, the committee may report the bill again in the hopes of reversing the earlier result. In the second case, the recommittal motion requires the committee to report the bill back immediately with certain specific changes made. The minority frequently uses this device when it adopts a constructive alternatives strategy; at this point it can introduce its ideas and, in effect, press them to a vote. Recommittal efforts are guaranteed to the minority, and the Rules Committee cannot abrogate that guarantee in its rule. The recommittal motion out of the way, the House moves to voting on final passage.

Voting on the floor can take place by a formal roll call as well as by the three methods available during Committee of the Whole deliberations. One-fifth of the members can demand that the roll be called, and this is usually done on all important legislation if for no other reason than to make a formal record of those in favor and those opposed. There are other ways for a legislator to make his position known at the roll-call stage. He can announce a "pair" with another legislator; that is, each lawmaker declares his position on the pending matter, one for and the other against, but neither is actually present to vote that way. Or, less frequently, a "live pair" may be used, with one member, though present, pairing with an absent colleague who holds the opposite point of view on the issue in question. There are obvious strategic implications in this latter practice, for the live pair device permits one vote to be neutralized when a man, physically present, agrees not to vote. In a close contest one or two votes may make the difference between victory and defeat. In any event, by actually answering the roll when it is called or by forming a pair any member can make his position a matter of public record.

At the conclusion of the roll call voting, under the rules, any member of the winning side can offer a motion to reconsider, but only one such motion may be entertained. Such a motion is offered immediately after the vote on final passage — before any one in fact changes his mind — and is almost always tabled (set aside) by a voice vote.

RULES AND PROCEDURES IN THE SENATE

Over in the smaller Senate, a somewhat simpler set of rules performs the same functions as do the House procedures. The same general considerations need to be kept in mind in discussing the Senate rules. First, the rules are often not neutral and are used for strategic purposes to pass or, more often, to defeat legislation. Each side in any contest will use the rules as it sees fit in order to advance its purposes. Second, the rules clearly affect the distribution of power; as with the House, Senate procedures build the fragmentation which characterizes the chamber permanently into the system. The rules protect the power base of the committees and they enhance the position of minorities. The advantage lies with those opposed to change; victory at any of the multiple veto points kills a bill. To pass, legislation must move over all the hurdles successfully, and proponents must mobilize their strength at each stage of the process if they are to prevail.

Even more than in the House, strict adherence to the rules would prevent the Senate from accomplishing anything. Recourse to the niceties of the rules is seldom made; for the most part the technicalities are overcome by the widespread use of unanimous-consent agreements. In most instances, senators are willing to let matters come to a decision, even if they anticipate that it will be an unfavorable decision. The informal norms of reciprocity work to keep to a minimum the invocation of the full potential of the rules for the purpose of obstruction; only when members feel very intensely about some issues are they likely to go all out, using any and all provisions of the rules, to prevent consideration and eventual passage.

Introduction Bills are introduced during the morning hour — a period set aside at the beginning of each day during which senators may make short speeches, usually limited to three minutes; present petitions and memorials; or report bills from committee — by legislators who are present on the floor, are recognized, and who usually make speeches explaining the purposes of their proposals. Cosponsorship is permitted, so that a senator will often introduce legislation on behalf of himself and a number of cosponsors. The extent of cosponsorship gives an immediate indication of the support already in existence for a bill; a large number of cosponsors means that the construction of a legislative coalition, through bargaining and compromise, is well under way. Cosponsorship has the additional advantage of reducing the number of bills and resolutions introduced. In the Eighty-eighth Congress (1963–1965), 3,947 introductions were made, only about one-fourth as many as in the House.[13]

Upon introduction, a bill is referred to the appropriate committee, as specified in the rules that define committee jurisdictions, by the presiding officer. Occasionally, there is a conflict over jurisdiction — as in the case when the Foreign Relations Committee asserted its right to have a bill embodying the Food for Peace Program referred to it instead of to the Agriculture Committee — which will ultimately be settled by majority vote on the floor or by a decision to send the bill to more than one committee (a practice forbidden under House rules). Because such conflicts can arise, proponents of a bill will attempt to draft it in a fashion to ensure its referral

---

[13]Froman, 1967, p. 101. A further reason for the smaller number of bills introduced in the Senate is that the small size of the chamber means that there are few lawmakers who feel a need to "do something" or who introduce legislation on behalf on constituents even though it has no chance whatever to pass.

to a committee likely to look upon it favorably. Such disputes are rare, however, and the rules protect the jurisdictions of most committees on most matters.

Committee consideration Senate committees, like those in the House, serve to screen legislation, eliminating undesirable proposals, and to guide the formulation and content of those bills which seem to embody needed policy proposals. They hold hearings, "mark up" the bill, and report the committee draft when their work is complete. As the chief agents of specialization the committees command substantial respect from the nonmembers, who in most cases are prepared to accept the decisions of the experts. If they are unwilling to do so, there are a number of ways to bypass the committee, though these extraordinary procedures are unlikely to produce satisfactory results.

In the first place, there is a discharge provision in the rules, one which differs from that available in the House. Any senator can move to discharge the committee of a particular bill. He must introduce his motion during the morning hour, and a variety of dilatory tactics including insistence that the *Journal* be read in full are available to prevent the member seeking to introduce a discharge motion from gaining recognition for that purpose. The motion can be considered only after it lies over for one legislative day. This last is of importance, for the Senate rules distinguish between a legislative day and an ordinary calendar day. A new legislative day begins following adjournment; if there is a recess, not an adjournment, the legislative day continues on the following calendar day.[14] By preventing adjournment, supporters of the committee action can delay consideration of the discharge motion. After the passage of a legislative day, the Senate *may* vote to take up the discharge motion, to pass it, to take up the bill once discharged, and to pass the bill. At each of these four stages, all of which must be crossed if the bill is to pass, a filibuster (see pp. 133–134), by which under the rules providing for unlimited debate opponents of the measure can try to "talk it to death," is possible. Given the difficulty of ending debate, it is easy to see why discharge motions are seldom offered and almost never successful. There have been six discharges since 1789 (Froman, 1967, p. 131).

Alternatively, committees may be bypassed by the use of "nongermane" amendments (or "riders," as they are often called). On any legislation other than appropriations bills, any proposal, even one that has not been previously introduced, can be attached as an amendment. In this fashion, the Civil Rights

[14]For instance, in 1956, an attempt to discharge the Judiciary Committee of a civil rights bill was thwarted by this tactic. The legislative day of July 16 lasted until July 26, the day before final adjournment (adjournment sine die) of the session; thus there could be no morning hour and no introduction of the discharge motion. Opponents of the bill objected to all unanimous-consent requests to have a morning hour during this period. The motion was finally introduced on the 26th, but since under the rules it is required to lie over for one legislative day, and since a motion to take it up immediately is subject to a filibuster, adjournment came before any action could be taken. See Shuman, 1957.

bill of 1960 reached the floor as an amendment to a bill for the relief of a school district in Missouri; likewise in 1965, Sen. Everett Dirksen (R., Ill.) brought his proposal to reverse the Supreme Court's decision applying the "one man, one vote" reapportionment formula to both houses of state legislatures to the floor on a trivial resolution proclaiming National American Legion Baseball Week. The nongermane amendment thus circumvents the committee of jurisdiction and, since as an amendment it need not face a motion to consider, it avoids a possible filibuster on whether to take it up.

Yet there are reasons why the rider device is not often used. A nongermane amendment is, under the rules, subject to a nondebatable motion to table; a majority can set it aside immediately and thus there is little reason to use the procedure unless proponents of the amendment have the votes to pass it. Moreover, there are two opportunities for opponents to filibuster, one on adoption of the amendment and another on passage of the bill to which the amendment is attached. Finally, informal pressures militate against the use of the rider; to bring issues to the floor via the rider practice is to undercut the committees as well as the leadership, which has the responsibility of scheduling Senate business, and the lawmakers realize that working relationships would be destroyed if ordinary procedures were frequently disrupted. Thus, there is a reluctance to utilize the rider device, unless a majority that feels strongly about some issue has no other way to get its proposal to the floor.

Another way to get matters to the floor is under suspension of the rules. A motion to suspend can be introduced by a single senator who, after one legislative day has elapsed, can move to consider the suspension motion. This last is debatable and can evoke a filibuster, but if it comes to a vote, a simple majority is sufficient to pass it. Suspension proceedings are virtually always reserved for appropriations matters; since the rules provide that amendments to such bills must be germane and, in addition, must not add new expenditures or new legislation, it is necessary to find some way to cut through these restrictions. Suspension of the rules provides a way to adjust appropriations bills on the Senate floor (Froman, 1967, p. 135).

Finally, Senate rules make it possible to place bills passed by the House directly on the calendar, thus bypassing the standing committees. When the House sends a bill to the Senate, it is read twice and referred to committee. Objection by any senator to the second reading of the bill requires that the bill lie over for one legislative day. After an adjournment, when a new legislative day begins, a single senator's objection to "further proceedings" on the bill causes it to be placed directly on the calendar. Two filibusters remain possible, on the motion to consider the bill and on final passage. If the Senate is prepared to wait for the House to act, placing a House-passed bill on the calendar provides a way to avoid a hostile committee. This tactic was the one used to keep the Civil Rights bills of 1957 and 1964 out of the Senate Judiciary Committee, chaired by James Eastland (D., Miss.).

In the Senate, then, the rules protect the autonomy of the committees to a somewhat lesser degree than do House procedures. A determined majority, using in particular the nongermane amendment or the placing of a House-passed bill on the calendar, can circumvent a committee more readily than can a similar House majority employing the discharge petition or other devices. The major line of defense in the Senate is, of course, the filibuster, which can be broken only by a two-thirds vote. The fact remains, however, in the Senate as well as in the House, that the reluctance to go "out of channels," fostered by the informal norms governing behavior, together with the difficulty of using the alternative procedures permit a minority to use a number of devices, especially the committee, to delay or defeat a bill. Such power enhances the bargaining position of the bill's foes, for they may exact substantive concessions as the price for abandoning the strategic positions which the rules allow them to occupy.

On the floor It should be repeated that these are extraordinary procedures, used only infrequently when the legislative stakes are high. Ordinarily, simpler, less controversial procedures obtain. Most bills, when reported by a standing committee, go on to the Calendar of General Orders, the main Senate calendar.[15] The smaller upper house does not require a "traffic cop" like the House Rules Committee. Rather, the majority-party leadership, usually after consultation with the leaders of the minority, determines the schedule. Considerable effort goes into setting the agenda in a fashion acceptable to all senators, and many decisions are taken by unanimous consent. The Senate, unlike the House, often considers several bills on the floor at the same time, shifting back and forth from one to another. In short, these relatively informal, unstructured procedures preclude delay in taking up bills reported by the committees.

Like the House, the Senate has procedures for expediting noncontroversial legislation. Each Monday, after the morning hour, a call of the calendar has privileged status, though by unanimous consent the call may be dispensed with or made at some other time. Bills are taken from the calendar, unless there is objection, and discussed under a rule which imposes a limit of five minutes on the participation of each senator. If an objection is lodged, the bill is ordinarily passed over, though it may be considered anyway by a motion passed by a simple majority vote. The parties maintain committees to keep tabs on bills of this variety and to object to them on behalf of their colleagues. In this way, matters on which there is little or no conflict are handled without delay.

On major legislation, after the morning hour on the day agreed upon by the leaders, a motion to consider the bill is offered. It is usually agreed to by unanimous consent; if not, a simple majority can vote to take up the matter,

---

[15] There is also an Executive Calendar, used for presidential nominations and for treaties.

though it is possible under the rules to filibuster the motion to consider. Consideration takes place under flexible rules; often unanimous-consent agreements allow the Senate to move to consideration of other bills or to go into executive session to consider nominations made by the President. Under a rule adopted in 1964, debate on the pending business is required to be germane for a three-hour period, but this rule, too, is frequently waived by unanimous consent. Senate floor proceedings, in sum, are designed to suit the convenience of the members, even at the cost of eliminating long periods of debate on a single topic. The informality of Senate debate is underscored by the relaxed use of a quorum rule. When a quorum call is ordered, the Senators are counted as they enter the chamber, but they often do not stay and the break in the proceedings created by the call often leads to reduced rather than increased attendance. In general, except as the time to vote on major legislation draws near, few senators are likely to be found on the floor; many a "major" speech has been made to no more than a half a dozen or so colleagues present in the chamber.

Debate also proceeds under the rule of unlimited debate, which provides in effect that any senator may speak as often and as long as he likes. Since it is seldom if ever certain how much talk will go on, it is most difficult to estimate when debate will end and voting commence. The strategic implications of this rule are, of course, tremendous; debate may be used to prevent the Senate from ever coming to a decision, that is, the filibuster becomes a major weapon, in potential at least, to defeat a bill. Especially late in a session, when the rush to adjournment is on, the "talkathon" is a powerful weapon; by continuous discussion and refusal to enter into unanimous-consent agreements, the conduct of Senate business can be brought to a halt. The price for restoring the ordinary routine is agreement to drop consideration of the bill at which the extended debate aims. This is the tactic that Southern Democrats for years employed against civil rights legislation.

On other occasions, a sort of "selective" filibuster may be used for the purpose of stalling a bill without tying up the Senate. In these instances, those opposed to the legislation will permit other matters to be taken up by unanimous consent, but will continue to discuss the item of their concern. Extending debate in this way may provide time to mobilize a coalition to defeat the bill, or to exact concessions in the provisions of the bill to make it more acceptable. The liberals, mostly Northern Democrats, used the former against a proposed constitutional amendment on reapportionment in the Eighty-eighth Congress (1963–1964), talking while they assembled a coalition to block the proposal (Keynes, 1969). Southern opponents of the 1957 Civil Rights bill watered it down considerably by debating until the proponents of the bill, recognizing that they could not break the filibuster, agreed to weaken the bill as a price for passing any civil rights legislation at all (Shuman, 1957, pp. 970–974). The mere threat of a filibuster may be enough to cause committees to remove offensive provisions as they mark up the bill.

Finally, extended debate may be used by a small group, which lacks the

one-third of the votes necessary to sustain a filibuster, as a device to dramatize their cause. By holding up the business of the Senate, they hope to gain
publicity for their views, attention which may be of value in some future
contest over policy. This tactic, more than any other, probably motivated the
1962 filibuster, conducted by a hopelessly outmanned band of liberals, against
a bill giving control of communications satellites to a private, nongovernmental corporation rather than to a public one.

Amendments are, of course, in order during floor consideration. The
rules require that amendments be submitted in advance, in contrast to House
practice, so that the senators will be on notice that an attempt to alter the
bill will be made. Amendments, like the bills themselves, are considered
under the rule of unlimited debate and thus cannot come to a vote until all
members have had an opportunity to say all that they want to; that is, a
filibuster is possible here as well. This suggests that it is crucial for debate to
end and voting to begin if the Senate is to move its business forward. In most
instances, this is not difficult, for the lawmakers are willing to let matters
proceed. Frequently, if senators do not run out of things to say in the natural
flow of events, the party leaders and those most involved with the bill will
negotiate an agreement to end debate and vote at some specific time; the
date set will be sufficiently far in the future to permit all members ample
opportunity to make their speeches. The agreement is presented to the
Senate as a request for unanimous consent and is preceded by a quorum call
to allow any lawmaker a chance to object. One objection, of course, makes
termination of debate by this means impossible. On all but the most controversial legislation, such unanimous-consent requests are acceded to,
though the date set may have to be renegotiated to guarantee all a reasonable
chance to speak.

Where debate—"extended discussion" or an "educational campaign,"
as it is euphemistically put—is used to prevent a vote, that is, where a filibuster occurs, one other method for closing if off is available. This is, of
course, rule XXII, the most famous Senate rule, which allows cloture—the
ending of debate—to be invoked by two-thirds of those present and voting.
The procedure here is straightforward; any member can circulate a cloture
petition which he files with the presiding officer after sixteen senators have
signed it and which is read to the chamber. After a wait of two calendar
days, a vote is taken and a two-thirds affirmative vote ends debate,[16] and
brings the bill to a vote.

The simplicity of the procedure belies the difficulty of amassing the two-
thirds of the vote needed to pass a cloture motion. Complicated negotiations
are required to draft a bill which such a large coalition will feel strongly
enough about to vote to cut off debate. Moreover, in the light of the tradition
of unlimited debate, some senators oppose cloture as a matter of principle,
quite apart from their views on the bill at hand. Perhaps such an attitude

---

[16]More accurately, debate ends after each senator has had a chance to speak for one hour on the bill
or any pending amendments thereto. Not all members will take advantage of this opportunity.

stems from a recognition that the filibuster will, at some time, prove useful to all groups in the Senate, and the feeling that to end one now may set a precedent which will prevent the use of the filibuster, when it counts, in the future. Senators, then, must feel strongly about the bill at issue before they will support cloture, and in many cases it is unlikely that two-thirds of them will view the matter with sufficient intensity. In any event, from 1917, when the first cloture rule was adopted, through early 1971, votes were taken on fifty-three cloture motions; eight of these successfully cut off debate. Cloture was invoked most recently on the Civil Rights Act of 1964, the Voting Rights bill of the following year, and the open housing legislation of 1968, the only three successful cloture votes—in nineteen tries—in the area of civil rights (Froman, 1967, pp. 119–120; *Congressional Quarterly Weekly Report,* Mar. 12, 1971, p. 549). Where cloture fails, the bill is in effect killed.

The cloture rule, in sum, pervades the conduct of Senate business. Its requirement of an extraordinary majority of two-thirds of the legislators to pass bills—this is what unlimited debate entails—means that a firmly committed minority, of about thirty-four to forty-nine members, can block the wishes of a simple majority of up to sixty-two or sixty-three senators. The bargaining, which precedes floor consideration and also takes place while a bill is being debated, recognizes this fact; to assemble a coalition which can win against a filibuster may require major concessions, in terms of the legislation's major provisions, to potential nonstop talkers. The threat of a filibuster may often be as effective as actually engaging in one. In short, legislative strategy revolves around the ultimate recourse of a minority to the rule of unlimited debate.

Yet the tendency may be to overestimate the impact of the filibuster, especially given the virtual impossibility of assessing precisely the effect of a threat—real or imagined—to engage in lengthy discussion. For one thing, the filibuster is used with restraint; extended debate seldom ties up the Senate, even on much highly controversial legislation. In 1969, for instance, a strong minority opposed to President Nixon's "Safeguard" Antiballistic Missile program refused to filibuster even though it seemingly had the votes to do so, presumably in order not to disrupt or disorganize national defense policies.[17] Indeed, Wolfinger (1971, p. 117) suggests that the device is reserved "for bills involving salient and emotional issues, of which the prime contemporary example is civil rights." And even here, as noted above, since 1964 three such bills have passed the Senate after cloture was successfully invoked.[18] Finally, in the same vein, modern Presidents—from Eisenhower

[17]The crucial vote on an amendment denying funds for ABM deployment failed by a 50-50 vote (excluding a gratuitous vote by Vice President Agnew, unnecessary because under the rules an amendment requires a clear majority; that is, a tie kills the proposal).

[18]Wolfinger (1971, pp. 120–121) also suggests that, assuming no legislation would be enacted that had not passed the House and that was not supported by a Senate majority, only one civil rights bill was blocked by the filibuster: a 1946 measure establishing a fair employment practices commission, which passed the House and gained a simple, but not the needed two-thirds majority on a Senate cloture vote.

to Nixon—have not appeared sufficiently threatened to make serious efforts to support reform of rule XXII (Wolfinger, 1971). Thus, while a determined minority can, and sometimes does,[19] block Senate action, and while the threat of a filibuster may influence the legislative deliberations, the evidence available indicates that the operation of rule XXII does not often frustrate Senate majorities.

When debate ends, by whatever means, the voting begins, and may take three forms: voice, division (or standing), or roll call. There is no teller vote, as there is in the House, and moreover, also in contrast to House procedure, there can be only one vote on any bill or amendment. Thus, a demand for a roll call must come in advance of any balloting; one-fifth of those present may insist on a roll call under the rules, but in practice, under the norm of reciprocity, any senator desiring a roll call will be granted one by his colleagues.[20] A recommittal motion is in order in the Senate, after amendments have been voted upon and before final passage, but the practice is not often utilized. A lawmaker can record his position by the use of pairs— general or "live"—as in the House, or by simply having his position announced by a colleague. Under Senate rules, a member of the winning side, but only one, may move to reconsider, and this is done immediately after the vote, before the winning coalition leaves the floor, and is routinely tabled by a voice vote.[21]

RULES AND PROCEDURES PERTAINING TO CONFERENCE COMMITTEES[22]

Discussion of the rules and procedures of the two houses of Congress should make clear that there exist multiple centers of influence, defeat at any of which will doom the chances of a bill for eventual passage. There remains one other feature of the congressional system to discuss, for unless the House and Senate enact identical bills, a rare happening, a conference committee—a joint committee of the two chambers—is necessary to har-

[19]Most recently, in September 1970, a constitutional amendment altering the electoral college arrangements for selecting the President, which had passed the House, died in the Senate although, if votes for cloture can be equated with support for the substance of the amendment, it appeared to have the backing of a simple majority of senators.

[20]Froman, 1967, p. 124. On some occasions, getting a roll call may be crucial to the result; on matters of personal interest to legislators, such as salary increases, members may be unwilling to support publicly positions they would take on voice or division votes. In 1967, in order to avoid having to vote on its own salaries, Congress established a system whereby the President, acting on recommendations of a commission of experts, could propose increases which would go into effect automatically unless vetoed by Congress. Even here, however, opponents of increases are able to force a vote and thus compel the representatives publicly to cast ballots for higher pay.

[21]For an example of a rare instance where the outcome was reversed on a motion to reconsider, see Froman, 1967, pp. 125–126.

[22]This section relies heavily on Froman, 1967, chap. 9. See also Paletz, 1970.

monize the differences in the legislation. And if the bills cannot be reconciled, or if either house rejects the final version of the measure, the policy at stake, despite having come so far across so tortuous a course, will fail to become law. The requirement that both House and Senate pass bills in identical form not only imposes additional obstacles in the policy-making process, but also opens up a number of strategic possibilities as well.

The presiding officers—the Speaker of the House and the President pro tem of the Senate—formally appoint the conference committee members to represent their respective chambers when the members of the chamber agree to a conference. In practice, the appointment power rests with the chairman and ranking minority member of the standing committee of jurisdiction; they select the majority and minority conferees, respectively. While most bills, amended by the other house, do go to conference, other possibilities exist. If a conference poses difficulties, backers of a bill may seek to accept all amendments of the other chamber rather than submit the bill to a conference committee; otherwise the amendments will be rejected and a conference sought. Usually the choice is made by house leaders and accepted by the unanimous consent of their colleagues. In the House of Representatives, however, prior to 1965, one objection necessitated getting a rule from the Rules Committee granting privileged status to a Senate-amended bill. The rule could be denied, as it was for the 1960 aid to education bill, which subsequently died; or if granted could instruct the House conferees to accept or reject particular Senate amendments. In 1965, at the same time it was enlarged, the Rules panel was stripped of its power to control the path of a bill to conference; the Speaker, in consultation with the party leadership, may at his discretion entertain a motion, which may include specific instructions, to send a bill to conference. An objection to unanimous consent requires that the motion be put to a vote and a simple majority will sustain the motion. The power to move legislation to conference, in short, now rests with the party leaders rather than with the Rules Committee, which, as noted, may not cooperate with the leadership.

Another interesting strategy is available here. If the Senate amendments to a House-passed bill are quite different from the original provisions, and if the legislation goes to conference, then a major portion of the process of House consideration can be circumvented. That is, if Senate amendments deal with topics not included in the initial House bill, the conference will deal with material not examined by a House standing committee, on which no hearings were held, which was not debated or voted upon on the floor. One example of such an effort occurred in 1964, when the Senate attached a Medicare program to a House bill which included only a small increase in social security payments. Proponents of a social security–financed medical insurance program, blocked in the House by the implacable opposition of Chairman Wilbur Mills (D., Ark.) of the Ways and Means Committee, sought to take the bill to conference with instructions to accept the Senate amendments. The Rules Committee instead reported a rule which left the House conferees uninstructed; no agreement was possible in conference and the bill—Medicare and the increased social security benefits—failed (Froman, 1967, pp. 149–152). Under the 1965 rules changes, the leadership rather than the Rules Committee controls the terms under which a bill goes to conference, but the tactic remains available nonetheless. Such a technique is the House's method, comparable to the Senate placing a House-passed bill directly on the calendar, of avoiding a potentially hostile standing committee.

The drama which surrounds these intricate parliamentary maneuvers should not lead us to forget that they are extraordinary events, and that most bills follow a more normal routine. The chamber which acts second, and makes changes in a bill, returns it to the house of origin, which may accept the alterations, or reject them and request a conference. In the latter case, the presiding officers, as noted, choose the conferees to represent their respective houses, almost always appointing the senior members of the legislative committee which handled the bill initially. Both parties are always represented in the chamber's delegation. Negotiations ensue, and any compromises reached must be accepted by a majority of the conferees from each chamber; that is, voting is by house, not by individuals, and the conference report must be approved by a majority on each side.

When the conferees reach agreement, as they do in a vast majority of cases,[23] they send the conference report, embodying the agreed-upon language, to the two houses, where it is privileged business. In the House, the report must lie over one day, or if immediate consideration is desired, the Rules Committee must grant a rule. If the report embodies new legislation, that is, includes topics not in the bill as originally passed, the Rules Committee must report a rule waiving points of order against the bill. Otherwise, as privileged matter, the report goes to the floor without having to go to the Rules panel. In the Senate, the privileged status of the conference report means that the motion to consider the report is nondebatable, and thus there cannot be a filibuster, though a majority vote may defeat the motion. Acceptance of the report, however, is debatable and can be filibustered; this means that on controversial matters, such as civil rights, the House will have to accept the Senate version of the bill without change to avoid a conference and a possible filibuster. In both chambers, the report cannot be amended and the final vote is in effect a "take-it-or-leave-it" one. If the report is rejected, the bill dies, though the conferees may reconvene and try to work out new terms; if accepted, the bill goes to the President for his signature.

[23] Agreement was reached on eighty-five of eighty-nine bills sent to conference in the Eighty-eighth Congress (1963–1964). Froman, 1967, p. 158. See also Steiner, 1951.

SUMMARY

The congressional rules and procedures define the context within which the legislature conducts its business, within which the major features of the system — the committees and the political parties — operate. Though much of what has been discussed here is the unusual and complicated, we should not forget that most of what Congress does is carried out under a routine that avoids controversy. Unanimous consent is the usual order of the day; the full potential of the rules is exploited only in those rare instances where a large number of lawmakers feel very strongly about a major issue of national policy. Otherwise, for the vast bulk of the subjects which the legislature treats, negotiation proceeds to construct coalitions without recourse to the extraordinary procedures.

Although the rules in the smaller Senate are substantially less complex than those in the House, procedures in both chambers help shape the strategy and tactics necessary to produce legislative results. In each house, first of all, the rules protect the autonomy of the independent standing committees; it is very difficult, though a determined majority may do so, to bypass a substantive panel. The alternative procedures are exceedingly hard to exploit, and moreover, legislators evince a reluctance to invade the province of the specialists, largely in the hopes of promoting respect for their own expertise. In the House of Representatives, the committee on rules poses special problems, particularly when it operates independently of the party leadership. In short, the committees dominate the prefloor stage of legislative activity protected to a notable degree by the formal rules. On the floor, particularly under the unlimited-debate rule in the Senate, other opportunities for delay and defeat are available to the foes of legislation. From dilatory tactics aimed at preventing consideration of a bill to those which seek a negative vote on final passage or even on a conference report, there exist obstacles which a measure may be unable to surmount.

Generally speaking, the rules and procedures of Congress institutionalize a decentralized, fragmented system of power, a system characterized by multiple centers of influence (or veto points) at each of which a bill may meet its doom. Thus the rules are not neutral, but give an advantage to the forces seeking to prevent change; in contrast to proponents of legislation who must overcome every hurdle, those in opposition can sustain the status quo with a triumph at any single veto point. Much of the controversy over the rules (to be discussed in Chapter 14) reflects this fact; those who benefit from current power distributions defend the procedures that confer the advantages while those lawmakers who feel deprived seek to enhance their positions through altering the rules.

Finally, the rules, by decentralizing authority, ensure that bargaining will be the way in which the legislature is able to resolve conflicts. Because no single senator or representative, or even any small group of lawmakers, has the power to dominate congressional proceedings, negotiation and compromise become the chief modes of developing agreement. Coalitions of those who man the influential posts, which the rules help to define, are required if bills are to move through the congressional system, and bargaining, marked by mutual concessions, is the way such coalitions are assembled. The effect of this process of coalition building is seen in the content of legislation as well. Extremism, whether vice or virtue, marked change, whether to the left or to the right, will seldom generate the support needed to muster the majorities, sometimes extraordinary ones, which the rules require. Rather, as the discussion of lawmaking and oversight (in Chapters 10 to 12) will reveal, the need to build coalitions, broadly based, imposes a need to moderate demands, and change, when it occurs, will be gradual or incremented in character. In sum, the rules of the congressional system must be taken into account if we are to understand not only *how* Congress works but also *what* Congress is able to accomplish.

CHAPTER SIX

Informal Norms and Organization

Our discussion, to this point, has stressed the simultaneous operation of two broad sets of forces within the legislative system. On one hand, there are features of the system—the highly autonomous standing committees and the formal rules of procedure—which institutionalize a fragmented, decentralized distribution of the power to affect congressional activity. On the other hand, there are forces—inherent in the organization of Congress along political party lines—which seek to overcome fragmentation and to integrate (or centralize) the actions of the system. We have suggested that the parties can, at best, only partially counteract the divisive tendencies of congressional organization and process, mainly because they lack the ability to enforce discipline on their nominal partisans.

This is the case, to a great extent, as a result of the legislators' desires; few congressmen are willing to trade the freedom to decide and act as they see fit for the yoke of party discipline. It has become customary, over the years, for representatives and senators to resist efforts to convert the parties into powerful agencies able to compel compliance. Only in rare instances are legislators punished for behavior inimical to party unity.[1] In short, tradition in Congress works against the imposition of party discipline in an effort to stimulate the party-loyalist orientations of the lawmakers; such a tradition,

---

[1]One example, noted on p. 105, of party discipline was the loss of seniority imposed upon Reps. Albert Watson (S.C.) and John Bell Williams (Miss.) by the House Democrats in reprisal for their open support of the Republican candidate for President. For other instances, see Huitt, 1957.

widely respected, militates against greater centralization of the legislative system.

Other examples of the importance of tradition in the operations of Congress have been presented in the previous chapters. Seniority, nowhere described in the formal rules of either house, is the basis for choosing committee chairmen. The filibuster, though available in many circumstances, is reserved for the few instances in which a large minority feels very strongly about a particular issue, as do Southerners about the civil rights question. In general, there are many opportunities to exploit the rules for narrow personal or partisan purposes, but congressmen customarily refrain from taking advantage of these opportunities. The deference accorded to committee specialists has also been noted; the experts' views carry considerable weight with their colleagues.

All this suggests that custom (or tradition) is important for any understanding of the ways in which the legislative system operates. More formally and precisely put, this means that our knowledge of the congressional process will be enhanced by consideration of the norms, or folkways, of the House and Senate. Norms consist of sets of expectations which the legislators hold about how the occupants of particular positions in Congress should, and should not, behave. As Matthews (1960, p. 92) puts it, the folkways of the Senate consist of its "unwritten rules, its norms of conduct, its approved manner of behavior." The existence of such informal, unwritten rules reduces the level of conflict in Congress and facilitates the legislature's production of its outputs. Put another way, the norms support the decentralized distribution of influence which characterizes both chambers of Congress. Disruption of this pattern "is prevented through the existence of certain general norms of conduct which are widely held and widely observed . . . and which function to minimize internal conflicts" (Fenno, 1965, p. 70). The newly elected lawmaker is taught (learns through the socialization process) the norms by "word and example" of his more senior colleagues (Fenno, 1965, p. 71). In this way, the newcomer is prepared to assume the major roles of the legislative system while, at the same time, congressional operations are able to proceed with a minimum of disruption.

Several sets or clusters of folkways deserve attention. The first of these is a set of norms which pertains to general modes of behavior and which applies to all members of the chamber. A second set of norms prescribes some limits to the activities of the major congressional subsystems—the committees and the political parties; the House and Senate, in other words, have recognizable expectations about how the committees and parties should act. Finally, the subsystems themselves, especially the committees, develop internal norms, informal but generally accepted ways of conducting their business. There also exist, especially in the larger House, a variety of informal groups, based on regional, ideological, and other affinities, which contribute to the nature of legislative role orientations and behavior.

FOLKWAYS OF THE HOUSE AND SENATE

In each house of Congress there exist norms, of general applicability, which define the form and the style of interpersonal relationships among the members of the chamber. As noted, these constraints on behavior help make the legislative process run more smoothly. The norms assume importance from the perspective of the individual lawmaker as well. Conformity to the folkways is widely believed to be the most certain avenue to positions of congressional influence and authority; those who "play by the unwritten rules" seem to win the favor of their colleagues while those who ignore the norms seem to wield less power over, and to gain less recognition from, their fellow legislators. Thus, a representative's role orientation toward the folkways—whether he is a conformist or a maverick—appears to have an impact on his career prospects.

The norms Matthews (1960, Chap. 5) has specified a group of important chamberwide norms in the Senate, and members of the House seem to observe a similar set of behavioral guidelines (Fenno, 1965, pp. 70–76; White, 1956, Chap. 7). First among these is the norm of *apprenticeship;* the freshman legislator is expected to remain in the background while he learns what is expected of him. He should endure his status as a novice without complaint. He will sit at the foot of the table when his committee meets, he will get the least desirable office, and he will be asked to perform "more than his share of the thankless and boring tasks of the Senate, such as presiding over the floor debate . . . (Matthews, 1960, p. 93). Furthermore, he is expected to refrain from participating in the debate—"to be seen but not heard"—until the time is right, until it is clear that he has something positive to contribute. This norm is less binding in the House than in the Senate. Given the two-year term of representative, it is recognized that he may have to speak out, in order to gain some publicity, as a part of his reelection efforts; his comments, however, are expected to be pertinent to the issue under discussion. Those who violate the norm are likely to incur the displeasure of those who outrank them in seniority.

As a second norm, the beginning senator or representative is enjoined to devote himself to *legislative work,* to be a "workhorse, not a show horse." On the whole, the lawmaker is to avoid being a headline hunter, though some publicity for electoral purposes is deemed necessary and appropriate. Rather, he should commit himself, his time and energy, to carrying on the dull, routine, but difficult work essential to advancing the chamber's business. Related to this is pressure to *specialize*—to become an expert on some topic or narrow range of issues—to the virtual exclusion of all but the most superficial knowledge of the much broader set of other issues. Recognition as an expert, a man who "does his homework" and knows what he is talking about, wins respect from legislative colleagues and enables the specialist to make a meaningful contribution to the resolution of matters pending in the house.

There are other folkways as well. In as highly political an institution as the United States Congress, it is unreasonable to hope that conflict can be avoided entirely. The norms of *courtesy* and *reciprocity* help to keep the inevitable differences of opinion which divide the lawmakers from becoming so severe that the personal relationships among the members, on which the ability to conduct business may depend, are permanently damaged or destroyed. Courtesy refers to the perceived need to keep political differences from degenerating into personal dislikes. It is, of course, perfectly appropriate to disagree with a colleague over the substance of policy; it is highly undesirable to let such disagreements lead to personal animosity. The seniority rule, as noted, eliminates one source of antagonism by reducing the choice of committee chairmen to fixed practice. Similarly, conventions about the conduct of debate contribute to the same end. Remarks are never made directly to another lawmaker, rather all comments are addressed to the presiding officer; nor are fellow representatives mentioned by name, rather references are to the gentleman from Indiana or to the senior Senator from Pennsylvania.[2] Similarly, personal attacks are studiously avoided. The nearest thing to an insult which finds its way into the *Congressional Record* is a comment like the one attributed to Rep. John W. McCormack (D., Mass.) (Smith, 1964, p. 146): "I have a minimum high regard for the gentleman."[3] The norm of courtesy, finally, calls for a legislator to pay a compliment to one of his colleagues whenever possible; thus birthdays, anniversaries of the beginning of congressional service, the completion of action on a bill, and other such events become occasions for an outpouring of praise which often crosses party lines.[4]

---

[2] The following comments, from the debate on a bill to establish a Council on Environmental Quality, are typical.

> *The Speaker:* The gentleman from Hawaii is recognized for one hour.
> *Mr. Matsunaga:* Mr. Speaker, I yield 30 minutes to the gentleman from Ohio.
> *Mr. Gross:* Mr. Chairman, will the gentleman yield?
> *Mr. Dingell:* I am glad to yield to the gentleman from Iowa.
> *Mr. Dingell:* Mr. Chairman, I yield such time as he may consume to my distinguished friend, the gentleman from Ohio.
> *Mr. Aspinall:* Mr. Chairman, I do not want to appear as a wet blanket to what appears to be more or less of a love feast going on. . . . *Congressional Record,* Sept. 23, 1969, pp. H8263–H8273.

[3] When an acrimonious exchange does occur, it is frequently edited out of the *Congressional Record.* For instance, on one occasion when he was defeated on an amendment, Sen. Frank J. Lausche (D., Ohio) is reported to have charged that he had been "blitzed by orders which came down from the mountaintop," that is, that his supporters had been pressured by outside political forces. The Majority Leader, Mike Mansfield (D , Mont.), retorted: "I think the Senator from Ohio is off his rocker." The *Record* contained the following exchange. Mr. Lausche: "I know when I am outvoted on the basis of merit and I know when I am blitzed on the basis of fear of the elections." Mr. Mansfield: "I think the Senator from Ohio is off base in making a statement to that effect." See the Associated Press dispatch, "Senators Maintain Courtesy Tradition by Altering Record," *New York Times,* Saturday, Dec. 8, 1967, p. 55, col. 3.

[4] The speech of Senate Majority Leader Mike Mansfield upon the passage of the Housing and Urban Development Act of 1969 illustrates the use of compliments.

> *Mr. Mansfield:* Mr. President, the Senator from Alabama deserves the highest commendation of the entire Senate for his able and competent management of the housing program extension just adopted overwhelmingly. Senator Sparkman yields to no one in his knowledge and understanding

Reciprocity also enables members of Congress to work together more effectively. This folkway encourages the exchange of favors among the legislators: where one lawmaker can, at no real cost to himself, give aid to a colleague, he is expected to do so. Logrolling, the swapping of favors or reciprocal actions sometimes known as "backscratching" or "trading off," is the order of the legislative day. Votes are traded; neither side in any controversy will take advantage of the rules to "sneak" a bill through; "if a senator *does* push his formal powers to the limit, he has broken the implicit bargain and can expect, not cooperation from his colleagues, but only retaliation in kind" (Matthews, 1960, p. 101).[5] In short, a congressman should be helpful if he can, but at the very least he should refrain from taking advantage of others. Reciprocity combined with courtesy work to keep conflict impersonal and within bounds; acceptance of these norms limits personal, as opposed to political, antagonisms and enables legislative activity to proceed in an atmosphere relatively free of interpersonal strife.

A final norm, that of *institutional patriotism,* should be noted here. Each representative should evince loyalty, display an emotional commitment, to his chamber. Senators, with obvious pride, declare their house to be "the world's greatest deliberative body"; members of the House make the same claim on behalf of the lower chamber. While the national lawmakers may disagree about which is the superior house of Congress, most will assert the

---

of this Nation's housing needs. He has been constantly in the forefront, I might say, in bringing new and imaginative ideas into the field of housing. We are again in his debt.

Joining the distinguished chairman of the Banking and Currency Committee in guiding this measure through to swift passage was the distinguished Senior Senator from Utah (Mr. Bennett), the ranking minority member of the committee. Joined by the Senator from Texas (Mr. Tower), their thoughtful views on the matters involved contributed a great deal to the high caliber of the entire debate. So to Senator Bennett and to Senator Tower both we are extremely grateful.

Likewise we are indebted to the Senator from Wisconsin (Mr. Proxmire) for once again bringing devoted efforts to bear on this measure. As usual, his contribution was immeasurable. The same may be said for the Senator from New York (Mr. Javits).

Finally, the Senate appreciates the contributions of the Senator from Minnesota (Mr. Mondale), the Senator from Iowa (Mr. Miller) and the many others who joined the discussion. The Senate may again be proud of a fine achievement obtained with efficient and orderly action. *Congressional Record,* Sept. 23, 1969, p. S11165.

[5] Senator Russell Long (D., La.) took advantage of the rules in 1967 to pass a social security bill which included restrictions on welfare payments to families with dependent children. "Soon after the Senate convened at 9 A.M. Senator Long moved to bring the Social Security bill up for consideration—not by name but by its calendar number. With three quick voice votes and no debate in the virtually empty chamber, he whipped the bill through to approval." None of the major opponents of the provision were on the floor; freshman Sen. Joseph D. Tydings (D., Md.) who was to guard against such a contingency did not recognize the bill by its calendar number. When the majority leader returned to the floor, he declared: "What was done is fully within the rules and regulations of the Senate, but I think the way it was done raises a most serious question so far as the rights of any individual is concerned. There is such a thing as decorum and dignity in this body." Mansfield did secure a unanimous-consent agreement rescinding the vote, but only after promising to permit another vote on the bill the following day. Senator Long, thus, averted a threatened filibuster. See John W. Finney, "Senate Liberals Caught Napping," *New York Times,* Dec. 15, 1967, p. 1, col. 1. Whether this episode contributed in any way to Long's removal, one year later, from his post as Assistant Majority Leader (Whip) is unknown, but such behavior is most certainly not condoned by the Senate folkways.

superiority of the legislative to the executive or judicial branches. In a sense, loyalty to Congress is a product of the simultaneous operation of all the folkways; all serve to focus the legislators' attention on the internal workings of each house, to facilitate friendly or at least cooperative relationships among the members, to create an esprit de corps which discourages actions which would bring discredit on the institution.[6]

Functions of the norms Most observers agree that these traditions serve useful purposes for Congress. In general, the operation of the norms reduces the probabilities that the legislative system will be disrupted to the point that it is incapable of acting. That is, the legislative customs enable Congress to act, to get things done. The norm of legislative work provides an incentive to pay attention to the business at hand; specialization encourages the division of labor and the development of expertise which so complex an institution as Congress requires. In the same vein, the apprenticeship notion reduces participation in debates, for only those recognized as experts are expected to speak on the floor. In the Senate, with its rule of unlimited debate, this may help keep too many discussions from consuming too much time. Apprenticeship, requiring as it does that new lawmakers defer to their elders, coupled with the norms of courtesy and reciprocity minimizes the inevitable frictions which occur in a highly political body. Furthermore, by limiting personal animosities, these same folkways help to create the conditions in which bargaining and compromise, the basic techniques of congressional conflict resolution, can be conducted most effectively.

Yet it should be noted that these traditions also contribute to the decentralized character of the legislative system. Values of deference, reciprocity, specialization, and courtesy lend support to the authority of the independent standing committees. These folkways discourage dissident lawmakers from challenging the positions of the committee experts. The norm of institutional patriotism inhibits proposals for reform. To attack the status quo is to cast doubt on the quality of the legislative institution. The existence of such constraints as these makes difficult the lot of the political party; any efforts to strengthen the party's ability to unify its members are guaranteed to encounter hostility engendered by adherence to the norms. The traditions and habitual patterns of thought and action constitute a sort of legislative culture which sustains the independence of committee chairmen, regional leaders, and even some members of the formal party apparatus.

[6]The few instances in recent years when discipline was meted out by Congress to its own members seem to have been responses to "conduct unbecoming to a member of Congress." Thus the Senate censured Joseph R. McCarthy (R., Wisc.) for his abuse of the investigatory powers and Thomas Dodd (D., Conn.) for his use of campaign contributions to cover personal expenses. Similarly, the House refused to seat Adam Clayton Powell (D., N. Y.) because of his failure to pay a libel judgment against him and, perhaps, because of his generally flamboyant conduct. Where the reputation of Congress has not appeared to be at stake, critics have charged the lawmakers with extreme reluctance to act to ensure ethical conduct.

Observers of Congress also agree that the pressure to adopt a conformist orientation toward the norms is not entirely successful in ensuring compliance. Certain types of lawmakers, motivated by particular forces, find conformity most difficult (Matthews, 1960, pp. 102–114). Previous training seems to make a difference; legislators with experience in executive political offices (governors, federal executives, and local government officials) seem less able to restrain themselves and often violate the norms. Those with political ambitions—senators seeking the Presidency or representatives eager to move to the upper house—need to be seen and heard to advance their candidacies. A competitive constituency, where elections are won or lost by a few votes, may require the incumbent to protect his electoral prospects by speaking out or aggressively championing some district-oriented project. Liberals, whose ideology requires them to act on behalf of social change, also find conformity frustrating and are more apt to behave in ways inconsistent with the culturally accepted routines.

The "inner-club" controversy Where students of Congress do not agree is on the effects of nonconformity. One school of thought argues that there exists an "inner club" in the Senate whose membership is composed of those who conform to the norms and which wields a disproportionate share of senatorial power.[7] Those who accept the folkways are accepted into the club; those who will not, for whatever reasons, are kept at arms length from the centers of power. Matthews (1960) finds, for example, that those who conform—who speak infrequently and who accept the norm of specialization—are the most effective senators, the ones who get a higher proportion of their legislative proposals passed. His data are reproduced in Table 6-1 and

[7]For views supporting the existence of a "Senate Establishment," see White, 1956; Matthews, 1960; and Fenno, 1965. Sen. Joseph Clark (D., Pa.) felt that an inner club existed and attacked it on the Senate floor and in print. See Clark, 1963; 1964, chap. 6.

TABLE 6-1 *Floor speaking, index of specialization, and legislative effectiveness (83rd and 84th Congresses)*

	Index of legislative effectiveness, %			
	High	*Medium*	*Low*	
Level of floor speaking:				
High	0	33	67	100% (9)
Medium	3	68	29	100% (31)
Low	15	59	26	100% (39)
Index of specialization:				
High	23	69	8	100% (13)
Medium	10	62	28	100% (29)
Low	8	51	41	100% (39)

SOURCE: Matthews, 1960, table 44, p. 115. Reprinted by permission of the University of North Carolina Press.

show that high specialization and a low level of participation on the floor lead to higher effectiveness.[8] Specifically, a higher proportion of infrequent speakers (15 percent) than of more frequent debators (0 percent) ranked among the most effective senators. Similarly, highly specialized lawmakers saw 23 percent of their bills passed, on the average, as compared to the passage of only 8 percent of the bills offered by the least specialized senators.

One other piece of evidence is available. Nonconformists, so the inner-club argument holds, are denied access to the powerful positions in Congress, including assignment to the major legislative committees. To test this proposition, Swanson (1969) has examined the rates at which various types of senators advance toward the top of the committee hierarchy. He finds that in contrast to the conformists—ideological conservatives and moderates—the mavericks—mainly liberals—moved onto the important committees very slowly. Recognized nonconformists such as Proxmire (Wis.), Clark (Pa.), Douglas (Ill.), and Morse (Oreg.) were without major committee assignments after eight years of senatorial service while their more conformist-oriented colleagues in most cases received choice posts. Moreover, these liberals voted heavily in favor of Senate reforms—liberalizing the cloture rule and altering the committee structure—which were directed at weakening the hold of the inner circle. In short, as Swanson declares, "those liberal senators, like Joseph Clark, who make a habit of challenging overtly the rules and traditions practiced by the Establishment, are likely to be ignored when prime committee posts are distributed."

Other less clear-cut forms of punishment may be meted out to nonconformists. Jewell and Patterson (1966, pp. 374–375) point to some examples. Those who do not play according to "the rules of the game" may encounter "selective inattention"; they will be avoided in the corridors or in debate; their ideas and proposals will be ignored. Similarly, those who violate the norms may meet "process sanctions"; their bills may be lost or temporarily misplaced, quite inexplicably. By these devices, the members of the club indicate to those outside the legislative culture that their behavior is not appreciated. In sum, the inner-club position holds, with Fenno (1965, p. 71), that "Members who learn [the norms] well and whose behavior demonstrates an attachment to them are rewarded with increased influence. Conversely, members who seriously and persistently deviate from them are punished by diminution of their influence."

A more moderate view of the establishment is advanced by Huitt (1961b) in a study of "the outsider in the Senate." While acknowledging the existence

[8]The index of floor speaking is the number of speeches which each senator made during the Eighty-third and Eighty-fourth Congresses. The index of specialization is the proportion of all bills and resolutions introduced by each senator referred to the two committees receiving the largest number of the bills he sponsored. The assumption is that the more specialized a senator is, the more concentrated, in policy terms, will be the bill he offers, and the narrower the range of committees to which his bills will be referred. The index of effectiveness is the proportion of all the bills and resolutions a senator introduced which actually passed the Senate. All these measures, as Matthews, 1960, App. D, pp. 274–275 and 278–279, recognizes, are simple and possibly subject to distortion.

of an inner circle in the Senate, Huitt suggests that it is not so intolerant of the nonconformist; the outsider orientation is, in other words, a legitimate one. No sanctions are imposed on the recalcitrant lawmaker; as in the case of William Proxmire (D., Wis.), there is a recognition that personality, ideological conviction, or constituent pressures may lead a senator to reject the folkways. While damaging the reputation of Congress is unacceptable behavior, nonconformity with the folkways can be tolerated. Moreover, Huitt suggests, mavericks are useful to the system: they provide access for outside groups whose demands might otherwise be unregistered; they provide an extreme point of view which makes the middle ground, which the leaders adopt, seem more reasonable. In short, while Proxmire, as a case in point, has "unquestionably paid a price for choosing the Outsider role," he seems to consider the cost acceptable. Though he may be more removed from the centers of Senate power, the Wisconsin Democrat gains a freedom to act, unrestrained by the norms, which he finds satisfying. Outsiders then, in Huitt's view, are functional for the system, and the inner club recognizes this and refrains from invoking specific sanctions against those, like Proxmire, who assume the nonconformist orientation.[9]

Implicit in the view that the outsider's behavior is widely accepted in the Senate and that no overt sanctions are imposed on nonconformists, so long as their activities do not reflect upon the integrity of the chamber, is the question of the actual significance of the establishment. Nelson Polsby (1964, 1969) makes the point explicit, arguing that there is no clear evidence that an inner club exists. First, he suggests, discussions of the Establishment do not agree on who is a member and who is not. Senators, such as Robert A. Taft (R., Ohio), Robert S. Kerr (D., Okla.), and Lyndon B. Johnson, contrary to club norms, have sought higher office without having to forfeit their status as "Senate men"; others, Hubert H. Humphrey (D., Minn.) and Lyndon Johnson for instance, have urged reform of Senate practices and not visibly lost their colleagues' regard. Nor do members of the club seemingly possess similar personalities or differ in personality terms from the outsiders.

Second, Polsby argues, those who do conform do not seem to act antagonistically toward those who do not conform. All senators are accommodated with respect to scheduling and disposition of Senate business. No members of the upper house seem to be completely without influence in some areas; that is, power is shared with the mavericks. Outsiders do not seem to have reduced ability to affect legislative outputs. In short, Polsby suggests, it is difficult to decide who is "in" and who is excluded from the inner circle and it is hard to find evidence that those who are "out" suffer from their status. Those who choose an outsider orientation, that is, are not deprived of influence within the chamber where seniority and specialization lead to influence quite apart

[9]Matthews, while admitting that "a few" outsiders may serve useful purposes in the Senate, argues that the members of the chamber tolerate the orientation but do not consider it legitimate, and that the outsider's "immediate and direct influence in the Senate is usually slight." See Matthews, 1961a, and Huitt's (1962) response.

from membership in any inner club. More recently, Polsby (1969) goes on to argue, the emergence of the Senate as a primary source of national party leaders, including presidential candidates, has undercut the "club mentality." An increasing number of senators have chosen to focus on national issues, and to master the intricacies of procedure in order to act with respect to these issues, thus reducing the conformity to the folkways.

To summarize: There is widespread agreement among students of Congress that there exists a set of norms—apprenticeship, specialization, courtesy, and the like—which color much of what the legislators do. Whether these folkways merely facilitate the conduct of business or contribute as well to the allocation of legislative influence is a more debatable issue. While there exist fragments of evidence—differences in legislative effectiveness and in progress toward gaining important committee posts—which suggest that conformists are rewarded for paying attention to the norms,[10] more data is surely needed to resolve the question conclusively. And in any event, each legislator recognizing that the folkways do exist must decide how to relate to them, whether or not to conform. More accurately, since role orientations are related to specific situations, he will have to choose the conditions under which he feels it necessary to behave in ways that his colleagues will not approve.

NORMS RELATING TO LEGISLATIVE SUBSYSTEMS

The norms with chamberwide applicability, just discussed, constitute only one set of legislative customs and expectations, defining the relationships among the senators and representatives as members of their respective chambers. A second set of folkways, also pertinent to any understanding of congressional outputs, relates to the relationships between the houses, as single units, and the major subsystems within each chamber, the standing committees and the political parties. The central point to note is that the committees and parties, whatever their formal powers, whatever they assert to be within their provinces, operate under constraints, embodied in a set of normative expectations, that the full chambers impose upon them.

Norms about committees Only recently have scholars begun to investigate the expectations which the House and Senate hold about their standing committees. In this section, we will treat the relationships between the House and

---

[10]Other pieces of evidence would include the defeat of Joseph Clark by Robert Byrd (W. Va.) for the post of secretary of the Senate Democratic caucus, in a situation in which the liberals seemed to have the votes to win. Presumably some senators sympathetic to the liberal cause voted against the maverick Clark. Similarly, the rise of Edward M. Kennedy (Mass.) to Democratic Assistant Majority Leader in the Senate seems to have been aided by his conscious effort, in contrast to his brothers whose eyes were just as clearly focused on the White House, to become a "Senate man" by conforming to the norms. When Byrd and Kennedy met, in a 1971 contest for the latter's position as Whip, the former won the post, perhaps suggesting the strength of the Southern, conservative segment of the Establishment within the Democratic Party.

two of its panels; these are probably typical of the *kind* of traditions which each house holds about its committees, though, of course, the *content* of the norms may differ for particular committees.

Because it is "a highly visible, well-identified, and much talked about" subsystem, members of the lower house have some well-defined notions about the place of the Appropriations Committee in the legislative system.[11] One group of these ideas prescribes the committee's part in achieving the goals of the chamber. First, since the legislature's major functions include enacting laws, the committee is expected to do its part to that end. Specifically, this means that when the chamber authorizes programs, Appropriations is to fund those programs; the committee can give greater or smaller amounts, but it cannot fail to supply some money for the purposes supported by a majority of the full chamber. At the same time, and somewhat contradictorily, the House expects Appropriations to try to save money, that is, to be as economical as possible. This imposes an incremental strategy on the committee; it will economize as much as it can but without impairing the programs and projects that the parent body desires.

Beyond this, the committee is expected to oversee the executive branch. Because Appropriations controls the purse strings, it has advantages over other panels, strategically less well placed, which it is expected to exploit. The committee can, of course, decide how much money particular agencies should have; it can, through informal contacts, reach agreements with the bureaucrats; and its hearings provide an opportunity to scrutinize executive conduct. These powers enable Appropriations to impose legislative priorities on the mammoth executive establishment. Finally, the committee is expected to uphold the position of the lower house in its dealings with the Senate. Appropriations members, as conference participants, are to sustain the more economical stance of the lower house in their negotiations with the more "spendthrift" senators.

A second set of norms defining the relationships of the Appropriations panel to the parent body relate to the autonomy of the committee; Fenno describes these as "maintenance" expectations. The "most basic" of these is that "whatever House-prescribed goal the committee seeks to achieve it should always act as a dependent subsystem of the House of Representatives" (Fenno, 1966, p. 20). Such behavior permits the chamber-committee relationship to remain predictable. Specifically, the prescription entails a number of injunctions. For one thing, the committee should follow consensus-building procedures; that is, decisions should be reached through a process of bargaining and accommodation which ensures that all interested parties receive a fair hearing for their views. The committee, in addition, should appropriate,

---

[11]These paragraphs summarize Fenno (1966, chaps. 1–2) who (p. 4) suggests that the power of Appropriations plus its high level of contact with the parent chamber accounts for the clear-cut expectations held by the latter. The members of the House may not hold such precise views about less important and active committees.

not legislate. Policy choices, under the division of labor arrangements that characterize the House, are the province of the standing committees, and Appropriations should limit itself to deciding how much money is required to implement those choices.[12]

A third maintenance expectation requires that the committee act as a collector and distributor of information. If the full chamber has access to information, it can in the last analysis enforce its will on the committee. Finally, the House expects the Appropriations Committee to observe the integrative chamberwide legislative norms. Thus the members should act as specialists, devote themselves to legislative work, and, following the notions of reciprocity and courtesy, cooperate with their colleagues—their fellow panel members, the party leaders, the rank and file—in order to achieve committee and chamber goals. In short, the Appropriations members should act as "responsible legislators," men who will adhere to the legislative culture.[13]

The House, moreover, possesses sanctions with which it can guarantee that its committees, including Appropriations, acknowledge their ultimate dependence upon the parent body. In the case of Appropriations, the House can, if it chooses, alter the jurisdiction of the committee; if the committee behaves irresponsibly, it can be stripped of its authority to deal with certain specific matters. In the same vein, if the committee is uncooperative, the House can bypass it, often using the device known as "backdoor spending" by which programs are financed directly or indirectly from the federal Treasury without Appropriations Committee scrutiny. Control is more often exercised, less visibly, through the effort to ensure that the representatives who win places on the committee will conform to the expectations of the full House. The size of the committee has been altered to increase its responsiveness; aspirants for committee positions are screened to make sure that those who are appointed will act responsibly.

Other sanctions are also available. The House can simply refuse to defer to the experts and can amend the committee bill, if it is deemed inappropriate, on the floor, making it conform to more widely held views. Finally, the non-members can control the committee by defining its procedures. If Appropriations is perceived as failing to supply information, the House can require more budget items be considered annually, thus ensuring the committee will generate data on those items. As noted, points of order can be lodged against committee bills. Or new procedures can be required, as they were in 1958, aimed at increasing the quantity and the clarity of information available to nonmembers. In sum, the House expects the Appropriations Committee to

[12] While Appropriations does sometimes include substantive provisions, that is, does legislate, in money bills, it does so with the approval of the full chamber. The latter reserves the right to refuse to waive points of order against a money bill which contains legislation. Restraint is necessary if overt conflict between the substantive committees and Appropriations is to be avoided.

[13] For a discussion of the idea of the "responsible legislator" and its relevance to the committee assignment process, see Chapter 3, pp. 64–65, and Masters, 1961.

act to support the attainment of House-prescribed goals; if the expectations are violated, the House retains the ultimate authority to impose its will. From the perspective of the committee and its members, these folkways limit the freedom to act. Power is given to the committee, but it can be taken away. Committee activity must not jeopardize that power, and must as a consequence, go on within the limits which the House expectations about that activity impose.

The House Ways and Means Committee operates within similar, rather clearly defined, constraints (Manley, 1965, 1970). Its jurisdiction over revenue matters—taxation, the national debt, social security, and international trade—makes the committee a major focus for members of the parent chamber; many have a stake in the committee's decisions. In consequence, while Ways and Means is granted considerable autonomy, in deference to its expertise, it is nevertheless expected to be particularly responsive to the full House. Indeed, the price of that autonomy, and of the closed rule under which many of the committee's bills are considered, is a sensitivity to the views of interested representatives. The basic goal of the committee is to produce "widely acceptable" legislation (Manley, 1970, p. 232). As with Appropriations, a subtle chamber-committee relationship exists between the House and Ways and Means; the former grants the latter substantial freedom in the clear expectation that the committee will accommodate member views and under the ultimate sanction of rejecting committee proposals that do not reflect majority sentiment.

Taxing and spending are at the heart of government operations, and it is not surprising that the House of Representatives has the most visible set of expectations about its panels that deal with these topics. Other committees, dealing with important but less central matters, appear to have relatively less clearly defined norms within which to operate. Fenno (1970) reports that, in contrast to Appropriations and Ways and Means whose members defer to the full chamber to preserve their own power positions, members of other committees receive less explicit guidance from the parent chamber. The House retains, of course, the ability to defeat these committees' bills on the floor, but given its relative lack of concern with the substance of these panels' decisions does not hold as clear-cut expectations about the style of committee activity. Thus, such committees as Foreign Affairs, Education and Labor, Interior, and Post Office and Civil Service pay as much heed to other forces as to the House itself. Thus, congressional committees appear to function under varying sets of expectations, norms that in varying degrees impose limits on the ability of each panel to achieve the goals which its members seek to attain.

Norms about parties Expectations about the relationship between congressmen and their political parties also exist, though the content of these norms is not entirely clear. At the very least, it is clear that members are expected to act on behalf of the party when it is possible to do so. It is also obvious, as noted in Chapter 4, that tradition works against the enforcement of party discipline; the few sanctions available are invoked only in extreme cases. The folkways seem, moreover, to approve defection from the party on grounds of constituency pressure—where a vote with party would produce electoral troubles at home—or on grounds of conscience—where a vote with party would require a vote against personal conviction. Despite this normative acceptance of defection, the party remains an important, and in many instances the most important, influence on a legislator's vote (see Chapter 12). On numerous occasions, members of Congress follow the general expectation by voting with the majority of their fellow partisans. The point to remember here is that the parties, like the committees, operate within a set of expectations which help to specify the relationships between the legislative system and its component subsystems.

COMMITTEE NORMS

Congressional committees work within two sets of norms: chamberwide folkways which affect interpersonal contacts among the lawmakers, and expectations about how the committees should contribute to the output activities of Congress. House and Senate committees develop their working "rules of the game," which define how they will comply with the broader folkways. These "rules" are unwritten and informal and constitute a set of norms which help to establish acceptable ways in which the committee can meet its obligations to the parent chamber. While only a few panels have been examined carefully, sufficient research is available to permit some discussion of these intracommittee customs.

Fenno's (1965; 1966, chaps. 3–5) work on the House Appropriations Committee provides a convenient starting place. First of all, there exists a set of *personal goals or expectations* which individual committee members hold and which they can realize only if the committee retains its acceptance in the House as a whole, that is, only if the panel meets the expectations of the full chamber. Quite clearly, the Appropriations Committee is an influential body; its decisions influence many substantive policy areas. Given this broad range of concerns, it is not surprising that members of Appropriations are better informed than those assigned to other panels; they are in the "middle of things." Additionally, they possess power and prestige: they are able to effect national economic policy, to demand a hearing in any policy conflict where funds will be required, to work for constituency-oriented programs and projects, and to exert control over the agencies of the executive branch. These powers make the committee members important and eager to sustain their advantageous position.

To get and keep these satisfactions, the committee members are prepared to labor long and hard. The committee fosters the "style of hard work" whereby the members diligently develop and make use of their expertise, out of the glare of publicity. Only by dint of hard work can they manage to retain the rewards they seek; maximum effort enables them to withstand and prevail over competing centers of influence. This style, in turn, becomes satisfying, an end in itself, for it contributes to committee unity. Long hours require personal contact and understanding; these lead to friendships, feelings of solidarity, and a sense of attachment to the committee. Where the satisfactions are great, the work involved becomes worthwhile. In short, committee members believe their style of work permits them to derive the benefits they desire from committee service, and they endeavor to make this clear to new legislators coming on to the panel.[14]

In sharp contrast, other goals motivate the members of other committees. Fenno (1970) suggests that policy content rather than legislative influence per se is central to the Foreign Affairs and Education and Labor Committees in the House. The former is especially concerned to formulate and pass the foreign aid bill while the latter wrestles with a host of substantive issues. Still another member perspective is illustrated by the Interior and Post Office Committees. The chief goal fostered on these panels is the reelection of the members; the committees act to advance the constituency interests of those who serve and, thus, to enhance their political prospects. Committees develop work styles to suit the aims that their members desire to accomplish.

Congressional committees also develop *traditional goals, ends which they seek to promote.* Appropriations members seek, first of all, to maintain—for Congress, and for themselves as the relevant experts—the "power of the purse." Thus they resist any efforts, such as "backdoor-financing" schemes, which might reduce the power of the legislative branch to determine what federal monies are spent for what purposes. Likewise, Appropriations members style themselves as the "guardians" of the Treasury; it is their task to prevent raids on federal funds. It follows that the committee views with suspicion all budget requests, assumes that there is extra money tucked away in them, and, in the vast majority of cases, appropriates less than was requested. In fact, during the 1947–1962 period, the committee reduced nearly three-fourths of the agency budget requests which it examined.[15]

These three norms—protect the power of the purse, guard the Treasury, and cut budget estimates—pose problems of adaptation, especially in the light of the high levels of member identification with Appropriations. The desire

[14]The House Ways and Means Committee has member goals similar to those of Appropriations. Panelists are among the most prestigious and influential representatives; Democratic members also serve as the party's Committee on Committees. Members identify with Ways and Means and adopt a style of work required to master the complexities inherent in consideration of revenue legislation. In so doing, they preserve for themselves central positions in the legislative system (Manley, 1965; 1970, chaps. 2–3).
[15]Fenno, 1966, Table 8.2, p. 354. Another 18.4 percent of the requests were unaltered; thus about 92 percent of all agencies received the precise amount requested or less.

to economize inevitably entails conflict with broader norms in general and with the standing committees in particular. The latter, quite understandably, want programs funded, want to spend. Appropriations wants to cut budgets, wants to save, and feels compelled to reexamine what the substantive committees have done. Tension is endemic to the system and cannot be avoided. Yet conflict between the authorizing panels and Appropriations remains at a tolerable level. The Appropriations Committee respects the House expectation that programs be supported. It cuts budgets, but does so at the margins, reducing estimates but not to the point the programs are endangered. Thus the conflict, in Fenno's (1966, p. 126) words, remains "episodic and piecemeal" rather than "persistent and cumulative." The committee tends, overall, to meet House norms and thus to avert any sustained campaigns against its position.

Antagonism is not so easily avoided, however, with regard to another House expectation—that projects in members' districts win support. Such constituency activities are, of course, held to be crucial to the reelection prospects of many lawmakers. In recognition of these needs, the Appropriations Committee has adopted another norm, one that is in a sense incompatible with the goal expectations outlined above. The committee recognizes that it must serve the constituency needs of House members. Appropriations men realize that they cannot both protect the Treasury and fund local programs; they adapt by backing dams, post offices, and the like in their colleagues' districts, but try to be moderate in this respect. They recognize that a failure to yield to the parent chamber might undermine the committee's position and they modify their own goals accordingly.

It is possible to specify functionally comparable goals, which Fenno (1970) calls the "strategic premises" of committee activity, for other panels as well. We have already noted the thrust of the Ways and Means Committee to preserve its autonomy and influence by writing revenue bills that will be accepted by the full chamber. The constituency-oriented Interior Committee follows the classic "pork barrel" politics of giving each member something he desires for his district while at the same protecting the interests of the "private users of land and water resources," the major constituents of most committee members. The policy-oriented committees also display distinctive goals: Foreign Affairs seeks to advance foreign aid while Education and Labor, unable to agree on the substance of policy, engages in partisan conflict and pursuit of individual members' personal policy preferences. These characteristic premises, Fenno (1970, pp. 29–52) argues, reflect member goals and the environment in which the committee operates, and are sustained by the norms of individual behavior that exist on congressional committees.

There is, then, a third set of norms which impinges on committee activity. Not only do committees seem to have traditions about what the members can expect to derive from committee service and about the goals the committee should seek, but there are *folkways governing how these personal expecta-*

tions and committee purposes can be attained. That is, the committees also have process, or maintenance, expectations. Again, the House Appropriations Committee provides a case in point; other committees appear to have process norms functionally equivalent, though not necessarily identical in content.

In the first place, Appropriations has a clearly defined role structure, with sets of expectations about the behavior of the occupants of the various positions.[16] Thus the committee has informal rules about the use of subcommittees, the powers of leaders—chairman and ranking minority member of the full committee and the subcommittees—the place of newcomers to the committee, and the desirability of committee "integration." The full committee agrees that autonomous subcommittees should be the chief decision-making units. A set of norms guides the operation of the subcommittees; they are to specialize in particular appropriations topics (e.g., foreign operations, Defense Department, public works, and so on); and the members are to work hard, to observe the tradition of commitment to legislative chores. The subcommittees have their own form of reciprocity; each is expected to defer to the experts in return for deference to its expertise. Decisions are to be reached through compromise, and once taken are to be supported by all ("subcommittee unity"). Moreover, under the norm of "minimal partisanship" the subcommittee members are to work together to produce sound legislation without the intrusion of partisan motivations into their deliberations. The subcommittees, in short, are enjoined to develop internal cohesion through observation of these normative modes of procedure.

Likewise, the full-committee and subcommittee leaders are to behave in specified ways. The former are to control matters through their powers to choose subcommittee personnel. The chairman and ranking minority member tend to balance subcommittees with those who have special constituency reasons for service on a particular unit and those who are "disinterested," that is, have no personal constituency motive for service on a given subcommittee. Such a balance fosters adherence to broader norms, for it encourages support for members' constituency projects and, at the same time, a desire to trim budget requests. The full-committee leaders, in addition, may also involve themselves in subcommittee affairs by serving on them as regular participants or as ex officio members by virtue of their leadership posts. Finally, the full-committee chairman can abolish a subcommittee if he deems this course necessary to permit Appropriations to achieve its goals.

Subcommittee leaders are expected to act to reinforce these procedural norms. They are encouraged to work harder, to become extremely well informed, to specialize in the matters which their subcommittee treats. They are also expected to encourage decision by compromise, without the rancor of partisanship, in an atmosphere characterized by smooth, friendly relations

[16]The Appropriations Committee, or any other, can easily be treated as a political system, defined as the members plus their permanent staff, as described in Chapter 1. This discussion summarizes Fenno, 1966, chap. 4.

among the subcommittee personnel. On the other hand, the newcomer to the committee is expected to serve a period of apprenticeship, to remain inactive and quiet while he learns the ways of the panel. The roles of committee and subcommittee leader, member, and novice are, thus, normatively specified.

The fact that these roles fit together, "mesh" in Fenno's words, means that Appropriations is a well "integrated" committee, that is, that it minimizes intracommittee conflict and works efficiently to achieve its goals (Fenno, 1963). High levels of integration mean high conformity to the norms and a close parallel between expected behavior and real action. High integration, more importantly, leads to power in the parent body; as noted, if the experts stand firm and united, they are very likely to prevail when policy is enacted. Power, in turn, means that Appropriations members can meet their personal expectations. The committee has been able to achieve such strong integration for a number of reasons. First is a widely shared agreement, described previously, on committee goals. Next, the nature of the committee's business is helpful. It is far easier to reach negotiated settlements on matters of dollars and cents than with regard to issues involving principles; it is far simpler to make monetary concessions than to appear to yield on matters of principle. Moreover, since the appropriations process is an annual one, the members make such decisions over and over and the repetition reinforces the desirability of integration and the need for predictable decision-making norms.

The Appropriations members' acceptance of the commitment to legislative work, noted above, also contributes to committee integration; the desire to conform to House and committee expectations, to act as responsible legislators, encourages cooperation among committee members. Moreover, since the committee is important and prestigious, it is attractive; legislators eagerly seek to win seats on Appropriations; very few members leave it voluntarily.[17] Thus, the committee membership is stable and marked by a high commitment to committee goals. These conditions of constant involvement with the same colleagues, all working for shared ends, facilitate integration. In a sense, a sort of circular process is at work: Appropriations, as an integrated and powerful committee, is attractive to its members who adhere to norms designed to sustain the integration, and thus the power, of the panel. If integration permits the meeting of expectations, then integration becomes a value in itself.

Appropriations does not rely solely on voluntary compliance with the norms to sustain committee integration; a number of control mechanisms exist as well. Perhaps the most important is the socialization process. During the period of apprenticeship which new members are expected to observe, the senior men show their juniors how things are done. It is made clear, by word and example, that the novice is to accept the traditional modes of behavior. The process of appointment to major committees, such as Appropria-

---

[17] See Table 3-1, p. 60, for rankings of committee prestige.

tions, stresses, as we have seen, the search for responsible lawmakers who, free from strong ideological commitments and intense constituency pressures, can be flexible and adaptable. Thus most newcomers to Appropriations are receptive to the learning process. Those who are not may find that they cannot win appointment to desirable subcommittees, are cut off from needed information, or are virtually excluded from meaningful participation in committee affairs. Senior members can easily employ such sanctions against the dissident. Those who choose to conform, by contrast, find that sooner or later their patience will be rewarded by acceptance and influence within the committee.[18]

The remaining committees that Fenno (1970) treats reveal differing degrees of adherence to the norms relating to specialization, participation, and partisanship. Foreign Affairs, for instance, shows only a little specialization; while it has an elaborate subcommittee structure, its main business, the foreign aid program, is handled in the full committee, and the development of expertise is thereby inhibited. The absence of deference to expertise reduces the need for a norm of apprenticeship; participation in committee deliberations is widespread. Involvement, however, is not partisan, for Republican and Democratic members alike share support for the foreign aid principle.[19]

The structure of norms on the Interior Committee reflects the panel's focus on constituency affairs. The few, relatively large subcommittees have moderate expertise, and in deference to specialization are granted some autonomy. Full-committee deliberations seek to generate legislation that will serve the constituency interests of all members, thus enhancing their reelection prospects, and to this end, participation is open to all. The imposition of an apprenticeship folkway would limit the members' ability to work for their districts and thus no such norm exists on Interior. A fully developed set of committee rules, scrupulously observed, further facilitates

[18]The House Ways and Means Committee, also a major and prestigious body, protects its position in the chamber in a fashion similar to that of Appropriations. Integration—fostered by norms of restrained partisanship and membership responsibility—sustains the committee's influence. Integration is fostered by the style of its chairman—Wilbur D. Mills (D., Ark.)—which encourages reciprocity, devotion to committee work, and a sense of committee unity. As an integrated body the committee is attractive and powerful; to sustain this position in the chamber requires acceptance of, and behavior in conformity with, integrative norms. New members are socialized through an apprenticeship system. In sum, intracommittee traditions influence members' activities and their observance permits the members to attain positions of importance in the legislature. See Manley, 1965; 1970.

The Senate Appropriations Committee has similar norms, leading to a well-integrated panel. Senate panelists adhere to notions of reciprocity, courtesy and deference, specialization, and nonpartisanship. A modified form of apprenticeship is also observed, modified because newcomers to the committee may be relative senior senators and thus unwilling to remain completely silent. On the Senate committee, see Horn, 1970, chap. 3.

[19]At the start of the Ninety-second Congress (1971), Chairman Thomas E. Morgan (D., Pa.) reorganized the Foreign Affairs Committee, seemingly clearing the way for greater subcommittee autonomy, increased expertise, and perhaps for an expansion of committee concerns beyond the fairly narrow confines of the foreign aid program.

the accommodation of the maximum number of constituency interests. Adherence to the norm of nonpartisanship serves the same purpose; interparty conflict would only reduce the opportunities for constituency service.

The Education and Labor Committee displays still another pattern. Its mix of permanent and temporary subcommittees discourages specialization; no autonomy inheres in the permanent panels. Committee members are free to pursue their personal policy preferences everywhere, in subcommittee or full committee. No reciprocity is shown to the views of others. The resulting mode of conducting business is chaotic, with most members pursuing a course of "policy individualism." The lack of consensus on the substance of policy or on the means of generating policy agreements leads, almost inevitably, to division along partisan lines; Education and Labor is unable to contain partisan conflict, which often spills over on to the House floor.

In summary, congressional committees develop in differing degrees internal norms that help them serve their members' personal aims, their obligations as committees, and the expectations which the full house holds about their behavior. Some committees, like House Appropriations and Ways and Means, are well-integrated panels, they possess clear sets of normatively prescribed goals and processes by which those goals are to be attained. Committee integration—characterized by a clearly defined role structure, and norms of specialization, reciprocity, subcommittee unity, and minimal partisanship—is the means to achieve these objectives. New members are taught that the best route to influence—to the achievement of personal goals—is conformity to the committee traditions; representatives who deviate are punished, denied the opportunity to exert influence. The behavior of committee members, in short, cannot be fully understood without consideration of the norms or expectations which impinge upon them inside the committee itself.

Other committees are less integrated but no less influenced by internal norms. These panels vary in the extent to which their members defer to their colleagues' expertise, in the degree to which the members willingly serve a period of apprenticeship, and in their ability to mute or restrain partisan conflict. Given a concern for reelection and constituency service, which typify the House Interior and Post Office Committees, and perhaps Agriculture as well (Jones, 1961), representatives would find themselves blocked by such folkways. Similarly, a focus on policy matters, as Foreign Affairs, and Education and Labor display in the House, seems to lead to lessened integration. In general, it seems plausible to hypothesize that acceptance of norms which create integration and committee cohesion enhances the power of a committee and its members, enabling them to avoid or defeat most serious challenges to their legislation. Nonconformist orientations toward committee norms may weaken the position of the committee vis-à-vis the nonmembers.

INFORMAL ORGANIZATIONS

Folkways are only one sort of informal "rules of the game" which seem related to the workings of the legislative system. Another set of influential forces emanates from a number of informal organizations which may act as supplements to, or competitors with, the committees and the political parties. Though nowhere described in the formal rules, these groups may have significant effects on the lawmaking, oversight, and representational activities of Congress. It must be confessed, however, that little is known about the precise impact of these organizations.

Various types of informal groups exist. The most nebulous of these are friendship or social groups. Not surprisingly, small groups of legislators meet in the gymnasium, cafeteria, or for social purposes; these groups cross party lines, and may contribute to the creation of friendships and alliances which may, in turn, influence subsequent behavior (Clapp, 1964, pp. 44–45). In the same vein, groups such as the classes (freshman beginning service in the Ninetieth or Ninety-first Congresses, for instance); Senate and House breakfast prayer groups; or discussion clubs such as the Republican SOS, Acorns, and Chowder and Marching Society meet frequently, may well engage in political conversations, and as a result "under certain circumstances . . . may have important policy implications" (Jewell and Patterson, 1966, pp. 403–407, at p. 404).

More important are the avowedly ideological or policy-oriented informal groups, the best known of which is the liberal Democratic Study Group. The DSG is informal only in the sense that it operates outside the rules of the House; otherwise it is highly organized with officers, an executive committee, and a series of task forces charged with developing policy positions on a variety of issues such as food and agriculture, consumer affairs, health and welfare, and international affairs and defense policy (Kofmehl, 1964; Ferber, 1971). *Congressional Quarterly* (Weekly Report, Oct. 10, 1969, pp. 1940-1945) reports that 125 Democrats serving in the Ninety-first Congress (1969-1970) were or had been DSG members. The organization does research, plans strategy, and maintains its own whip system in order to pass legislation. Its activities are financed by dues collected from the members. The group has had some success in passing liberal bills and continues to work for congressional reform, favoring, for example, the election of committee chairmen rather than continued use of the seniority criterion. Southern Democrats have their own caucus, and the liberal and moderate Republicans have their Wednesday Club which has its own staff and serves as a source of information for its members (Groennings, 1970).

Also worthy of note are the state delegations. Members representing the same state recognize that they have interests in common which transcend party lines; they meet more or less regularly to discuss ways to promote the well-being of their states, often acting in concert to promote particular projects of interest to them all. The House delegation from Washington collaborated and succeeded in locating a publicly owned, nuclear power plant in their state (Kessel, 1964). Other state delegations seem to cohere on roll call votes to a marked degree (Truman, 1956; Matthews and Stimson, 1970; Clausen, 1970).

These informal, unofficial groups—social, class, ideological groups, and state delegations—do a number of things for their members (Fiellin, 1962). They serve, first of all, as agents of socialization. New legislators learn the norms from their senior colleagues in these informal groups; they are taught what expectations others hold about their enactment of the legislative role. Moreover, social agencies of this sort help a freshman lawmaker adapt to his new position. The newcomer may feel alone and adrift in a large, and in many ways impersonal, body; from his fellows in social groups he may receive friendship and attention which reassure him about his standing in Congress. Other, more tangible, benefits may also flow from membership in unofficial groups. For example, information may be transmitted via informal agencies as well as by way of party or committee leaders; through the unofficial groups, a legislator can find out the intentions of others or pass along his own views to his congressional colleagues.

A related function which unsanctioned groups perform is to provide cues and structure for ambiguous situations. For instance, when the parties are divided or inactive, when there is no precedent to guide a congressman, he may turn for advice to members of these informal groups. In fact, these bodies take on their greatest significance in precisely those circumstances when other influences are inconsistent or nonexistent. Moreover, when active and unified, informal groups may enhance the bargaining power of the bloc. The greater the number of votes involved and able to be committed the more the committee and party leaders will have to consider making concessions in order to win them. Bloc solidarity also offers protection of a sort against constituency pressures; if the group stands together, each member can justify his position in terms of the views of the others. Such unanimity may, however, provide support for behavior which is deviant with respect to chamberwide norms or which is detrimental to the conduct of legislative business. For example, Fiellin (1962) points out that the New York House Democrats, forming what their critics have called the "Tuesday-to-Thursday Club," supported each other in taking long weekends away from the capital. This stress on politicking at home leads, in the opinion of these critics, to a consequent neglect of congressional obligations.

In sum, informal groups perform a number of useful services for their members. When other agencies are inactive or divided, or when their positions are ambiguous or badly communicated, individual lawmakers may turn to social, ideological, or state delegation groups for information, advice, and support.

SUMMARY

This chapter has suggested that there is a dimension to the legislative system which consideration of the more formal aspects of the system—the committees, parties, and rules of procedure—does not take into account adequately. Informal features of the system—norms of a number of types and unofficial groups—influence the nature of role orientations and the legislative behavior of representatives and senators. Folkways of several sorts constrain individual lawmakers. One type specifies more or less clearly the desirable modes of interpersonal relationships which should enable members of a particular chamber to go about their work relatively free from the personal animosities which, if present, might inhibit the bargaining and compromise upon which congressional decision making ultimately rests. And the available evidence, though not conclusive, points to conformity to these chamberwide norms as one avenue to legislative power and influence.

A second set of traditions defines the position of the committee and party subsystems in Congress. These beliefs specify the limits on the autonomy of the standing committees; even those substantive panels that are granted substantial independence do not possess absolute freedom. The committees are expected to act in keeping with the broad goals of policy enactment which motivate the legislature. The parent chamber retains the final authority to control the committees, and the latter, in recognition of their ultimate dependence, generally conform to the expectations of the full house. In sum, these norms grant wide but not unlimited discretion to the committees to act as specialists on the matters within the panel's jurisdiction. A similar set of customs, consistently honored, while indicating the general importance of party loyalty, at the same time legitimizes disloyalty on the grounds of electoral or personal considerations.

A third, and final, set of norms contributes to the pattern of decision making internal to congressional committees. Each panel tends to develop a characteristic normative structure that facilitates the members' ability to seek their desired ends and that helps to define the committee's relationships to nonmembers, both within and without the legislative system. The available evidence indicates that when a committee can face the parent chamber united behind its proposals, displaying a cohesiveness which norms such as dedication to legislative work and minimization of partisanship foster, it is in a strong position to make its views prevail. In the absence of such unity, committee bills are likely to be amended substantially when they reach the chamber floor. In short, norms of all three kinds, if observed, impose constraints on individual lawmakers' behavior at several stages in the legislative process. When to observe these norms—whether to conform or to assume a nonconformist orientation in any particular situation—is a crucial decision for each member of Congress, for to play the maverick role may have serious consequences for his long-run career prospects. Moreover, role conflict is

highly likely to arise given these normative constraints; conformity will earn rewards from legislative colleagues, but may be costly in terms of his standing with his constituents. How the representative resolves such conflicts in any given legislative context will, presumably, influence his behavioral response to that situation.

Informal groups possess a similar potential for influence. To the extent that a lawmaker uses a social or policy-oriented group, or his state delegation, as a reference point or as a source of cues on what is appropriate action, a countervailing force to committee or party loyalty is introduced into the legislative system. While the limited data available suggest that unofficial groups come into play most often when competing pressures are absent or inconsistent, on occasion such bodies provide alternative focal points to the formally defined features of the system. To understand how Congress produces outputs, in any given situation, will require analysis of the activity and effectiveness of these groups about which the rules are silent.

More broadly, this chapter is the last in a series designed to describe the nature of the legislative system. It is this system which converts inputs from the environment into the outputs of policy, oversight, and representation. What emerges from the treatment of the major formal and informal features internal to the system is the picture of Congress as a decentralized institution where power is shared widely, but not necessarily equally, among the members. Put another way, there exist in the national legislature multiple centers of influence, but these points are not equally accessible to all.[20] Some senators and representatives are clearly more powerful and more important than others.

This dispersion of authority is sustained in a variety of ways. The committees have carved out substantial independence for themselves. The formal rules buttress this autonomy; they define virtually exclusive committee jurisdictions, they make it difficult for the committees to be circumvented, and they, in effect, compel decision making by negotiation. The informal norms, to a considerable degree, contribute to this fragmentation of the congressional system. The traditions of specialization, reciprocity, and commitment to legislative work, taken together, sustain a decision-making process which operates through bargaining characterized by deference to recognized experts and by mutual respect among dedicated lawmakers. In short, the committees, the rules, and the norms interact to create a system where power is widely diffused.

On the other hand, integrative, centralizing tendencies are unable to overcome the divisive forces. The congressional parties lack the sanctions necessary if they are to impose party discipline; the norms operate to weaken partisanship and to justify defection. The rules favor the status quo; they

---

[20] For a discussion of the Senate as moving from a "decentralized" (rather than "centralized" or hierarchical) toward an "individualistic" body, see Ripley, 1969*b*.

require the proponents of change to win at successive stages of the legislative process, while those content with things as they are need only carry the day at one of the many veto points. The expectations about committees do work to prevent anarchy—the committees are held responsible for moving toward broadly defined chamber goals—but these norms also leave wide latitude to the standing panels. In short, the parties, as the chief centralizing agencies in Congress, remain ill-equipped to assemble the fragments of legislative power into a more tightly organized pattern than presently exists.

In other words, in the language of the systems approach employed here, when role conflicts occur, as they inevitably must, the members of Congress tend to resolve them in favor of decentralizing rather than integrating features of the system. Specifically, party loyalty frequently loses out to committee or informal group pressures; congressmen prefer to continue to operate under the existing rules, which sustain decentralization, than to work for procedural change; legislators find it advantageous to conform to the norms rather than to act more expeditiously. In sum, the contemporary Congress displays strong orientations toward the fragmenting attributes of the system. The sources of inputs—demand and supports—to such a system is the next topic to be considered in Part 2, and in Part 3 we turn to a consideration of the ways in which a decentralized system converts these inputs into outputs.

PART

2

Inputs to the Congressional System

CHAPTER SEVEN

The Executive and Congress

The previous chapters have described the nature of the congressional system, its structures and processes, its formal and informal features. The upshot of that discussion is the argument that influence in Congress is widely shared. Individual legislators are more often positively oriented toward the norms, rules, or committees than to party, with the result that their behavior reflects these decentralizing forces. Compromise through negotiation becomes the chief mode of resolving conflict; bargaining creates majorities which can enact their preferences. To discover which kinds of majority, composed of what sorts of lawmakers, will emerge on any given issue requires examination of the specific orientations which are operative in any particular situation. Put another way, the question relates to the ways in which the inevitable role conflicts are resolved. In a presidential election year, for instance, where party and committee pressures produce a conflict situation, congressmen may be more inclined to support party in order to help make a record on which their candidate can run successfully; at other phases of the electoral cycle, legislative activity may instead reflect a desire to preserve committee autonomy. The point, to put it as succinctly as possible, is that behavior stems, in part, from the orientations toward the *internal* attributes of the legislative system which the situation at hand activates.

But such internally generated forces are far from being the only relevant influences on the actions of congressmen. The legislative system does not exist in a vacuum; rather it responds to a variety of demands originating outside the halls of Congress. These demands from the environment, more-over, are not merely verbal requests for some form of action. Various bases of influence, often substantial, are available to those outside the legislature who would have Congress act in some particular fashion. Not only does the senator or representative have to relate himself to the internal aspects of his chamber, but he must decide in what ways he will respond to initiatives originating outside Congress and in what fashion he will resolve conflicts be-tween these external demands and his orientations toward the features of the legislature itself. The lawmaker must decide, to note one specific case, how he will act when the President or an interest group urges one course of action upon him while simultaneously his committee colleagues argue for a different form of behavior. This chapter, and the next two, examine the major sources of inputs to Congress—the executive, the interest groups, the courts, and the public—noting the resources each has available in seeking to influence Congress, and the techniques by which those resources are employed.

THE PRESIDENT AS "CHIEF LEGISLATOR"

It has become a commonplace observation that the President provides the main stimulus to congressional activity. The Chief Executive, so the expecta-tion appears, is to lead and the legislature is to respond to his exercise of leadership. Popular response to the President appears to reflect his success as a problem solver; in the same vein, public opinion rewards Congress when the legislative branch acts on presidential requests and finds its performance less satisfactory when it hinders executive proposals (Davidson et al., 1966, chap. 2). The White House, then, is widely seen as the locus of policy initia-tive, and its occupant, as "chief legislator," is expected to press for action on such initiatives.[1] These presidential proposals, and the efforts of the execu-tive to advance these suggestions, constitute a major set of demands upon Congress.

The President has been successful in winning for himself a central place in the pattern of public expectations for a number of reasons. For one thing, the nation has faced problems which transcend local boundaries. Issues which world wars, economic dislocations, industrialization, and urbanization raise have all seemed to demand national resolution, and the citizenry has come to look to Washington for solutions for such major challenges. The Chief Execu-tive, moreover, is the only federal official elected by the nation as a whole and it seems natural that popular attention and expectations should focus on him rather than on 535 senators and representatives chosen in widely dif-fering constituencies. Finally, a number of twentieth-century Presidents—

---

[1] Most treatments of the President include a discussion of his relationship to Congress and most assign to him the task of providing legislative leadership. See *inter alia,* Corwin, 1957, chap. 7; Koenig, 1964, chap. 6; Rossiter, 1960, pp. 28–30; Johnson and Walker (eds.), 1964, pp. 199–228; Haight and Johnston (eds.), 1965, chap. 9.

Wilson, the two Roosevelts, Truman, and others—have capitalized on the increased expectations about the responsibilities of government in general, and the national government in particular, to assert the power of the executive branch. In short, the people expect the President to provide leadership and modern Presidents have responded by attempting to exercise such leadership.[2]

Congress, too, has come to expect presidential leadership and to complain when the White House does not live up to these expectations. If the public— which will judge the legislators as well as the President—looks to the Chief Executive for leadership, then it is essential that Congress be clear on what the President wants it to do. In Neustadt's (1955, p. 1014) words, Congress needs a guide to "the wants of its biggest customer."[3] Related to this is the need, given the relative scarcity of legislative resources, for a starting place; congressmen prefer working from drafts which the executive provides to developing bills "from scratch" with minimal outside assistance. Similarly, Congress cannot deal with all bills proposed and the President's program establishes priorities; Congress is prepared to organize its activities around presidential preferences. Finally, the suggestions of the Chief Executive help the legislators calculate his potential response to their actions. The President possesses the veto and other resources and what he wants done, as embodied in his program, will indicate where and when he is likely to exercise these powers. For all these reasons, then, Congress has been more than willing to let initiative pass to the President and to react to his proposals.

In sum, by implicit but common consent, the President is now expected to define the workload of Congress, to set the agenda of the legislature. Such an arrangement reflects popular sentiment and has advantages for the lawmakers. The result is that the President's program, constituting roughly 5 per-cent of the total number of bills pending before Congress, consumes the bulk of congressional energies and constitutes the greatest number of public laws enacted (Berman, 1964, p. 70). Demands from the President, then, are the largest source of inputs to the legislative system.

The Chief Executive, moreover, has substantial assistance in formulating his program; a vast establishment, centered in the Executive Office of the President (the White House Office), is at his disposal[4] Through the

---

[2]The prevalence of such notions can be seen in the recurring use, by the party out of power, of a theme relating to the need to "get the country moving again," to deal with the great issues, in recent presidential election campaigns. Greenstein (1966, pp. 30–36) suggests that this mode of response may reflect the psychological functions which the President performs for Americans, especially that of "providing citizens with a *vicarious means of taking political action.*"

[3]Cf. also Neustadt (1954). This paragraph draws heavily on Neustadt's work.

[4]This presidential establishment includes the Office of Management and Budget, the Council of Economic Advisors, the National Security Council, other boards and agencies, and a host of special assistants, legal counsel, and other policy advisors. Moreover, the President will draw on the advice of numerous individuals and groups outside the White House Office, including the Cabinet, various commissions and task forces, numerous interagency committees, and a network of personal acquaintances and political associates. Cronin and Greenberg (eds.), 1969, present a convenient summary of presidential resources.

process known as "central clearance," the program is assembled and its progress through Congress observed and encouraged. The Office of Management and Budget, before 1970 called the Bureau of the Budget, has much of the responsibility here, acting, of course, on behalf of the President, with his concurrence, and subject to his immediate control. The Office aids the Chief Executive in formulating his proposals; it acts as a clearinghouse, sorting out ideas, fitting them together, consulting with legislative leaders when necessary, and coordinating the drafting of specific bills. What survives this winnowing process is transmitted to the legislature in the President's State of the Union, Budget, and additional special messages.

The Office of Management and Budget (OMB) continues to act as a clearinghouse during congressional consideration of the President's recommendations. Executive agencies are expected to submit their proposals to OMB for approval; if clearance is not forthcoming the bureaus are to refrain from presenting their ideas to Congress. Similarly, legislative committees will frequently submit draft bills, before reporting them, to OMB in order to assess their compatibility with the President's program. Measures deemed inconsistent, and thereby unacceptable to the executive, may be revised in committee in the hopes of avoiding hostile action, perhaps including a veto. The Office also evaluates legislation which Congress passes in terms of the President's program, often preparing veto messages for his use should he conclude that he cannot sign a particular bill. The important point, however, for present purposes, is that the Chief Executive, aided and abetted by considerable expertise, submits his program which becomes the central focus of congressional activity.

PRESIDENTIAL INVOLVEMENT
IN THE LEGISLATIVE PROCESS

The President does not limit his involvement in the legislative process to setting Congress's agenda; rather, in a variety of ways, some direct, some indirect, he intervenes in that process to work for the enactment of his program. In this section we explore the bases of the President's authority, that is, the resources that he can bring to bear on members of Congress. Before turning to these bases of executive power, it is well to note that this power is not without limits; there are constraints on the President's ability to impel Congress to pass his program, or even substantial parts of it.

Limits on presidential leadership Some features of the executive-legislative relationship are fixed, and no amount of presidential leadership can alter them. The President must, of necessity, work within the limits that these "givens" impose. For one thing, the basic nature of the congressional system is not likely to change very much or very rapidly. While occasionally alterations which make the leadership task easier do occur such as the adoption of the 21-Day Rule, for the most part the context within which the President must work is a constant. This means, in the light of the analysis of the system presented in Part 1, that the Chief Executive must maneuver his proposals through a decentralized system—characterized by bicameralism, independent committees, specific rules of procedure, widely observed informal norms, and weak political parties—in which action may occur only after considerable exertion. Similarly, the leaders—their personalities, beliefs, modes of activity —are largely given: the committee chairmen are selected automatically under the seniority rule; the party leaders are chosen without overt intervention from the White House.[5] In sum, the President must deal with the structures, processes, and personnel of Congress largely as he finds them; he cannot alter these features of the system to suit his own convenience.

In the same vein, the President is powerless to change some of the pressures to which members of Congress must respond. For instance, the constituencies—the states and districts—which elect the lawmakers are, in many ways, constants. The demographic attributes of the constituencies are fixed; the kinds of people—their occupations, their socioeconomic status, their ethnic backgrounds, and the like—who live in the various districts change slowly if at all. Local party organizations are largely immune from presidential control; as we have seen, they, rather than national leaders, control affairs in their own areas. To the extent that legislators react to local sentiments they may be forced to resist executive blandishments. This situation will require the President to try to exert influence on congressmen who may be unwilling or unable to lend him support.

Finally, events—both foreign and domestic—lie outside of presidential control. Civil disturbances, a decision of the Supreme Court, strains among the members of an international treaty organization, or the collapse of a regime to which vast quantities of aid have been committed will tax the leadership skills of the President. He will, no doubt, attempt to interpret such occurrences to suit his purposes, but he will have to take account of the fact that these events did take place. And in some cases, events may change the entire character of an administration. Harry Truman could not, because the North Koreans invaded the South, commit himself to domestic affairs as he clearly would have preferred; the Korean war came to dominate the 1950– 1952 years of the Truman administration (Neustadt, 1960, pp. 123–146). Thus, the President will have to contend with forces generated by the legislative system, the nature of constituency pressures, and the flow of events, forces that lie outside of his power to shape to any great degree.

Opportunities for presidential leadership Within these limits there remain a number of possibilities for presidential leadership. The most immediate

[5] In a recent Republican leadership contest, occasioned by the death of Senate Floor Leader Everett M. Dirksen, President Nixon studiously sought to avoid open involvement in the fight between Hugh Scott (Pa.), the eventual winner, and Howard Baker (Tenn.). He assumed a similar neutrality in the 1971 rematch between the same contenders when Scott won by a narrow margin.

targets for executive influence are, of course, the lawmakers themselves; through direct contacts, either personally or through his personally selected intermediaries, the President can seek to win support for his policy proposals. That is, the Chief Executive can try to mold congressional opinion directly by working on the preferences of individual legislators, seeking to reinforce the positions of those already sympathetic to his cause and to convert into supporters those who are undecided or even hostile to him.

Congressional opinion may be altered in a second, and related, fashion. A legislator's views may reflect his own preferences, but in a representative institution they may also reflect the congressman's perceptions of what those he must represent— those upon whom his continuance in office is dependent, his constituents—believe is desirable.[6] As we shall see subsequently, the legislator may have considerable difficulty in assessing the opinion of the "folks back home"; nonetheless he must, especially if his is a delegate or politico orientation toward his obligations as representative,[7] consider what the residents of his state or district appear to believe or desire. This fact provides the President with another opportunity for influence: he can attempt to shape the legislator's perceptions of constituency sentiment. More specifically, to the degree that he can make a convincing case to a lawmaker that the latter's constituents favor some particular policy alternative, he can hope to win the lawmaker's support.

Finally, the President can try to influence congressional opinion indirectly by working through constituency opinion. While it is no doubt easier to persuade a member of Congress that he needs to act in a certain fashion because his constituents want that action than it is actually to create or mobilize district opinion favorable to his proposals, the President may embark on the latter course. If he can get local citizens aroused enough to write or otherwise press their views on their representatives, these lawmakers may feel compelled to act in keeping with these expressions of popular sentiment. The entire citizenry need not always be mobilized; it may be sufficient for the President to enlist elite opinion— the sentiments of important local groups or individuals—in his cause. If such elites—upon whom the local representative may depend for campaign assistance or other aid—urge a senator or representative to support the President, these lawmakers may well respond positively to such communications.

The success of the Chief Executive in moving his program through Congress— by influencing legislative sentiment directly or by mobilizing constituency pressures—will depend as well on his personal leadership talent: his ability to take advantage of the opportunities available and his skill in working around the fixed elements which confront him. There is no reason to expect all Presidents to be equally well prepared for the task of leading

---

[6]The distinction between personal preferences and perceptions of constituency views follows Miller and Stokes, 1963.

[7]See above, pp. 20–21, for a discussion of the legislators' representational role orientations.

Congress. Some Presidents, Dwight Eisenhower for example, have been unwilling to exert strong leadership with respect to the legislative branch; others, like Lyndon Johnson, have been less restrained in intervening in the legislative process. Some Chief Executives have served in Congress and come to the White House with a solid understanding of the workings of the legislature; others, lacking such experience, are less well prepared to deal with Congress. In general, Presidents will differ in their abilities to recruit backing for their programs; some will be temperamentally more suited than others to engage in the activities, discussed below, which constitute the President's resources in dealing with the legislature. Thus, the President's success in working with Congress will reflect the flexibility of congressional opinion and constituency sentiment, and his own abilities to exploit these opportunities.

Formal bases of presidential power Within the limitations which the available opportunities and his own skills impose, the Chief Executive's ability to intervene successfully on behalf of his program rests in part on the formal bases of influence which the Constitution provides and in part on the informal resources which his political position makes available. On the formal side, Article 2, section 3 of the U.S. Constitution states that the President "shall from time to time give to the Congress information of the state of the union, and recommend to their consideration such measures as he shall judge necessary and expedient. . . ." From this injunction has come the practice of the annual State of the Union and Budget addresses supplemented by a large number of special messages which, taken together, constitute the program of the administration and which, as noted, dominate the agenda of Congress. This same constitutional provision empowers the Chief Executive to call the legislature into special session to consider his proposals. Neither power is of much value to the President as neither goes beyond giving him a form to set forth his program. President Harry Truman did get some political mileage out of a special session which he convened in 1948; he launched his successful reelection campaign of that year by challenging what he labeled the "do-nothing Republican Eightieth Congress" to enact legislation embodied in the GOP platform. The failure of Congress to act provided Truman with a central campaign theme, but not with the bills he wanted enacted.

Of greater importance is the veto power (Article 1, section 7) which the President possesses. He can, if he sees fit, prevent a simple majority of Congress from acting. Within ten days after passage he may return a bill to Congress, detailing his objections to it; a two-thirds majority in each house can override the veto. When Congress is not in session, the President can kill legislation simply by withholding his signature from it, that is by exercising the so-called "pocket veto." Presidents have used this important restraining power sparingly over the years, though the frequency of the veto has increased during recent years as the scope of federal government involvement in the social life of the nation has enlarged. Overall, through 1966, more than 2,200 vetoes were cast, and of these Congress has overridden a mere seventy-three. Thus the Chief Executives' restraint has been matched by a virtually unblemished record of making the veto stick. If he holds his fire for important targets, the President has a strong chance to bring down his game. More difficult to assess is the extent to which the possibility of a veto, real or anticipated by Congress, causes the legislators to shape their bills in a way designed to head off such a threat. In any case, the veto power does provide the White House with one means to attempt to bring the legislative product into line with presidential desires.

The positive power to suggest, even when coupled with the negative power to block action, does not provide the President with a very strong legal position from which to lead Congress; as we shall note, he has additional resources to put to work. But on the constitutional point, it is worth noting that the Twenty-second Amendment, which limits the President to two terms in office, may impose constraints on executive leadership in the last years of a President's second term. Because he is leaving office, so the argument runs, he will no longer have the influence to move his program through the legislature. What little evidence there is, however, does not readily support this view: President Eisenhower was, if anything, strong during the final years of his administration; nor did Lyndon Johnson's influence, already damaged by opposition to his Vietnam war policies, appear to decline precipitously following his announcement that he would not seek reelection.

Informal bases of presidential influence: the power to persuade[8] As the preceding paragraphs suggest, the formal powers of the President are of little help in and of themselves. When combined, however, with a variety of informal avenues of influence, they give the Chief Executive a rather formidable arsenal of weapons with which to press for congressional accession to his demands. His task, of course, is to win enough votes for his proposals to enact them into law, and he undertakes this chore with the initiative on his side and with the crucial ability to do favors for many, if not all, members of Congress. These advantages provide the bases for presidential leadership; they belong to any Chief Executive, and they can be used to win legislative backing.

In addition, particular Presidents may have other resources. For one thing, the state of his "professional reputation" and "public prestige" will affect the persuasive power of the incumbent. Reputation refers to the feeling on the part of those whom the President seeks to influence that he has the ability and the determination to employ his advantages, that is, that he will hold up his end of any bargains, implicit or explicit, which he undertakes.

[8]The phrase "the power to persuade" is Neustadt's (1960, especially chaps. 3–5); much of what follows rests on his work.

Prestige implies that the President will be able to rally public sentiment behind his cause. The greater the Chief Executive's reputation and prestige, the more difficult it will be for the individual congressman to resist requests from the White House, for to engage in open combat with a determined and popular President is to court disaster. The essence of presidential influence, then, is (in Neustadt's words) "the power to persuade," the ability, using all his advantages to "persuade people to do the things they ought to have the sense enough to do" (or what the President thinks they ought to do) without persuasion (Harry S. Truman, quoted in Neustadt, 1960, pp. 9–10).

Whatever the extent of the President's advantages, he may seek to use them, most directly, to alter the personal preferences and the perceptions of constituency opinion held by the individual lawmaker—in Dahl's (1950, p. 22) phrase, to change his "view of reality." The President can argue in terms of substantive considerations or potential political repercussions, trying to influence the legislator's views of (preferences concerning) policy moves required to deal with any situation or to change the evaluation (perception) of possible constituency response to the actions considered by the representative. To the extent that these efforts succeed, the President may rally voting support in Congress. He can, first of all, direct his arguments to the entire legislature. He can use speeches, special messages, press conferences, letters to the legislative leadership which are released for publication, and the reports of presidential "task forces" to interpret events and argue for a desired policy.[9] The effort here is to provide a persuasive argument, or at least an acceptable rationale, for backing his requests.

The President may also direct his attention to specific subgroups of congressmen. He may appeal to his party colleagues in terms of party loyalty or the need to establish party positions to use in a forthcoming electoral campaign. He may focus attention on the most important committee by means of letters to the members or through the testimony of high-ranking executive personnel at the committee's hearings. In addition, committee or subcommittee members may be briefed by the relevant executive agency.[10] Furthermore, the managers of a bill may be willing to make legislative concessions in order to win backing from those favored by accepted amendments.[11] Such tactics may serve both to win votes and to divide the opposition.

[9] Haviland, 1958, documents President Eisenhower's use of most of these devices in his attempts to rescue the 1957 foreign aid bill.

[10] The House Foreign Affairs Committee, for example, has established permanent "consultative" subcommittees for the explicit purpose of receiving briefings from executive agencies. See Carroll, 1966, pp. 336–338.

[11] For instance, the Manpower Development and Training Act of 1962 was passed by a coalition forged only after Republican support was won over by casting the program within the framework proposed by the American Vocational Association. See Sundquist, 1968, pp. 85–91. Similarly, the Senate Foreign Relations Committee headed off potential opposition to the Japanese Peace Treaty by accepting in advance a "reservation" declaring that the treaty should in no way be read to give Senate approval to the Yalta agreement. In this way, a potentially explosive issue was defused without affecting the substance of the treaty. See Cohen, 1957, pp. 23–24, 166–168.

A third method of altering the preferences and perceptions of congress-men is to deal directly with them as individuals. The president can do this himself; he can call congressmen to the White House for private conversa-tions or he can personally phone them to ask for support; or he can make favorable references to a particular representative in his public statements in order to win the "goodwill" and hopefully the vote of the lawmaker.[12] Conversations with individual legislators can be used to persuade them, in terms of the national or local interest, of the wisdom of the President's policy, or to suggest to them that their political futures necessitate backing the Presi-dent. Or such meetings may serve as negotiating sessions where an "arrange-ment" between the Chief Executive and the lawmaker is consummated.

In such situations, it is upon the President's ability to do favors, to provide goods and services, that his persuasive power rests. Among other things, he can employ his veto to the advantage of some legislator or in other ways use his influence over pending bills to assist the man whom he seeks to influence. He may also make use of his patronage power, offering to appoint political associates of the congressmen to federal posts within the state or district. In this way he may help the legislator solidify his local political situation.[13] The President can, in the same vein, give or withhold election assistance; he can, if he chooses, endorse congressional candidates, pose for pictures with such men, or make personal appearances in their districts. If he is highly regarded such electoral aid may benefit the local legislative nominee. While it is not clear precisely to what extent these bases of per-suasion are used — bargains struck are not likely to be explicit or widely publicized — these advantages do enable the President to work, from a posi-tion of strength, to win support for his legislative program.

The President, of course, will not make all these contacts, engage in all such negotiations, personally; he will have the White House Office, among other instrumentalities, at his disposal. The Executive Office of the President has within it a number of men — the exact size of the contingent depends upon the preferences of the particular incumbent — responsible for legislative liaison. Lawrence F. O'Brien, who served Presidents Kennedy and Johnson as chief contact man with Congress, received substantial publicity as an effective presidential assistant.[14] Relying heavily on personal acquaintance with many legislators — enabling him, or his coworkers, to persuade by means of numerous personal contacts on Capitol Hill — and only as a last resort on

[12] For instance, Chairman Wilbur Mills of the House Ways and Means Committee was assiduously "wooed" by Presidents Kennedy and Johnson in the hopes of moving such important bills as the recipro-cal trade bill (1962) and Medicare (1965) through Mills' panel.

[13] Such efforts are not always appreciated or effective. In the 1971 supersonic transport fight, on the day of a crucial Senate vote, President Nixon sent Margaret Chase Smith (R., Me.) a letter informing her that he had reversed a decision, made during the Johnson Presidency, to close a naval shipyard in her state. Mrs. Smith made the letter public, and voted against the President. See *The New York Times*, Mar. 25, 1971, p. 24.

[14] On O'Brien, see Morgan, 1962, and the interview with O'Brien in *Congressional Quarterly Weekly Report*, July 23, 1965, pp. 1434–1436.

pressure, O'Brien converted his close relationship with the President into support for the Kennedy-Johnson program. President Richard Nixon turned to a former member of the House to manage his congressional relations, bringing Clark McGregor (Minn.) to the White House as Counsel to the President. McGregor operated far less obtrusively than had O'Brien. Each Chief Executive will create his own organization to assist him in persuading congressmen to go along with his policy proposals; whatever the specific form it takes, the liaison organization will serve as a chief communications device by which presidential-legislative accommodations will be worked out.

Through the use of these methods, then, the President may seek to shape the preferences and perceptions of the congressmen by appeals aimed at the legislature as a whole, at specific subgroups within each chamber, and at the individual members themselves. But he cannot use all these approaches simultaneously; he must pick and choose from among them those techniques which will enable him to assemble a legislative majority. The tactics selected must be used carefully; they should be effective without smacking of the heavy-handed pressure which is likely to arouse congressional hostility and to cost the President support.[15]

The President can also employ many of those same techniques to operate through the legislative system. He or his executive-branch associates can seek to influence party leaders and committee chairmen and, in turn, through them win support from the rank-and-file congressmen. Party leaders, as noted previously (pp. 105–107), have a variety of weapons which they can use for the benefit, or to the detriment, of members of Congress. That is, the party leaders possess rewards and sanctions with which they can attempt to influence legislative action. If the President can win the wholehearted backing of these leaders he may also be able to secure support from others who can be persuaded by the leaders. Similarly, the committee chairman has perquisites which he can employ to affect the fate of legislation referred to his panel (see pp. 67–69); he can, if he wishes, use these resources to bargain with members of his committee for support for proposals he favors. Thus if the Chief Executive can enlist the chairman in his cause, he may also win backing from the committee members. The legislative system, then, provides the President with focuses for his efforts to influence Congress. To the extent that he can win the support of those who control the levers of power within Congress, he may also be able to win the votes of those subject to the operation of that power.

We have suggested that the President can seek to shape the preferences and perceptions of representatives and senators directly or indirectly through the legislative system. In addition, he can try to affect them by mobilizing constituency opinion; he can attempt to arouse mass opinion, elite opinion,

---

[15] Haviland, 1958, p. 709, reports that President Eisenhower's "threat" that a special session might be necessary if Congress did not appropriate the full amount of the 1957 foreign aid authorization antagonized the Democrats in Congress.

or the former through the latter. Such efforts should be particularly successful with legislators whose representative orientation focuses on their state or
district or whose style of representation is that of a delegate or politico. The
same devices mentioned earlier, such as radio and television speeches, remarks at press conferences, and public appearances in general — in short,
the ability to command attention, to "make news" — will permit the Chief
Executive to appeal directly to the people, asking them to communicate
with their representatives in support of his position. If such requests arouse
a large response, the pressure on some legislators may be the decisive influence on their vote decisions. President Eisenhower's speech to the nation
on behalf of the Landrum-Griffin Labor Reform bill provides an example of
the potential effectiveness of an appeal "over the heads of Congress." One
study of the act concludes that the President's speech was "the deciding
factor for a number of congressmen. . . . "[16]

The President may also try to shape congressional opinion indirectly by
enlisting the support of elite opinion. If newspapers in a state or district
editorialize with near unanimity for a particular policy, the representative
who takes his cues from the press rather than from mass opinion may be led
to back the President. He may do so because he finds the editors' arguments
persuasive or because he believes these views typical of the electorate, but
either interpretation may convince him that a vote for the President's
proposal is the wisest course of action. President Kennedy's meetings with
editors from the individual states seem to have been designed to win newspaper support for the policies of his administration. The President may also
try to operate in similar fashion through other segments of elite opinion.

Finally, the President may try to use elite opinion to arouse the average
citizen. The executive branch may try to coordinate the activity of interest
groups in order to generate the maximum amount of public pressure on Congress. In the Landrum-Griffin fight, noted above, the White House, at the
behest of the President, acted as "coordinator of effort and clearinghouse of
ideas and planning in the attempts [of management groups] to generate public
support for labor reform legislation" (McAdams, 1964, p. 74). Or a special
conference of "opinion makers" may be convened to accomplish the same
purpose. If the national opinion leaders can be won to the administration's
position, they may carry the message to the general population, which in
turn may bring pressure to bear on Congress.[17]

The President and foreign policy   The advantages which permit the President
to intervene in the legislative process on behalf of his program are heightened

---

[16]McAdams, 1964, p. 198. President Richard Nixon seems to have had arousing "the silent majority,"
as he called it, in mind, perhaps as a means of muting his congressional critics, when he delivered his
election-eve speech defending his policies for ending the Vietnam war on Nov. 3, 1969.

[17]For a study of one such attempt, the 1958 Conference on Foreign Aspects of U.S. Security, convened
in Washington to develop popular support for foreign aid, see Rosenau, 1963.

in the foreign policy area. Congress has been, in recent years, unable to mount a serious challenge to executive hegemony in the making of American policy in the international sphere; this reflects an imbalance in influence potential which is less pronounced in the domestic policy sphere. For one thing, the Chief Executive has vastly greater informational resources and technical expertise at his disposal than does Congress as an institution, much less individual members whatever their commitment to specialization on foreign affairs. The far-flung network of foreign service officers, military attachés, civilian intelligence officers, and other overseas personnel funnel their communications to the President via their particular executive agencies. Thus substantial data is available to the President, data which he may, by invoking the idea of "executive privilege,"[18] refuse to make available to Congress or to the appropriate legislative committee. The Chief Executive can, as a result, bring considerable expertise to bear on Congress, and the latter has often felt obliged to defer to that formidable show of intelligence.

Moreover, as the constitutionally designated Commander in Chief, the President need not consult Congress, formally at least, before acting. Thus, for instance, Presidents Truman, Eisenhower, Kennedy, and Johnson all committed American troops in one way or another to fight in Asia. In some instances, the need to act rapidly virtually precludes prior consultation with the legislature. President Truman had to commit American forces to the defense of South Korea promptly in order to avert loss of the country; there was simply not time to engage in deliberations on the matter in Congress.[19]

In general, in the foreign policy sphere, the President can do what Congress cannot accomplish: he can get all the interested parties—the diplomats, the military as well as the politicians—together for intensive, but secret, discussions leading to the making of foreign policy choices. The process by which these decisions are made, as Huntington (1961, pp. 135–166) points out, may be legislative in character—that is, such decisions may be the result of long negotiations, leading to compromise, among the interested parties—but they are made within the executive branch, with a minimum of legislative participation.[20] Congress will, in most cases, have to ratify such choices, by appropriating the requisite funds, for instance, but the lawmakers will be hard put to resist the proposals of a united executive branch. Put another way, this means that it will be difficult for an individual lawmaker to sustain a legislative, as opposed to a presidential, role orientation on foreign policy matters.

Even where Congress makes a determined effort to reassert for itself a major voice in the making of foreign policy, as the Indochina war situation

[18]Under the "executive privilege" idea, the President, or those under his direction, need not reveal information which he deems "in the national interest" inappropriate to make public.

[19]On Truman's decision, see Paige, 1968.

[20]Huntington (1961) argues that "the locus of decision is executive; the process of decision is primarily legislative" (p. 147). Congress, he suggests, performs a lobbying function by making its views known, but does not possess the "decisive" authority in strategy making (p. 145).

impelled it to do beginning in 1968, the legislative branch has been unable to make much headway against the executive. Though the challenge of Sen. Eugene McCarthy (D., Minn.) surely contributed to Lyndon Johnson's refusal to run for reelection, the subsequent assault on the Nixon administration's policies—which saw repeated attempts to impose specific deadlines for withdrawal of the American presence in Vietnam, to cut off funds for specific military ventures, to block deployment of the antiballistic missile (ABM) system, to prune the defense budget, and to reduce American overseas troop commitments—had at best a marginal impact on the nation's foreign policy. No doubt the rising chorus of congressional criticism contributed to the President's sense of the political necessity for disengagement from Southeast Asia, but the form and pace of that disengagement have been his own creations. Nor was he deterred from extending the fighting into Laos and Cambodia when he believed it was necessary to do so. Similarly, the overall defense posture of the nation reflects presidential far more than legislative preferences. Thus, it is difficult to conclude that Congress's 1968 to 1971 efforts to stake out an important foreign policy influence for itself have borne much fruit. At most, it may be that the congressional opposition has exerted a restraining influence on the executive; the substance of policy, however, seems fundamentally to reflect the President's choices.

Furthermore, in moving foreign policy programs through Congress, the President has been highly successful in muting partisan hostility to his proposals by employing the tactics commonly referred to as bipartisanship. There has been little agreement as to the precise meaning of the term; here we will use it to denote the attempt by the President, through consultation with the leaders of the party out of power, to win enough opposition support to enact the desired policies. Bipartisanship may also entail some form of commitment to keep the issue out of subsequent election campaigns or to refrain from trying in other ways to gain partisan advantage from the agreement, but the essence of bipartisanship is the effort to win backing through consultation.[21] Bipartisanship can operate only when there is time for consultation, when the opposition has acknowledged foreign policy leaders, and when these leaders are willing to work with the administration.[22] Collaboration of this sort is likely to require the President to permit the opposition to get its "trademark" on the bill through participation in its drafting or by insisting on specific amendments, thus permitting them to display their impact

[21]On bipartisanship, see Westerfield, 1955, and Crabb, 1957.
[22]The classic example of successful bipartisanship is the cooperation which developed in the late 1940s between the Truman administration and the Republican minority led by Senator Arthur H. Vandenberg (Mich.). See Westerfield, 1955; Crabb, 1957; and Jewell, 1962. For Vandenberg's own view of bipartisanship, see Vandenberg, 1952. For a more recent example involving the House of Representatives, see Haviland, 1958.

on the shape of policy.[23] Despite the problems involved, bipartisanship, by which "politics stops at the water's edge," has proved to be an effective device for minimizing party conflict and for recruiting legislative allies for the President's foreign policy program.

The use of bipartisanship and other tactics has enabled the Chief Executive to dominate the legislature with respect to international relations. This can be seen most clearly in James A. Robinson's review of the conditions surrounding the making of twenty-two important foreign policy decisions during the 1933–1961 period (reproduced in Table 7-1). Here it is evident that despite high congressional involvement in sixteen of the twenty-two instances and the need for congressional action (legislation or a resolution) in seventeen cases, the legislature initiated only three decisions and exerted "predominant influence" over only six policy choices. Furthermore, Congress was unable to assert authority despite the availability of relatively long periods in which to decide; there was a "short" decision period in only two situations. In sum, Congress has most often deferred to the President, limiting itself to amendment and legitimation of foreign policies developed within the executive branch and adopted by the President as his own.

The extent of presidential influence over the foreign policy choices of individual lawmakers is also demonstrable. Table 7-2 displays the change in position on foreign affairs legislation which stemmed from the change, in 1960, of national administrations. President Kennedy, succeeding the Republican Eisenhower, was able to gain more support from twenty-one members of his party and two GOP legislators while thirty-two others (five Democrats and twenty-seven Republicans) moved further away from the internationalism which they had supported in the previous administration.[24] Thus the Chief Executive can move some, but relatively few, members, mainly of his own party, toward his views, but the large numbers whose votes remained unchanged should make clear the limitations on the effectiveness of presidential leadership.

Thus, presidential strategy aims at winning votes for and, in the long run, agreement on policy by the most economic use of available tactical moves. The President may try to enlist the support of a majority in a variety of ways. He may, for example, start with the bulk of his own party and try to add to them enough opposition votes to enact the legislation he desires. He may make legislative concessions, attempt to rally public opinion, or if he finds votes difficult to obtain, make use of his techniques of personal persuasion.

[23]Thus the Truman administration let Senator Vandenberg, in guiding the Vandenberg resolution of 1948 through the Senate, tie American participation in "collective security arrangements—the major purpose of the resolution—to the popular concept of strengthening the United Nations," Jewell, 1962, pp. 119–123.

[24]A comparison of voting in the Truman (Eighty-first Congress) and Eisenhower (Eighty-sixth Congress) administrations reveals a comparable shift took place when the Democrats were turned out of office in 1952. See Kesselman, 1965.

TABLE 7-1 *Congressional involvement and decision characteristics*

	Congressional involvement (high, low, none)	Initiator (Congress or executive)	Predominant influence (Congress or executive)	Legislation or resolution (yes or no)	Violence at stake (yes or no)	Decision time (long or short)
1. Neutrality Legislation, the 1930's	High	Exec.	Cong.	Yes	No	Long
2. Lend-Lease, 1941	High	Exec.	Exec.	Yes	Yes	Long
3. Aid to Russia, 1941	Low	Exec.	Exec.	No	No	Long
4. Repeal of Chinese Exclusion, 1943	High	Cong.	Cong.	Yes	No	Long
5. Fulbright Resolution, 1943	High	Cong.	Cong.	Yes	No	Long
6. Building the Atomic Bomb, 1944	Low	Exec.	Exec.	Yes	Yes	Long
7. Foreign Service Act of 1946	High	Exec.	Exec.	Yes	No	Long
8. Truman Doctrine, 1947	High	Exec.	Exec.	Yes	No	Long
9. The Marshall Plan, 1947–1948	High	Exec.	Exec.	Yes	No	Long
10. Berlin Airlift, 1948	None	Exec.	Exec.	No	Yes	Long
11. Vandenberg Resolution, 1948	High	Exec.	Cong.	Yes	No	Long
12. North Atlantic Treaty, 1948–1949	High	Exec.	Exec.	Yes	No	Long
13. Korean Decision, 1950	None	Exec.	Exec.	No	Yes	Short
14. Japanese Peace Treaty, 1952	High	Exec.	Exec.	Yes	No	Long
15. Bohlen Nomination, 1953	High	Exec.	Exec.	Yes	No	Long
16. Indochina, 1954	High	Exec.	Cong.	No	Yes	Short
17. Formosan Resolution, 1955	High	Exec.	Exec.	Yes	Yes	Long
18. International Finance Corporation, 1956	Low	Exec.	Exec.	Yes	No	Long
19. Foreign Aid, 1957	High	Exec.	Exec.	Yes	No	Long
20. Reciprocal Trade Agreements Act, 1958	High	Exec.	Exec.	Yes	No	Long
21. Monroney Resolution, 1958	High	Cong.	Cong.	Yes	No	Long
22. Cuban Decision, 1961	Low	Exec.	Exec.	No	Yes	Long

NOTE: The assignment of each case to different categories represents a "judgment" rather than a "calculation" on the part of the author.
SOURCE: Reproduced with permission from Robinson, *Congress and Foreign Policy Making*, Homewood, Ill.: The Dorsey Press, 1967, rev. ed. p. 65.

TABLE 7-2   *Changes in attitude toward foreign policy from 86th to 87th Congress, House of Representatives, by party*

	Toward internationalism	*Toward isolationism*	*Not shifting*
Democrats	21	5	204
Republicans	2	27	94

SOURCE: Mark Kesselman, "Presidential Leadership in Congress on Foreign Policy: A Replication of a Hypothesis," *Midwest Journal of Political Science,* vol. 9 (1965), p. 405. By permission of Wayne State University Press. Copyright 1965 by Wayne State University Press.

Or, the Chief Executive, as is so often the case with civil rights, may cast the issue in nonpartisan terms and attempt to win backing from both parties by appeals based on the merits, the national interest, or the moral necessity involved. The President will employ the methods which, in each legislative situation, he believes are most likely to produce victory.

While the President is confronted by factors—the legislative system, events, and the demographic characteristics of constituencies—which lie largely beyond his control, he has a variety of advantages and leadership techniques which he can use, directly or indirectly, to influence the preferences and the perceptions of constituency opinion held by individual members of Congress. His success in dealing with the legislature is likely to determine, especially in domestic affairs where his position is weaker than it is with regard to foreign policy, his ability to have his policies enacted.

Some additional caveats The advantages enumerated above constitute an imposing list of opportunities and techniques, but in fact their use and success is limited. For one thing, not all the available techniques can be employed by the President in the same instance—some of them may be mutually exclusive. It is unlikely, for instance, that any policy issue can simultaneously be made a partisan and a nonpartisan question; the President must calculate in which of these two guises his desired policy is most likely to pass. Then, the President cannot intervene too frequently, for his credit with members of Congress is not inexhaustible. Congressional sensitivity to accusations of domination by the executive branch is likely to inhibit legislative response to unlimited presidential appeals. The Chief Executive, therefore, will have to assign priorities to the bills which make up his program. He must decide what bills are worth intervention in congressional affairs and which are not; he may wish to preserve enough credit to permit him to deal effectively with any emergency which might arise.[25] Thus the particular issue involved and

[25] Just how much "credit" a President actually has is difficult to assess; all are criticized for improper involvement with Congress. Critics of the late President Kennedy accused him of being too reluctant to use his influence to advance his legislative program; some argued that Lyndon Johnson overextended himself and asked too much of Congress; some observers criticize Richard Nixon for investing his limited resources in the wrong issues (e.g., the deployment of an antiballistic missile system and the Supreme Court nomination of Clement Haynsworth).

the importance the President attaches to it will influence the extent to which he throws his weight into a struggle with Congress.

EXECUTIVE AGENCIES AND CONGRESS

Our discussion, to this point, implies that the President is the whole story. This is, of course, not the case; rather the broad range of departments, agencies, and bureaus which compose the executive branch are, at one time or another, some more frequently than others, involved in direct contacts with Congress. They may act on behalf of the President or work at cross-purposes with him, but in either case they "lobby" Congress, making demands upon the legislature as well as providing support for it. From the perspective of Congress, this means that the representatives and senators can count on receiving a good deal of attention from the bureaucracy.

Administrative lobbying The administrative agencies possess considerable opportunity to influence the members of Congress. In the first place, they can provide services for lawmakers, services which reduce the burdens which the legislators must bear. As previously noted, congressmen receive large numbers of requests for information and intervention in administrative affairs from their constituents. The bureaucrats recognize that they are, in many instances, better equipped to meet such requests and, furthermore, that helping the congressmen to satisfy their constituents may earn "goodwill" and perhaps even policy support for the agency or bureau. This activity can be time-consuming—in 1963, the Department of State directed 23,000 letters to members of Congress, most of them in response to requests initiated by the lawmaker's constituents (Robinson, 1967, p. 150)—but the results may be worthwhile. At least, as Robinson puts it, the State Department assumes "that the more satisfactorily it handles constituent-initiated requests, the more likely it is to obtain the support of the members on policy," and also "that nonpolicy goodwill is transferred to and reinforces policy relations. . ." (Robinson, 1967, pp. 162–163).

In addition to assisting congressmen in answering their mail, the executive agencies provide a variety of other services (Robinson, 1967, chap. 5; E. de Grazia, 1966, esp. pp. 310–315). They will help individual legislators prepare speeches to be given in Congress or outside the chambers. The bureaus will also aid a lawmaker by arranging for publicity in his local newspaper, media exposure designed to enhance his standing with his constituents. Finally, and perhaps most importantly, when a decision is made which affects a representative's district, the agency will inform him immediately, often letting him make the public announcement. This lets him cast the event in the most favorable light, in order to make the most of it. Again the aim of such services is to earn the high regard of congressmen in the hope that such goodwill will provide a capital against which the agency may draw support for the specifics of its program.

The executive bureaus, like the President's White House staff, have established offices specifically charged with responsibility for congressional liaison. These offices provide direct links between the executive and Congress, channels that serve purposes beyond the provision of the sorts of services enumerated above. Through the liaison networks, the agencies transmit information relevant to policy questions which are up for decision; the best data available to a legislator may come from the agency. Moreover, such information may permit the lawmaker to gauge more accurately the intentions of the decision makers in the executive branch. Agency data, in short, may be crucial to a congressman, and the agency hopes he will find ways to express his gratitude for having received this useful material.

Finally, from the congressional perspective, such channels of communication allow messages to be *sent* as well as received; that is, the representative can express his views to the policy makers via the liaison networks. Friendly congressmen, sympathetic to a bureau's cause, may send along suggestions about strategy to move its programs ahead. Liaison activities may provide the agencies with other useful information. Such communications may inform the executives about the current status of legislation as well as the prospects for passage. Congressional research, which committee staffs conduct, may develop data of use to the executive, studies which liaison men may obtain from legislators. In short, liaison activities constitute a two-way communications link which not only enables the executive branch to lobby legislators— to persuade them of the wisdom of its position— but also permits the agencies to inform themselves about congressional activities.

More important, liaison activities seem to have policy payoffs. Robinson (1967, pp. 161–170) reports that satisfaction with State Department information processing services is associated with approval of the substance of American foreign policy. Specifically, the more a lawmaker approved of the Department's performance—answering requests for policy information, volunteering information, and in general conducting effective information services—the more inclined he was to support the programs that the Department favored. This was especially true among Democrats, the party out of power; Republicans, already predisposed to back the policy of President Eisenhower, did not respond as readily to the information services provided them. Liaison efforts may, thus, be particularly useful in winning support from members of the opposition, who may be more dependent than members of the administration party on information which the executive agencies supply.

The administrative agencies recognize that liaison activities can serve their interests— by earning goodwill or even policy support— and they devote substantial resources to their contacts with the legislature. In fiscal 1963, for instance, as Table 7-3 reveals, the ten executive departments employed 500 persons whose jobs related to securing information for Congress. These activities consumed more than 1.8 million man-hours and a payroll of nearly 5.5 million dollars.[26] There was considerable variation in the size of the liaison operation, but each department invested considerable resources in such activities. In short, the executive branch appreciates its opportunities to advance its interests in Congress and takes advantage of them.

Liaison activities are, moreover, only a part of the picture; other contacts between administration and legislature abound. On the more formal side, agencies present their views in testimony before the substantive committees (or subcommittees) which authorize their programs and before the appropriations panels which fund them. This can be a time-consuming enterprise; in one six-month period, for example, Secretary of Defense Robert S. McNamara spent a total of 74.5 hours, on twenty different occasions, giving testimony to eight different congressional committees.[27] Other department personnel spend comparable amounts of time at legislative hearings. Other formal communications include the filing of annual reports, often required by statute, which spell out the accomplishments of the agency and attempt to justify whatever new departures it proposes to take. Research is also conducted and these studies, like the reports, are useful in pointing to needs with which the agency would like to deal.

[26] For other, similar data, see Robinson, 1967, pp. 161–170, and E. de Grazia, 1966, p. 306.
[27] *Organization of Congress, Hearings before the Joint Committee on the Organization of Congress, 89th Congress, 1st Session* (Washington, D.C.: Government Printing Office, 1965), p. 446.

TABLE 7-3   *Executive investment in liaison activities, by department, fiscal year, 1963*

Department	Personnel involved in congressional information	Man-hours expended in congressional information	Total congressional information costs
State	68	329,794	$ 711,373
Treasury	16	195,957	155,901
Defense	230	433,119	2,409,900
Justice	39	79,800	269,987
Post Office	28	44,000	374,440
Interior	17	392,830	291,079
Agriculture	13	33,035	113,685
Commerce	29	48,032	280,781
Labor	23	149,678	289,500
HEW	37	154,917	536,292
Total	500	1,856,162	$5,432,938

SOURCE: Pipe, 1966, from charts 1 and 2, pp. 16 and 17. Reprinted with permission from the *Public Administration Review,* vol. 26 (1966).

The greatest number of contacts between agency and Congress, and probably the most crucial ones, are not the formal ones of the hearing room or the printed report but rather those which occur in a variety of informal settings. Memoranda and phone calls are exchanged by agency and congressional personnel. A departmental budget officer may clear his requests with the clerk of the subcommittee which must pass on them (Fenno, 1966, pp. 303–313). Conversations at social events provide opportunities to exchange ideas and information. Such informal contacts may lead to an "understanding" between an agency or bureau and the committee—legislators and staff—to which it is ultimately responsible; the agency may discover what the response of the committee will be to its ideas and how much of what it wants the congressmen on the committee are willing to give. What occurs at the hearing and in the committee room, when the bill is marked up, may be little more than a ratification of agreements previously reached through informal contacts.

These formal and informal contacts, including liaison activity, provide executive agencies with opportunities to persuade and bargain with the members of Congress who make the ultimate policy choices. The bureaus, in an effort to build support for their views, may attempt to mobilize outside, public sentiment and interests (Freeman, 1965, pp. 84–87). They may use publicity, in a fashion not unlike the way in which the President operates, to stimulate those segments of the public with whom they deal to support their views. Agencies, charged with specific responsibilities, work closely with groups in society—the Bureau of Indian Affairs has intimate contacts with the Association on American Indian Affairs; the Interstate Commerce Commission with the railroad and trucking industries; the Defense Department with military contractors and such organizations as the Navy League and the Air Force Association; and so on—and to the extent that they can stimulate these "clientele" groups to support their views, the executive agencies can bring additional pressure to bear on Congress.[28]

In short, executive bureaus make demands upon Congress. They do so by means of formal presentations and reports, by means of extensive liaison operations, by means of informal contacts and friendships between key agency and congressional personnel, and by means of outside group activities. Pressures generated in these ways are designed to alter the preferences and perception of legislators, and to do so in ways similar to the methods which the President employs.

Intraexecutive differences If this activity, which may be considerable, is carried out on behalf of the President's program it may be most helpful to his success. Bureau lobbying may increase the likelihood that Congress

---

[28] Agencies theoretically could seek to arouse mass public opinion, as does the President. In fact, the general populace is unlikely to become involved with the sorts of issues of interest to single bureaus, and attention is thus focused on elite opinion.

will go along with the Chief Executive's requests, for it may be difficult for lawmakers, especially those positively oriented toward the Executive, to resist the combined weight of the united expertise of the administration. Often, however, the executive branch is divided rather than unified; agencies frequently disagree among themselves or dissent from the President's views. When this occurs, the demands on Congress emanating from the bureaucracy will be divided, creating role conflict for legislators and requiring them to choose among competing executive interests.

Such choices are posed because agencies do not always get what they want from the executive branch. Bureaucrats—not unreasonably, given their long experience running particular programs—may feel that they know more than the political appointees, who change as administrations change, who are their nominal superiors. Thus when the central clearance process and the ultimate presidential decisions about the content of the administration program do not provide the agency with the resources which its leaders feel necessary, they may feel compelled to take their case directly to Congress, in a sense circumventing the President.

Pressures from clientele groups may lead to the same course of action; the agency may feel a deeper commitment to those whom it regulates or deals with than to the administration. The Interstate Commerce Commission, for instance, has been accused of promoting the interests of the railroads rather than seeking to regulate the industry (Huntington, 1952). The armed services, within the Department of Defense, seem to be prepared to compete in consort with their defense contractors to gain a larger slice of the defense budget than the President desires them to have (Huntington, 1961, pp. 384–404). The combined preferences of agency and nongovernmental groups may lead to efforts to subvert the President's program.

The bureaus, thus, may work against presidential desires; with the support of legislative and outside allies, they may use their lobbying opportunities to try to substitute their own preferences for those of the Chief Executive. The import of their testimony and reports,[29] the communications transmitted via the liaison networks, and the ideas exchanged through personal contacts will

---

[29]Budget hearings before the committees often place the agency witness in a role-conflict situation: as a representative of the executive branch he is expected to defend the President's requests; as an agency man he would help to get more from Congress. The hearings see what Wildavsky calls a "formalized game" played out. "The agency official is asked whether or not he supports the amounts in the President's Budget and he says 'yes' in such a way that it sounds like yes but everyone present knows that it means 'no' . . . A committee member will then inquire as to how much the agency originally requested from the Budget Bureau. There follows an apparent refusal to answer in the form of a protestation of loyalty to the Chief Executive. Under duress, however, and amidst reminders of Congressional prerogatives, the agency man cites the figures. Could he usefully spend the money, he is asked. Of course he could. The presumption that the agency would not have asked for more money if it did not need it is made explicit. Then comes another defense of the administration's position by the agency, which, however, puts up feeble opposition to congressional demands for increases." Aaron Wildavsky, *The Politics of the Budgetary Process,* pp. 88–89. Copyright © 1964 by Little, Brown and Company (Inc.). Reprinted by permission. For another example, see Fenno, 1966, pp. 275–276.

be to urge the congressional committee members to include agency rather than presidential views in the authorization and appropriations legislation they consider. In extreme cases, the agency may become so entrenched in the legislative process, given the strength and strategic locations of legislative supporters, that it is independent of presidential or other executive control.

The classic example of an agency protected by Congress against executive supervision is the U.S. Army Corps of Engineers. Though the formal organization chart shows the Corps in the Defense Department, "Congress expects the Corps to be *directly* responsible to it" (Maass, 1951, p. 105). In practice, this means the Engineers report to the Committee on Public Works in each House. "The Corps concurs heartily in this relationship. The Engineers call themselves 'the engineer consultants to, and contractors for, the Congress of the United States'" (Maass, 1950, p. 106). A succession of Presidents have sought to subordinate the Corps and to transfer much of its river development activity to the Department of the Interior, but the Engineer-legislative alliance has held firm against such executive desires (Maass, 1952). There have been other instances in which agency-congressional cooperation and mutual support has literally wrested control over a part of the executive branch from the President. To cite one additional case, Nieberg (1962) reports that during the Eisenhower years, the Democratic members of the Joint Atomic Energy Committee practically took over the Atomic Energy Commission, an executive agency, which worked with the congressmen against other bureaus within the executive branch.

For his part, the President may be unwilling as well as unable to discipline the recalcitrant agencies. Efforts to exert control may undermine the morale of bureau employees with consequent effects on performance. More importantly, intervention in agency affairs may antagonize the clientele groups as well as the congressional allies of the agency; the support of these interests may be essential on other issues, and the President may choose not to risk offending them. Similar considerations inhibit the use of the Presidential power to remove agency heads, and such controversial figures as J. Edgar Hoover (FBI), Gen. Lewis Hershey (Selective Service System), and William McChesney Martin (Federal Reserve Board) have been permitted to serve long years in their posts despite the likelihood that some Presidents would have preferred to see other men in those jobs.

More often, the President attempts to make the central clearance procedures work. And, in truth, most agencies would prefer to work through OMB; if they can successfully make their aims a part of the administration program, the full resources of the executive branch will be potentially available to back the agency requests. If the bureau loses in the formulation of the President's program, however, its independence, buttressed by its allies in Congress and outside, may enable it to recoup during the legislative process.

In sum, executive departments, agencies, and bureaus, like the President, make demands on Congress; they want program authority and funds to operate their activities. These executive units work for what they want in a variety of ways; through lobbying Congress, attempting to persuade the legislators of the wisdom of their views and to work out arrangements under which the lawmakers will support their aims, through liaison activities, formal and informal contacts, and mobilization of clientele pressures. If agency desires coincide with the preferences of the President, congressmen may face a united executive and be hard pressed to resist. Often, however, agencies will not be satisfied with what the President proposes for them and they will work against the Chief Executive's program, utilizing their lobbying resources to persuade the crucial legislators to heed their advice, not that of the President. Where intraexecutive differences cannot be resolved at the central clearance stage, the demands on Congress from the executive branch will be inconsistent.

EXECUTIVE SUPPORTS FOR CONGRESS

The executive branch, whether unified or divided, does more than simply make demands upon Congress. Inputs to a system, it will be recalled,[30] include not only demands for specific outputs but also supports—actions and sentiments directed toward the system—which are essential for the survival of the system. If environmental actors cease to regard the system as legitimate, it cannot continue to function and will be modified or go out of existence entirely. In this light, many of the exchanges between the executive and Congress can be seen as supports by which the former assists the latter to perform its duties and thus contributes to the preservation of the legislative institution.

For one thing, in attempting to persuade—to alter the congressmen's preferences and perceptions—the President and the executive agencies provide useful information, data without which the lawmakers might be unable to deal effectively with the issue at hand. This is not to say that the executive is not selective in supplying factual material, providing that which will enhance its ability to persuade, but merely to suggest that the information transmitted is of value to members of Congress. Not only does such data help the representatives give intelligent consideration to policy questions that confront them, but it also allows them to communicate with interest groups and concerned segments of the public. To the extent that these groups—also in the environment of the legislative system—feel that Congress is doing its job satisfactorily, they will support the institution and thus contribute to its survival.

In providing other services for lawmakers, agencies help, indirectly at least, the legislative system sustain its legitimacy. Agency aid, provided

---

[30]See Chapter 1, pp. 5, 7, and 8, for a discussion of support.

through liaison operations, in dealing with constituent requests enables members of Congress to respond quickly and effectively to citizen communication. Rapid response to such inquiries may earn the legislature the support of the populace, support forthcoming specifically as a result of services rendered. Executive acclaim of legislative action serves the same ends. Presidents are quick to lavish praise on Congress when it enacts elements of the administration program; bill-signing festivities become "love feasts" with the Chief Executive often distributing, with abandon, encomiums and ceremonial pens used in signing the legislation. The effect of such ritual may be to underscore the importance of Congress in the larger political system.

More broadly, the executive seeks to work with the legislature, to win its backing of the presidential program through positive, persuasive effort rather than through subversion of the congressional system. Even in the foreign policy sphere, where, as we have seen, the Commander in Chief and other powers have placed the President in a strong position relative to Congress, the Chief Executive tries to gain legislative approval for his policy initiatives. Thus Presidents Eisenhower and Johnson obtained congressional resolutions before taking steps to commit American troops to the Middle East and Southeast Asia. In short, the executive branch contributes to the support of the congressional system in general by dealing with it in a way calculated to preserve its legitimacy and in particular by providing specific information and services which enable it to foster favorable attitudes from other environmental forces. Put another way, inputs from the executive include support as well as demands.

SUMMARY

The President and the executive branch provide the most important set of inputs to the legislative system. The Chief Executive, by common consent, sets the agenda of Congress; the legislative workload revolves around the administration program. Not only does the President set congressional priorities, he also intervenes in the legislative process to push for the enactment of his proposals. Using a variety of formal and informal resources, he seeks to win legislators to his cause, bargaining and persuading in an effort to assemble a majority sympathetic to his position. In the realm of foreign affairs, in particular, the Chief Executive is in a powerful position vis-à-vis Congress.

Nonpresidential agencies of the executive branch complicate the picture. The departments, bureaus, and commissions possess substantial resources of their own with which to try to influence legislative action. If they commit these resources to support the President—and they are likely to do so if they are content with the outcome of the central clearance procedures—the demands made upon Congress will be powerful indeed; if, however, the agencies lobby against the President's proposals, demands on Congress will be inconsistent and, as a result, less forceful. The executive branch in making proposals to the legislature provides support as well, contributing to the legitimacy and, thus, the continued existence of the congressional system.

The members of Congress, for their part, will have to contend with demands from the executive. How the senators and representatives respond will depend, in part at least, on the sort of orientation they hold toward the executive. Those who are legislative-oriented will prefer to substitute congressionally determined priorities for those of the Chief Executive, or to give the administration program thorough scrutiny. We may hypothesize that members of the political party which does not control the Presidency, legislators from safe districts and/or with high seniority, lawmakers who have attained positions of committee leadership, and those who assume a district-oriented focus on representation will be least likely to heed executive entreaties or yield to presidential blandishments.

On the other hand, some congressmen will prefer to work for the implementation of executive-determined goals, to work, that is, to pass the President's program. It seems probable that members of the party that controls the White House; lawmakers from electorally marginal districts, whose political futures may be closely tied to presidential accomplishments; nonleaders on congressional committees; and those with a national, as opposed to a state or district, representational focus will be inclined to assume an executive orientation and be responsive to the President's leadership initiatives. It remains, of course, for the executive branch to assemble a majority in support of the administration program, perhaps beginning with those legislators who assume an executive role orientation.

Where the executive branch is divided, where the demands reaching Congress are inconsistent, the lawmakers may experience role conflict; they will have to choose whether to work for the President or to back the agency requests.[31] We might expect that members of the committee which has numerous contacts with a particular agency, legislators whose constituencies are particularly affected by the agency's activities, and legislators in the opposition party will defend the agency position. Conversely, representatives without legislative or constituency concerns for an agency, especially those of the President's party, should be more prepared to assist the Chief Executive in controlling the various segments of his administration. Whether a lawmaker is President- or agency-oriented in any given situation will also depend on the circumstances surrounding that situation. However role conflict of this sort is resolved, members of Congress must work under constant pressure from

---

[31] Many situations will be more complicated than a simple conflict between the president and an executive agency. As we will see in Chapters 10 and 11, contests will frequently be between coalitions, each containing elements from the executive, legislature, interest groups, and the interested public. For the present, the essential point is that the legislators experience role conflict stemming from incompatible demands made by various parts of the administrative branch.

the executive branch, demands from the President himself and from the various departments, agencies and bureaus which are a part of the administrative apparatus of government. Satisfactory performance in meeting these demands will earn support for the legislative system from those who initiated them, and it is this support which is essential for the survival of the system.

CHAPTER EIGHT

The Lobbyists and Congress

The Chief Executive has emerged, in the twentieth century, as a major source of inputs to the legislative system. His program defines the congressional workload to a very great extent; he and the agencies of his administration make extensive demands on Congress and work vigorously in support of those demands. This central position of the executive branch, however, should not obscure the deep involvement of other environmental actors in the legislative process. This chapter treats a second persistent source of inputs, the interest (or pressure) groups.[1] Interest groups are ubiquitous; they are involved in a great proportion of legislative decisions, and their presence makes it easy to conclude that they are extraordinarily powerful participants in legislative deliberations. The argument advanced here, however, is that while pressure groups are indeed deeply enmeshed in congressional affairs, they are not as dangerous as is sometimes suggested.

In fact, *lobbying*—the name given to group efforts to exert influence and to win desirable legislative outcomes—serves useful purposes for Congress. For one thing, organizational activities provide a communications link between Washington and the "grass roots," that is, between the lawmakers and various segments of the public. Messages flow in both directions across this network, enabling group members to make their sentiments known to their elected

---

[1]The labels "interest" and "pressure" groups will be used interchangeably, and not pejoratively, for stylistic purposes.

representatives and also providing them the opportunity to ascertain the views of the members of Congress. This link may be especially crucial in light of the fact, noted in Chapter 2, that the lawmakers are recruited from a very narrow base in society; the participation of groups, especially those purporting to speak for labor and farm interests whose members are only infrequently elected to Congress, may increase the possibility that points of view which otherwise would not be heard will be taken into account in congressional deliberations. In short, pressure groups provide inputs to Congress which account, in part, for the outcomes of the legislative decision process.

THE CLASSIC IMAGE

Yet to say that interest organizations exert influence is not to attribute to group activities an excessive control over what Congress does. The classic image of lobbying does, however, portray the interests as using undue power to promote their private goals at the expense of the national or public good. Nongovernmental organizations—business groups, labor unions, farm associations, veterans and professional societies, and the like—possess, so the argument runs, vast resources which they employ to wrest from the legislature decisions which promote their interests or to block measures that embody policies inimical to those interests.[2] As Berman (1964, p. 104) puts it: "Lobbies do not find it difficult . . . to administer one defeat after another to Presidents who champion a positive legislative program." Defending against hostile action, of course, may be simpler than mobilizing the resources required to push substantive legislation through to passage.[3]

Interest groups, and the lobbyists in their employ, have numerous opportunities to exert their influence, given the character of American politics in general and the legislative system in particular. American political parties are decentralized; real authority rests with the state and local organizations. Thus if an interest group is concentrated in particular constituencies—as, for example, are the auto workers union in Detroit and the farm associations in the agricultural areas of the Middle West—it can involve itself in the activities of the parties. A group may, in these circumstances, seek to control the nomination process; it may commit sizable sums of money and numbers of its personnel to securing a place on the ballot for a candidate sympathetic to the group's cause. Or, alternatively, the association may stay aloof from nominating politics, but work assiduously for one or the other nominee in the gen-

[2] If a formal definition is necessary, interest groups may be considered as private, nongovernmental organizations which seek to influence the nature and content of governmental activities, that is, to shape the nation's public policies. Our concern here, of course, is with the demands that the pressure groups make on Congress for particular outputs and with the supports for the congressional system that the groups supply.

[3] For a recent statement of this view, see King, 1965.

eral election. Thus, pressure groups may gain influence by working to ensure that the voters send men favorably disposed to their goals to Washington.

Beyond the electoral process, the legislative system affords opportunities for group influence. The dependence of lawmakers, especially those from marginal districts, on local party organizations provides avenues for groups to use to make their appeals to the congressmen. Like the President and executive-agency personnel, lobbyists seek to persuade legislators of the wisdom of acting in keeping with the group's views. The groups attempt, in other words, to alter the senators' and representatives' personal preferences and their perceptions of constituent sentiments. At base, organizational influence rests on a presumed ability to reward those who support the group's position and to punish those who do not go along. Such ability, according to the classic image, permits interest associations to wage campaigns, not unlike those that the President conducts, for their preferred bills at every stage of the legislative process.

The interest organizations may draft bills; they give testimony at committee hearings; they exploit informal contacts with important legislators; they collect information, through the conduct of research, that they can supply to congressmen in the hope of persuading the latter; and they may seek to organize voting blocs to supply the needed majorities in the House and Senate. In a fragmented legislature like Congress, where the subsystems are autonomous and the integrative forces are weak, there are multiple points at which pressure groups may seek to exert influence.

These same points of access also provide opportunities for indirect influence exercised by arousing the populace to pressure their representatives. Public relations campaigns, employing the mass media, may be conducted to cause citizens to write their congressmen in support of specific proposals which a group favors. Interest organizations may also engage in advertising ventures designed to generate "goodwill" that can, if necessary, be converted into pressure at some later point in time. Thus, the aircraft industry, to cite one case, uses commercial messages to stress its contribution to the American space effort not because it hopes to stir up demand for rockets and satellites but in order to demonstrate its value to the nation. Respect for the industry may be convertible into popular backing on particular issues of concern to the aerospace corporations. In sum, the conventional view of interest groups holds that the decentralized character of the legislative branch makes possible both direct and indirect approaches by lobby organizations.

In its pure form this classic image sees lobbyists, in virtual control of legislative activities, skulking about the Capitol Hill corridors, browbeating lawmakers helpless to resist group power, and in general securing whatever it is they want from Congress. In a less extreme form, this view holds that the legislature serves to legitimate decisions reached by accommodation among the concerned groups. As Latham (1952a, p. 390) states: "The legislature referees the group struggle, ratifies the victories of the successful coalitions, and records the terms of the surrender, compromises, and conquests in the form of statutes."[4]

CONTEMPORARY LOBBYING

But opportunities for the exercise of power, which most certainly do exist, must not be mistaken for the ability to dictate the outcome of legislative activity. Though there remains a need for considerably more research on the place of interest groups in congressional decision making, a few recent studies suggest that these associations play a more modest part in the legislative drama than that which the classic image assigns them: they play, in most instances, supporting rather than starring roles. This is not to say that pressure groups are unimportant and need not be considered; on the contrary, their presence must be taken into account. The point is merely that they do not dominate the stage to the extent some observers believe they do, and that their activities represent only part of the story and need to be viewed in conjunction with the parts of other actors.

Lobbyists versus legislators The classic image holds that in the struggle between lobbyists and legislators the former hold the upper hand. In fact, recent research, especially that of Milbrath (1963) and of Bauer, Pool, and Dexter (1963), finds that the balance of power, in the contemporary era at least, lies with the congressmen.[5] The lawmakers can seldom be compelled to act contrary to their own interests; lobbyist contacts depend upon the willingness of the legislator to tolerate them. To put it most simply, current investigation indicates that members of Congress control their relationships with the representatives of interest groups; the legislators determine what the nature of such relationships will be in most cases.

Again, this is not to deny that private organizations do engage in the activities that the traditional view attributes to them, but rather to suggest that few lobbyists believe these influence techniques are effective and that few are willing to undertake them. For example, most groups stay out of the electoral process in all but the most marginal ways. Taking sides in a campaign is a risky venture. There is much to be gained by supporting a winner, especially if the group can justifiably take credit for the victory. A lawmaker who be-

---

[4]See also Latham, 1952b. Other important treatments which stress the importance of groups include Bentley, 1908; Truman, 1951; and Gross, 1953, especially chaps. 2–3.

[5]Milbrath (1963) and Bauer et al. (1963) provide much of the data on which this chapter rests. For other works which lend credence to the position advanced here, see Matthews, 1960, chap. 8; and Scott and Hunt, 1966.

lieves that he owes his office, in part at least, to group activities is likely to be receptive to the group's point of view. Conversely, however, there is much to be lost in backing a loser; the incumbent is highly unlikely to be favorably disposed to an interest that openly lent its resources to his opponent. Most groups, faced with these choices, prefer to hedge their bets, and they avoid direct commitment to any particular candidate, preferring to wait and try to influence whomever the voters put into office (Truman, 1951, pp. 288–320).

Another, and perhaps more crucial, reason for avoiding the electoral process is that groups, most often, cannot deliver the vote to the candidate of their choice. Studies of American voters indicate that the single most important factor in national, partisan elections is the individual's "party identification," that is, his long-standing, deeply rooted sense of belonging to one or the other of the political parties. As a result of this commitment, learned early in childhood, most citizens vote repeatedly for the same party, election after election.[6] In such circumstances, groups will be hard pressed to move many voters from their habitual patterns, and to support the candidate of the minority party, in all but the most competitive districts, is to invite defeat. Thus, while group leaders, especially union officials, acting for themselves as individuals, not on behalf of their organizations, may endorse candidates, most associations prefer to adopt official stands of neutrality and to avoid open identification with either nominee. Moreover, when they do get involved, "political contributions are not forthcoming unless there is already considerable similarity in outlook and interest between donor and recipient" (Milbrath, 1963, p. 283). In short, election aid, if given at all, goes to candidates already committed to the group's cause.

In the same vein, groups do try to arouse the public, including of course their own membership, to communicate with—that is, to bring pressure to bear upon—the legislators. They do try to stimulate letter-writing campaigns, trying to flood Washington with messages urging the recipients to vote for, or otherwise back, the group's position. If the organization can create the image of widespread public approval of its goals, it may persuade some lawmakers, and even a very few may be of critical importance in a close contest, to work for its aims. Yet this is hard to accomplish; few people will take the time to write and congressmen are quick to detect, and discount, a campaign of "inspired" mail in which all the texts are identical or in which all the correspondence is of the "form letter" variety. Such efforts are expensive and their results problematical.

Even more costly and less likely to succeed are the public relations campaigns aimed at creating "goodwill." These efforts aim at creating a climate of public opinion favorable to the group, which can serve as the basis for subsequent communications endeavors relating to specific issues. But as Milbrath (1963, p. 251) points out, such efforts may invite countercampaigns which undercut the initial enterprise. Moreover, people are preoccupied with per-

---

[6]See, *inter alia,* Campbell et al., 1960, pp. 146–167, on the idea of party identification.

sonal, more specific matters, and they may not respond at all to group efforts.

The most effective of these indirect approaches to legislators is the use of constituents and friends to carry the word to Washington (Milbrath, 1963, pp. 241–242). A resident of the lawmaker's district or a personal acquaintance, or preferably someone who is both, may be able to get a message to a congressman, perhaps without the latter being aware of the source of the views presented. In some cases, the intermediary may make the appointment and the lobbyist may accompany him in order to talk directly to the representative. The cost of sending a lawmaker's friends or constituents is likely to be substantially less than that of mounting an extensive letter-writing or public relations campaign, and it is not surprising that lobbyists prefer the former tactic to the latter methods.

In fact, when asked to rate the effectiveness of various techniques (on a scale from 0–10) for influencing congressmen, Milbrath's sample of Washington lobbyists tended to downgrade both the methods of keeping channels of communication open which the conventional wisdom identifies as important and the use of indirect forms of petition and pressure. These data are arrayed in Table 8-1, and they make clear the lobbyists' preferences for direct, per-

TABLE 8-1 Lobbyists' ratings of techniques of influence

Technique	Rating score	
	Mean	Median
(a) Methods of keeping channels open:		
Campaign work	2.28	0.92
Contributing money	1.88	0.85
Entertaining	1.59	1.17
Giving a party	1.24	0.88
Bribery	0.10	0.10
(b) Type of communication through intermediaries:		
Contact by constituents	5.90	5.79
Public relations campaigns	5.55	6.14
Letter and telegram campaigns	4.55	4.29
Contact by a close friend	3.76	2.77
Publicizing voting records	2.05	1.00
(c) Means of direct communication:		
Personal presentation of viewpoints	8.13	9.15
Presentation of research results	7.40	7.91
Testifying at hearings	6.55	5.83

SOURCE: Lester W. Milbrath, *The Washington Lobbyists.* © 1963 by Rand McNally & Company, Chicago, from Tables XI-I, XII-I, XIII-I. As Milbrath notes: "Neither measure of central tendency [the mean or median] is quite suitable. The full distribution of the ratings is the best guide to the data." These are given in the tables indicated.

sonal presentation of group views. We will return to this point shortly, but here the essential fact is that the lobbyists disavow the use of such crude techniques as bribery and entertainment and have rather low expectations about the efficacy of getting involved in electoral politics (see also Dexter, 1969a, pp. 6–7, 38). Communication through intermediaries ranks somewhat higher though still considerably below direct personal contacts. Using constituents to deliver messages and engaging in public relations campaigns are the tactics in this group which lobbyists prefer. In short, the modes identified as typical by the classic image, while they are sometimes used, do not appear to be the main devices for influencing legislators upon which group representatives rely.

One reason for the lobbyists' disinclination to use such techniques seems to be their lack of the resources necessary to put these methods into operation. In their detailed study of the formation of reciprocal trade policy, Bauer, Pool, and Dexter (1963, Part IV) have documented the weaknesses of the groups which sought to influence trade legislation. To begin with, these interests had limited financial bases from which to operate; while large sums were expended by all groups, no one organization had sufficient funds "to enable it to act in decisive fashion" (Bauer et al., 1963, p. 345). Moreover, groups interested in particular issues like foreign trade find it difficult to agree on goals or tactics and thus are less successful than they might be in pooling the money available to the set of associations involved. Actual opposition among concerned groups and lack of effective coordination among potential allies limits the ability of the parties to the controversy to make good use of the resources they do possess. In the same vein, the interest associations suffer from the unavailability of skilled personnel; low pay and unstable career expectations lead the best men to leave the field for more attractive employment elsewhere (Bauer et al., 1963, p. 345).

Inadequate resources—little money and few talented employees—thus limit the ability of interest groups to capitalize on the available opportunities to influence lawmakers. These same shortages prevent lobbies from generating the information which would let them reach members of Congress. The ability to provide services, including data gathering, "unlocks legislative doors" and permits the lobbyist to make his case persuasively, and it is precisely this function which lack of resources makes difficult to perform. Exacerbating the problem is the necessity to commit much of the time, energy, funds, and personnel that are available to dealing with the clientele rather than the policy makers; group representatives must perform services for their employers and members of the clientele group; they must also work to convince these people that they are doing good work. As a result, there may be precious little time left to lobby effectively, much less to plan ahead; "most pressure group activity is emergency fire fighting" (Bauer et al., 1963, p. 349; see also Milbrath, 1963, chap. 7).

Contributing to this general weakness of lobbying as traditionally viewed is the relative immunity of congressmen to application of political pressure. Senators and representatives are the targets of many, perhaps excessive, and competing demands, not merely those from particular pressure groups. We have already noted the prominence of demands from the executive branch. Out of the welter of messages he receives, messages which stress numerous positions and goals, the legislator is quite often free to respond to whichever pressures he chooses (Dexter, 1969b, chap. 8). Somewhat paradoxically, many and inconsistent communications may create the conditions of freedom; the lawmaker, asked to do all things for all people, must inevitably please some and displease other initiators of pressure, including interest groups, and thus can act to suit himself. Since, on controversial matters at least, he will win some applause and earn some approbation no matter what he does, he can behave as he sees fit. Put in other terms, role conflict may not be entirely distasteful to the congressman; where the demands are more or less in balance, the legislator may "play them off" against one another and do as he pleases.

The relative inattention of his constituents contributes to the congressman's freedom of choice. He knows that, except for a small number of highly salient issues, few voters in his district will know where he stands on any given question. His electoral success depends more on creating the impression that he is doing a good job overall than on any specific act or set of acts. As noted (Chapter 2), issues seldom play a crucial part in the election contest. The decentralized character of the legislative system further enhances the independence of the lawmaker from organizational demands. Given the multiple decision points in Congress, he can act in keeping with group demands occasionally, but as he chooses at other, more crucial, times. For instance, it is not uncommon for legislators to vote to recommit, and thus kill, a bill, but then, if the recommittal motion fails, to vote for the proposal on final passage. For all these reasons, representatives can ignore or give only minimal attention to the importunings of interest groups. From the vantage point of the latter, the conclusion of Bauer, Pool, and Dexter (1963, p. 324) is that lobbying, of the sort which the conventional image envisages, is "unimportant compared to other functions of pressure groups."

"Lobbying as a communications process"[7] All this does *not* mean that interest organizations and their lobbyists are uninvolved in, or not central to, the legislative process, but only that their involvement is not usually of the sort postulated by the traditional view. More specifically, lobbying seems to focus more on aiding legislators already sympathetic to the group's aims than on pressuring those opposed or undecided to move toward the group's position. As one study (Bauer et al., 1963, pp. 350–357) puts it, interest associations are inclined to run "service bureaus" for those with whom they are in agreement.[7]

[7]The phrase is Milbrath's 1960; 1963, Part 3.

Groups thus become elements, sometimes important ones, in coalitions composed of executive branch personnel, congressmen, and concerned segments of the public, which work for particular legislative actions. The contest is likely to be among a number of similar coalitions rather than a struggle of group against legislature.

The job of the group representative, in these circumstances, becomes that of a communications specialist transmitting the views of his employers to decision makers in Washington and seeking to persuade, without recourse to heavy-handed pressure, those whose minds are still open to the wisdom of his organization's cause. As Milbrath summarizes it,

> . . . lobbyists spend most of their time receiving and sending communications. Most of this they do from the seclusion of their own offices. Some communications are passed via personal conversation with members of Congress . . . , but these consume little time. Very few are transmitted or facilitated through entertainment. Most lobbyists spend at least some time traveling about visiting local groups attempting to improve communication with the people who support them and to stimulate the flow of communications from the grass roots to governmental decision makers.[8]

This is an image far different from that painted by the conventional treatment of the lobbyist.

From the perspective of the legislative system, we need to examine the ability of groups to present demands to Congress and to intervene in the congressional process in support of those demands. The chief aim of most lobbyists, recognizing the inappropriateness of pressure tactics, is to seek *access* to legislators, that is, to secure a hearing for the group's views (Truman, 1951, pp. 264–265 and chap. 11; see also Dexter, 1969*a,* pp. 121–122). Access constitutes the establishment of a communications channel over which the group representative can transmit messages to the lawmaker. Without access, without the opportunity "to make his pitch," the lobbyist is unlikely to win friends or influence congressmen. Thus, he strives to keep open a line of communication to those legislators whom he would like to help or whose aid he would like to solicit.

Gaining and retaining access is not an easy task; resistance from congressmen may be high. First, as noted, the lawmakers are bombarded with messages from a multitude of sources, and thus pick and choose to whom they will listen. To be heard, the lobbyist must make his message stand out in competition with the noise of rival communications. Next, what Milbrath (1963, pp. 209–211) calls the congressman's "perceptual screen" is likely to impede meaningful access. Given that legislators, like all individuals, possess

---

[8]Lester W. Milbrath, *The Washington Lobbyists.* © 1963 by Rand McNally & Company, Chicago, p. 121. Dexter (1969 *a*, p. 79) underscores this point: ". . . information is the commodity above all others which the lobbyist . . . needs."

beliefs and values which color their outlook, the interest group may find that the messages it sends will be distorted or misread, that "something is lost" in the transmission. Lawmakers, in short, may see in a group communication what they want to see rather than what they were intended to see.[9] Thus, access is useful to the extent that messages sent over the channel are received *and* understood.

Access, where available, provides the lobbyist with his preferred mode of attempting to alter legislators' preferences and perceptions, the method of direct presentation. The data in Table 8-1 reveal the degree to which group representatives favor these methods over more indirect ways. Furthermore, in keeping with the service bureau idea of group operations, access is used to help rather than to pressure congressmen. The lobbyist seeks to build credibility and a reputation for integrity and trustworthiness. Through the presentation of useful information, produced by sound research, in a straightforward fashion, the lobbyist hopes to win the confidence of the representative. To the extent the lawmakers with whom he communicates come to rely on him, to believe in his reliability, the lobbyist's chances to persuade are enhanced.

Thus when he makes his presentation, the organization spokesman tries to be pleasant and nonoffensive. He takes as little of the lawmaker's valuable time as possible, attempting to be "succinct, well organized, and direct" and to appear "well prepared and well informed." The arguments he makes should be supported by factual data, should reflect his personal convictions, and should generally be of the "soft-sell" variety. Moreover, lobbyists believe it desirable to leave a written summary of the views presented with the congressman. In this low-keyed manner, the group representative hopes to create a climate in which the lawmaker feels that he should not only listen to the group position but also take it seriously. Direct, person-to-person, communication is preferred, but the groups also feel that testimony at public hearings is necessary, serving both as a supplement to private conversations and as a device to gain publicity for their views (Milbrath, 1963, pp. 220–228). Dexter (1969a, pp. 65–71) makes much the same point: most lobbyists feel they must "always be straightforward with congressmen and senators." Moreover, it is better to focus on a single issue rather than on a full program; legislators prefer to discuss specific items rather than ideologies. Thus, some organizations—particularly unions, teachers' groups, and the League of Women Voters—undermine their potential influence by acting as "missionaries" for a broad set of social concerns.

Access, through which the interest groups hope to win support for their goals, thus becomes the chief avenue for group success. It is important to note, in this connection, that access itself is unequally divided among the

[9]For discussion of this "selective-perception" phenomenon by which individuals focus on some aspects of a message and ignore other parts of the same communication, see Newcomb et al., 1965, chaps. 6–7; Secord and Backman, 1964, pp. 27–32; and Klapper, 1960, pp. 19–25 and 64–65.

groups seeking to influence Congress. Not all interests have access, and not all those which do have it with equally crucial people in the legislature. Looked at in another way, influence in the legislative system, while widely diffused, is not equally distributed. Some lawmakers, notably committee and party leaders, are more powerful than their colleagues. The ability to communicate effectively with those men is highly advantageous, for if they support the group's cause, they may bring additional backing with them.

Also relevant here is the tendency for groups to make use of access only with respect to legislators whom they perceive as already on their side or, at worse, uncommitted. "Most lobbyists, most of the time, act to reenforce, strengthen, and reassure congressmen and staff who tend to be on their side. They rarely *argue* with known enemies" (Dexter, 1969a, p. 73). Even within these limits groups seem to be conservative in their choice of tactics; in the area of reciprocal trade policy, Bauer, Pool, and Dexter (1963, p. 351) report observing "no more common mistake than that of failing to push people who were movable because it was assumed that they were on the other side" (see also Dexter, 1969a, p. 67). This suggests, in the same vein, the importance of timing; when to try to exploit access becomes a critical decision for the lobbyist. Since he can make use of his access only infrequently, he wants to make his appeal at exactly the right moment—not too early in the contest, before there is any impetus for the congressman to announce his position, or too late, when the legislator is already firmly committed. If his message is timely, the chances that it will be heard, and perhaps heeded, are increased. In short, getting to the right man at the right time is an essential ingredient of successful lobbying.

To summarize, this section has suggested that the classic image of lobby activity is highly inaccurate and misleading. The lobbyist, so recent research reveals, is less the master of the legislator, and more his subject. Because the congressman is the target of many groups, and because his constituents are usually unaware of his specific acts, he can define the "pressures" to which he will respond to suit his own aims and opinions. In such circumstances, the lobbyist can merely seek to gain and hold access to influential legislators, access which will permit him to communicate directly with the congressional decision makers. Group representatives prefer direct contact of an informal, low-pressure variety to other means of influencing senators and representatives; they also find these techniques more effective.

The task of the pressure groups, then, becomes one of keeping channels of communication open. This can be accomplished most successfully by establishing a "trusting" relationship with individual congressmen, a relationship sustained by the provision of information and the performance of other services. If a legislator can rely on a lobbyist he will probably listen to his views. Over the years, mutually satisfactory arrangements are likely to develop between the pressure group and those in Congress friendly to the group's aims. The group provides aid to lawmakers working for goals which it shares; its influence comes from having its friends in the right place to shape legislative decisions.

This can be seen clearly if one looks at the composition of the Senate Finance Committee which in 1969 faced the issue of oil depletion allowances —tax benefits for the oil and gas industries—which had become a major symbol for those attacking the American tax structure as inequitable. The committee had among its members many friends of these industries, which naturally opposed the loss of their favorable tax position.[10] For example, the chairman of the committee, Russell Long (D., La.), represented an oil-producing state, had long championed industry interests, and had "personal financial holdings in oil." The second ranking Democrat, Clinton Anderson, also represented an oil state, New Mexico, had personal interests in oil and consistently voted to protect the depletion allowance. Other committee Democrats—Talmadge of Georgia, Fulbright of Arkansas, and Harris of Oklahoma —came from states which produce oil and gas, and these men display records of persistent support for measures aimed at protecting these industries.

On the Republican side of the committee were a number of generally conservative, probusiness senators. Such men as Wallace Bennet (Utah), Carl Curtis (Neb.), Miller (Iowa), and others consistently voted for positions which aid or protect industry in general. Other GOP members— Fannin of Arizona and Hansen (Wyo.)—were from oil- or gas-producing states. Little or nothing is known about the part that industry interest groups played in the fight over the oil depletion allowance, but it seems reasonable to assume that they backed those members of the committee who refused to go along with a sharp cut in the allowance written into the tax bill which passed the House of Representatives.[11] In any event, little pressure would seem required in such situations; groups can devote their available resources to assisting their legislative allies.

To repeat, this stress on the supportive rather than on the aggressive posture of interest associations does not mean that these other techniques of influence are obsolete or useless. Lobbyists do, as noted, resort to the use of intermediaries and public relations campaigns, even though the high cost and relative inefficiency of such methods lead them to prefer direct personal contacts. Moreover, groups do get involved in elections, do try to use entertainment and other less desirable means to curry the favor of legislators. Further, lobbyists can and do get favors, but these are usually "one-shot"

---

[10]This treatment relies on "Industry Has Strong Friends on Finance Committee," *Congressional Quarterly Weekly Report,* Sept. 26, 1969, pp. 1787–1795.

[11]Late in 1969, the Finance Committee proposed, and the Senate passed, an oil depletion allowance of 23 percent, down from the 27½ percent given in the existing law, but above the 20 percent limit set in the House bill. The conference committee settled on 22 percent.

benefits—a contract, a favorable tax ruling, a pardon—rather than broad policy decisions (Dexter, 1969a, p. 113). There are, however, limits on the availability of even these specific achievements: ". . . few important officials will risk serious jeopardy to their reputations by repeated acts of favor to some personal friend" (Dexter, 1969a, p. 117). And, finally, bribery is not unheard of: in 1956, Sen. Francis Case (R., S. D.) reported on the Senate floor that a lobbyist representing natural-gas interests had made a $2,500 campaign contribution a few days before a vote on a bill easing the regulatory controls over the natural-gas industry; as a result Case voted against the bill, and when it passed, President Eisenhower felt obliged to veto it. Similarly, in December 1969 ex-Sen. Daniel Brewster (D., Md.) was indicted for having accepted $24,500 in bribes from a lobbyist employed by a Chicago mail-order house to influence his votes on legislation proposing increases in postal rates. Yet, on the whole, the burden of current knowledge supports Dexter's (1969a, p. 112) conclusions that "only on rare occasions" can a lobbyist "really 'provide,' or 'offer,' that is to say, sell or rent influence" to his employer. For the most part, demands on the legislative system from lobbyists are legitimate; members of Congress can control their relationships with the group representatives.

LEGISLATIVE USE OF LOBBIES

In some cases, the influence relationship is actually reversed. Rather than act to influence lawmakers, using whatever access is available, interest groups may respond to initiatives taken by congressmen. That is, legislators with particular causes to promote will seek to enlist pressure groups in their efforts. The senator or representative, of course, seeks to take advantage of whatever resources the organization is willing to commit to his support. He may seek to rally the public, or at least the group's membership, behind his proposal, using the group itself to conduct the grass-roots campaign. He may want to take advantage of the group's contacts with his fellow legislators. He may hope to get needed research from an interest association, data which will reduce his dependence on the executive branch or less reliable sources.

In order to be able to call on organizations in this fashion, a legislator may go to some lengths to court the groups; the congressman has resources which he may use to build "credit" with a lobbyist. For one thing, a member can provide information to a group; he can "leak" to the group the decisions taken in executive sessions of congressional committees, inside information which may keep the lobbyist from being caught unawares by committee action. Knowing what is coming may permit the interest representative to make plans accordingly. Similarly, a member of Congress can do much to publicize group goals and activities; he can insert material favorable to the interest in the *Congressional Record;* he can place items which promote the group where they may be read by his legislative colleagues. He can, in addition, lend his own standing and prestige to organizational membership and financial or publicity drives by making speeches, statements, writing letters, or otherwise permitting the group to exploit his membership in Congress. In the same vein, the lawmaker may hold committee or subcommittee hearings on bills that a group favors even though such legislation has no real chance to pass; the group, testifying at such hearings at least gets a public forum in which to call its views to the attention of interested parties—the executive, legislators, and concerned members of the nongovernmental public. Finally, and most importantly, the legislator can intercede with the bureaucracy on behalf of a group, seeking to expedite consideration of the organization's claims. As noted (Chapter 7, pp. 184–187), the executive branch is quite prepared to respond to congressional requests as a part of its effort to court the lawmakers. This executive responsiveness enables the senators and representatives to assist the lobbyists.

Thus the legislator possesses some devices—mainly informational and publicity-generating resources—that he can use to earn the "goodwill" of interest groups, favorable sentiments which he hopes to convert into specific action in response to his initiatives. On the other side of the coin, the congressman also has sanctions that he can use to discipline uncooperative groups (Matthews, 1960, pp. 188–190). Most important is his control over access. As we have seen access is the lobbyist's most important asset and the legislator can, if a group and its representative do not respond adequately, close off that access; he will not be in when the group spokesman calls; he will not return those calls. An even stronger tactic, to attack directly, is also available. Given the prevalence of the classic image of pressure-group activity, it is not surprising that such associations are vulnerable to open attack, charges which the public is disposed to believe. A charge of improper action will find a receptive audience and the group will be well advised to prevent, if possible, any lawmaker from leveling such accusations. In sum, there is much that a member of Congress can do that will incline a lobbyist to give aid when he is asked to do so.

To cite one example, Bauer, Pool, and Dexter (1963, pp. 354–357) describe an incident in 1954 when an interest group, the Committee for a National Trade Policy, organized at President Eisenhower's request, wound up working for Sen. Albert Gore (D., Tenn.) in support of a more liberal reciprocal trade bill than the President desired. The initial contact came from Senator Gore's office and the group worked as "an auxiliary service bureau for a senator with whom it was in complete agreement. Its staff provided him with information, they helped him in writing, they arranged for statements of support . . . , and they even assumed the task of approaching a half-dozen amenable Republicans, something a Democratic senator could not well do." In short, lawmakers may, on their own initiative, get invaluable assistance from interest organizations willing to help out.

THE REGULATION OF LOBBYING

One theme of the discussion to this point is that the nature of the legislative system is such that lobbyists can generate little of the pressure which the conventional view of the group process attributes to them. The superior position of the lawmakers enables them to control their relationships with interest organizations and to impose a set of norms—rules of the lobbying game—which makes the process one in which groups work with their supporters far more often than they intimidate fearful opponents.[12] Supplementing these informal controls, moreover, is a set of legal restrictions, imposed on lobbying by Title III of the 1946 Legislative Reorganization Act and other statutes. Such laws, however, have not proved particularly effective, but they do contribute to imposing limitations on what groups can do in their efforts to influence the government.[13]

These statutes have outlawed such undesirable activities as bribery; tried to limit the amounts of money spent in election campaigns; attempted to keep federal government employees out of lobbying sorts of activity; and, most importantly, sought to bring group efforts to influence congressional action out into the open. In this last connection, a number of requirements have been imposed on those engaged in lobbying. For one thing, all persons and organizations that seek to influence congressional consideration of legislation must register with the clerk of the House of Representatives or the secretary of the Senate. They must also file information, on a quarterly basis, relating to how much money has been received and spent and the purposes for which the funds were used. More specifically, lobbyists, if their *principal purpose* is to influence legislation must keep records of the names of each individual who contributes $500 or more to the organization or who receives $100 or more from the group, and this data and the purposes for which the disbursements are made must also be filed quarterly. Reports, based on this information, are to be printed in the *Congressional Record*. All these provisions, so the argument runs, should prevent pressure groups from exercising excessive influence by making them operate under the watchful eye of the public.

Unfortunately, these statutory provisions have not had the desired effects; they have been found deficient in several respects. First, the Supreme Court

[12]See Milbrath, 1963, pp. 324–327, for a discussion of these informal limitations on lobbying.
[13]For a more detailed review of the efforts to regulate the lobbying process by statute see *Congressional Quarterly Service*, 1968, especially pp. 11–26; and Zeller, 1958.

has constricted the applicability of the registration and disclosure laws. In the case of *United States v. Harriss et al.,* 347 U.S. 612 (1954), the Court held that only those persons and organizations that solicited, collected, and disbursed money for the *principal purpose* of influencing legislation were required to register and to file statements of their expenses. Associations for whom relations with Congress are only a subsidiary concern need not make public their financial receipts and expenditures. The Court held, furthermore, that the law was applicable only to direct, immediate efforts to affect legislative outcomes and not to indirect methods such as "grass-roots" lobbying or other approaches through intermediaries. Finally, Congress has never seen fit to establish an agency with power to enforce the lobby-control laws in any systematic fashion, and pressure on groups to comply has been at best irregular. Thus, while these statutes do compel the publicizing of some of the most obvious activities of interest organizations, the loopholes they contain have reduced their impact considerably; the intentions of those who framed them have not been met. The essential point, however, remains that together with the built-in controls inherent in the system, the regulatory laws create a situation in which lobbying is surely far less perilous for the nation than the classic image would lead one to believe.

PRESSURE-GROUP SUPPORT FOR THE LEGISLATIVE SYSTEM

The systems approach reminds us that interactions between groups in the environment and Congress, like those between the executive and legislative branches, include not only demands for outputs but also supports for the system. To reiterate, support consists of feelings, favorable or hostile, and actions in keeping with those sentiments which may either sustain or undermine a system. If support declines, the system will have to adapt in order to recoup its losses; if support fails precipitously, the system may become the object of more antagonism than it can endure and it will be destroyed. It is clear that the U.S. Congress is in no such imminent danger, and it should be recognized that interest groups contribute to the legislature's ability to maintain a high degree of support, and thus legitimacy, and a central place in the political process.

Interest organizations buttress the legislature in a number of ways. For one thing, they most often refrain from attacking the system, that is, they avoid actions that would undermine confidence in Congress. They do not, as we have noted, often have recourse to bribery. This may only be because they realize that there is little, if anything, to be won by the use of such methods, but the effect is to reduce the frequency of acts which would serve to undermine confidence in the legislature. The paucity of allegations of illegal, or even immoral, relationships between lobby group and lawmaker, and the willingness of Congress to act when such situations do arise,[14] seem to give people—government officials, group members, and the general populace—the feeling that their demands will receive a fair hearing in the legislature.

Correlatively, interest associations, like the executive-branch personnel, tend to operate through the system, that is, they make use of the opportunities that Congress offers to try to persuade the lawmakers to respond. They do not seek to subvert the system; rather they attempt to win gains from Congress. Put another way, groups work to alter legislators' preferences and perceptions of constituency opinion, not to discredit the institution. In this fashion, group activities contribute to the survival potential of Congress.

More specifically, interest groups provide much substantive aid for lawmakers. Information is a prime example; data that groups generate may be the sole independent counterweight available to legislators under pressure from the executive branch. The desire to build trusting relationships, previously noted, creates a need for lobbyists to supply reliable information to their contacts in Congress; information which gives the senators and representatives a source other than the executive. In the same vein, such data enables congressmen to respond effectively to constituent requests, action which should increase satisfaction with legislative performance. Interest groups provide other assistance as well; they may write speeches for lawmakers, contact other members of Congress or influential citizens, or in other ways solicit backing for a legislator's goals. The entire set of ways a group can function as a "service bureau" for congressmen constitutes supports for the legislative system; by enabling the lawmakers to play their roles more effectively, groups contribute to the maintenance of confidence in the legislature's utility and, thus, to its survival.

Overall, then, organizational activity is useful for Congress. It helps the legislature reach decisions, resolve societal conflicts, by providing a number of supportive services. Moreover, to the extent that an association feels that legislative decisions are at least tolerable, it may help create acceptance of these decisions by encouraging its members to back policies which the group had a hand in shaping. In short, by providing a mechanism for transmitting various points of view to Washington, by assisting in the consideration of various alternative courses of action, and by promoting acceptance of the decisions which are taken, interest groups make a substantial contribution to the continued viability of Congress.

SUMMARY

Pressure-group activity, or lobbying, seems on the whole to be a persistent feature of legislative politics in the United States. Numerous associations of a

---

[14] Witness the 1968 censure of the late Sen. Thomas Dodd (D., Conn.) for improper use of campaign contributions.

highly varied character make demands upon, and also provide supports for, Congress; the centrality of organized groups in the legislative process is not to be denied. The main thrust of this chapter, however, is to suggest that the classic image of group involvement, which holds that governmental action is in some sense the resultant of the intersection of group goals and influence is misleading; contemporary research more realistically assigns to groups a more modest part in the drama of policy making. Rather than decisive influences, pressure organizations emerge as one source of inputs, out of a number of such sources, to which the legislator must relate as he performs his congressional chores. Groups may be important, but the ways in which their influence is felt are far more limited than is often believed.

The present approach stresses the constraints on interest activity. It is harder than many people realize for groups to use the electoral process to reward their friends and punish their enemies; nominations cannot easily be managed and votes are very difficult to deliver. Public relations campaigns, aimed at directing heavy and unremitting pressure at congressmen are extraordinarily costly and meet virtually immovable obstacles in public apathy and indifference. Some indirect methods of communicating with congressmen, the use of friends and constituents as intermediaries, are more effective and less expensive, and lobbyists appear to prefer these techniques to the more difficult massive efforts.

The most preferred tactic, according to the lobbyists' own testimony, is direct personal contacts. Access to lawmakers is not employed to bribe or pressure, but rather to persuade on the merits; persuasion that features solid research support if possible and an inoffensive style of presentation. Such low-key, "soft-sell" techniques are essential because in the relationship between lobbyist and lawmaker, the latter deals from a position of strength. The group spokesman is short on resources and power, he is dependent upon the congressman. As a result, he is most likely to run a "service-bureau" operation, seeking to aid legislators already committed to his views to advance their cause. From the representative's viewpoint, public inattention coupled with inconsistent demands from a variety of sources permits him to act as he sees fit; ironically, role conflict may produce freedom of action. Thus the legislator can control his relationship with the lobbyists, for he can cut off access and in most instances the group will not possess sanctions to use against him.

If this is so, we would expect that congressmen would have little to fear from pressure groups, and this, in fact, appears to be the case. One typical senator reports that "lobbies are the most valuable instrument in the legislative process" (quoted in Matthews, 1960, p. 117). The late Rep. Clem Miller (1962, p. 133) concluded that "pressure groups . . . are essential to the American political process," and that "they are generally neither sinister nor malicious. . . . " Interviews with numerous members of the House of Representatives led another student of Congress to conclude that legislators feel that they can "use the lobbyists' help properly without being improperly used themselves" (Clapp, 1964, p. 206). In short, senators and representatives believe that, in general, interest-group demands not only are in keeping with the constitutionally guaranteed right of petition but also serve to articulate points of view which need to be heard. Moreover, they believe that group participation improves the quality of legislative performance.

If this view is truly widely held, we might further predict that members of Congress would assume a facilitator, or at least a neutral, role orientation rather than the posture of a resister toward interest groups. The data in Table 8-2 on the role orientations of representatives verify this prediction. Our hypothesis is especially true for Republicans, where only 6 percent fall into the resister category. Even among the Democrats more than two-thirds were either neutral or favorably disposed toward group involvement. This party difference probably reflects the fact that so many associations speaking for business and professional interests work with GOP lawmakers and are welcomed as supporters. The main point, however, remains that the members of Congress do assume identifiable orientations toward interest groups.[15]

Pushing our speculation a step further we might suggest that orientation toward group activity should be related to a legislator's behavior with respect to congressional outputs. For example, a facilitator might be expected to respond to group appeals rather than to presidential or executive pressure when confronted with the necessity to choose between the two. Or he might be found allied with an executive-interest coalition when sympathetic to its cause. A resister, on the other hand, could be expected to resolve a conflict between the administration and a pressure group in favor of the former, or might be less willing to cast his lot with a group-centered coalition. The existence of a substantial proportion of neutrals, while it lends credence to the view that most congressmen are not fearful about group influence, should also remind us that the largest number of lawmakers do not align themselves,

[15]For a more detailed discussion of congressmen's orientations toward interest groups, see Davidson, 1969, pp. 165–174.

TABLE 8-2   Interest-group role orientations among congressmen

Orientation	All (%)	Democrats (%)	Republicans (%)
Facilitator	29	24	38
Neutral	49	45	56
Resister	21	31	6
Total	99	100	100
N	(85)	(51)	(34)

SOURCE: Data collected by Roger H. Davidson, David M. Kovenock, and Michael K. O'Leary and made available by the Interuniversity Consortium for Political Research.

in general terms, for or against interest organizations. Rather they seem to be prepared to pick and choose according to the situation at hand and in the light of their other role orientations. Relevant considerations would, of course, include the party affiliation and issue position of the President, and the views and activities of the relevant congressional committees, legislative parties, constituents, and the involved pressure groups.

From this often enormous quantity of almost certainly conflicting pressures, the lawmaker must select the set of inputs to which he will respond. Such choices will inevitably involve the resolution of role conflict. Though interest groups, we have argued, are seldom able to determine legislative outcomes, and most often confine themselves to supporting the legislators committed to their views and to persuading the undecided, nevertheless, in attempting to understand the forces which affect the behavior of congressmen and thus the outputs of the legislative system, we can ill afford to ignore the inputs originating with the numerous pressure groups operating in the environment of Congress.

CHAPTER NINE

Intermittent Pressures:
Public Opinion and the Courts

The interactions between Congress, on the one hand, and the executive branch and the pressure groups, on the other, are without doubt the major source of inputs to the legislative system, but they by no means exhaust the pressures to which the lawmakers must respond. This chapter outlines the ways in which the public, as individuals rather than as organized groups, and the federal judiciary pose challenges which Congress must meet. While these demands and supports are less constant, less persistent, nonetheless the citizenry and the judges do act in ways which require legislative reaction. The essential point remains, here as in the previous chapters, that members of Congress will assume orientations toward the public and the courts, as toward the other sources of inputs to the system, and that knowledge of those orientations may help us understand the ways in which congressmen act and the fashion in which Congress performs its lawmaking, representational, and oversight tasks.

PUBLIC DEMANDS ON CONGRESS

The public, as the concept is employed here, refers to citizens acting as individuals and communicating their demands and supports to the legislature. It is, of course, true that interest groups organize popular sentiment and act on behalf of their members. Our concern at this point is to treat the unorganized populace, to suggest the ways in which single citizens can and do influence the behavior of Congress. That is, citizens do not always channel their attempts to influence legislative outcomes through pressure groups; often they communicate directly with their elected representatives.

The inputs from the public take two forms. One is the demand for "services," for what the lawmakers refer to as "casework." Constituents want information, aid in their dealings with the bureaucratic apparatus, and other things which are not related to policy matters. The vast bulk of mail directed to congressmen, as much as three-fourths of it by some estimates, is of the service variety. Most callers at the legislator's Washington or district offices do not express their views on policy matters or request that the representative assume a particular stance on any given issue. These service requests are not intermittent; rather they are constant and heavy; and as such become a major preoccupation of the congressional offices. Large amounts of time, energy, and staff resources are committed to dealing with such demands. The largest proportion of the lawmaker's representational activities is directed to handling appeals of the casework type, and we will deal with this topic in Chapter 13.

Policy demands The second set of inputs from the public, and the one which will concern us here, pertains to public policy. Some individuals do try to express their policy views directly to their elected representatives. These demands *are* intermittent; in general, few Americans feel, and respond to, the urge to let their congressmen know what is on their minds relative to the major substantive issues of the day. This results from a number of causes. For one thing, issues tend to be remote, complex, and as a result, often unintelligible to many citizens. The authors of *The American Voter*, for instance, found that only about 12 percent of the electorate responded to the stimuli of the 1956 election campaign in what they describe as an "ideological" fashion. That is, only one voter in eight conceptualized his choice in terms of a liberal-conservative dimension along which the candidates could be located with regard to their stands on the central campaign issues. While many of the remaining voters explained their choices in terms of "group benefits"—e.g., "the farmer prospers under Republican administrations"—or in terms of "the nature of the times"—e.g., "things go well when the Democrats are in power"—all of which are, in a vague sense, "issue-oriented" responses (Campbell et al., 1960, chap. 10), only the more sophisticated, ideological concern is likely to lead a citizen to communicate his views to his elected representatives. Even the 1964 presidential campaign, in which the Republican challenger, Sen. Barry M. Goldwater (Ariz.), explicitly offered "a choice not an echo" in issue terms—in strong contrast to more normal campaigns in which policy choices are muted rather than highlighted—was perceived as an ideological, or issue-based, contest by only a third of the electorate (Field and Anderson, 1969).

Attachment to party, not consideration of the issues, seems to account for choices in legislative as well as presidential elections, especially in the former. One study of the off-year 1958 congressional voting found little interest in, or knowledge about, the campaign. Only 7 percent of the voters mentioned issues in explaining their vote intentions. One-fourth of the electorate claimed to have heard of or read about both congressional candidates, while nearly a half (46 percent) admitted to having neither heard nor read about any nominee. In the same vein, more than 50 percent did not know which party was the majority in the national legislature. Unconcerned about the substantive issues at stake, most voters fall back on attachment to party as their decison-making device; most vote Republican or Democratic consistently election after election, for Congress as for President (Stokes and Miller, 1962). Legislative candidates, recognizing the irrelevance of specific policy choices to much of the electorate, prefer to avoid explicit discussion of the issues and instead focus on more general appeals.[1]

Given the low levels of interest in the issues, even during the heat of election campaigns, it should not surprise us to discover that few citizens become involved enough to communicate their views to public officials, including members of Congress. The available evidence suggests that from a seventh to a fifth of Americans have ever written a letter to a national legislator; and a far smaller proportion write regularly (Woodward and Roper, 1950; Dexter, 1956; Lane, 1959, pp. 67–74). Moreover, since most contacts with congressmen, whether by mail or by direct personal visit, are not concerned with policy questions—one estimate suggests that only about one-fourth of the mail is issue related (Tacheron and Udall, 1966, pp. 282–283)—it seems safe to conclude that only 5 or so percent of the citizenry actually seek to let their representatives know where they stand on issues of public policy. And when this small flow of mail is spread across a number of questions which Congress considers simultaneously, it is clear that the legislators are hardly inundated with the policy views of their constituents.

This is not to say, of course, that members of Congress never receive an abundance of correspondence that pertains to policy. There are some issues which seem to strike a responsive chord among large numbers of citizens, prompting them to write to express their views or to make a voting choice. Matters with direct, immediate personal consequences for voters seem to be of this sort; such things as wars, which disrupt families and ordinary routines of life, and severe economic dislocations, which have profound effects on purchasing power and social status, may lead individuals to break their customary habits and to act politically on the basis of these issues. Other subjects, "style issues"[2] such as capital punishment, the humane slaughter

[1]See Chapter 2, pp. 46–47, for a discussion of the place of issues in legislative elections. We face a "chicken-and-egg" problem here; there is no way to tell whether legislative candidates avoid the issues because the public is not interested and does not respond, or whether the public pays scant attention to issues because the politicians do not stress them.
[2]"Style issues" are those which have minimal material content; they reflect the feelings and emotions more than the reality of the voter's position in society. See Berelson et al., 1954, pp. 184–185.

of animals, fluoridation of local water supplies, and the like seem to arouse emotion, and thus to encourage issue-based political activity, among significant segments of the populace to an extraordinary degree.[3] Such citizen involvements do occur, but the crucial point is that they do not take place very frequently.

The "information gap" In fact, the lawmakers have a difficult time in ascertaining what the residents of their states and districts believe about most current issues. As we have seen, they receive only a few policy-related communications. Moreover, those messages they do receive come from atypical sources; citizens with better educations, higher economic status, more leisure time, and confidence in their ability to transmit their views communicate far more often than do individuals with less opportunity and capacity. The policy preferences of these upper-class letter writers are scarcely likely to be typical of a cross section of the lawmaker's constituents. Congressional mail on the reciprocal trade issue, for instance, favors protectionism, while the actual distribution of opinion, as measured by reliable surveys, supports the free-trade principle (Bauer et al., 1963, p. 103). The same type of distortion seems to occur with respect to other issues. Moreover, the mail that does come, even that from the high-status portion of the public, often is obscure, of unclear meaning, frequently asks for things that the legislator cannot do, and in many instances arrives too late to be effective, reaching Washington after the congressman has made commitments that cannot easily be altered (Dexter, 1963b).

Nor are other, alternative sources of data about constituents' issue positions more reliable than the content of letters. Newspapers are a poor guide to public opinion; their editorial content tends to reflect the specialized viewpoints of their owners, publishers, and editors, sentiments which are highly unlikely to reflect the attitudes of the average reader of the daily press. More and more, members of Congress are making use of some form of public opinion poll, but even here the results are mixed (Marasculio and Amster, 1964). Good polls—that is, those which are carefully conducted, based on representative samples of constituents and employing sound questions—are expensive, and only a few legislators are willing to pay the cost of such surveys. Easier to carry out, and substantially cheaper, are questionnaires sent, usually at no cost under cover of the franking privilege, to all postal patrons in the lawmaker's district. Such "polls," however, do not yield reliable results; the questions asked are often loaded, seemingly written to elicit opinion favorable to the legislator's own views rather than to ascertain the true distribution of constituency sentiment. Even where the questions are fairly worded, the returns are not unbiased, for not all segments of the local population are equally likely to respond. The better-educated, higher-

[3]For a suggestion that such issues may serve to allow individuals to express, or "externalize," basic personality needs, see Lane and Sears, 1964, pp. 75–76.

status citizens—precisely those who are likely to write letters to their representatives—are the most likely to make the effort to return the questionnaires, and as we have seen, the views of this group are not typical of those who are less apt to respond. Similarly, the views presented in personal conversations—in Washington or in the district—are unlikely to give the member of Congress a representative sample of constituent sentiment; only an atypical few will seek him out for an individual expression of opinion (Dexter, 1963*b*).

In sum, the congressmen suffer from what we may describe as an "information gap"; they face grave difficulties in discovering what are the preferences of their constituents. Local citizens are often not interested at all in the issues pending in Congress, and the mail, personal contacts, newspaper views, or poll respondents are not likely to be typical even of those district residents who are concerned. Most lawmakers, thus, operate on the basis of uncertain intelligence, unsure of which constituents, with what points of view, are watching their behavior with respect to which policy questions. Moreover, as Bauer, Pool, and Dexter (1963, pp. 419–420) put it, ". . . a congressman determines—consciously or unconsciously—what he hears."

> . . . an anticipatory feedback discourages messages that may not be favorably received from even getting sent. A congressman very largely gets back what he puts out. In his limited time, he associates more with some kinds of people than with others, listens to some kinds of messages more than to others, and as a result hears from some kinds of people more than from others. He controls what he hears both by his attention and by his attitudes. He makes the world to which he thinks he is responding. Congressmen, indeed, do respond to pressures, but they generate the pressures they feel. (Reprinted by permission of Aldine-Atherton, Inc.).

This means, in effect, that senators and representatives are relatively free to act as they please, secure in the knowledge that "there is no district viewpoint *as such* to be represented on the overwhelming majority of issues" (Dexter, 193*b,* p. 9). On those questions, constituents simply are not concerned and thus make few, if any, demands on the legislators. It is only the rare issue on which the lawmaker can be quite clear about what his constituents want and can expect reprisals if his behavior deviates markedly from those expectations.[4] In the remaining situations, he can largely ignore public opinion and pay relatively greater attention to demands from other sources.

On the other hand, there is certainly no unbridgeable gulf between constituents and congressman. Several factors tend to make lawmakers attentive to, and supportive of, the views of the voters in his state or district.

---

[4] Among the major, recurring issues of public policy, civil rights seems to be a matter about which citizens feel strongly, communicate their views, and gain substantial conformity to those sentiments from their elected representatives. See Miller and Stokes, 1963; and Cnudde and McCrone, 1966.

For one thing, the representative may share the sentiments of those who put him in office. His background and experience, and thus the values which he holds, may lead him to hold policy preferences similar to those which characterize the district. The black lawmaker from the urban ghetto or the representative from the Midwest wheat belt need not receive a flood of messages from his district to know what his constituents believe about the poverty or farm programs. Such shared values, then, may lead to a coincidence of views, even in a situation of intermittent communications.[5]

There remains, in addition, a pervasive uncertainty about subsequent elections; the lawmaker, in the absence of clear data on constituent sentiments, can never be entirely sure whether his action on policy matters will affect his reelection prospects. Thus, in deciding what to do in any given situation, he will take into account his relationship with his local party organization, the competitiveness of the two parties in his locality, the kind of people who reside in the district, and his own feelings—however intuitive and emotional—about the mandate given him by the voters. He will, of course, also consider whatever information he possesses about his constituents' interest in, and sentiments about, any given issue (Matthews, 1960, chap. 10). All of this provides no clear guide to action, but it does seem to require each legislator to think about possible local repercussions that his behavior may induce; this ensures some policy linkages, though clearly not perfect ones, between Washington and the states and districts.

Role orientations Different lawmakers respond to the necessity to relate to their constituencies in different ways; they assume differing role orientations toward the policy demands emanating from "back home." As data from one study of the House of Representatives reveal (Table 9-1), significant

[5]This does not appear to occur with regard to civil rights. Cnudde and McCrone, 1966, suggest the congressmen vote as they do on such matters not because they share their constituents' views but because they perceive those preferences and, given the high salience of the issue, act accordingly.

TABLE 9-1   *Representative role orientations among congressmen*

Orientation	All (%)	Democrats (%)	Republicans (%)
Trustee	28	28	27
Politico	46	51	38
Delegate	23	17	32
Undetermined	3	4	3
Total	100	100	100
N	(87)	(53)	(34)

SOURCE: Data collected by Roger H. Davidson, David M. Kovenock, and Michael K. O'Leary, and made available through the Interuniversity Consortium for Political Research.

proportions of congressmen seem to assume trustee, politico, and delegate orientations.[6] The important point, for present purposes, is that nearly seven of ten members of the House acknowledge some obligation to act on behalf of their constituents. This group includes about one-fourth who, as delegates, seek to mirror district sentiment and the largest single contingent, the politicos, who pick and choose, following constituency dictates when they feel the district is alert, and pursuing a more independent course on those occasions when the issue lacks local visibility.

These differing orientations reflect varying circumstances in which the legislators find themselves (Davidson, 1969, pp. 126–135). As Table 9-1 makes clear, party affiliation is relevant here; Democrats are more likely to adopt trustee and, especially, politico orientations, while Republican representatives seem to prefer the delegate posture. Constituency conditions, as might be expected, are also important. Lawmakers from closely competitive districts are found assuming the delegate stance; their colleagues holding safe seats feel freer to act as trustees. Position in Congress—seniority levels and possession of a leadership post—also influences role orientation; senior lawmakers and leaders show less regard for constituent opinion and select the trustee posture more often than their freshmen and nonleader colleagues, who more frequently opt for the delegate orientation.[7]

Thus, policy demands from the public, as opposed to requests from the same source for services, are intermittent. This appears to be the case because the average citizen is not sufficiently involved or observant to find out what the issues are or where his legislator stands on those matters, and to take action on the basis of this information. The flow of communications to Washington is so slight in most situations that the congressman has great difficulty in ascertaining his constituents' policy views. The messages he does receive are unlikely to be representative of district sentiment. Only in extraordinary circumstances can he expect to confront a concerned and aroused citizenry. Despite the necessity to operate on this basis of limited information, members of Congress do assume varying role orientations toward the public. Some—more than a fourth—profess to be unconcerned about popular views and act as trustees, the remainder acknowledge the need to defer to the electorate on at least some policy matters, either as politicos or as delegates. Though data are largely lacking, we would expect that delegates would spend more time trying to assess constituent views, and

[6]Dexter, 1963b, provides further evidence of the existence of these orientations. For additional discussion of these types, see Chapter 1, pp. 20–22.

[7]It is difficult to untangle all these relationships; as Davidson (1969, p. 135) points out, these variables are interrelated. Low-seniority lawmakers tend to be from electorally marginal districts, as are nonleaders; conversely, seniors and leaders often represent safe districts. Leaders, of course, tend to have high seniority. Perhaps the best way to put it is to argue that those legislators who, from the vantage point of the outside observer at least, are least secure—who face a tough reelection fight, have served for short periods, and who have not advanced to leadership positions—are most likely to assume the delegate orientation. The more secure—who win reelection by a comfortable margin, have had long tenure, and who have attained leadership posts—feel freer to act as trustees.

would behave more in keeping with those views than would their colleagues of the trustee persuasion. We will return to such questions, in the broader context of representation, in Chapter 13.

PUBLIC SUPPORTS FOR CONGRESS

Although policy demands from the public are erratic and hard to assess, nonetheless the legislative system, if it is to survive, depends upon continued support from the populace, that is, the citizenry must at the very least tolerate Congress—consider it legitimate—or, preferably, hold positive views of the institution. If supports, the favorable sentiments and actions consequent to them, fall below some critical, though undefined, level, the system will be unable to endure and will undergo radical change or cease to exist. Easton (1965a, pp. 124–126; 1965b, parts 3–5) distinguishes two sorts of supports— diffuse, or general feelings of acceptability not tied to any definite referent; and specific, or positive reactions resulting directly from particular outputs. Supports from the executive branch and the interest groups, as noted, tend to be of the specific variety; the President, bureaucrats, and lobbyists seem favorably disposed toward Congress because it has, over the years, responded sufficiently to their demands.

By contrast, popular support is more likely to be of the diffuse sort, stemming more from generally favorable feelings than from positive reactions to the legislature's specific accomplishments. This is in keeping with the low issue-content of citizen political opinion; those who are largely unaware of day-to-day legislative activity are hardly apt to judge the institution in terms of its particular outputs. Rather it appears that Congress receives support as one branch of a widely venerated governmental apparatus. Americans believe their political arrangements—their "democratic" political system—to be "good" ones, perhaps even the best possible way to organize a national state. At least, heavy majorities, larger than those in other nations, of United States respondents say that the national government "improves conditions," that they are "proud" of their governmental and political institutions, and that they expect to be treated "equally" by their government.[8] More importantly, most Americans possess a "sense of civic competence," a feeling that the government is accessible and that they, as citizens, are capable of exerting influence on it (Almond and Verba, 1965, pp. 136– 145). Though most citizens are never moved to seek to influence the national institutions, they feel that the government would be responsive if they exerted their control. They can support, in other words, a government which they believe to be good, working well, and attuned to their interests. As a result,

[8] Almond and Verba, 1965, pp. 48 (Table 2.3), 64 (Table 3.1), and 71 (Table 3.3). The percentages holding these views are 76, 85, and 83, respectively.

support for all branches—executive, judicial, and legislative—remains high, well above the threshold level.

There has not been, in fact, a serious challenge to the legitimacy of Congress, something not the case with respect to the other branches. Franklin D. Roosevelt confronted the Supreme Court with the so-called "court-packing" plan when the judiciary refused to uphold the constitutionality of a number of New Deal legislative measures; he was, however, rebuffed. The Constitution was amended, limiting the President to two elected terms of office, perhaps as a result of Roosevelt's four successful election campaigns. Congress has avoided such outside attacks: its members have been prompt to move against their colleagues who behave in ways, contrary to the norm of "institutional patriotism," which threaten to discredit the legislative institution; congressmen have responded to adamant demands (e.g., for civil rights legislation in the 1957–1965 period) seemingly in time to head off any very great loss of confidence in the national legislature. In short, while there are periods characterized by the impulse to reform, Congress has not been confronted by a major assault on its basic framework.

Despite this relative freedom from overt attack, there is suggestive evidence that Congress lags behind the other branches of government in popular esteem. A survey of student opinion, conducted by the Harris Poll in 1965, indicated that 39 percent of those interviewed had a "great deal" of confidence in Congress while the comparable figures for the executive branch and the Supreme Court were 49 and 65 percent, respectively.[9] More generally, congressional popularity has ebbed and flowed (Table 9-2); the proportion of the public rating the legislature's performance excellent or good has varied from 26 percent (1971) to 65 percent (1965). Moreover, the opinion distribution has shifted markedly from one year to the next, probably reflecting an indifference toward congressional activity. On the whole, given this lack of concern, the public probably responds to legislative visibility; that is, when Congress is active, does things, passes bills, it earns citizen approval. Such seems to have been the case in 1964 and 1965, and to a lesser extent in 1966, when a sizable portion of the Kennedy-Johnson program was enacted. In 1963 and especially in the period after 1968—when the government, including the legislature, struggled with only marginal success to resolve the Vietnam situation and to curb inflation—congressional outputs were not forthcoming, and the legislature's standing with the public declined as a result.

Other evidence supports this view of a public that evaluates Congress with an unenthusiastic tolerance. Davidson and Parker (1970) find modest support for Congress: 12 percent of a national sample gave the legislative branch a high rating; 25 percent felt it did not perform well; and the re-

[9] As reported in Davidson, Kovenock, and O'Leary, 1966, p. 50. Another survey, this one of 115 members of the Washington press corps, found that the journalist also ranked the President ahead of Congress. See Davidson et al., 1966, pp. 42–44.

mainder, nearly two-thirds of the respondents, displayed mixed reactions about its operations. These authors (1970, p. 11) conclude that "most citizens seemed to harbor positive but measured feelings about Congress. . . . " Many "are neither alienated enough to hold predominantly negative attitudes nor marginal enough to hold no attitudes at all. They have not, however, participated to the point that they can apply discriminating or critical judgments to the political regime" (p. 25). Thus, there appears to exist a wide, but perhaps shallow, reservoir of support for Congress among the American people.

There are at least two possible explanations for this rather indifferent acceptance of Congress. For one thing, diffuse support, simply because it has few specific referents, does not evoke passion. Those citizens relatively well satisfied with the national government give it their loyalty in toto without much genuine involvement in politics, while by contrast those who are relatively less well off tend to look at the government, including the legislative branch, with a more jaundiced eye. Davidson (1970) presents data that provide indirect support for this view. The "mainstream" Americans—the better educated, whites, and those with higher incomes— express a normative preference for lawmakers who assume a tribune orientation. That is, the "haves" willingly settle for representatives who will voice citizen interests. The "have-nots"— the poor, blacks, and those with less education— tend to prefer the inventor ideal, that is, their focus is on solutions to their problems, not merely on being heard. In short, neither group has much reason to get wildly excited about Congress; the numerical superiority of the former accounts for the overall positive evaluation of the national legislature.

TABLE 9-2 Popular evaluations of Congress

Year	Rating		
	Excellent-good (%)	Fair-poor (%)	Not sure (%)
1963	33	60	7
1964	59	33	8
1965	64	26	10
1966	49	42	9
1967	38	55	7
1968	46	46	8
1969	34	54	12
1970	34	54	12
1971	26	63	11

NOTE: The question was: "How would you rate the job which has been done by Congress this past year—excellent, pretty good, only fair, or poor?"
SOURCE: Harris Poll, as reported in *Louisville Courier Journal,* Jan. 13, 1969, p. *B*3, and *Congressional Quarterly Weekly Report,* Mar. 5, 1971, p. 506.

A second possibility is that the legislature is evaluated in terms of popular feelings about the President (Davidson et al., 1966, pp. 59–63). The Chief Executive, as noted previously, is the focal point of a citizen's attention to politics and the government. Opinion data show a correspondence between the public's evaluations of the two branches: when citizens feel the President is doing a good job, they rate the legislature high as well; when they are dissatisfied with the Chief Executive's performance, they give Congress low marks at the same time. Further evidence in support of this view comes from periods of "divided government," when one party controls the White House and the other dominates Capitol Hill. In those circumstances, people who identify with the President's party rate Congress higher than do the partisans of the "out" party, even though the latter controls the legislature. This suggests that "persons of the President's party blithely assume that their party is the government-in-power and that they evaluate all federal institutions accordingly" (Davidson et al., 1966, p. 62). The public seems to expect Congress to aid and abet the President. When Congress acts in this fashion it is rewarded with popular approval; otherwise the legislature is held in lower esteem.

In sum, citizen support for the national legislature is mainly diffuse support. It fluctuates widely, but though apparently unenthusiastic still well within the acceptable limits; even at periods of negative assessment—usually when the government as a whole is inactive or when Congress appears to thwart the President—Americans do not seem to question the basic legitimacy of the congressional institution. Thus there has been no serious attempt to reorganize Congress or to alter its position in the constitutional pattern; at least there has been little or no popular response to the suggestions for reform—made by academic observers as well as by lawmakers themselves—which have been proposed frequently in recent years.[10] Whatever thrust for reform may be generated, while it may win public backing, is not likely to originate in the environment of the legislative system, but rather will in all probability begin at the elite level.

DEMANDS FROM THE SUPREME COURT

Congress also receives demands from the third branch of government—from the federal judiciary and especially from the U.S. Supreme Court. Demands from the courts, however, are of a somewhat different kind than those which originate with the executive, the interest groups, or the public. These latter

[10]It is worth noting that Congress seems sensitive to possible attrition in support, perhaps through the operation of the feedback mechanism. When support declines, the legislators seem prepared, as in 1946 and 1970, to adopt reorganization legislation that gives the impression, perhaps only illusory, of improving the ability of Congress to act on the issues of the day.

are addressed directly to the legislature, requesting that Congress take, or refrain from taking, some particular action. Demands originating in the courts reach Congress in a more circuitous fashion; in the course of deciding cases, the federal judiciary occasionally issues rulings interpreting the Constitution or congressionally enacted statutes. The content of these rulings poses challenges for the legislature, for the decisions may run counter to the lawmakers' interpretations and intentions.

Put another way, the argument is that the courts, and particularly the Supreme Court at the pinnacle of the federal judiciary, act as policy makers in a way generally held to be reserved for the elected branches of government. The power of "judicial review," the authority to interpret the Constitution and statutes and to declare the latter "null and void" when inconsistent with the former, lies at the base of the court's policy-making position. The courts can thus, using the vehicle of specific cases, render decisions which impose limits on what Congress can do, or which enunciate substantive decisions of a sort that the legislature might otherwise be expected to enact.[11] For instance, while it was clearly within the province of Congress to outlaw segregation in the public schools, a majority of the lawmakers were, for almost a hundred years following the Civil War, unwilling or unable to act on this topic. It remained for the Supreme Court, in the landmark case, *Brown v. Board of Education,* to declare, specifically and unequivocally, that segregated schools, even if there were "separate but equal" facilities for different races, were not permissible under the Constitution. Likewise, the Court rather than Congress has been the chief architect of national policies requiring legislative reapportionment and forbidding prayer in the public schools.[12]

Such policy decisions pose problems for Congress; the Court, having prevented the legislature from acting or having interpreted congressional action in a way inconsistent with legislative intent, in essence makes demands on Congress to accept its dictates. The senators and representatives must decide whether to permit the judicial determination to stand or whether to take steps, usually through passage of legislation, to reassert legislative policy priorities. Thus, constitutional amendments were introduced in the Senate to reverse Court holdings with regard to reapportionment and prayer in the public schools. Though neither has yet passed, the purpose of each was to reject the demands for such policies and to substitute the legislature's point of view for that of the judiciary.

The courts do not always make demands of this indirect sort; rather, history suggests that there are recurring periods in which the judiciary seems to render opinions that threaten congressional policy-making prerogatives

---

[11] The Supreme Court, it should be noted, can make policy by the slenderest of majorities, a 5 to 4 vote.
[12] On the courts as national policy makers, see *inter alia,* Schubert, 1960, 1965; Peltason, 1955; Rosenblum, 1955; and Dahl, 1958.

with respect to major issues—e.g., civil rights—which concern major political interests in the nation. The legislature, for its part, is seldom willing to accept court-announced policy initiatives passively, especially when important political relationships are altered. Congress often takes, or seems ready to take, counteractions to reverse the courts; thus, there have been cycles of conflict between court and Congress, with the former making demands by acting as a policy maker in ways which threaten the latter. The legislature acts to reassert its preeminence, and the judiciary, recognizing its inability to compel a hostile Congress, tends to retreat, to mitigate its challenges, in such circumstances.[13]

The tension of the 1954–1959 period illustrates the nature of this inter-branch conflict.[14] The Supreme Court's decision in the *Brown* case, as noted, outlawed segregation in the nation's public schools; Southern congressmen objected to the ruling for obvious reasons and were joined in opposition by other lawmakers who, following a "strict constructionalist" philosophy, felt that the courts should leave policy making to the elected branches of government. Little, however, was undertaken to limit the powers of the Court or to reverse the specific ruling of the Court.

When the Supreme Court embarked on a series of cases relating to the "internal-security" or "Communists-in-government" issue, the antagonism toward the judiciary erupted. On June 17, 1957—a date immediately dubbed "Red Monday" by the foes of the Court—the Court decided four cases in ways that limited the government's ability to deal with what were referred to as "security risks." One case, *Watkins v. United States,*[15] was a direct challenge to Congress itself; the decision held that the legislative power to investigate was limited, that congressional inquiries could be so vague as to deprive a witness of his rights under the due process clause of the Fifth Amendment to the Constitution. In *Yates v. United States,* 354 U.S. 298 (1957), the Court overturned the convictions of fourteen American Communist leaders, convictions obtained under the Smith Act, the major antisubversion law on the federal statute books, authored by Rep. Howard W. Smith (D., Va.), the chairman of the powerful House Rules Committee. Finally, in *Service v. Dulles,* 354 U.S. 363 (1957), the State Department was ordered to reinstate an employee who had been discharged because of doubtful loyalty. Coming on the heels of the *Jencks v. United States,* 353 U.S. 657 (1957), decision, in which the Court held that a defendant was entitled to examine FBI files which supposedly contained detrimental information, the "Red Monday" cases stirred the opponents of judicial power into action. A series of other decisions during this same Court term further exacerbated Court-Congress relations.

13On relations between the Supreme Court and Congress, see Murphy, 1962; and Pritchett, 1961.
14This account follows Murphy, 1962, parts II and III.
15354 U.S. 178 (1957). The second case, *Sweezy v. New Hampshire,* 354 U.S. 234 (1957), applied similar restrictions to state legislative investigations.

A legislative coalition, composed of segregationists and security-minded conservatives and opposed to the Court's use of its powers of statutory interpretation to enunciate policy, sought to impose checks on the judiciary. For one thing, a bill was introduced in Congress to reverse the Jencks doctrine, a bill which removed the requirement, set forth in that case, that FBI files, however confidential, had to be made available to defendants in security cases. Other legislation was also proposed for the purpose of overturning other decisions which some legislators found objectionable. In addition, Sen. William E. Jenner (R., Ind.) introduced a bill to reduce the appellate jurisdiction of the Supreme Court by placing five categories of cases— including those dealing with the loyalty-security issue and those involving state antisubversive laws[16]—beyond the purview of the federal courts.[17] A watered-down version of the "Jencks bill" passed Congress overwhelmingly, and while the provisions of the legislation did not really narrow the Court's original holding very much, its passage was symptomatic of the hostility toward the judiciary present on Capitol Hill. The more restrictive Jenner bill failed in the Senate by a single vote.[18]

The extent of legislative antagonism was not lost on the judges of the Supreme Court. During its 1958 and 1959 terms, the Court backed off; without so much as acknowledging the legislative criticisms, a series of decisions indicated that the justices were prepared to draw back from the logical implications of their earlier opinions (Murphy, 1962, chap. 10). These later holdings indicated that the Court was going to move slowly, if at all; they included a restatement of the investigatory power, giving state and federal legislatures wide latitude to seek needed information, and a broader mandate for governmental agencies to remove suspected subversives from their payrolls. These decisions had the desired result; they effectively defused congressional attacks on the judiciary. This is the usual pattern: legislative counterattacks forcing the Court to reduce its activism, to be considerably more discreet in its policy-making activities.

Major confrontations between Court and Congress, such as that of the 1954–1959 period, are rare; more common are minor skirmishes in which the

---

[16]The Supreme Court had, in *Pennsylvania v. Nelson,* 350 U.S. 497 (1956), struck down the Pennsylvania sedition act and by implication similar statutes in more than forty other states on the grounds that in passing the Smith Act, a federal antisubversion law, Congress had "preempted" the area for the national government, thus superseding the state acts on the same topic.

[17]The Supreme Court, under the Constitution, has "original jurisdiction" over a small set of cases; all other cases fall within the Court's "appellate jurisdiction," that is, reach the Court on appeal from lower courts. Congress controls the types of cases that the Court can hear on appeal, and, theoretically at least, can restrict the sorts of cases appealed to the Supreme Court. Thus one way to circumvent the Court is to change its jurisdiction. Another, of course, is to enact statutes which effectively substitute congressional for judicial preferences. A third way, difficult and seldom used, is to amend the Constitution, as was done when the Sixteenth Amendment was enacted to permit the levying of income taxes, which the Court had forbidden in *Pollock v. Farmers' Loan & Trust Co.,* 157 U.S. 429 (1895).

[18]Five other "anticourt" bills passed the House during this period, but were subverted in the Senate. Murphy, 1962, chaps. 7–9.

legislators act to overturn objectionable judicial rulings. For instance, the Court was overruled on twenty-one separate occasions between 1945 and 1957 ("Congressional Reversal of Supreme Court Decisions," 1958). In seven instances the Court, seemingly moved by sympathy for the social objectives embodied in the legislation, misread congressional intentions, placing too heavy an emphasis on a single, "central purpose." To correct this undue stress on one facet of what the lawmakers viewed as a multipurpose statute, Congress passed new laws clarifying its aims and suggesting that other goals were also central to its intent in enacting the original bill. In another major set of cases, the Court's ruling upset a "common understanding," and all the interested parties, satisfied with the understanding, urged Congress to act to restore the status quo ante. Where the major interests involved do not agree, Congress is substantially less likely to act and Court rulings will more probably survive legislative scrutiny.

In sum, conflict between the judiciary and the legislature is intermittent, reaching crisis proportions only infrequently, but breaking out in less visible controversies at shorter intervals. Where Court decisions make policy that Congress could make—where the Court "usurps" congressional prerogatives, that is—where the justices misread legislative intent, or where the judiciary disrupts satisfactory working relationships, Congress is likely to respond by acting to reverse the Court. Such legislative action constitutes the congressional response to the demands implicit in Court rulings.

Though these clashes occur rarely, the individual senators and representatives will probably hold orientations toward the federal courts.[19] Some will be pro-Court, tending to feel that Congress should, in most instances, defer to judicial declarations; others will be anti-Court, feeling that the legislature, as an elected body, should reassert its own priorities in the event of conflict with the judges. Others, perhaps most congressmen, will respond more to the situation at hand than to the Court in general. For one thing, the justices change as time passes, and with alterations in personnel come new policy-making tendencies. In the 1930s, for example, a "conservative" Court thwarted the New Deal, and incurred the wrath of the "liberals." Two decades later, the liberal Warren Court pushed ahead with its antisegregation and reapportionment policies, and it was the conservative elements in Congress which opposed the Court.[20] Moreover, the kind of policy at stake, and its effects on differing constituencies may well influence the orientation of individual lawmakers toward the Court. Major issues—such as civil rights and school prayers—which are deeply felt by his constituents may incline a congressman

[19] It must be admitted that there is virtually no data to support the speculation of this paragraph.
[20] Richard Nixon's appointments of Warren E. Burger, a "strict constructionalist," as Chief Justice and Harry A. Blackmun and his nominations—both eventually rejected by the Senate—of Clement Haynsworth and G. Harrold Carswell, both "conservatives," indicate that a President, given several new members to appoint, may alter the character of the Court. Nixon's intentions seem clear: to turn the Court to the political right.

to take an anti-Court stance, while less visible and emotional questions may permit a pro-Court orientation. Behavior in these circumstances, then, is likely to reflect both basic feelings toward judicial power and the situational context of the moment.

JUDICIAL SUPPORTS FOR CONGRESS

If judicial-legislative clashes provide material for headline writers, this should not obscure the fact that controversies of the sort described occur only very rarely. The Court only seldom gets "out of line" with the lawmaking majority as indicated by voting alignments in Congress; on such occasions, as we have seen, conflict follows. Ordinarily, however, the Court reflects, is a part of, the dominant political coalition of a particular political era, and as such serves far more often to legitimize the policy choices of that alliance than to assert its own distinctive preferences (Dahl, 1958). In other words, the actions of the courts, in the vast preponderance of instances, support the legislative outputs of Congress, as approved by the President.

Where conflict occurs, it may be the result of the inability of the Chief Executive to place men sympathetic to his policy views on the Supreme Court bench. For instance, though the average turnover on the nation's highest court is one new justice every twenty-two months, Franklin Roosevelt had to wait for more than four years before he was able to replace even one of the appointments made by his Republican predecessors. The court fight of the 1930s then, was, in part at least, the product of historical accident which kept a conservative court intact during a period of rapid, and liberal political change. One would guess that such clashes will occur very infrequently. Richard Nixon, coming to office at a time which appears to some observers to be the first stage of an era of political change comparable in some respects to the New Deal period, had four court vacancies to fill during his first term as president; his nominations reflect his desire to reshape the Court. In short, most often the Court reflects the political coloration of the elected branches and its decisions tend to ratify the decisions of those branches.

The basic supportive nature of Court action can be seen in another way. During the whole history of the exercise of judicial review down to 1958, according to Dahl's (1958) calculations, the Court held only eighty-six provisions of a mere sixty-four acts of Congress to be unconstitutional. These pronouncements came in only seventy-eight of the thousands of decisions that the justices have rendered; the overwhelming majority of Court rulings pose no challenges for Congress. To be sure, these figures understate the degree to which the Court makes demands upon the legislature, for some clashes have resulted from statutory interpretation by the judiciary. Yet controversy over the meaning of laws is only a little more common than disagreements over constitutionality; the conclusion remains that most judicial actions are consonant with legislative policy determinations, that the Court supports rather than undercuts Congress. Judicial acceptance of most of the legislative output unquestionably contributes to the survival of the congressional system.

SUMMARY

The public and, in its own special, indirect way, the judiciary, make demands upon Congress. These demands, however, are substantially less sustained than those originating with the executive or interest groups. Individual citizens are seldom worked up over specific issues of public policy and, as a result, they seldom bother to communicate their policy views to their representatives in the House and Senate. Consequently, the lawmakers do not often possess reliable information concerning the substantive positions that their constituents take; none of the most readily available sources—the mail, the press, postcard opinion polls, or personal contacts—provide reliable data on district sentiments. The congressmen are, thus, except on the most salient issues—which are few and far between—left to their own devices in deciding how to act. Yet because there is no certainty about when the "folks back home" will become aroused, members of Congress must relate to their constituents; some act as delegates, agents for those who elect them; others assume a trustee orientation, using their own independent judgment; and the remainder, a majority, act as politicos, choosing when they will mirror their constituents' opinions and when they will go their own way.

The Supreme Court, the highest of the federal courts, also makes demands upon Congress in the form of decisions which challenge the legislature's intentions in enacting statutes or which impose judicially determined policies in subject-matter areas where Congress assumes it should be the preeminent decision maker. Such holdings require the lawmaker to act, in each situation, to defend judicial power—a pro-Court orientation—or to assert congressional power—an anti-Court orientation. Knowledge of the individual legislator's feelings about the judiciary should help us to understand the congressional system's response to demands originating in the judicial branch.

Both the general public and the federal courts lend support to the congressional system as well; each tends, in the overwhelming proportion of cases, to sustain legislative activity. The citizenry, indifferent to specific issues most of the time, accepts Congress as an integral part of a revered governmental apparatus. While popular opinion about legislative performance vacillates, seemingly with the visibility of congressional action and the degree of legislative support for presidential programs, the level of support has remained well above the danger point, at which the legitimacy of Congress would be jeopardized. Likewise, the courts uphold most legislative activity, usually deferring to the policy enactments of the elected branches. Only very rarely does the judiciary act to substitute its policy preferences for those of the lawmakers; most often the Court is part of the dominant national political coalition. In short, while attention centers on controversy, the more normal situation is for the public and the judiciary to support Congress, not to challenge its legitimacy.

We have now added intermittent pressures and supportive opinion from the public and the courts to the more persistent inputs to the legislative system from the executive and interest groups. The congressional environment, thus, is the origin for a relatively large number of demands and supports for the legislature; each lawmaker in considering how to perform the basic output functions of Congress must take account of the desires of the President, the pressure groups, the public, and the courts. Since these sources of inputs will hardly ever be in complete agreement, the senator or representative will inevitably experience role conflict; he will have to decide to which environmental influence he will respond. His orientations toward each of these forces—reflecting among other things his own beliefs, his prelegislative experiences, and his appraisal of the political importance of these elements— as well as the nature of the situation in which he must act, will be relevant to his ultimate choice.

Also involved in behavioral decisions, of course, will be the individual lawmaker's position within the legislative system—his party affiliation and post, if any, within the party hierarchy; his committee assignment and any leadership position on the panel; his relationship to the rules of procedure; and his involvement with the norms and informal organizations of Congress. Put another way, the congressman is beset by pressures from inside and outside the system and he must act after resolving, in some fashion or other, the conflicting demands from this set of forces. The relative strength of his orientations toward the structures and processes internal to the system, described in Part 1 of this book, and toward the inputs from external sources, treated in Part 2, will, given the situational context at hand, go far toward determining how the individual lawmaker will act, and the sum of individual actions, in a sense, constitutes what Congress will do. To use another image, the behavior of congressmen is, in effect, the resultant of the intersection of sets of forces internal and external to the legislative system. The ways in which the senators and representatives behave, and thus the modes by which Congress produces its outputs of policy decisions, oversight, and representation, are the central topics to which we now turn, in Part 3 of this volume.

PART

3

Outputs of the Congressional System

CHAPTER TEN

Lawmaking 1: Getting to the Floor

To this point, we have identified the major forces—both within and without the legislative system—to which the senators and representatives must relate. The internal features of Congress—the structures of the legislature, the rules that govern the ways in which the legislature operates, and the processes by which inputs are converted into outputs—are characterized by fragmentation and decentralization. The ability to influence congressional decisions, in other words, is widely shared, especially in the smaller Senate where a relatively large number of committee and subcommittee assignments allows each lawmaker to find a niche in which he can wield substantial influence over legislative outcomes. Each lawmaker, however, must contend with the party leaders and must operate within the rules, both formal and informal.

The external environment of Congress directs demands, but also extends supports, to the legislature. While these environmental forces—the executive, the pressure groups, the unorganized public, and the judiciary—have been treated separately and sequentially, it must be remembered that all may be, and the first two mentioned almost always are, active simultaneously and seldom with unanimity on the same side of any issue. On most questions before Congress, the individual lawmaker will be urged to follow one course of action by some parts of the executive branch, some involved interest groups, and some segments of the concerned citizenry. Similar sets of influences will implore him to act in other ways.

The representative must, as a result, resolve such conflicts on all but the most trivial issues. And he must do so under conditions of uncertainty and imperfect information. In effect, he must answer a number of questions either explicitly or implicitly before he acts: (1) How will any proposed behavior affect his standing within Congress? With his fellow partisans? With those with whom he serves on committee? With those with whom he associates informally? (2) How will any proposed action affect his political future? his relationships with local political leaders? with important groups and individuals in his constituency? (3) How will the things he might do affect his position in the Washington community? with the President? with the various agencies and bureaus? with the lobbyists? The answers to such queries will, in the light of his own beliefs and values and within the situational context at hand, go far toward determining how the lawmaker acts. This is not to say these are "rational" calculations, but only to suggest that some assessment of the costs and benefits of any action is likely to precede the action itself.

To put it another way, role conflicts will be settled according to the weight attached to, or the strength of, the congressman's various role orientations. The behavior of the lawmakers, and in a sense the outputs of Congress, will flow from the resolution of these inevitable conflicts. It is to this concern—the congressional performance of these lawmaking, or policy-making, oversight, and representational activities—that this and the succeeding chapters are addressed. Basically we will look to see the conditions under which, and the processes by which, Congress produces the outputs expected from it. Such legislative activity will, to repeat, reflect the forces, internal and external to the system, operative at any time and the orientations of the senators and representatives toward those forces.

LAWMAKING: SOME GENERAL CONSIDERATIONS

We begin with the lawmaking function because, first of all, the legislators themselves seem to consider it the most important of their activities. One study of the allocation of congressmen's time indicates that nearly two-thirds (64.6 percent) of the lawmaker's workweek is devoted to "legislative" tasks, including committee work and general duties.[1] Policy making (or lawmaking), of course, embodies, in Easton's (1965a, p. 50) oft-quoted phrase, "authoritative allocations of value." In other words, legislative enactments distribute and redistribute resources, imposing costs and conferring benefits, taking from some interests and citizens and giving to others. Medicare, for example, exacted higher social security taxes from working people under sixty-five

---

[1] Saloma, 1969, Table 6.5, p. 184. Note that the lawmakers' staffs, by contrast, commit only 14.3 percent of their time to "legislative support" (p. 185). Thus it appears that the average legislator delegates other activities to his staff while retaining the lawmaking chores as his own obligation.

years of age in order to provide medical services for the elderly. Other legislation may give symbolic rather than tangible rewards. The Voting Rights Act of 1965 made it public policy that all Americans, regardless of color, should have equal access to the ballot box; for many, however, such a pronouncement had only psychic value, for they still encountered obstacles to full electoral participation. Policy decisions, as incorporated in congressional actions, offer benefits and assess costs unequally, and much of the political conflict which surrounds proposals reflects the competition of the interested parties for favorable allocations.

Nor is lawmaking activity unrelated to the oversight and representational outputs of Congress. While we will treat each separately, it should be remembered that each legislative function is closely intertwined with the others. Laws set down guidelines for administrative agencies, expectations that are enforced through oversight activities. Control and representation bring lawmakers into contact with those who carry policies into effect and those who feel the effects of policy; such contacts may indicate the need for new laws to remedy defects in existing statutes or to improve the quality of their administration. In short, policy choices stimulate feedback (see Chapter 1, pp. 6–7 and 22) which, in the form of new or renewed demands, may require congressional reconsideration of current allocations.

The content of legislative policies, we will argue, is highly likely to reflect the decentralized character of the institution which makes them, and it may be worthwhile, at this point, to review some of the features of the congressional system that shape the policy-making process. While the ultimate decisions are made on the floor, most often by a roll call vote, the real choices more frequently come before a bill reaches the floor. The central fact is, of course, that the autonomous committees make the major choices and that these are merely ratified at a later point in the proceedings by the entire chamber. What was true in Woodrow Wilson's (1956, p. 66) time remains largely true in the contemporary Congress: ". . . there is one principle which runs through every stage of procedure, and which is never disallowed or abrogated—the principle that the Committees shall rule without let or hindrance." In short, the "real work" of Congress is concentrated in the committee rooms.

While basically correct, Wilson may have exaggerated to some extent; there are limits to what the committees can do. The norms of both houses impose some constraints on the committees; the panels are limited by the operation of general expectations about appropriate behavior. These limits are broad; the idea of reciprocity suggests great tolerance for the activities of others, but if a committee goes too far, the rules provide for ways to circumvent it. Only in the rare case where a determined majority feels itself thwarted by a committee espousing a minority position will these techniques prove useful.

Such conditions are not often met, and the result is that the committees possess considerable latitude to act as they see fit and to convert their determination of policy into the judgment of the full chamber. In this process, the committee chairman looms large. He has substantial control, again within rather broad limits, of what his committee (or subcommittee) does and how it goes about its business, and the committee decisions will often reflect his values (or "biases") and his orientations toward the lawmaking function of the legislature.

What all this means, in sum, is that the first series of steps in the process of policy formulation is the necessity for proposals to move through the committee stage. Committee consideration, especially in the prestige panels, may go far to determine congressional output. The remainder of this chapter explores the process by which the committees of Congress handle legislation prior to sending it to the floor for the final phases of policy making.

The committees, as noted, do not operate in a vacuum. Rather, they are limited in several ways. We have already seen (Chapter 6) how individual committees develop their own particular work styles reflecting the goals of the members, the operating premises of the committee, and the expectations, often constraining, of the full chamber. These normative patterns limit the ways in which the various panels approach their lawmaking chores. In addition, there are situational restraints as well; the panels are influenced by the same forces which impinge on Congress as a whole (Saloma, 1969, pp. 99–107). For one thing, the partisan division within the legislature may be crucial; the closer the division between the parties the more limited is policy output likely to be.[2] For another, the nature of the opposition to particular proposals may be important; the more intense the minority, the more willing it may be to exploit all the intricacies of the rules to block a bill. Related to this is the extent of public involvement. The more involved the public becomes, the more difficult it will be for a committee simply to ignore and thus bury a bill. The commitment of the President is relevant also. If a legislative item ranks high on his list of priorities, he may use his limited resources to secure its passage; proposals less crucial to his program will, to a far greater extent, be left to the mercy of the congressional committees. In short, norms, rules, and situations all structure the committees' treatment of policy initiatives.

ROLE ORIENTATIONS TOWARD LAWMAKING

Before turning to the lawmaking process it will be well to indicate that members of Congress approach that process from differing perspectives, that is, hold different orientations toward the policy-making function. Two

---

[2]Manley (1970, p. 381) concludes: "Far from discounting the policy importance of elections, a study of Ways and Means leads to the conclusion that electoral stability or change is very significant in the subsequent policy-making process and the outputs of that process."

orientations dominate this set of purposive roles: the tribune and the ritualist (see Table 10-1). The former refers to a focus on the citizenry; the tribune sees himself as a spokesman for the people, as a man who must, above all else, serve popular needs and desires. His primary referent, thus, is outside the halls of Congress. The ritualist, on the other hand, responds first and foremost to forces internal to the legislature; his focus is on interpersonal relationships with his colleagues and on the rules and procedures, both formal and informal, which govern his chamber. The ritualist is, as a result, likely to act in accord with the norms, as a specialist on a narrow range of topics.

The remaining purposive role orientations are less common; no frequency exceeds 10 percent of the representatives' choices. The inventor, for instance, the man who sees himself as the creator of new policies, is only infrequently found in Congress. Given the widespread acceptance of presidential initiative in the legislative process, it is not startling to discover that congressmen do not generally feel obligated to formulate overarching solutions to the great issues of politics. More surprising, perhaps, is the scarcity of lawmakers selecting the broker orientation. In a legislature where bargaining is the chief mode of conflict resolution, it is certainly reasonable to expect significant numbers to see their role "not only to compromise and arbitrate, but also to coordinate and integrate conflicting interests and demands" (Wahlke et al., 1962, p. 256). Yet only a handful of House members see such activity as their primary task. Finally, virtually no representatives gave responses which fell into the opportunist category; apparently few lawmakers serve in Congress without becoming in some way involved in the work of their chamber. The norms of hard work, specialization, and institutional patriotism, of course, discourage the candid admission that one's real concerns lie outside the legislative halls.

These role orientations, it must be pointed out, are not mutually exclusive; a congressman can clearly hold more than one. For example, it is surely

TABLE 10-1   *Purposive role orientations among congressmen*

Orientation	All (%)	Democrats (%)	Republicans (%)
Tribune	47	40	59
Ritualist	41	45	35
Inventor	7	11	0
Broker	4	4	3
Opportunist	1	0	3
Total	100	100	100
N	(87)	(53)	(34)

SOURCE: Data collected by Roger H. Davidson, David M. Kovenock, and Michael K. O'Leary and made available through the Interuniversity Consortium for Political Research.

possible for a tribune to represent the people by acting as a ritualist or a broker. He may seek to advance popular interests as he perceives them, by working within the context which the rules and folkways prescribe or by attempting to negotiate compromises which yield him part of what he desires to attain. Conversely, the ritualist may argue that in following the dictates of the procedural rules and norms he can best work for those who elected him; moreover, he may do so by engaging in brokerage activities. In fact, the compatibility of the broker role with the tribune and ritualist orientations may account for the low frequency with which lawmakers talked about the former; negotiating and compromising may simply be normally associated with each of the other orientations.

Davidson's (1969, pp. 78–97) study, in addition, suggests some of the characteristics associated with the various purposive orientations. First of all, as Table 10-1 indicates, party affiliation makes a difference. Democrats, perhaps reflecting the large Southern component within the party, are more likely to focus on internal process and thus to assume the ritualist stance; Republicans, by contrast, perhaps because of their minority status, are more often externally oriented and, in consequence, more frequently tribunes. Prelegislative experiences also matter. Lawyers are more likely then legislators with business backgrounds to be ritualists; in view of the legal concern for proper procedures, this is predictable. Finally, position within Congress is relevant. Freshmen representatives, nonleaders, and non-Southerners, especially those representing suburban districts, tend to be tribunes while more senior lawmakers, those from the South, and those in leadership positions more often select the ritualist orientation. Newly elected members, without the experience that comes with seniority, uninitiated in the ways of the chamber, not yet leaders, and perhaps representing well-educated and relatively interested constituents—such as tend to reside in suburban districts—are likely to be closely attuned to those who elected them and thus to be tribunes. With the passage of time, as they acquire seniority and experience in the House, these lawmakers tend to focus more on the internal issues and more frequently to assume the ritualist posture. In any case, the evidence suggests that the legislator's background and his position within Congress affect the purposive role orientation he adopts. Furthermore, we may assume that his orientation, in turn, influences the ways in which he approaches his congressional duties.

DRAFTING THE BILL

In the light of all these factors—the lawmaking situation at hand and his orientations toward his policy-making duties—the congressman acts on specific measures. These proposals, as is the case with most policy initiatives, seldom originate in Congress but rather come in the form of demands from outside the legislative chambers. The President is the chief source of policy inputs and he is supported by coalitions of political interests, including executive branch personnel, interest groups, and interested citizens, as well as members of Congress.[3] These proposals are designed to win legislative approval; much thought goes into assembling winning political coalitions and into mobilizing that backing behind bills that can pass. Thus the drafting process is the first stage of the legislative struggle, and the first tactical goal of sound draftsmanship is to write a bill that the committee to which it is referred will treat sympathetically.

In drafting their proposals, policy advocates have the committee of reference, and especially its chairman and ranking minority member, very much in mind. Put another way, the form as well as the content of a bill are intimately related to its prospects for clearing the committee hurdle, and strategic choices are made accordingly.[4] Legislation that wins the widest range of support, inside as well as outside the legislature, is the ideal, of course. How best to achieve these objectives—congressional acceptance without undue policy retreat—is the draftsmen's strategic problem.[5] A number of issues must be faced in this connection.

What to ask for? The first difficulty which the legislative strategists must confront is the question of what to ask for. The quantity of authority or money to seek may prove a thorny issue; the problem is to balance what is needed to accomplish the policy aims to be embodied in the bill against what Congress, or more accurately the crucial committee in each house, is likely to give. To ask for too much is to risk being defeated and getting nothing; conversely, to demand too little is to risk a congenital inability to achieve the desired goals.

Similarly, there is the problem of how to allocate the power or funds sought. Should a new agency be created to run the new program or is there an existing agency or department which is both willing and able to do the job? If the relevant congressional committees have a high regard for a particular bureau, it may enhance the bill's prospects to give the authority to that agency. To follow this course, however, is to face the possibility that a new policy will become caught up in the web of bureaucratic procedures which characterize an ongoing organization and, as a result, will not be im-

[3]To mention one, and perhaps atypical, example, the Economic Opportunity Act of 1964, a central element in the War on Poverty, crystallized in the executive branch where a task force headed by R. Sargent Shriver, Director of the Peace Corps, drafted a bill after paying "explicit attention . . . to outside clienteles" and devoting considerable effort to "win over numbers of businessmen, economists, local officials and welfare workers." President Johnson sent the bill to Congress accompanied by a message urging its passage. See Bibby and Davidson, 1967, pp. 230–238, quotation at p. 235.
[4]On the tactical choices at the drafting stage, Gross, 1953, pp. 198–218 remains the best source. Much of what follows draws on this work.
[5]On the handling of such problems, see Bibby and Davidson, 1967; Eidenberg and Morey, 1969, chap. 4; and Bailey, 1950, chap. 3.

plemented in the most desirable fashion. On the other hand, if the committee is hostile to an existing agency, or if the bureau seems ill-equipped to handle the program, it is preferable to create a new administering agency.[6] The difficulty, of course, may come where the committee favors an organization in which the proponents of the policy have little confidence. One way out of such a dilemma is to draft the bill with greater or lesser specificity. Where confidence in the potential administering agency is low, greater care may be taken to write legislation very specifically so that there is minimal discretion left to the bureaucrats. More general and more vague provisions are acceptable where the administrative prospects are favorable.

Finally, there is the not insignificant matter of securing the resources to carry out the new policy. Generally, this question relates to a formula for raising the needed revenues and for distributing them. It is clear that legislative provisions which do not adequately allocate the burdens will be opposed by interests which feel discriminated against and by the congressmen who speak for those interests. Draftsmen must seek acceptable distributions of the costs and benefits of the programs they seek to advance.

The form of the legislation A second set of issues pertains to the proper form in which to cast the measure. It may be possible, in a few situations, to avoid a bill altogether. A resolution or an item in an appropriations measure may have the same effect as an authorization and arouse little or no opposition; John F. Kennedy attempted to establish a department of urban affairs by using his authority to propose executive-branch reorganizations, but Congress rejected this move, and an equivalent department was later created by formal legislative action. Almost all major policy moves, excluding perhaps some in the foreign policy sphere and a few instances where policy flows from judicial determination, must receive a congressional stamp of approval and thus must move through the legislative process, beginning with committee consideration.

Perhaps the central choice for the bill's drafters is whether to have an omnibus bill or a series of narrower measures. The former, consisting of a set of related but separable proposals joined together in a single bill, has certain appealing attributes. For one thing, the linking of several policies is likely to attract considerable attention. This visibility may be enough to arouse and sustain citizen and group interest sufficient to win committee approval and eventual passage. By the same token, however, great publicity may stimulate the bill's opponents to organize and, as a result, may hinder the legislation's progress. Moreover, some provision, with no chance of passage as a single item, may gain approval as a less central and controversial part of a larger package.

[6]In drafting the Economic Opportunity Act of 1964, a mixed strategy was followed in this regard. The Job Corps; VISTA, a domestic version of the Peace Corps; and the controversial community-action programs were to be administered by a new agency, the Office of Economic Opportunity (OEO) but the Neighborhood Youth Corps was to be run by the Labor Department. Bibby and Davidson, 1967, p. 237.

An omnibus measure, in addition, may facilitate the bargaining (or "log-rolling") which is the chief mode of legislative decision making. Joining a number of items together may help assemble a winning coalition, for each potential ally can be given some provision to secure its support. Each member — whether the President, executive bureau, interest group, or legislator— has some stake in moving the bill ahead and should act accordingly. In the same vein, a multifaceted bill may contain extra provisions, added solely for the purpose of being jettisoned in negotiations with the opponents of the legislation. These superfluous items can be sacrificed, as bargaining counters, in order to protect the major sections which embody the goals most important to the bill's proponents.[7] Finally, the prospects for gaining referral to a friendly committee are enhanced in an omnibus bill, for judicious drafting may enable an entire piece of legislation to be sent to a favorably disposed panel where some items, if introduced separately, would go to hostile bodies.

On the other hand, a narrowly focused bill may have comparable advantages. By restricting public attention, a narrow-gauge bill may avoid controversy; its concerns may not be of sufficient interest to a large enough group for it to become a matter of importance. It may advance, through the efforts of those backing it, while other matters occupy the center of the committee, or chamber, stage. Moreover, the task of drafting is simplified in the more limited context of a restricted purpose bill. The choice of an omnibus or more specific piece of legislation will, of course, reflect the calculations of the drafters as to the form most likely to achieve their policy objectives; the nature of the committee to which the bill will be referred, including the position of the chairman within the panel, will be among the considerations taken into account.

How specific a bill? A final set of questions which the drafters must consider pertains to the specificity of the various statutory provisions proposed. The amount of detail included in a draft bill may affect congressional treatment. The absence of specificity may keep a coalition intact; too much detail, especially in the usual situation of limited resources, may cause those who feel slighted by the draft proposals to join the opposition.[8] Conversely, however, too little detail may appear to be deception, an effort to confuse

---

[7]This seems to have been the tactic of President Kennedy in proposing what eventually became the Civil Rights Act of 1964. Speculation has it that such provisions as the fair employment practices section were included for bargaining purposes only, with no real hope that they would survive. That they were included in the final version, so the argument runs, is attributable to a failure on the part of the opposition leadership in the Senate, notably Richard Russell (D., Ga.), to calculate correctly the extent of support for the bill. Rather than use the threat of a filibuster to exact concessions, as they had done in 1957, the opponents tried to defeat the whole bill, only to discover, when it was too late, that the proponents had the votes to invoke cloture—cut off debate—and pass the bill. See *Congressional Quarterly,* 1968, p. 58; Sundquist, 1968, pp. 259–271, and on the 1957 bill, Shuman, 1957.

[8]Unable to satisfy all the welfare groups interested in having their own pet programs incorporated in the community-action title of the Economic Opportunity Act (1964), the drafters of the bill simply deleted all specifications from the act, and "Congress did not seem to notice the omission." Bibby and Davidson, 1967, pp. 236–237.

the issue and to mislead the opposition. In the same vein, there is the matter of precision and intelligibility. The greater the specificity, perhaps desirable to make legislative intentions clear and to limit the discretion of those who will administer the programs, the greater the risk that the text will be so precise as to be unintelligible to many legislators, who as a result may be skeptical about the bill. Finally, bill writers usually seek to keep the linkages between the various sections of the legislation as loose as possible; where interconnections are minimal, elimination or modification of one section—either during committee or chamber deliberations, or in judicial proceedings which follow passage—will not affect the remaining sections.

Thus, drafting a bill has numerous tactical implications; what is included in the bill, the form in which the provisions are cast, and the detail in which policy proposals are spelled out all contribute to the ways in which Congress treats a policy request. The draftsmen's choices may affect the committee to which the legislation is referred, thus determining the identity of the chairman who will wield substantial influence over the bill's fate. The terms of the draft will provide the basis for the initial phase of negotiations leading to the creation of coalitions for and against the policy at issue. What is sent to committee, in short, sets the frame of reference for much of the legislative process which follows referral.[9]

IN COMMITTEE: HEARINGS

The draft, when completed, is introduced in each house and referred to the committee that under the rules has jurisdiction over the subject matter contained in the bill. Occasionally, as noted previously, two or more panels may claim jurisdiction and the full chamber may have to decide to which committee the bill will be sent. Most often, however, there is no controversy and the legislation goes directly to the appropriate committee. Here it is at the mercy of the panel, and particularly of the chairman, for the extraordinary procedures that make it possible to circumvent the committee—discharge, suspension of the rules, and the like—are seldom invoked. Most proposals are not taken seriously, having been introduced for the satisfaction of some political interests rather than in the hope of passage; the key to the committee's intentions is whether or not hearings are held. At the hearing stage, the maneuvering for political position continues. Without hearings, a bill will not pass, though if they are held they by no means guarantee passage.

[9] To the extent that members of Congress are involved in the drafting stage, usually as participants in a supporting coalition, we may expect them to act in keeping with their role orientations toward law-making. Thus, tribunes and inventors would be likely to stress the content of the policies written into legislation, resisting strategic compromises which would limit the substantive provisions of the bill. On the other hand, ritualists and, perhaps, brokers would be more inclined to urge the draftsmen to put together a bill which could survive the rigors of the congressional process, including the stage of committee consideration, even at the expense of content.

Purposes Hearings serve a number of useful purposes.[10] The most common justification is that they perform an educational function for congressmen and for the public. The testimony of expert witnesses and those who will be affected by the policy embodied in the legislation will provide the lawmakers with needed information about the bill and its possible consequences. As Fenno (1966, pp. 324–341) puts it, the hearings allow interested lawmakers to seek political intelligence, to discover who will be affected, and with what results, by proposed legislation (see also Wildavsky, 1964, pp. 84–90). Similarly, hearings theoretically make the same information available to interested citizens. In fact, there is little evidence to suggest that a significant proportion of the populace is attentive to them. The hearings do, however, place substantial quantities of data in the public record.

Secondly, and more importantly, the hearings provide the interested parties—the testifying witnesses and their congressional interrogators—with a major opportunity to present their views, to argue as persuasively as possible for their favored policies. From another vantage point, the hearings provide a propaganda forum for those with a stake in the outcome of the committee's deliberations. Group spokesmen can justify their positions; congressmen need to know where the groups stand in order to make their own political calculations. Similarly, the hearings enable senators and representatives to record their own views, accompanied by suitable justification or rationalization. All participants thus help to "make a record" that may serve their interests at later stages of the policy process.

Hearings also facilitate coalition formation by making clear where the various concerned parties stand and by establishing what needs to be done—through negotiations—to cement an alliance sufficient to pass the bill. Grounds for agreement can be discovered in the committee room; compromises to resolve disagreements may also become clear at this stage. Committee revisions, which follow the completion of hearings, may constitute the "contract" among the coalition members on the basis of which they cooperate to work for passage of their desired policies.

On another front, hearings serve to legitimate, or rationalize, the policy decisions that Congress takes. The participants in legislative deliberations are more likely to accept their results as binding if the decisions are reached after an acceptable process has been followed. The hearings, at which all have an opportunity to present the "facts" as they see them, to have their say, and to attempt to persuade the legislative decision makers of the wisdom of their cause offer a legitimate procedure by which to arrive at policy choices. In sum, the hearings serve as a "safety valve" by which most interested parties are allowed to be heard, and thus contribute to making policy in an "acceptable fashion." The high levels of support for Congress, noted above, probably

---

[10] A number of sources treat the committee hearings. Among the best are Gross, 1953, chap. 15; Clapp, 1964, pp. 297–305; and Fenno, 1966, pp. 280–303, 324–343.

flow in part from the widespread acceptance of the fairness of congressional hearings.

Finally, the hearings serve tactical purposes in the campaign for policy enactment. Long hearings, held at the discretion of the committee or subcommittee chairman, may slow the decision-making process enough to permit the political situation to be assessed clearly. By prolonging consideration of a bill, time to build a winning coalition may be gained; the arguments that the witnesses advance may serve the same purpose. Similarly, individual congressmen may avoid commitment, preferring to wait until the hearings conclude and the facts are fully available. For all these reasons—informational, political, and tactical—the hearings are a central feature of the lawmaking process.

Closed hearings Not all hearings are conducted in the kind of open public sessions that facilitate the informational aspects described above; some are held in private, behind closed doors. On some matters, notably relating to the military, executive sessions are essential to protect classified information. More controversial—few would object to privacy for security reasons—is the view that closed hearings encourage candor and serious discussion and, at the same time, remove the lawmakers' temptation to "play to the gallery," to seek publicity rather than to give the bill careful scrutiny. In the same vein, closed hearings may provide a device for excluding interests inimical to the position of the committee chairman, or at least may minimize the attention given to the views of those interests. As many as one-third of committee meetings are not public,[11] though not all private meetings hear testimony; some, perhaps most, are held to amend the bill.

The 1970 Legislative Reform Act sought to open committee hearings more fully. The act included provisions calling for public meetings to conduct regular business as well as to hold hearings and requiring greater publicity for what occurs at such sessions. Thus, Senate committee hearings are to be open except when they consider matters that are confidential or pertain to the national security; House panels are to meet in public unless a committee majority, not just the chairman, decides that an executive session is required. Roll calls taken in both Senate and House committees are to be recorded and announced or printed in the panel's report. Finally, the act permits radio and television coverage of House committee hearings, as has been the case in the Senate, under conditions specified by the committee itself. Thus, individual committees will determine the extent to which the Reorganization bill's intention of reducing secrecy is achieved; it remains too early to see any clear-cut impact of the reform legislation on committee practice. Whether

---

[11] Figures compiled by the *Congressional Quarterly* reveal that between 1953 and 1970, the proportion of closed committee meetings varied from 30 percent (1959) to 43 percent (1968); the average for the 18-year period was 37 percent. Committees vary widely in their use of closed sessions; in 1970 the range was from all executive sessions (House Appropriations) to 7 percent closed meetings (House Education and Labor). See *Congressional Quarterly Weekly Report,* Feb. 12, 1971, pp. 387–389.

changes do occur will depend to a large degree on the willingness of rank-and-file committee members to enforce the new rules against recalcitrant, and still enormously influential, chairmen, thus risking the subsequent reprisals of the latter.

The role of the chairman Whether hearings are open or closed to the public, the committee or subcommittee chairman remains the central figure in the drama. The chairman's preeminent position in his panel enables him to control the hearings, staging them carefully to advance his ideas against those of his committee colleagues, if he chooses to do so (Gross, 1953, pp. 284-298). He decides first of all when to hold the hearings, whether to move fast before the opposition can mobilize or whether to go slowly to give his backers sufficient time to generate support. His discretion includes control over the duration of the hearings as well; he may cut the hearings short when he feels a winning coalition has been formed or to guarantee enough time for full-chamber consideration and, presumably, passage.

The chairmanship also confers the power to use the committee staff as the chairman dictates; this is especially true where staffing is on a partisan basis, with minimal assistance given to the minority (Ripley, 1969*b,* pp. 200-212). The chairman is thus able to use the staff in support of his own views: staffers can conduct research for the purposes of developing justifications for their employer's stand; they can help him conduct the hearing by providing him with questions intended to make witnesses favorable to his position look good or to embarrass those opposing the chairman.

The chairman exercises considerable influence over the hearings in other ways as well. While all interests that want to be heard usually are permitted to testify, the chairman controls the order in which they will appear and the amount of time each will be allotted. He can, if he wishes, give witnesses with whom he agrees a prominence which permits their testimony to overshadow that which hostile witnesses present.[12] Seldom is the chairman's intention stated as clearly as that of Wilbur D. Mills of the House Ways and Means Committee, who told the press that he would hold hearings on President Nixon's 1971 revenue-sharing proposal "not for the purpose of promoting it, but for the purpose of killing it." Similarly, the chairman usually is the first to question the witnesses and, in turn, recognizes others on the committee to continue the interrogation. He is thus able to ensure to a great degree that the witness is questioned in a fashion suitable to himself. He may go so far as to bypass dissident panel members, denying them the opportunity to participate at all.

---

[12] For instance, in Sen. J. William Fulbright's (D., Ark.) celebrated Vietnam hearings, held before his Senate Foreign Relations Committee in 1968, the antiwar witnesses were the first to testify while the proadministration forces were placed at the end of the hearings. In this way, the former got substantial attention in the mass media while the latter appeared only when media coverage began to wane.

The testimony In the light of the foregoing considerations, it is not surprising that the testimony of witnesses before congressional committees is not entirely devoted to the objective statement of the "facts." Rather, as might be expected, the hearings are used by those who appear as propaganda opportunities where they can advance their own ideas and challenge the positions of their opponents. From this perspective, the lawmakers might be able to gain a balanced view of the issues at stake from listening to all the opinions expressed, but there are limitations on the effectiveness of this possibility. For one thing, not all interested parties are represented at committee hearings; unorganized interests such as the poor or disadvantaged are not prepared— either financially or intellectually—to give testimony. For another, the legislators have their own opinions, and are as much concerned to justify their views as to explore the various policy alternatives in detail. Such biases are apparent in the questions put to the witnesses.

Prior to the questioning, the witnesses, beginning most often with executive-branch personnel representing the President and the departments and agencies involved in the programs being proposed and following with the spokesmen for a wide variety of interest groups, read prepared statements either in full or in part, with the full text inserted in the record. The questions, which follow the statements, are friendly or hostile depending on the coincidence of opinion of witness and lawmaker. The intent of the latter is usually to develop information and argumentation in support of his own position. As Keefe and Ogul (1968, p. 209) put it, the interrogation mainly seeks to gain "propaganda advantage, to intensify old loyalties, and to fill out the record." Thus, among the potential uses of hearings, the information-gathering function appears to be a subordinate one (see also Huitt, 1954, and Lutzker, 1969).

Yet it is well not to overstate this point. While it is probably the case that many program initiatives are so broad and complex that it is virtually impossible for interested committee members to explore all of the bill's intricacies, the hearings remain the major opportunity for senators and representatives to satisfy themselves of the wisdom of legislative proposals. This they do by the process of "sampling for information" (Fenno, 1966, pp. 332–341), that is, by focusing their attention on those aspects of the bill that they feel most able to comprehend. Thus, the lawmakers will ask about budget increases or new programs rather than about all items in a bill; they will be interested in program implications for their own states and districts rather than in the broader, nationwide ramifications of the measure; and they will attempt to gauge the qualities of the administrator who will run the program, often in personal terms, rather than to evaluate his technical competence. If they are satisfied on these counts, if they are reassured by this "sample of data," the congressmen are likely to accept the entire piece of legislation, including, of course, those items about which they know relatively little.

The intent of the representative is often easily inferred from the nature and content of his questions. Some inquiries straightforwardly seek information. Others reflect the lawmakers' viewpoints. A friendly interrogation may seek to lead the witness; in extreme form, the legislator may make a lengthy statement of the view that he and the witness share, to which the latter responds only by agreeing totally with the position that the "question" espouses. On the other hand, antagonistic interrogation may seek to impeach the witnesses' veracity, challenge his expertise, or subvert his argument.[13] In short, the participating congressmen will attempt to use the hearings for their own purposes, whether these are broadly political or narrowly informational.

Occasionally, committees will go to some lengths to persuade seemingly reluctant witnesses to testify. The effort may be inspired by a need to obtain otherwise unavailable information, but more often it reflects the search for tactical advantage. Such testimony may permit clarification of the issues; if the opposition can be forced into the open, its position may be made explicit and ways found to undercut its arguments. Failure to appear may seem to

---

[13]Some examples of these various tactics can be seen in the following excerpts from the hearings on the 1968 foreign aid bill, *Hearings* before the Committee on Foreign Affairs, House of Representatives, Ninetieth Congress, Second Session on HR 15263 (Washington, D.C.: Government Printing Office, 1968).

Mr. Hays (D., Ohio): Mr. Battle, Greece is in your area of responsibility?

Mr. (Lucius D.) Battle (Asst. Secretary of State for Near Eastern and South Asian Affairs): Yes, sir.

Mr. Hays: Are you the man who made the policy decision to give the fascist dictatorship in Greece more military equipment?

Mr. Battle: We have not made that decision.

Mr. Hays: There is several million dollars worth on the books.

Mr. Battle: I thought you meant in addition to that. . . . We have not made a decision to resume full military assistance. There is an item carried in the budget . . . on a contingency basis in the hope that they will move toward constitutional government. . . .

Mr. Hays: We have made a decision to recognize them which was done sort of covertly.

Mr. Battle: It is a question of what is meant by recognition here. This is a very complicated legal thing.

Mr. Hays: Why don't we get uncomplicated and just do it simply and say "you are a bunch of nogoodnicks and we don't recognize you?" (Part 2, pp. 259–260)

***

Mr. Fraser (D., Minn.): I have been impressed with what I have been able to learn of the orientation training school in Hawaii. . . . it would seem desirable that this kind of center be established for each of the major regions.

Mr. (William S.) Gaud (Administrator, Agency for International Development): Yes.

Mr. Fraser: . . . I have the impression that in your business . . . that the more money you can put into the education and operationally oriented research, orientation and in-service training, the more rapidly everybody concerned becomes more able to deal conceptually with these very difficult problems of development.

Mr. Gaud: I agree with you. . . . We do relatively little of this and I am sure that it would improve our operations if we could do more of it. . . .

Mr. Fraser: So from your point of view, this all centers on money. . . ?

Mr. Gaud: Yes, sir.

Mr. Fraser: Well, I hope we can give you the support that you need in those areas. (Part 3, pp. 480–481).

indicate that the witness, and the interest he represents, has something to hide, and the lawmakers can play upon their ability to create such an impression to encourage testimony from those they would like to hear and question (Gross, 1953, pp. 293–294).

The testimony of the witnesses, however reluctantly they may have agreed to appear, and the questions that the committee members put to them are recorded verbatim, and in most cases the hearing is published. The printed text, however, is not always a completely accurate transcript; for several reasons, congressmen may edit the record. For one thing, classified information may be deleted to preserve security.[14] Revisions may also be required to "correct errors," that is, to remove objectionable or questionable commentary or to excise a particularly acid exchange among committee members and the witness. What is left constitutes both a source of information, tó the extent that the hearing stressed its data-gathering function, and a propaganda document designed to propagate specific opinions concerning the policy issue at stake.

Participation One important point to make clear about the hearings is that they are very often poorly attended by the committee members themselves. Clapp (1964, pp. 265–266) estimates that from one-third to one-half of the members— the "hard core" of seniority leaders and the present and aspiring subject-matter experts— regularly turn up to listen to the testimony.[15] And not all of these are able to participate in each hearing; even though a legislator is genuinely interested in the topic under discussion, he may feel compelled to assign higher priority to constituency and representational activities or, expecially in the case of the more heavily burdened senators, he may have another, more important, hearing at the same hour. Other legislators will stay away because they are indifferent to the subject in question. It is not unusual to find a single congressman conducting a subcommittee hearing, particularly if the issue involved is less than earthshaking in its import.

We may speculate that participation levels in committee hearings reflect the legislators' role orientations toward committee work. The senior members, having achieved positions near the top of the committee hierarchy, will

---

[14]The following, less-than-revealing, dialogue occurred during the foreign aid hearings of 1968, cited above, note 13.

Chairman Morgan (D., Pa.): General, on page 3 of the statement you refer to the fact that Pakistan is receiving both military and economic aid from Red China and (security deletion).

General (Theodore J.) Conway: Yes, Mr. Chairman, they are.

Chairman Morgan: (Security deletion).

General Conway: Yes, sir, Mr. Chairman (security deletion).

Chairman Morgan: (Security deletion).

General Conway: Not thus far, Mr. Chairman. (Part 5, pp. 794–795).

[15]Carroll (1966, p. 28) reports that "Probably less than ten members of the thirty-two man Committee on Foreign Affairs . . . persistently and actively participate in the deliberations of the group." Such participation levels probably characterize most congressional committees, especially the least prestigious ones.

probably be motivated by leadership orientations or aspirations and thus take part in panel deliberations. Similarly, lawmakers with shorter tenure, who have developed expertise through their commitment to subcommittee work, are likely to get involved because of the expert roles they are able to play. On the other hand, those who possess neither leadership positions nor substantive knowledge are likely to look elsewhere for their legislative satisfactions— to other committees, or to constituency service, for example.

To summarize, committee hearings serve a variety of purposes, not all of them related to the information-gathering rationale most often given to justify the questioning of witnesses. More importantly, the hearings serve as political testing grounds where the possibilities for the creation of coalitions capable of mobilizing a majority are explored. The committee chairman dominates the scene, managing the hearings and utilizing the committee's staff resources as he sees fit, and the hearings may be intended to advance his policy views. The testimony that witnesses present may reflect these facts; it is designed for propaganda and bargaining as well as for informational purposes.

Member participation in hearings is low; only those with positive orientations toward their committee assignment are likely to bother to take part in the panel's deliberations. Yet for those who do participate, the hearings are likely to offer opportunities consistent with their views of the lawmaking process. For the tribune, the hearing provides a public forum where he can speak for those he seeks to represent; it allows him to articulate his conception of popular needs. The ritualist, whose focus is on the rules and norms, has less need to involve himself deeply in the hearings. For him it is enough that they be held, that the ritual be observed; he is more concerned that people have the opportunity to testify, that decisions be reached through proper procedures than with what specific witnesses have to say. For these reasons, he may have less incentive to attend and participate.

Interrogation may serve other orientations as well. The inventor may acquire knowledge; he may get new ideas for innovative solutions to policy problems from the witnesses. The broker may ease his task by discovering, on the basis of the testimony presented, the grounds on which to negotiate a compromise. And even the opportunist, whose interests lie outside the halls of Congress, may find the hearing gives him a chance to gain publicity through his questioning of the witnesses. In short, the legislator's orientation toward lawmaking may be related to the way he approaches the committee hearing.

IN COMMITTEE: THE "MARK-UP"

The hearings concluded, the committee or subcommittee meets in closed session to "mark up" the bill, that is, to amend or revise the draft which was originally referred to the panel. Unfortunately, given the nonpublic character of such deliberations, little is clearly known about the exact nature of the proceedings, but it does seem evident that the basic decisions are made in these executive sessions. The information gleaned from testimony heard at the hearings may be taken into account during these sessions, but it is equally likely that the witnesses serve merely to reinforce the lawmakers' previously held preferences. In any event, the product of the "mark-up" process goes a considerable distance in determining the policy output of Congress on any particular topic.

The committee or subcommittee chairman is the central figure in this phase of activity, as he is at other stages. Under his direction, the bill is read section by section, or even line by line. Discussion of the various provisions and amendments to the existing text are in order as the reading proceeds. Where clarification is needed, the chairman may call upon the committee staff to present their research results; his control over the staff may mean that their reports serve to buttress the chairman's views. Quite often, a skillful chairman can lead the committee members toward agreement by consensus, without recourse to formal voting on amendments.

For example, Wilbur D. Mills (D., Ark.), Chairman of the House Ways and Means Committee, is an acknowledged master at achieving his goals within the committee, usually winning committee approval for legislation that can pass the full House (Manley, 1965; 1969; 1970). Moreover, he seems able to manage affairs to his liking without the use of sanctions, punishments meted out to those who refuse to go along. His influence rests, rather, on more positive bases. For one thing, Ways and Means members recognize Mills' great expertise. He is clearly the master of the intricacies of committee business; few, if any, of the rank and file are his equals on this score. Mills' leadership is, in addition, held legitimate by those on the panel; his chairmanship, by itself, and his conduct in that position, have earned him the approval of his leadership. Thirdly, Mills is adept at bargaining, and he has used his ability to confer rewards to establish "positive relationships with most of the members," relationships which entail considerable member deference to his initiatives. Finally, Manley suggests that most committee members identify with Mills, value their relationships with him, and seek to act in ways which will preserve the association. One such behavior, of course, is to agree with him. Taken together, these resources give Mills great influence and enable him to generate agreements in Ways and Means sessions.

Votes cannot, however, always be avoided, and here the chairman wields additional authority. He casts, in many committees, the proxy votes of absent members, an obvious gain for the position he favors.[16] The same bases of influence which lead to consensus also work to deter rank-and-file panelists from voting against their chairman; this is clearly the case where the committee norms encourage minimal partisanship and genuine efforts to reach agree-

[16] The Legislative Reorganization Act of 1970 barred the practice of proxy voting unless an individual committee adopts a rule permitting the use of proxies. It remains to be seen whether committee majorities will move to impose the restriction on their chairmen.

ment. Even with these advantages, the chairman is sometimes outvoted. Committee voting, in keeping with the character of executive sessions, is seldom recorded; Manley's (1965) investigation of the Ways and Means Committee, however, turned up forty instances in which the voting positions were recorded, and in these cases, Chairman Mills was defeated on only seven occasions.

Not all chairmen, to be sure, are able to take advantage of their advantages as skillfully as Mills. Two recent chairmen of the House Education and Labor Committee, Graham Barden (D., N.C.) and Adam Clayton Powell (D., N.Y.), and A. Willis Robertson of the Senate Banking and Currency Committee have acted in a much more heavy-handed fashion in order to obtain their goals in committee. Barden, for instance, in seeking to block enactment of federal aid to education programs, made no effort to keep his committee to its task. He permitted extended discussion and debate, often failed to call committee meetings, adjourned those he did call if a quorum was not present, deprived the panel members of strong committee staff, and in general, sought to evade the responsibility to act. As a result of such behaviors, the consensus which typifies Ways and Means was notably absent on Education and Labor under Barden (Fenno, 1963; 1970. See also McAdams, 1964; Wilson, 1960; Sundquist, 1968, pp. 346–369; and Bibby and Davidson, 1967, chap. 5).

In short, through various means the committee chairman usually controls the product of his committee. Through persuasion, pressure, or compromise, he is often able to develop a text which is satisfactory to him. Whatever the precise pattern, the final draft reflects the negotiations among the ranking members of the panel, buttressed by the staff specialists on the issue at hand, and the experts on the committee. When these members agree, the remainder of the committee is virtually certain to go along.[17] In some cases, the "mark-up" produces a bill so different from what was initially referred to the committee that the output, labeled a "clean bill," is given a new number and introduced, usually by the committee chairman, as a distinct piece of legislation. In any event, the "mark-up" process determines the policy proposals on which the full House and Senate will act.[18] On occasion, the committee draft may include changes from the original which are designed to impede passage, to make the legislation unacceptable to the majority of the full chamber. That is,

[17]Horn (1970, chap. 5) outlines the process on Senate Appropriations. There the actual mark-up may be preceded by a number of highly informal meetings. The first of these may involve the staff working on matters under the jurisdiction of a particular subcommittee setting down and calculating areas of agreement and matters of controversy. There follows a "pre-mark-up" between the subcommittee chairman and the ranking minority for "coordination" at which, Horn estimates, the various subcommittee pairs decide from 80–99 percent of the outstanding issues. The formal subcommittee mark-up serves mainly to ratify these agreements and to permit the remaining subcommittee members to present their views. The full committee mark-up accepts most of the subcommittee recommendations, treating those few controversial items that remain unresolved.

[18]When a subcommittee conducts the hearings and marks up the bill, there may be an intermediate step interposed. The subcommittee sends the revised bill to the full committee—which may simply approve it, or decide to hold additional hearings and open the bill up for additional discussion and amendment. In the latter case, the process is similar to that described in the text.

the alterations try to create a bill so extreme in its provisions that it cannot be passed on the floor.[19]

COMMITTEE DECISIONS

The content of committee decisions, of course, varies from panel to panel and from issue to issue, and is difficult to generalize about; however, a few common elements can be identified and, in addition, decision patterns on a few committees can be specified. First of all, situational factors, noted previously, enter into the legislators' calculations. On one hand, a bill may have no real chance of passage, and the entire committee process—from drafting through the "mark-up"—may merely serve to lay the groundwork for action at some future point in time when conditions change. This seems to have been the strategy of the Medicare supporters in the period before 1964; they knew they could not get a bill out of Ways and Means in the face of the opposition of Chairman Mills. On the other hand, pressure to act may be nearly irresistible and the committee may feel compelled to act. Medicare seems to have reached this point after the 1964 elections gave the Democrats a two-to-one majority in the House; at least, Chairman Mills became a convert at this point and moved the bill quickly through his committee when the Eighty-ninth Congress convened (see, *inter alia,* Sundquist, 1968, chap. 7).

Committee norms are also intimately related to committee output. We have already suggested (Chapter 6) that certain traditional ways of handling committee business seem to develop, and it follows that these folkways will influence the pattern and content of panel decisions. For example, the House Appropriations Committee stresses its obligations to guard the federal Treasury; this norm, in turn, leads to a policy of cutting budget requests. When coupled with the House-imposed expectation that programs will be funded, this leads to an interesting decision pattern: Appropriations tends to give *less* than the administering agencies want but *more* than they received during the previous fiscal year (Fenno, 1966, pp. 352–358). The data, set forth in Table 10-2, make this clear; while only 8 percent of the committee decisions gave agencies more than they requested for the current year, nearly seven out of ten decisions awarded agencies more than they had received in the prior fiscal year.

Another feature of the House committee decision pattern is the incremental character of the changes made by the panel, alterations with regard both to agency requests and to the previous year's allocation. These data are arrayed in Table 10-3, and reveal that most committee choices did not move

---

[19] Southern opponents of federal aid to education pursued such a strategy in the Education and Labor Committee, voting *for* the so-called Powell amendment, which forbade any federal aid to school districts practicing segregation, in order to write a bill which they knew could not pass. See Fenno, 1963, pp. 222–224.

TABLE 10-2 House Appropriations Committee decisions for thirty-six bureaus, 1947–1962

Committee decisions	Number of decisions	% of decisions
(a) Appropriations as related to estimates		
Increases over estimates	46	8.0
Same as estimates	106	18.4
Decreases below estimates	423	73.6
	575	100.0
(b) Appropriations as related to previous year's appropriation		
Increases over last year's appropriation	398	69.2
Same as last year's appropriation	22	3.8
Decreases below last year's appropriation	155	27.0
	575	100.0

SOURCE: Richard F. Fenno, Jr., *The Power of the Purse,* Tables 8.1 and 8.3, pp. 353 and 355. Copyright © 1966 by Little, Brown and Company (Inc.). Reprinted by permission.

TABLE 10-3 House Appropriations Committee decisions: percentage changes, thirty-six bureaus, 1947–1962

(a) Appropriations as a percentage of estimates

% of estimates received	Number of decisions	% of decisions
Over 110.0	7	1.2
100.1–109.9	39	6.7
100	106	18.4
90.0–99.9	300	52.2
80.0–89.9	76	13.2
Below 80.0	47	8.2
	575	99.9

(b) Appropriations as a percentage of previous year's appropriation

% of last year's appropriation received	Number of decisions	% of decisions
Over 150.0	29	4.9
110.1–150.0	171	29.7
100.1–110.0	198	34.4
100	22	3.8
90.0–99.9	86	15.0
80.0–89.9	28	4.9
Below 80.0	41	7.1
	575	99.8

SOURCE: Richard F. Fenno, Jr., *The Power of the Purse,* Tables 8.2 and 8.4, pp. 354 and 356. Copyright © 1966 by Little, Brown and Company (Inc.). Reprinted by permission.

the agency's appropriation far from what it had requested, or what it had received a year earlier. Thus, in more than three-fourths of the cases, the committee's allocation for an agency was within 10 percent of the bureau's request, most falling within the 90–99.9 percent range indicating a small cut in the estimate. Similarly, more than half the decisions gave agencies a sum within a 10 percent range of the previous year's appropriation. On the whole, then, Appropriations cuts requests marginally but allows agency expenditures to increase from year to year. "The Committee thereby cuts the budget but permits a conservative growth" (Fenno, 1966, p. 357). Committee action is thus in keeping with its internal norms and the external pressures it receives. We might guess that ritualists and brokers will be most content with this type of decision pattern; their concern with the "rules of the game" and the discovery of acceptable policy choices should be satisfied with the achievement of consensus. Inventors and tribunes, on the other hand, given their greater concern for specific policy positions, may well be less pleased with these sorts of policy outcomes.

The dollars and cents decisions of Appropriations make that committee more amenable to systematic analysis of its decisions; yet the choices of other committees also seem to fall into discernible patterns. The House Ways and Means Committee, for instance, produces legislation with a conservative bias (Manley, 1970, pp. 239–247). Because the committee seeks to preserve and extend its own influence, it must respond to the expectations of the parent chamber; because the full House has most often in recent years contained a conservative majority, composed of Republicans and Southern Democrats, Ways and Means has reported bills that reflect the voting alignments in the House. Thus, Manley (1970, p. 246) suggests, in the light of the committee's belief that it must, if it is to sustain its central position of influence, reflect House majorities, "new policy changes have . . . been slow in coming and temperate in content."

The foreign policy committees also display characteristic output patterns. House Foreign Affairs operates in an executive-dominated policy environment and gives special emphasis to the foreign aid program; while disagreeing about how to respond to other executive requests, the committee is in solid agreement that the President's foreign aid proposals must go through. Thus, Foreign Affairs acts affirmatively and authoritatively on aid, but is less able to pass on other aspects of American foreign policy (Fenno, 1970). The Senate Foreign Relations Committee, in the period 1947 to 1956, seemed to act on the basis of a norm of internationalism; that is, its decisions reflected a willingness to commit the United States to expanded participation in the affairs of the world. New members, as they joined the panel, were socialized to this norm, and in many cases they cast fewer "anti-internationalist" votes than they had prior to receiving the Foreign Relations assignment. In fact, Farnsworth (1961, p. 155) concludes that "the most effective way to destroy anti-internationalist sentiment in the Senate, other than defeat at the polls, is to make those senators holding such attitudes members of the committee."[20]

Other committees, those which deal with what Lowi (1964) calls "distributive" policy concerns, seem to have developed what might be called "something-for-everyone" decision rules, reflecting the logrolling or mutual non-interference attributes of committee decision making. The House Interior Committee, for instance, aims at legislation that permits its members to get some project for their constituencies; the panel minimizes partisanship in order to optimize the distribution of benefits to the legislators. This constituency service contributes to the reelection prospects of the committee members and the committee's image of "routinized, expert deliberations" carries considerable weight when Interior bills reach the floor (Fenno, 1970). The House Agriculture Committee behaves in a related fashion. Organized around subcommittees for each of the major farm commodities, the committee tends to agree on a general bill which incorporates the separate subcommittee proposals for their own products. Partisanship often erupts when the bills reach the floor, but within the committee bargaining or logrolling, which gives each interest something of what it wants, seems to prevail (Jones, 1961). We may speculate that ritualists and brokers, with their concern for procedures and convention, will prefer service on such committees and will be more willing to subscribe to the decisions reached through compromise and negotiation. Tribunes and inventors, by contrast, with their strong interests in the substance of policy, should find membership on this type of committee less satisfying and should be less willing to withhold their dissenting views.

This evidence, admittedly sketchy, suggests that committee decisions are not random, but rather fall into identifiable patterns, reflecting a customary way of doing business perhaps altered by the exigencies of the situation during the period of decision. On the whole, committees deal with the bills before them in typical, but individualized, ways, patterns that reflect the particular combination of member expectations, chamber norms, committee goals, and panel premises that characterizes each committee.

THE COMMITTEE REPORT

In some cases, of course, committee consideration, even after hearings are held, may lead to a decision not to have a bill. A majority of the members

---

[20]The internationalist orientation of the committee persisted into the mid-1960s when, under the chairmanship of J. William Fulbright (D., Ark.), disenchantment with the Vietnam war and, to a lesser extent, with the foreign aid program led the panel to assume a more critical posture toward heavy American overseas commitments. To some extent, this shift may reflect the quarrel between Fulbright and President Lyndon Johnson over Vietnam. This altered perspective has been carried over into the Nixon administration.

may conclude that existing policies and programs are adequate; they may be unable to agree on the specific provisions of substitute measures; or they may recognize that their proposals would meet defeat on the floor. In other cases, including most of the important bills, especially those that are part of the President's program, the committee will send out a bill, as marked up, with its recommendation. Occasionally, the panel will report a bill which it opposes, attaching a recommendation against passage. At other times, the committee will report out a piece of legislation without indicating any position. Finally, of course, the panel may recommend passage; the committee's affirmative judgment will facilitate acceptance by the full chamber.

A committee report accompanies the bill to floor and becomes one focus of attention during floor consideration. The report contains the text of the legislation and the arguments that the committee majority believes will sustain its "mark-up" decisions. If there is division within the committee, the report will also include any separate views that those opposed to the bill, as reported, choose to file. The report thus becomes a campaign document, a place where those concerned can find the views of the recognized substantive experts on the topic in question and a source of argumentation for those who want to buttress their own positions. In this way, the proponents of various policy alternatives seek to use the report to rally support for their preferences.

The report serves other purposes as well. It is designed, quite intentionally, to be read by others outside the legislative system. For one thing, it is written to establish clearly "congressional intent" in passing the law. The courts, in adjudicating controversies about any statute will refer to the report to discover what Congress desired the bill to accomplish; judicial interpretation often reflects legislative intentions. Similarly, the report aims at executive-branch personnel who will administer the act. Oversight activities, among other things, seek to guarantee "proper" implementation of congressionally enacted policies, and the report often contains explicit statements about how the committee, which will oversee administrative performance, expects the bureaucracy to run the program. The report thus helps the committee communicate with those inside and outside Congress.

SUMMARY

In a highly decentralized legislative system like the American Congress, the committees assume great importance; policies, embodied in legislation, that cannot survive the stage of committee consideration cannot, of course, become law. Much lawmaking activity, as a result, is directed toward assembling coalitions of interests through a variety of bargaining procedures which can, first of all, move a proposal through the relevant House and Senate committees. Efforts to build alliances begin with the drafting of proposals. Provisions of the bill—reflecting the drafters' decisions about what to include, in what form to cast the desired items, and how specifically to spell out the proposals—will be designed to maximize support and to minimize opposition. Some sections may be included solely to serve bargaining purposes, to be discarded in order to retain provisions of higher priority.

The hearings are also important in coalition building. They do serve to ventilate the issues—providing an opportunity for the legislators and interested citizens to inform themselves—but they also offer interested parties—the executive, pressure groups, concerned citizens—a platform from which to state their views and to set forth the conditions under which they will join one or another of the competing coalitions. Moreover, even those who eventually lose out may accept their defeat more gracefully if they have had an opportunity to argue their case; the hearings give them such a chance. What purposes the hearings serve will depend, to a considerable degree, on the desires of of the committee or subcommittee chairman, who exercises substantial control over them.

The chairman is equally important in the "mark-up" phase of the committee consideration. Here, behind closed doors, coalitions are cemented and, if there is to be a bill at all, the panel's preferred form for the legislation is determined. The chairman dominates the proceedings, though in many cases he produces agreement through the give and take of negotiation. In some committees, this process assumes an identifiable pattern, reflecting the operative committee norms, and the decisions of the committee reflect this pattern. Situational exigencies, of course, may lead a panel to depart from its usual type of decision.

The behavior of individual representatives during committee consideration will reflect their role orientations toward committee work in particular and toward lawmaking more generally. Seniority leaders and subject-matter experts along with those who aspire to such statuses will make up the bulk of the "efficient element," or active core of members, which controls the committee-deliberation phase. Others are less likely to participate in committee business. Among the congressmen who are involved, it seems likely that ritualists and brokers, reflecting the importance to these orientations of finding acceptable policy solutions within the confines of the rules and procedures of the system, will ask fewer questions of witnesses, will be satisfied with a bargaining mode of conflict resolution, and will be prone to accept such settlements without audible dissent. Their concern, after all, is more with the process of decision making than with the content of the policy choices. Tribunes and inventors, on the other hand, as befits their focus on actors outside the system, can be expected to stress solutions to policy problems. As a result, they should ask more questions, be more unhappy with "watered-down compromises," and be less willing to remain silent if unsuccessful in committee.

In any event, the lawmaking process continues when the committee makes its report; each bill still must survive on the floor. Although strong panels can often reasonably expect to have their judgments and decisions sustained in the full chamber, nonetheless there are pitfalls which must be circumvented. The committee report provides the focus for continuing the struggle before the full membership of the House and Senate, and to this second phase of the policy-making battle we now turn.

CHAPTER ELEVEN

Lawmaking 2: On the Floor

If a bill clears the committee stage of consideration and is reported—and, of course, most legislation dies without ever emerging from the committee of jurisdiction—it must still survive the floor-consideration phase of the legislative process. While its chances may be considerably improved, there remain formidable obstacles to overcome before final passage is assured. The bill must first get to the floor for debate and decision; it must survive the amending possibilities which exist for its opponents; and it must win, perhaps several times, at the voting stage. Bills passed by one house may fail in the other; often a conference-committee compromise is essential for bills which do gain approval, in different form, from both chambers. All may come to naught, of course, if the President decides to veto rather than to sign legislation that reaches his desk. This chapter seeks to explicate and analyze the steps in the process by which a bill becomes a law and to suggest ways in which the legislators' role orientations may contribute to their responses to pending legislation as it moves through the legislative system. Put in other words, the transformation of demands into outputs will reflect the role perspectives of the lawmakers engaged in the conversion process.

FROM COMMITTEE TO FLOOR: A REVIEW

It may be worthwhile, at this point, to review the course that a bill must traverse before floor consideration actually occurs. These matters have been treated in Part 1, but can be briefly summarized here. First of all, there are ways to circumvent the standing committees entirely or to rescue legislation languishing in committee chambers. Both houses of Congress have discharge procedures by which a majority of the membership can bring a bill directly to the floor; each also makes provision for suspending the rules and passing legislation. In the House the Calendar Wednesday technique provides a way to overcome committee hindrance while in the Senate legislative proposals may reach the floor as nongermane amendments (riders) or by placing a House-passed bill directly on the calendar without referral to committee. These tactics are available, but it should be remembered that the norms of reciprocity and courtesy make most lawmakers loath to resort to such extraordinary procedures.

Once a Senate committee releases a bill, for whatever reason, it goes directly on the calendar from which it will be called up for consideration according to the terms of an agreement between the leaders of the political parties. The larger House interposes the Rules Committee between substantive committee and calendar. That panel must grant a rule before floor consideration can take place. A small but significant number of bills expire because the committee refuses to give a rule or because the rule is rejected by a majority vote of the full membership. The rule, which is most often accepted, defines the conditions under which debate is held—how much time will be devoted to deliberation, what sorts of amendments will be in order, and whether points of order will be waived. Only after the Rules Committee has acted will the bill come up for discussion on the floor. As in the case of the Senate, House party leaders, through consultation, decide when floor consideration will occur.

Thus, there are impediments which may prevent legislation favorably reported by a standing committee from reaching the floor. Most important bills, embodying major policy proposals, do get on the proper calendar and are available for debate on the floor. Some measures, especially in the closing rush immediately prior to adjournment may, however, never be called up for discussion. In any event, much jockeying for strategic advantage may go on between the committee and floor phases of consideration.

DEBATE AND AMENDMENT

Very little systematic evidence on the nature and effects of congressional debate exists; nonetheless some general conclusions can be advanced. There is, for one thing, a general consensus among Capitol Hill observers that only very rarely does floor discussion influence the outcome of legislative deliberations. In other words, the coalitions for and against the committee draft generally hold firm during debate; members are seldom compelled by the power, clarity, or persuasiveness of congressional oratory to change their vote intentions. On some occasions, however, particularly when the contest is exceptionally close, a critical few votes influenced during debate may determine the fate of a major bill or amendment. Thus, while debate infrequently changes many votes, what occurs on the floor may be crucial under special circumstances.

More often floor speeches are not delivered in the hopes of altering legislators' positions, but rather for a variety of other purposes. Discussion may aim at those outside the legislative halls; floor statements permit a congressman to get his views on record, perhaps satisfying interest groups or concerned citizens that he is taking a "correct" stand. Statements may be directed at others within the chamber, but their intent is mobilizing and arousing the speaker's allies rather than converting the opposition. That is, a presentation on the floor, to the extent that other lawmakers listen to it, is more likely to provide them with a rationale, or specific supporting arguments, for the views they already hold than to cause them to change their minds (Clapp, 1964, pp. 140–142; Berman, 1964, pp. 248–256; Keefe and Ogul, 1968, pp. 256–268). Similarly, a speech backing a colleague's bill, whether or not effective in any way, may build credit for the speaker, giving him some claim, however informal and implicit, on the colleague's support at some future date (Matthews, 1960, p. 247).

These functions, rather than the influencing of votes, underlie congressional debate in both the House and the Senate, despite the somewhat differing styles of discussion in the two chambers. In the lower house, given its size, debate is tightly structured and is conducted under the conditions set forth in the rule granted by the Rules Committee. Thus, even on major bills, the time allotted for debate is unlikely to exceed four hours and more often will be a two-hour period. The standing committee which reported the bill dominates the debate. The chairman and ranking minority member frequently manage the contending forces, pro and con. Each gets one-half the available time to assign as he sees fit; each will use part of the time himself and dispense what remains to others, his committee colleagues and perhaps other influential members of the chamber. Thus the experts, the senior men on the committee of jurisdiction, who are presumably well versed in substance of the issues involved, monopolize the discussion.[1]

In the small, less-formal Senate, debate proceeds more leisurely but with less focus on the topic at hand. Even under the unlimited-debate provisions of the rules, however, not all of the senators participate. One study (Lehnen, 1967) reveals that on a sample of ten issues during 1961 anywhere from two to sixty-nine Senators spoke on the floor, the average being seventeen or

---

[1] The frustration of those who wish to speak but are not given any time may be at least partially alleviated by granting of "special orders," under which the member is allowed to address the House for extended periods at the close of the day. On other occasions, a representative may get the floor for one minute during which he may read a sentence or two of a speech and request permission, granted by unanimous consent, to insert the whole document in the *Congressional Record*.

eighteen. Among this less than one-fifth who took part in normal debate only about one-half, that is, ten or eleven senators, spoke more than two percent of the debate, or at least twice as much as a random distribution of speaking would predict. In short, a very few members do most of the talking on the Senate floor. In addition, of these few debaters about half are the committee experts on the topic, the other half being concerned senators eager to participate.

The norms or folkways of the Senate (see Chapter 6) seem to contribute to the restraint which most members display with regard to floor participation. Lehnen's evidence suggests that freshmen, serving their apprenticeship, speak less than the more senior members. The norm of specialization, with its injunction to senators to focus their attention on a limited range of topics, also seems relevant. Across the ten issues examined only fourteen members spoke a minimum of two percent of the debate on three or more bills; forty-five contributed two percent on one or two measures; and forty reached that level of participation on no issues. The first-mentioned group—whom Lehnen (1967, p. 515) labels "generalists"—includes a number of senators who would be expected to speak frequently. The mavericks, those who refuse to conform to the chamber norms, are clearly visible within this group; such men as Wayne Morse (D., Ore.), William Proxmire (D., Wis.), John Williams (R., Del.), and Jacob Javits (R., N. Y.) spoke a substantial amount on a broader-than-average range of issues. Likewise, as Matthews (1960, pp. 109–110) has suggested, men with presidential ambitions, in order to play to audiences outside the legislative halls, will feel it essential to speak out on many matters. Thus, in 1961, such presidential possibilities as Hubert Humphrey, Estes Kefauver, and Stuart Symington were found in the generalist group. In addition, as expected, senators with experience as political executives, especially as governors of large, industrialized states, were less willing or able to conform to the norms and spoke more frequently than did the senators without such experience.

Over and above orientation toward the folkways of the legislature, we may speculate that a legislator's role perspective on the lawmaking process will be related to his participation in floor debate. Those members of Congress whose view of the policy process necessitates that they present their own ideas, to speak either for their constituents or for "the people" (tribunes) or to advance their proposed solutions to the problem in question (inventors), will be more likely to feel a need to take part in floor debate. Conversely, the ritualists, brokers, and opportunists should participate less since they perceive less reason to get their opinions in the record. Similar arguments should lead the former groups to be more active than the latter at the amendment stage of the floor proceedings.

It is, in fact, at this later amending phase that debate may be most important, though even here that importance should not be overemphasized. For, as with general debate, proposing amendments may serve purposes considerably removed from any immediate intention to improve the quality of a piece of legislation. Amendments may serve to placate constituency or other interests; their demands can be made for them without real hope of having these changes accepted. The mere offering of such amendments may also permit the making of a record: individual lawmakers can state their personal views and the minority can propose its alternatives to the majority position.

Amendments may be necessary to sustain a majority coalition. If it appears that the needed votes may be lacking, changes in the provisions may give those with some doubts about the bill additional incentives to join, or remain in, the potential majority. Floor discussion may, in these circumstances, contribute to communicating the coalition's intentions to its members. Thus, floor statements may help to inform a bill's supporters how to vote on these amendments. Similarly, some amendments may touch upon topics previously undiscussed and here, too, the debate may help clarify meaning as well as provide cues about how to respond to the proposal to both sides in the legislative contest. It is in this rather limited way that, on specific amendments, floor discussion may be pertinent to the substantive results of Senate or House consideration of legislation.

More often, however, amendments, for whatever reason they may be proposed, pose no serious challenge to the provisions of the bill and, as a result, debate on them tends to be directed to external audiences not to those within the legislative system. The chamber norms contribute to this common situation; specialization and reciprocity, taken together, lead to the view that bills should "be written in committee, not on the floor." That is, the committee experts are presumed to know best, and where they agree that an amendment should be rejected (or accepted), the rank-and-file legislators are likely to feel constrained to accept this judgment. This premise makes it exceedingly difficult for foes of a bill to attack it at various points in an effort to undermine it by indirection rather than to defeat it by frontal assault. In the House, as noted, the rule under which the measure is considered by the whole membership may preclude amendments entirely. In the upper house, while such restrictions on offering amendments do not exist, the norms alone serve to limit effectively the number of amendments offered with serious intent. The deference shown to committees, and their preferences, is often at a peak for panels which are well integrated and unified on the floor.

These proceedings—general debate and the discussion of particular amendments—are recorded in the *Congressional Record*, but this journal is not a perfect transcript of what actually occurs on the floor (Mantel, 1959; Neuberger, 1958). The law requires that floor activity be recorded "substantially verbatim"; yet practice permits serious departures from this standard. For one thing, the record can be revised. Remarks in the House never uttered on the floor can be inserted and appear as if they had, in fact, been addressed to those present. In both House and Senate, permission is freely given for the orators "to revise and extend" their comments, adding new material, deleting old, correcting grammar and syntax, and otherwise perfecting their statements.[2] The *Record* thus becomes one place where a man can think "I wish I had said that," and then appear to have indeed uttered the words.[3]

The *Congressional Record* includes considerably more than the proceedings on the floor. The "Daily Digest" contains a summary, in statistical terms, of what the legislature has accomplished to that point in the session. Announcements of committee meetings and reports of those already held are printed, thus providing an additional source of information for the members. More useful, for political if not lawmaking purposes, is the appendix to the *Record* where individual representatives can place extraneous materials: "editorials, reports, speeches, poems, essays, letters, recipes, and testimonials" (Clapp, 1964, p. 154). The legislator may also reprint in the appendix his newsletters, his voting record, or his tabulations of responses to a questionnaire sent to his constituents. Items may be inserted to please district interests or individual voters back home; these or other items may be inexpensively reproduced from the *Record* and mailed—free, using the franking privilege—to constituents. Since his reelection prospects seem to reflect creating a favorable impression on the residents of his district, this opportunity to use the journal may contribute to the advantages with which the incumbent enters his reelection campaign. (See Chapter 2.)

In sum, when a bill reaches the floor following committee consideration, much of what takes place is directed to those outside the legislative system rather than toward the congressmen themselves. Only those whose role orientations—as committee leaders or experts, or as tribunes and inventors with respect to policy making—incline them toward participation are likely to find much satisfaction in floor activity. Similarly, the *Congressional Record* serves primarily as a communications link to groups outside of Congress. This is not to argue that floor proceedings never alter legislative outcomes, but only to suggest that this is an infrequent occurrence. Debate most often serves to reinforce existing commitments, but on occasion, in an especially close fight, floor discussion may make a difference. It seems reasonable, then, to concur in Clapp's (1964, p. 140) judgment that floor debate "rarely influences many . . . votes." Nor is debate particularly enlightening; as Matthews (1960, p. 243) puts it, legislators "do not debate, they talk"; they give speeches, but do not exchange views.

---

[2] In the Senate record, what was actually said is distinguished from what was inserted after the fact by the size of the type used.

[3] More seriously, the differences between what is actually said on the floor and what appears in the *Record* may be relevant if the statute is challenged in the courts. The inaccuracy of the journal may make difficult the judiciary's efforts to interpret the law consistently with congressional intent, for that intent may be hard to assess from a reading of the *Record*.

CONGRESSIONAL VOTING

When debate ends, the main point of congressional decision, the calling of the roll, is reached. In the House of Representatives, this means that the Committee of the Whole—in which the lower chamber carries on most of its deliberations, including preliminary action on amendments, under relaxed quorum requirements (see Chapter 5)—rises and the House reverts to its regular quorum rule.[4] Here, on the floor, the ultimate policy choice is made; here the bill is accepted or rejected; here the nature of the system's output is specified. Put another way, when the roll is called, the coalitions for and against the bill are identified. While it is often the case that the outcome is known in advance, only when the members of Congress state their "ayes" and "nays" do their positions become a matter of public record. Roll calls do not, however, necessarily represent the personal convictions of the legislators. Votes may reflect party or constituency appeals rather than individual lawmakers' assessment of the issues at hand; the congressman may feel the need to support a position which his own judgment may suggest is incorrect because he wants to support his party or because he fears electoral reprisals if he fails to back the view popular in his constituency.[5]

Interpersonal relationships among legislators influence vote decisions. The norms of each chamber, especially those of apprenticeship, specialization, and reciprocity, enhance the stature of the experts of the standing committees. These men frequently decide early in the policy-making process and others, the nonspecialists, look to them, especially if they share the same party affiliation, for advice, much of which may be accepted uncritically. One senator (quoted in Matthews, 1960, p. 251) reports "I try . . . to read the report on a bill before voting on it, but I must admit that I have voted on many hundreds of bills solely on the basis of what other senators told me about them." Other legislators may look to their personal staffs or to the committee staff for cues about how to vote. Some will promise to vote one way if their ballots will be decisive but will go their own way if the contest is already settled.[6] These sorts of decisions reflect the division of labor in

---

[4] Voting in the Committee of the Whole is by voice, standing, and teller votes, which often go unrecorded. In 1970 the Reorganization Act permitted twenty House members to demand a recorded teller vote. While relatively noncontroversial items may be shouted through by voice vote, once the House is in regular session rather than sitting as the Committee of the Whole, virtually all major issues are resolved by roll call voting.

[5] In the unsuccessful 1970 battle to confirm the nomination of Judge G. Harrold Carswell to the Supreme Court, a number of Southern Senators seem to have supported the nominee despite reservations about him because they needed to support a candidate from their region. Reported *Time* magazine: "Even many Southerners felt insulted that Nixon had chosen Carswell to represent them. 'I'm voting for the guy,' said one Southern Democratic Senator, 'but it's great to see the Republicans stewing in their own juice. They made this bed.'" Quoted in Bloomington (Ind.) *Sunday Herald-Times*, Apr. 19, 1970, p. 11.

[6] In the Carswell fight, Sen. Winston Prouty (R., Vt.) appears to have promised the Republican leadership to vote for confirmation if his vote was needed; since the battle was lost by the time his name was called, he opposed the nominee. Ripley (1967, p. 74) reports that the Speaker of the House can often count on as many as ten of the "pocket votes" if he needs them.

Congress: the experts in one area give advice on that topic and must get counsel on most, if not all, other matters (see Matthews, 1960, pp. 249–256).

Individual votes Nonetheless, examination of the factors which seem related to the vote choices of individual members of Congress may achieve considerable insight into congressional alignments. On most, but not all, issues party affiliation remains "more influential than other pressures on Congress" (Turner, 1951, p. 33; see also Turner-Schneier, 1970, chap. 2; Shannon, 1968, chap. 3). Legislators' votes also may reflect other factors— their own social backgrounds (e.g., their training and experiences prior to service in the legislature), their political situations within the legislative system, and the kinds of constituencies they represent. Which elements within each of these categories are most important will vary from issue to issue and from one time period to another. Such shifting patterns of coalition formation are exactly what we would expect to find in a representative assembly characterized by multiple centers of influence and decision making through negotiation and compromise.

As noted previously (Chapter 4), political party provides a central point of reference for many members. Other things being equal (which they seldom are), lawmakers prefer to vote with their parties, especially if their side occupies the White House. We have also pointed out, however, that congressional norms condone defection when constituency interests or individual conscience dictate voting against the party position. Thus, partisanship remains an important but not inviolable basis for intralegislative conflict; on many questions each of the contending coalitions has its base in one of the two parties and each seeks to hold its partisans in line while adding enough defectors from the most vulnerable members of the opposition to offset any losses from its own ranks which may nonetheless occur.

Table 11-1 indicates the limited nature of party competition and loyalty in recent years. Column 2 suggests that between one-third and one-half of the roll calls are party votes on which majorities of the two parties oppose one another; on the remaining votes—at least one-half and sometimes as many as two-thirds—the divisions are along other than party lines.[7] Note that the two most recent Congresses showed a diminution of partisan conflict; by 1967 the relatively high interparty polarization that marked the surge of new social legislation passed during the Kennedy-Johnson administration of the mid-1960s had receded substantially. And in the Ninety-first Congress, where a Republican President confronted a Congress controlled

[7] Using a more restrictive definition of a party vote—when 90 percent of one party votes against 90 percent of the other—Turner (1951, p. 24) found that only 17.1 percent of all rolls during the 1921–1948 era could be so classified. Schneier's (1970) revision of Turner reveals a reduction in the number of party votes, defined by Turner's restrictive criterion, in recent years. The percentage of roll calls on which 90 percent of one party opposed a similar proportion of the other varied from 8.0 (1959) to 1.3 (1966). Similarly Shannon's (1968) study of the Eighty-sixth and Eighty-seventh Congresses found that 5.1 percent of the roll calls were strict party-line votes.

TABLE 11-1   Party voting in Congress, 1963-1970

Congress	Roll calls	Party votes (%)	Democratic unity (%)	Republican unity (%)
91st (1969–1970)				
Senate	663	35	58	59
House	443	29	59	61
90th (1967–1968)				
Senate	596	33	57	60
House	478	36	63	70
89th (1965–1966)				
Senate	483	46	60	65
House	394	47	67	69
88th (1963–1964)				
Senate	534	41	64	66
House	232	52	71	72

NOTE: Party votes refers to the percentage of all chamber roll calls on which a majority of voting Democrats opposed a majority of voting Republicans. Party unity indicates the percentage of the time the average member voted with the majority of his party on party votes.
SOURCE: *Congressional Quarterly Weekly Reports,* Jan. 29, 1971, pp. 237–241; Dec. 29, 1967, pp. 2662–2666; Oct. 30, 1964, pp. 2588–2592.

by the Democrats, party lines were blurred still further. Where the parties did oppose one another, each could count on the loyalty of about two out of three of its members. In the Ninety-first Congress, for instance, the average senator voted with the majority of his party on about six of every ten roll calls.[8] These data reveal the incomplete character of party unity; lawmakers vote with their parties more often than not, but defection is common and widespread.

The minority party, lacking control of the Presidency, has been found to be less cohesive than the majority (or President's) party (Truman, 1959, pp. 72–90 and 172–190). As previously discussed, the Chief Executive frequently intervenes in the legislative process on behalf of those bills central to his program. On such occasions, as the data in Table 11-2 indicate, and particularly with respect to domestic policy matters, his party gives him considerably more support than does the opposition. For instance, in the Ninety-first Congress, President Nixon won support from the average Republican senator and representative 60 and 63 percent of the time, respectively; he won the votes of the typical Democrat in the Senate 42 percent of the time, while the

[8]These averages mask wide individual variations. In the Ninety-first Congress, for example, Sen. William Proxmire (D., Wis.) and two Republicans—Sens. Roman Hruska (Neb.) and Clifford Hansen (Wyo.)—led their respective parties, voting *with* the majority of their colleagues 86 and 89 percent of the time, respectively, on party votes. On the other hand, Sens. Spessard Holland (D., Fla.) and Clifford Case (R., N.J.) voted *against* majorities of their own parties on 63 and 69 percent, respectively, of the party roll calls. See *Congressional Quarterly Weekly Report,* Jan. 29, 1971, pp. 237–241.

TABLE 11-2   *Presidential support, by parties; selected Congresses*

Congress	President	Domestic policy		Foreign policy	
		Democratic support (%)	Republican support (%)	Democratic support (%)	Republican support (%)
91st (1969–1970)	Nixon (R)				
Senate		42	60	63	74
House		50	63	59	54
90th (1967–1968)	Johnson (D)				
Senate		53	47	59	57
House		67	49	66	44
87th (1961–1962)	Kennedy (D)				
Senate		63	36	68	45
House		73	37	76	45
86th (1959–1960)	Eisenhower (R)				
Senate		34	69	55	69
House		38	66	60	60

NOTE: The figures in the table refer to the average percentage of roll call votes by members of each party cast in agreement with the stated position of the President on each type of issue.
SOURCE: *Congressional Quarterly Weekly Report,* Jan. 29, 1971, pp. 218–231; Oct. 26, 1962, pp. 2035–2046; *Congressional Quarterly Almanac,* vol. 16 (1960), pp. 106–116, and vol. 15 (1959), pp. 108–124.

average Democrat in the lower chamber cast 50 percent of his votes in keeping with the President's preferences. In the prior Congress, Lyndon Johnson received greater support from House and Senate Democrats than from the Republican contingents in either house.

On some issues, especially in the foreign affairs domain, party differences are less clear-cut. In the Ninety-first Congress, for example, House Democrats viewed Mr. Nixon's foreign policy proposals more favorably than did the House Republicans (Table 11-2). In general, however, issues on which the administration stakes its prestige; matters of economic policy, including measures dealing with the tax structure, welfare programs, and the regulation of industry; and votes on organizational and procedural matters internal to the legislative system tend to array the two parties against one another (Jewell and Patterson, 1966, p. 430). Other issues which tend to evoke controversy along partisan lines include reciprocal trade, conservation, and farm policies (Turner, 1951, chap. 3; Turner-Schneier, 1970, chap. 3). Froman (1963, chap. 7) has suggested one reason for such differences: the two parties have their bases in different types of constituencies. Democrats in Congress tend to represent districts with fewer owner-occupied dwelling units (i.e., more homes occupied by renters), greater concentrations of urban population, more nonwhite residents, and greater population density. These kinds of districts have "liberal" populations which tend to elect "liberal" Democrats. In the same vein, those representatives chosen in atypical districts (i.e., Democrats from Republican-type areas) are most likely to bolt their party and vote with the opposition.[9]

There may, moreover, be differences between the two parties which account for greater loyalty among Democrats. More than their Republican counterparts, the Democrats seem to display a greater flexibility, a greater willingness to accommodate other interests within their own party (Mayhew, 1966). Specifically, Democrats whose constituencies seem to demand particular policies can count on the voting support of their colleagues whose districts have no real stake in the decision. Republicans, by contrast, who feel the need for specific programs, are often left to stand alone by their "disinterested" fellow partisans, who seem to prefer to vote a conservative, economizing position rather than to support a colleague. That is, mutual support, perhaps a concomitant of the specialization and reciprocity norms, lead Democrats to back one another's proposals while Republicans are more prone to divide along ideological lines rather than to "logroll" within the party ranks.

The time dimension also affects the impact of party on congressional voting. As time passes, the partisan perspective on particular issues may alter; events occur which may cast particular policies in a new light. The example of the shift in Republican votes to enact civil rights legislation has already been cited. In foreign affairs, once a Republican occupied the White House, GOP support for the foreign aid program dramatically increased while Democratic backing for the aid principle declined sharply (Rieselbach, 1966, chap 2; Kesselman, 1965). In the same vein, changes in the social, economic, and political climate in the Southern United States eroded the votes of Democrats from that region for the lowering of tariffs through reciprocal trade agreements (Jewell, 1959a; Watson, 1956). Some issues, such as social security, become noncontroversial as the years go by and the party which initially opposed them comes to support them with a fervor almost equal to that of the original proponents of the idea.[10]

In short, while party seems to influence the votes of individual congressmen to a greater extent than other factors, it is by no means always decisive. Many other features of the legislative system compete with party for lawmakers' attention; in such role-conflict situations, party loyalty wins out often but not inevitably. We may predict, for instance, that the stronger the attachment to party, that is, the more powerful the orientation toward playing a

---

[9] A number of examples come immediately to mind: the large number of Southern Democrats representing rural, low-density areas who vote frequently with the conservative Republicans; and Republican senators—for instance, Javits (N.Y.) and Case (N.J.)—whose states are urban, industrial, and densely populated, and whose voting records resemble those of Northern Democrats more closely than the records of many of their fellow Republicans. For comparable data on the House, see Shannon, 1968, chap. 7.

[10] The disavowal of presidential candidate Barry Goldwater's proposals to make social security voluntary and to sell the Tennessee Valley Authority to private enterprise by numerous Republicans testifies to such a change in partisan outlook. Goldwater's views, which would have struck a responsive chord in the 1940s, were no longer acceptable in the mid-1960s.

loyalist role, the greater the likelihood that a member of Congress will vote the party line. Similarly, the more a legislator feels the need to act on behalf of "the people" (as a tribune or inventor) the less need he will feel to back his party when party and conviction conflict; conversely, ritualists and brokers, once the formalities have been observed, should be more apt to align themselves with their partisan leaders and experts.

When members defect from party position, as they often do, their votes may reflect a variety of contending forces. For one thing, their personal experiences, their political socialization, may leave them with values and beliefs which lead them to vote a more conservative (or liberal) position than their fellow partisans. The data in Table 11-3 indicate that where one is born and raised seems to have a lasting impact on legislative voting. Those whose homes were in small-town, rural America seem to have developed a more parochial, provincial outlook on issues of public policy; at least, they tend to vote a more conservative position than their legislative colleagues from larger, metropolitan areas. Note also that place of birth makes a difference no matter what region the lawmaker represents, regardless of his party affiliation, and quite apart from whether he is chosen in a rural or urban congressional district.

Other studies reveal a similar effect for additional social-background attributes. Andrain (1964) found younger senators; those with occupational experience in law, journalism, and teaching; and those of Catholic, Episcopalian, and Presbyterian religious affiliation more favorable toward civil rights legislation than senators with contrasting personal attributes. In foreign affairs, Catholics appear more inclined to vote for foreign aid bills than non-Catholics (Fenton, 1960; Rieselbach, 1966) and representatives with business backgrounds are more supportive of the aid program than those with other occupational experience (Rieselbach, 1966). What a man was before he became a politician, thus, may influence how he acts once in elective office.

TABLE 11-3 *Size of birthplace, constituency type, and support for the conservative coalition*

Size of birthplace	Northern Democrats		Southern Democrats		Republicans	
	Metropolitan	Nonmetropolitan	Metropolitan	Nonmetropolitan	Metropolitan	Nonmetropolitan
Rural, small town	14.7	24.4	60.0	67.3	69.8	73.4
(under 10,000)	(23)	(32)	(23)	(46)	(28)	(73)
Urban	7.6	9.8	47.9	53.1	56.6	68.7
(10,000 and over)	(62)	(24)	(15)	(14)	(25)	(59)

NOTE: The cell entry is the mean percentage of support for the conservative coalition for each category of congressman. The number of cases is given in parenthesis.
SOURCE: Rieselbach, 1970.

In addition, the legislator's position in Congress may influence his vote decision. Committee service, and the consequent exposure to committee norms, may inculcate specific values which find expression when the roll is called. Thus, the Senate Foreign Relations Committee members tend to back internationalist foreign policy proposals and programs (Farnsworth, 1961). In the House, Foreign Affairs committeemen favor foreign aid legislation to a greater degree than do nonmembers; Armed Services panelists take a dimmer view of reciprocal trade than do those serving on other committees (Rieselbach, 1966). Identification with, or a strong, positive orientation toward, the committee to which he is assigned may thus lead the lawmaker to espouse a position characteristic of many members of the committee; integrated committees may give cues which carry weight with their members.

More difficult to assess is the effect of a second political factor, the nature of electoral competition with the congressman's state or district. By one view, a hard-fought contest, where the winner gains his victory with less than 55 percent of the vote,[11] serves to depress the representative's spirit of adventure. That is, when his margin is narrow, the winner is less likely to take an extreme position and more likely to be cautious, for if he is indiscreet, alienation of even a small group from his electoral coalition may cost him his seat. Conversely, this line of reasoning predicts that those from safe seats, where electoral competition seldom if ever poses a severe threat, will feel freer to disregard constituents' or party wishes and to vote as they see fit without fear of reprisals at the polls. Some data support these contentions: MacRae (1958) found that Republicans from marginal areas were more sensitive to constituency characteristics than those from safe districts, that is, their votes tended to reflect the demographic attributes of the electorate. No such relationship existed for Democrats. Froman (1963) found that those from competitive seats and those whose districts were atypical of their parties were more likely to eschew extreme voting positions than their party colleagues from safe, typical districts (see also Shannon, 1968, chap. 6).

Huntington (1950) has produced contrary evidence. He argues that the closer the election contest, the greater the tendency for the candidates to take dissimilar stands, as each seeks to mobilize his own partisans rather than to entice the "middle-of-the-road" voters. This leads Democrats to assume a "liberal" stance while Republicans adopt a "conservative" line. Miller (1962) produced evidence in support of this view: congressmen representing safe districts are more sensitive to constituent opinion than those from more

---

[11] Conventionally, seats where the winner amasses more than 60 percent of the vote are classified as "safe"; those where he wins with from 55 to 60 percent as "intermediate"; and those where his victory is secured with less than 55 percent as "marginal" or "competitive." For a suggestion that such a classificatory scheme oversimplifies reality, that what is "safe" in one state or for one office may, in fact, be "competitive" in another state or for a different office, see Schlesinger (1960).

competitive areas. Thus, while it is uncertain what the precise effect of a legislator's electoral situation is on his voting behavior, there is support for the notion that constituency conditions may induce caution and defection from extreme party positions. Moreover, we would predict that such tendencies would be more pronounced among those congressmen who assume a district-oriented focus of representation and those who adopt a delegate orientation toward their constituents. Nationally oriented lawmakers and trustees should be more likely to vote against constituent interests and for party, even if their electoral situations are marginal.

This discussion suggests a third category of relevant forces for interpreting congressional voting. The representative's response when the clerk calls the roll may reflect the nature of his district as well as his orientation toward the district's residents. Substantial quantities of research reveal relationships between constituency characteristics and congressional roll call behavior. Such relationships are most visible in situations or on issues when party pulls are reduced or nonexistent; in such circumstances the representative falls back on his knowledge of the "folks back home" as a guide in casting his vote. In other instances, there will be direct role conflict between the wishes of the party leaders and the legislator's perception of constituent interests; here he may choose to support the latter at the expense of the former.

Among the most visible of these constituency factors is region: there are clear differences within each party among the members from particular sections of the nation. On the Democratic side of the aisle, in both the House and the Senate, the differences between Northerners and Southerners are well known. Northern Democrats tend to be more liberal than their colleagues from below the Mason-Dixon line on numerous issues. Civil rights is, of course, primary among these topics (Andrain, 1964; MacRae, 1958), but similar regional differences have been found on social-welfare topics (MacRae, 1958; Marwell, 1967), agricultural policy (MacRae, 1958), and foreign policy issues (Grassmuck, 1951; Jewell, 1959a; Westerfield, 1955; Key, 1949), including foreign trade (Watson, 1956; Rieselbach, 1966) and foreign aid (MacRae, 1958; Rieselbach, 1966; Shannon, 1968).[12] On each of these items, the Southerners hewed to a more conservative line, resisting efforts to enlarge the scope of federal government activity and to increase the size of federal expenditures in these areas.

The Republicans have been split along regional lines as well, though the cleavage has been much less clear-cut than the division among the Democrats. Most often, the intra-Republican conflict has seen Eastern senators and representatives break away from the larger, dominant Midwestern wing

---

[12] In gross terms, *Congressional Quarterly* reports that over the past dozen years the percentage of roll call votes in Congress which saw a majority of voting Southern Democrats in opposition to a majority of voting Northern Democrats varied from 40 (1960) to 21 (1962). The 1960–1970 average was 31 percent. See *Congressional Quarterly Weekly Report*, Jan. 29, 1971, p. 254.

of the party to vote a more liberal line on civil rights (MacRae, 1958) and to support a more internationalist foreign policy (Westerfield, 1955; Marwell, 1967; MacRae, 1958; Rieselbach, 1966). This coastal-interior split is less clearly seen because during most of the contemporary era, the Republicans have been the minority party and, as such, less cohesive than the majority (Truman, 1959); this greater fluidity of voting alignment may obscure the operation of regional forces.

Other constituency factors seem important as well. The urban-rural division is also reflected in roll call voting. Urban congressmen have been found to differ from the representatives of rural areas on a number of measures including prohibition, farm programs, civil rights (Turner, 1951, 1970; MacRae, 1958), foreign aid, foreign trade, and immigration (Havens, 1964; Rieselbach, 1966). Urban legislators seem more willing in all these domains to see the government become actively involved in dealing with social and economic issues, that is, they take a more liberal, in the conventional sense of that term, view of what policy decisions are required. Similarly, lawmakers from high socioeconomic status districts and those whose constituents are well educated have been discovered to be supportive of foreign aid bills; so have the representatives of constituencies containing substantial proportions of German, Irish, and other immigrant stock (Rieselbach, 1966; Turner, 1951). In short, especially when party pressure is reduced, congressmen's votes reflect the demographic features—the region, economic and educational character, urban or rural nature, ethnic composition, and the like—of their constituencies.

There are numerous reasons why a member of Congress can be expected to pay heed to his perceptions—however accurate or inaccurate they may be—of his district, its inhabitants, and their desires. For one thing, if his goal is to remain in office—and reelection is a paramount consideration for a vast majority of national legislators—then he must seek to retain the support of his constituents. Next, he may share the basic outlook of the district electorate; he may be a farmer elected in an agricultural area or a union leader chosen in a blue-collar, working-class district, and as such he may "know" without direct communication from the district what its inhabitants desire. Finally, the lawmaker may adopt a district-oriented focus, a trustee style, or both as his guiding premises. To the extent that any or all of these considerations operate, it is not surprising that on some occasions the congressman will "vote his district" rather than his party or his committee.

Lastly, we may note that an individual legislator's personality, ideology, or even his idiosyncracies may influence his response when the roll is called. Admittedly, information on such matters is hard to obtain; the standard data sources on social-background or constituency attributes do not help much with regard to such personal factors. Yet there is fragmentary evidence on the point. Two studies (Froman, 1963; Anderson, 1964) compared the voting records of holdover legislators (incumbents) in successive Congresses with the performances of new men—of the same party and representing the same districts—in the same Congresses and found the former to be more consistent than the latter. Put another way, when a new man comes to Congress—even though he is of the same party and from the same constituency as his predecessor—his votes will differ from those of the man whom he has succeeded to an extent not seen in the votes of the man who wins reelection. It appears, then, that the new man, though his objective circumstances resemble markedly those of the previous incumbent, brings to Congress something of himself—personal characteristics, beliefs, values—quite apart from party and constituency features, which influences his response to the issues on which he must vote.

The individual voting choice, thus, appears as a complex act, influenced by the congressman's party affiliation, his prelegislative experiences, his political situation of the moment, the nature of the constituency he represents, and his own particular set of personal attributes. Out of this welter of often conflicting forces he must make his choices; he will decide—perhaps unconsciously, perhaps with full awareness—on an orientation toward his party, his committee, his district, his politics, his conscience; and from these orientations and the resolution of conflicts among them will emerge his vote decision. Where these forces largely push in the same direction—e.g., where party, committee, and constituency all seem to favor the same course of action—his choice will be easy (Turner, 1951; 1970); where there are sharp differences among those to whom he pays heed, the legislator's choice will be difficult, his behavior less predictable, and his vote often at odds with the desires of his party leaders, committee colleagues, or constituency interests.

Much of this complexity can be seen in Table 11-3 which relates party, background characteristics (place of birth), and constituency features (region and metropolitanism) to representatives' support for the Southern Democratic-Republican conservative coalition. Each of these factors contributes to the voting records. Party contributes most—the differences across the rows of the table between Northern Democrats, on one hand, and the Southern Democrats and the Republicans, on the other, are the largest—but the other elements are important as well. Support for the coalition is minimized among Northern Democrats born in larger cities and representing metropolitan areas and is maximized among Southern Democrats and Republican representatives born in small towns and elected in nonmetropolitan districts. Thus, while party loyalty—the loyalist orientation—is strong, conflicting pulls from social-background experiences and constituency produce deviations from strict adherence to the party line. We should also remember that the interplay of these forces varies from issue to issue and with the passage of time; party cleavages dominate some issues at some periods of time, while on other matters or in other eras, lines of division in Congress reflect constituency or other forces.

Voting patterns The discussion to this point has focused on the forces moving individual lawmakers to vote with or against their political parties, to act as party loyalists or as mavericks. Much effort has gone into the attempt to specify these forces, but this should not be permitted to obscure the fact that legislative outcomes reflect the sum total of individual votes; policy decisions are made by majorities constructed from the votes of single representatives. Thus, a few words are in order about the patterns which these individual votes form. We have already noted possible lines of cleavage other than party which may characterize congressional conflict. One of these is the regional factor. On some issues like foreign aid, at least during the 1950s and early 1960s, clear-cut sectional alignments are visible. Coastal lawmakers of both parties were, in this era, the chief proponents of the aid program; interior legislators were notable among the opponents of the aid principle (Rieselbach, 1966; Shannon, 1968). Moreover, civil rights divisions commonly fall along a North-South line.

Similarly, we have pointed out the possibility that when party is divided or inactive, votes may reflect an urban-rural division, or, more precisely, may indicate conflict between metropolitan and less densely settled areas. Turner (1951, chap. 4), for instance, has found that while the city-farm dimension is less powerful than party or regional pressures as an explanation of congressional voting, nonetheless such a cleavage did appear on roughly one-fifth of all the roll calls examined, and was independent of other forces impinging on the lawmakers from city and country. Similarly, MacRae (1958, pp. 260-267) discovered that urban representatives were, in the Eighty-first Congress, more liberal on welfare legislation than their colleagues from more rural parts of the country. This is not surprising given the tendency of such measures to benefit big-city populations. Finally, urban lawmakers have, within both parties, been more supportive of foreign aid and reciprocal trade bills than have farm-district congressmen (Smuckler, 1953; Rieselbach, 1966).

The most well noted and probably most frequent nonpartisan cleavage in Congress is the so-called conservative coalition which unites Southern Democrats and Republicans in opposition to the liberal proposals most effectively backed in the national legislature by Northern, most often Democratic, interests. Table 11-4 presents a picture of the coalition's strength. The coalition, it can be seen, appears on anywhere from one-tenth to nearly 30 percent of the roll calls in a given Congress; it comes into existence somewhat more often in the Senate than in the House, perhaps because it is sustained by the "inner club" in the upper chamber. When the Southern Democratic–Republican alignment occurs, it has a mixed but generally strong record of success: its victories occurred, in the past decade, on about six of every ten roll calls on which the alliance was consummated. Thus, when party loyalty breaks down it is frequently because the Southern Democrats choose to make common cause with the Republicans rather than with their Northern brethren.

TABLE 11-4   The conservative coalition in Congress, 1963–1970

	Coalition roll calls	Coalition victories (%)	Southern Democratic support (%)	Republican support (%)	Northern Democratic support (%)
91st (1969–1970)					
Senate	27	65	62	60	18
House	20	71	66	65	17
90th (1967–1968)					
Senate	21	68	62	61	21
House	22	67	65	70	13
89th (1965–1966)					
Senate	27	46	62	60	19
House	22	28	65	74	13
88th (1963–1964)					
Senate	18	46	68	63	17
House	12	67	64	69	12

NOTE: Coalition roll calls refer to the percentage of all roll call votes on which a majority of voting Southern Democrats and a majority of voting Republicans combine to oppose the voting majority of Northern Democrats. Coalition victories are the percent of coalition roll calls on which the coalition wins. The support figures are the percent of the time the average legislator in each party-regional category votes with the coalition on coalition roll calls.
SOURCE: *Congressional Quarterly Weekly Reports,* Jan. 29, 1971, pp. 242–247; Nov. 1, 1968, pp. 2983–2990; Dec. 29, 1967, pp. 2649–2661; and Nov. 27, 1964, pp. 2741–2750.

The coalition does not appear randomly, nor are its victories spread evenly across the variety of issues which Congress considers. Rather the conservative alliance emerges more on some matters than on others. In 1969, for example, the coalition was activated most frequently in the Senate on taxation and spending matters, where it won twenty of twenty-seven contests including a minimizing of the reduction of the oil-depletion allowance granted to the oil industry.[13] The coalition was often visible on foreign affairs and defense matters; the most notable of its ten victories (in fifteen contests) was its successful struggle to carry President Nixon's antiballistic missile program through the Senate. As might be expected, the coalition is also active in the civil rights field; in 1969, it won all four of the Senate battles which it waged. Thus, in recent years, the conservative coalition has achieved considerable results in pushing a "hard line" in foreign relations and in imposing restrictions on the scope of federal government activities in the areas of social welfare and civil rights.

Despite its accomplishments, however, the coalition is no more cohesive than the political parties. As the right-hand columns of Table 11-4 indicate,

[13] The data for 1969, used in this and subsequent paragraphs in this section, are from *Congressional Quarterly Weekly Report,* Jan. 16, 1970, pp. 158–165. They do not differ appreciably from data for earlier years available in appropriate numbers of the *Congressional Quarterly*.

the average Republican and Southern Democrat supports the coalition on about two-thirds of the coalition roll calls; the average Northern Democrat casts one vote in five with the conservative alliance. These figures, as might be expected, mask wide differences among individual lawmakers. For example, in the Ninety-first Congress such Southern Democratic senators as Fred Harris (Okla.), Ralph Yarborough (Tex.), Jennings Randolph (W. Va.), and J. William Fulbright (Ark.) opposed the coalition on more than half of the coalition votes; some Republicans—notably Clifford Case (N.J.), Jacob Javits (N.Y.), Richard Schweiker (Pa.), and Edward Brooke (Mass.)—cast more than 60 percent of their votes in opposition to the coalition. Conversely, some Northern Democrats—such as Alan Bible (Nev.), Clinton Anderson (N. Mex.), and Gale McGee (Wyo.)—support the coalition more than twice as frequently as the average for their Northern colleagues. Coalition lines, thus, are no more solid than those of the parties; as an informal alliance, it has even fewer means than the parties to ensure the backing of its "members." The conservative coalition remains, nonetheless, the most potent of the nonpartisan alignments in Congress.

In general, when lines of division do not coincide with partisan cleavages, there appears a configuration which approximates a "liberal-conservative" split. The liberal cause draws its heaviest support from Northern Democrats, buttressed by some Republicans from the urban areas, particularly the Eastern metropolitan centers in New York, New Jersey, and Pennsylvania. Southerners of both parties, many representing rural districts, together with the bulk of the Republicans vote most often for conservative policy alternatives. Put in other terms, it appears, by inference at least, that Eastern, urban Republicans on the one hand, and Southern rural Democrats on the other, are the legislators most apt to be impelled—by ideology or constituency pressures—to defect from their respective parties and to vote with the opposition. When such forces operate, the conservative coalition replaces the party alignment as the organizing feature of congressional roll-call voting. There remain, of course, a substantial number of votes so lacking in controversy that they are essentially bipartisan in character.[14] Even here, those who are in the minority may be moved by their orientations toward lawmaking (tribune or inventor) or constituency (district focus or trustee style) to bolt the more commonly held position.

Committee success Another pattern in voting on the floor of Congress which should be mentioned here is the success which the committees achieve. If the arguments advanced in this book—that congressional decisions are often

---

[14]Roughly two-thirds of all roll calls—68 percent in the Ninety-first Congress, 63 percent in the Nintieth Congress, and 54 percent in the Eighty-ninth Congress—are bipartisan in character, according to the *Congressional Quarterly* definition. Roll calls are so classified when voting majorities of the two parties adopt the same position. See *Congressional Quarterly Weekly Report,* Jan. 29, 1971, pp. 248–252; and Dec. 29, 1967, pp. 2643–2647.

committee decisions; that the more integrated committees, which play down partisanship and which stand united behind panel decisions, are likely to prevail on the floor—are accurate, then we would expect that at the floor stage the full chamber would approve the committee's recommendations. Assumption of a committee-leadership or expert orientation should hinge on the legislator's ability to exert influence over that narrow range of topics within his area of specialization; if he cannot carry the day in this domain, there would be little incentive to adhere to the norms which encourage reciprocity.

The available evidence on this topic supports the expectation that the full chamber is reluctant to overturn the committees' recommendations. Fenno (1966, pp. 448–470, 590–614) has provided detailed data for one pair of committees, the appropriations panels in the House and Senate. These bodies, moreover, especially the House committee, are exceptional in that they go to the floor in a strong position. They are prestigious, well-integrated, minimally partisan groups; these advantages are precisely those which promote full-chamber acceptance of committee recommendations. The pattern of committee decisions, of course, seeks to meet House expectations and, thus, to facilitate approval at the floor-consideration stage. The House panel also has procedural leverage: its reports are privileged, going directly to the floor without requiring a rule from the Rules Committee; it can obtain, on occasion, a waiver of points of order against its bills, thus minimizing the prospects of reversal on the floor. The House panel has other advantages as well. Consideration of its bills occurs in the Committee of the Whole, with its quorum requirement of 100; the fifty-member committee may dominate such proceedings. The rules for voting in the Committee of the Whole permit many votes to be taken by voice, standing, or teller, and the experts' influence may be at a peak for these unrecorded ballots. Finally, the rules governing the amending process help protect the committee's interests, for they permit the committee to get a roll call if it loses in the Committee of the Whole, but deny such an opportunity to its opponents.

All things considered, then, Appropriations is able to guard its proposals on the floor. Additionally, final passage comes quickly, most often within four or five days of the release of the committee report. Such prompt action serves to make difficult the opponents' task in assembling an anticommittee majority; fast consideration will minimize both the flow of information and the situational changes which might encourage rank-and-file lawmakers to vote against the specialists of the committee. In such circumstances, the debate, which the committee members tend to dominate, focuses on the committee's success in meeting the chamber's expectations about panel performance: ". . . the committee's arguments in terms of hard work, expertise, and unity function to maintain House confidence. . ." (Fenno, 1966, p. 444).

Given these strengths, it is not surprising to discover that the Appropriations Committee defends its recommendations with substantial effectiveness. The data, appearing in Table 11-5, reveal that in nearly nine of ten cases the full House accepts committee figures without change. Not surprisingly, this high level of overall success conceals some interesting variations. Where the committee loses, its failure may reflect the mood of the House. During some periods, the committee will guard the Treasury ferociously and amendments aimed at increasing committee recommendations will predominate, for those dissatisfied with committee action will seek to reverse the budget cuts on the floor. Such was the case, for instance, in years like 1947 and 1953, when the Republican committee majority wielded a sharp knife and the Democrats sought to repair some of the damage through the amending process. Conversely, when economy is foremost in the minds of many legislators, as was the case in 1951 and 1957, floor amendments will seek to reduce appropriations, even below the levels that an economy-minded committee proposes. Constituency interests seem, in addition, to lead some members to propose raising appropriations; this seems especially true of Public Works and Interior Department bills which contain large numbers of "pork-barrel" projects sought eagerly by elections-conscious legislators.

Finally, committee unity, as expected, is related to committee success. Where the committee was united, it won a vast majority of its floor tests; where partisan divisions erupted, the committee was far more likely to be reversed. When challenged on a roll call vote, committee unity is likely to crumble; in only six of thirty-six roll calls on Appropriations matters did 70 percent or more of the membership stand together; moreover on twenty-one of these votes the committee recommendation was amended. That there were only thirty-six roll calls during the fifteen-year period which Fenno analyzed testifies to the committee's success in averting roll calls. When roll calls could

TABLE 11-5   *Congressional action on appropriations committee recommendations for thirty-six bureaus, 1947 to 1962*

	Number of decisions	% of decisions
House action		
Accept committee recommendations	517	89.9
Decrease committee recommendations	30	5.2
Increase committee recommendations	28	4.9
	575	100.0
Senate action		
Accept committee recommendations	510	88.5
Decrease committee recommendations	15	2.6
Increase committee recommendations	51	8.9
	576	100.0

SOURCE: Richard F. Fenno, Jr., *The Power of The Purse,* Tables 9.4 and 11.11 pp. 450 and 597. Copyright © 1964 by Little, Brown and Company (Inc.). Reprinted by permission.

not be avoided, however, committee unity fell before partisan politics, a situation which significantly reduced the committee's ability to sustain its budget figures. Thus, when voting "for the record" was required, other orientations—toward party, constituency, interest groups, for example—came to undermine the norm of committee unity.

While the more relaxed Senate rules do not present the same opportunities to the upper house's Appropriations Committee, nevertheless, that panel carries the day for its recommendation to virtually the same extent as its House counterpart (see Table 11-5). The norms of specialization and reciprocity, especially potent in the smaller, more individualized Senate, promote deference to the Appropriations experts. One difference between the chambers, however, should be noted: in keeping with its "court-of-appeals" function, where the Senate does reverse its committee it is more likely to vote an increase in appropriated funds. As in the House, both the mood of the times and constituency pressures affect the Senate's response to committee proposals; the upper house nonetheless is inclined to view its task as one of correcting injustices found in the House bill, and thus to raise fund levels where this appears necessary.

Other, more general, evidence leads to a similar conclusion: the committees, at least those in the House, regularly carry the day on the floor. The data in Table 11-6 indicate that on the whole the full chamber sustains the committees' position; House panels "win" in nine of ten instances.[15] While floor success is widespread—no committee lost more than one-fifth of its measures—there are variations among the House panels. Dyson and Soule (1970) conclude that committee integration, the ability of committee members to put aside partisan disagreement and to vote together in support of their panel's bills, is critical for avoiding defeat on the floor. Education and Labor, already identified as a highly partisan body, thus ranks near the bottom in defense of its positions. Similarly, these data support Fenno's view that Appropriations does not do as well when its proposals must face a roll call. On the other hand, such bodies as Foreign Affairs and the often-controversial Internal Security (formerly Un-American Activities) Committee manage to vote as a unit and to win passage for their legislation.

What we know, then, suggests that, with some variation among the panels, congressional committees regularly win chamber approval for their decisions. In the House, the rules and norms contribute to this success; the folkways seem crucial in the Senate. In both, the committees seem able to manipulate the decisional context so that committee-loyalist orientations and conformity to the norms produce deference toward committee suggestions. Where other orientations—to party, interest group, or constituency—are activated, the

---

[15] Dyson and Soule (1970) define "winning" as the majority of a committee and the majority of the full House assuming the same position on a roll call vote. Decisions taken by other than record votes are thus excluded from their analysis, but it seems reasonable to believe that important matters, those in which the committees have an important stake, will face a floor vote.

prospects for committee victory decline markedly. It appears that unified, well-integrated committees like the Appropriations panels or the House Ways and Means Committee will be able to win approval for their views on the floor. Where competing pressures are great, however—ideological, partisan

TABLE 11-6   House committee defeats on floor roll call votes, 1955–1964

Committee	Number of bills	Number of floor defeats	Defeats (%)	Rank, by successes
Rules	6	1	16.7	18
Ways and Means	81	4	4.9	5
Appropriations	176	25	14.2	16
Armed Services	49	2	4.1	4
Un-American Activities	5	0	0.0	1
Judiciary	42	3	7.1	9.5
District of Columbia	22	4	18.2	20
Foreign Affairs	52	2	3.8	3
Agriculture	66	9	13.6	15
Interstate and Foreign Commerce	43	3	7.0	8
House Administration	7	1	14.3	17
Science and Astronautics	14	1	7.1	9.5
Public Works	34	2	5.6	7
Government Operations	15	2	13.3	14
Merchant Marine and Fisheries	8	0	0.0	1
Interior	37	2	5.4	6
Education and Labor	53	9	17.0	19
Banking and Currency	56	6	10.7	13
Post Office and Civil Service	29	3	10.3	12
Veterans' Affairs	10	1	10.0	11
Total	805	80	9.9	

NOTE: Successes (column 4) are calculated by the authors in terms of defeats (columns 2 and 3); that is, the most successful committees are those which suffered the fewest defeats.
SOURCE: James W. Dyson and John W. Soule, "Congressional Committee Behavior on Roll Call Votes: The U.S. House of Representatives, 1955–1964," *Midwest Journal of Political Science,* vol. 14, 1970, Tables 3 and 4, pp. 636 and 638. Reprinted by permission of the Wayne State University Press. Copyright 1970 by Wayne State University Press.

feelings on the House Education and Labor Committee, or constituency interests on the House Agriculture Committee, for instance— the floor stage may well see much of a committee's work undone by amendment or outright defeat.

CONFERENCE COMMITTEES

When the voting is over, and bills embodying public policy decisions passed, there will be often, especially on major legislation, the need to resolve in conference committee the virtually inevitable differences between the versions passed in each house. Unless agreement can be reached, and the bill reduced to identical language acceptable to both chambers, it cannot become law. Whenever the house which first passed the bill refuses to approve any alterations made in the other chamber, a conference becomes necessary; the conference committee is an ad hoc panel, representing both House and Senate, created to find the appropriate grounds for agreement.

The fact that on important matters a conference is likely to prove necessary influences floor consideration of some bills. Strategists working for particular policies take this into account; they may, for instance, accept restrictive or otherwise undesirable amendments without a floor fight in the hopes that the offensive provision can be quietly scrapped in conference. Conversely, where they have the votes to win, they may insist on a roll call vote in order to put on record the views of the chamber, thus bolstering the position of their chamber's conferees. Because conference deliberations, in keeping with the style of the legislative system, are characterized by negotiating and compromise, proponents of a particular view may purposely include some provisions in their bill for use as bargaining counters, items which can be dropped in conference in order to protect the bill's central features. Anticipation of a conference thus may shape the tactics to be employed on the floor. In some instances, notably on civil rights bills, strategy dictates all measures to avoid a conference; rather than hold out for specific items, the Senate will be under pressure to accept the House version, thus avoiding a conference and, perhaps crucially, a filibuster against the conference committee's report.

When disagreement occurs and a conference is required, the respective House and Senate presiding officers possess the formal power to appoint the conferees (or managers) for their chambers. In practice, however, by custom, the real choices are in the hands of the committee that considered the bill. This means that senior committee experts and leaders dominate the delegations. For example, Fenno (1966, pp. 643–644) reports that on appropriations matters, a five-man group, consisting of the chairman and ranking minority member of the full committee, the two ranking majority members and the ranking minority man on the subcommittee of jurisdiction, usually represents the House in conference. Delegations from other committees are similarly composed of the more senior panelists. Senate conference-committee membership, though often larger than the lower chamber's unit, is likewise drawn heavily from the upper reaches of the seniority ladder. Conference-committee composition of this type has led to criticism of the "unrepresentative" character of the panels (Clapp, 1964, pp. 277–279).

Conference committees meet behind closed doors in executive session, no formal records of their deliberations are kept, and thus information on committee proceedings is scanty. It seems probable, however, that the guiding premises that Appropriations Committee conferees follow (Fenno, 1966, pp. 617–620) apply to other conferences as well. Each delegation is expected to defend the interests of its parent chamber but at the same time to guarantee that the issues in question are resolved. That is, interchamber quarrels should not be permitted to prevent enactment of some legislation on a topic dealt with in each house. Only rarely, in other words, will a conference committee doom legislation by failing to compromise the House-Senate conflicts.[16]

Decision making in conference, operating within those expectations, may reflect a number of factors. One side may be better prepared and, in a sense, overwhelm the other; a dominant personality, a lawmaker with a deep commitment, may tip the balance by the sheer force of his participation; superior "interpersonal skills — of advocacy, compromise, stubbornness, bluster and threat" — may prove decisive (Fenno, 1966, pp. 642–652, at p. 650). The degree of unity within the chamber's delegation may affect its position; if deeply divided one house's conferees may be unable to resist the importunings of the other side. External pressures may be important: managers with the full confidence of the parent chamber may be in a strong position to stand firm for their house's position. On the other hand, particularly toward the end of a session, the need to act, often buttressed by the urgings of the majority-party leadership, may require one side's conferees to yield more readily than they would wish.

The most common tactic appears to be the attempt to stand firm on the important features of the bill. Often the stubborn side will point to a roll call vote which indicates the depth of the full chamber's commitment. In some cases, instructions may be given the conferees either informally during debate or directly by roll call vote; in extreme instances, while the conference is in progress, the managers from one chamber will return to the parent body for

---

[16] In 1962, a seemingly petty quarrel between two octogenarian appropriations committee chairmen — Clarence Cannon (D., Mo.) in the House and Carl Hayden (D., Ariz.) in the Senate — threatened to bring the entire appropriations process to a halt. In that year, Chairman Cannon, on behalf of his committee, proposed to change the place where the conference committees met, traditionally on the Senate side of the Capitol. The Senate rejected this proposal, and for six months no conference committees met. Eventually, the dispute was settled: a neutral meeting ground agreed upon, and the normal process resumed. This incident clearly revealed the tension underlying the House-Senate relationship, tension which surfaces from time to time to influence conference-committee deliberations. For a full treatment of the 1962 episode, see Pressman (1966).

instructions. Either way, specific directives strengthen the bargaining position of the conferees. Understandably, because basic decisions are made in conference, interest groups and the executive branch may lobby for decisions favorable to them. To the extent that they have strong role orientation to such groups, individual conferees may be expected to yield to such requests. Committee staff may also be consulted during committee deliberations.

The results of committee negotiations are most often compromises, apportioning the disputed provisions between the two chambers. The usual situation is one in which the managers work within the framework of the bills passed in the House and Senate. On occasion, however, the drafts are so different that there is considerable opportunity for the conference to produce new legislation, much of which was not seriously considered in either chamber; Steiner's classic study (1951, pp. 174–176), though now two decades old, reports that only three of fifty-six conferences produced bills that included much substantially new material. Most often, these committees operate within the rules that preclude them from going beyond the areas in dispute and altering provisions on which the two houses are in agreement. Where they do go "beyond their authority," they are usually sustained if the chamber in question is satisfied with the committee product.

The relative strength of House and Senate in conference-committee negotiations is an open question, although the most recent evidence leads to the judgment that the latter's position prevails more frequently. Steiner (1951, pp. 170–172) concluded that of the fifty-six bills studied, the House "won" on thirty-two occasions, that is, the final product was more like that initially passed in the lower chamber in these instances. Senate influence was greater on fifteen occasions, while influence was equally divided in the remaining nine cases. Fenno's more recent study (1966, pp. 661–670) directly contradicts Steiner's findings. Where the latter found the House supreme in appropriations conferences, the former found that the Senate won, in the sense that the conference agreed on a dollars-and-cents amount closer to the upper house's figure than to the original sum appropriated in the House of Representatives, on 56.5 percent (187 times) of the 331 contests between 1947 and 1962; the House won 30.5 percent of the time (101 instances); and the conference split the difference exactly on the remaining 13.0 percent (43 times) of the decisions. Fenno speculates that the Senate's success stems from the closer relationship of its conferees to the full chamber, enabling them to stand firm, fully confident that the parent body will sustain them. Lacking this confidence, the House managers, more often at odds with chamber majorities, feel compelled to retreat more often than not.

A study by Vogler (1970), covering 295 conferences in five Congresses over a twenty-year period, provides a general picture consistent with Fenno's data on appropriations conferences. Overall, the Senate won in 65 percent of the cases while the House conferees carried the day in the remaining 35 percent of the joint meetings. There is, however, as the data in Table 11-7 reveal, considerable variation in the outcomes of conferences involving the relevant pairs of House and Senate committees. Of the fifteen pair analyzed, eight reached decisions generally closer to the Senate bill, three achieved settlements approximating the House position, and four tended to strike a balance between the views of the two chambers. Vogler speculates, following Fenno, that the closer Senate-committee relationship enables the upper chamber's conferees generally to sustain their views. However, where House conferees feel the need to respond to interests in the environment of the legislative system—constituents or, perhaps, organized interest groups—they may be more committed to their position. The conferences relating to legislation from the Interstate Commerce, Interior, and Judiciary commit-

TABLE 11-7 *Congressional conference-committee output, selected Congresses, 1947–1966*

Committee		Conference settlement generally closer to bill as passed by
Senate	*House*	
Aeronautics and Space Sciences	Science and Astronautics	Senate
Agriculture	Agriculture	Senate
Appropriations	Appropriations	Senate
Armed Services	Armed Services	Senate
District of Columbia	District of Columbia	Senate
Finance	Ways and Means	Senate
Post Office and Civil Service	Post Office and Civil Service	Senate
Public Works	Public Works	Senate
Foreign Relations	Foreign Affairs	Both Chambers
Banking and Currency	Banking and Currency	Both Chambers
Government Operations	Government Operations	Both Chambers
Labor and Public Welfare	Education and Labor	Both Chambers
Commerce	Interstate and Foreign Commerce	House
Interior and Insular Affairs	Insular Affairs	House
Judiciary	Judiciary	House

NOTE: The table rates the relative success of conference committee subsystems drawn from particular pairs of committees with jurisdiction over the same subject-matter areas.
SOURCE: David J. Vogler, "House Dominance in Congressional Conference Committees," *Midwest Journal of Political Science,* vol. 14, 1970, Table 2, p. 316. Reprinted by permission of the Wayne State University Press. Copyright 1970 by Wayne State University Press.

tees—that is, where the House conferees do the best—are precisely of this sort. A particular project in his own district is far more important to a representative than any specific item in his state is to a senator; thus, the former is encouraged to stand firm on constituency-oriented matters while the latter is more willing to compromise to get a bill.

In any case, when a majority of the conferees from each side agree on a set of provisions, the conference committee rises and reports its decisions back to the two chambers. While the House and Senate can reject the committee's report, they seldom do so, for the odds favor the conference committee should a contest develop (Paletz, 1970). For one thing, the folkways sustain the managers. They are the experts to whom deference is owed, and to challenge them is to invite invasion of the specialist's bailiwick by rank-and-file lawmakers—a result to be avoided if the notions of division of labor and reciprocity are to be preserved. In the House of Representatives, the formal rules help as well. Conference reports are considered for one hour only, the time completely under the control of leader of the conferees, usually the full- or subcommittee chairman most directly concerned with the bill. Moreover, in both chambers, the report must be accepted or rejected in toto; there can be no objections to single provisions, and most legislators are loath to send an entire bill back to conference to adjust at most a few items. When challenged, at least in the appropriations area where there are some data (Fenno, 1966, pp. 670–676), the evidence suggests that the conference committee is sustained in the vast majority of the cases. When the final votes are cast, and the conference reports adopted in both houses, the bill, and the policy it contains, are ready for presidential scrutiny.

THE SUBSTANCE OF CONGRESSIONAL POLICY OUTPUTS

It is considerably more difficult to generalize about the content of congressional policy outputs than to speak about the process by which these outputs are produced. Yet, after all, it is through its substance that legislation, by whatever systemic process it is enacted, has its ultimate impact on the citizens of the nation. Thus, it seems worthwhile to try to suggest something about the substance of congressional policy making and, moreover, to make an effort to move beyond the obvious assertion that, because the legislature must enact most governmental outputs, Congress has a significant influence on the nature of those enactments. This, of course, need not be the case.

Since it is generally recognized that Congress reacts to executive proposals, that the President requests and Congress responds, it may be well to begin with a look at the shape of the legislature's reaction to executive policy initiatives. Table 11-8 presents data that give a general picture of the overall

TABLE 11-8 Congressional response to presidential policy initiatives

Year	President	Foreign policy			Domestic policy					
		Total requests	Requests passed	% passed	Total requests	Requests passed	% passed	Total requests	Requests passed	% passed
1970	Nixon	30	19	63.3	180	78	43.3	210	97	46.2
1969	Nixon	34	7	20.6	137	48	35.0	171	55	32.2
1968	Johnson	36	23	63.9	378	208	55.0	414	231	55.8
1967	Johnson	48	28	58.3	383	177	46.2	431	205	47.6
1966	Johnson	50	26	52.0	321	181	56.4	371	207	55.8
1965	Johnson	54	39	72.2	415	284	68.4	469	323	68.9
1964	Johnson	32	28	87.5	185	97	52.4	217	125	57.6
1963	Kennedy	61	22	36.0	340	87	25.6	401	109	27.2
1962	Kennedy	40	33	82.5	258	100	38.8	298	133	44.6
1961	Kennedy	43	24	55.8	312	148	47.4	355	172	48.5
1960	Eisenhower	41	22	53.7	142	34	23.9	183	56	30.6
1959	Eisenhower	59	32	54.2	169	61	36.1	228	93	40.8
1958	Eisenhower	40	20	50.0	194	89	45.9	234	109	46.6
1957	Eisenhower	66	40	60.6	140	36	25.7	206	76	36.9
1956	Eisenhower	52	16	30.8	173	87	50.3	225	103	45.8
1955	Eisenhower	51	32	62.7	156	64	41.0	207	96	46.4
1954	Eisenhower	26	17	65.4	206	133	64.6	232	150	64.7

SOURCE: Congressional Quarterly Almanac, vols. 10–26, 1954–1970.

congressional response to the President's program.[17] The pattern is one of variable legislative acceptance of presidential leadership that ranges from passing nearly seven out of ten of Lyndon Johnson's 1965 requests to passing barely one-fourth of the proposals made by John Kennedy two years earlier. On the whole, those Presidents with large electoral, and healthy congressional, majorities—e.g., Johnson in 1965 and Eisenhower in 1954—do best, while those who must confront an opposition majority in Congress—Eisenhower after 1954 and Nixon in 1969 and 1970—and those with slender mandates from the voters—Kennedy and Nixon—find the legislature more reluctant to move their programs ahead.

In the substantive areas, it is clear that Presidents win more victories on foreign policy matters than on domestic issues. This reflects the superior position of the executive vis-à-vis the legislative branch with regard to international relations and questions of national defense (see Chapter 7). In fourteen of the seventeen years between 1954 and 1970, the Chief Executive produced more response to his foreign than domestic policy recommendations;[18] moreover, no individual President had a lower success rate on international matters in more than a single year. Thus, the legislative branch seems more willing to defer to executive expertise in the realm of international politics. Such a conclusion ought not, however, obscure the fact that some Congresses have been more willing than others; presidential rates of success in foreign affairs range from about one-fifth (Nixon in 1969) to better than 87 percent (Johnson in 1964).

Moreover, there are rather pronounced differences in congressional deference to the Chief Executive with regard to specific aspects of the nation's international relations. On matters directly related to military preparedness—e.g., weapons procurement and deployment, force levels, and other items that flow from the Commander-in-Chief power—Congress, until recently, has shown little inclination to seek to impose its judgments on the President. The Indochina war has altered this situation somewhat; the Senate, in particular, has been restive, seeking to limit the executive's authority to conduct operations in Southeast Asia beyond congressional scrutiny. The effect of this campaign to alter the relations between the branches with respect to military affairs has been less tangible than psychological; while

---

[17] These figures must be taken as approximations. For one thing, the President may ask for something he knows Congress will not grant; a present request may start a process that will culminate in passage at some, perhaps distant, future time. Second, Congress may alter a proposal to barely recognizable form, but if the President initially suggested it, he will get credit for its passage. Finally, a President's success ratio will reflect the controversiality of his program; his "score" may be inflated if his requests include a large proportion of relatively less important proposals. In short, the data in Table 11-8 are only suggestive of the records of the Chief Executives.

[18] In addition, *Congressional Quarterly*, using a different mode of calculation than that in Table 11-8, found that the President's rate of congressional approval for his foreign policy proposals exceeded that for domestic policy in each of the seven years from 1947 to 1953. See *Congressional Quarterly Almanac*, 1953, p. 87.

unable to alter American policy in any real sense, the Senate has enunciated a claim, that it can perhaps act on in the future, to an enlarged involvement in the formulation of policy.

Other facets of American foreign relations reflect congressional involvement to a considerably greater extent. In 1971, the Selective Service Act was allowed to expire while the legislature wrestled with an in effect gratuitous amendment setting a specific date for United States troop withdrawal from Indochina. While Congress has continued to extend the reciprocal trade program, thus empowering the President to negotiate tariff agreements with other nations, it has been willing to impose quotas on imports opposed by the Chief Executive. Some individual legislators, in addition, have been involved in working to persuade foreign governments voluntarily to limit exports of some commodities, notably Japanese textiles and Italian shoes, to this country, a step intended to head off legislation imposing quotas. Finally, Congress has repeatedly in recent years made deep cuts in the foreign aid budget and, in addition, altered the allocation of funds between military and economic assistance. In sum, in many areas the nation's foreign policy bears the indelible stamp of congressional involvement.

This same conclusion is even more justified in regard to domestic policy. While we cannot outline the substance of policy on every major matter here, a few examples should suffice to illustrate the indisputable influence of Congress on the shape of a multitude of governmental activities on the home front. For one thing, the legislature has virtually exclusive control over a host of decisions involving individual constituencies, the area that Lowi (1964) refers to as the distributive arena of policy. Such things as river and harbor development, agricultural assistance, post office construction, and a host of other matters fall within the domain of the legislature. Presidential efforts to modify if not eliminate the system of farm price supports or the program of federal aid to school districts that serve the children of government employees have continually come to naught. Where the Chief Executive seeks to inhibit legislative policy making on such topics through use of the veto power, he runs the maximum risk of having his veto overridden, as President Nixon discovered in 1970 when Congress upset his rejection of the Hill-Burton Act providing for aid to localities in building and modernizing hospitals. Thus, where the classic bargaining (or "logrolling") pattern of choice permits the legislators to enact measures that allow them to serve their states and districts, Congress remains in substantial control of national policy.

A comparison of President Nixon's 1970 and 1971 legislative programs further illustrates the impact of Congress on the Chief Executive's policy initiatives (*Congressional Quarterly Weekly Report,* Mar. 26, 1971, pp. 702–707). Thus, for example, the President broadly restructured his revenue-sharing proposals, including a more than tenfold increase in the funds to be made available, in order to win the support of Wilbur Mills and John Byrnes, the chairman and ranking Republican of the House Ways and Means Committee, who had scuttled the revenue-sharing idea during the 1970 congressional session. Similarly, though he had vetoed a comparable bill only months earlier, in 1971 Mr. Nixon asked Congress to spend federal funds to enable cities and states to create temporary "public-service" jobs for the unemployed. In response to legislation in the environmental protection field that was stronger than his original suggestions, the President in 1971 urged Congress to pass a series of laws imposing stricter controls on those who threatened to pollute the environment. In addition, the administration backed away from an earlier request to limit the extension of the Office of Economic Opportunity, popular in Congress, to a single year and instead proposed to extend the poverty program for two years. Finally, the important welfare reform package was extensively "rewritten and modified" in an attempt to mollify the conservatives in the Senate, where the 1970 version of the plan had died.

Another set of 1971 administration proposals simply reintroduced ideas, presented the previous year, on which Congress had not acted at all. Included was a series of bills on health care and another group dealing with consumer affairs. It is worth noting also that the administration accepted the authority, which Congress had granted, despite the President's rejection of it, to impose wage and price controls as a method of bringing inflation under control. Secretary of the Treasury John Connally did, however, indicate that there was no intention to use the legislatively conferred power. While by no means a complete catalog of legislative-executive interactions, these examples should make clear that domestic policy reflects congressional activity. Thus, Congress, and especially the opposition party, is often busy, as *Congressional Quarterly* (*Weekly Report,* Mar. 26, 1971, p. 702) described the Democrats in 1971, "offering proposals, counterproposals, and alternatives on almost every issue: . . . economy, education, pollution, health, consumer affairs and transportation."

More generally, the 1971 examples should leave little doubt that Congress is far more than a conveyer belt on which demands originating outside the legislative system move quickly, easily, and in unaltered fashion to enactment. Rather, the process of producing policy outputs involves the redesign of programs, the alteration of specifications, and often the abandonment of blueprints during congressional consideration. Lawmakers who orient themselves toward their constituencies, as delegates and politicos; toward their committees, as leaders and experts; toward the substance of policy, as tribunes and inventors; toward interest groups, as facilitators; and toward their political party, as loyalist members of the opposition—all seem unwilling to defer to outside expertise. Instead, they prefer to strive to construct solutions to the country's problems that reflect their own notions of what national priorities should be. The results of congressional deliberations, i.e., the legislature's policy outputs, often are given shape as much by these ideas of senators and representatives as by the proposals that Congress receives initially.

SUMMARY

Congressional decisions—whether taken anew or merely ratifications of understandings reached earlier in the legislative process—are formally made on the House and Senate floors. A bill, once released by committee and reaching the floor, is available for debate and amendment. In general, discussion on the floor has at best marginal effects; it is far more likely to reinforce existing sentiments than to convert the speaker's opponents. As a result, attendance at floor sessions is usually light, and the debaters direct their remarks to audiences outside the congressional system. Amendments also serve political purposes as often as they are intended to work changes in pending measures. The amending process, like general debate, is controlled by the committee leaders and experts whom the norms single out as the most crucial participants. The committees of original jurisdiction are able, for the most part, to manage the debate and amending phase to protect their own interests; this is particularly true of the prestigious, highly cohesive panels. The proceedings, recorded in the *Congressional Record,* are, thus, often aimed at external groups rather than at fellow congressmen; only rarely do floor actions alter legislative outcomes.

When the debate concludes, voting begins, and the verdict is rendered. Individual votes reflect the operation of numerous forces: interpersonal relations among legislators; party loyalty and/or pressure, especially when the party controls the Presidency; the legislators' precongressional or social-background experiences; the lawmakers' current political situations; and the kinds of districts that they represent. While party remains the main pole around which congressional conflict revolves, on some occasions other factors—region, metropolitanism, or other constituency attributes—underlie the central cleavage. On a significant proportion of roll calls a liberal-conservative alignment has appeared, pitting Northern Democrats and Eastern Republicans, with their roots in urban districts, against a conservative coalition of Southern Democrats and the remaining Republicans, reflecting a set of rural interests. Finally, it should be noted that voting patterns may reflect the position of the committee reporting the bill; to the degree that the panel is integrated and respected, it may be able to count on the full chamber, out of respect for expertise, to uphold its recommendations.

The power of the senior committee leaders and experts is even more pronounced during conference-committee consideration of measures that pass the two houses in different forms. The senior specialists dominate conference-committee membership and deliberations; they act to defend the interests of their respective chambers but at the same time to reach agreement. When the conferees agree on a report, the chamber rules, formal and especially informal, enable them to win approval for the product of their deliberations with relative ease. The report, hammered out in private negotiating sessions, usually reflects a compromise between House and Senate versions, but occasionally when those versions differ markedly, the conference has wide latitude to draft virtually new legislation. In such situations, of course, the influence of the managers is enhanced.

The behavior of senators and representatives during the long, often arduous, lawmaking process—from drafting and introduction to final voting and conference consideration—should, we predict, reflect the differing role orientations of the congressmen. Tribunes and inventors should participate more during floor action than ritualists, brokers, or opportunists. Party loyalists should vote the party line more faithfully than mavericks. The stronger the orientations of individual members of Congress toward interest groups (facilitators) or the executive branch (proexecutive), the more they should respond to appeals from such sources; where these pleas run counter to party, we should find greater crossing of party lines. Similarly, where constituency pressures are activated and work against party loyalty, lawmakers with district and delegate orientations should defect more than their nationally oriented, trustee colleagues. Where demands from these sources coincide, the legislators' choices should be simplified; where the demands are incompatible, the resolution of role conflict may be difficult, psychologically and politically. Since the latter situation often obtains, the behavior of congressmen is not always predictable; especially in a decentralized system, which places a premium on bargaining and compromise, the shifting lines of coalitions may be hard to follow. Role conflicts assume differing intensities on different issues, leading lawmakers to behave differently as situations alter. In such circumstances, despite our knowledge of some regularities in legislative behavior, we can never be entirely certain in what precise fashion, and with what specific result, the processes described in this and the preceding chapter will convert demands on Congress into policy outputs. Yet, we can be certain that there will be a sufficiently diverse distribution of role orientations toward the various objects within and without the congressional system to ensure that those policy outputs will emerge from the legislative process bearing the unmistakable imprint of the American national assembly.

CHAPTER TWELVE

Congressional Oversight

Lawmaking is unquestionably the most dramatic and newsworthy form of legislative activity; nothing about Congress's work can compare in visibility with the enactment of major measures embodying new policies with regard to labor-management relations, civil rights, urban problems, medical care, or a host of other issues with which the lawmakers must deal. The clashes of competing interests, the struggles between contesting coalitions over policy are without doubt the high points of legislative activity. Yet the drama of substantive decision making, symbolized by the casting of roll call votes, is only the surface portion of the congressional iceberg; the major part of the legislature's undertakings go on hidden from view. As we have seen, the critical phases of policy making itself may occur in executive sessions where committees or subcommittees mark up their bills in full expectation that they will pass the full chamber.

In addition, much legislative energy is expended on matters at most only tangentially related to policy issues. One such feature of the congressional workload, one further set of demands which must be processed, is the range of activities which cluster under the rubric of legislative oversight. In the words of the Reorganization Act of 1946, the standing committees of Congress are enjoined "to exercise continuous watchfulness" over the executive branch's administration of the laws of the land. This injunction has justified legislative involvement across the whole spectrum of bureaucratic behavior. Put another way, this means that oversight extends to bureaucratic planning as well as to administrative implementation of congressionally enacted statutes; it operates in advance of agency decisions and it reviews these choices after they have been made.[1]

The potentially deep concern of senators and representatives with the executive branch reflects the central place which bureaucracy has assumed in mid-twentieth-century America. National solutions to nationwide problems have inevitably led to the creation of an enormous administrative establishment; the conditions of modern life—war, depression, urban problems, and the like—have seemed to necessitate national intervention in problems held in earlier eras to be beyond the purview of the federal government. The complexity of modern issues, the inability of legislation to specify precise forms of behavior for each conceivable contingency, requires Congress to grant discretion, often very wide, to executive agencies and bureaus; governmental operatives are entrusted the tasks of setting and applying "fair standards," of developing "reasonable procedures," of acting in the "public interest." Because it is necessary to write such vague prescriptions into enabling statutes does not mean that congressmen have no concern about the substance of the procedures established or the nature of the standards set. It is precisely these concerns which lead legislators to engage in oversight activities, for bureaucratic discretion means bureaucratic policy making and lawmakers are, quite understandably, unwilling to yield their policy-making authority without restriction to administrators within the executive branch.[2]

OVERSIGHT: SOME GENERAL CONSIDERATIONS

To begin with, we should note that oversight serves a variety of legislative purposes. Among these are *policy* aims; Congress, or at least interested members of each chamber, can seek to ensure that administration of laws is in keeping with the intent of the legislature in initially enacting the bills. That is, it is possible that policy goals which moved the legislature to act in the first place may be subverted in their implementation by the bureaucracy; executive-branch personnel may not seem to carry out the statute in a way which will satisfy the demands which the legislation was intended to assuage. Oversight provides the opportunity for Congress to inquire into the ways in

---

[1] Some authors (Harris, 1965; Jewell and Patterson, 1966) have distinguished among "oversight," "supervision," and "control" in an effort to identify the various ways in which Congress and the executive branch relate to one another, in order to separate involvement in decision making from ex post facto review of administrative behavior. In the present chapter, oversight is used to refer to the whole gamut of legislative-executive relationships; such usage seems appropriate because of the virtually constant character of congressional "watchfulness."

[2] This is to say nothing more than, in practice, no distinction between policy making and policy implementation can be sustained. The old idea that Congress sets policy and the administration carries it out simply does not describe contemporary reality.

which the statute is being executed, and the lawmakers may discover departures from legislative intent. For example, a clear case of interbranch conflict occurred over the implementation of the Juvenile Delinquency and Youth Offenses Control Act of 1961 (Moore, 1969). The chairman of the Special Education Subcommittee of the House Education and Labor Committee, Mrs. Edith Green (D., Ore.), expected the act to permit short-run, practical experiments in juvenile delinquency control; the administrators charged with operating responsibility, however, felt that long-run, overall planning for a "total attack" on delinquency was a preferable strategy. The ensuing struggle lasted more than three years and resulted in a compromise settlement: in exchange for extension of the authorizing legislation, the administrators agreed to act more in keeping with congressional wishes and to establish and maintain closer relationships with the appropriate congressional committees.[3]

Even where there is no distortion of legislative intent, oversight may reveal that a policy is not working, is not achieving the results that its passage envisaged. Congress is not immune to criticism; in the view of many observers such contemporary programs as farm price supports, school integration, and foreign aid are not accomplishing their objectives. Legislative control devices permit members of Congress to investigate, through a variety of techniques, the extent to which programs are attaining their intended goals. Where failures are detected, new legislation may be required to rectify the situation, to try new ways to bring about desired ends. Thus, it is clear that oversight relates to policy; "watchdog" activities of Congress may serve to single out those topics on which new legislation seems needed.

A second broad set of aims that oversight serves pertains to bureaucratic *efficiency*. Quite apart from legislative intentions, or from the success or failure of programs, administration of statutes may be inefficient, overly expensive or otherwise wasteful, unfair, or even occasionally dishonest or illegal, and oversight may ferret out such inequities and take steps to correct them (Macmahon, 1943; Harris, 1965; Saloma, 1969). In other words, administrative management may be faulty, agencies may be poorly organized, or bureaus may be inefficient in other ways, and oversight can both publicize these executive-branch failures and suggest methods for surmounting the disclosed difficulties. To cite one instance, the revelation that the Department of State was using money from a general "emergencies" fund to finance public opinion polls and then "leaking" the survey results to the press aroused a House subcommittee. The International Operations Subcommittee of the Committee on Government Operations held five days of public hearings, charged the Department with using funds for "self-aggrandizing publicity,"

[3]For a case in which ". . . the Executive Branch of the Government was effectively able to transform the legislative intent of Congress . . ." and eventually have its transformation incorporated into law, see McLellan and Clare's (1965) study of Public Law 480.

and in effect forced the Department to abandon its polling operations (Brown, 1961).

The fact that Congress has a mandate to see that federal programs are "faithfully, effectively, and economically carried out" (Harris, 1965, p. 1) should not lead to the conclusion that the charge is easily met. On the contrary, the watchdog chores are conducted in a complex, uncertain environment marked as much by informal relationships as by formal prescriptions. We have noted (in Chapter 7) that the flow of influence within the executive branch does not always follow the lines of the official organization chart. While agencies often cooperate with the President, on other occasions they work at cross-purposes to him; at times executive bureaus are more intimately tied to the legislature than to the administrative branch. Here we encounter what is, in effect, the reverse side of the coin: Congress must engage in its oversight activities in an atmosphere where a variety of interests are involved. The sort of "subsystems" (Freeman, 1965) or "whirlpools" (Griffith, 1951) which unite agency, legislative, and interest group into coalitions concerned with both policy formulation and administration in particular areas complicate congressional supervision and control. For a lawmaker to question the ties between, say, the Interstate Commerce Commission and the railroad industry (Huntington, 1952) or the Army Corps of Engineers and the Public Works Committees of Congress (Maass, 1950) may be a thankless task, for established relationships, involving in some cases one's legislative colleagues, may prove highly resistant to change.

In keeping with the decentralized character of the legislative system, oversight is carried on in an unsystematic, uncoordinated fashion. The charge of the Reorganization Act of 1946 was not to Congress as a whole but rather to each standing committee to keep tabs on the administration of laws within its subject-matter jurisdiction. Each panel thus guards its oversight prerogatives as jealously as it protects its lawmaking authority. Where there are overlapping jurisdictions, as between Armed Services and Foreign Affairs Committees in the international relations area, there will also be competing claims for oversight responsibilities; where committees differ in substantive outlook, this conflict will be reflected in their supervisory activities. For instance, in the 1968–1971 period, the Senate Foreign Relations Committee, highly critical of the military posture of both the Johnson and the Nixon administrations, was equally hostile toward the Pentagon's administration of its weapons-procurement machinery, pointing to "cost overruns"—actual construction costs in excess of budget estimates—totaling billions of dollars. The Armed Services panel, a staunch defender of administration policy, assumed at the same time the task of defending the efficiency with which these military programs were administered. Oversight, like policy making, reflects the fragmented nature of congressional organization and operation.

Of particular significance in this respect are the differing perspectives of the authorizing committees on the one hand and the appropriations bodies on the other. The former panels concern themselves primarily with the need for, or legitimacy of, particular programs; the latter focus on the financial requirements. The advantage lies with the appropriations committees, or, more accurately, with the House Appropriations subcommittees. They deal with matters of concern annually while the practice of authorizing programs for periods of several years renders substantive committee involvement episodic. The Appropriations panels commit substantial staff resources to oversight; the subject-matter committees seldom match this commitment (Carroll, 1966; Fenno, 1966). Recognizing their deficiencies, the Armed Services Committees have experimented with *annual authorizations* (Gordon, 1961; Dawson, 1962), but this practice has had little noticeable effect in enhancing the committees' ability to control or supervise the military establishment. Congressional oversight is, in reality, often oversight by House Appropriations subcommittees. The Senate committee, by custom and because of the more diffused workloads in the upper chamber, is usually content to yield much of its responsibility to its House counterpart (Fenno, 1966).

The effect of all this is to disperse the performance of the oversight function among the committees of Congress, but at the same time to concentrate it in the hands of those bodies, like the House Appropriations subcommittees, whose norms and practices make them willing to assume the role of overseer. Oversight, this is to say, is a committee responsibility, but there is a wide variation in the degree to which the many panels pursue this facet of legislative business. Situational factors, which direct attention to policy making, may reduce concern for oversight. The willingness of committee leaders or experts to focus on oversight rather than on more immediate policy choices or to countenance supervisory actions by junior panelists will influence the energy devoted to oversight. Even those legislators involved with control activities—those, that is, who assume something other than an oversight-indifferent orientation—may adopt an agency-orientation aimed more at protecting bureau autonomy than at imposing congressional, or even presidential, control over administrative behavior (see Chapter 1, pp. 19–20). There exists, then, no centralized organization of oversight; rather the uneven operation of a variety of factors leads to fragmented, decentralized, unsystematic congressional control of the executive branch.

In brief, then, oversight may facilitate the policy goals of the overseers; the stakes in watching the executive may be far greater than a simple desire to promote administrative honesty and efficiency, though these goals should not be discounted as unimportant for their own sake.

TECHNIQUES OF OVERSIGHT

These two broad sets of aims, policy and efficiency goals, may be sought through a variety of methods ranging from explicit statutory pronouncements to subtle and implicit communications over highly informal channels. Each technique is employed in ways designed to sensitize the executive-branch bureaucrats to the desires of those few legislators—the subcommitte or full-committee chairman, the subject-matter expert, or the party leaders— whose interests lead them to pursue an active role as overseers. This section will treat these modes of oversight in isolation, but this analytic necessity should not obscure the fact that a number of control devices may operate simultaneously.

Statutory controls One form of control, written into law, is Congress's prescription of the form or organization of the executive branch. In establishing policies, in devising programs, the legislature creates departments, agencies, or bureaus to carry them out and, further, may define the internal structure of these bodies. The more specific the enabling statutes, of course, the smaller is the discretion left to the agencies, and the more restricted are their policy-making opportunities. In some cases, specific offices are established. For example, as an extreme case, the Fish and Wildlife Act created in the Interior Department an Assistant Secretary for Fish and Wildlife which the Department argued was an unnecessary post (Harris, 1965, p. 25). More often, well-defined offices are set up in keeping with departmental desires. Included in policy choices, then, are congressional decisions about the creation of new administrative units and the form in which such units will be cast. In other instances, the legislature may assign new programs to old agencies or restructure existing bureaus to facilitate congressional control. In 1952, the State Department's Passport and Visa Offices were transferred to a newly created Bureau of Security and Consular Affairs in order, presumably, to facilitate legislative committee control of passport policy (Harris, 1965, p. 24). In short, where their purposes are served, lawmakers are perfectly prepared to define the structure of administrative agencies with care and precision.

Nor does Congress always stop there; on occasion, the legislature prescribes specifically interagency or executive-legislative relationships. Statutes may define the relationship between superior and inferior; regulatory commissions are designed to operate beyond the control of the President, the nominal head of the executive branch; lines of control may be established that give bureau chiefs independence from the departmental secretary. The effect of such prescriptions, of course, is to muddy the lines of authority within the executive hierarchy, but congressional control may, at the same time, be made easier by enactments of this sort.

In the same vein, various forms of mandatory consultation may be written into law. Congress may require one agency to inform others about its decisions, sometimes before these are implemented; to exchange data with other bureaus; to secure the approval of some outside agency or officer; or to consult with an "advisory committee" established, by law, to oversee the agency (Cotter and Smith, 1957; Harris, 1965). Again, congressional purposes are likely to be of both the policy and the efficiency variety. In a number of instances, the lawmakers will go further still in restricting the bureaucrats' freedom of action and will set forth, in statutes, procedures that administrators are to follow in the course of their daily routines. Such subjects as "contracts for public buildings, personnel transactions—pay, allowances, travel, etc.—public lands, purchasing practices, supply, printing, and conduct of legal business" are dealt with in congressional enactments (Harris, 1965, p. 43) and executive officials must act within the limits that these laws impose. Specifics of this kind seem aimed at promoting efficiency and eliminating waste in bureaucratic operations; they also make clear that Congress is in control of the administrative establishment. Much day-to-day administration of federal programs, thus, goes on within the confines of statutory controls.

The legislative veto A special form of statutory control is the legislative veto, which in its various forms permits Congress, or more often its committees or even subcommittees, to block action that the executive—the President, departments, or bureaus—proposes to take. In general, the relevant laws require that administrative decisions be submitted, in advance, to some set of legislators whose disapproval prevents the steps in question from being taken. Obviously, the requirement of prior concurrence enhances the legislature's ability to promote policy compliance, efficiency, or both.

One example of the operation of the legislative veto is the provision, in the acts permitting the President to reorganize the executive branch, that such plans be submitted first to Congress for approval. If within sixty calendar days, either the House or Senate votes, by simple majority, against the proposal, the plan is defeated (Cotter, 1966; Harris, 1965).[4] In 1962, President Kennedy, having failed to persuade Congress to create a department of housing and urban development by statute, sought to accomplish the same end under the reorganization power. He thus proposed, using his reorganization power, to combine a number of federal agencies concerned with urban problems—the Housing and Home Finance Agency, for example—into the new Cabinet-level department, only to have the House of Representatives veto the plan by an overwhelmingly negative vote, 264 to 150 against the reorganization (Parris, 1969).[5] Between 1946 and 1966, a period spanning

[4]Under the 1939 Reorganization Act, the legislative veto could be imposed only by a concurrent resolution, that is, one passed by both chambers. Subsequent renewals of the law permit either house, acting alone, to kill reorganization plans. See Cotter, 1966, and Cotter and Smith, 1957.

[5]Among the reasons for the plan's defeat were congressional resentment over the President's efforts to accomplish indirectly that which he had been unable to attain by legislation, and, more importantly, the antiadministration stand taken by Southern Democrats when Mr. Kennedy's intention to appoint a Negro, Robert C. Weaver, as Secretary of the new Department became known. Changes in the political climate—the heavy Democratic majorities in Congress after the 1964 presidential contest and the muting of the race issue accomplished by the passage of the Civil Rights Act of 1964 and presidential silence about the identity of the new Secretary—permitted Lyndon Johnson to propose, and Congress to create, the new Department, by law, in May, 1965 (Parris, 1969).

the presidencies of Truman, Eisenhower, Kennedy, and Johnson, Congress rejected twenty-one of eighty-four, or one-fourth, of the executive's reorganization plans; Truman was treated somewhat more harshly than his successors (*Congressional Quarterly*, 1965). Similar provisions have been inserted into legislation in other subject-matter areas.[6]

The principle of the legislative veto has not only been extended to other topics, but its operation has been simplified and committees have been given the opportunity to exercise the veto on behalf of the full chamber. In the latter case, no resolution need be passed by either house. One device, no longer used however, required certain executive agencies to "come into agreement" with congressional committees before implementing particular decisions. A 1944 statute, for instance, required the Navy Department to secure the advance approval of all proposals for land acquisition or lease (Harris, 1965, p. 243). Similarly, in 1955, the Defense Appropriation Act contained the proviso that no business enterprise run by the federal government could be terminated and transferred to private enterprise, if, within ninety days, either Appropriations Committee disapproved the step (Carper, 1960). Presidents Eisenhower and Johnson, in recent years, opposed such provisions, on constitutional grounds, as illegal delegations of authority, and vetoed or protested several bills that included "come-into-agreement" sections. The constitutional argument revolves around the question of whether the separation-of-powers doctrine precludes this form of congressional participation in program execution.

A related device also in effect providing individual committees with veto power over administrative proposals is the annual authorization scheme, by which no funds are to be appropriated for specific projects which have not first been authorized by the proper congressional committees. In 1959, to cite one instance of a common practice, the Military Construction Authorization Act for fiscal 1960 included a section providing that "No funds may be appropriated after December 31, 1960 . . . for the procurement of aircraft, missiles or naval vessels unless the appropriation of such funds has been authorized by legislation enacted after such date." Thus, no funds could be spent for weapons other than those approved by the Armed Services Committees of the House and Senate (Dawson, 1962; Gordon, 1961); this annual authorization procedure greatly enhances the ability of the substantive committees, in contrast to the appropriations bodies, to review, criticize, and amend programs in the course of extending them for the subsequent year. Such reviews, of course, may serve both substantive policy and ef-

---

[6] For instance, the Alien Registration Act of 1940, as amended, permits Congress to counter the attorney general's decisions in deportation cases by concurrent resolution (Harris, 1965, pp. 233–234). Similarly, Congress can, also by concurrent resolution, block the transfer or exchange of nuclear material or restricted data by the United States to foreign nations (Green and Rosenthal, 1963, pp. 87–89, 142–146).

ficiency goals.[7] This device has also been controversial, but for practical not constitutional reasons; no one seriously denies Congress's *right* to engage in annual reassessment of ongoing programs, but objections have been lodged to the impairing of bureaucratic planning— in terms of rationality and efficiency— that yearly authorizations, with their uncertain outcomes, introduce (Saloma, 1969, pp. 143–144).

Although not formally a veto power, another common statutory requirement which Congress imposes on the executive bureaus, the requirement that they submit advance reports to appropriate legislative committees, has the same effect. These laws specify that the agency must report proposed actions in advance, thus giving the committee time to inform itself about the matter, to make its views known, and, if necessary and desirable, to take steps to block the administrative proposal. For example, the Internal Revenue Service is statutorily compelled to inform the Joint Committee on Internal Revenue Taxation of its intention to make tax refunds of more than $100,000 thirty days prior to making payment of the claim (Harris, 1965, p. 259); the Joint Committee on Atomic Energy makes similar demands for prior information on both the Atomic Energy Commission and the Defense Department (Green and Rosenthal, 1963, pp. 89–103; Thomas, 1955, p. 153). While not mentioning the veto power specifically, these provisions obviously give the congressional experts opportunity to exert their influence in a way not unlike the formally prescribed veto authority.

In a variety of ways, then, described as the legislative veto, Congress has equipped itself, if members wish to do so, to intervene in bureaucratic affairs to impose particular policy aims or to encourage more rational, efficient administrative procedures.[8] The legislature, or at least some influential legislators, have at their disposal, as a result of these techniques, the means to control administrative behavior to a considerable extent; that they do not always employ these weapons to the fullest degree in no way reduces the potential for meaningful legislative oversight of the executive branch.

"Power of the purse": appropriations and the audit Perhaps the single most important tool of congressional oversight is the appropriations power, the power to approve the expenditure of all federal funds, which Congress possesses. The ability of the Appropriations Committees, and especially the House panel, to curtail the financial resources available for programs is a powerful inducement to the administrators of those programs to listen

[7]For another instance, this one requiring annual authorization for the National Aeronautics and Space Administration, see Saloma (1969, pp. 147–149). Interestingly, the Science and Astronautics Committee of the House voted 25–0 for the proposal, while only fourteen of the fifty Appropriations panelists supported the provision (ibid., p. 149).

[8]A number of sources, including Cooper (1956), Schauffler (1958), Rhode (1961), and Cooper and Cooper (1962), treat in detail the issues raised by the various forms of the legislative veto.

carefully to the views of the committee leaders and experts. A concomitant of this is, of course, that control over money is often control over policy, for a committee which disapproves of a policy, or the way a policy is carried out, is unlikely to be generous with the limited funds available. Where money is given, that is, policies are fostered; where it is withheld, program implementation must be limited. The point should not be overstated, however, for as noted (Chapter 9) the Appropriations Committees operate within the full-chamber expectation that authorized programs will be funded, and thus committee action is limited to incremental alterations rather than basic changes. Within these limits, however, even a 5 percent budget slash may prove crucial for successful policy implementation.

We have seen, in Chapter 7, how the executive branch, operating through the Office of Management and Budget,[9] formulates the budget which the President submits to Congress. Following the Chief Executive's economic message, the House Appropriations Committee, by custom acting prior to Senate panel consideration[10] divides the budget into some twelve to sixteen bills, each of which is treated by the Appropriations subcommittee with jurisdiction over the relevant section of the budget. Subcommittee treatment resembles that accorded any bill: hearings are held, the bill is marked up in executive session, the draft is approved by full committee, and then is sent to the floor.[11] In the course of this consideration, the subcommittees conduct much legislative oversight.

The subcommittee hearings provide the chief means of formal control; they produce a direct confrontation between agency personnel seeking to justify their use of funds appropriated in the past and to win new, and often larger, sums from the committee, and the legislators, fearful of bureaucratic distortion of congressional intent and administrative profligacy, seeking to "guard the Treasury" and to reduce expenditure levels. The hearings, thus, become a contest, one in which the Appropriations Committee frequently bends the executive departments to its will. But the struggle goes on within limits—the victor gains increments, large in dollar amounts on occasion, but small in terms of the total sums involved. This reflects the political facts of life, for the committee must support programs, and, as a result, seeks not to eliminate but to modify requests, often in the name of economy and efficiency.

[9] The Office of Management and Budget, created in 1970, assumed the functions that the Budget Bureau had performed, and the new office will presumably provide central direction for the budgetary process. It is, however, too early to judge what, if any, changes in the process this reorganization of the Executive Office of the President (White House Staff) may produce.

[10] The Constitution provides that revenue measures, those raising government revenues, begin in the House of Representatives; the tradition has developed that the lower chamber also initiate the process by which federal funds are expended.

[11] Two extraordinary books—Wildavsky (1964) and Fenno (1966)—treat the budgetary process in great detail, and the paragraphs which follow rely heavily on these two works. Other useful studies include Wallace, 1960, Huzar, 1950, and Wilmerding, 1943.

The subcommittees approach the hearings with particular images of the administration (Wildavsky, 1964, pp. 47–56; Fenno, 1966, chap. 7). As protectors of the purse strings, the congressmen are suspicious of the bureaucrats, assuming that they have "vested interests" in seeking additional funds. The lawmakers tend to assume, further, that executive estimates are inflated, that there is "fat" in the budget, to permit the agencies to pursue the expansionist goals. The job of the committee, as experts, is to ferret out the unnecessary requests, to pare the programs down to reasonable size. Thus, of course, the result is reduction of estimates in the vast majority of cases.

The problem which confronts the subcommittee specialists is where to cut. Information is needed about where the budgetary "soft spots" are, about which specific items are enlarged, and it is the absence of reliable data that poses difficulties for the overseers. In this context, the legislator, though confident that he is better informed than his House colleagues not on the subcommittee, acknowledges that he is at a relative disadvantage in challenging the agency experts who appear at the budget hearings (Fenno, 1966, pp. 344–349). Moreover the agencies will try to take advantage of their clienteles, the nongovernmental beneficiaries of the agency programs, to make a favorable case for the effectiveness of these programs and for the efficiency with which they have been run; nonbureaucratic witnesses may appear at hearings to buttress the agency's presentation. The lawmakers, thus, have problems in assessing and evaluating bureau requests.

In this situation, the legislators employ a number of strategies. First, and foremost, they "sample for information"; unable to assess many items accurately, they focus their questioning in the hearings on those topics about which they are best informed. They will inquire, for one thing, about budget items that are increased, about those programs that are expanding, seeking to judge the administrator's explanation and justification of the need to grow. Other items more stable in size will remain largely undiscussed in the hearings. Similarly, the congressman will look at agency adherence to committee instructions—sometimes written into law, sometimes transmitted informally—and failure to follow legislative suggestions will be used to justify reduction of the bureau's budget. Another tactic is to use that part of executive activity which takes place in the legislator's district as a focal point for interrogation. Constituency matters are basic to the representative's concerns and here he can judge with some clarity the agency's claims of accomplishment; if the program does not work well in his district, he is prepared to assume it is producing similarly unsatisfactory results elsewhere and, thus, that it is a prime target for appropriations cuts. Finally, the sample for data is likely to include a personal evaluation of the administrator. If the lawmakers have confidence in him, if he appears to know his agency and its operations thoroughly, if his presentations at the hearings are forthright and clear, then the members of the subcommittee come to respect the bureau chief. Where such respect cannot be won, then another locus for budget reductions has been established. In general, if he is satisfied on those items in his sample, items about which he feels most able to judge with assurance, the legislator tends to generalize to the entire agency operation and to be less eager to cut its budget (Fenno, 1966, pp. 332–341; see also Jernberg, 1969).[12]

In addition, the contest is a cumulative one, with the same contestants participating over a number of years. Thus, budgeting becomes, as Wildavsky (1964, p. 11) puts it, "experiential"; legislators and bureaucrats learn about one another, learn the other's techniques, their strengths and weaknesses. The participants in the hearings learn each other's needs, and the budget process assumes a more or less standard pattern: a suspicious committee, moved by its custom of cutting estimates, seeks to find places where money can be saved while the agency attempts to rebut the subcommittee's arguments for reduction. This gives the appropriations process its basic incremental pattern in which marginal adjustments, usually downward, are made where the congressmen can justify them. Put another way, the conflict revolves around the agency's budgetary "base," consisting of those accepted programs and policies about which the lawmakers do not inquire and which they expect to continue to finance. The agency personnel seek to defend, and enlarge, the base; the legislators endeavor to hold down budgetary growth; and controversy focuses on those portions of the budget about which there is no basic agreement (Wildavsky, 1964, pp. 16, 102–123).

The hearings concluded, the subcommittee marks up the appropriations bill, making whatever reductions it can.[13] We have noted (in Chapter 11) the pattern of the House committee's decisions—really the decisions of the individual subcommittees: estimates are reduced, but agencies get more than they had in the previous fiscal year. Here it remains to note some of the methods by which the reductions are achieved. One tactic is to focus on efficiency by including restrictions on money to be spent for administrative personnel. Limits are sometimes imposed on the number of people who can be employed at certain salary grade levels; or the amount of money for salaries in specific ranks may be curtailed (Carroll, 1966, pp. 166–169). In this way, the committee can seek to assure itself that there will not be "too many chiefs and not enough Indians" in agency operations. Saving money is seen as possible, then, through restricting the administrative apparatus.

---

[12]For their part, the agency people recognize these tactics, and prepare for them. They rehearse for budget hearings, they seek to perform well in key legislators' districts, they pay considerable heed to subcommittee instructions; in short, they seek to generate that very confidence that the lawmakers are looking for. On these matters, see Wildavsky, 1964, chap. 3, and Fenno, 1966, chap. 6.

[13]While it is clear that cutting is the main goal of the appropriations subcommittees, the point should not be overstressed. There are conditions under which the committees are willing, or even eager, to spend freely. Some legislators commit themselves to a cause—"To me forestry has become a religion. . . . "—and lawmakers fight to nourish the faith with additional funds (Wildavsky, 1964, pp. 48–49). In other instances, the need to support constituency interests—one's own or one's colleagues'—leads to spending rather than saving. These conflicts, most resolved in keeping with the budget-cutting norms, need nevertheless to be noted here.

On the policy side, the subcommittees may seek a number of shortcuts to savings. One device is to ask the agency to outline its own priorities; those items ranked low on the scale become prime targets for reduction, and, moreover, reduction with a built-in rationale, for the legislator can say that the agency, in effect, made the choice (Wildavsky, 1964, p. 106). Congressmen may also make recourse to outside forces—a budget-cutting or economy mood; similar and strong sentiments among the nonmembers of the subcommittee; the political climate at large—which compel limitations on spending, perhaps in the name of balancing the budget. Cuts induced in any of these ways reduce the funds available for program implementation. In some cases, not knowing where or how to cut leads to simpler but more drastic actions, for example the "across-the-board" or "meat-ax" reduction by which every line item in the budget is reduced by a fixed percentage, thus effecting savings at the expense of agency administration and programs alike.

While House consideration takes place, the Senate Appropriations Committee is waiting in the wings. Senators, with their more diversified committee assignments, have less time to inform themselves and to pore over budget requests than do their House committee counterparts; thus, analysis of the budget is less intensive in the upper chamber. Rather, the Senate panel considers itself as a "court of appeals" to which agencies that feel greatly aggrieved by House decisions can take their cases. The administrators use this opportunity to marshal the evidence on those programs which they feel the House bill has most seriously endangered and Senate subcommittee interrogations tend to focus on these items. The Senate often responds to such bureaucratic entreaties by raising appropriations above the House figure, setting the stage for a compromise, at an intermediate figure, in the conference committee. Senate consideration, then, is of a special sort—less thorough, less focused, less careful—providing a chance for the agencies to recoup some of the most damaging losses suffered during House deliberations (Fenno, 1966, pp. 564–572).[14]

Throughout this entire process, the Appropriations Committee staff in each chamber assumes a central importance. In contrast to those of many other committees, the appropriations staffs are characterized by permanence and professionalism, by a distance from the most partisan aspects of legislative politics. The House committee has a staff of twenty to twenty-five employees,[15] appointed by the full-committee chairman and working for him

---

[14]Horn (1970, pp. 77–82) argues that the view of the Senate Committee as a court of appeals is an "increasingly outdated thesis." Rather there is variation among Senate Appropriations subcommittees: a few do little or nothing until the House has acted, but most take initiatives without waiting for action in the lower chamber. While the court-of-appeals view accurately describes the situation in the 1940s and early 1950s, by 1965 more than half the Senate subcommittees acted on a *de novo* rather than on an appeals basis.

[15]This is the permanent staff; the committee also hires a variety of temporary, investigative staff help. These work mainly for the chairman of the full committee (Fenno, 1966, pp. 152–155).

or for a particular subcommittee chairman. The staffer thus may experience role conflict born of a need to serve two masters (Fenno, 1966, p. 151). The staff's job, as conceived by the legislators, is to assist in budget cutting. The Senate committee's staff, numbering in the neighborhood of thirty, is equally important; these employees "are at least as influential as those attached to the House group. That is to say they are very influential" (Fenno, 1966, p. 557).

Both staffs are highly integrated, working smoothly with one another and, most importantly, with the legislators for whom they labor. They are experts in their fields, and the subcommittee experts come to rely on them to a considerable degree. The staffers study budget estimates, look for places where reductions may be imposed, and advise the legislators on where to probe during budget hearings. They may travel—either with the lawmakers or alone—to visit agency installations for an "on-the-scene" assessment of bureaucratic performance and efficiency. More basic, perhaps, is the staff members' search for information through informal contacts with agency personnel; such channels may provide useful data for the budget-hearing confrontation. In a context where information is a scarce resource, where the lawmakers grope for data with which they can countervail the executive expertise, the skilled professionals of the committee staffs come to exert substantial influence at all stages of the budgetary process.

One other congressional resource, the General Accounting Office (GAO) is worth noting here (Harris, 1965, chap. 6). Created by the Budget and Accounting Act of 1921, the GAO, headed by the Comptroller General, is independent of the executive branch and is charged with auditing the books of federal agencies and with submitting reports on their expenditures to Congress. Subsequent legislation specifically declared the GAO "an agent" of the legislature, thus guaranteeing the lawmakers a data source of their own. The GAO tends to support the efficiency goal of legislative oversight, for its focus is on "the soundness of the agency's accounting and financial management system and the efficiency of its operations generally" (Harris, 1965, p. 155). In so doing the GAO compares agency policies with legislative intent; judges the propriety of agency transactions; and interprets the rights and obligations of agency administrators. Thus, the GAO's influence extends well beyond simple accounting procedures, and the Office, potentially at least, is a major asset for a system which suffers from a chronic information shortage.

In all these ways, then, the Appropriations Committees, and especially the House panel, seek to exploit their control over the expenditure of federal funds to keep a rein on the administration of congressionally enacted policies; the committees employ both program and efficiency criteria to guide the oversight of the executive branch. Budgetary controls are relatively subtle devices; external constraints make the process an incremental one which sees the committees most commonly cut small amounts from agency requests;

bureaucrats seek to defend or enlarge their share of the budget while the lawmakers seek, by a variety of tactics and with the aid of a well-qualified staff, to hold the line, or at least to slow the rate of administrative growth. In so doing, they impose limitations on agency discretion and the threat, real or potential, of budget cuts, serves to encourage administrators to pay heed to the desires of the lawmakers. The contest, in short, matches the agency's wish for discretion and flexibility against the congressmen's need to manage and control.

Controls over personnel Another focus for legislative oversight is on *who* works in the bureaucracy rather than on what administrators do. This form of control is in part embodied in the statutes, enacted by both chambers, which define the conditions for employment under the civil service system and, in part, exercised by the Senate's "advice-and-consent" power to approve the President's nominations of individuals to fill a variety of high-level executive positions, including the Cabinet secretaries, federal judges, and ambassadors to foreign nations. In either fashion, control over the personnel of the national government gives Congress the ability to place in particular bureaucratic positions types of individuals that the legislature finds acceptable. Acceptability involves more than finding men and women of talent who can be expected to perform well; it entails consideration of a variety of practical and political criteria as well.

Turning first to the prescription of standards for federal employment under civil service leads directly to the two Post Office and Civil Service Committees of Congress. These are low-prestige committees, with rapid membership turnover as those who acquire seniority move on to more desirable assignments; they lack the commitment to their tasks which characterizes the more highly regarded panels. Yet these bodies have considerable potential, for with the personnel of the federal executive rests much of the prospects for policy success (or failure) and governmental efficiency (or lack thereof). To the extent that sound administrators—who, given the discretion that inheres in the agencies and bureaus, are in reality political decision makers—can be recruited, the effectiveness of federal programs will be enhanced.

The legislation which the Civil Service Committees process is of several sorts. First, some bills define the scope of civil service coverage, establishing merit systems for various classifications of employees and exempting other groups. Those exempt positions, of course, are available for patronage use. Congressional acts also set pay scales, define job classifications, and treat "such subjects as eligibility, examinations and appointments, apportionment, hours of work, leaves of absence, training, employee ratings, employee relations, medical and other services, awards, promotions, lay off and separation, and retirement" (Harris, 1965, p. 198). Of central importance are provisions defining the composition of various boards and commissions:

statutes require some to maintain partisan balance, preventing their being "stacked" exclusively with members of one party; other laws dictate that employees be apportioned geographically among the regions of the nation; others guarantee that veterans of military service be given preference when vacancies are to be filled. Such statutory controls go far to specify who may work for the federal government and under what conditions the work will be conducted.[16]

Personnel measures also deal with the procedures for removing federal employees. Aside from defining a variety of grievance procedures, congressional enactments have, occasionally at least, tried to specify ways to reduce the size of the executive establishment, often acting by attaching riders to appropriations bills (Harris, 1965, pp. 212–218). Congress has, for example, imposed limits on the number of employees who can perform personnel-management work, setting a ratio (usually around 1 to 125) of such employees to total agency employees. So-called "Jensen riders" [after Rep. Ben F. Jensen (R., Iowa)] were attached to a number of appropriations bills in the early 1950s. These sought to limit bureaucratic growth by forbidding agencies to fill vacancies; no one would be fired, but no new employees could be added to the job rolls. Another variation on this theme is the "Whitten amendment,"[17] which set a ceiling on the number of permanent employees that specified departments and agencies could have on the payroll; the restriction led to a vastly enlarged use of "temporary" employees, hired to perform necessary tasks.

Finally, Congress has been concerned with exercising some control over the activities of executive personnel outside of regular working hours. In 1939, the legislature excluded by law the employment in federal service of any person holding membership in groups seeking to subvert the government — Communists and fascists, though primarily the former. During the 1950s, some committees of Congress, notably the House Un-American Activities (now Internal Security) Committee and the Senate Permanent Investigations Subcommittee of the Government Operations panel, pursued the question of "subversives in government" through the use of legislative investigations.[18]

---

[16]This power can, if Congress so chooses, be pushed to the extreme of defining a job so carefully that only a single individual is eligible to fill it. For instance, Corwin (1954, note 20, p. 417) cites the following statute:

> Provided further, that of the vacancies created in the Judge Advocate's Department by this act, one such vacancy, not below the rank of Major, shall be filled by the appointment of a person from civil life, not less than forty-five nor more than fifty years of age, who shall have been for ten years a Judge of the Supreme Court of the Philippine Islands, shall have served for two years as a Captain in the regular or volunteer army, and shall be proficient in the Spanish language and laws.

The man for whom this provision was intended was a constituent of the chairman of the House Military Affairs Committee and the chairman of the House conferees on the Military Organization bill, of which this language was a part. Needless to say, Congress seldom goes to such lengths to control low-level government appointments.

[17]Named after Rep. Jamie Whitten (D., Miss.) who introduced the first such restriction in 1950.

[18]On these investigations, see Carr, 1952, Rovere, 1960, Buckley, 1962, Buckley and Bozell, 1954, and Goodman, 1968.

More ordinary forms of political activity have also been limited; a series of laws, the Hatch Acts, have imposed restrictions on bureaucrats' political involvement in election campaigns. The initial intent of such proscriptions seems to have been a desire to protect administrative personnel from being forced, as a condition for holding their posts, to contribute time, energy, or money to the party in power, but one side effect of the laws seems to be an isolation of federal employees from day-to-day politics that other persons, in nonfederal employment, do not have imposed upon them. In all these ways, then, legislative enactments circumscribe the working conditions and, to a degree, the private lives of those in the federal service. The nature of these controls, without doubt, influences the kinds of people who work for the government as well as the ways in which these employees perform their jobs.

A much more dramatic, though probably less pervasive, way in which Congress controls the personnel of the federal establishment is the Senate's power to confirm the President's nominations for several thousand executive positions, ranging from Supreme Court justices to third class postmasters. Two generally applicable criteria—(1) technical competence: the nominee's possession of the requisite talent, ability, and skill to perform the job for which he has been proposed; and (2) freedom from conflict of interest: the nominee's ability to perform without incentive to place private monetary reward ahead of his bureaucratic responsibilities—ostensibly guide Senate response but partisan politics lurks near the surface of the chamber's consideration. Politically unsatisfactory appointments are opposed with arguments cloaked in the language of competence and conflict of interest.

Technical-competence issues have been raised in the Senate in a number of cases: against President Eisenhower's nomination, as Ambassador to Ceylon, of Maxwell Gluck, a businessman whose main qualification seemed to be a large contribution to the Republican campaign chest (Heard, 1960, pp. 147–148); against Lyndon Johnson's selection of Francis X. Morrisey, an unknown lawyer with close connections to the Kennedy family, for a federal judgeship; and against the nomination by President Richard Nixon of Judge G. Harrold Carswell, who had seen a large number of his opinions reversed by the Supreme Court, to the High Court. While Gluck was eventually approved, the Morrisey nomination was withdrawn and that of Carswell defeated on a roll call vote. In each instance, politics—ideology, party factionalism, desire to embarrass the Chief Executive, or some combination of these factors—seems to have moved some senators to oppose the nomination; the technical-competence argument provided a convenient rationale for a negative stand.

Issues of conflict of interest are less decisive at the confirmation stage; nominees usually anticipate objections on such grounds by selling their stock holdings or placing them in "blind trusts," the management of which goes on without the knowledge of the executive officeholder. The Senate seems unwilling to approve appointments of men, usually industrialists, whose firms do substantial business with the government and who retain interests in those companies. Charges involving conflict of interest more often are leveled by congressmen and others seeking political advantage, to force incumbents from office. Secretary of the Air Force Harold Talbott was compelled to resign in 1955 when he was charged with promoting his personal interests by taking advantage of his official position; Navy Secretary Fred Korth met a similar fate in the Kennedy administration; and Justice Abe Fortas was forced to resign from the Supreme Court in 1969 in the face of like charges.

Occasionally, ideological issues break into the open. Senate liberals, Wayne Morse (D., Ore.) prominent among them, waged an unsuccessful fight in 1959 to block confirmation of Clare Booth Luce as Ambassador to Brazil on the grounds that some campaign statements that she had supposedly made some years before were so extreme that they disqualified her.[19] Liberal coalitions blocked the promotion of lower court judges John J. Parker (1928) and Clement Haynsworth (1969) to the Supreme Court; in each case judicial decisions and personal philosophies were used to mobilize opposition to the nominees. Similarly, President Eisenhower's nomination of Charles E. Bohlen as Ambassador to the Soviet Union aroused substantial opposition among Senate conservatives who objected to Bohlen's presence at the Yalta Conference as indicating approval of the decisions taken at that World War II heads-of-state meeting (Rosenau, 1962).

These controversies, however dramatic, should not obscure the basic fact that the Senate accepts the vast majority of presidential nominations. In the twentieth century, three Cabinet appointees and three Supreme Court nominees have been rejected;[20] a handful of other controversial choices have been withdrawn before coming to a vote. During the Truman, Eisenhower, and Kennedy administrations (1947 to 1963) only twelve nominations were defeated (*Congressional Quarterly*, 1965, p. 102a). This strong tendency to acquiesce in presidential choices should not be taken to mean that the Senate is derelict in its obligation to give "advice and consent"; rather it should be interpreted to reflect a careful job of prior consultation by the President. The Chief Executive will, before sending his nomination to the Senate, take steps to gauge potential legislative reaction. He will clear his choice with his party leaders and will refrain from making appointments whose prospects for confirmation look dim. In such circumstances, controversies will be limited to those cases in which prior clearance is ignored or the extent of senatorial opposition miscalculated.[21]

---

[19]Mrs. Luce's triumph was short-lived; in her "victory" statement, she attributed the opposition to her appointment to Senator Morse's "having been kicked in the head by a horse," a comment which created such a furor that she resigned before ever having assumed her post.

[20]For a useful, though somewhat dated, treatment of the pre-1952 experience, see Harris, 1953.

[21]It was reported that President Nixon failed on both these counts in his rejected nominations of judges Haynsworth and Carswell to the Supreme Court (see Harris, 1971). In any event, these rebuffs to Southern "strict constructionalists" and the President's assertion, whether or not correct, that his nominees were the victims of regional prejudices testify to the importance of political and ideological concerns as well as the need for proper consultation in matters of senatorial confirmation.

On appointments for positions in particular states, in particular federal judgeships and postmasterships, the Senate has exacted an extensive veto power over the President through the informal device of "senatorial courtesy." If the senator (or senators) of the same political party as the Chief Executive objects to a nomination for a position within his state, if he declares the nominee "personally obnoxious" to him, the Senate, acting in accord with the norms of reciprocity and personal courtesy, will decline to confirm the President's choice. This informal rule serves to enhance the senators' patronage power; it enables them to block appointment of their political foes to important positions, and perhaps, if their own views win acceptance at the White House, to reward their own party associates with prominent posts. In one classic case, two federal judgeships in Illinois remained unfilled while Senator Paul Douglas and President Truman refused to accept one another's choices and were unable to reach an accommodation (Galloway, 1953, p. 577). Presidential consultation and clearance of his proposed nominations with the relevant senators means, in practice, that "senatorial courtesy" is seldom invoked, but its existence serves as a reminder of the potency of the upper house's influence over executive appointments.

In a wide variety of ways, then, Congress can exert control over the personnel of the federal executive branch. Both houses, acting through the normal lawmaking process, can define the qualifications and conditions for government employment for millions of workers under the civil service. The Senate, in giving its advice and consent, can influence the identities of those who hold the top executive positions. Controls of both sorts, though ostensibly concerned with who will serve, nonetheless contribute to what is done (policy) and how it is carried into effect (efficiency).

Control through investigation Still another oversight device, and a sometimes controversial one, is the congressional investigation. Sometimes using special committees,[22] more often employing its standing committees, Congress looks into a wide range of problems, outside[23] as well as within the government. The central purpose of such inquiries is, of course, to provide information on which to base its performance of its lawmaking function; there can be little doubt that the legislature needs to know current conditions if it is to enact policies to deal with contemporary problems. In the same vein, investigations may serve to expose inefficiency or mismanagement within the executive branch, serve, that is, the oversight function. Little criticism would be

---

[22]Special investigating committees pose difficult issues. By informal rule, or custom, the chairmanship of the special panel is entrusted to the lawmaker who proposes the investigation initially; this norm creates opportunity for junior legislators to gain visibility and exercise power, but at the same time may make an impartial inquiry most difficult, for it is not immediately clear that a man who stimulates an investigation is the best person to conduct it.

[23]Among the most famous investigations of nongovernmental problems are Sen. Estes Kefauver's (D., Tenn.) inquiry into organized crime in America and the exposure by the so-called McClellan committee on crime and corruption within certain labor unions.

directed toward investigations if they were always clearly limited to these purposes.[24]

Investigations have a long history, dating back to a 1792 inquiry into the causes of the massacre of more than 600 American soldiers by Indians in the Ohio Territory. A House investigating panel determined, among other things, that the commander of the force, General Arthur St. Clair, "nearing sixty and tortured with gout, had three horses shot from under him as he was being assisted to the saddle" (Taylor, 1961, p. 34). From that time forward, congressional committees have sought to uncover "the facts" about a very broad set of questions in pursuance of their lawmaking and oversight responsibilities. While the right of Congress to investigate has not been seriously challenged, the issue of what, if any, limitations on the investigatory power exist has never been precisely, or entirely satisfactorily, resolved. A series of court decisions, beginning with the case of *Kilbourn v. Thompson,* 103 U.S. 168 (1881), gives evidence that the judiciary has been reluctant to specify the rights and obligations of investigating committees.

On the whole, it appears that the courts will define the investigatory power on a case-by-case basis. Among the issues relevant to such determinations are the extent to which the investigation was pertinent to congressional functions, the degree to which questions put to witnesses are related to legitimate legislative goals, and the possibility that the constitutionally guaranteed privileges and immunities of witnesses may be violated. The issue seems clearly posed — the recognized need of Congress to know *versus* the equally clear need to protect the rights of those from whom information is sought — but precisely how the balance between these competing goals is to be struck remains uncertain. The courts have asserted that the investigatory power is not "omnipotent," but to date have refused to state clearly the nature of those limitations (Taylor, 1961, chap. 4).

Abuses of the power to investigate receive publicity well beyond the frequency of their occurrence; the vast majority of investigations are conducted well within the judicially imposed limitations. The inquiry into the effectiveness of defense mobilization during World War II, headed by Sen. Harry S. Truman (D., Mo.), is often held out to be a model of a fair and judicious use of the investigatory power (Riddle, 1964). Acknowledging both the need to investigate agency performance and the decorum of most proceedings, it remains the case that abuses, and the potential for abuses, continue to be the most controversial feature of legislative investigations. Some inquiries seem to relegate the acquisition of information to a subsidiary place, instead serving to promote a variety of political purposes. For one thing, the investigation may seek to defend or protect an agency rather than to probe its administration; the hearings may be used as a forum for the friends of the bureau to make a case for the soundness with which its programs have been run; in a few

[24]On investigations generally, see Taylor, 1961, and Barth, 1955.

cases, such a sympathetic inquiry may be designed to preempt a more hostile one that another committee might otherwise undertake. Another noninformational purpose of investigations is to glorify the chief investigator, or at least to enhance his public image. The famous Army-McCarthy hearings of 1954 seem, in retrospect, to have produced little useful data on the Army's administrative practices; rather they appear to have been part of Sen. Joseph McCarthy's more general campaign against the "liberal establishment" in Washington (Rovere, 1959; Taylor, 1961).

It is the violation of the civil rights of witnesses, however, which remains the central abuse to which the critics of investigations point. Armed with power to subpoena witnesses and evidence, and to charge the uncooperative with contempt of Congress, committeemen are not always willing to afford witnesses with the same protections they would have in a court of law. Witnesses have not always had the right to counsel; the opportunity to cross-examine those who give damaging evidence against them; or the chance to avail themselves of the privilege, guaranteed by the Fifth Amendment to the Constitution, against self-incrimination. Senator McCarthy's widely used phrase, "Fifth-Amendment Communist," assumed a refusal to answer a question to be an admission of guilt rather than the right of a witness to avoid giving evidence which might be used against him in a subsequent proceeding. An investigator, seeking publicity for himself or his cause, may make charges, which the witness has no chance to rebut, that damage the witness' reputation unjustly, charges which may be remembered even though no formal proceedings are even convened or long after the charges have been disproved. In recognition of these possibilities, in 1955, the House of Representatives adopted a code of fair practices, though one without enforcement provisions (Heubel, 1957).

The issue is, thus, how to balance the legitimate need of Congress to seek out information with the obligation to protect the individual witness's civil liberties. The investigation, despite its potential for misuse, remains a highly valuable technique for a legislative body which suffers from limited information, and which feels inferior to executive-branch expertise. At present, restraints on investigators are mainly self-imposed; further abuses will, in all probability, lead to additional, involuntary restrictions being imposed on committee information-gathering activities.

Informal controls A final set of oversight techniques involves neither statutory requirements nor hearing-room confrontations. Instead they reflect a variety of informal, and sometimes "off-the-record," contacts and communications. The success of these contacts, the understandings reached between agency and subcommittee as their result, may reduce the more routine dealings to a formality, to a ratification of understandings previously reached. To begin with, the lawmakers may ask questions or give suggestions during a hearing to which the administrators feel compelled to respond; if compliance is not forthcoming, the subcommittee may treat the agency harshly in future years. Statements incorporated in committee reports have a similar effect; though legally these are mere obiter dicta, the bureaucrat is loath to ignore them, for to do so is to invite committee reprisal. Issues raised in informal contacts between agency and committee staff lead to the same end: the administrators seek to please the lawmakers and, thus, to avert subsequent budget cuts (Harris, 1965, p. 9; Kofmehl, 1962, pp. 127–131).

Executive personnel are attuned to the content of these informal communications, of course, because of the formal sanctions which underlie them. In order to avoid the imposition of punishments—less money, more restrictions, or less authority—bureau personnel seek to anticipate the reactions of the lawmakers, that is, the former plot their courses of action taking into account what they believe the latter to want (Friedrich, 1937, pp. 16–18; Wildavsky, 1964, pp. 74–83; Freeman, 1965, pp. 69–70). To reduce uncertainty still further the agency may initiate contact with the relevant committee or subcommittee, seeking in effect to get advance approval for its proposed actions, or at least attempting to get a better gauge of what the representatives' responses are likely to be. Friendships are sought, in the interests of understanding, confidence, and predictability, on a social as well as a professional level. Legislators' visits to agency installations may be eagerly sought by the lawmakers and bureaucrats, not only as "fact-finding" tours but also as opportunities for informal discussion (Fenno, 1966, pp. 303–313). Agreements reached, in advance, through such communications channels or mutual confidence developed in this way may go far toward removing conflict from the formal executive agency–legislative committee dealings.

CONGRESSIONAL OVERSIGHT: SOME LIMITATIONS

All the ways and devices, discussed previously, give Congress the opportunity to oversee (control, supervise) the federal executive branch. In practice, however, a number of forces serve to limit the effectiveness of the legislative "watchdog" operations. Legislators are reluctant to undertake the overseer role; their orientations seem to run in other directions for the most part. Those lawmakers who do make a commitment to oversight labor under a number of handicaps which reduce their effectiveness.

Effective oversight, of course, requires a sufficient number of legislators to commit a significant proportion of their resources to the job; otherwise control will be haphazard and incomplete. Individual congressmen, as we have seen, must face severe role conflict in this regard; each must decide how, when, and in what ways he will divide his time and energy among the three major output functions: lawmaking, oversight, and representation. Policy making remains the most dramatic legislative activity; to chart new directions is, for many, more gratifying than the often painstaking chore of sifting budgets or studying bureaucratic regulations. Oversight, it appears, often comes off second-best in competition with the various representational activities. As we shall see (Chapter 13), in more detail, constituent relations assume a prominent position for many congressmen for the instrumental need, at the very least, to win reelection. A legislator cannot act as policy maker or overseer if he neglects his constituency obligations to the point where he is turned out of office. Thus, a large proportion of senators and representatives appear to assume an oversight-indifferent orientation, resolving their role conflicts in favor of lawmaking and representation rather than the supervisory function.

Scher (1963) suggests a number of specific reasons for such a choice. First is a restatement of the point made above: "Congressmen tend to see opportunities for greater rewards in the things they value from involvement in legislative and constituent-service activity than from participation in oversight activity" (p. 531). Second, they "tend to view the agencies as impenetrable mazes and to believe that any serious effort at penetrating them poses hazards for the inexpert Congressman which outweigh any conceivable gain to him" (p. 532). This latter variation on the theme that the costs of oversight exceed the benefits to be derived suggests the problems of the generalist pitted against the expert. Even those who, within the legislative system, are classed as specialists lack the technical "know-how" to challenge the bureaucrats; the availability of competent staff aid in some circumstances is insufficient to offset the bureaucrats' advantages.

Another set of restraining influences relates to the individual lawmaker's reluctance to intrude on operative legislative-executive relations, to disrupt ongoing "subsystems" (Freeman, 1965). Where congressmen have "mutually rewarding relationships" with administrators, they prefer not to endanger them by forceful oversight (Scher, 1963, pp. 533–534); where they can obtain desired goals through personal involvement they see no need to employ formal committee procedures to gain their ends (Scher, 1963, p. 534). Disturbing such subsystem relationships may, negatively, invoke sanctions from the nongovernmental—interest groups or constituency interests—participants in such arrangements. To damage or even challenge the widely accepted association between, say, a regulatory agency and its clientele (i.e., those whom the agency regulates) may invite reprisals (i.e., campaign opposition or loss of financial contributions) from the clientele. Because, then, they can get what they want through other means or because the costs may appear too great, members of Congress are reluctant to interfere with established legislative–executive–outside group arrangements.

Scher (1963, pp. 537–540) also cites two other pressures which may reduce legislators' inclination to act as overseers. For one thing, members of the President's political party may expect greater rewards from cooperating with the Chief Executive than from critical examination of his appointees' performance; party loyalists may seek to protect the President rather than to run the risk of embarrassing him. Finally, there is the fact of committee and congressional routine; as lawmakers, for the reasons listed, turn away from control and supervision, their habitual mode of operation comes to omit oversight. The watchdog role, unrewarding as it is perceived to be, atrophies as the potential overseers look elsewhere for their professional satisfactions. All these forces lead a majority of legislators, *ceteris paribus,* to be oversight-indifferent, or if involved to become agency-oriented, either through membership in a "subsystem" or out of party loyalty.

But other things are not always equal; there exist forces and opportunities that stimulate an orientation which seeks active oversight of the executive branch (Scher, 1963, pp. 540–550). In general, when there are advantages to be gained through supervisory activity, congressmen will turn their attention away from lawmaking and representation toward control. More specifically, a chance to embarrass an opposition President, to win partisan advantage, may be a spur to legislative oversight. Likewise, if they perceive the Chief Executive as threatening congressional prerogatives, the representatives may seek to bring the agency, especially the regulatory commissions, more firmly under control by means of intervention, through oversight, into agency affairs. Outside interests, pressure groups in particular, may provide incentive for involvement with the bureaucracy. If legislators cannot satisfy important constituency or other groups by the normal, personal means, the pressure to use formal, oversight techniques will build. Similarly, when there is a push, originating within or without the legislative system, for policy revision, congressmen may seek to influence agency decision makers through formal oversight proceedings. Finally, when functioning relationships appear to be endangered, by possible exposure of ineffectiveness or policy failure, those lawmakers with a stake in maintaining the status quo may launch a "defensive" or "protective" investigation, sometimes labeled a "whitewash" by its critics, designed to neutralize the potential disruption.[25] In other words, in search of political advantage, or in response to strong demands from outside sources, oversight may appear worth the investment of time and energy to a number of lawmakers. On balance, however, Scher (1963, pp. 550–551) concludes that the legislator's most common but not constant calculation that his resources are better spent on other matters "explains his frequent preference for leaving the agencies alone as well as his periodic willingness to examine them closely."

Even should such calculations lead a legislator to assume a positive orientation toward oversight—and they most certainly will for some members of

[25] When, for instance, in 1970, critics of Supreme Court Justice William O. Douglas moved to impeach him, or in other ways to force his retirement, the House Democratic party leadership quickly created a special panel to investigate the charges against Douglas, presumably preferring to have a sympathetic rather than a hostile body conduct the inquiry. Not surprisingly, the panel exonerated Justice Douglas.

Congress[26] — he may encounter other obstacles that inhibit such activity. Major features of the congressional system contribute to this situation. We have already noted the pull of political party; an interested congressman may abandon oversight rather than challenge the leaders of his party. The autonomous committees also operate, in some circumstances, to discourage active exercise of control (Bibby, 1966). The attitude of the panel chairman and how he decides to employ his powers go far toward determining the kinds and extent of control that his committee exercises. If the chairman is policy oriented, he will steer the panel in that direction; if he is a minority chairman — if his preferences do not dominate the group — he will restrain panel activity in all sectors, including oversight. If, conversely, he is a "service chairman," seeking to facilitate the chosen work of his colleagues, he will leave them free to engage in control activities.[27] The chairman's preferences with regard to subcommittees and staffing affect committee oversight performance as well. To the degree he allows subcommittees to become independent, to carve out their own areas of expertise, they will have more freedom to engage in supervising the executive agencies within their jurisdictions. Similarly, the larger the staff resources, in general and for individual subcommittees in particular, the greater the potential assistance available to those lawmakers concerned with control duties. In all these ways, then, the chairman, and how he chooses to manage his committee, may constrain the oversight possibilities of even those committee members eager to assert their supervisory prerogatives.

Even if, in spite of all these obstacles, a legislator finds himself in a position to engage in oversight, he must still face formidable handicaps. For one thing, and especially critical in the appropriations process, administrative operations are extraordinarily complex, involving as they do technical and scientific matters, numerous programs, and large numbers of items entailing the expenditure of great sums of money. We have already indicated how, in the face of these difficulties, congressmen must "sample for information," probing mainly those concerns about which they have some knowledge and ignoring those topics, a large number, about which they lack a firm basis for purposeful questioning. Oversight, thus, becomes, of necessity, a highly selective activity with a concentrated focus on a very few items.

One study (Sharkansky, 1965) indicates clearly the nature of this selectivity.

---

[26] We may hypothesize that medium-to-low seniority congressmen, having served their apprenticeships, may find oversight an attractive opportunity to put their developing expertise to work and to begin to exercise power in some area, however limited, of their concerns. As these men gain in seniority, and achieve full-fledged expert status, and, perhaps, leadership posts, their attention should turn more toward the policy-making outputs of Congress.

[15] Bibby (1966, pp. 80–82) points out the example of J. William Fulbright in this connection. Chairman of the Senate Banking and Currency Committee, the Arkansas Democrat was, as now, more interested in foreign than in domestic policy, and, focusing his interest on the former, he left the committee pretty much free to "run itself." In such circumstances, the interested Banking and Currency members could engage in oversight without interference from the chairman.

Examining one subcommittee—the House Appropriations subcommittee charged with responsibility for the various programs of the Department of Health, Education and Welfare—and its treatment of four quite different HEW agencies—the Children's Bureau, the Office of Education, the Food and Drug Administration, and Howard University—the author found, first, that oversight attention tends to focus on the agencies "more prominent . . . in the public eye" (p. 627). The Office of Education and the Children's Bureau have the largest budgets, are involved with more programs, and grew at faster rates, and the subcommittee paid more heed to them than to the less visible bureaus. Witnesses from these agencies were asked more questions about more budget items than were the spokesmen of the less well-known ones. Next, severity of treatment—cutting budgets and placing specific instructions in subcommittee reports—tends to follow attention, especially in the case of the Office of Education, an "adventurous" agency, whose administrators were both evasive in budget hearings and prone to disregard prior committee instructions. Finally, none of the agencies escaped all intensive questioning, perhaps because the overseers wanted to avoid creating the impression among the bureaucrats that there was nothing to fear from the subcommittee, or perhaps because they hoped to discover some "errant administrative behavior" (p. 628).

Another basic problem, beyond the lack of information and the consequent need to question selectively, that overseers must face reflects their own "frame of reference." Dexter (1963a) in examining congressional activity in the sphere of military affairs, found that the lawmakers tended to set their sights low; they preferred to leave broad policy decisions to the military and to deal, instead, with more mundane matters such as the acquisition and disposition of military land holdings. In fact, he describes the House Armed Services Committee as "primarily a real estate committee" (pp. 310–312). Lacking the necessary expertise to challenge the executive experts, the overseers have adopted a focus on efficiency to the virtual exclusion of evaluating the effectiveness of policy choices. The longer the former focus dominates legislative thinking, the more the tradition of avoiding a challenge to the experts becomes inculcated, and the more difficult it becomes to assert congressional control over the policy features of administrative behavior.

However suspicious of the bureaucrats he may become, so long as he lacks basic data from which to proceed and so long as he feels himself inadequate to investigate, the legislator's supervision of the executive will remain peripheral rather than central. One counterweight which might strengthen the lawmaker's hand is the availability of a strong and specialized committee or personal staff. Such a resource, however, is seldom available. The committee chairman, as noted, controls the staff and he may choose to assign it tasks other than those pertaining to oversight; if he is a loyal party supporter, he may be disinclined to delve into the affairs of his party's administration. Moreover, only a few committees make much provision for nonpartisan staffing which would provide the minority party, whose members might be expected to have the greatest incentive to act as supervisors, the basis to take seriously its role as critic of the majority's administrative behavior.[28] Even the Appropriations Committees, known for their well-qualified staffs, are unable to develop the sort of expertise required to counter executive specialists. One proposal, frequently voiced, would increase the staff resources available to committees in an effort to redress the balance between the two branches (Saloma, 1969, pp. 159–168).

One remaining difficulty should be noted here; in spite of whatever countervailing power that Congress may generate, the administration, under the doctrine of "executive privilege," can refuse to inform the legislature. One of the by-products of the St. Clair investigation in 1792 was a rule, not invoked in that instance, established by President Washington and his Cabinet that, in Thomas Jefferson's words, "The Executive ought to communicate [to Congress] such papers as the public good would permit, and ought to refuse those, the disclosure of which would endanger the public" (Taylor, 1961, pp. 39–40). Since then Presidents have repeatedly invoked the privilege, asserting their power to withhold from the legislature those documents which they believe should remain confidential "in the public interest." To cite an acute instance of the congressional problem, in its 1955 inquiry into possible financial irregularities in the contract negotiations for private construction of a utility plant for use of the Atomic Energy Commission, the so-called Dixon-Yates Affair, the legislature was refused information by a number of government officials, including the Budget Director, the chairman of the Atomic Energy Commission, the chairman of the Securities and Exchange Commission, and the chief special assistant to the President (Rourke, 1960, p. 685). The publication, in 1971, via a "leak" to the *New York Times* and other newspapers, of the so-called "Pentagon Papers" makes indisputably clear how much information a "top secret" classification can withhold from the legislative branch.[29]

While there is little controversy over the principle that some documents and data should remain secret, the application of the principle has generated considerable interbranch friction. Congress asserts its right and need to know what the executive branch is doing and argues that the bureaucrats often go beyond the topics—scientific or military matters, for example—on which secrecy is acceptable to suppress data in the interests of partisan advantage,

---

[28] For a discussion of the partisan feature of committee staffing, see Chapter 3, pp. 77–79.
[29] The papers, running to forty-seven volumes protected by a "top secret" classification, revealed that a substantial amount of executive-branch deliberation, contingency planning, and basic-policy decision making about the American involvement in Indochina was conducted beyond the purview of Congress. The Nixon administration, though it might have expected to profit politically from the papers' revelations, sought to restrain the press from publishing the documents, arguing in effect that publication would compromise executive privilege, the right to protect a free and full flow of information and opinion among executive-branch personnel. The Supreme Court, however, by a 6–3 vote, ruled otherwise, upholding the freedom of the press from prior restraint upon publication.

to make the administration look good, or to conceal things that might reflect adversely on it. The phrases "news management" and "credibility gap," characteristic of current political debate, indicate the nature of the congressional challenge to executive information policies. The issue is not, of course, clear-cut; Congress has recognized that secrecy has its uses, has enacted statutes protecting executive-branch data from disclosure, and has often employed closed meetings to conduct its committee business. The issue, unlikely ever to be resolved definitively, is how to balance competing needs for "publicity and privacy in the operations of democratic government" (Rourke, 1960, p. 691); how to maximize the availability of information without compromising operations which must, of necessity, remain covert.

For all these reasons, oversight is often, but not always, in Redford's phrase (1960, p. 255), "spotty, spasmodic, and sometimes cursory." Faced with a vast establishment to review and armed with limited resources—in effect, generalists challenging specialists in the latters' own bailiwick—it is not surprising to find that Congress has compiled an uneven oversight record. This is not to argue that congressional control is nonexistent—of course, it is strong in many areas and on many topics—but rather to suggest that, given the balance of resources, legislative oversight is not as careful or consistent as those (e.g., Huntington, 1965) who propose or desire greater congressional attention to the oversight function would wish.

There remains one more problem, a systemic issue, to consider. Since congressional oversight is, in reality, committee oversight, and since the committees operate, to a large degree, independent of one another, supervisory actions, like other forms of congressional activity, are carried out in an uncoordinated, disintegrated fashion. Decisions taken by two committees, each pursuing its oversight mandate, may be inconsistent with one another; even two subcommittees of the same parent body may reach incompatible conclusions. This form of behavior is consistent with other modes of decision making in a fragmented, decentralized system, but the point remains that Congress makes little or no effort to coordinate its oversight activities in some meaningful pattern.

Nowhere is the difficulty more visible than in the appropriations process. The extraordinarily complex and abstruse issue of how to allocate scarce national financial resources among the multiplicity of federal programs is never faced; rather a series of some fifteen or so separate money bills is passed in series, one at a time, without serious effort at fitting them together. Each appropriations subcommittee makes its own decisions, from its own perspective, and, as we have seen, usually wins chamber approval of these decisions. Not until the last bill is passed, often well into the fiscal year involved, can the total expenditures which Congress has voted be calculated. The rank-and-file legislators, asked to vote on these measures, must answer the roll without much knowledge of what they will be asked to approve in subsequent appropriations legislation, and are thus virtually incapable of taking a comprehensive view of federal revenues and expenses.

Congress has, in the past, recognized the problem of uncoordinated budgets and has experimented, unsuccessfully, with integrative devices. The Legislative Reorganization Act of 1946 created the Joint Committee on the Legislative Budget to study the President's budget message and to report out a resolution containing Congress's fiscal proposals. This was done in 1947 and in 1948, but in neither year, once faced with specific appropriations bills, could the legislature live with the budget estimates it had set for itself. Members of the appropriations committees, though on the Joint Committee, were reluctant to share their powers; the joint body was poorly staffed; and political circumstances—a Republican congressional majority facing a Democratic President—did not facilitate the experiment; the idea was abandoned in 1949 (Carroll, 1966, pp. 198–200).

A year later, in 1950, another venture sought to remedy the well-perceived lack of budgetary coordination in the House of Representatives. At that time, instead of treating a series of appropriations measures, the full Appropriations Committee combined all subcommittee recommendations into an omnibus bill which ran to 427 printed pages and, as eventually passed, entailed expenditures in excess of twenty-nine billion dollars. This experience led to a quick return to more customary practice. The omnibus bill was on the House floor for five weeks; the Senate, in its appellate capacity, had to wait until the lower chamber completed action before going to work; no money appeared to have been saved; and Congress could do little except urge the President to save money (Carroll, 1966, pp. 203–206). For more than twenty years, since 1950, the budget has been treated piecemeal, and Congress has denied itself any chance to look at the revenue and expenditures issues from a broad, coordinated perspective. By the same token, it is virtually impossible to fix the responsibility for budgetary difficulties which do develop.[30] What is true of appropriations politics is most probably also the case with other committees dealing with other topics.

SUMMARY

A second set of demands on Congress is for oversight of the administrative branch of the federal government. These demands may originate outside the legislative system from those—the President, interest groups, and concerned

---

[30]Carroll (1966, pp. 207–208) argues that "Congress prefers confusion." Local projects can be funded, power exercised by subcommittee members, responsibility avoided, and, as a result, movements to centralize budgetary politics have been resisted. Mistakes can be remedied in supplemental or deficiency appropriations bills, which make coordination that much more difficult, but which preserve the legislators' freedom to act.

citizens—interested in the application of policy decisions by the bureaucrats or from the same or similarly located sources concerned with promoting administrative efficiency. Members of Congress, of course, often share these goals. Oversight—that is, control, supervision, or review of the executive branch and its activities—is that set of congressional behaviors taken in response to these demands.

Senators and representatives have a number of potential weapons with which to engage in oversight: they can write a variety of provisions, including the legislative veto, into law; they can use their "power of the purse" to restrict administrative discretion; they can set standards for federal employment and in other ways control the personnel of the executive branch; they can launch investigations to determine the nature of administrative conduct; and they can seek to keep the bureaucrats in line through informal contacts buttressed by the threat, often merely implicit, of formal sanctions. The opportunities for oversight, and the devices available for its conduct, thus are many and varied.

Yet despite these possibilities, and despite the fact that it is frequently conducted vigorously and with the desired effects of inhibiting adventurous bureaucrats, congressional oversight, nonetheless, encounters certain problems which prevent it from working as adequately as it might. The opportunities available for involvement before, during, and after administrative actions, to put it in other words, cannot be exploited to the maximum possible degree. For one thing, the inevitable role conflict over where a legislator should expend his energies is often resolved in favor of other forms of activity; concern with lawmaking and representation, seen as more rewarding, lead large numbers of legislators to assume an oversight-indifferent orientation. Moreover, those concerned with overseeing the executive may be agency-oriented—that is, eager to protect working relationships with bureaucratic units—rather than determined to exert legislative control. The corps of potential "watchdogs" is, in consequence, relatively small, except for those few occasions when political capital appears within reach from oversight.

Even those with a pro-Congress orientation toward control, who want to impose congressional priorities on executive agencies, have a series of difficult hurdles to leap. They lack information, especially that which the bureaucrats prefer to keep from them; they lack the tradition of forceful supervisory activity, focusing on the superficial rather than on the basic issues; they may be constrained by their committee seniors, who may, preferring to work on other matters, keep staff and other sources out of the potential overseers' hands. And, finally, Congress is ill equipped to make systematic use of that control which is conducted. For all these reasons, then, oversight is less effective than those who believe Congress should make a greater commitment to supervision and review would wish it to be.

The point should not be overstated however. Though selective in character, where operative oversight is highly effective, the channels—formal and informal—exist over which lawmakers can make their views known to the agencies and bureaus. From the bureaucratic perspective, it is well to consider legislative opinion carefully, for Congress, within the limits noted, can and does seize opportunities to enforce its will. And inevitably a number of lawmakers will find adequate rewards in the exercise of oversight to ensure that some members of Congress, able to alert their less-concerned colleagues, will be watching all facets of agency activity.

CHAPTER THIRTEEN

Legislative Representation

Lawmaking and oversight do not, by any means, exhaust the output activity of senators and representatives. A third category, and perhaps the most basic one, of legislative responsibility encompasses the various tasks that congressmen undertake to represent their constituents. We have already (Chapter 1, pp. 20–21, and Chapter 9, pp. 214–217) noted that the demands for representation may be of two general sorts: requests for specific policy choices—that is, for particular lawmaking outputs—and requests for services generally devoid of policy content. Much of what the former demands entail has been mentioned elsewhere in this book; here we will pull these threads together in a clearer statement of the relation between the legislator's substantive decisions and his constituents' policy preferences. Secondly, this chapter will explore the congressmen's responses to the multitude of requests for favors and services with which the residents of his state or district almost literally deluge him.

Before dealing with these topics, two points need to be made. One is that we are offering no explicit definition of representation, for to do so would require entry into a normative thicket which it seems best to avoid at this juncture.[1] Put another way, our values concerning what *should be* the proper relation between legislator and constituents go far toward shaping our definition of what representation is. Should a lawmaker back policy

---

[1] We will, however, venture on this treacherous path in Chapter 14.

proposals that those living in his district favor even if he believes them unwise, or should he do what he holds to be correct in the face of adverse views "back home"? Should a member of Congress spend his time performing services for his constituents, or should he ignore these relatively unimportant chores and instead concentrate his efforts on policy making or oversight duties? These are very hard questions—congressmen answer them only with great difficulty—and how we respond to them affects directly what we believe about representation. To avoid these thorny issues, we will here treat representation as the set of interactions involving demands of both a substantive and a service variety between the electorate and the elected, between the congressman and those who send him to Washington, D.C.[2]

The second matter pertains to the distinction between representational outputs and those of lawmaking and oversight: these are not mutually exclusive forms of activity; rather there are clear interrelations among them. Demands for specific policy initiatives, most obviously, raise the question of a lawmaker's support for various measures in general, and of his vote, in particular; likewise demands for services may suggest to him that new legislative departures are required to eliminate the situation stimulating the demand. Service requests ("casework") often reflect dissatisfaction with administrative performance and they may well lead the congressman to focus his attention on overseeing agencies which seem to arouse considerable constituent discontent. Representation, thus, assumes a central importance for legislative outputs: not only does it permit (or require) the lawmaker to serve, in some fashion, those who elected him, but it also provides needed and useful information for his policy-making and oversight roles (Olson, 1966).

Representation, then, refers to the requirement that Congress, elected by the citizenry, should in some fashion work to protect the interests of the electorate, speak for them, and act on their behalf. Failure to do so—failure, that is, to represent—will, in systemic terms, lead to a loss of support for the legislature. An institution, Congress or any other, which does not respond satisfactorily to the expectations that people hold about it will soon cease to have the respect of the populace and will find that its pronouncements will no longer be regarded as legitimate. The system will, in such circumstances, either have to adapt, that is, redefine its mission and readjust its procedures, or it will be unable to survive (see Chapter 1, pp. 5-6 and 17-18).

POLICY REPRESENTATION

Policy representation refers to the belief that the legislator should act to advance the interests of the people. At issue is the extent to which there is

[2]Among the many books that treat representation in philosophical terms, see especially de Grazia, 1951, and Pitkin, 1967. On the definitional problem, see Fairlie, 1940, and Gilbert, 1963.

some form of correspondence between the lawmaker's behavior and the desires of those whom he has been chosen to represent. Any analysis of the constituency-congressman relationship must focus on several topics: *Who* is to represent? *How* is representation to be effected? The first question involves a discussion of the recruitment process by which representatives are selected and retained in office; the second deals with the behavior, in this instance in the congressional context, of the representative, how he relates to the residents of his constituency.

Who is to represent? In Chapter 2 we have suggested that the American electoral process, and the constitutional arrangements which define it, determine substantially the sorts of men and women who sit in Congress. For one thing, the units of representation are fixed: the states in the Senate, the congressional districts, composed under recent judicial decisions of as nearly equal as possible populations, in the House of Representatives. Electoral schemes, moreover, require that the lawmakers seek election in single-member districts. In practice, given the decentralized character of political parties in this country, this means that each individual candidate, particularly in House races, is on his own; he must organize his own campaign, choose the themes which that campaign will stress, raise his own funds to defray his election expenses, and generally count on marginal aid at best from his national party. He may, in many cases, have to endure these rigors in both a primary and a general election campaign, and, of course, repeat the process every two or six years if he desires, as most national lawmakers do, to remain in office.

Not all Americans are equally equipped to survive this winnowing process and thus only a small group, and an atypical one, successfully runs the electoral gamut and sits in Congress. In demographic terms, that is, the members of the national legislature are in no sense a cross section of the citizenry, or even of the electorate. They are drawn from the upper reaches of the social structure: they have more education, better jobs paying higher salaries, and are more often members of "prestige" churches than those who elect them; they are more often white, not black; middle-aged, not under forty; of Anglo-Saxon, not Southern or Eastern Eurpoean, ancestry. These differences assume importance because beliefs about politics and policy differ among the social strata; those who serve in Congress, that is, bring to that service different perspectives on public issues than would a more faithful representation of the American people as described in the United States census of population.

Representation in action: focus and style Once in office, lawmakers must act on the basis of some set of orientations toward those whom they are to represent. Eulau and his collaborators (1959) have identified two facets of this legislature-constituent connection: focus and style. Focus refers to the geographic unit that the representative feels he is to serve. We would expect, perhaps, that the single-member district and the other localized electoral arrangements already noted would lead large numbers of lawmakers to assume a district- (or state-) areal role orientation, that is, to feel that their primary obligation is to act to benefit the local citizens, to whom their subsequent reelection efforts will need be directed. In fact, however, a substantial proportion of members of the House of Representatives profess to place the "national interest" above or on a par with constituency interests (Davidson, 1966; 1969). Table 13-1 presents data on this point. While the balance tips toward relating to district first, a full half of the sample rated the nation over or equal to the district as the focus of representational responsibility. This was particularly true among Democrats; Republicans were more inclined to select the district as their primary point of reference.

A number of factors seem to help explain these orientations and the interparty differences among them. Electoral margin is an obvious place to look: as we might guess, representatives from closely competitive districts, presumably fearful of losing their seats, feel a greater need to hew the line, as they perceive it at least, that their constituents set (Davidson, 1969, pp. 126–132). The larger number of "safe" Democrats explains part of the party difference revealed in Table 13-1. In addition, freshmen legislators, again presumably cautious lest some blunder nip their careers in the bud, orient themselves to their district to an extent not found among their seniors; in part, however, this relationship reflects the fact that freshmen come disproportionately from marginal districts, where, after all, newcomers are most likely to win (Davidson, 1969, pp. 133–135). Uncertain electoral status and low seniority are precisely the characteristics that should instill legislators with a sensitivity to their districts, and to find that these attributes go with a district orientation is not remarkable. The argument here is not that district focuses are uncommon, but only that they do not dominate congressional

TABLE 13-1   *Areal role orientations among congressmen*

Orientation	All (%)	Democrats (%)	Republicans (%)
District dominant	42	38	50
Nation and district equal	23	19	29
Nation dominant	28	34	18
Nongeographic	5	7	0
Undetermined	2	2	3
Total	100	100	100
N	(87)	(53)	(34)

SOURCE: Data collected by Roger H. Davidson, David M. Kovenock, and Michael K. O'Leary and made available through the Interuniversity Consortium for Political Research.

thinking, to the exclusion of broader perspectives, in the way often described (Hacker, 1961; Rosenau, 1963; Huntington, 1965). Moreover, even though the members of Congress as a group are not representative of the population in a statistical sense, both the local (district or state) and national orientations are present in the legislature in considerable proportion.

The second component of representation in practice, style, relates to the manner in which the congressman feels he must act for his constituents. We have previously seen (Chapter 1, p. 19, and Chapter 9, pp. 219–221) that there are three types of representational orientations: the delegate posture, which requires the lawmaker to "mirror" the sentiments of the district as best he can; the trustee stance, which asserts the legislator's independence and his obligation to do what he believes right and proper regardless of what the residents of his district wish him to do; and the politico role, which sees the representative shift back and forth between the delegate and trustee positions as the political situation at hand dictates. Some 70 percent of all members of the House, it will be recalled, acknowledge the need to pay heed to district views on at least some occasions, that is, assume either delegate or politico orientations. As with focus, the adoption of stylistic orientations reflects a number of factors: Republicans, congressmen from marginal districts, and those with low seniority seem more attuned to their constituents than Democratic, safe-seat, or senior legislators. Nor are these two dimensions of the representation-orientation unrelated; as might be expected, certain patterns of focus and style go together. A trustee, for example, prepared to risk the ire of his constituents and to follow his own judgment regardless of the consequences, might be expected also to look to a broader set of concerns, the national interest, rather than to adhere slavishly to the whims of those residing in his geographical district. And this appears to be the case; Davidson (1969, p. 126) found that nearly three-fourths (73 percent) of the trustees placed national above district interests. Conversely, nine out of ten (90 percent) of the delegates were district oriented, indicating that those who see their task as following constituency guidelines also define constituency in congressional-district terms. The central point, again, is that while local claims are widely respected in Congress, there remains a not insubstantial number of legislators who are prepared, at the verbal level at least, to substitute their personal views for those of their constituents, renouncing if necessary the interests of their districts in favor of some, to them at least, more generally beneficial national position.

All this should lead us to expect some, but by no means perfect, correspondence between what voters feel desirable and what lawmakers choose to do. The earlier discussion, in Chapter 9, indicating the intermittent character of popular demands on Congress, underscores this point, for it suggests that the public is often uninterested in what goes on in Washington, and uninformed about the behavior of individual representatives. Miller and Stokes, in their study of representation (1963), conclude that this considerable ignorance among the electorate vitiates a major criterion for responsible representation: the ability of the citizen to punish the representative who fails to act appropriately. A citizen cannot vote an incumbent out of office for policy reasons unless he is aware of the legislator's actions.

From the Washington vantage point, the congressman suffers from a comparable disadvantage, for he has great difficulty in establishing what positions the residents of his district hold. He gets relatively little policy-oriented mail on all but a few issues which excite the public; much of what he does receive is pressure-group inspired, and as such, cannot be taken completely at face value. Even the ordinary mail is unlikely to reflect constituent sentiment accurately, given the known propensity of upper-status, better-educated citizens, with their own special points of view, to write more often than those with less skill or leisure time to facilitate communicating with members of Congress. Personal visits from constituents or lobbyists from local organizations, newspaper editorials, and other sources of information have similar biases. Moreover, few legislators have the inclination or, more importantly perhaps, the funds to engage in reliable opinion-polling operations; rather they may use less expensive postcard surveys, the results of which are likely to be misleading given the tendency for some groups in society to respond to such polls while other, equally numerous, groups tend to ignore them. It is in this sense, then, that we have characterized the citizen-congressman link as marked by an "information gap" with each side relatively uninformed about what the other is doing or thinking. It is more noteworthy, perhaps, seen in this light, that we find senators and representatives displaying so much concern for district sentiment than that we discover some departures from a close link between constituency and Congress.

Put in other language, the representative function is carried out in a "mixed" fashion; there exist legislators of both the delegate and trustee persuasions, those who focus on the local district and others whose main concern is with some broader, national set of priorities. Two factors, which Miller and Stokes (1963) build into a model of representation, may account for the varying forms which the citizen-legislator link assumes. Given the situation of relatively poor communications and the lack of information on both sides, the congressman in choosing his course of action, in deciding how to respond to the policy choices confronting him, will fall back on (1) his own preferences, (2) his perceptions of what his constituents believe, or (3) some combination of preferences and perceptions. Figure 13-1 displays the paradigm that Miller and Stokes employ. Note that the delegate relationship assumes a strong, direct association between the constituency's collective opinion and the representative's roll call vote (as an indicator of his policy choice).[3] The lawmaker's vote should reflect what the citizens "back home"

[3]In terms of Figure 13-1, this stresses the linkages (F) and (B)–(D). The delegate posture might reflect the direct correspondence between constituency views and congressman's behavior, quite apart from the accuracy of the latter's perception of the former. That is, the lawmaker may conform to citizen desires more or less by accident. Alternatively, and more in keeping with commonsense notions about representation, the lawmaker may correctly, whether relying on good or bad data, perceive what his constituents want and act accordingly.

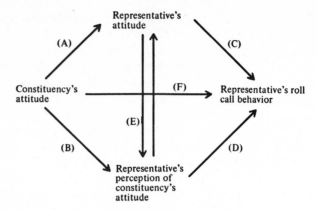

FIGURE 13-1   Connections between a constituency's attitude and its representative's roll call behavior (Source: Miller
and Stokes, 1963, reprinted by permission of *The American
Political Science Review*).

want and his (correct) perception of local sentiments. The trustee orientation,
to the extent it exists, should reveal a direct connection between the representative's attitude and his behavior; this linkage would occur quite apart
from the correspondence between constituency opinion and legislator's vote
and without reference to the legislator's perception, whether accurate or
not, of that constituency opinion.[4]

In fact, Miller and Stokes (1963) found that different linkages were
important on different policy domains; their analysis focused on three
topics: civil rights, social welfare, and foreign policy. Civil rights is a subject
about which Americans clearly feel very strongly: many seem to feel that the
drive of blacks for equality threatens established residential, educational,
and employment patterns; others, with equal passion, believe that only
strong action will end discrimination. It is not surprising, in the light of the
high visibility of civil rights issues as well as the emotion these subjects
arouse, that congressional behavior reflects popular involvement, that is, that
the delegate mode of representation seems operative. The data in Table 13-2
indicate the strength of these relationships. Note, in Column 1 of the table,
that with regard to civil rights, the lawmaker knew to a large extent how his
constituents felt (correlation coefficient = .63), that his perception of
their sentiments was closely related to his votes (.82), and that his personal
preference and his perception of his district together are still more strongly
connected to his vote (.88). These figures suggest clearly that the congressmen knew what their constituents believed and that they voted in keeping

---

[4]In Figure 13-1, linkage (C) should be strong; (A) not necessarily so, since some representatives will
vote their convictions regardless of district viewpoint; and the (B)-(D) chain unimportant because of the
trustees' willingness to vote against measures that they perceive their constituents to favor.

with these beliefs despite the fact that their personal convictions and the district views were only moderately (.39) related.

The picture on issues of social welfare and foreign policy, especially the latter, indicates greater leeway for lawmakers, that is, that they can more often assume a trustee orientation in these areas. In the international relations sphere (column 3 in Table 13-2), congressmen and constituents held opinions bearing little relationship to one another (coefficient = .06); likewise, there is no appreciable correspondence between the constituency's attitude and the lawmaker's roll call behavior (−.09). These facts indicate that the legislator has a good deal of freedom to act as he pleases in this policy area. In fact, his votes reflect his own attitude (.42), in keeping with the trustee notion, and his perception of his district's opinion (.49). This latter connection suggests that even on the relatively remote foreign policy topics many congressmen try, though unsuccessfully, to "vote their districts"; they fail because their perceptions do not correspond to reality (correlation = .19).[5] Social welfare falls in an intermediate position. Again, the connections among what the district residents think, what the legislator thinks, and what the legislator believes his constituents think are low, though not

[5]For a reanalysis of the Miller-Stokes data, using different and more complex correlational methods, see Cnudde and McCrone, 1966.

TABLE 13-2 *Congressional representation*

Correlation coefficient	Issue domain		
	Civil rights	Social welfare	Foreign policy
1. Constituency's attitude and representative's attitude	. 39	.21	.06
2. Constituency's attitude and representative's perception of constituency attitude	.63	. 17	.19
3. Representative's attitude and representative's roll call votes	.77	.61	.42
4. Representative's perception of constituency attitudes and representative's roll call votes	.82	.54	.49
5. Both representative's attitude and perception of constituency with representative's roll call	.88	.70	.56
6. Constituency's attitude and representative's roll call votes	.57	.28	−.09

SOURCE: Miller, 1962; Miller and Stokes, 1963, reprinted by permission of *American Political Science Review*.

as weak as with foreign affairs.[6] The links between the representative's personal view and his perception of his district are more closely related to his vote; we might conclude that this situation fits the politico orientation, with the congressman relatively free to vote his convictions but seeking to follow his view of what his constituents want.

In general, this evidence suggests that such constituency control of legislators' behavior as exists operates through the lawmakers' attempts to act consistently with their perceptions of constituency attitudes. In some cases, such as civil rights matters, these perceptions are accurate; the citizens are concerned and the congressmen know it and respect that concern. On many more issues—social welfare and foreign policy, for instance—the legislators act in keeping with their views of constituent sentiment despite the fact that, in actuality, the local residents are relatively ignorant and apathetic (Stokes and Miller, 1962). Although they have considerable freedom to act as they see fit on most matters, the lawmakers conform to the delegate mold of representation to a degree not really necessary.

A number of possible explanations exist for this closer-than-necessary connection between congressional policy choices and constituency opinion. For one thing, though only a few people are sufficiently well informed to make meaningful electoral choices on policy grounds, this small group may be enough to determine the outcome in a marginal district (Miller and Stokes, 1963). The legislator's record needs to be tailored to suit those critical to his reelection. Other constituency groups, again particularly in competitive areas, may further limit the legislator's freedom to act as trustee (Matthews, 1960, pp. 237–239). The local party may make its support contingent on the congressman's adoption of certain issue positions. A relatively homogeneous population may have a similar effect: a representative will be justifiably fearful of offending the farmers (or workers, or other types of voters) who dominate his district; he is likely to try to please them quite apart from his own preferences. The legislator's own views—his beliefs, values, group attachments—will influence the way he represents his state or district; to the extent he shares these values and beliefs with his constituents, he will act as a delegate almost without knowing it, or perhaps, while feeling that he is acting on his own.

In related fashion, uncertainty about district views, fear about possible electoral reprisals may lead the senator or representative to assume a stance close to that which he perceives his constituents to take. He may worry that a mistake—a poor policy choice on his part—may arouse his constituents and, thus, to avert such a possibility he may seek to build a record which cannot be attacked. Therefore, his votes may reflect the potential for constituent control even though that record is never well known in the district. Similarly, the lack of detailed information about his record may not be the

---

[6]The Miller-Stokes data were collected before the Vietnam war era. It seems likely that major international issues would lead to a far stronger linkage between constituency and congressional opinion and behavior.

equivalent of voter ignorance; the electorate may have a vague general image of the lawmaker, whether he is performing well or unsatisfactorily. This image may reflect his legislative record and, in recognition of this fact, the congressman may cater to his perception of district desires in an effort to create a favorable impression (Miller and Stokes, 1963).

Congressmen may, moreover, react to the uncertainty which surrounds them by overestimating the awareness of the electorate. Not surprisingly, as public figures to whom the mass media and others attend, they feel in the public eye to an unrealistic extent. For example, Kingdon (1968) found that electoral winners, and again those from marginal constituencies in particular, tend to overestimate their own visibility and the issue orientation of the electorate. Believing the citizenry to be informed, aware, and responsive to his actions, the incumbent will, accordingly, try "to anticipate their reactions to his decisions" (p. 145) and will pay attention to their wishes, at least as he sees them. Finally, in the absence of real information on public preferences but fearful of a possible misstep, the member of Congress may need to make an "educated guess" about his constituent's beliefs. He may base his estimate on the nature, in demographic terms, of those who reside in his district, assuming that their attitudes reflect their social characteristics (Rieselbach, 1966). Some such relationship as this may account for the somewhat larger associations (in Table 13-2) between constituency's opinion and the legislator's roll call votes than between the constituency and the legislator's personal opinion.

For these reasons, rooted in uncertainty about the political future, congressmen seek to act as delegates, to relate their performance in Congress to local district sentiment. Knowledge about these sentiments is likely to be better for those from safe districts, where the majority is more easily identifiable, and for those who are most familiar with their constituencies (Miller, 1962). Even with such relatively better data on the home district, many lawmakers feel a need to act as agents beyond what the actual link to the district seems to require. While there are some—trustees and those whose focus is national—who argue that they have no obligation to vote in keeping with district preferences, the vast majority of congressmen do act with constituency interests clearly in mind.

Policy representation: an overview If we combine these findings with some of the data on legislative voting behavior (presented in Chapter 12), we may develop a paradigm of voting choice which may serve as an overview of policy representation as well. The paradigm appears in Figure 13-2.[7] The

---

[7] A word of caution about the paradigm is in order. The arrows in the figure do not necessarily represent the same magnitude; some may be more important than others, some may be irrelevant in particular instances. Even if values could be assigned to any of these linkages, there is no certainty that the pattern would remain meaningful from one issue to the next or as time passed. All that we are suggesting is that the factors enumerated in Figure 13-2 should be able to account for much of the variation in voting alignments, and each of the arrows points to a relationship which may prove fruitful as an explanation of the vote specifically and of representation more generally.

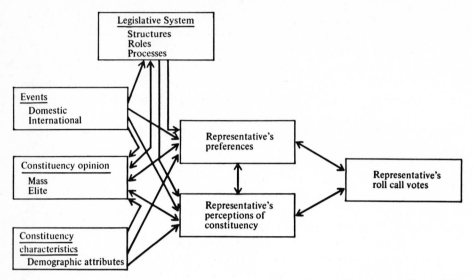

FIGURE 13-2   A paradigm of congressional vote decisions (Source: Rieselbach, 1966, p. 171).

lawmaker's stance appears, in a sense, as the resultant of a complex set of forces.[8] First of all, the representative may act as a trustee following the dictates of his own conscience. Then, he may adhere to his perception of constituency opinion and act as a delegate. Or finally he may respond, when the roll is called and policy choices must be made, with a shifting combination of the two, balancing his own judgment against the perceived need to "vote the district," acting, that is, as a politico.

Preferences and perceptions, in turn, are affected by external stimuli. The legislator is first of all a part of the legislative system; he belongs to a political party; he is a member of one or more committees; and he is subject to the operation of formal rules, informal norms, and a variety of communications links. Such influences may assume primacy in a given policy choice, causing the legislator, to the extent he responds to them, to respond to nonconstituency forces, to act, that is, more as a trustee than as a delegate. Second, the legislative system is itself deeply embedded in the larger political system, and the representative's behavior may be influenced by what the other branches of government, the executive and judicial, do or by what the representative expects them to do. Demands from the President or the courts may, in other words, require a lawmaker to abandon the delegate posture.

A congressman's preferences may also be shaped by events—the situational context—outside the legislative system. Certain policy requisites may be

[8] The discussion which follows draws on Rieselbach (1966, pp. 170–180), which presents a more detailed elaboration of the paradigm.

seen to flow from the failure of present programs, foreign or domestic. These same occurrences may have indirect effects: an event may convince the leadership of one or both political parties that some response is necessary and the leaders, in turn, may urge the rank and file of their parties to support them.[9] Then, as we have seen, constituency opinion may be related to the legislator's preferences and thus to his vote. His contacts with his constituents may persuade him that a particular course of action is desirable. A distinction between mass and elite opinion is appropriate in this context: one congressman may take his cues from the general population or some segment of it; another may be influenced by the "opinion makers" of his constituency.[10] The views and arguments of the opinion-leading elite may be quite different from those that average citizens voice, and thus these two sources of information may be incompatible, perhaps compelling the lawmaker to choose one or the other of the recommended courses of action.[11]

Again, events may affect legislative preferences indirectly by way of constituency opinion or the legislative system. A national or international occurrence may go virtually unnoticed until the congressman is alerted to it, and its consequences, by demands from constituency opinion—mass, elite, or both—or by pressures originating within Congress itself.

Finally, as we have noted, the gross (demographic) characteristics of his constituency may influence the lawmaker's preferences. His attitudes may be influenced by the kinds of people—in ethnic, religious, racial, class, or occupational terms—who reside in his district; or they may reflect the fact that he shares one or more of these attributes with his constituents. In either case, his preferences may reflect the district's major features, and may do so without any knowledge of or concern for the actual distribution of constituency opinion.[12] District characteristics may also affect congressional preferences indirectly, exerting influence through constituency opinion. The existence "back home" of some particular group may, in fact, generate a widespread community viewpoint on some issue, which when communicated to Washington may influence the attitudes of the representative.

The legislative system, events, constituency opinion, and constituency

[9]The McClellan ("Labor Rackets") committee's revelations of alleged labor union corruption and misuse of funds are pertinent here. In addition to affecting the preferences of some legislators, these disclosures, though for differing reasons, persuaded the leaders of each party that reform legislation was essential (McAdams, 1964, pp. 11–13, 36–40, 268–269).

[10]Rosenau (1963, p. 6) defines "opinion makers" as those "who occupy positions which enable them to transmit, with some regularity, opinions about . . . issues to unknown persons."

[11]Identification of subtypes of constituency opinion may allow us to assert another mode of district influence on legislative behavior. Looking at mass opinion only, Miller and Stokes (1963) found little relationship between constituency attitude and legislator's vote, especially on foreign policy and social welfare issues (see Table 13-2); it may be that some congressmen choose to listen to the views of the elite rather than those of the mass.

[12]Here is another way in which constituency may be important, may be indirectly represented, despite the absence of any correlation between the actual state of constituency opinion and the roll call behavior of the representative.

characteristics may also have similar effects on the individual lawmaker's perceptions. All these may provide him with an indication of the possible response of his constituents to action he contemplates taking. For example, the functioning of the legislative system may shed light on the state of public opinion. The testimony he hears presented to his committee may affect the congressman's views of mass opinion. If he reads articles or speeches inserted in the *Congressional Record,* his conception of elite opinion may alter. Or he may accept, as indicating the feelings of his own constituents, the interpretation that the legislative leadership presents of the state of public sentiment. While admittedly there are no data on these speculations, it is at least plausible to argue that the representative's perception of constituency opinion may be shaped in part by such cues coming from the legislative system.

Likewise, events may have an impact on the perceptions of the lawmakers, who may estimate the reaction of their constituents to a particular happening, and the probable consequences, electoral or otherwise, for themselves which may flow from this response. Election results may permit the congressmen to gauge the views of those they represent.[13] The connection between constituency opinion and perception requires little further elaboration: many legislators seem to act consistently with their perception of district attitudes. They may be responding to mass or elite opinion, or to the threat of interest-group pressures, but they act in keeping with what they see the district, however they conceptualize it, to desire. Finally, and in much the same fashion, aggregate constituency characteristics may influence the perceptions and the vote of a legislator. Because some group, say union members, reside in his district in large numbers, the representative may gauge labor's reaction to his behavior and act in ways to avert any adverse reaction. He may do so without any real information about the concern, if any, or the opinions of labor about the issue at hand. In all these ways, the member of Congress may act in keeping with his perceptions of what the residents of his district believe and what they are likely to do in consequence of these beliefs.

As a last point, we should note that some of the arrows in the paradigm point in both directions, suggesting that "feedback" processes are involved (see Chapter 1, pp. 6–7 and 22). Once a legislator has gone on record in favor of a policy, his position may harden, for to vote "nay" at some later time would be to display his inconsistency. Once his preferences become set, his perceptions of constituency opinion may shift to lend support to his attitudes. And when his votes and preferences become known to his constituents, those

[13]The argument, heard frequently after both the 1960 and 1968 presidential elections, that the narrow margins of victory indicated a desire on the part of most Americans to "go slow," "to consolidate," may have decreased the willingness of some congressmen to push ahead vigorously with a variety of new programs. Indeed, policy departures in the 1960s followed, for the most part, the 1964 landslide victory of Lyndon Johnson.

who respect his judgment or expertise may alter their opinions. Or those who disagree with his stand may cease to communicate with him, thus introducing an additional bias into his perceptions of constituency opinion. In short, his actions help to shape the representative's preferences and perceptions. "Congressmen, indeed, do respond to pressures, but they generate the pressures they feel" (Bauer, Pool, and Dexter, 1963, pp. 415–421, at p. 420).

The paradigm in Figure 13-2, then, reveals that the vote decisions, and thus the policy-representational behaviors, of individual members of Congress grow out of their own preferences and their perceptions of constituency opinion, or a combination of these two factors.[14] These preferences and perceptions, in turn, are shaped by the lawmaker's position in the legislative system, by events, by the opinions and demographic characteristics of his constituency, or by some combination of these elements. A number of these potential influences are likely to operate simultaneously, and how the senator or representative resolves these role conflicts will determine the form his policy representational activity takes. We cannot, to be sure, specify what form the resolution will take for any single legislator on any particular issue, or at any point in time. We can, however, suggest that congressmen of a delegate persuasion will tend to act in keeping with their perceptions of constituent wishes, responding to district opinion, gross constituency attributes, and the perceived impact of events on the district.

By contrast, the trustee will rely on his own personal preferences, directly or as they reflect his interpretation of events or his position in the legislative system. To the extent that he acts consistently with his conscience, his view of the immediate situation, or with his party or committee membership, the trustee will play down district considerations and stress instead a broader, national orientation. The politico will follow a middle course, shifting from conformity with his view of district expectations to an independent stance, and varying in the weight he gives to national and local perspectives, as the situation seems to warrant.

CONSTITUENT SERVICES

The previous discussion should not obscure the fact that policy demands are intermittent; orientations—style and focus—toward policy representation are in part a product of uncertainty and are formed in the absence of much reliable information about constituent preferences. The contrast between

[14] It must be confessed that it is often difficult to distinguish between preferences and perceptions. The essence of the distinction lies in the extent to which the legislator acts on the basis of his own values. If he works for what he believes to be "good" or "desirable," we may say he follows his preferences; if he takes a course dictated by his view of what constituent response will be, then perceptions are important. Of course, and this is the rub, it is often impossible to tell when preferences affect perceptions—when, that is, the lawmaker perceives his constituents to favor what he himself prefers—and vice versa.

policy demands and the situation with regard to constituent services can hardly be overemphasized. Demands for nonpolicy performance are constant and frequent; members of Congress, almost without exception, feel that such requests should be honored, both as a matter of principle and as a matter of political necessity. Davidson and his collaborators (cited in Olson, 1966, p. 343) found that more than three-fourths (78 percent) of the members of the House of Representatives whom they interviewed believed that their constituents required and were entitled to help in their dealings with the mammoth federal government. Moreover, in the view of many, if Congress does not provide such assistance it will not be available elsewhere. Representation of this "casework" variety is viewed as fundamental, a responsibility which the legislature cannot shirk.

Casework It is no exaggeration to suggest that with virtual unanimity lawmakers respond to demands for services as mandated delegates with a strongly local orientation. Most congressmen feel that such requests must be taken seriously; the vast majority seek to respond quickly and accurately to each case. Electoral arrangements provide one motivation to do so. We have noted earlier that reelection prospects reflect not so much a detailed awareness of the legislator's specific actions as a general image that he is working hard and effectively to promote citizen interests. Service to constituents is one obvious way for the legislator to make that impression, however vague and nonspecific it may be, a positive one. Long after the voters have forgotten where he stood on any particular policy matter, they may cast a ballot for (or against) him on the basis of their sense of how "good" a job he is doing. Service work, many lawmakers believe, will provide, far more than will strict attention to the lawmaking or oversight functions, that "decisive margin of goodwill, votes, campaign funds, and assistance which enables a member to remain in Congress" (Olson, 1966, p. 341).

There are other, less self-serving, justifications for a heavy commitment to service work (Galloway, 1953; Saloma, 1969). For one thing, performing this sort of service does provide the average citizen with an opportunity for redress of grievances that he cannot get from any other source. The cost of bringing legal action is enormous; the administrative branch is not likely to be overly willing to acknowledge its own failings, and, thus, Congress can most easily and effectively give aid to citizens with complaints against bureaucratic impersonality and inefficiency. This is to suggest nothing more than that "casework" is "worth doing." Put another way, the direct tie between constituent and congressman permits local perspectives to be recognized; the President represents the national interest while the lawmaker, bound to his district, can discover and articulate the impact of such national orientations on the varying localities of the country. In a sense, such a commitment to localism—regional, state, or local—rather than to national interest keeps the government "closer" to the people than it might otherwise be.

More important, perhaps, the performance of service tasks contributes to the lawmaking and oversight activities of Congress. Former Sen. Joseph S. Clark (D., Pa.) justifies intervention in administrative affairs on behalf of constituents as "an effort to humanize what is inevitably a hardened bureaucratic process" (1964, pp. 63–64). Knowing that improper or unfeeling treatment of citizens may lead to imposition of congressional directives, executive personnel may seek to avoid such legislative involvement by dealing effectively with complaints from citizens; this form of "anticipated reaction" may reduce the need for formal oversight. Similarly, the concentration of public objections on a few agencies or programs may serve to single out prime targets for oversight; where complaints are rife, the benefits from oversight are likely to be large and the potential for the commitment of scarce resources to such control activities likely to be increased.

In the same vein, citizen requests may inform the policy-making process. Clapp (1964, pp. 77–94) reports, after conducting round-table discussion with members of the House of Representatives, that many legislators feel that communications from constituents help them to identify "laws that need revision and agencies that would benefit from reorganization" (p. 79). Service requests also provide information of value in lawmaking; knowing what is on constituents' minds, what is bothering them, may give the congressman a sense of what needs to be done—policy departures or administrative simplification—to alleviate citizen difficulties. Without such knowledge, policy making might display reduced sensitivity to popular needs (Saloma, 1969, p. 182).

Finally, Saloma (1969, pp. 182–183) argues that the service function contributes to the continuing independence of Congress. The constituency tie, buttressed by the local election arrangements, means that the President, or the national party organization acting on his behalf, will lack the sanctions to enforce party discipline on Congress. From the legislative vantage point, this means that lawmakers can, through cultivation of constituency interests, gain long tenure and the expertise necessary to confront the bureaucracy. Without the ability to turn congressmen out of office, the executive must work with the legislature; it cannot subjugate Congress through a centralized party system but must bargain with autonomous congressmen. In this way, the service chores, and the independence they sustain, contribute to the fragmented character of the legislative system.

Mail—often running to several thousand letters per week—brings the bulk of the requests for services; a few are made in person, sometimes in Washington, sometimes upon the legislator's return home. Olson (1966, pp. 347–349) indicates that the requests are of seven broad types. The largest of these is communications bearing on legislative matters. This fact does not contradict the assertion made earlier that policy demands are intermittent, for many of these incoming messages do not urge the correspondents' views on the legislator; rather they contain requests for information concerning his positions. Of those letters which do contain some policy preferences, a greater number, perhaps a majority, are "inspired" mail, that is, form letters or preprinted postcards prepared by interest groups. Congressmen tend to discount such messages, assuming that they do not reflect the same depth of concern as a personal letter drafted by the writer himself. Mail related to legislative matters thus is burdensome without, in compensation, providing much information on constituent sentiments.

A second major category of requests, specific cases, requires some form of intervention into bureaucratic affairs. The lawmaker, or more likely a member of his staff acting for him, must contact a specific agency to ask for help in locating a missing social security check, in speeding up the processing of an application for a federally guaranteed loan, or in facilitating any of the large number of dealings that constituents have with the Washington bureaucracy. The staff, as we shall see in greater detail below, assumes a central importance in the handling of casework; it is, from the congressional point of view, highly desirable to maintain a large and experienced staff, for with long tenure comes the acquaintance with the administrators that permits meaningful contact to be made. Expertise for casework may be as essential as specialization for policy making. Knowledge and technical competence are requisites for successful processing of service requests, for these involve the lawmaker and his office in matters spanning the entire broad spectrum of programs that federal agencies run. And as the federal government expands in size and scope of activity, these skill requirements must inevitably enlarge as well, or the lawmaker will find himself unable to handle his case load.

Involvement with the executive branch is not, however, without its limits; too frequent contact is likely to have diminishing returns, for at some point the administrators may begin to resent congressional "interference," feeling that "pressure" is being applied to influence the outcome of administrative proceedings. To avoid the impression of excessive involvement, some, but not all, congressmen will limit their contacts with the agencies to requests for information as to the status of some pending matter. The legislator's interest, of course, may be more than sufficient encouragement for the bureau to expedite its consideration of the matter. While a few members of Congress continue to represent their constituents personally before agency boards or panels, many more refuse to act as counsel for residents of their states or districts. Nor is a congressman's influence equal in all areas. He is more likely to be effective in the areas over which the committees on which he serves have jurisdiction; on these topics his interest is backed up by the sanctions at the disposal of the panel with oversight responsibilities. The effective treatment of specific requests, however, even within these often self-imposed limits, is a basic obligation that most lawmakers assume.

There are other types of service requests which constituents direct toward their representatives in Congress. Many citizens merely seek information, about federal programs, about federal regulations, about research conducted by the government. To handle these demands, legislators turn to the agencies involved for help and find the bureaucracy quite willing to oblige. We noted (in Chapter 6) how the executive engages in liaison work to enhance its standing with and influence over the legislature; one form that such executive "lobbying" takes is to assist members of Congress in meeting constituent requests. The agencies devote thousands of hours of work to this end; they supply literally millions of publications for legislators to distribute (Clapp, 1964, p. 77). Such contributions to easing the service burden may earn the agency some legislative goodwill.

Another group of district-based requests pertains to employment. The federal government is, of course, a major employer, and people desiring such jobs ask their representatives to supply information on application procedures or, in some cases, to intercede on behalf of those who have applied. Congressmen do have influence over the filling of some jobs, including postmasterships; they make appointments to the various service academies, though they tend to rely heavily on competitive examinations; and they may have some marginal involvement in filling a few Capitol Hill posts like doormen and pages. People eager to have these positions will contact their representatives, and the latter, desiring to respond, will devote substantial time and energy to the difficult chore of obtaining such appointments. Senators may make use of "senatorial courtesy" in this connection, but the effort to negotiate arrangements—bargaining not only with the executive but also with local political party leaders—is strenuous and the results uncertain.

A smaller but perhaps more demanding number of requests involve district projects. A local group will ask for aid in securing a community-action program, an urban-renewal project, a reclamation or other rivers and harbors project, or one of the many other forms of largesse that the federal government has to distribute. District business enterprises want government contracts, and the legislator may get credit for the economic benefits that flow from such awards. Conversely, the congressman will struggle valiantly to avert closing of federal installations within his district (Carper, 1960); the blame for such losses may be placed at his doorstep. Success or failure with respect to these highly visible projects, with their effects on sizable numbers of constituents, may go far to shape the district's image of its representative.

Finally, there is a set of miscellaneous requests that for all their relative novelty consume substantial amounts of time. The high school class needs arrangements—tours, gallery passes, hotel rooms, and the like—for its Easter trip to the Capitol. The lawmaker will want to greet, and be photographed with, the class. The stamp collector wants a special first-day cover; the numismatist wants something special from the United States mint; others want special types of souvenirs. All write their congressman, expecting some response; all do get something, often compliance with their requests, from Washington, even at considerable cost to an overworked congressional office.

Thus the demands for services are many and varied, but all require a substantial commitment of scarce resources. No single case, by itself, is likely to be of critical importance, but taken in toto, service requests provide the legislator with an unsurpassed opportunity to create and sustain that generalized image of competence and concern which seems so crucial to a successful political career. It is for this basic reason that most, if not all, members of Congress act with a local focus and a delegate style with respect to constituency services. Each letter, each request, must be answered courteously and with dispatch;[15] every effort should be made to satisfy the constituent. Given such premises, representation in its district facet becomes a high priority item on the congressman's agenda.

There are differences of opinion as to how much of his time the average lawmaker commits to constituent service. On one hand, Clapp (1964, p. 60) concludes, on the basis of discussions with numerous representatives, that "it is not uncommon for members of the House to devote the major portion of their time and energy to the nonlegislative portion of their jobs." By contrast, Saloma's survey, admittedly based on an imperfect sample,[16] of 150 congressmen indicates that the typical lawmaker spends considerably more time on his legislative work than on constituency service. There is no quarrel, however, about the workload of the representative's staff; both authors suggest that most congressmen assign vast proportions of staff resources to varying kinds of communications with district residents. Table 13-3 presents some data on legislative workloads. What seems clear is that regardless of how much of his own time he commits to constituency relations, the lawmaker delegates to his staff much of the responsibility for responding to demands originating in the district.

The congressional office Indeed many members of Congress, particularly in the House where constituency demands seem more burdensome (Olson, 1966, p. 344), organize their personal offices, allocate their staff resources, to

---

[15]Senator Stephen M. Young (D., Ohio) was a notable exception to the usual pattern of seeking to avoid offending any constituent regardless of how antagonistic his communication might be. As examples of Young's inclination to meet vituperation more than halfway, consider the following: "You are . . . lower than a snake's tail." "Folks like you who claim that many Protestant ministers are Communists . . . are like individuals who hoist their skirts from imaginary mice." "I unhesitatingly assert you have not read the bill, have not read any committee hearings and reports relating to surgical and medical care for the elderly. You have probably been impressed by some pamphlet or book received from one of your insurance companies. . . . I will cast my vote in accord with my study and information and my conscience." One man wrote "protesting that Mrs. John F. Kennedy had had a horse transported free to this country from abroad. What would happen if *he* tried to do that?" To which the Senator replied: ". . . acknowledging your letter wherein you insult the wife of our President, am wondering why you need a horse when there is already one jackass at your address." Quoted in *The Reporter*, vol. 27 (1963), p. 18.

[16]Saloma (1969, note 34, p. 184) reports that Republicans and freshmen congressmen are overrepresented in his sample; fewer Democrats and seniors than expected responded to his questionnaire.

maximize their ability to handle constituent services with dispatch. In the office of Rep. John V. Tunney (D., Calif.) the ten employees, the maximum permissible under the House-imposed ceiling, were assigned their duties as follows:

Administrative Assistant: handles purely administrative matters.

Legislative Assistant: legislation, press, and utility work.

Senior Secretary: casework.

Assistant Secretary: casework.

Personal Secretary: handles personal correspondence.

Secretary: runs robotype machines, puts out newsletters, etc.

Two Part-Time Assistants: college girls who do miscellaneous clerical work.

Two District Secretaries: each runs a district office (Olson, 1966, p. 360. Reprinted by permission of The American Enterprise Institute).

A glance at these office assignments indicates the extent to which staff personnel are given constituency-related duties; even the designated *legislative* aide has "press" and "utility" responsibilities which seem to be more in the line of constituency service activities than directly related to policy making.

Moreover, not all members take full advantage of the allowances available for their offices. In 1963 (Olson, 1966, p. 360; Clapp, 1964, p. 63), only about one congressman in five had the full complement of office personnel available under House rules; conversely, another one-fourth employed under half the maximum personnel allowable. While the budget for staff salaries runs to about $50,000 annually for each lawmaker, only a small proportion spend this

TABLE 13-3 Congressional workloads, by function

Function	Congressman		Congressional office	
	Hours/week	%	Hours/week	%
Legislative	38.0	64.6	30.8	14.3
Constituency service	16.3	27.6	53.5	24.7
Correspondence (mixed constituency service and education)			88.6	40.8
Education and publicity	4.6	7.8	22.4	10.3
Other			21.4	9.9
Total	58.9	100.0	216.7	100.0

SOURCE: From John S. Saloma, III, *Congress and the New Politics,* Tables 6.5 and 6.7, pp. 184–185. Copyright © 1969 by Little, Brown and Company (Inc.). Reprinted by permission.

amount in full. Thus, while a common complaint is that the lower chamber lacks adequate staff support, the fact is that only a few members use all of what they have. On the Senate side, the problem is severe but somewhat less acute. To meet somewhat lower demand levels, senators have, on the average, from thirteen to fifteen staff employees; office monies are apportioned on the basis of state population (Olson, 1966, p. 356). The member of the upper chamber has some perquisites not available to his House counterpart. For one thing, the Senate authorizes each member to hire one legislative assistant; no such slot is identified in the House, though some members create a comparable position. Additionally, senior senators can divert some of the burden, either legislative or constituent service, to committee staff. With seniority goes some committee power; committee or subcommittee chairmen control staff appointments which they can use to place loyal employees on the payroll. These staffers can, and do, help out the lawmaker with his personal chores. But even in the Senate, it seems clear that the great bulk of office resources go to handle constituency relations.

The congressional office, in both chambers, has become a complex operation involving considerable sums of money. In addition to the funds for salaries, previously noted, a full panoply of allowances is granted to sustain office work, both in Washington and in the home state or district (Olson, 1966, pp. 361–365; Clapp, 1964, pp. 62–77). Among the goods and services which the lawmakers are empowered to obtain are stationery (House members, in 1970, got $3,500 per year), stamps ($700 annually for airmail and special delivery postage), equipment, and long-distance telephone calls. Other funds are given to employ summer interns, often selected from among a legislator's constituents, who are not counted against the allotted number of staff employees. The franking privilege, which permits first-class mail to be sent free, is an indirect subsidy. In general, reaction to these arrangements is mixed; some legislators consider these funds sufficient to run their offices while others feel that they are grossly inadequate. Those who feel the need for additional money will spend their own funds; some will use honoraria received for giving speeches to various groups around the country to supplement their office allowances even though the acceptance of such fees may leave them open to charges of conflict of interest.[17]

Still other money is available to maintain district offices; House members, in 1963, received $1,200 for the rental of space, and another $600 to supply the office (Clapp, 1964, pp. 74–77). A few members, representing large states or far-flung districts, maintain more than one constituency office; more than 100, on the other hand, have no district office at all. Local operations, while providing an additional channel of communication for constituents, seem to play a relatively minor part in the legislator's handling of his job. The staff assigned to the district receives constituents—the congressman himself may do

---

[17] The Senate, in recognition of this problem, has recently begun requiring full disclosure of all honoraria in excess of $300. A similar House requirement went into effect in 1972.

so when he is in the district—but most casework requests are handled in Washington.

Of special significance is the problem of travel to and from the home state or congressional district. Most congressmen feel the need to be seen "back home" acutely; they feel that visibility in the district adds to their stature, contributes to their images, and thus contributes to electoral victory. Presence in the constituency, of course, also provides an additional opportunity to meet local people, hear their complaints, and discuss the issues with them. In recognition of this need to return home, each lawmaker receives reimbursement for a number of trips—most recently, five in the House and six in the Senate—to and from the district. Many congressmen, particularly those from marginal areas, find this allowance insufficient; they feel they must go back to their districts far more often. Olson (1966, pp. 362–364) reports some members made more than thirty trips home a year. Senator Gale McGee (D., Wyo.) made sixty-eight trips over and above those allowed him in one six-year term; these extra journeys were financed either out of his own pocket or, despite the obvious potential for conflicts of interest, by private organizations as fees for speeches, articles, or other services.[18]

The congressional office, given its focus on constituency matters, has become the prime agent of response to district demands and, moreover, has become a highly systematized operation. Sophisticated equipment is used to facilitate the accepted need to deal with each and every incoming communication. Though, as noted, each member of Congress is free, within the limits of the available money, to organize his office as he sees fit, some standard practices have developed. For one thing, the staff handles most of the mail; the legislator sees only those letters that the staff feels warrant his attention. The remaining messages—those asking for the lawmaker's opinions, requesting information, or "inspired" form letters, for instance—are handled by automatic machinery; the robotypewriter and the automatic signature machine not only produce the response, but also make it look, to the uninitiated at least, as if it were individually typed and personally signed. The case requests are parceled out among the staff with only the most difficult finding a place on the legislator's desk. In short, each office develops its own routines, though these have some common features from one office to the next, for handling the heavy load of constituency requests; these routines, in keeping with the role orientations of the congressmen,[19] determine how the constit-

[18]This need for money for travel, for other forms of campaigning, and for a host of additional purposes is a serious and pervasive problem, one to which we will return in Chapter 14.

[19]We would hypothesize, for instance, that ritualist and opportunist orientations toward lawmaking would lead to greater commitment of staff resources to constituent services. By contrast, the inventor, with his focus on problem solving, might be tempted to use a greater proportion of his budget for legislative assistance. Similarly, the delegate-representational style should lead to a heavy investment in constituency services while the trustee posture might be expected to lead to a greater commitment to substantive concerns. Such differences, however, would probably be slight, for all members desire reelection and attention to service demands serves this cause well. All we suggest is that, given the eagerness to stay in office, some orientations should be accompanied by a somewhat stronger involvement—personal and staff—in policy making and/or oversight.

uency-service burden is allocated between principal and agents, and how much time the representative will commit to these demands and how much he will reserve for other—lawmaking and oversignt—activities.

Publicity and constituent education Constituency, without doubt, bulks large in the lives of representatives in the nation's capital. Indeed, so great is the opportunity to enhance one's position through efficient performance of requests from the district, that should the flow of such demands slacken, the congressman devotes considerable energy to stimulation of service requests. This reflects the legislator's conviction that visibility, remaining in the public eye, is crucial to electoral success; this, in turn leads him to use a variety of educational, or "public relations," devices to reach his constituents. Some of these techniques may be specifically designed to increase the volume of communications to the congressional office (Clapp, 1964, pp. 83–84). As the data in Table 13-3 reveal, both lawmaker and his staff commit about one-tenth of their time to publicity and educational activities.

The forms of such activities are numerous. Among the most common is the newsletter; Saloma (1969, pp. 174–175) reports that approximately 80 percent of the lawmakers circulated newsletters, and several used more than one variety. These are sent to selected mailing lists or to all postal patrons residing in the district. The content of the newsletters, of course, differs widely, but the tendency is to focus less on policy matters—though issues perceived to be of central concern to constituents are treated in some detail—and more on the general level and range of the congressman's activities on behalf of the local citizens. Moreover, the newsletters are taken seriously and prepared with care; the average member spends six hours of his time and commits more than twenty-eight hours of staff time to writing, editing, and mailing each newsletter (Saloma, 1969, p. 175). Moreover, local newspapers often reprint the letters, thus enlarging the potential audience.

The questionnaire, soliciting constituents' opinions on a range of policy issues is another device often used; some 60 percent of Saloma's (1969, p. 175) respondents report sending them to the district either on a selective or on a constituency-wide basis. We have already noted (Chapter 9) the limitations of the questionnaire as an information-gathering instrument—poor question construction and nonrandom patterns of response, for example—but the mere distribution of them, whether or not the recipient reads or responds to them, is another opportunity to enhance the congressman's image of concern for the district and the sentiments of its inhabitants. The importance attached to the questionnaire can be seen in the twenty hours devoted to its preparation and the 118 hours, on the average, committed to the tabulation of results. The latter are often inserted in the *Congressional Record;* included in the news-letter, perhaps a special one for the specific purpose; or released to the press.

Congressmen, and especially members of the House of Representatives, often feel that they receive insufficient media coverage; they believe the press, television, and the other means of mass communications neglect the legislature in favor of the executive (Clapp, 1964, pp. 96–102). Although they recognize the central position of the Presidency in the competition for popular attention, few legislators are prepared to accept their secondary position and most seek actively to stimulate press and other media coverage. They regularly issue press releases, especially to papers in their home states and districts; they cut television and radio tapes, and supply these free of charge to local stations. The House of Representatives has facilities, provided at nominal cost, and advisory personnel to help with the preparation of broadcasts; media specialists in the employ of the political parties provide similar assistance. More than half of those whom Saloma (1969, p. 174) surveyed gave regular reports to their constituents, averaging eight radio broadcasts and four television appearances each month during congressional sessions. While many regret the need to commit so many scarce resources to supplementing media coverage, these expressions are "almost inevitably followed by solemn assertions that it really *is* necessary" (Clapp, 1964, pp. 96–97).

Other methods—aimed at image building—are also used (Clapp, 1964, pp. 104–110). Film and record libraries are assembled and various items made available to local schools, civic and fraternal organizations, and other interested groups; committee prints—hearings and reports—may be sent to interested citizens as may other government publications; local newspapers are carefully scanned and letters of congratulation—to school graduates, newlyweds, new parents—often accompanied by recipe books or the widely circulated *Infant Care* are mailed; letters of condolence go to the families of the recently deceased. Trips to the district, for whatever central purpose, are used to fill as many speaking engagements as time and energy permit. In all these ways, the congressman strives to make clear to his constituents that their welfare is basic to him and that he is constantly active on their behalf.

The line between education and self-serving publicity is, of course, a difficult if not impossible one to draw precisely. The range of legislator-constituent communications outlined in the preceding paragraphs does without doubt convey a considerable amount of information from Washington to the localities; this is the case even if there are other than informational goals underlying these activities. Saloma's (1969, pp. 176–177) survey reveals the mixed focus of these publicity operations. The largest single category, comprising 38 percent of House respondents and 44 percent of the senators, was labeled "promoter," indicating that the lawmaker is "principally concerned with enhancing his own image and advancing self-interest through" his communication with the district. At the other extreme is the "educator" who sees information transmission more as an end in itself than as a means to self-aggrandizement; a mere 9 percent of House and 3 percent of Senate respondents fall in the "educator" group. Intermediate, with a specialized educational goal, is the "persuader," who seeks to move his constituents toward his own opinions or to sustain and reinforce those who already agree with him; the "persuader" attempts to develop support for his personal views, not really to provide the citizenry with the basis on which to make independent judgments.[20]

Saloma (1969, p. 177) further finds that party affiliation relates to the pattern of communication that the lawmaker adopts: Democrats in both chambers tend to be promoters while Republicans incline toward the persuader orientation. In addition, as he accrues seniority, the legislator tends to shift from the promoter to the persuader posture. We may speculate, with respect to more general representational role orientations, that the trustee, especially if he focuses on the national rather than on the state' or district level, should be most likely to try to act as an educator; the delegate, on the other hand, should be more concerned with promotion and persuasion. Similarly the inventor, in contrast with those who assume ritualist, broker, or opportunist orientations toward lawmaking, should evince greater concern with the educational features of his district communication as a means of generating support for his proposed solutions to national problems. In any event, if the performance of constituent services, the response to district demands, reveals imperfect commitment to the ideals of citizen representation and popular education, it is because this aspect of legislative output, like so many features of a decentralized system, serves multiple purposes for the members of Congress.

ROLE CONFLICT

The high priority which congressmen place on responding to demands for constituency services, when juxtaposed against similar commitments to policy making and oversight, suggests the strains, the role conflicts, which may plague individual lawmakers. Each of these broad categories of output activities requires substantial attention from Congress as an institution; no one seriously denies that each output function is within the province of the legislature or that it is reasonable to expect Congress to perform in each area. Each senator or representative, however, cannot perform all possible roles with equal facility; he will inevitably have to confront numerous sets of conflicting expectations and to select the ways in which he will allocate his personal and staff resources among the competitors for his attention. With respect to output activity, each must decide whether to devote himself to policy making, oversight, or representation, for no single individual can commit himself equally and simultaneously to all three concerns. The set of

---

[20]Saloma's data (1969, pp. 176–177) reveal that 39 percent of House members and 47 percent of Senators assume the persuader stance, either alone or in combination with the promoter posture. The remaining lawmakers, 15 and 6 percent in House and Senate, respectively, are designated "reticents," indicating that they engage in no consistent pattern of educational, persuasive, or promotional activities.

chapters in Part 3 of this book has indicated that for most lawmaking and the constituency service aspect of representation seem to take precedence over policy representation and surveillance of the executive agencies.

This is true for several reasons. In the first place, there is simply no time to master the intricacies of substantive policy issues and at the same time to develop a clear understanding of the complexities of administrative agency behavior. Electoral realities, chamber norms, personal preferences, and a variety of other forces seem to impel a majority of lawmakers to choose to work at the former rather than the latter. Understanding is limited, moreover, even within the specialized concerns of a single committee; there is just too much detailed data for one man to consume within the confines of the topics with which any single committee deals. It might be possible to develop expertise as a combined lawmaker-overseer if the full resources of a legislator's staff could be utilized for such a purpose; but, as noted, political survival dictates to many members of Congress that constituent demands receive top priority. Again oversight tends to be neglected as a result of these considerations. Observers of Congress continually debate the relative merits of the distribution of legislative resources among the output activities—and we will return to this problem in the next chapter—but the essential point here, regardless of one's normative posture, is that congressmen cannot cope satisfactorily with all three output functions; they are forced by physical limitations of time and capacity to allocate their energies among them.

However the representative defines his role with respect to output activities—whether he adopts the constituency–service, legislative-specialist, or oversight–indifferent pattern, which we hypothesize as common, or any of the virtually infinite permutations and combinations of role orientations available to him—he will have to face other forms of role conflict. These may, as the chapters in Part 2 suggest, take the form of incompatible demands from outside the legislative system; the President, executive agencies and bureaus, interest groups, and, less consistently, the courts and interested individual citizens may urge alternative solutions to a single problem upon him. To the extent that he responds to one set of demands, he must perforce reject others. How he acts within his chosen orientations toward output activities, in other words, will reflect how he evaluates these demands from the system's environment.

There remains, in addition, a set of role conflicts stemming from forces internal to the legislative system. The lawmaker's political party, acting through its leadership, may take a stand and plead for his vote; his committee, acting in accordance with its internal norms, may do likewise; chamber norms may impose certain restrictions upon him; informal groups or individual friends may make claims upon his loyalty; and the legislator must choose to which of these appeals he will respond. Again, the basic conclusion is obvious: quite apart from role choices toward output functions, the congressman must define *how* he will act with respect to the tasks he has set for himself. Finally, all or most of these forces may be operative simultaneously. To cite one of many possible examples, a senator or representative may have to choose between the President and an interest group alliance, on the one hand, and his committee and other pressure groups, on the other; or, more generally, two competing coalitions—each composed of elements within and without the legislative system—may seek his support. How he responds to their appeals—how he resolves his role conflicts, that is—will reflect the weights and values that, in the last analysis, he assigns to their demands.

The demand model ought not, however, be overdrawn; the legislator is not simply buffeted by conflicting pressures. There are ways to reduce, if not eliminate, the inability to satisfy all those concerned with his behavior. Not all potential sources of pressure will be involved in each particular case. The public, for instance, is little involved with most policy issues and even less concerned with most oversight of administration. Where he perceives the public to be aroused, the lawmaker will do well to respond; where it appears relatively indifferent, he is free to look elsewhere for cues about appropriate behavior (Miller and Stokes, 1963; Jones, 1961). Similarly, the President may decide, for reasons of indifference or as a tactical maneuver, to assume a "hands-off" stance toward some question. On other matters, notably foreign policy issues, pressure groups may have little or no interest (Cohen, 1959). Where such circumstances exist, the flow of demands on Congress is proportionately reduced.

Another conflict-reducing technique is to take advantage of the multistage character of the legislative process (Jones, 1961). A congressman may respond to, if not satisfy, one set of demands at one stage and another set subsequently. He may, for instance, introduce a bill at the request of some environmental group even though he is fully aware that it will not emerge from committee, much less pass; he may propose an investigation or otherwise challenge administrative actions with little or no expectation that much change will occur. Similarly, he may attempt to have a demand-satisfying provision written into a bill in committee; he may respond to another set of demands when the bill is up for amendment; and his votes on recommittal motions as well as on final passage may align him with still other interests. He has multiple opportunities to try to support differing points of view. Finally, the multiplicity of demands may, paradoxically, provide freedom (Dexter, 1963b; Bauer, Pool, and Dexter, 1963); playing one group or set of demands against another may permit the lawmaker to follow his own preferred course of action confident that he will have some allies no matter what he chooses to do.

We should not, however, infer from these considerations that role-orientational choices are always "either-or" decisions. They may be explained in such terms, but they do not often occur in so clear-cut a fashion. As we have seen, commitment to one activity may well yield payoffs in another. Involvement in constituency services often requires intervention in bureaucratic affairs that, in turn, may give insight into the operations of the executive branch and facilitate oversight. Listening to constituent requests may provide some clues about public needs which legislation may be able to satisfy. Nor should we conclude that lawmakers assume their role orientations irrevocably. Rather, we should remember that events external to the legislative system may create new conditions; an election may pass the Presidency to the other party or may elevate a new man to an important committee chairmanship; the passage of time may alter the perspective from which the member of Congress views some problem. These changes may well bring about significant alterations in individual orientations and in the distribution of orientations within the legislature.

The problem of role conflict is not that a lawmaker must do one thing to the exclusion of all others, but rather that he must do one thing (or a very few) well while he treats the other tasks more superficially. The problem is not that he must respond to one set of pressures only, but that in responding to one set he must act contrary to other interests. The outputs of the legislative system will reflect the distribution of these choices and responses. So long as a significant number of senators and representatives commit themselves to each output, so long as a meaningful contingent in Congress responds in some fashion to widely held demands, the system will perform adequately. To the extent that one function is neglected, to the degree that major demands go unheeded, a loss in support may result, with serious consequences for the future of the legislature.

FEEDBACK

The operation of feedback provides a built-in corrective device for any imbalance which may develop in the distribution of the system's activities. Feedback, as described in Chapter 1 (pp. 6–7 and 22) refers to the process by which the outputs of the system exert influence on the actors in the environment, stimulating them to make new demand inputs and to give greater or lesser support to the system. Output failure—unwillingness or inability to legislate, oversee, or represent—may thus be costly in systemic terms. Rejection of such policies as Medicare leads to increased demands for implementation, demands expressed by more groups and citizens, more executive personnel, and more legislators. Unsatisfactory policy choices may produce similar results. The rather moderate civil rights bills of 1957 and 1960 did not come close to satisfying the aspirations of black Americans who in increasing numbers, supported by white allies, adopted sit-in and other protest techniques unused to that point in time. Such actions, and the resistance of some citizens to them, served to enlarge the pro-civil rights coalition which made more insistent demands on Congress. Coupled with the change of

administrations, the Democratic sweep of 1964, and the persistence of the
prorights forces, these new demands, or at least many of them, were included
in the civil rights act of 1964 and the voting rights bill of the following year.

Congressional failure adequately to discharge any one of the output
functions may automatically lead to demands for action in that area. Congress's minimal involvement in the nation's policies with regard to Indochina.
its deference to the executive in military matters generally, especially after
the April 1970 commitment of American troops to Cambodian soil, made
Congress as well as the President a focus for the discontent that erupted
following the change in the character of the war. While we do not know much
about the motivations of those involved, we may speculate that the public
outcry, and especially that on the nation's campuses, not only led the Chief
Executive to impose geographical and time limitations on the Cambodian
venture but also reinforced the position of those in Congress who were
determined to reassert legislative prerogatives in the foreign policy sphere.
It may be that inattention, popular demands for action, or public dissatisfaction with past failures may all lead legislators who are looking for career
opportunites to move into the particular area involved. So long as there are
demands for action in all areas and support, either personal or institutional,
to be won for response to such demands, apparently Congress will not long
neglect any of its output responsibilities.

Feedback may also account for heightened legislative responsiveness to
inputs from the environment. If, and the "if" is basic, external interests—
whether concerned with foreign or with domestic matters—can organize
effectively and can take their demands into the political arena they should
find willing spokesmen for them within the legislative ranks. Congressmen are
concerned not only with enhancing their own political futures, but also with
locating places where they can serve and where they can exercise political
power. Organized interests may not only threaten them with early and un-
desired retirement from office, but also may offer opportunities to take
meaningful stands and to move forward in meeting national needs. Again,
insofar as the lawmakers perceive such openings, they are likely to seize them,
thus bringing new expressions of concern into the legislative process. In this
sense, feedback may serve as the steering mechanism by which Congress,
sooner or later, acts to meet pressing national issues and to preserve support
for the congressional system.[21]

This speculation should serve to remind us that the legislative system is
not rigid and unchanging but is flexible and in flux. The formal and informal
characteristics of the system are often, though seldom dramatically, altered;
the actors internal to the system change with elections and with the assumption of new political roles by new generations; the actors external to the

---

[21] We will ignore the prospect, not altogether an unthinkable one, that Congress will fail to perceive
widely held, deeply felt demands and will persist in pursuing actions which undermine its support and
threaten its very survival.

system come and go, wax and wane in influence, imposing new demands in keeping with new circumstances and responding in new ways to the system's outputs. Change may not be rapid—the Congress of the 1930s bears a marked resemblance to the contemporary legislature—but it does occur. The question, frequently and hotly debated, is whether Congress can adapt sufficiently and rapidly enough to retain its essential strength. It is to this issue, and a rather bewildering variety of answers to it, that we turn in the concluding chapter.

SUMMARY

A third set of expectations about the outputs of the legislative system focuses on the representative character of Congress. While definitions of representation vary, in keeping with normative concerns, there exists a widely shared belief, among congressmen as well as outside the legislative halls, that Congress must serve those who elect its members. The legislature is expected to act both as the policy representative of the electorate and as a service bureau, a point of contact between citizen and government, quite apart from specific policy decisions.

In the area of policy representation, despite the rather atypical men which the electoral process rewards with places in Congress, the lawmakers focus their actions to a considerable degree on the narrow confines of their own states and districts. A large majority thus assume a delegate or politico representational style and a district or combined district-national focal orientation. They do so, moreover, in the face of persuasive evidence that their local constituencies are at best only vaguely aware of any specific actions they take. The legislators' uncertainty, rooted in the ultimate authority of the citizenry to retire them from office, leads them to pay more attention to local matters than might otherwise be necessary. The extent of this concern varies from issue to issue, from one situation to the next, and in response to the activation of one or more relevant participants in Congress or in its environment.

With regard to nonpolicy representation, constituency service, the record is clearer: virtually all members of Congress feel a strong need to respond to requests of all kinds from back home. There is little doubt that a general, vague but perhaps pervasive, image of their performance is at the base of their reelection prospects. Moreover, casework helps people, gives them access to the vast federal establishment available nowhere else. Service chores also provide information, about public needs and administrative conduct, which facilitates the lawmaking and oversight aspects of the legislative responsibility. The burden is heavy, but the lawmakers feel, as a general rule, that it must be met, and many commit the largest portion of their office and staff resources to citizen services. Related to constituency service is the need to initiate communication with the district, not just to respond to messages flowing to Washington. The lawmakers handle this facet of their duties in several ways: many use a variety of public relations devices to promote their own interests; others seek partisan goals, seeking to persuade those who will listen of the correctness of their personal views; some combine the promoter and persuader goals; and a few, the smallest number, define their task as constituent education, for its own rather than for the lawmaker's sake.

Taken together, the two types of representational activities underscore the conclusion about the nature of support for the legislative system reached in Chapter 9. Such support as representational outputs produce is less likely to be specific, is less likely to flow directly from particular policy outputs. Rather, support will more often be diffuse, reflecting the sort of nonspecific, generalized feelings of legislative competence which result from successful response to constituent demands for services. Many citizens, of course, will continue to give support as a matter of habit, as they have been taught (socialized) to do, quite apart from any of Congress' outputs.

Representational activities, of both types, compete with lawmaking and oversight for the congressmen's attention and energies. Role conflict is widespread and most often resolved in favor of legislative specialization and constituent service. Though it is clear that some role orientations are more attractive, the operation of the feedback cycle points to opportunities for legislators to serve and, simultaneously, to gain advantage. Thus, those functions and interests that are insufficiently treated should, with the passage of time, be the areas most attractive to ambitious legislators. Whether this self-correcting process is adequate to keep Congress not only relevant but also effective in the era of "continuing crisis" is a question, heretofore studiously avoided, to which we must now direct our attention.

PART

4

Congress and the Future

CHAPTER FOURTEEN

Congressional Reform: Proposals and Prospects

To this point, the purpose of this book has been to analyze and describe the workings of the American Congress as precisely and objectively as possible. While points of controversy have been noted, no serious effort has been undertaken to specify the sorts of changes in congressional operations which numerous critics have proposed. Rather, within the framework which the systems perspective provides, we have sought to generalize about the nature—the structures, roles, processes, both formal and informal—of the legislative system, the inputs—of support as well as demands—from the environment to the system, and the interaction of these two sets of factors in the system's production of outputs. Such concerns have led us to examine the committees, political parties, formal rules, and the legislative culture inside Congress; the transactions between the executive branch—the President and the agencies—the interest groups, the courts, and the public, on the one hand, and Congress on the other; and the ultimate products—outputs of lawmaking, oversight, and representation—that the legislative system generates in response to the inputs it receives. We have, in addition, suggested a number of propositions, which existing data seem to justify, linking the role orientations of the legislators toward these various facets of the system with the lawmakers' behaviors; where data is lacking or inconclusive, we have speculated about such relationships. In all this, our aim has been to portray the system's functioning with the maximum care and specificity possible.

As soon as we move from the empirical world itself to judging that world in terms of its desirability, its "goodness" or "badness," we confront a difficult set of issues. These are the value questions which cannot be answered with certainty, for what appears as acceptable to one observer will be hopelessly inadequate to another. That is, the values about "correctness" or propriety of a particular institutional arrangement or practice that the student brings to his subject will determine much of what he sees when he looks at the object of his inquiry. Specifically, with regard to Congress, this premise suggests that our evaluations of the legislature's performance, and the reform proposals which flow from those evaluations, will reflect what we believe Congress ought to be doing. An example of differences among observers of the national scene may serve to illustrate how one's overall view of Congress's effectiveness as well as of the legislature's place in the larger political system flows directly from one's premises about what that system should be doing.

At the close of the Eisenhower administration in the late 1950s, two students of American national politics recorded their impressions of the state of the nation; from their reports it is hard to believe that each was looking at the same institutions. The first author, James McGregor Burns, viewing the political process rom a liberal (in the common, colloquial sense of the term) perspective found inaction, an unwillingness or inability to meet the challenges of the times, to be the hallmark of the era. In *The Deadlock of Democracy* (1963), Burns argued that the President, the motive force in national politics, the man most likely to propose and implement solutions to pressing national problems, was unable to act; the legislature, with its archaic rules and customs, dominated by Southern conservatives eager to preserve the status quo, hamstrung the innovative Chief Executive. Thus the deadlock, the inaction, flowed directly from a Congress which would not permit action, which blocked imaginative ideas required to deal with continuing crises in urban affairs, civil rights, foreign policy, and other areas. The solution which Burns envisaged was to restructure national political institutions, especially to enhance the power of the political parties, so that the President, with certain support from his partisans in the legislature, would be free to respond creatively to emerging national problems. Liberation of the President was the key, in Burns's view, to breaking the policy impasse into which the country had fallen.

On the other hand, James Burnham, a conservative (in the contemporary usage of that term), looked at national politics and saw a startling different picture. Far from a weak President, unable to provide necessary leadership, Burnham, in *Congress and the American Tradition* (1959), saw a dangerous drift away from the proper relationships between the branches of government toward executive *domination* of the political process. Far from being able to block undesirable executive initiatives, Congress had surrendered much of the authority, which the framers of the Constitution had intended it to exercise, to the Chief Executive. In consequence, Burnham argued, the American political process has become seriously out of balance, with Congress reduced to a subsidiary position, out of keeping with the tradition of legislative supremacy which the Founding Fathers had intended to prevail. The solution, of course, is to restore Congress to its proper authority, to dismantle the Presidency and the executive establishment such that Congress can impose its policy preferences and exercise control over the bureaucracy.

The reform proposals of each author are considerably more detailed and specific than this discussion indicates; we will treat concrete suggestions for change in a subsequent section. For now, the essential point is that the observer's values—what he wants to see as the political system's outputs—color the lenses through which he views that system; the reforms he proposes are designed to bring about the desired results. The liberal is in general interested in change; when change does not occur rapidly enough to suit him, he seeks to alter the system to favor action and to reduce the requirements that innovation come slowly. The conservative, conversely, is most frequently opposed to rapid change, preferring to move slowly and to minimize the disruption of the existing patterns.

Lest there be any doubt that suggestions for reforms reflect desired political outcomes, we need only look at the changes in perspective that the Indochina war introduced within a decade of the publication of the Burns and Burnham books. When the President, utilizing the powers that the liberals have been willing to grant him and that the conservatives have been reluctant to see him exercise, involved the nation in a war that liberals felt was useless and that conservatives felt was essential to national defense,[1] the positions of the two groups seemed to reverse. The liberals, erstwhile defenders of executive initiative, took the lead in a movement to reassert congressional power as a check on the President; the conservatives, heretofore critical of unchecked exercise of executive power, rallied to the cause of the Chief Executive.[2] In short, as this example clearly illustrates, policy preferences dictate what is the preferred form of political organization, and reform ideas are advanced to facilitate those policy goals.

From a slightly different perspective, this suggests that reform must be viewed in a political context (Wildavsky, 1964, pp. 128–135). That is, different structures, rules, and processes will inevitably lead to different policy results,

---

[1]The issues, pro and con, relating to the war in Vietnam and Cambodia are obviously complex and value laden, but they are not directly relevant to the argument advanced here that political reforms are proposed to bring about specific political results.

[2]Thus, in the Senate a liberal coalition, including Senators John Sherman Cooper (R., Ky.), Frank Church (D., Id.), J. William Fulbright (D., Ark.), Jacob Javits (R., N.Y.), and many others attached the so-called Cooper-Church amendment to the Military Sales Act of 1971 by which the President was forbidden to spend money to support American troops in Cambodia after June 30, 1970, without prior consultation with Congress. An even stronger proposal, to end the war by denying all funds for military activity in Indochina, was advanced by Senators George McGovern (D., S.D.) and Mark Hatfield (R., Ore.), but was rejected on the Senate floor. Nonetheless, the change in perspective remains clear: it is the liberals, customarily supportive of presidential leadership, who have led the effort to restrict that leadership because, on this issue at least, they do not like the direction in which the Chief Executive has taken the nation.

and proposals for reform, justified in terms of efficiency, are unlikely to strike a responsive chord unless they promise to provide satisfactory policy outcomes as well. Congress is, as we have seen, a decentralized political system in which bargaining is the central mode of conflict resolution. However inefficient the process or unsatisfactory the results produced may appear to outside observers, those who wield power under existing institutional arrangements are likely to remain, as they presently are, unwilling to support reforms which will weaken their own influence within the system (Davidson et al., 1966; Ripley, 1969; Clapp, 1964). Change which alters the conditions in which bargaining occurs will be resisted by those to whose advantage, actual or perceived, the negotiating process seems to work. Thus reform, values, and politics are interwoven and difficult to disentangle, and all that we can do in this chapter is to suggest some of the basic value positions and the reforms which go with those postures. We cannot hope to resolve the issues of reform definitively.

One additional point needs to be made here. The discussion that follows assumes that Congress will continue to exist as a component of a larger political system which, though it may change in degree, will be of the same basic kind as it is at present. While some "radical" criticism of American institutions has emerged in recent years, it seems unlikely that a major "revolution," a major attack on the federal Constitution, will find much support. Moreover, what the radical critics would create to replace existing institutions is so unclear that analysis of their ideas is most difficult. Thus, the present discussion assumes that the familiar structures and processes will retain their basic shapes and that the major issues of reform, including reform of Congress, will be on the advisability of altering the political system with an eye to improving its performance of those things that observers wish the national government to do.

SOME PERSPECTIVES ON THE
CONGRESSIONAL SYSTEM

Since models of the congressional system relate directly to perspectives on the larger political system of which the legislature is a part, it is well to begin with the broader view, to explore the implications of these more general images for Congress, and then to turn to the specific reform ideas proposed to translate each model into reality. The major dimension around which these models revolve relates to the balance of power between the legislative and executive branches; the chief quarrel which divides the reformers into distinct camps is over how much control over Congress the President should exercise, and vice versa. One school of thought, the presidential-dominance models, stresses the need for executive leadership while the opposite view, the congressional-supremacy models, holds that the critical element is the ability of the legislature to seize and hold governmental initiative. We shall explore these conceptions, in turn, indicating the place of Congress in each.[3]

Presidential-dominance models There are a number of variations of the presidential-dominance model but the central feature of each is the vast power of the executive to propose and to carry out programs. The "executive-force" scheme stresses, among other things, that the President assumes responsibility as "chief legislator" and "chief administrator," that is, that he advances policy proposals and manages the execution of those programs within the bureaucracy. Congress, on the other hand, devotes its energies to passing upon, perhaps with some modifying influence, the President's program and, in so doing, to legitimizing that program. In other words, Congress is expected, in this scheme of things, to yield the lawmaking function as well as that part of its oversight function which is motivated by a desire to influence policy. The legislature should, conversely, focus its attention on the efficiency component of oversight, striving to guarantee that programs are run honestly, with an eye to saving money, but without undue "interference" with policy implementation. Moreover, the legislative branch should serve as a link between citizens and government: presenting their views to the executive in the course of congressional deliberations on executive measures, performing services on their behalf, and educating them about the content of national policy.[4] Thus this model looks to Congress to yield policy making and implementation to the executive and, instead, to concentrate upon oversight and representation.[5]

A second major variation on the theme of presidential dominance is the "responsible-party" model. Like the executive-force notion, those who espouse the responsible-party doctrine believe that the president, elected by the entire electorate, is most likely to provide the requisite leadership for solving the problems of the contemporary world. They propose, as the vehicle for executive domination, to centralize and discipline the political parties, so that the chief executive will have a certain majority in Congress to pass his policy proposals. The British parliamentary arrangements seem beneficial in this respect; the president, like the prime minister, would possess, through his leadership position, the ability to win approval, and to control the carrying out, of his preferred programs. As in the previous case, Congress, having surrendered its basic lawmaking powers, and the policy-related part of its

[3]For other ways of categorizing these executive-legislative relationships, see Davidson et al., 1966, pp. 17–34, and Saloma, 1969, pp. 37–47.
[4]For arguments supporting notions of a "strong" or dominant Presidency, see Rossiter, 1960, Lippmann, 1954, Harris, 1965, and Dahl, 1950. For a description of this model, and a virulent attack upon it, see de Grazia, 1965.
[5]In this and subsequent discussion, we have oversimplified to a considerable degree; here, for instance, the argument is not that Congress should *never* engage in policy making, but rather, on the whole, should commit itself to oversight and representational activities.

oversight mission as well, would expend its efforts primarily on oversight for efficiency purposes and all forms of representation. Specific reforms, which we will discuss in the next section of this chapter, flow from each of these visions of the political process (Burns, 1949; 1963; Americal Political Science Association, 1950).

Congressional-supremacy models The reverse perspective, following the line that Burnham (1959) advances, sees Congress as the dominant force in national politics. This view, sometimes labeled the "literary" or "whig" theory (Davidson et al., 1966; Saloma, 1969), holds that the legislature ought to exercise all powers in all areas of concern; that is, in the terms of systems analysis, Congress should be preeminent with respect to all three output functions—lawmaking, oversight, and representation. In stark contrast to the executive-dominance models, under the notion of legislative supremacy, the President would have considerably less initiative and would commit himself substantially more to execution of congressionally determined policies—efficient administration in keeping with legislative intent, moreover. Congressmen, elected in small areas by relatively homogeneous populations, are better suited to exercise these powers, are better equipped to represent and to serve the citizenry, for whose benefit government is to operate (de Grazia, 1965, 1966). Since all proponents of this view agree that Congress currently does not possess this range of authority, the reforms they suggest aim at reinvigorating the legislature, at restoring it to its proper place in the political process.

Intermediate positions: bargaining models There are, as might be expected, a number of intermediate positions between the extremes of presidential- or legislative-supremacy models. The identifying feature of these approaches is one of balance, each branch possessing some bases of power and influence, and each is required to work out solutions through bargaining, negotiation, and compromise with the other.[6] Since the two branches do, in effect, represent two constituencies, one more liberal than the other (Kendall, 1960), it is reasonable to expect interbranch conflict and to require a mode of conflict resolution that does not totally subordinate or completely suppress either side. Thus, policy struggles are fought out between competing coalitions—each composed of executive-branch personnel, hopefully including the Chief Executive; legislators; and interest groups and interested citizens from outside the formal governmental institutions—through a multistage process from initiative through debate and passage to implementation. The battle

---

[6]This view—often called the pluralist perspective in light of its recognition that there exist multiple centers of influence, none able to dominate the others, which must accommodate their diverse interests through negotiation and compromise—is most often identified with Robert A. Dahl and Charles E. Lindblom. See Dahl, 1950, 1956, 1967; Dahl and Lindblom, 1953; and Lindblom, 1959, 1965, 1968. See also Wildavsky, 1964.

will be waged at each step until nearly total acceptance of the outcome by most major participants. Specific outcomes result from the strength and the skill of the various elements. An adept President can, in many cases, use the bargaining advantages he possesses to move his administration's program through to acceptance; a less adroit Chief Executive will find himself frustrated, in Congress or elsewhere, by the opposition (Neustadt, 1960). Variations of the model depend, of course, on whether the observer prefers to see the balance tipped toward a particular set of participants; reform proposals are similarly intended to enhance the bargaining position of favored participants.

One specific variation deserves mention because it has been advanced by members of Congress, generally liberal ones (Clark, 1964, 1965; Bolling, 1965; Miller, 1962). While granting that decisions often emerge from complicated negotiating processes, these legislators seek to broaden the distribution of bargaining levers within Congress itself. The position of committee chairmen, buttressed by the seniority rule and autocratic powers inherent in the top committee post; the domination of party leadership positions by members of the Establishment; and the operation of informal norms and restraints all serve to preclude junior lawmakers from equal participation in the congressional phase of policy making. These senators and representatives propose to "democratize" Congress, to enlarge, that is, the number of legislators who can exert influence over subjects under congressional consideration; the reforms they propose are intended to produce more widespread and meaningful rank-and-file participation in legislative deliberations. In general, like other bargaining models, these modifications recognize that the political arrangements facilitate competition for the exercise of lawmaking, oversight, and even representational functions (Davidson, 1966), and seek to alter the balance of power among the competitors.

CONGRESSIONAL REFORMS

Each of the basic orientations carries with it specific reform proposals, designed, of course, to bring about the desired institutional arrangements and with them the reformers' desired policy and other outputs. There are two basic positions relating to Congress and congressional reform at the center of these quarrels:[7] one, to which the proponents of presidential dominance subscribe, favors those changes necessary to increase executive ability to control Congress; the other, held by the believers in legislative supremacy, aims at enlarging congressional power and influence vis-á-vis the executive. The intermediate positions pick and choose among the

[7] In what follows we will limit the discussion to those reform proposals which directly affect Congress and will ignore suggestions intended primarily to alter the Presidency or the political parties.

reforms that the two polar schools of thought suggest depending on which way they seek to shift the executive-legislative balance; the latter views tend to favor incremental alterations designed to shift the balance in one or another direction. Here we shall review the two major positions, indicating the major reforms in the congressional system that each proposes.[8]

Strengthening the President The changes in congressional practice which the proponents of the various presidential-dominance models prefer seek to improve the Chief Executive's ability to advance his, most often liberal, program through Congress. The legislature's power to obstruct, the current impediment to the desired state of affairs, must consequently be reduced. The reformers propose to move on a number of fronts, electoral and systemic—to increase the probability that the legislature will enact the demands of the President, will be responsive to inputs originating in the system's environment. Congress would, as we have noted, be left to deal with oversight and representational problems.

One target of these reformers is the electoral process which, in their view, elevates conservatives—out of touch with, and lacking in sympathy for, the President's more liberal constituency—to positions in Congress. Assuming that the customary mode of apportionment contributes to this result, favoring rural, and presumably conservative, interests, the forces for change have favored court-enforced reapportionment as a means to increase the representation accorded urban, presumably liberal, interests. Fair apportionment, based on population equality, would give the President additional votes in the House, liberalizing the more conservative chamber. While it seems true that the House is less liberal than the Senate (Froman, 1963), as the evidence of the impact of the widespread reapportionment of the 1960s slowly accumulates, it seems unlikely that redistricting will have the hoped-for results. The number of rural seats has been marginally reduced, to be sure, but the chief beneficiary seems to have been suburban rather than central-city areas of the nation; in consequence, there has not appeared an upsurge of those with proexecutive role orientations voting for the President's program regularly in the House.[9] Current population trends, moreover, give little hope to those who would prefer to see more urban seats in Congress.[10]

[8]We will present an overview of these positions, but the reader should not be led to conclude that all reformers agree on each item or that all would insist on the adoption of a reform package in toto.
[9]The only period during the decade of the 1960s in which the Chief Executive had a clear proexecutive, party-loyalist majority in the House occurred in the Eighty-ninth Congress (1965–1966) as a result of the Lyndon Johnson–Democratic landslide victory in the 1964 presidential contest. This was, of course, well *before* the major impact of the 1963 *Wesberry v. Sanders* congressional reapportionment decision of the Supreme Court. Subsequent elections have wiped out this propresidential legislative majority.
[10]Tabulations of the 1970 census indicate that not only have urban centers lost population relative to the suburban areas, but that at least half of the twenty-five largest cities have suffered a net population loss. This will be reflected in the apportionment of the 1970s which should show more suburban seats. Surburban legislators cannot readily be classified, as a group, as conservatives or liberals.

A second electoral reform designed to enhance Congress's responsiveness to executive policy demands is extension of the House member's term of office from two to four years. Such a change might have a number of advantages—it would reduce the lawmaker's dependence on the electorate and on financial contributors to his campaign fund; it could free him from the most onerous burden of casework and thus enable him to do more oversight—but the principal gain, in this context, would be to make congressmen more susceptible to presidential leadership. It seems clear to many observers that lawmakers elected with the President, on his "coattails," tend to exhibit loyalty to him; thus if all legislators were so chosen, and only in this fashion, they might be expected to display greater loyalty to party and President than congressmen chosen in years when there was no presidential contest.[11] When in 1966, President Johnson proposed extension of the congressional term, no majority could be found in support of the idea.[12]

Finally, we should note the program of those reformers in favor of the responsible-party model of executive domination. As a result of their grand design of centralizing the national political parties, great alterations in the electoral scheme would ensue (Burns, 1963; American Political Science Association, 1950). In effect, the new and powerful national party committees would control the fate of their own congressional candidates. No longer would the candidate be on his own; rather the national agency would control campaign finance and would manage a national campaign on national issues. If the ultimate power to control the nomination—to exact loyalty pledges in advance or to punish the recalcitrant incumbent—rested with the President and his national committee, a member of the President's party in Congress could oppose his chief only upon pain of retirement from office in the ensuing election. Thus the President, in the fashion of the British prime minister, would have a virtually certain congressional majority in support of his program.

These reformers also propose a multitude of changes intended to alter the internal dynamics of the congressional system in ways that promote executive control of the system's outputs. Their focus includes the committee system, and the position and mode of selection of panel chairmen; the political parties; and the formal rules of procedure. Changes in these structural features would in all likelihood have an impact on the informal norms and organizations of Congress; thus, these changes, if adopted, would basically

---

[11] Those who fear such a possibility, but who seek some of the advantages of a longer term, have proposed various "staggered" term arrangements, in the fashion of Senate elections. For a full discussion of the extended term proposals, see Jones, 1967. Chapter 2, pp. 50–52, discusses the coattail effect within the more general context of congressional elections.

[12] Davidson et al. (1966, pp. 96–98) found a majority of the legislators they polled to favor a longer term. When, however, confronted with the need to adopt a specific proposal to embody some form of the four-year term, that majority failed to materialize. See also Jones (1967). The Senate was less than enthusiastic about the proposal, feeling that the extended term of service might give members of the House the "free" opportunity to challenge incumbent senators without risking the loss of their seats.

alter the nature of the legislative system. In general, the thrust of the total package of changes is to reduce the ability of various minorities to block the President's program; to facilitate, that is, the movement of the program through the legislative obstacle course.

With respect to the committees, a number of suggestions have been made, the most basic of which pertain to the powers of chairmen in general and, more particularly, to seniority as the mode of choosing the chairman. The goal of the proposed changes is to give the President and his political party leaders in Congress greater control over committee conduct, to reduce, that is, the independence and autonomy which currently characterizes the committee subsystems. One route to this goal is to reduce the powers of the chairman as panel leader, making him more responsive to the majority of committee members. A regularized set of rules, carefully adhered to, that permits the majority to call meetings, place items on the agenda, and bring matters to a vote even in the face of opposition from the chairman is often proposed. While it is true that committee majorities do possess such powers on some panels, many members seem loath to use them in view of the chairman's available sanctions. If, however, the perquisites of the chairman—his ability to set up subcommittees and appoint their chairmen, and to control staff and committee funds, for instance—were reduced, the rank and file should be more willing to challenge him.[13] If the President could, under such circumstances, command a panel majority, he would be able to move his proposals through committee to the floor.

A second method of gaining control of the committees, and a more basic one in the view of those fostering executive domination, would be to ensure that the chairman, especially if he continued to wield substantial authority, was a party loyalist. The seniority system, automatically rewarding electoral survival and longevity, works against this goal, and becomes a prime target for reform. A number of alternatives have been offered: election of chairmen by committee members on a secret ballot, slection from among the three most senior majority-party members, or choice on the basis of other than seniority criteria. Again, abandonment of the seniority rule in favor of any more open selection process would permit the Chief Executive, given a committee majority favorable to his program, to have a sympathetic panel chairman in charge of the elements of that program. A small but potentially significant step was taken when the Ninety-second Congress convened in 1971. Both political parties decided that criteria other than seniority might be used in the selection of House committee chairmen. The recommendations of the respective committee on committees would be submitted to the party caucus for

---

[13] The Legislative Reorganization Act of 1970 contains a small step toward reducing the chairman's powers. The bill bars giving "blanket" proxies to the chairman, the usual beneficiary of the practice, or other committee members. Proxies, limited to specific votes, are still permissible. As initially voted, the bill prohibited all proxy voting, but the House had second thoughts and amended the bill to narrow the use of proxies only marginally.

ratification. The new procedure was not implemented, however, and the senior panelist sat as chairman on each committee in 1971–1972.[14]

To the extent that the committees of Congress are brought under control, the authority of the second major subsystem within the legislature, the political party, is enhanced. As a concomitant of the perceived need for stronger parties and greater centralization, the executive-dominance reformers propose some specific steps to buttress the position of the parties. Party leaders, according to this view, should resolve their role conflicts in favor of assuming the orientation of "President's men" on Capitol Hill; they should, that is, commit themselves, their energies, and the resources at their disposal as majority leaders to advancing the administration's program. Party agencies should be devoted to the same end and empowered to foster those goals. The caucus should be able to exercise power on behalf of the majority of its partisans; it should control committee assignments, for example, rewarding the faithful and meting out punishments to the disloyal. Policy committees should be able to set forth party positions, subject to review and ratification by the full-party membership meeting in caucus; at the immediate operating level, the policy committee should be empowered to schedule party-sponsored bills for floor consideration. If linked to responsible parties able to punish dissenters through control of the nominating process, such reforms should create powerful parties capable of steering their programs through the legislature.

The reformers seeking to smooth the congressional path of executive policies look to changing the rules of procedure as well. Here, too, the goal of the proposals is to reduce the ability of minorities, entrenched at particular veto points within a decentralized system, to block administration programs. In the House, the chief focus is, as might be expected, the Rules Committee, and the major reform suggested is to reinstitute and make permanent the 21-Day Rule under which the Speaker can, over committee objections, call up measures for floor consideration after the bill has been in the panelists' hands for more than twenty-one days. The provision has been in effect twice in the past, most recently in the Eighty-seventh Congress, but has not survived renewed conservative strength and was stricken from the rules on each occasion after two years in operation. Another rule change applicable to all committees is the proposal to alter the discharge rule, lowering the number of signatures required from the present 218, a majority of the full chamber, to some more readily attainable number, such as 150. Such changes would reduce the ability of the committees to block passage of measures favored by majorities in the full house.

[14]In a direct test of support for modifying the seniority, on July 28, 1970, the House voted 196 to 28 against the idea of selection from the top three committee seniors and 160 to 73 against the simple statement that seniority should not be the only consideration in the choice of committee chairman. These votes support the findings of Davidson et al. (1966), Clapp (1964), and Ripley (1969b) that there exists no significant sentiment among the lawmakers themselves to replace the seniority criterion.

On the Senate side, the reformers' main target is the obvious one, unlimited debate, the filibuster, and the cloture rule. The proponents of executive domination desire to eliminate the possibility that a bill commanding majority support will nonetheless become so mired in extended debate that it cannot be passed. Thus, they propose, first of all, to impose limitations on debate; the suggestions include eliminating the "morning hour," leaving more time to deal with substantive legislation; limiting the amount of time any senator can hold the floor;[15] imposing requirements intended to make debate germane to the issues at hand; reducing the opportunity for filibusters by making the motion to take up a bill nondebatable and, thus, removing one opportunity to talk the measure to death;[16] and, finally and most importantly, altering the cloture rule to allow a smaller majority—both 60 percent of those present and voting and a simple majority (50 plus 1 percent) have been proposed—to terminate debate. Each of these changes would curtail a minority's potential to tie up the Senate in the interest of defeating specific bills.

A few remaining, miscellaneous ideas have been advanced. In both chambers, steps have been proposed to limit the dilatory tactics available to minorities; for instance, the need to have the *Journal* read each day could be eliminated. A more extreme idea would require that Congress as a whole complete action on executive proposals within a specific period of time, say, six months, after the measure had been sent from the White House to Capitol Hill. In these and a variety of other ways, the place of Congress in the national political process would be altered: fragmentation of power would be diminished and centralization created; committee independence would be restricted, the parties strengthened, and the rules altered; all to permit executive leadership to carry the day.

Still other proposals have been put forward to guarantee that policy formation and implementation would rest in executive hands. To eliminate the possibility that Congress might intrude in this area through positive steps enacted in legislation, the executive-dominance forces propose to expand the President's veto power to include the item veto, that is, the power to disapprove specific provisions selectively rather than to reject a bill in its entirety. Such a move would obviate one legislative strategy for asserting congressional policy-making initiatives, that of including a small number of items, opposed by the Chief Executive, in bills containing major programs that he favors on the assumption that he will accept a few undesirable provisions rather than risk losing major matters of central concern.[17]

---

[15] Clark (1964) proposes that no senator be permitted to speak for more than two hours unless he is managing the bill or receives unanimous consent.

[16] Filibuster possibilities would remain on actual passage of legislation and on acceptance of conference reports.

[17] Such strategy dictates linking a variety of proposals into a single omnibus bill, accomplished at the drafting stage or by amendment on the floor. The Voting Rights Act of 1970 is typical of the successful operation of the strategy. Congress appended a provision granting eighteen-year-olds the right to vote to the bill, despite President Nixon's announced view that such a change required a constitutional amendment, and the Chief Executive signed the measure, though with considerable reluctance, and sought an early court test of the constitutionality of changing the voting age by statute.

Moreover, the reformers propose steps that would effectively preclude Congress, or its committees and interested members, from engaging in oversight of the executive branch for policy, as opposed to efficiency, reasons. Administrative agencies should, according to this view, receive broad discretionary grants of authority to carry out policy, including, for example, funding for several years in advance. Conversely, Congress' use of restrictive practices, such as the legislative veto with its multifaceted devices for giving the legislature the opportunity to exercise prior clearance of bureaucratic actions, would be curtailed or eliminated. Thus, the ability of Congress to affect policy, at the implementation phase, would be removed, and the Chief Executive left relatively free to make policy and see it conducted according to his wishes.

All these suggestions, whether adopted wholly or in part, singly or in combination, would basically alter the position of the congressional system in the larger political order. Policy choice and conduct would essentially be left to the executive while Congress would focus its attention on oversight to promote efficiency and on representation of public concerns. Such dramatic alterations in the system would, no doubt, bring other less visible changes as well. Without the opportunity to shape policy, different sorts of individuals would probably find legislative service congenial; tribunes and inventors, for instance, would seem less likely to find Congress a meaningful place to advance their programmatic goals. The norms would also change; there would be little payoff in legislative specialization and commitment to congressional work; focus of concern might be expected to move from lawmaking to oversight and representation as the opportunities to serve and to exert influence become more plentiful in those domains. Other possible alterations exist, but cannot be specified precisely or remain even beyond speculation in the absence of reform in the direction of executive dominance.

Such reform, however, does not seem probable. Generally favored by academics, these proposals have been circulated, without finding many proponents, since the 1940s. To effect them would require, in many cases, amending the Constitution, not an easy chore in any situation but all the more difficult in view of the need for congressmen to vote to dismantle their own bases for influence over a significant segment of national political concerns. It is hardly surprising, therefore, that senators and representatives, for the most part, have been unwilling to take such suggestions seriously. If the demands for structural change grow sufficiently strong, the legislators might find it necessary to consider wholesale change, but given public disinterest in reform and the preference of others outside the legislative system for trying to make it work rather than seeking basic alterations, such demands seem unlikely to develop. Into the 1970s, at least, all participants seem to prefer incremental to radical change.

Strengthening Congress The executive-dominance models, whatever their precise form, seek to promote rapid enactment and speedy implementation of policy changes. There remain, however, considerable numbers of people, more frequently of a conservative persuasion, who believe that rapid adoption of new programs is undesirable, who feel that change when it comes should follow slow and careful deliberation and should, in general, follow only from the support of substantial majorities of all segments of American society (Burnham, 1959; de Grazia, 1965, 1966). They argue, in other words, that the legislative system should be less, not more, responsive to demands from the system's environment. Their position is that Congress has been eclipsed by the executive, contrary to tradition and expediency, and they believe that Congress must be restored to preeminence across the full range of its responsibilities, that is, with respect to all three output functions.

In general, the proponents of congressional dominance seek to enhance the power of minorities; this follows from their conviction that change—new policies and programs—should come only after all significant segments have agreed that it is needed, only, that is, after consensus has been reached on the wisdom and desirability of the change. Thus, any reforms, such as those that the proexecutive schools of thought suggest, which serve to prevent various interests from being heard, from pressing their sentiments, should be resisted. A fragmented, decentralized legislative system with its multiple points of access and influence, is a positive benefit and should not only be preserved, but also extended. Changes that the congressional supremacists propose toward this goal span the full range of system features: the electoral process, the internal attributes of Congress, interchange between Congress and the various actors outside the legislature, and the system's outputs.[18]

With regard to the electoral arrangements, the pro-Congress forces resist both reapportionment and any effort to impose national, disciplined political parties. Indeed, the very "localism," the concern for local as opposed to national interests, which those who believe in executive power deplore is a positive virtue for the backers of legislative dominance. Reapportionment, reflecting simply population equality, and the forced subscription to a national party's platform, compelled by the ability to inflict electoral defeat, would prevent or at least minimize the representation of diverse interests, especially those incapable of representation in population terms. Thus, an election system, not unlike that presently operative, in which each candidate remains free to build his own organization, raise his own funds, take his own issue positions, and appeal to whatever groups he deems appropriate targets, is desirable, for in this fashion will the widest possible array of differing viewpoints find expression in Congress.

With respect to the internal mechanisms of the legislature—the commit-

---

[18]It is perhaps worth noting, again, that there exist many varieties of opinion on the need to strengthen Congress with differing perspectives on the need to subordinate the executive to the legislative branch. Our purpose here is to review some of the specific proposals and the intentions of their proponents. See the proposals of the House Republican Task Force on Congressional Reform and Minority Staffing (McInnis, 1966) for clear evidence of the wide range of ideas within a single political party.

tees, parties, and formal rules—those in favor of congressional supremacy seem relatively well satisfied with existing arrangements, seeking in the main to resist the efforts of those who would reduce committee autonomy, impose centralization by means of strengthened political parties, and foster both these objectives through changes in the rules of procedure. Thus any proposals to alter the seniority system or the basic powers of committee chairmen are opposed. Positively, individual committees can be made better able to resist the executive, to formulate and espouse alternative arguments to counterbalance those that the President advances, if they have more and better staff resources and increased information, independent of the executive. The need for better data is pervasive and we will return to it in a subsequent section. With regard to staff assistance, provision of more professionals, capable of sophisticated research, would enable the committee experts to come up with superior ideas or more persuasive arguments for their own positions. The minority should have its own staff, under its own immediate control; this could enhance the minority's ability to state its views, its differences with the majority, clearly and persuasively. Such changes would imply a diminution of partisan staff in favor of a concentration on obtaining skilled, professional aid.

Improved committee procedures might further improve the committee's products, making them better able to survive comparison with executive proposals. Less carefully stage-managed hearings, for instance, at which all concerned interests could be heard, would permit the airing of more points of view in greater detail. More open hearings might provide better information for the committee members; new information resources might have the same result. Adequate opportunity for panel deliberation, possible if constraints on member behavior were relaxed, might also improve the output of the committees. More carefully prepared reports, growing out of the improved hearings and extended consideration, circulated to the full chambers well in advance of floor treatment, might raise the quality of debate and, ultimately, of the congressionally enacted measures. Especially if joined to procedural reforms designed to open up floor proceedings to wider participation and more careful discussion, these alterations in committee practice could allow the legislature to assert itself more effectively in opposition to the executive.

To achieve this same purpose, the congressional supremacists look with considerable disfavor on suggestions to centralize the parties or to amend the rules to allow for accelerated congressional action. Those who prefer legislative domination resist imposition of disciplined parties within Congress; such things as strong party caucuses or strengthened policy committees would reduce the chance for various interests, out of favor with party leaders, to be heard. Such agencies might move too quickly, running roughshod over minorities that deserve to have a say. The political parties should remain loose confederations which do little more than facilitate the organization of

Congress at the start of each session. Similarly, the elimination or restriction of Rules Committee power in the House, the Senate filibuster, or other veto points available to minorities would bring about change too rapidly, would mute voices which need to be heard, and the congressional supremacy forces resist the 21-Day Rule or alteration of the cloture procedures.

On the whole, the pro-Congress elements are satisified with, or at least propose few major changes in, the basic procedural and structural organization of the congressional system insofar as domestic policy matters are concerned. To be sure, they would like fuller debate in the House of Representatives as well as greater opportunity to propose amendments without restriction—both changes would slow things down and simultaneously give alternative positions more chance to be expressed—but these and other similar ideas do not radically alter the outlines of the system. In the foreign policy sphere, however, they feel that the balance of power has shifted dramatically toward the executive and that legislative prerogatives need to be reasserted. They favor, as a result, limitations on the President's ability to make arrangements with foreign nations through executive agreements, thus bypassing the senatorial right to give advice and, especially, consent to such commitments embodied in treaty form. To this end, these observers supported the so-called Bricker Amendment to the Constitution, designed to limit presidential discretion in international relations, which in 1954 failed by a single vote to obtain the necessary two-thirds majority in the Senate. This viewpoint opposes broad grants of authority for executive establishment of foreign trade policy, holding that Congress should make such determinations. With regard to both the foreign and the domestic policy areas, Congress suffers from an information deficit and its data-gathering capacity needs to be enlarged considerably to broaden and strengthen congressional initiative in programmatic matters.

Turning from lawmaking to oversight reveals another area where Congress's position vis-à-vis the executive can be greatly improved, according to the legislative supremacists. As it stands, the bureaucracy is so vast and so complex that the lawmakers are unable to oversee it with much success either to influence policy or to promote efficiency. The most extreme version (Burnham, 1959) of the reformer's vision sees the answer in the dismantling of the executive branch, reducing it to a size which congressional watchdogs could control effectively. For example, social security might be made voluntary, publicly owned power projects such as the Tennessee Valley Authority sold to private industry, and other programs turned over to states or localities. Only absolutely essential programs would remain under federal management and the legislature could oversee these with a minimum of difficulty.

Other reformers recognize the improbability of implementing such ideas and focus instead on a series of smaller but nonetheless significant changes that could substantially enlarge congressional oversight capacity. For one thing, the power of the purse, the control over the federal budget, could be expanded to an appreciable degree. One tack here is to improve the budget process within the present framework, that is, to enable Congress, acting through the appropriations committees in the two chambers, to do a better job in dealing with the executive budget. Superior information would both give more insight into bureaucratic activities and reduce dependence on executive sources, no doubt biased toward protecting and enlarging existing programs. More staff committed to budgetary control and an expanded General Accounting Office auditing of executive accounts might also enable financial decisions to be made with a fuller assurance that the legislators making them were indeed exercising independent judgment, well aware of what the agencies had accomplished in the past. Such steps as these would reduce the need for budgetary overseers to sample for that information which they can most easily comprehend—about agency performance in their own constituencies or relating to broad assessments of the administrator's competence, for example—and to generalize from that limited data to overall evaluations of agency activities. The more thorough the review, so this argument runs, the greater the legislature's ability to ensure that bureaucratic behavior conforms to congressional intent and to the canons of efficient administration.

Another major set of proposals in this same vein relates to promoting budget coordination, to give Congress an opportunity to compare income and expenditures completely, to provide the lawmakers with a chance to see the budget in full rather than in piecemeal fashion. The latter is presently the case, in the view of the critics as well as many more impartial observers. While the President submits a single, unified budget, Congress, or rather its appropriations committees, immediately splits the fiscal program into a dozen or more bills which are then given separate, unrelated treatment. At no point does the interested lawmaker have occasion to see how the full budget looks and to compare total proposed expenditures with available revenue. Rather the full picture is not visible until all appropriations measures have been passed; the last bills in the series become major targets for reduction as the sums committed in the earlier bills begin to mount. What is cut at one point can, of course, be restored later in supplemental appropriations bills, a fact which may encourage cuts for partisan reasons in the full knowledge that such reductions will not permanently impair desirable programs. What is needed to remedy such defects, to reduce Congress's competitive disadvantage when facing executive experts in the narrow confines of the latter's specialization, to give the legislature the opportunity to set its own broad priorities for the commitment of federal revenues is to coordinate, centralize to some degree, the congressional consideration of the budget (Committee for Economic Development, 1970).

Several ideas have been advanced to achieve this goal. One proposal (Cotter, 1966, pp. 80–81) calls for converting the Bureau of the Budget, currently the main coordinating device *within* the executive branch, into a "joint agency" of the President and Congress, thus giving the latter data on executive-agency requests as well as the opportunity to contribute to the original form of the budget. That there is little support for this notion is clear from the 1970 congressional approval of a reorganization plan that merged the Budget Bureau into the broader Office of Management and Budget, a development that has seemingly exacerbated Congress's need to develop countervailing influence against the executive. Other suggestions look to creation of a legislative budget, perhaps formulated by a congressional budget office, setting forth the lawmakers' vision of national priorities. Revival of, and further experimentation with, such devices as the Omnibus Appropriations bill, found wanting in an earlier brief trial, might permit more careful congressional budgetary consideration. Greater use of the joint-committee or subcommittee device, resisted at present, might broaden congressional perspectives; such panels could involve the legislative special-ists from both chambers, regardless of their major committee assignments, thus reducing the duplication of effort that exists under current practice and bringing greater expertise to bear on major problems (Carroll, 1966, pp. 224–228).

Carroll (1966, pp. 211–224) has also proposed the use of select committees, specially chosen for specific, narrow-gauge issues, as "study and coordinating" bodies. Such panels might also tap the skills of the most talented members, quite apart from major assignment and independently of the seniority criterion, and could provide the forum in which agreement on priorities (as well as consensus on the substance of policy) might be reached. Finally, enhanced cooperation between the staffs of various committees might improve coordination, especially between the substantive and the appropria-tions bodies; to the extent information and ideas could be exchanged through staff contacts among concerned committees there might occur a broadening of congressional perspective. All such proposals for increased coordination are intended, in various ways and employing various devices, to enhance legislative power by broadening the vantage point from which Congress views the executive branch, and as a result giving the legislators occasion to impose their view of national needs, to allocate available budgetary resources in keeping with their own formulation of national priorities.[19] Drawing more legislators into the budget process might, in addition, enlarge the range of interests with access to the budgetary power of Congress.

Such reforms all assume that the goal is to perfect existing oversight of the budget. Wildavsky (1966), however, concluding that such proposals are unlikely to win acceptance or to work if adopted, suggests that Congress

[19]It should be noted, however, that coordinating procedures, if controlled by the executive, might deprive Congress of effective management of the "purse strings." For example, Carroll (1966, pp. 232–237) suggests centralized political parties as an alternative coordinating device, one which would assuredly improve the position of the executive vis-à-vis Congress.

break out of the traditional mode of budgetary control. His proposals would substitute a "radical incrementalism" for the "annual budgetary process as it is now known" (p. 148). The new procedure would eliminate the need for Congress to review each budget item each year; rather each figure would remain fixed until the agency involved asked the legislature to alter it. Congressional inaction could not put a program out of business; there would be no need for "emergency" resolutions at the start of a new fiscal year permitting agencies to continue to spend, on a monthly basis, at the previous year's rate; there would be no need to request supplemental appropriations. The burden of proof would, in effect, pass from Congress to the agencies which would have to come forward with a persuasive justification for changing the funding level at which they were then operating.

Such a procedure would permit Congress to focus its resources, to deal with "emergent problems" raised by the agencies or by the legislators themselves. Those programs requiring attention could be examined with considerable care, and decisions could await considerable study; there would be no time deadline, as in the annual appropriation procedure, compelling fast action. Lawmakers could dig deeply into a few problems and make better-informed judgments about them. Innovation would be stimulated, for successful programs could quickly be expanded and failures rapidly terminated, as evidence about results came to the attention of lawmakers with sufficient time to consider the data. Moreover, "radical incrementalism" might heighten executive sensitivity to legislative views; bureaucrats might find themselves called to appear at budget hearings at any time, not merely at one phase of the budgetary cycle, and they might be more inclined to "keep in touch" throughout the year.

Above and beyond fiscal controls, Congress's oversight capacity could be enlarged in other ways. As noted in Chapter 12, Scher (1963) has suggested a relative neglect of oversight, because in the calculations of many lawmakers involvement with the executive agencies provides insufficient payoffs to justify the effort. One possibility to remedy this situation would be to take steps to generate incentives, perhaps of a partisan character, for engaging in "continuous watchfulness." If, for instance, the minority contingent on a committee with oversight responsibility had its own staff, these lawmakers might undertake more searching examination of the bureaucracy than would their majority-party colleagues, fearful of embarrassing a President of their own party (Cleveland, 1966). In the same vein, Rep. Robert M. Michel (R., Ill.) has proposed that the minority have permanent control of the Government Operations Committees in the House and Senate; here, too, the opportunity for partisan gain might encourage the out-party to venture into administrative arrangements where the majority may fear to tread (1966). What seems required here is to upgrade oversight, using partisan advantage or other inducements to persuade members of Congress that the exercising of control is worth the expenditure of scarce personal and staff resources.

Reform suggestions pertaining to the control function are numerous and varied. A few other examples will indicate the range of the critics' ideas. One device is to create an oversight calendar in each chamber; this would set aside a minimum of two days each month on which committee reports on control activities might be presented and debated (Cotter, 1966, p. 81). Enlarged standing-committee staffs, especially if the new positions were filled with skilled professionals, might improve the quality of substantive panel review of administrative behavior. The more committees—policy and money panels—involved in oversight the more thorough the coverage is likely to be. Various reformers have picked up the idea, first advanced by the late Sen. Estes Kefauver (D., Tenn.), of instituting a "question period," after the British experience, during which the departmental secretaries would appear on the floor of Congress to explain, defend, and discuss the practices within their respective domains (Horn, 1960). Finally, we may note the more extreme proposal of E. de Grazia (1966, pp. 316–321) that the liaison practices, so effective on behalf of the executive, in effect be inverted, placing congressional agents within every executive agency; such liaison men, with access to all that goes on inside the bureau to which they are assigned, would surely provide the overseers better data and a more accurate knowledge of agency performance than is presently available to Congress.[20] All such proposals, singly or in combination, might enable the legislature to be more fully informed about administrative behavior, and in consequence, to control that behavior more carefully. Moreover, involvement of more legislators as watchdogs—whether of the budget or substantive policy matters—would enlarge the range of viewpoints brought to bear on departmental conduct.

A final set of reform ideas relates to improving the quality of congressional representation, either with respect to policy, to the performance of constituent services, or to both. One set of proposals seeks to give lawmakers more and better information on district opinion, and includes more personal staff, in Washington or "back home," for assignment to constituency matters. Also advice and assistance on the sound use of polling techniques would enable congressmen to gauge local opinion more reliably, correspondingly reducing the need to rely on communications from an atypical segment of the constituency. A congressional recess fixed in advance, for, say thirty days in midsummer, would permit the lawmaker to return home to take soundings of public opinion for himself.[21] Such proposals would reduce the isolation that many legislators feel in Washington; life in the capital, as Chapter 2 suggests, creates a tendency to look away from constituents, and renewing the link with the district might serve to counteract, in part at least, the tendency to drift away from the electorate.

Another group of proposed changes would shift the focus of representation

[20] For other, similar suggestions, see A. de Grazia, 1966, p. 17, and Pipes, 1966.
[21] A provision for an annual summer recess for the House of Representatives was included in the Legislative Reorganization Act of 1970.

away from constituent services toward a policy-spokesman stance. According to this view, lawmakers, heavily overburdened by nonpolicy-related case-work, neglect policy representation (and policy making and oversight as well). That is, they resolve their role conflicts, of necessity, in favor of constituent services. The resulting neglect of policy, and oversight to a lesser extent, has contributed to the executive's ability to dominate Congress. Thus changes are needed to restore legislative vitality. One proposal would entail lightening the casework load by limiting the kinds of activities that lawmakers could legitimately perform on behalf of their constituents. Thus, the formal rules might be amended to forbid congressmen from contacting administrative agencies on nonlegislative matters (Saloma, 1969, pp. 189–190). The effect of such changes, however, might be more pronounced for congressional offices than for legislators themselves, for as indicated (in Chapter 13) the lawmakers tend to delegate most casework to their staffs.

A variant on this theme of reducing the constituent service demands is the "ombudsman" idea (Gellhorn, 1966; Anderson, 1968). Following the practice used in the Scandinavian countries, some Americans, Congressman Henry S. Reuss (D., Wis.) among them, have suggested creating an office of administrative counsel, an investigative arm of Congress charged with responsibility for dealing with citizen complaints. A central staff of some twenty experts would possess the resources, unavailable to many individual offices, to deal effectively with constituent requests, and could relieve legislators of much time-consuming service activity. Moreover, a central agency would soon routinize such investigations, given the need to perform similar tasks repeatedly on behalf of all members of Congress, effecting a saving in time and energy. Legislative contact with constituents, so essential politically in the minds of lawmakers, could be retained by limiting the ombudsman to acting on requests from congressmen and by requiring that the results of all inquiries be channeled to the citizen through the representative's office. In this way, the legislator could get credit and contact without performing the onerous legwork necessary to obtain results.

It is probably a genuine reluctance to surrender these representational duties of constituency service that has caused Congress to adopt a cautious approach to instituting these changes—both the self-denying prohibition against deep involvement in administrative affairs and the ombudsman notion. Indeed, Davidson (1966) has argued that the executive branch poses a major challenge to Congress's domination of citizen-government communication channels. Much of the legislature's strength rests on its capacity to articulate popular views, sentiments peculiar to regions and localities as well as some national perspective. Moreover, failures in just this regard—the muting of too many voices which need to be heard—motivate critics of the congressional supremacy persuasion. The data, presented in Chapter 2, clearly indicate that congressmen do not represent, in demographic terms, some segments of American society. Davidson (1966, p. 399) finds that Congress "is defective in its representation of the sciences, the professions (except for law), and the learned institutions." The bureaucracy, the civil service, recruits extensively from precisely these areas, creating a situation in which the executive may understand such interests, may represent them, in ways that Congress cannot. The danger in these circumstances is that the legislature will find itself left out as crucial decisions are made by the experts in the executive and in the outside world. Broadening the base of legislative specialization—with more information and more staff expertise—and sensitizing lawmakers to other interests—through providing more contact with constituent groups, for instance—could serve to keep Congress as the central link in the flow of communications from citizen to government.

The thrust of all these proposals—which, of course, are not always mutually consistent, not capable of simultaneous adoption—is to assert a need to alter the balance of power between the executive and legislative branches in favor of the latter. Whether he wants to make Congress the supreme national decision maker or merely to redress a perceived imbalance in influence, the reformer seeks to enhance the legislature's ability to perform in all areas—lawmaking, oversight, and representation. To the extent that congressional performance is extended in all these areas, the individual legislator's role conflicts will intensify, for he cannot now be effective in all areas and to extend his responsibilities will certainly exacerbate his difficulties. For the reformer's hopes to be realized would require not only more opportunity for congressional initiative and control, but also a balance among the commitments of senators and representatives to the various facets of the legislative task. As with the propresidential reforms, however, much of the debate here is purely academic; Congress has over the years shown itself to be singularly reluctant to undertake wholesale reform, even to reassert its own prerogatives. Rather, change has come slowly and piecemeal.

Incremental change Each school of thought seeks to alter the basic institutional arrangements of American national politics in pursuit of a particular vision of the sorts of decisions each desires: liberals promote executive dominance in order to bring about change more rapidly; conservatives favor congressional supremacy to retard change. Neither perspective, as a broad view, has found many supporters; reform of Congress *has* occurred, more frequently than is often realized, but it has come in incremental fashion in pragmatic response to national needs and political pressures. In 1911, for instance, when undue centralization seemed to threaten a variety of interests, the Speaker of the House, the chief symbol of centralized authority, was stripped of his powers. There emerged, in the following years, the fragmented legislative system, described in these pages, featuring a negotiating and compromising style of decision making. Such reforms as have been adopted have been aimed at readjusting the conditions for the exercise of bargaining power, have been intended, that is, to strengthen the hand of some interest without basically restructuring the congressional system. For example, when the committee structure appeared too fluid, the 1946 Reorganization Act rationalized the system by merging committees and redefining panel jurisdictions. When science and astronautics surfaced as topics in need of attention, in the post-World War II era, committees were created in each chamber to wrestle with these issues.

When political conditions provided the opportunity, in the early 1960s, proponents of policy change moved to take advantage of the situation. The House Rules Committee was enlarged to make the passage of liberal legislation more likely. The 21-Day Rule was imposed, in 1964, to limit the Rules panel's ability to hold up bills; simultaneously that body was deprived of its authority to prevent bills, passed by the House, from going to conference. Two years later, the 21-Day Rule was repealed, but the limitation relating to conference committees was continued. Thus, in the ebb and flow of political maneuvering there remains an accretion of reform which over time alters the character of the legislative system. It seems likely, therefore, that a decentralized system, resolving its internal conflicts by negotiation and compromise, and bargaining with the executive, neither able to dominate nor willing to be dominated by him, will continue to exist. Reform will occur, but it seems unlikely to be dramatic; rather new procedures and relationships will evolve in response to external demands and internal needs.

Congress itself, reflecting the variety of interests and ideologies of its members, seems "little concerned with *planned* change or 'reform'" (Ripley, 1969, p. 215, emphasis added). The lawmakers show no interest in either the executive-force or the congressional-supremacy models;[22] their complaints about the system reflect their personal frustrations, not any fervor for systemwide reform. Somewhat paradoxically, the congressional perspective on congressional reform—as lawmakers themselves (Clark, 1964, 1965; Bolling, 1964) or academic observers (Ripley, 1969b; Davidson et al., 1966; Clapp, 1964) report it—superficially resembles the executive-dominance proposals; but in the unlikely event its ideas were accepted the effect would be additional division of legislative authority.

Specifically, the lawmaker's own suggestions would democratize Congress, would diffuse power more widely than present practice, would increase the freedom and influence of individual legislators. One formulation of such reforms, most directly associated with ex-Sen. Joseph S. Clark (D., Pa.),

---

[22]During the years that this was being written (1969–1971), the Senate was making a rather concerted effort to reassert its authority in the spheres of national defense and foreign policy. Its opposition to the Vietnam war was clear; its doubts about weapons procurement and other defense policies were evident in its concern with excessive cost of numerous weapons. Whether the basic policy-making processes in these areas will, as a result of these senatorial assertions, be fundamentally altered remains to be seen; it is simply too early to be sure that civilian counsel will outweigh the voice of the military in policy deliberations.

constitutes a systematic attack on the inner club, especially the Senate Establishment, that operates to the detriment of outsiders and those of low seniority. The reformers' main objective is to broaden the leadership structure, involving more lawmakers and permitting a majority of the party members to make policy and enforce discipline. A regular party caucus; a new steering committee, empowered to make committee assignments with "the best interests of the party and program in mind" (Clark, 1964, pp. 172–173) and to discipline recalcitrant partisans;[23] and a revitalized policy committee, to formulate programs after considerable deliberation, would all contribute to weakening the power of the senior members and making the party more responsive to a majority of its membership.

A number of rules changes would, in this view, be necessary to enable the party majority to act once party policy had been determined. The same changes attractive to proponents of the executive-force approach seem useful here: minority power would be weakened by, among other things, reimposing the 21-Day Rule, simplifying the discharge procedure, and modifying the seniority procedure in the House, and by eliminating the use of dilatory tactics,[24] enforcing a germane debate rule, subjecting committee chairmen to the will of panel majorities, and liberalizing the cloture rule to curtail the filibuster in the Senate. In all these ways the Establishment's power would be restricted; in its place majorities presumably would govern.

The difference between these proposals and the similar ones that the executive supremacists favor is the link to the national political parties. Where the party-responsibility advocates would subordinate the legislature to the decisions of a national party, in which, of course, leading lawmakers would participate, the internal congressional critics have no desire or intention of yielding legislative prerogatives, in full or in part, to agencies external to the legislative system. Congressional leaders would not speak for outside interests but rather would be chosen by, and act on behalf of, legislative majorities. As a result, more legislators would be involved, more bargaining might be required to build majority coalitions, and power in Congress might be even more widely diffused than it has been in recent years. Such reforms might well make conflict resolution more difficult; they might slow down the decision-making process substantially.

The antiestablishment assault accomplished little on a broad scale; moreover, it seems to have spent itself, and its major proponents have left

---

[23]For House Democrats, this would remove the committee-assignment responsibility from the Ways and Means Committee members.

[24]Specifically, under the proposed reforms, it would no longer be possible to require a full reading of the *Journal,* the "morning hour" would be curtailed, and committees would be permitted to sit when the Senate is in session (rather than the present requirement that unanimous consent be obtained). With these impediments removed, the majority would have greater opportunity to work its will, unencumbered by minority-imposed roadblocks.

Congress or have muted their criticism. What remains is a more pragmatic, less ideological, feeling that individual legislators might win still more power and greater opportunity for its exercise. Thus, reform sentiment focuses on proposals to reduce workloads; in the Senate, it is suggested, no man should serve on more than two committees or chair more than one subcommittee.[25] More staff is sought, especially if the added employees would be responsible to individual lawmakers. Another aim is reform of committee procedures, reducing the arbitrary use of chairmanship prerogatives and guaranteeing all—even the most junior minority member—a chance for full participation in committee business. Such more regularized operations would maximize the impact of individual congressmen. The leadership might do more to inform legislators about scheduling and other facets of chamber business; each man would be better able to protect his own interests if fully aware of what was pending. Each of these ideas would have the effect of strengthening the position of single legislators, increasing the possibility for each to gain, protect and exercise authority over some facet of congressional affairs. In stark contrast, there does not appear to be appreciable interest in Congress in the dramatic reforms—changes in seniority, party centralization, committee autonomy, and the four-year term, for instance—that engage the attention of critics external to the legislative system.

The lesson is again clear: reform occurs incrementally, in response to demands and in appropriate political circumstances, not in planned fashion. There has been a trend to individually exercised power, particularly in the smaller Senate. The cloture rule was, however marginally, altered to allow two-thirds of those present and voting, rather than two-thirds of all senators, to terminate debate. More basic, the so-called Johnson Rule, adopted by the Democrats under Majority Leader Lyndon B. Johnson and subsequently accepted by the Republicans as well, under which no senator can serve on more than a single major committee until all senators have one such good assignment, spread the opportunity for important service more widely among the chamber's membership. Reform will, in all probability, continue to come about slowly, in small steps. Only a major assault, with broad popular support, seems likely to compel more rapid change; Congress might then, as it has so often in the past, act, meeting the demands at least part way, to disarm its critics.

General problems: staff and information Throughout this discussion, two major defects in congressional operations have been mentioned repeatedly. Limitations on staff and information resources have been widely recognized,

---

[25] In January 1971, House Democrats decided that committee chairmen should not also chair more than one subcommittee, thus opening up some forty subcommittee chairmanships to junior representatives and reducing, to a degree at least, the direct authority of the full-panel chairman.

and reform proposals often begin with remedies in these areas. Increased staffing has much to recommend it; more employees could provide more help wherever the individual lawmaker chooses to invest his energies. He could use additional aid to improve the basis on which he acts as a policy maker; House members could profit from a specifically designated legislative assistant comparable to that provided for senators. Similarly, more help, if available, could be assigned to oversight activities; extra manpower might generate more information about administrative behavior. Finally, added staff could enable hard-pressed congressional offices to improve the speed and efficiency with which they respond to requests for constituent services. That members of Congress could easily find useful purposes to which to put more staff seems beyond question.

Yet enlarged staffs, however attractive they seem in theory, do not provide a simple solution to the problem of strengthening the legislature's capacity to handle its responsibilities; indeed some skeptics hold that more assistance would create additional burdens rather than alleviate present ones. For one thing, as Gross (1953, p. 422) points out, "imaginative staff aides often uncover new problems, new opportunities, and new challenges. They tend to create—or at least attract—heavier burdens." Thus more staff might create greater, not lesser, competition for the congressman's limited attention. Additionally, there are limits to the manageability of individual offices; too many employees may convert the lawmaker into an office manager, to the detriment of his more basic tasks. Controlling a large staff, keeping it operating in furtherance of the legislator's purposes, minimizing the tendency for a staffer to "play congressman" (Saloma, 1969, p. 163), will tax the skills of the most talented lawmaker.

Other doubters fear a large staff, not under tight rein, might engage in unrestrained partisanship at the expense of more important data-gathering, idea-generating functions; this threat seems particularly acute with regard to investigative staff for committees where the temptation to seek partisan gain may be difficult to resist. Finally, too much bureaucratization of legislative offices, too many intermediate links between congressman and those with whom he must deal, may color the legislator's perceptions of the world, may in effect make him the captive of his staff. In short, added staff would not be an unmixed blessing; its effectiveness would depend upon the ability of the congressman to master it, to bend it to his will. In any event, there must surely be a maximum size beyond which the staff cannot grow without subverting the role of the congressman as it presently exists.[26]

A second major strand in congressional reform is the widely recognized lack of independent and reliable information from which the lawmakers, overseers, and representatives suffer. Legislative initiative in policy making

---

[26]One limitation is simply physical; there currently exists office space sufficient only for a minimal increase in the personal and committee staffs of Congress.

is hampered by insufficient data; congressmen often feel a need to defer to the executive whose expertise far exceeds theirs. Oversight possibilities seem limited because members of Congress cannot penetrate the complexities of administrative procedure; they do not know what questions to ask to gauge accurately bureaucratic performance. Representation, too, may suffer from an inability to go to the right place or from the difficulty required to dig out the answers to constituent questions once the location of the data is uncovered.

In all these areas, with respect to all functions, Congress cannot compete effectively with the executive (Dechert, 1966, pp. 185–203). Executive privilege—by which the President can, in the "national interest," decide to withhold information from Congress—and national defense requirements limit the data available; it is in the nature of interbranch competition and suspicion that the executive personnel tend to enlarge the areas in which they feel they must not release information. In effect, the bureaucrats tend to believe "what Congress doesn't know can't hurt us," and legislators find them unresponsive even to direct interrogation at committee and subcommittee hearings.[27] Moreover, the executive is able to put its own construction on events in a way that constricts legislative opportunity to advance alternative proposals: the executive briefs the press and other mass media in "off-the-record" or "not-for-attribution" sessions, releasing only what information it deems advisable to reveal, interpreting what it does make available to suit its own purposes. Moreover, news, appropriately structured, is sometimes "leaked" to the media. The net result is that congressmen must act in situations which effectively foreclose the options available to them.

Beyond this dependence on the executive as a source of data, with all its impediments to full disclosure, the nature of the legislative system contributes to the congressional information deficit. A decentralized system, with numerous centers of autonomous power, each with lines to different information sources, leads to fragmentary, uncoordinated, or often unavailable data; data collected in one place, for one set of purposes, is simply not made accessible to other congressmen in other locations with other purposes in mind (Saloma, 1969, pp. 214–218). Thus, the individual lawmaker is left to make difficult decisions, on complex and controversial issues, with minimal information, less even than he might get with a modicum of difficulty, less certainly than he would need to decide with some acceptable degree of "rationality."

Two sets of proposals have emerged as ways to remedy this grave defect in Congress's deliberation and decision making. The first seeks to expand the presently available information sources. Additional staff—personal and committee—for research purposes would help provide additional data. More funds for existing agencies such as the Legislative Reference Service of the

---

[27] For a rather plaintive lament about executive secrecy by an experienced lawmaker with previous administrative-branch service. Symington, 1970.

Library of Congress or the General Accounting Office, would enable these to investigate along more fronts and with greater depth and diligence. Other learning experiences—for instance, foreign travel, on-the-site visits to federal installations, time to read and money to buy books—could be promoted (Robinson, 1966). Extended usage of outside consultants or congressionally created task forces, comparable to those that the President has employed for many years, has been suggested, as has the establishment of a "congressional institute of scholars" or some similar "university-type organization" (Dechert, 1966, p. 207). All such ideas seek to enlarge the data-gathering and interpreting assistance available to the legislators.

Far more radical, and seemingly more promising in the long run, is a second set of proposals urging Congress to harness computerized information-storage and retrieval systems for legislative purposes (Janda, 1966, 1968; Chartrand, Janda, and Hugo, 1968; Saloma, 1969). Indeed, Congress may be compelled to move on this front merely to keep abreast of the executive, notably the Defense Department, which has pioneered in the use of electronic equipment in policy-making activities; without adaptation in this sphere, the legislature may find its information deficit too severe ever to make up. The lawmakers concerned with policy decisions and oversight must understand such things as cost-efficiency analysis, planning programming budgeting, and operations research—techniques that executive agencies have used and will continue to employ on an expanded scale in the future—if they wish to wield influence in these areas. Adjustment to the new technology may well be an imperative if the legislative system is to survive.

Janda (1966, 1968) suggests that a relatively simple and inexpensive information-processing system for Congress can serve the legislature in many phases of its task.[28] It is far from inconceivable that each congressman can have on his desk a remote terminal, tied to a central computer, that he can use as he chooses to call for information on topics of interest to him. The data he asks for, via the terminal-computer link, will be before him, in typewritten form, in a matter of moments. This is an important point; the legislator can choose what he wants to know; his freedom to specialize, to follow his own orientations, to focus his energies where he wishes, need not be impaired; he runs little risk of being overwhelmed by information which is of no use to him. The options, dictated by political and value considerations, remain open; the information system is the lawmaker's servant, not in any sense his master.

Such information storage and retrieval arrangements could serve in numerous ways. To cite only a few examples, the task, often arduous, of

---

[28] A word on what computer-based information systems *cannot* do is in order here. Computers are not decision makers and they cannot perform the intellectual task of choosing among alternative courses of action. They can, however, by making readily available information which may clarify those alternatives, and the legislator's calculations, make the decisions more "rational" in the sense that the decision maker has before him as much of the relevant data as are stored in the information system.

determining the existence, content, and location of bills on subjects of interest could be vastly simplified. A "legislative history" can be compiled and stored in the computer: when a bill is introduced it can be indexed by subject, its text or an abstract of its contents recorded, its sponsors noted, the committee to which it is referred listed. As action on the proposal occurs it, too, can be added to the history; hearings can be cited or abstracted and amendments incorporated as they are voted. At any point, a lawmaker can get an up-to-date status report on any measure; indeed a general inquiry might turn up the existence of a bill, perhaps in the other chamber, unknown to some member. The availability of such data should prevent any congressman from being caught off guard. He can easily find out where legislation is and can take time to work up his position before he must act; he need not rely so extensively on word-of-mouth assurances from the experts, party colleagues, or house leaders. Computerized information retrieval might also provide data on lobbyists—who they are, whom they represent, what legislation they are interested in, where to reach them, and so forth—on the contents of present law, the United States Code having already been stored on magnetic tape for computer processing; or on the results of studies undertaken by such agencies as the Legislative Reference Service of the Library of Congress or the Government Accounting Office, which could easily be stored for electronic retrieval. The ready availability of information, from these or other sources, would enable lawmakers to make policy choices based on considerably more data than presently seems to enter their calculations.

Computerized information storage could strengthen Congress's exercise of oversight as well. Looking at the budget, for example, past agency performance could be easily recorded as could previous years' appropriations. A lawmaker could thus prepare for budget hearings more effectively; he could ascertain which agencies have recouped their losses through supplemental appropriations, he could compare past estimates with past expenditures, he could discover agency personnel utilizations, and he could establish a host of other facts about agency programs and their results. All of this might serve to reduce his need to "sample" for information, might permit him to engage in more penetrating analysis across the range of agency activities.

Representation might also benefit from electronic data processing. Successful modes of handling constituent service requests could be stored and recalled when similar cases arose. Summaries and analyses of communications on policy matters—letters, newspaper editorials, interest-group petitions, opinion-poll results—could be reviewed before action was taken. The lawmaker could also reflect on his own past voting record on particular topics. Thus, he could make his perceptions of constituency sentiment more precise before he voted on major issues; he might still act in keeping with stronger orientations toward other participants in the process—internal to Congress or in its environment—but his calculations about the potential gains and losses should be more accurate. Finally, the representative's ability to commu-

nicate with, or educate, his constituents would be enhanced if mailing lists—
of all voters, of those in his party or particular interest groups, of potential
contributors, of those with particular substantive concerns—were stored for
easy access; this might well reduce the effort required to get a message to the
right people at the right time so that its impact would be maximized.[29]

Both sets of proposals—for expanded data generation and for more rapid
processing and wider dissemination of existing information—have the
potential, according to their proponents, to strengthen Congress's position
relative to the executive. The former set would decrease the dependence
upon the bureaucracy for information; the latter would make it possible for
more lawmakers to have more data on a greater number of topics. Both sets
of changes should make Congress more efficient as well; more information,
reflecting more points of view, would better prepare legislators for lawmaking, oversight and representational activities. Yet, it should be noted,
such reforms—particularly the use of computers—might bring about unintended and unanticipated consequences.[30] For example, more readily
available data on many subjects might encourage more congressmen to
ignore the norms of specialization and of deference to substantive experts
on the grounds that they could now exercise independent judgment; the
collapse of these folkways might, though not certainly, leave Congress less
able to resist executive initiatives. On the other hand, failure to adapt to
changing circumstances, to adopt new techniques, may leave the legislature
less able to meet its responsibilities—less capable of producing acceptable
outputs—and thus serve to undermine support for the congressional system.

SUPPORT: ISSUES OF SECRECY AND ETHICS

It has been a recurrent theme of this volume that a system, legislative or other
type, must retain the support—favorable sentiments and actions—of those
with whom its members interact if it is to survive. If substantial numbers of
those in the environment no longer consider it legitimate, the system's outputs

---

[29]There are, of course, numerous other potential uses for electronic data-processing arrangements.
One which should be mentioned is automated voting, currently successfully in use in a number of states.
The chief advantage of such an arrangement would be to save time; roll calls which require a half-hour
or more—and there are hundreds of them, including quorum calls, each year—could be handled in from
three to five minutes by computer. However, use of such a procedure might require more time spent
on the floor—now the lawmaker knows he has a half-hour or so to make his way to the chamber after
the bells announce the roll call—and might reduce flexibility by eliminating the possibility to wait and
see how the totals stand before casting a vote.

[30]Perhaps the fear of such unexpected results, for personal careers as well as institutional stability,
accounts for the reluctance of lawmakers to take the steps proposed in this section despite their clear
recognition of their informational problems. On their views, see Davidson et al. (1966). The House
refused to include the establishment of a joint House-Senate committee to study the development of a
computer system in the 1970 reorganization bill.

are unlikely to be accepted, its existence no longer tolerated. Support, it will be recalled, is of two varieties, specific and diffuse. The former refers to positive sentiments generated by particular outputs, in a sense appreciation of services rendered; the latter pertains to rather vague, undifferentiated feelings of loyalty quite apart from specific actions of the system. Congressional reformers have pointed to alleged defects in the legislative system, the consequence of which, if no remedies are forthcoming, may be a loss of support.

As we have seen, the major actors involved in legislative politics have continued to sustain the congressional system. The executive, the interest groups, and the interested segments of the public have preferred to endeavor to make the system work—to foster action on their demands through persuasion and pressure—rather than to try to alter it in any fundamental way. Even the liberals, anxious to promote more rapid policy changes, have not sought to discredit Congress in their efforts to reform the institution; instead they have couched their proposals in perfecting rather than in denigrating language. More concretely, with respect to specific support, Congress's policy outputs have, on the whole, been sufficiently responsive to demands for specific programs to nourish hopes that it can be encouraged to enact acceptable policies in the future. Congress has, in other words, legislated "ideas whose time has come" often enough to sustain generally high levels of specific support.[31]

Much support, however, is of the diffuse sort; the socialization process inculcates acceptance of the American political process, including Congress, and the populace has retained a basic loyalty to it despite the previously noted low level of detailed knowledge about specific issues that the average citizen possesses. Congress has come under fire on two counts—the secrecy which shrouds many aspects of its operations and the ambiguous ethical character of some legislators' actions—which in the view of those who propose reforms may undermine public confidence in the legislative institution. With respect to secrecy, the basic criticism is that the public is unable to inform itself adequately on what Congress is doing and on the behavior of individual legislators. Among the factors that the critics cite is the tendency for a number of committees to meet in executive session; the House Ways and Means Committee never holds public meetings, other committees average about one-third closed sessions. Also the panels have been loath to permit modern media coverage—radio and television broadcasts, for instance—of

---

[31]For instance, in August 1971, confronted by the agitation of the woman's liberation movement, the House of Representatives discharged the Judiciary Committee by an overwhelming 332 to 22 vote and passed, 350 to 15, a constitutional amendment barring discrimination on the basis of sex. The amendment had languished for forty-seven years; no hearings had been held in the twenty-one years that Rep. Emanuel Celler (D., N.Y.), a passionate enemy of the proposal, had chaired the Judiciary Committee. The Senate placed the amendment directly on the calendar, bypassing the Judiciary Committee, and guaranteeing more prompt floor consideration.

those meetings which are open. Floor proceedings, especially the use of the Committee of the Whole, have also come under attack; until 1971, no roll call votes were taken in the Committee of the Whole where crucial decisions may be made. The inability of the concerned citizen to place responsibility for various actions accurately, so the critics argue, may erode public support for the legislature by encouraging the notion that Congress and its members have something to hide.

Congress, in fact, has taken steps to remedy these alleged defects. The House, in 1970, included in the Legislative Reorganization Act provisions exposing both committee and floor proceedings to additional public scrutiny. Permission was granted to televise, broadcast, and photograph committee hearings within limits that place discretion on the admission of the media in the hands of individual panels; the provision would make possible but not guarantee broad coverage of hearings. The same bill included a provision that would require recording and publication of members' votes in committee sessions; under existing rules only the totals not the stands of single members were made public. At the same time, however, the House refused to move too far and rejected a proposal to require a majority of a committee to vote to close committee meetings. Thus, the House has proposed to take a few steps to remove the cloak of secrecy which surrounds committee deliberations but has reserved the opportunity to continue to meet in private when the members deem it essential to do so.[32]

One other step has also been taken that promises to shed light on congressional operations, this time at the floor-consideration stage. Prior to the 1970 bill, no roll call votes were recorded in the Committee of the Whole; votes were of the voice, standing, or teller variety. Under the new provision, if twenty members demand it, the names of those participating in teller votes would be recorded as they walked up the aisles. This step would reduce the possibility for lawmakers to try to minimize role conflict by taking contradictory stands at different stages of the legislative process. They could no longer readily vote one position in the privacy of committee or Committee of the Whole and take another stand for the record at the time of final passage. The floor reform, like those in committee, was justified, their proponents argued, in terms of support. As Rep. Charles Gubser (R., Calif.), a sponsor of the antisecrecy proposal to record teller votes, put it: the nation's youth, "the taxpayers, the poor, the rich, men of all races view Congress with a minimum high regard" (quoted in Hunter, 1970). Making legislative action more visible would help to raise the level of popular approval of Congress.

A second and perhaps more serious area in which Congress has come

---

[32]The opponents of even these marginal changes in committee openness argued, in effect, that such publicity would encourage committee members to play to the gallery, that the presence of media representatives would disrupt ongoing committee routines. In the language of systems analysis, these reforms would undermine the norms of hard work and commitment to legislative business.

under attack is the issue of legislative ethics; doubts about the detachment of congressmen have been raised, and proposals to ensure that lawmakers are as free as possible from conflicts of interest, that their actions are intended to advance the public good and not their own financial positions have been advanced. There have always been occasional instances of congressional wrongdoing (Wilson, 1951), but on the whole these have been relatively few and far between. In the 1960s, however, a series of incidents have reinvigorated the reformers' determination to dispel popular uncertainty about congressional ethics. To the extent, of course, that doubts about the honesty, the freedom from self-serving behavior, of congressmen exist, support for the legislative institution, the acceptance of its outputs as legitimate, is likely to be seriously eroded.

It seems clear that the pressures of legislative life contribute to a situation in which the individual representatives and senators constantly must confront issues of ethics. Public expectations are high; the citizens seem to believe that their elected representatives must be beyond reproach (Mitchell, 1958). At the same time, the strains of virtually continual campaigning, with its consequent fund requirements for travel to and from the home district as well as for more directly election-related costs, are severe. Living expenses are high as well. Some legislators maintain residences both in their home state or district and in Washington; the social life in the nation's capital is demanding with its constant round of entertainment. Thus, despite salaries in excess of $40,000 annually, members of Congress find the need for money a central feature of their political and personal lives, and many seek ways to supplement their incomes. Secondly, the character of the legislative task, especially its policy-making and representative features, requires the lawmaker to listen to the requests and importunings of many groups and organizations. The notion that Congress should serve all, should stay in touch with the populace, in effect, requires access to the system for multiple interests. It is not surprising that those with policy concerns seek to exploit this available access to further their own goals; in doing so, they may sometimes offer inducements which fall between outright corruption—graft and bribery—and the understandable need of legislators to earn outside income. It is this so-called "gray area" that poses the ethical dilemma of Congress (Getz, 1966).

The list of recent controversies illustrates the difficult situation that the lack of clear and specific ethical standards can pose. In 1967, Sen. Thomas J. Dodd (D., Conn.) was censured by his Senate colleagues for misuse of campaign funds; he admitted having diverted money raised for his reelection battles to defray his personal expenses. In the same year, the House excluded Rep. Adam Clayton Powell (D., N.Y.) from the Ninetieth Congress; he was in defiance of the courts in his home state, having refused to pay a libel judgment rendered against him, and had placed his wife on his congressional payroll although she was not physically in Washington or performing legislative tasks.[33] On the whole, however, lawmakers prefer to leave the disciplining of fellow members to the courts or to the voters.[34]

Far more pervasive, however, are the conflict-of-interest situations in which a lawmaker must render judgments, on laws and oversight problems, about matters in which he has a personal stake. Can a representative—e.g., Robert Watkins (R., Pa.)—with a personal interest in the trucking business act impartially as a member of the House Commerce Committee which oversees the Interstate Commerce Commission, the agency that regulates truckers? Can a lawmaker—Rep. Sam Gibbons (D., Fla.), for instance—who serves on the House Ways and Means Committee help write fair tax laws when his law firm lists among its clients "six of the country's largest insurance companies, the nation's number two car-rental corporation, and the South's biggest grocery chain" (Sherrill, 1970, p. 6)? What is the impact on a senator's— George Murphy (R., Calif.), for example—behavior if he receives a $20,000 annual retainer, a travel credit card, and half the rent on his apartment from a major corporation for "public relations" work? What is the public to think when a senator—Russell Long (D., La.)—whose personal and family income from oil exceeded $2 million in a 6-year period leads the fight to retain favorable tax treatment for the oil industry from his position as chairman of the Senate Finance Committee? These sorts of questions, more frequently asked of late, have increased the concern of Congress with its own standards of conduct (Sherrill, 1970).

Some steps have been taken. Each chamber now has a Select Committee on Standards and Conduct charged with policing the ethics of its members. The Senate panel was created in direct response to the "Bobby Baker scandal" which revealed that the secretary to the Senate Democratic majority had taken advantage of his position to amass a vast fortune.[35] Two years later, in the wake of the Powell affair, the House established a similar body. Neither

---

[33] Indeed, it might be argued that Congress acted in these two instances only because Powell and Dodd violated the norms of institutional patriotism and reciprocity. Powell, in addition to being black, a flamboyant maverick, was excluded by a coalition of partisan Republicans, Southern and border state Democrats, those who believed him to have disgraced the legislature, and those moved by a deluge of constituency mail. Eventually, the courts upheld his claim that he had been illegally denied his seat and he was seated, though fined and, more importantly, stripped of his seniority and, thus, of his committee chairmanship. Powell was defeated in his party's primary in 1970. Dodd's "sin" was a scathing attack on the select committee investigating the charges against him; he later repented, throwing himself on the mercy of his colleagues, and escaped with a censure. The Connecticut Democrats denied him renomination at their 1970 state convention. See Getz (1966).

[34] There have been some indictments growing out of alleged illegal conduct. Ex-Senator Daniel Brewster (D., Md.) is to be tried on charges that he sold his vote on a postal rate bill to mail-order interests for $24,500. Former Rep. Thomas F. Johnson (D., Md.) is serving a sentence imposed for accepting $17,500 for his help in trying to save a saving-and-loan firm from federal prosecution.

[35] Baker's operations came into public view when one vending machine company filed suit in federal court charging that Baker had used his position to influence a defense contractor to give its vending machine contract to a firm in which Baker had a personal stake. Baker's own assessment was that he was worth more than $2 million, with interest in a number of profitable corporations (Getz, 1966, pp. 118–119).

committee, according to the critics, has done much to remedy the situation;[36] neither has adequate enforcement powers or has demonstrated a willingness to do more than the bare minimum required to avoid open scandal.[37] Secondly, in 1958, Congress enacted a code of ethics for all government service; the code, however, has no enforcement provisions and imposes no penalties for transgressions. Its rules range from the hortatory—"Uphold the Constitution . . ." and "Give a full day's labor for a full day's pay"—to the vague injunction to "Engage in no business with the government, either directly or indirectly, which is inconsistent with the conscientious performance of . . . governmental duties."

There also exist a set of conflict-of-interest statutes, revised and updated in 1962. These laws outlaw bribery and corruption, proscribe compensation for appearances by legislators before federal agencies, ban direct contracts between congressmen and the government, and prohibit receipt of salary as direct compensation from an outside source as payment for services rendered. Finally the legislature moved toward financial-disclosure requirements intended to reveal the lawmakers' major interests and sources of income, and, thus, to indicate to what potential conflicts they may be exposed. Representatives publicly reveal from what businesses they receive income in excess of $1,000 annually or in which their holdings are valued at $5,000 or more, *if* the source of income was engaged in *"substantial"* business with the federal government or was under federal regulation; they also report their connections with organizations from which they received an income of $1,000 or more. The public disclosures of senators are limited to lecture fees and honoraria; all fees in excess of $300 are to be reported. Legislators in both chambers file additional data, but these remain sealed and are opened only under extraordinary circumstances. In general, then, the interested public can discover some but by no means all of the potential conflicts of interest under which national lawmakers work.

The critics believe that considerably more needs to be done; they are unwilling to accept the present internal arrangements, especially the weak code of ethics, or to rely on the electorate to control wrongdoing and punish transgressors.[38] Some favor a more strongly worded code of conduct (Wilson,

[36] The House, in fact, defeated a motion creating the committee on a voice vote, and reversed itself only when the absence of a quorum necessitated a roll call vote (Getz, 1966, p. 136).

[37] For instance, in 1969, the House Ethics Committee refused to launch an investigation of the *Wall Street Journal*'s report that Rep. Seymour Halpern (R., N.Y.), a member of the House Banking Committee, had received a series of unsecured loans totaling more than $100,000 from several major banks.

[38] The voters do seemingly respond to charges of unethical conduct on occasion. In 1966, charges that Sen. A. Willis Robertson (D., Va.), chairman of the Senate Banking and Currency Committee, was too close to banking interests may have contributed to his defeat. Robertson sponsored legislation to provide an exemption from the antitrust laws for two banks which desired to merge; the bank responded by sending out letters urging that stockholders give their "thanks" to Robertson, presumably in the form of campaign contributions (Sherrill, 1970, p. 22). Two years later, Sen. Edward Long (D., Mo.) was retired from office following *LIFE* magazine's report that he had received substantial sums from the Teamsters Union for "referral fees."

1966). Others propose to extend the scope of the conflict-of-interest statutes, broadening the coverage of the self-denying ordinances these laws contain. The New York City Bar Association study of congressional ethics (1970) suggested a blanket prohibition, effective six years after election, of the practice of law by legislators; nor should members' law firms represent clients that the members themselves cannot serve. Moreover, some reformers want to extend the prohibition against accepting compensation from outside sources to cover bonuses, stock options, and other forms of indirect payment; they would prevent legislators from acting as agent or attorney in any legal proceeding to which the government is a party, not simply those before the U.S. Court of Claims, as is presently the rule; they suggest that lawmakers should receive no pay for representing outside groups before Congress as they cannot now be compensated for appearances before executive agencies; they propose a postemployment ban, like that imposed on former executive employees, on exlegislators' dealings with the federal government (Getz, 1966, chap. 2).

Finally, there have been advanced a number of proposals for disclosure statutes under which every lawmaker would make public annual reports on his sources of outside income. Senator Clifford Case (R., N.J.) has for a number of years pushed to require each member of Congress to reveal the donors of all gifts, including campaign contributions; to report all income from outside sources; to issue an assets-and-liabilities statement; and to record all sales and purchases of stocks, bonds, and real estate. The argument for disclosure, either as a supplement to, or in the place of, restrictive statutes rests on the extraordinary difficulty in determining when genuine conflict of interest exists. It is certainly possible for congressmen to share viewpoints with his constituents, or some segment of them, and to act on behalf of those interests without engaging in improper conduct. The line between public and private interest, in other words, is not always easy to draw precisely, and disclosure laws might have the virtue of revealing what direct financial stakes a member has in the issues on which he must act. Politicians, including legislators, it must be noted, are not uniformly revered by the American public, and all these steps—codes of conduct, conflict-of-interest laws, and disclosure statutes—might reduce the possibilities for unethical behavior, might render congressional decisions more impartial, and might, in consequence, raise the popular esteem, so essential for system survival, in which Congress is held. Support might be increased, uncertainty about the legislature might decline, if congressional activities were less secret and carried on in accordance with broader, more clearly and carefully defined ethical standards.

CONCLUSION

The present, and concluding, chapter has explicated and explored some of the normative issues inherent in the analysis of the legislative system. We have put off consideration of such questions because while we can deal directly with some matters pertaining to how and why Congress acts as it does, the responses to inquiries relating to whether legislative behavior is *good or bad,* appropriate or unacceptable, flow directly from the observer's values. Thus, liberals, moved to seek social change rapidly, find Congress too slow to act, and too reluctant to take needed policy departures. On the other hand, conservatives, preferring to minimize social change, perceive the legislature as too dominated by a proliberal executive and too fast to indulge in unneeded and untested social experimentation. The reform proposals of each ideological position, as well as those of intermediate schools of thought, then, reflect the policies their proponents seek to advance and must be viewed within the political context of the policy consequences that their acceptance might entail.

Liberals tend to favor an "executive-force" model of government in which Congress would yield its policy-making functions to the President and would instead focus its attention on representation and oversight to ensure efficiency. Conversely, conservatives prefer legislative supremacy and would increase congressional authority over all categories of outputs. Intermediate positions reflect a recognition that Congress is essentially a bargaining system that resolves conflicts through negotiation and compromise; the reforms they espouse are incremental in character, entailing relatively modest changes designed to redress the balance among contending interests. Legislators themselves, to the degree that reform concerns them, reflect this view and prefer changes which enhance their positions as individual members of Congress. The multitude of reform ideas, from whatever value position they are put forth, reflect a concern with making the legislature properly responsive to a favored set of interests and demands. Other proposals seek to shore up inputs of support for Congress and aim at reducing the secrecy which surrounds congressional operations and at improving the ethical climate within which the lawmakers act.

There can, of course, be no definitive answers to normative questions of the sort raised here. All that can be said is that those who are unhappy with the legislative product will continue to suggest ways that congressional operations can be improved to suit their own purposes. It seems clear also that Congress itself is unlikely to leap at wholesale changes of any variety and will reform itself slowly and painstakingly as it has in the past, acting when the lawmakers themselves are persuaded that change is necessary or cannot be resisted. The current question, broadly put, is whether Congress can adapt sufficiently and rapidly enough to retain its essential strength. Those who value a strong legislative system as a counterbalance for an increasingly powerful executive in a basically pluralistic political order hope that it can.

Bibliography

Abram, Michael, and Joseph Cooper: "The Rise of Seniority in the House of Representatives," *Polity,* vol. 1, 1968, pp. 52–85.

Alford, Robert: *Party and Society* (Chicago: Rand McNally, 1963).

Almond, Gabriel A., and Sidney Verba: *The Civic Culture* (Boston: Little, Brown, 1965).

American Political Science Association, Committee on Political Parties: *Toward a More Responsible Two-party System* (New York: Rinehart, 1950).

Anderson, Lee F.: "Individuality in Voting in Congress: A Research Note," *Midwest Journal of Political Science,* vol. 8, 1964, pp. 425–429.

Anderson, Stanley V. (ed.): *Ombudsmen for American Government?* (Englewood Cliffs, N.J.: Prentice-Hall, 1968).

Andrain, Charles F.: "A Scale Analysis of Senator's Attitudes toward Civil Rights," *Western Political Quarterly,* vol. 17, 1964, pp. 488–503.

Bailey, Stephen K.: *Congress Makes a Law* (New York: Columbia University Press, 1950).

Baker, Gordon E.: *The Reappointment Revolution* (New York: Random House, 1966).

Barber, James D.: *The Lawmakers: Recruitment and Adaptation to Legislative Life* (New Haven: Yale University Press, 1965).

Barth, Alan: *Government by Investigation* (New York: Viking Press, 1955).

Bauer, Raymond A., Ithiel de Sola Pool, and Lewis A. Dexter: *American Business and Public Policy* (New York: Atherton, 1963).

Bell, Roderick, David V. Edwards, and R. Harrison Wagner (eds.): *Political Power* (New York: Free Press, 1969).

Bentley, Arthur F.: *The Process of Government* (Chicago: University of Chicago Press, 1908).

Berelson, Bernard, Paul F. Lazarsfeld, and William N. McPhee: *Voting* (Chicago: University of Chicago Press, 1954).

Berman, Daniel: *In Congress Assembled: The Legislative Process in the National Government* (New York: Macmillan, 1964).

Bibby, John F.: "Committee Characteristic's and Legislative Oversight of Administration," *Midwest Journal of Political Science,* vol. 10, 1966, pp. 78–98.

—— and Roger Davidson: *On Capitol Hill: Studies in the Legislative Process* (New York: Holt, Rinehart and Winston, 1967).

Bolling, Richard: *House out of Order* (New York: Dutton, 1965).

Bone, Hugh A.: "An Introduction to the Senate Policy Committees," *American Political Science Review,* vol. 50, 1956, pp. 339–359.

——: *Party Committees and National Politics* (Seattle: University of Washington Press, 1958).

Brown, MacAlister: "The Demise of State Department Public Opinion Polls: A Study in Legislative Oversight," *Midwest Journal of Political Science,* vol. 5, 1961, pp. 1–17.

Buckley, William F., Jr.: *The Committee and Its Critics* (New York: Putnam, 1962).

—— and L. Brent Bozell: *McCarthy and His Enemies* (Chicago: Regnery, 1954).

Bullock, Charles S., III: "Apprenticeship and Committee Assignments in the House of Representatives," *Journal of Politics,* vol. 32, 1970, pp. 717–720.

—— and John Sprague: "A Research Note on the Committee Reassignments of Southern Democratic Congressmen," *Journal of Politics,* vol. 31, 1969, pp. 493–512.

Burnham, James: *Congress and the American Tradition* (Chicago: Regnery, 1959).

Burns, James M.: *Congress on Trial* (New York: Harper, 1949).

——: *The Deadlock of Democracy* (Englewood Cliffs, N.J.: Prentice-Hall, 1963).

Campbell, Angus: "Surge and Decline: A Study of Electoral Change," *Public Opinion Quarterly,* vol. 24, 1960, pp. 397–418.

——, Philip E. Converse, Warren E. Miller, and Donald E. Stokes: *The American Voter* (New York: Wiley, 1960).

——, ——, ——, and ——: *Elections and the Political Order* (New York: Wiley, 1966).

Carper, Edith T.: *The Defense Appropriations Rider* (University, Alabama: University of Alabama Press, 1960).

Carr, Robert K.: *The House Committee on Un-American Activities, 1945–50* (Ithaca: Cornell University Press, 1952).

Carroll, Holbert N.: *The House of Representatives and Foreign Affairs,* rev. ed. (Boston: Little, Brown, 1966).

Chartrand, Robert L., Kenneth Janda, and Michael Hugo (eds.): *Information Support, Program Budgeting and the Congress* (New York: Spartan Books, 1968).

Clapp, Charles L.: *The Congressman: His Work as He Sees It* (New York: Doubleday Anchor, 1964).

Clark, Joseph S.: *The Senate Establishment* (New York: Hill and Wang, 1963).

——: *Congress: The Sapless Branch* (New York: Harper and Row, 1964).

——: "Making Congress Work," in Clark (ed.), *Congressional Reform: Problems and Prospects* (New York: Crowell, 1965), pp. 344–360.

Clausen, Aage R.: "Home State Influence on Congressional Behavior," paper presented to the 1970 Annual Meeting of the American Political Science Association.

Cleveland, James C.: "The Need for Increased Minority Staffing," in Mary McInnis (ed.), *We Propose: A Modern Congress,* Selected Proposals by the House Republican Task Force on Congressional Reform and Minority Staffing (New York: McGraw-Hill, 1966), pp. 5–19.

Cnudde, Charles F., and Donald J. McCrone: "The Linkage between Constituency Attitude and Congressional Voting Behavior: A Causal Model," *American Political Science Review,* vol. 60, 1966, pp. 66–72.

Cochrane, James D.: "Partisan Aspects of Congressional Committee Staffing," *Western Political Quarterly,* vol. 17, 1964, pp. 338–348.

Cohen, Bernard C.: *The Political Process and Foreign Policy* (Princeton: Princeton University Press, 1957).

———: *The Influence of Non-governmental Groups on Foreign Policy-making* (Boston: World Peace Foundation, 1959).

Committee for Economic Development: *Making Congress More Effective* (New York: 1970).

Congressional Quarterly Service: *Congress and the Nation, 1945-1964* (Washington, D.C.: Congressional Quarterly, 1965).

———: *Legislators and the Lobbyists,* 2nd ed. (Washington, D.C.: Congressional Quarterly, 1968).

———: *Revolution in Civil Rights,* 4th ed. (Washington, D.C.: Congressional Quarterly Service, 1968).

"Congressional Reversal of Supreme Court Decisions, 1945-1957," *Harvard Law Review,* vol. 71, 1958, pp. 1324-1337.

Cooper, Joseph: "The Legislative Veto: Its Promises and Its Perils," in Carl J. Friedrich and Seymour Harris (eds.), *Public Policy: Yearbook of the Graduate School of Public Administration,* vol. 7 (Cambridge: Harvard University Press, 1957), pp. 128-174.

——— and Ann Cooper: "The Legislative Veto and the Constitution," *George Washington Law Review,* vol. 30, 1962, pp. 467-516.

Corwin, Edward S.: *The President: Office and Powers* (New York: New York University Press, 1957).

Cotter, Cornelius P.: "Legislative Oversight," in Alfred de Grazia (coord.), *Congress: The First Branch of Government* (Washington, D.C.: American Enterprise Institute, 1966), pp. 25-81.

——— and J. Malcolm Smith: "Administrative Accountability to Congress: The Concurrent Resolution," *Western Political Quarterly,* vol. 9, 1956, pp. 955-966.

Crabb, Cecil V.: *Bipartisan Foreign Policy: Myth or Reality?* (Evanston, Ill.: Row, Peterson, 1957).

Cronin, Thomas E. and Sanford D. Greenberg (eds.): *The Presidential Advisory System* (New York: Harper and Row, 1969).

Cummings, Milton C., Jr.: *Congressmen and the Electorate* (New York: Free Press, 1964).

——— and Robert L. Peabody: "The Decision to Enlarge the Committee on Rules: An Analysis of the 1961 Vote," in Robert L. Peabody and Nelson W. Polsby (eds.), *New Perspectives on the House of Representatives* (Chicago: Rand McNally, 1963), pp. 167-194.

Dahl, Robert A.: *Congress and Foreign Policy* (New York: Harcourt, Brace & World, 1950).

———: *A Preface to Democratic Theory* (Chicago: University of Chicago Press, 1956).

———: "The Concept of Power," *Behavioral Science,* vol. 2, 1957, pp. 201-215.

———: "Decision-making in a Democracy: The Supreme Court as a National Policy-maker," *Journal of Public Law,* vol. 6, 1958, pp. 279-295.

———: *Pluralist Democracy in the United States: Conflict and Consent* (Chicago: Rand McNally, 1967).

——— and Charles E. Lindblom: *Politics, Economics and Welfare* (New York: Harper, 1953).

Davidson, Roger H.: "Congress and the Executive: The Race for Representation," in Alfred de Grazia (coord.), *Congress: The First Branch of Government* (Washington, D.C.: American Enterprise Institute, 1966), pp. 377-413.

———: *The Role of the Congressman* (New York: Pegasus, 1969).

———: "Public Prescriptions for the Job of Congressman," *Midwest Journal of Political Science,* vol. 14, 1970, pp. 648-666.

———, David M. Kovenock, and Michael K. O'Leary: *Congress in Crisis: Politics and Congressional Reform* (Belmont, Calif.: Wadsworth, 1966).

——— and Glenn R. Parker: "The Pattern of Support for Congress," paper prepared for the 1970 Annual Meeting of the American Political Science Association.

Dawson, Raymond H.: "Congressional Innovation and Intervention in Defense Policy: Legislative Authorization of Weapons Systems," *American Political Science Review,* vol. 56, 1962, pp. 42-57.

Dawson, Richard E.: "Political Socialization," in James A. Robinson (ed.), *Political Science Annual,* 1966 (Indianapolis: Bobbs-Merrill, 1966), pp. 1–84.

Dechert, Charles R.: "Availability of Information for Congressional Operations," in Alfred de Grazia (coord.), *Congress: The First Branch of Government* (Washington, D.C.: American Enterprise Institute, 1966), pp. 167–211.

de Grazia, Alfred: *Public and Republic* (New York: Knopf, 1951).

———: *Republic in Crisis: Congress against the Executive Force* (New York: Federal Legal Publications, 1965).

———(coord.): *Congress: The First Branch of Government* (Washington, D.C.: American Enterprise Institute, 1966).

de Grazia, Edward: "Congressional Liaison," in Alfred de Grazia (coord.), *Congress: The First Branch of Government* (Washington, D.C.: American Enterprise Institute, 1966), pp. 297–335.

Deutsch, Karl W.: *The Nerves of Government* (New York: Free Press, 1963).

Dexter, Lewis A.: "What Do Congressmen Hear: The Mail," *Public Opinion Quarterly,* vol. 20, 1956, pp. 16–27.

———: "Congressmen and the Making of Military Policy," in Robert L. Peabody and Nelson W. Polsby (eds.), *New Perspectives on the House of Representatives* (Chicago: Rand McNally, 1963), pp. 305–324. *(a)*

———: "The Representative and His District," in Robert L. Peabody and Nelson W. Polsby (eds.), *New Perspectives on the House of Representatives* (Chicago: Rand McNally, 1963), pp. 3–29. *(b)*

———: *How Organizations Are Represented in Washington* (Indianapolis: Bobbs-Merrill, 1969). *(a)*

———: *The Sociology and Politics of Congress* (Chicago: Rand McNally, 1969). *(b)*

Dixon, Robert G., Jr.: *Democratic Representation: Reapportionment in Law and Politics* (New York: Oxford University Press, 1968).

Drew, Elizabeth Brenner: "Mr. Passman Meets His Match," *The Reporter,* vol. 31, Nov. 19, 1964, pp. 40–43.

Dyson, James W., and John W. Soule: "Congressional Committee Behavior on Roll Call Votes: The U.S. House of Representatives, 1955–1964," *Midwest Journal of Political Science,* vol. 14, 1970, pp. 626–647.

Easton, David: *A Framework for Political Analysis* (Englewood Cliffs, N.J.: Prentice-Hall, 1965). *(a)*

———: *A Systems Analysis of Political Life* (New York: Wiley, 1965). *(b)*

———and Robert D. Hess: "The Child's Political World," *Midwest Journal of Political Science,* vol. 6, 1962, pp. 229–245.

Eidenberg, Eugene, and Roy D. Morey: *An Act of Congress* (New York: Norton, 1969).

Eulau, Heinz, John C. Wahlke, William Buchanan, and LeRoy C. Ferguson: "The Role of the Representative: Some Empirical Observations on the Theory of Edmund Burke," *American Political Science Review,* vol. 53, 1959, pp. 742–756.

———and Katherine Hinckley: "Legislative Institutions and Processes," in James A. Robinson (ed.), *Political Science Annual, 1966* (Indianapolis: Bobbs-Merrill, 1966), pp. 85–189.

Evans, Rowland, and Robert Novak: "The Johnson Style," in Lawrence K. Pettit and Edward Keynes (eds.), *The Legislative Process in the U.S. Senate* (Chicago: Rand McNally, 1969), pp. 177–199.

Fairlie, John A.: "The Nature of Political Representation," *American Political Science Review,* vol. 34, 1940, pp. 236–248 and 456–466.

Farnsworth, David N.: *The Senate Committee on Foreign Relations* (Urbana, Ill.: University of Illinois Press, 1961).

———: "A Comparison of the Senate and Its Foreign Relations Committee on Selected Roll Call Votes," *Western Political Quarterly,* vol. 14, 1964, pp. 168–175.

Fenno, Richard F., Jr.: "The House Appropriations Committee as a Political System: The Problem of Integration," *American Political Science Review,* vol. 56, 1962, pp. 310–324.

———: "The House of Representatives and Federal Aid to Education," in Robert L. Peabody and Nelson W. Polsby (eds.), *New Perspectives on the House of Representatives* (Chicago: Rand McNally, 1963), pp. 195–235.

———: "The Internal Distribution of Influence: The House," in David B. Truman (ed.), *The Congress and America's Future* (Englewood Cliffs, N.J.: Prentice-Hall, 1965), pp. 52–76.

———: *The Power of the Purse* (Boston: Little, Brown, 1966).

———: "Congressional Committees: A Comparative View," paper read to 1970 Annual Meeting of the American Political Science Association.

Fenton, John H.: *The Catholic Vote* (New Orleans: Hauser Press, 1960).

Ferber, Mark F.: "The Formation of the Democratic Study Group," in Nelson W. Polsby (ed.), *Congressional Behavior* (New York: Random House, 1971), pp. 249–269.

Field, John Osgood, and Ronald E. Anderson: "Ideology in the Public's Conceptualization of the 1964 Election," *Public Opinion Quarterly,* vol. 33, 1969, pp. 380–398.

Fiellin, Alan: "The Functions of Informal Groups in Legislative Institutions," *Journal of Politics,* vol. 14, 1962, pp. 72–91.

———: "Recruitment and Legislative Role Conceptions: A Conceptual Scheme and a Case Study," *Western Political Quarterly,* vol. 20, 1967, pp. 271–287.

Finney, John W.: "Senate Liberals Caught Napping," *New York Times,* Dec. 15, 1967, p. 1, col. 1.

———: "Pressures Grow as the (ABM) Issue Becomes Partisan," *New York Times,* June 29, 1969, Section IV, p. 2, col. 6.

Fishel, Jeff: "Party, Ideology, and the Congressional Challenger," *American Political Science Review,* vol. 63, 1969, pp. 1213–1232.

Fox, Douglas M., and Charles H. Clapp: "The House Rules Committee's Agenda-Setting Function, 1961–1968," *Journal of Politics,* vol. 32, 1970, pp. 440–443.

——— and ———: "The House Rules Committee and the Programs of the Kennedy and Johnson Administrations," *Midwest Journal of Political Science,* vol. 14, 1970, pp. 667–672.

Free, Lloyd A., and Hadley Cantril: *The Political Beliefs of Americans* (New Brunswick, N.J.. Rutgers University Press, 1967).

Freeman, J. Lieper: *The Political Process: Executive Bureau-Legislative Committee Relations,* rev. ed. (New York: Random House, 1965).

Friedrich, Carl J.: *Constitutional Government and Politics* (New York: Harper, 1937).

Froman, Lewis A., Jr.: *Congressmen and Their Constituencies* (Chicago: Rand McNally, 1963).

———: *The Congressional Process: Strategies, Rules, and Procedures* (Boston: Little, Brown, 1967).

——— and Randall B. Ripley: "Conditions for Party Leadership: The Case of the House Democrats," *American Political Science Review,* vol. 59, 1965, pp. 52–63.

Galloway, George B.: *The Legislative Process in Congress* (New York: Crowell, 1953).

Gawthrop, Louis C.: "Changing Membership Patterns in House Committees," *American Political Science Review,* vol. 60, 1966, pp. 366–373.

Gellhorn, Walter: *Ombudsmen and Others: Citizens' Protectors in Nine Countries* (Cambridge, Mass.: Harvard University Press, 1966).

Getz, Robert S.: *Congressional Ethics* (Princeton, N.J.: Van Nostrand, 1966).

Gilbert, Charles E.: "Operative Doctrines of Representation," *American Political Science Review,* vol. 57, 1963, pp. 604–618.

Goodman, Walter: *The Committee: The Extraordinary Career of the House Committee on Un-American Activities* (New York: Farrar, Straus, and Giroux, 1968).

Goodwin, George, Jr.: "The Seniority System in Congress," *American Political Science Review,* vol. 53, 1959, pp. 412–436.

———: "Subcommittees: The Miniature Legislatures of Congress," *American Political Science Review,* vol. 56, 1962, pp. 412–436.

——: *The Little Legislatures: Committees of Congress* (Amherst: University of Massachusetts Press, 1970).

Gordon, Bernard K.: "The Military Budget: Congressional Phase," *Journal of Politics,* vol. 23, 1961, pp. 689–710.

Grassmuck, George: *Sectional Biases in Congress on Foreign Policy* (Baltimore: Johns Hopkins University Press, 1951).

Green, Harold P., and Alan Rosenthal: *Government of the Atom: The Integration of Powers* (New York: Atherton, 1963).

Greenstein, Fred I.: *Children and Politics* (New Haven: Yale University Press, 1965).

——: "The Psychological Functions of the Presidency for Citizens," in Elmer E. Cornwell (ed.), *The American Presidency: Vital Center* (Chicago: Scott Foresman, 1966), pp. 30–36.

Griffith, Ernest S.: *Congress: Its Contemporary Role* (New York: New York University Press, 1951).

Groennings, Sven: "The Wednesday Group in the House of Representatives: A Structural-Functional Analysis," paper presented to the 1970 Annual Meeting of the Midwest Political Science Association.

Gross, Bertram: *The Legislative Struggle* (New York: McGraw-Hill, 1953).

Gross, Neal, Ward S. Mason, and Alexander McEachern: *Explorations in Role Analysis* (New York: Wiley, 1958).

Hacker, Andrew: "The Elected and the Anointed: Two American Elites," *American Political Science Review,* vol. 55, 1961, pp. 539–549.

——: *Congressional Districting,* rev. ed. (Washington, D.C.: Brookings Institution, 1964).

Haight, David E., and Larry D. Johnston (eds.): *The President: Roles and Powers* (Chicago: Rand McNally, 1965).

Harris, Joseph P.: *The Advice and Consent of the Senate* (Berkeley: University of California Press, 1953).

——: *Congressional Control of Administration* (Garden City, N.Y.: Doubleday Anchor, 1965).

Harris, Richard: *Decision* (New York: Dutton, 1971).

Havens, Murray C.: "Metropolitan Areas and Congress: Foreign Policy and National Security," *Journal of Politics,* vol. 26, 1964, pp. 758–774.

Haviland, H. Field, Jr.: "Foreign Aid and the Policy Process, 1957," *American Political Science Review,* vol. 52, 1958, pp. 689–724.

Heard, Alexander: *The Costs of Democracy* (Chapel Hill: University of North Carolina Press, 1960).

Hermann, Margaret G.: *Some Personal Characteristics Related to Foreign Aid Voting of Congressmen* (Unpublished M.A. Thesis, Northwestern University, 1963).

Hess, Robert D., and Judith V. Torney: *The Development of Political Attitudes in Children* (Chicago: Aldine, 1967).

Heubel, Edward J.: "Congressional Resistance to Reform: The House Adopts a Code for Investigating Committees," *Midwest Journal of Political Science,* vol. 1, 1957, pp. 313–329.

Hinckley, Barbara: "Interpreting House Midterm Elections: Toward a Measurement of the In-party's 'Expected' Loss of Seats," *American Political Science Review,* vol. 61, 1967, pp. 694–700.

——: *The Seniority System in Congress* (Bloomington: Indiana University Press, 1971).

Horn, Stephen: *The Cabinet and Congress* (New York: Columbia University Press, 1960).

——: *Unused Power: The Work of the Senate Committee on Appropriations* (Washington, D.C.: Brookings Institution, 1970).

House Republican Conference: *The Republican Conference and Committees of the Conference in the United States House of Representatives, 90th Congress* (Washington, D.C.: n.d.).

Huitt, Ralph K.: "The Congressional Committee: A Case Study," *American Political Science Review,* vol. 48, 1954, pp. 340–365.

———: "The Morse Committee Assignment Controversy: A Study in Senate Norms," *American Political Science Review,* vol. 51, 1957, pp. 313–329.

———: "Democratic Party Leadership in the Senate," *American Political Science Review,* vol. 55, 1961, pp. 333–344. *(a)*

———: "The Outsider in the Senate: An Alternative Role," *American Political Science Review,* vol. 55, 1961, pp. 566–575. *(b)*

———: "The Internal Distribution of Influence: The Senate," in David B. Truman (ed.), *The Congress and America's Future* (Englewood Cliffs, N.J.: Prentice-Hall, 1965), pp. 77–101.

———: "Congress, the Durable Partner," in Ralph K. Huitt and Robert L. Peabody, *Congress: Two Decades of Analysis* (New York: Harper and Row, 1969), pp. 202–229.

Hunter, Marjorie: "House Backs End of Teller Votes on Amendments," *New York Times,* July 28, 1970, p. 1, col. 8.

———: "Recorded Teller Vote Credited with Defeat for SST Outlays," *New York Times,* Mar. 19, 1971, p. 24.

Huntington, Samuel P.: "A Revised Theory of American Party Politics," *American Political Science Review,* vol. 44, 1950, pp. 669–677.

———: "The Marasmus of the I.C.C.: The Commissions, the Railroads, and the Public Interest," *Yale Law Journal,* vol. 61, 1952, pp. 467–508.

———: *The Common Defense: Strategic Programs in National Politics* (New York: Columbia University Press, 1961).

———: "Congressional Responses to the Twentieth Century," in David B. Truman (ed.), *The Congress and America's Future* (Englewood Cliffs, N.J.: Prentice-Hall, 1965), pp. 5–31.

Huzar, Elias: *The Purse and the Sword* (Ithaca, N.Y.: Cornell University Press, 1950).

Hyman, Herbert: *Political Socialization* (New York: Free Press, 1959).

"Industry Has Strong Friends on Finance Committee," *Congressional Quarterly Weekly Report,* Sept. 26, 1969, pp. 1787–1795.

Jacob, Herbert: "Initial Recruitment of Elected Officials in the U.S.: A Model," *Journal of Politics,* vol. 24, 1962, pp. 703–716.

Janda, Kenneth, "Information Systems for Congress," in Alfred de Grazia (coord.), *Congress: The First Branch of Government* (Washington, D.C.: American Enterprise Institute, 1966), pp. 415–456.

———: *Information Retrieval: Applications in Political Science* (Indianapolis: Bobbs-Merrill, 1968).

Jernberg, James E.: "Information Change and Congressional Behavior: A Caveat for PPB Reformers," *Journal of Politics,* vol. 31, 1969, pp. 722–740.

Jewell, Malcolm E.: "Evaluating the Decline of Southern Internationalism through Senatorial Roll Call Votes," *Journal of Politics,* vol. 21, 1959, pp. 624–646. *(a)*

———: "The Senate Republican Policy Committee and Foreign Policy," *Western Political Quarterly,* vol. 12, 1959, pp. 966–980. *(b)*

———: *Senatorial Politics and Foreign Policy* (Lexington: University of Kentucky Press, 1962).

——— and Samuel C. Patterson: *The Legislative Process in the United States* (New York: Random House, 1966).

Johnson, Donald Bruce, and Jack L. Walker (eds.): *The Dynamics of the American Presidency* (New York: Wiley, 1964).

Jones, Charles O.: "Representation in Congress: The Case of the House Agriculture Committee," *American Political Science Review,* vol. 55, 1961, pp. 358–367.

———: "The Role of the Congressional Subcommittee," *Midwest Journal of Political Science,* vol. 6, 1962, pp. 327–344.

———: "Intra-party Competition for Congressional Seats," *Western Political Quarterly,* vol. 17, 1964, pp. 461–476. *(a)*

———: *Party and Policy-making: The House Republican Policy Committee* (New Brunswick, N.J.: Rutgers University Press, 1964). *(b)*

——: *Every Second Year: Congressional Behavior and the Two-year Term* (Washington, D.C.: Brookings Institution, 1967).

——: "The Minority Party and Policy-making in the House of Representatives," *American Political Science Review*, vol. 62, 1968, pp. 481–493.

——: *The Minority Party in Congress* (Boston: Little, Brown, 1970).

—— and Randall B. Ripley: *The Role of Political Parties in Congress: A Bibliography and Research Guide* (Tucson: University of Arizona Press, 1966).

Jones, E. Terrence: "Congressional Voting on Keynesian Legislation, 1945–1964," *Western Political Quarterly*, vol. 21, 1968, pp. 240–251.

Kabaker, Harvey M.: "Estimating the Normal Vote in Congressional Elections," *Midwest Journal of Political Science*, vol. 13, 1969, pp. 58–83.

Kammerer, Gladys M.: *The Staffing of the Committees of Congress* (Lexington, Ky.: Bureau of Governmental Research, 1949).

——: *Congressional Committee Staffing Since 1946* (Lexington, Ky.: Bureau of Governmental Research, 1951).

Keefe, William J., and Morris S. Ogul: *The American Legislative Process: Congress and the States*, 2nd ed. (Englewood Cliffs, N.J.: Prentice-Hall, 1968).

Kendall, Willmoore: "The Two Majorities," *Midwest Journal of Political Science*, vol. 4, 1960, pp. 317–345.

Kessel, John H.: "The Washington Congressional Delegation," *Midwest Journal of Political Science*, vol. 8, 1964, pp. 1–21.

Kesselman, Mark: "Presidential Leadership in Congress on Foreign Policy: A Replication of a Hypothesis," *Midwest Journal of Political Science*, vol. 9, 1965, pp. 401–406.

Key, V. O., Jr.: *Southern Politics* (New York: Knopf, 1949).

——: *Politics, Parties, and Pressure Groups*, 5th ed. (New York: Crowell, 1964).

Keynes, Edward: "The Senate Rules and the Dirksen Amendment: A Study in Legislative Strategy and Tactics," in Lawrence K. Pettit and Edward Keynes (eds.), *The Legislative Process in the U.S. Senate* (Chicago: Rand McNally, 1969), pp. 107–149.

King, Larry L.: "Washington's Money Birds," *Harper's Magazine*, August 1965, pp. 45–54.

Kingdon, John W.: *Candidates for Office* (New York: Random House, 1968).

Klapper, Joseph T.: *The Effects of Mass Communication* (Glencoe, Ill.: Free Press, 1960).

Koenig, Louis W.: *The Chief Executive* (New York: Harcourt, Brace & World, 1964).

Kofmehl, Kenneth: *Professional Staffs of Congress* (West Lafayette, Ind.: Purdue University Press, 1962).

——: "The Institutionalization of a Voting Bloc," *Western Political Quarterly*, vol. 17, 1964, pp. 256–272.

Kornberg, Allan, and Norman Thomas: "The Political Socialization of National Legislative Elites in the United States and Canada," *Journal of Politics*, vol. 27, 1965, pp. 761–775.

Kravitz, Walker: "The Influence of the House Rules Committee on Legislation in the 87th Congress," in Joseph S. Clark (ed.), *Congressional Reform: Problems and Prospects* (New York: Crowell, 1965), pp. 127–137.

Lane, Edgar: *Lobbying and the Law* (Berkeley: University of California Press, 1964).

Lane, Robert E.: *Political Life* (New York: Free Press, 1959).

—— and David O. Sears, *Public Opinion* (Englewood Cliffs, N.J.: Prentice-Hall, 1964).

Latham, Earl: "The Group Basis of Politics: Notes for a Theory," *American Political Science Review*, vol. 46, 1952, pp. 376–397. *(a)*

——: *The Group Basis of Politics* (Ithaca, N.Y.: Cornell University Press, 1952). *(b)*

Lawson, Murray G.: "The Foreign Born in Congress, 1789–1949: A Statistical Portrait," *American Political Science Review*, vol. 51, 1959, pp. 1183–1189.

Lehnen, Robert G.: "Behavior on the Senate Floor: An Analysis of Debate on the Senate Floor," *Midwest Journal of Political Science*, vol. 11, 1967, pp. 505–521.

Leuthold, David A.: *Electioneering in a Democracy: Campaigns for Congress* (New York: Wiley, 1968).

Lindblom, Charles E.: "The Science of Muddling Through," *Public Administration Review,* vol. 19, 1959, pp. 79–88.

———: *The Intelligence of Democracy* (New York: Free Press, 1965).

———: *The Policy-making Process* (Englewood Cliffs, N.J.: Prentice-Hall, 1968).

Lippmann, Walter: *The Public Philosophy* (Boston: Little, Brown, 1954).

Lipset, Seymour Martin: *Political Man* (New York: Doubleday, 1960).

Lowi, Theodore J.: "American Business, Public Policy, Case Studies and Political Theory," *World Politics,* vol. 16, 1964, pp. 677–715.

Lutzker, Paul: "The Behavior of Congressmen in a Committee Setting: A Research Report," *Journal of Politics,* vol. 31, 1969, pp. 140–166.

Maass, Arthur: "Congress and Water Resources," *American Political Science Review,* vol. 44, 1950, pp. 576–593.

———: *Muddy Waters* (Cambridge, Mass.: Harvard University Press, 1951).

———: "The Kings River Project," in Harold Stein (ed.), *Public Administration and Policy Development: A Case Book* (New York: Harcourt, Brace, 1952), pp. 533–572.

Macmahon, Arthur W.: "Congressional Oversight of Administration: The Power of the Purse," *Political Science Quarterly,* vol. 58, 1943, pp. 161–190 and 380–414.

MacRae, Duncan, Jr.: *Dimensions of Congressional Voting* (Berkeley and Los Angeles: University of California Press, 1958).

——— and Hugh D. Price: "Scale Positions and 'Power' in the Senate," *Behavioral Science,* vol. 4, 1959, pp. 212–218.

Manley, John F.: "The House Committee on Ways and Means: Conflict Management in a Congressional Committee," *American Political Science Review,* vol. 59, 1965, pp. 927–939.

———: "Congressional Staff and Public Policymaking: The Joint Committee on Internal Revenue Taxation," *Journal of Politics,* vol. 30, 1968, pp. 1046–1067.

———: "Wilbur D. Mills: A Study in Congressional Influence," *American Political Science Review,* vol. 63, 1969, pp. 442–464.

———: *The Politics of Finance* (Boston: Little, Brown, 1970).

Mantel, Howard N.: "The Congressional Record: Fact or Fiction in the Legislative Process," *Western Political Quarterly,* vol. 12, 1959, pp. 981–995.

Marasculio, Leonard A., and Harriet Amster: "Survey of 1961–1962 Congressional Polls," *Public Opinion Quarterly,* vol. 28, 1964, pp. 497–506.

Martin, Joseph W.: *My First Fifty Years in Politics* (New York: McGraw-Hill, 1960).

Marwell, Gerald: "Party, Region and the Dimensions of Conflict in the House of Representatives, 1949–1954," *American Political Science Review,* vol. 61, 1967, pp. 380–399.

Masters, Nicholas A.: "Committee Assignments in the House of Representatives," *American Political Science Review,* vol. 55, 1961, pp. 345–357.

Matthews, Donald R.: *U.S. Senators and Their World* (Chapel Hill: University of North Carolina Press, 1960).

———: "Can the 'Outsider's' Role be Legitimate?" *American Political Science Review,* vol. 55, 1961, pp. 882–883. *(a)*

———: "United States Senators—A Collective Portrait," *The International Social Science Journal,* vol. 13, 1961, pp. 620–634, reprinted in Samuel C. Patterson (ed.), *American Legislative Behavior: A Reader* (Princeton, N.J.: Van Nostrand, 1968), pp. 130–144. *(b)*

——— and James A. Stimson: "Decision-making by U.S. Representatives: A Preliminary Model," in Sidney Ulmer (ed.), *Political Decision-making* (New York: Van Nostrand, 1970), pp. 14–43.

Mayhew, David R.: *Party Loyalty among Congressmen: The Difference between Democrats and Republicans* (Cambridge, Mass.: Harvard University Press, 1966).

McAdams, Alan K.: *Power and Politics in Labor Legislation* (New York: Columbia University Press, 1964).

McClosky, Herbert, and Harold E. Dahlgren: "Primary Group Influence on Party Loyalty," *American Political Science Review,* vol. 53, 1959, pp. 757–776.

McInnis, Mary (ed.): *We Propose: A Modern Congress,* Selected Proposals by the House Republican Task Force on Congressional Reform and Minority Staffing (New York: McGraw-Hill, 1966).

McKaye, William R.: *A New Coalition Takes Control: The House Rules Committee Fight of 1961* (New York: McGraw-Hill, 1963).

McKinney, Madge M.: "The Personnel of the Seventy-seventh Congress," *American Political Science Review,* vol. 36, 1942, pp. 67–74.

McLellan, David S., and Donald Clare: *Public Law 480: The Metamorphosis of a Law* (New York: McGraw-Hill, 1965).

Meyer, John W.: "A Reformulation of the 'Coattails' Problem," in William N. McPhee and William A. Glaser (eds.), *Public Opinion and Congressional Elections* (New York: Free Press, 1962), pp. 52–64.

Mezey, Michael L.: "Ambition Theory and the Office of Congressmen," *Journal of Politics,* vol. 32, 1970, pp. 563–579.

Michel, Robert H.: "Reorganization of the Committees on Government Operations and Minority Control of Investigation," in Mary McInnis (ed.), *We Propose: A Modern Congress,* Selected Proposals by the House Republican Task Force on Congressional Reform and Minority Staffing (New York: McGraw-Hill, 1966), pp. 163–176.

Milbrath, Lester W.: *The Washington Lobbyists* (Chicago: Rand McNally, 1963).

———: "Lobbying as a Communications Process," *Public Opinion Quarterly,* vol. 24, 1960, pp. 32–53.

Miller, Clem: *Member of the House,* John W. Baker (ed.) (New York: Scribners, 1962).

Miller, Warren E.: "Presidential Coattails: A Study in Political Myth and Methodology," *Public Opinion Quarterly,* vol. 19, 1955–56, pp. 353-368.

———: "Majority Rule and the Representative System," paper presented to the 1962 Annual Meeting of the American Political Science Association.

——— and Donald E. Stokes: "Constituency Influence in Congress," *American Political Science Review,* vol. 57, 1963, pp. 45–56.

Mitchell, William C.: "Occupational Role Strains: The American Elected Public Official," *Administrative Science Quarterly,* vol. 3, 1958, pp. 210–228.

———: "The Ambivalent Social Status of the American Politician," *Western Political Quarterly,* vol. 12, 1959, pp. 683–698.

———: *The American Polity* (New York: Free Press, 1962).

———: *Sociological Analysis and Politics: The Theories of Talcott Parsons* (Englewood Cliffs, N.J.: Prentice-Hall, 1967).

Moore, John E.: "Controlling Delinquency: Executive, Congressional, and Juvenile, 1961–1964," in Frederic N. Cleaveland et al., *Congress and Urban Problems* (Washington, D.C.: Brookings Institution, 1969), pp. 110–172.

Morgan, Edward P.: "O'Brien Presses on with the 'Four P's'," *New York Times Magazine* Mar. 25, 1962, pp. 28ff.

Morrow, William L.: *Congressional Committees* (New York: Scribners, 1969).

Murphy, Walter: *Congress and the Court* (Chicago: University of Chicago Press, 1962).

Neuberger, Richard: "The Congressional Record Is Not a Record," *New York Times Magazine,* Apr. 20, 1958.

Neustadt, Richard E.: "Presidency and Legislation: The Growth of Central Clearance," *American Political Science Review,* vol. 48, 1954, pp. 641–671.

————: "Presidency and Legislation: Planning the President's Programs," *American Political Science Review,* vol. 49, 1955, pp. 980–1021.

————: *Presidential Power* (New York: Wiley, 1960).

Newcomb, Theodore M., Ralph H. Turner, and Philip E. Converse: *Social Psychology* (New York: Holt, Rinehart, and Winston, 1965).

New York City Bar Association, Report of the Special Committee on Congressional Ethics: *Congress and the Public Trust* (New York: Atheneum, 1970).

Nieberg, H. L.: "The Eisenhower AEC and Congress," *Midwest Journal of Political Science,* vol. 6, 1962, pp. 115–148.

Olson, Kenneth G.: "The Service Function of the United States Congress," in Alfred de Grazia, (coord.), *Congress: The First Branch of Government* (Washington, D.C.: American Enterprise Institute, 1966), pp. 337–374.

Paige, Glenn D.: *The Korean Decision, June 24–30, 1950* (New York: Free Press, 1968).

Paletz, David L.: "Influence in Congress: An Analysis and Effects of Conference Committees," paper presented to the 1970 Annual Meeting of the American Political Science Association.

Parris, Judith Heimlich: "Congress Rejects the President's Urban Department, 1961–62," in Frederic N. Cleaveland et al., *Congress and Urban Problems* (Washington, D.C.: Brookings Institution, 1969), pp. 173–223.

Patterson, Samuel C.: "The Professional Staffs of Congressional Committees," *Administrative Science Quarterly,* vol. 15, 1970, pp. 22–37.

Peabody, Robert L.: "The Enlarged Rules Committee," in Robert L. Peabody and Nelson W. Polsby (eds.), *New Perspectives on the House of Representatives* (Chicago: Rand McNally, 1963), pp. 129-164.

————: *The Ford-Halleck Minority Leadership Contest, 1965* (New York: McGraw-Hill, 1966).

————: "Party Leadership Change in the House of Representatives," *American Political Science Review,* vol. 61, 1967, pp. 675–693.

————: "Political Parties: House Republican Leadership," in Allan P. Sindler (ed.), *American Political Institutions and Public Policy: Five Contemporary Studies* (Boston: Little, Brown, 1969), pp. 181–229.

Peltason, Jack W.: *Federal Courts in the Political Process* (Garden City, N.Y.: Doubleday, 1955).

Pipe, G. Russell: "Congressional Liaison: The Executive Consolidates Its Relations with Congress," *Public Administration Review,* vol. 26, 1966, pp. 14–24.

Pitkin, Hanna F.: *The Concept of Representation* (Berkeley: University of California Press, 1967).

Polsby, Nelson W.: "Two Strategies of Influence: Choosing a Majority Leader, 1962," in Robert L. Peabody and Nelson W. Polsby (eds.), *New Perspectives on the House of Representatives* (Chicago: Rand McNally, 1963), pp. 237–270.

————: *Congress and the Presidency* (Englewood Cliffs, N.J.: Prentice-Hall, 1964).

————: "The Institutionalization of the House of Representatives," *American Political Science Review,* vol. 62, 1968, pp. 144–168.

————: "Goodbye to the Inner Club," *The Washington Monthly* (August 1969), pp. 30–34.

————, Mariam Gallaher, and Barry Spencer Rundquist: "The Growth of the Seniority System in the U.S. House of Representatives," *American Political Science Review,* vol. 63, 1969, pp. 787–807.

Press, Charles: "Voting Statistics and Presidential Coattails," *American Political Science Review,* vol. 52, 1958, pp. 1041–1050.

Pressman, Jeffrey L.: *House vs. Senate: Conflict in the Appropriations Process* (New Haven: Yale University Press, 1966).

Price, Hugh Douglas: "Race, Religion, and the Rules Committee: The Kennedy Aid-to-Education Bills," in Alan F. Westin (ed.), *The Uses of Power: 7 Cases in American Politics* (New York: Harcourt, Brace & World, 1962), pp. 1–71.

———: "The Electoral Arena," in David B. Truman (ed.), *The Congress and America's Future* (Englewood Cliffs, N.J.: Prentice-Hall, 1965), pp. 32–51.

Pritchett, C. Herman: *Congress versus the Supreme Court, 1957–1960* (Minneapolis: University of Minnesota Press, 1961).

Redford, Emmette S.: "A Case Analysis of Congressional Activity: Civil Aviation, 1957–58," *Journal of Politics,* vol. 22, 1960, pp. 228–258.

Reock, Ernest C., Jr.: "Measuring Compactness as a Requirement of Legislative Apportionment," *Midwest Journal of Political Science,* vol. 5, 1961, pp. 70–74.

Rhode, William E.: *Committee Clearance of Administrative Decisions* (East Lansing: Michigan State University Bureau of Social and Political Research, 1959).

Riddick, Floyd M.: *The United States Congress: Organization and Procedure* (Manassas, Va.: National Capitol Publishers, 1949).

Riddle, Donald H.: *The Truman Committee: A Study in Congressional Responsibility* (New Brunswick, N.J.: Rutgers University Press, 1964).

Rieselbach, Leroy N.: "The Demography of the Congressional Vote on Foreign Aid, 1939–1958," *American Political Science Review,* vol. 58, 1964, pp. 577–588.

———: *The Roots of Isolationism* (Indianapolis: Bobbs-Merrill, 1966).

———: "Congressmen as 'Small Town Boys': A Research Note," *Midwest Journal of Political Science,* vol. 14, 1970, pp. 321–330.

Riker, William H.: "The Paradox of Voting and Congressional Rules for the Voting on Amendments," *American Political Science Review,* vol. 52, 1958, pp. 349–366.

———: "Some Ambiguities in the Notion of Power," *American Political Science Review,* vol. 58, 1964, pp. 341–349.

Ripley, Randall B.: "The Party Whip Organizations in the United States House of Representatives," *American Political Science Review,* vol. 58, 1964, pp. 561–576.

———: *Party Leaders in the House of Representatives* (Washington, D.C.: Brookings Institution, 1967).

———: *Majority Party Leadership in Congress* (Boston: Little, Brown, 1969). *(a)*

———: *Power in the Senate* (New York: St. Martin's, 1969). *(b)*

Robinson, James A.: *The House Rules Committee* (Indianapolis: Bobbs-Merrill, 1963).

———: "Decision Making in Congress," in Alfred de Grazia (coord.), *Congress: The First Branch of Government* (Washington: American Enterprise Institute, 1966), pp. 259–294.

———: *Congress and Foreign Policy-making,* rev. ed. (Homewood, Ill.: Dorsey, 1967).

Rosenau, James N.: *The Nomination of "Chip" Bohlen* (New York: McGraw-Hill, 1962).

———: *National Leadership and Foreign Policy: A Case Study in the Mobilization of Public Support* (Princeton, N.J.: Princeton University Press, 1963).

Rosenbaum, David E.: "Liberal House Assignments a Rebuff to Southern Democrats," *New York Times,* Feb. 1, 1971, p. 18, col. 3.

Rosenblum, Victor G.: *Law as a Political Instrument* (Garden City, N.Y.: Doubleday, 1955).

Rossiter, Clinton: *The American Presidency,* rev. ed. (New York: Harvest Books, 1960).

Rourke, Francis E.: "Administrative Secrecy: A Congressional Dilemma," *American Political Science Review,* vol. 54, 1960, pp. 684–694.

Rovere, Richard H.: *Senator Joe McCarthy* (New York: Harcourt, Brace & World, 1959).

Saloma, John S., III: *Congress and the New Politics* (Boston: Little, Brown, 1969).

Sarbin, Theodore B.: "Role Theory" in Gardner Lindzey (ed.), *Handbook of Social Psychology,* vol. 1 (Reading, Mass.: Addison-Wesley, 1954), pp. 223–258.

Schauffler, Peter P.: "The Legislative Veto Revisited," in Carl J. Friedrich and Seymour Harris (eds.), *Public Policy: Yearbook of the Graduate School of Public Administration,* vol. 8 (Cambridge, Mass.: Harvard University Press, 1958), pp. 296–327.

Scher, Seymour: "The Politics of Agency Organization," *Western Political Quarterly,* vol. 15, 1962, pp. 328–344.

———: "Conditions for Legislative Control," *Journal of Politics,* vol. 25, 1963, pp. 526–551.

Schlesinger, Joseph A.: "The Structure of Competition for Office in the American States," *Behavioral Science,* vol. 5, 1960, pp. 197-210.

Schubert, Glendon E.: *Constitutional Politics* (New York: Holt, Rinehart and Winston, 1960).

————: *Judicial Policy-making* (Chicago: Scott, Foresman, 1965).

Scott, Andrew M., and Margaret A. Hunt: *Congress and the Lobbies: Image and Reality* (Chapel Hill: University of North Carolina Press, 1966).

Secord, Paul F., and Carl W. Backman: *Social Psychology* (New York: McGraw-Hill, 1964).

Shannon, W. Wayne: *Party, Constituency and Congressional Voting* (Baton Rouge: Louisiana State University Press, 1968).

Sharkansky, Ira: "An Appropriations Committee and Its Client Agencies: A Comparative Study of Supervision and Control," *American Political Science Review,* vol. 59, 1965, pp. 622-628.

Sherrill, Robert: "Why We Can't Depend on Congress to Keep Congress Honest," *New York Times Magazine,* July 19, 1970, pp. 5ff.

Shils, Edward A.: "The Legislator and His Environment," *University of Chicago Law Review,* vol. 18, 1950-51, pp. 571-584.

Shuman, Howard E.: "Senate Rules and the Civil Rights Bill: A Case Study," *American Political Science Review,* vol. 51, 1957, pp. 955-975.

Smith, Frank E.: *Congressman from Mississippi* (New York: Pantheon Books, 1964).

Smith, Howard W.: "In Defense of the Rules Committee," in Joseph S. Clark (ed.), *Congressional Reform: Problems and Prospects* (New York: Crowell, 1965), pp. 138-150.

Smith, J. Malcolm, and Cornelius P. Cotter: "Administrative Accountability: Reporting to Congress," *Western Political Quarterly,* vol. 10, 1957, pp. 405-415.

Smuckler, Ralph H.: "The Region of Isolationism," *American Political Science Review,* vol. 47, 1953, pp. 386-401.

Snowiss, Leo M.: "Congressional Recruitment and Representation," *American Political Science Review,* vol. 60, 1966, pp. 627-639.

Steiner, Gilbert Y.: *The Congressional Conference Committee* (Urbana: University of Illinois Press, 1951).

Stewart, John G.: "Two Strategies of Leadership: Johnson and Mansfield," in Nelson W. Polsby (ed.), *Congressional Behavior* (New York: Random House, 1971), pp. 61-92.

Stokes, Donald E., and Warren E. Miller: "Party Government and the Salience of Congress," *Public Opinion Quarterly,* vol. 26, 1962, pp. 531-546.

Stryker, Sheldon: "The Inter-actional and Situational Approaches," in H. Christiansen (ed.), *Handbook of Marriage and the Family* (Chicago: Rand McNally, 1964), pp. 125-170.

Sundquist, James L.: *Politics and Policy* (Washington, D.C.: Brookings Institution, 1968).

Swanson, Wayne R.: "Committee Assignments and the Nonconformist Legislator: Democrats in the U.S. Senate," *Midwest Journal of Political Science,* vol. 13, 1969, pp. 84-94.

Symington, Stuart: "Congress' Right to Know," *New York Times Magazine,* Aug 9, 1970, pp. 7ff.

Tacheron, Donald G., and Morris K. Udall: *The Job of Congressman* (Indianapolis: Bobbs-Merrill, 1966).

Taylor, Telford: *Grand Inquest* (New York: Ballantine Books, 1961).

Thomas, Morgan: *Atomic Energy and Congress* (Ann Arbor: University of Michigan Press, 1955).

Truman, David B.: *The Governmental Process* (New York: Knopf, 1951).

————: "The State Delegations and the Structure of Party Voting in the United States House of Representatives," *American Political Science Review,* vol. 50, 1956, pp. 1023-1045.

————: *The Congressional Party* (New York: Wiley, 1959).

Turner, Julius: *Party and Constituency: Pressures on Congress* (Baltimore: Johns Hopkins University Press, 1951).

——: *Party and Constituency: Pressures on Congress,* rev. ed., by Edward V. Schneier, Jr. (Baltimore: Johns Hopkins Press, 1970).

——: "Primary Elections as Alternatives to Party Competition in 'Safe Districts,'" *Journal of Politics,* vol. 15, 1953, pp. 197–210.

Tyler, Gus: *A Legislative Campaign for a Minimum Wage, 1955* (New York: Holt, 1959).

Vandenberg, Arthur H., Jr.: *The Private Papers of Senator Vandenberg* (Boston: Houghton Mifflin, 1952).

Vardis, V. Stanley: "Select Committees of the House of Representatives," *Midwest Journal of Political Science,* vol. 10, 1966, pp. 364–377.

Vinyard, Dale: "Congressional Committees on Small Business," *Midwest Journal of Political Science,* vol. 10, 1966, pp. 364–377.

Vogler, David J.: "House Dominance in Congressional Conference Committees," *Midwest Journal of Political Science,* vol. 14, 1970, pp. 303–320.

Wahlke, John C., Heinz Eulau, William Buchanan, and LeRoy C. Ferguson, *The Legislative System* (New York: Wiley, 1962).

Walker, David B.: "The Age Factor in the 1958 Congressional Elections," *Midwest Journal of Political Science,* vol. 4, 1960, pp. 1–26.

Wallace, Robert Ash: *Congressional Control of Federal Spending* (Detroit: Wayne State University Press, 1960).

Watson, Richard A.: "The Tariff Revolution: A Study of Shifting Party Attitudes," *Journal of Politics,* vol. 18, 1956, pp. 678–701.

Weinbaum, Marvin G., and Dennis R. Judd: "In Search of a Mandated Congress," *Midwest Journal of Political Science,* vol. 14, 1970, pp. 276–302.

Werner, Emmy E.: "Women in Congress: 1917–1964," *Western Political Quarterly,* vol. 19, 1966, pp. 16–30.

Westerfield, H. Bradford: *Foreign Policy and Party Politics: Pearl Harbor to Korea* (New Haven: Yale University Press, 1955).

White, William S.: *Citadel: The Story of the U.S. Senate* (New York: Harper, 1956).

Wildavsky, Aaron: *The Politics of the Budgetary Process* (Boston: Little, Brown, 1964).

——: "Toward a Radical Incrementalism: A Proposal to Aid Congress in Reform of the Budgetary Process," in Alfred de Grazia (coord.), *Congress: The First Branch of Government* (Washington: American Enterprise Institute, 1966), pp. 115–165.

Wilmerding, Lucius, Jr.: *The Spending Power* (New Haven: Yale University Press, 1943).

Wilson, Bob: "Congressional Ethics," in Mary McInnis (ed.), *We Propose: A Modern Congress,* Selected Proposals of the House Republican Task Force on Congressional Reform and Minority Staffing (New York: McGraw-Hill, 1966), pp. 253–259.

Wilson, H. H.: *Congress: Corruption and Congress* (New York: Rinehart, 1951).

Wilson, James Q.: "Two Negro Politicians: An Interpretation," *Midwest Journal of Political Science,* vol. 4, 1960, pp. 346–369.

Wilson, Woodrow: *Congressional Government* (New York: Meridian Books, 1956).

Wolfinger, Raymond E.: "Filibusters: Majority Rule, Presidential Leadership, and Senate Norms," in Nelson W. Polsby (ed.), *Congressional Behavior* (New York: Random House, 1971), pp. 111–127.

——and Joan Heifitz: "Safe Seats, Seniority, and Power in Congress," *American Political Science Review,* vol. 59, 1965, pp. 337–349.

Woodward, Julian L., and Elmo Roper: "Political Activity of American Citizens," *American Political Science Review,* vol. 44, 1950, pp. 872–885.

Yinger, J. Milton: *Toward a Field Theory of Behavior* (New York: McGraw-Hill, 1965).

Zeller, Belle: "Regulation of Pressure Groups and Lobbyists," *The Annuals,* vol. 319, 1958, pp. 94–103.

Index

Abram, Michael, 69
Abzug, Bella, 66
Access, 202–204
Acorns (discussion club), 160
Administrative lobbying, 184–187
Age of Congressmen, 31–32
Agency orientation, 15, 20, 192, 299
Albert, Carl, 65, 94, 95, 104, 110
Alford, Robert, 34
Almond, Gabriel, 22
Amster, Harriet, 217
Anderson, Clinton, 205, 279
Anderson, Ronald E., 215, 275, 378
Andrain, Charles F., 34, 272, 274
Anticourt orientation, 17, 230
Apportionment, 38–41, 366
Arends, Leslie, 99
Aspinall, Wayne, 83

Badillo, Herman, 66
Bailey, Stephen K., 241
Baker, Gordon E., 38, 39
Baker, Howard, 171
Baker, Robert, 392
Baker v. Carr, 40
Bankhead, William B., 104
Barber, James D., 35–36, 42
Barden, Graham, 83, 253
Bauer, Raymond A., 197, 200, 201, 204, 207, 217, 218, 339, 352
Bell, Roderick, 5, 7
Bennett, Wallace, 205
Bentley, Arthur F., 197
Berelson, Bernard, 28, 216
Berman, Daniel, 169, 195, 263
Bibby, John F., 45, 68, 92, 241–243, 253, 319
Bible, Alan, 279
Bicameralism, 10–11

Bipartisanship, 180–181
Blackmun, Harry A., 228
Boggs, Hale, 65, 95, 104, 110
Bohlen, Charles, 312
Boll Weevils, Democratic, 90
Bolling, Richard, 110, 365, 381
Bone, Hugh A., 102
Bowles, Chester, 65
Bozell, L. Brent, 310
Brewster, Daniel, 206, 392
Bricker Amendment, 374
Broker orientation, 19, 56, 84,
    239–240, 244, 259, 264, 272,
    294
Brooke, Edward, 31, 279
Brown, MacAlister, 298
*Brown v. Board of Education of
    Topeka,* 17, 225–226
Buckley, William F., 310
Bullock, Charles S., 66
Bureau of the Budget (*see* Office
    of Management and Budget)
Burger, Warren E., 228
Burnham, James, 360, 361, 364,
    372, 374
Burns, James F., 70, 360, 361,
    364, 367
Byrd, Robert C., 100, 149
Byrnes, John W., 84, 291

Campbell, Angus, 28, 50, 198, 215
Cannon, Clarence, 76, 285
Cantril, Hadley, 34
Carper, Edith T., 343
Carr, Robert K., 310
Carroll, Holbert N., 80–82, 175,
    250, 299, 306, 323, 376
Carswell, G. Harrold, 228, 267, 311
Case, Clifford, 269, 271, 279, 394
Case, Francis, 206
Casework, 215, 340–344, 355
Cellar, Emanuel, 116, 389

Chartrand, Robert L., 386
Chief Executive (*see* President)
Chisholm, Shirley, 31
Chowder and Marching Society,
    160
Church, Frank, 361
Clapp, Charles L., 45, 46, 54, 58,
    63–65, 88, 99, 101, 109, 119,
    120, 160, 212, 245, 250, 263,
    266, 285, 341, 343–346, 348,
    349, 362, 369, 381
Clare, Donald, 297
Clark, Joseph S., 63, 110, 146,
    147, 149, 341, 365, 370, 381, 382
Clausen, Aage R., 161
Cleveland, James C., 377
Closed rule, 121
Cloture, 133–134, 370, 383
Cnudde, Charles F., 218, 219, 333
Coattail effect, 50–52
Cochrane, James D., 78
Cohen, Bernard C., 175
Colgrove v. Green, 40
Colmer, William, 82, 123
Committee on Committees, 63–66,
    154
Committee of the Whole, 125–127,
    267, 280, 390
Committee assignment:
    criteria for, 64–67
    methods of, 63
Committee chairmen:
    powers of, 67–69
    seniority and, 69–73
Committee decisions, 254–257
Committee hearings:
    chairman and, 247
    closed, 246–247
    participation in, 250–251
    purposes, 245–246
    testimony, 248–250
Committee indifferent orientation,
    11, 84, 251

Committee leadership orientation, 11, 56, 67, 73, 80, 84, 251, 280, 292, 293
Committee "mark up," 251–254
Committee report, 257–258
Committee specialist orientation, 11, 55, 67, 77, 80, 84, 111, 251, 259, 280, 292, 293
Committee staff, 67, 77–80, 247, 253, 307, 319
Committee structure, types:
  anarchic, 83
  bargaining, 83–84
  oligarchic, 82
Conference committees, 62, 135–137, 284–288, 293–294
Conflict of interest, 311–312, 393–394
Conformist orientation, 13, 55–56, 146–149, 264, 282
Congress:
  committees of, 11–12, 57–85, 244–258
  as decentralized system, 57–58, 75–77, 84–86, 93, 111–112, 114–115, 131, 138–139, 163–164, 259–260, 299
  political parties in, 11, 12, 86–112
  as political system, 8–24
Congressional (campaign) committees, 103–104
Congressional committees:
  assignment to, 62–67
  chairmen of, 67–73
  general considerations, 58–62
  relations among, 80–82
  staff of, 77–80
  subcommittees, 74–77
  types of, 59–62
Congressional elections:
  apportionment, 38–41
  campaign finance, 44, 47

Congressional elections:
  campaigns, 45–48
  coattail effect, 50–52
  direct primary, 42–44
  issues in, 216–217
  nominations, 48–53
  voting and, 273–274
Congressional ethics, 391–394
Congressional intent, 258, 297
Congressional majority, 91–92
Congressional Record, 124–125, 143, 207, 208, 263, 265, 266, 293, 338, 348
Congressional reform:
  incremental change, 380–383
  information and, 384–388
  staff and, 383–384
  strengthening Congress, 371–380
  strengthening the President, 366–371
  values and, 360–362
Congressional system:
  defined, 9
  inputs to, 13–18
  models of, 362–365
  outputs of, 18–22
  rules of, 12
  structure of, 9–13
Congressmen:
  life in Washington, D.C., 53–54
  perceptions of constituency, 331–334, 336–339
  personality of, 10, 35–37, 275–276
  policy preferences of, 331–334, 336–339
  political backgrounds of, 10
  role orientations of (*see* Role orientations)
  social backgrounds of, 9, 28–34, 272–273
Connally, John, 292
Conservative coalition, 34, 277–279
Cooper, John Sherman, 361

Cooper, Joseph, 69, 303
Corwin, Edward S., 168, 310
Cotter, Cornelius P., 300, 301, 375, 378
Council of Economic Advisors, 169
Courts:
  demands on Congress, 224–229
  supports for Congress, 229–230
Crabb, Cecil V., 180
Cronin, Thomas E., 169
Cummings, Milton C., Jr., 51, 83, 119
Curtis, Carl, 205

Dahl, Robert A., 17, 57, 175, 225, 229, 363, 364
Dahlgren, Harold E., 30
Daley, Richard, 44
Davidson, Roger H., 45, 68, 70, 88, 89, 92, 168, 212, 219, 220, 222–224, 239–243, 253, 329, 330, 340, 362–365, 369, 379, 381, 388
Dawson, Raymond H., 299
Dawson, Richard E., 28, 302
Debate, 125–126, 132–135, 262–264
Dechert, Charles R., 385, 386
de Grazia, Alfred, 378
de Grazia, Edward, 186, 327, 363, 364, 372, 378
Delegate orientation, 21, 53, 55, 84, 219–220, 230, 292, 294, 330–331, 335, 336, 339, 347, 355
Demands, 13, 17, 167–190, 194–206, 214–221, 224–229
Democratic Study Group, 89, 160
Deutsch, Karl, 6
Dexter, Lewis A., 45, 197, 200–204, 206, 207, 216–218, 220, 320, 337, 352
Direct primary, 42–44

Dirksen, Everett M., 92, 100, 106, 111, 130, 171
District (state) orientation, 16, 53, 84, 192, 294, 329–331, 355
District- (state-) nation orientation, 17, 329, 355
Dixon, Robert G., Jr., 38
Dodd, Thomas, 145, 210, 391, 392
Douglas, Paul, 43, 147, 313
Douglas, William O., 318
Drew, Elizabeth Brenner, 76
Dulles, John Foster, 65
Dyson, James W., 282, 283

Eastland, James, 116, 130
Easton, David, 2, 4–6, 30, 221, 236
Education of congressmen, 32–33
Eidenberg, Eugene, 241
Eisenhower, Dwight, 51, 52, 65, 91, 92, 97, 98, 134, 173–175, 177–179, 181, 191, 206, 207, 270, 290, 302, 311, 312, 360
Elections (*see* Congressional elections)
Eulau, Heinz, 82, 328
Evans, Rowland, 97
Executive agencies and Congress:
  administrative lobbying, 184–187
  intraexecutive differences, 187–190
Executive office of President, 169, 176, 306
"Executive privilege," 179, 321

Facilitator orientation, 15, 212, 292, 294
Fairlie, John A., 327
Fannin, Paul, 205
Farnsworth, David N., 256, 273
Feedback, 6–7, 22, 237, 338–339, 353–356

Fenno, Richard F., 63–66, 68, 69, 74, 75, 77, 81, 83, 84, 141, 142, 147, 150, 152–158, 187, 188, 248, 253–257, 280–282, 284–288, 299, 304–308, 316
Fenton, John H., 272
Ferber, Mark F., 160
Field, John O., 215
Fiellin, Alan, 55, 161
Filibuster, 129–130, 132–135, 137, 284, 370, 374, 382
Finney, John W., 106, 144
Fishel, Jeff, 47, 48
Floor leaders, 95–98, 104, 105
Folkways of Congress (*see* Norms)
Ford, Gerald, 92, 95, 110
Fortas, Abe, 312
Fox, Douglas M., 119, 120
Free, Lloyd A., 34
Freeman, J. Leiper, 14, 187, 298, 316, 317
Friedrich, Carl J., 316
Froman, Lewis, 10, 107, 108, 114, 116–118, 122, 124, 128–130, 134, 137, 270, 273, 275, 366
Fulbright, J. William, 21, 65, 68, 205, 247, 257, 279, 319, 361

Galloway, George B., 313, 340
Gawthrop, Louis C., 60
Gellhorn, Walter, 379
General Accounting Office, 308, 375, 386
George, Walter, 97
Gerry, Elbridge, 39
Gerrymander, 39–41
Getz, Robert S., 391–393
Gibbons, Sam, 392
Gilbert, Charles E., 327
Gluck, Maxwell, 311
Goldwater, Barry, 51, 111, 215, 271
Goodman, Walter, 310

Goodwin, George, Jr., 60, 64, 70, 74, 76
Gordon, Bernard K., 302
Gore, Albert, 207
Grassmuck, George, 274
Green, Edith, 297
Green, Harold P., 61, 302, 303
Greenberg, Sanford D., 169
Greenstein, Fred I., 30, 169
Griffin, Robert P., 100
Griffith, Ernest S., 298
Groennings, Sven, 160
Gross, Bertram, 79, 241, 245, 247, 250, 384
Gross, Neal, 3
Gubser, Charles, 390

Hacker, Andrew, 38, 39, 330
Haight, David E., 168
Halleck, Charles, 91–92, 95, 110, 111
Halpern, Seymour, 393
Hansen, Clifford, 205, 269
Harris, Fred, 205, 279
Harris, Joseph P., 19, 296–298, 300, 302, 303, 308–310, 312, 316
Harris, Oren, 116
Harris, Richard, 312, 363
Hatch Acts, 311
Hatfield, Mark, 361
Havens, Murray C., 275
Haviland, H. Field, Jr., 175, 177, 180
Hayden, Carl, 285
Haynsworth, Clement, 183, 228, 312
Heard, Alexander, 311
Hebert, F. Edward, 65
Heifitz, Joan, 72
Hermann, Margaret, 37
Hershey, Lewis, 189

Hess, Robert D., 30
Heubel, Edward J., 315
Hinckley, Barbara, 52, 70, 71,
    73, 82
Holland, Spressard, 269
Hometowns of congressmen, 29–
    30, 272
Hoover, J. Edgar, 189
Horn, Stephen, 60, 79, 158, 253,
    307, 378
House of Representatives:
  Agriculture Committee, 65, 66,
    83, 159, 257, 284
  Appropriations Committee, 60,
    64–66, 74–76, 81, 119, 150–
    159, 254, 280–283, 299, 303,
    304, 320, 323
  Banking and Currency Com-
    mittee, 393
  calendars, 118–119, 122
  code of fair practices, 315
  Commerce Committee, 392
  Committee of the Whole, 125–
    127, 267, 280, 390
  differences with Senate, 10–11
  District of Columbia Committee,
    60, 69, 119
  Education and Labor Commit-
    tee, 65, 66, 68, 77, 83, 84,
    152, 154, 155, 159, 253,
    254, 282, 284, 297
  Foreign Affairs Committee, 66,
    81, 84, 152, 154, 155, 158,
    159, 175, 249, 250, 256,
    273, 282, 298
  Government Operations Com-
    mittee, 66, 297, 310
  Interior and Insular Affairs
    Committee, 65, 66, 77, 83,
    84, 152, 155, 158, 159, 256,
    287–288
  Internal Security Committee,
    60, 282, 310

House of Representatives:
  Interstate and Foreign Com-
    merce Committee, 116,
    287–288
  Judiciary Committee, 116, 118,
    287–288, 389
  Merchant Marine and Fisheries
    Committee, 60
  Post Office and Civil Service
    Committee, 66, 84, 152,
    159, 309
  Public Works Committee, 65,
    66, 84, 119, 298
  rules and procedures of, 115–127
  Rules Committee, 12, 60, 64,
    82–83, 95, 96, 107, 114,
    117–124, 131, 136, 137,
    262, 263, 280, 374, 381
  Science and Astronautics
    Committee, 303
  Speaker of, 93–95, 104, 105,
    108, 136
  Veterans' Affairs Committee,
    60, 119
  Ways and Means Committee, 60,
    63–66, 78–79, 84, 106, 114,
    119, 136, 152, 154, 155, 158,
    159, 176, 238, 247, 252–254,
    256, 283, 382, 389
Hruska, Roman, 269
Hugo, Michael, 386
Huitt, Ralph, 10, 36, 37, 58, 67,
    68, 87, 97, 101, 105, 147, 248
Hunt, Margaret A., 197
Hunter, Marjorie, 108, 390
Huntington, Samuel P., 34, 61,
    179, 188, 273, 298, 322, 330
Huzar, Elias, 304
Hyman, Herbert, 30

Informal organization, 160–161
"Inner club" in Senate, 146–149

Inputs (*see* Demands; Supports)
Interest groups (*see* Lobbying;
      Lobbyists)
Inventor orientation, 19, 84, 239,
      244, 259, 264, 272, 292, 294,
      347
Item veto, 370

Jacob, Herbert, 42
Janda, Kenneth, 386
Javits, Jacob, 264, 271, 279, 361
Jefferson, Thomas, 321
Jencks v. United States, 226
Jenner, William E., 227
Jensen, Ben F., 310
"Jensen riders," 310
Jernberg, James A., 306
Jewell, Malcolm, 12, 14, 16, 78,
      79, 102, 113, 147, 160, 180,
      181, 270, 271, 296
Johnson, Donald Bruce, 168
Johnson, Lyndon B., 37, 51, 63, 76,
      91, 97, 101, 102, 173, 174,
      176, 179, 180, 183, 191, 241,
      257, 268, 270, 290, 298, 301,
      302, 311, 338, 366, 367, 383
Johnson, Thomas F., 392
Johnson Rule, 63, 66, 383
Johnston, Larry D., 168
Joint Committee on Atomic
      Energy, 61, 189
Joint Committee on Internal
      Revenue Taxation, 79, 303
Joint Committee on the Legislative
      Budget, 323
Joint committees, 61, 376
Jones, Charles O., 49, 74, 83, 87,
      91, 102, 103, 110, 159, 257,
      352, 367
Jones, E. Terrence, 34
Judd, Dennis R., 48
Judiciary (*see* Courts)

Kabaker, Harvey M., 52
Kammerer, Gladys, 77
Keefe, William J., 248, 263
Kefauver, Estes, 313, 378
Kendall, Willmoore, 364
Kennedy, Edward M., 100, 149
Kennedy, John F., 91, 123, 178,
      179, 181, 183, 268, 270, 290,
      301, 302, 312
Kennedy, Robert, 42, 44
Kessel, John H., 161
Kesselman, Mark, 181, 183, 271
Key, V. O., Jr., 43, 44, 48, 117, 274
Keynes, Edward, 132
Kilbourn v. Thompson, 314
King, Larry L., 195
Kingdom, John W., 45, 47, 53, 335
Koenig, Louis W., 168
Kofmehl, Kenneth, 77, 316
Kornberg, Allan, 28
Korth, Fred, 312
Kovenock, David M., 212, 219,
      222, 239, 324
Kravitz, Walker, 119, 124

Lane, Edgar, 208
Lane, Robert E., 216, 217
Latham, Earl, 197
Lausche, Frank, 143
Lawmaking:
      amendments, 262–264
      in committee, 244–258
      conference committees and,
            284–288
      debate, 262–264
      defined, 18–19
      drafting legislation, 240–244
      floor consideration, 262–266
      general considerations, 236–238
      substance of, 288–292
      voting and, 267–284
Lawson, Murray G., 30

Legislative Apportionment (*see* Apportionment)
Legislative Reference Service, 77, 385
Legislative Reorganization Act of 1939, 301
Legislative Reorganization Act of 1946, 77–78, 80, 224, 295, 298, 323
Legislative Reorganization Act of 1970, 74, 108, 124, 126, 224, 246, 252, 368, 378, 390
Legislators (*see* Congressmen)
Leuthold, David A., 42–45
Library of Congress, 77, 386
Lindblom, Charles E., 364
Lippmann, Walter, 363
Lipset, Seymour Martin, 34
Lobbying:
  administrative, 184–187
  classic image of, 195–197
  as communications process, 201–206
  contemporary, 197–206
  regulation of, 208–209
  techniques of, 197–201
Lobbyists:
  in campaigns, 46
  inputs from, 15, 197–206
  nominations and, 44
  supports from, 209–210
  use by congressmen, 206–208
Long, Edward, 393
Long, Russell, 100, 144, 205, 392
Lowi, Theodore, 257
Lutzker, Paul, 248

Maass, Arthur, 14, 189, 298
McAdams, Alan, 83, 178, 253, 337
McCarthy, Eugene, 65, 180
McCarthy, Joseph, 36, 145, 315

McClellan, John, 313, 337
McClosky, Herbert, 30
McCormick, John W., 54, 90, 94, 104, 110, 143
McCrone, Donald J., 218, 219, 333
McGee, Gale, 65, 279
McGovern, George, 361
McGregor, Clark, 177
McInnis, Mary, 372
McKaye, William R., 119
McKinney, Madge M., 30
McLellan, David S., 297
Macmahon, Arthur W., 297
McMillan, John L., 69
McNamara, Robert S., 186
MacRae, Duncan, Jr., 34, 57, 273–275, 277
Magnuson, Warren, 106, 116
Mahon, George H., 65, 76
Mail, 331, 341–342
Manley, John F., 65, 68, 79, 84, 152, 158, 238, 252, 253, 256
Mansfield, Mike, 37, 90, 102, 143
Mantel, Howard N., 265
Marasculio, Leonard A., 217
"Mark-up" process, 129, 251–254, 295
Martin, Joseph, 110
Martin, Joseph W., 94
Martin, William McChesney, 189
Marwell, Gerald, 271, 274, 275
Masters, Nicholas A., 64, 151
Matthews, Donald, 10, 12, 29, 30, 32, 33, 53, 54, 60, 141, 142, 144, 146, 147, 161, 197, 207, 211, 219, 263, 264, 266–268, 334
Maverick orientation, 12, 88, 294
Mayhew, David R., 271
Meyer, John W., 51
Mezey, Michael L., 47
Michel, Robert M., 377

Milbrath, Lester, 15, 197–200, 202, 203, 208
Miller, Clem, 53, 88, 273, 365
Miller, Jack, 205
Miller, Warren, 16, 172, 211, 216, 218, 331–335, 337, 352
Mills, Wilbur, 84, 106, 114, 136, 158, 176, 247, 252–254, 291
Mitchell, William C., 2, 3, 54, 391
Moore, John E., 297
Morey, Roy D., 241
Morgan, Edward P., 176
Morgan, Thomas E., 158
Morrisey, Francis X., 311
Morrow, William L., 60
Morse, Wayne, 110, 147, 264, 312
Murphy, George, 392
Murphy, Walter, 17, 226, 227

National orientation, 17, 192, 329, 331, 335
National origins of Congressmen, 30
National Security Council, 169
Neuberger, Richard, 265
Neustadt, Richard E., 169, 174, 175, 365
Neutral orientation, 15, 47, 212
News management, 322
Nieberg, H. L., 189
Nixon, Richard, 51, 92, 98, 106, 134, 135, 176–178, 180, 183, 228, 229, 247, 257, 269, 270, 278, 290–292, 298, 311, 312, 321, 370
Nonconformist orientation, 13, 55, 146, 148
Norms:
chamber-wide, 142–145
committee, 153–159
defined, 12–13
functions of, 145–146

Norms:
about subsystems: committees, 149–152
parties, 152–153
Novak, Robert, 97

O'Brien, Lawrence F., 176–177
Office of Management and Budget, 169, 170, 188, 304, 375–376
Ogul, Morris S., 248, 263
O'Leary, Michael K., 89, 212, 219, 222, 239, 329
Olson, Kenneth G., 340, 341, 344–347
Ombudsman, 379
"One man, one vote" doctrine, 40–41, 130
Opportunist orientation, 19, 84, 239, 264, 294, 347
Outputs of congressional system (*see* Lawmaking; Oversight; Representation)
Oversight:
appropriations and, 303–309
controls over personnel, 309–313
defined, 19–20
for efficiency, 297–299
general considerations, 296–299
informal controls, 315–316
investigations, 313–315
legislative veto, 301–303
limitations on, 316–323
for policy, 296–297, 299
statutory controls, 300–301
techniques of, 299–316
Oversight-indifferent orientation 20, 55, 299, 317, 324

Paige, Glen D., 179
Paletz, David L., 288
Parker, Glenn R., 222

Parker, John J., 312
Parris, Judith H., 301
Parsons, Talcott, 2, 3
Party conference (caucus), 100–101, 104
Party identification, 50
Party indifferent orientation, 12
Party loyalist orientation, 12, 55, 88–89, 92, 106, 111, 140, 271–272, 276, 292, 294
Passman, Otto, 76
Patterson, Samuel C., 12, 14, 16, 77–79, 113, 147, 160, 270, 296
Peabody, Robert L., 83, 91, 95, 101, 107, 109, 110, 119, 122, 123
Peltason, Jack W., 225
Pennsylvania v. Nelson, 227
Percy, Charles, 43
Pitkin, Hanna F., 327
"Pocket veto," 173
"Pocket votes," 267
Policy committees, 101–103
Political parties:
    assets and liabilities of, 88–93
    conditions for leadership, 107–109
    conferences and committees, 100–104
    floor leaders, 95–98, 104, 105
    functions of, 87–88
    leadership change in, 109–111
    majority-minority status, 90–92
    patterns of leadership in, 104–105
    President and, 90–92
    structure of, 93–105
    techniques of leadership, 105–107
    voting and, 268–272
    whips, 98–100, 104, 106
Politico orientation, 21, 219–220, 230, 292, 330, 334, 336, 339, 355

Pollack v. Farmers' Loan and Trust Co., 227
Polsby, Nelson W., 12, 50, 69, 101, 148
Pool, Ithiel de Sola, 197, 200, 201, 204, 207, 218, 339, 352
Powell, Adam Clayton, 54, 68, 83, 145, 253, 390, 391
Powell v. McCormick, 54
Power to persuade, 174–178
Premark-up process, 253
President:
    as "chief legislator," 168–170
    Congress and, 167–193, 362–365
    foreign policy, 178–181
    inputs from, 14–15, 168–170
    outputs and, 288–292
    political parties and, 90–92
    supports from, 190–191
Presidential-bipartisan majority, 90–92
Presidential leadership of Congress:
    formal powers, 173–174
    informal powers, 174–178
    limits on, 170–171, 183–184
    opportunities for, 171–173
Presidential orientation, 15, 20, 192, 292
Presidential-partisan majority, 90–92
Press, Charles, 51
Pressman, Jeffrey L., 58, 285
Pressure groups (*see* Lobbying; Lobbyists)
Price, H. Douglas, 41, 57, 119
Pritchett, C. Herman, 226
Procourt orientation, 17, 230
Pro-oversight orientation, 20, 318, 324
Prouty, Winston, 267

Proxmire, William, 36, 110, 147, 148, 264, 269
Public opinion:
  "information gap," 217–219, 331
  inputs from, 16, 214–224
  policy demands from, 214–217
  support from, 221–224

Quorum, 125–126, 280

Race of congressmen, 31
"Radical incrementalism," 376–377
Randolph, Jennings, 279
Rayburn, Sam, 64, 104, 110, 123
"Red Monday" cases, 226
Redford, Emmette S., 322
Reform (*see* Congressional reform)
Religion of congressmen, 32–33
Reock, Ernest C., Jr., 40
Representation:
  congressional office and, 344–348
  constituent education and, 348–350
  constituent services, 339–350
  focus of, 328–331, 339
  policy and, 327–339
  style of, 219–221, 330–331, 339
Resister orientation, 15, 47, 212
"Responsible legislator," 64, 66, 151
Reuss, Henry S., 379
Rhode, William E., 303
Riddick, Floyd, 12, 114
Riddle, Donald H., 314
"Riders," 125, 129–130
Rieselbach, Leroy, 9, 14, 29, 34, 271–275, 277, 335, 336
Riker, William H., 57
Ripley, Randall B., 87, 90, 91, 93, 94, 98–100, 104–108, 163, 247, 267, 362, 369, 381

Ritualist orientation, 19, 55, 84, 239–240, 244, 259, 264, 272, 294, 347
Robertson, A. Willis, 68, 76, 253, 393
Robinson, James A., 64, 82, 83, 90, 116–122, 181, 182, 184–186
Role, defined, 3–4, 11
Role conflict, 4, 13, 21–22, 191–192, 213, 231, 235–236, 271–272, 294, 317, 324, 339, 350–353, 356, 380
Role orientations:
  toward committees, 11–12, 55–56, 67, 73, 77, 80, 84, 111, 250–251, 259, 280, 282, 292, 293
  toward courts, 17, 230
  executive, 14–15, 192–193, 294
  toward lawmaking, 19, 55, 84, 238–240, 244, 259, 264, 272, 292, 294, 347
  toward lobbyists, 15–16, 47, 212–213, 282, 292, 294
  toward norms, 13, 55–56, 146–149, 264
  oversight, 20, 55, 299, 317, 324
  toward political parties, 12, 55, 88–90, 92, 106, 111, 140, 271–272, 276, 282, 292, 294
  toward representation, 16–17, 21, 53, 55, 84, 192, 219–221, 230, 282, 292, 294, 329–336, 339–340, 347, 355
Roll call voting (*see* Voting)
Roosevelt, Franklin D., 169, 222
Roosevelt, Theodore, 169
Roper, Elmo, 216
Rosenau, James N., 178, 312, 330, 337
Rosenbaum, David E., 65
Rosenblum, Victor G., 225
Rosenthal, Alan, 61, 302, 303

Rossiter, Clinton, 168, 363
Rourke, Francis E., 321, 322
Rovere, Richard, 36, 310, 315
Rules and procedures:
   conference committees, 135–137
   House of Representatives:
      Calendar Wednesday
         procedure, 121–122, 262
      discharge petition, 116–117,
         262, 369, 382
      floor consideration, 124–127
      introduction of bills, 115–116
      privileged matter, 118–119
      suspension of rules, 117, 262
      voting, 125–127
   Senate: cloture, 133–134, 370,
      383
      discharge, 192, 262
      filibuster, 129–130, 132–135,
         137, 284, 370, 374, 382
      floor consideration, 131–135
      introduction of bills, 128–129
      privileged matter, 131
      suspension of rules, 130, 262

St. Clair, Arthur, 314, 321
Salinger, Pierre, 42
Saloma, John S., 236, 238, 297,
     303, 321, 340, 341, 346, 348–
     350, 363, 364, 379, 384–386
Saltonstall, Leverett, 100
"Sample for information," 305–306,
     319
Sarbin, Theodore, 3
Schauffler, Peter P., 303
Scher, Seymour, 317, 377
Schlesinger, Joseph A., 273
Schneier, Edward V., 268, 270
Schubert, Glendon E., 225
Schweiker, Richard, 279
Scott, Andrew M., 197
Scott, Hugh, 100, 171

Sears, David O., 217
Secrecy, 389–391
Select (ad hoc) committees, 62, 376
Senate:
   calendars, 131
   committees: Agriculture
      Committee, 65, 128
     Appropriations Committee,
      79, 81, 158, 253, 282, 299,
      303, 304, 307
     Armed Services Committee,
      80, 273
     Banking and Currency Com-
      mittee, 68, 76, 253, 319, 393
     Commerce Committee, 116
     Finance Committee, 79, 205, 392
     Foreign Relations Committee,
      21, 80, 128, 175, 247, 256.
      273, 298
     Government Operations Com-
      mittee, 36
     Interior and Insular Affairs
      Committee, 65
     Judiciary Committee, 116, 129,
      130
     Labor and Public Welfare
      Committee, 65
     Post Office and Civil Service
      Committee, 309
     Public Works Committee, 65, 298
     Rules and Administration
      Committee, 60
   differences with House, 10–11
   "Establishment," 12, 63, 146–
     382
   rules and procedures, 127–135
Senatorial courtesy, 313
Seniority, 69–73, 77, 88, 192, 368,
     382, 383
Service v. Dulles, 226
Sex of congressmen, 31
Shannon, W. Wayne, 268, 271,
     273, 274, 277

Sharkansky, Ira, 319
Sherrill, Robert, 392, 393
Shils, Edward A., 54
Shriver, Sargent, 241
Shuman, Howard E., 132, 243
Smith, Howard, 82, 123
Smith, Howard W., 119, 143
Smith, J. Malcolm, 300, 301
Smith, Margaret Chase, 176
Smuckler, Ralph H., 277
Snowiss, Leo M., 44
Social status of congressmen, 29, 32–34
Socialization, 4, 30–31, 141, 157–158, 161
SOS, Republican, 160
Soule, James W., 282, 283
Speaker of the House, 93–95, 104, 105, 108, 136, 380
"Special orders," 263
Sprague, John, 66
Standing committee, 59–60
Steiner, Gilbert Y., 137, 286
Stewart, John G., 37, 97
Stimson, James A., 161
Stokes, Donald, 16, 172, 216, 218, 331–335, 337, 352
Stryker, Sheldon, 3
Subsystems of Congress:
   committees, 11–12, 57–85, 244–258
   political parties, 11–12, 86–112
Sundquist, James L., 106, 175, 243, 253, 254
Supports, 13, 17–18, 190–191, 209–210, 221–224, 356, 388–394
Supreme Court, 17, 224–230
Swanson, Wayne R., 147
Sweezy v. New Hampshire, 226
Symington, Stuart, 385
Systems analysis, 2–8

Tacheron, Donald G., 216
Talbott, Harold, 312
Talmadge, Herman, 205
Taylor, Telford, 314, 315, 321, 322
Thomas, Norman, 28, 303
Torney, Judith V., 30
Tribune orientation, 19, 56, 84, 239–240, 244, 259, 264, 272, 292, 294
Truman, David, 91, 93, 98, 100, 111, 161, 197, 198, 269, 276
Truman, Harry, 51, 92, 169, 171, 179–181, 302, 312–314
Truncated majority, 91–92
Trustee orientation, 21, 56, 219–221, 294, 330–332, 335, 336, 339
"Tuesday-to-Thursday Club," 161
Tunney, John V., 345
Turner, Julius, 43, 268, 270, 275–277
Twenty-one Day Rule, 83, 95, 122–124, 171, 369, 374, 381, 382
Twenty-second Amendment, 174
Tyler, Gus, 83
Tydings, Joseph D., 144

Udall, Morris K., 216
Unanimous consent, 124, 131, 138
United States v. Harriss et al., 209

Vandenberg, Arthur H., 180, 181
Verba, Sidney, 221
Veto power, 173–174
Vinyard, Dale, 62
Vogler, David J., 286, 287
Voting:
   in committee of the Whole, 125–127
   committee success in, 279–284

Voting:
  conservative coalition, 277–279
  constituency and, 274–275
  electoral competition and,
      273–274
  on the floor, 127, 133, 135, 267–
      284
  individual votes, 268–276
  party and, 268–272
  patterns of, 277–279
  personality and, 275–276
  President and, 269–270
  social background and, 34, 272–
      273
  urbanism-ruralism and, 277

Wahlke, John, 3, 12, 15, 16, 19, 21,
      239
Walker, David B., 31
Walker, Jack L., 168
Wallace, Robert Ash, 304
Washington, George, 321
Watkins, Robert, 392
Watkins v. United States, 226
Watson, Albert, 105, 140
Watson, Richard A., 271, 274
Weaver, Robert C., 301
Wednesday Club, 89, 160
Weinbaum, Marvin G., 48

Werner, Emmy E., 31
Wesberry v. Sanders, 40, 366
Westerfield, H. Bradford, 180,
      274, 275
Wherry, Kenneth, 100
Whips, 98–100, 104, 106
White, William S., 12, 142, 146
White House Office (*see* Executive
      Office of the President)
Whitten, Jamie, 310
Whitten amendment, 310
Wildavsky, Aaron, 188, 245, 304–
      307, 316, 361, 364, 376
Williams, John, 264
Williams, John Bell, 105, 140
Wilmerding, Lucuis, Jr., 304
Wilson, H. H., 392
Wilson, James Q., 253
Wilson, Woodrow, 58, 169, 287,
      391
"Withinputs," 13
Wolfinger, Raymond E., 72, 135
Woodward, John L., 216

Yarborough, Ralph, 279
Yates v. United States, 226

Zeller, Belle, 208